# THE IRAN-CONTRA ARMS SCANDAL:
## Foreign Policy Disaster

# THE IRAN-CONTRA ARMS SCANDAL: Foreign Policy Disaster

## AN EDITORIALS ON FILE BOOK

Editor: Oliver Trager

**Facts On File Publications**
New York, New York • Oxford, England

# THE IRAN-CONTRA ARMS SCANDAL:
## Foreign Policy Disaster

Published by Facts On File, Inc.
460 Park Ave. South, New York, N.Y. 10016
© Copyright 1988 by Facts On File, Inc.

**Library of Congress Cataloging-in-Publication Data**

Main entry under title:

The Iran-Contra Arms Scandal

(An Editorials On File Book)
Includes Index
1. The Iran-Contra Arms Affair, 1986-
I. Trager, Oliver
II. Series
E876.I73 1987 973.927 87-15606
ISBN O-8160-1859-6

Printed In The United States of America

9 8 7 6 5 4 3 2 1

973.927
Ira c.2

# CONTENTS

# Preface

The Iran-contra arms scandal has garnered banner headlines for more than a year. The question that undid President Richard Nixon—"What did the President know and when did he know it?"—has come back to haunt President Ronald Reagan. But the questions raised by the Iran-contra affair may run deeper than those faced by Richard Nixon. Although not faced with impeachment or resignation, Reagan's popularity and effectiveness have been markedly undermined. It has been asserted that if the President knew that the shipments of military hardware to Iran were an effort to trade "arms for hostages" and that the profits from the sales were diverted to the contra rebels fighting to topple Nicaragua's Sandinista government, then he is as guilty as Nixon of deceiving the American public. But if he didn't know, his lack of stewardship is evident.

As the administration scrambled to extricate itself from the morass, questions continued to surface. How has the ability of the United States to deal with terrorism been transformed? How did Lt. Col. Oliver North acquire the power to run his secret White House operation? Did the National Security Council staff become too powerful and insular? Where did the diverted Iranian funds end up and how will the scandal affect the future of the contras? What role did Vice President George Bush play in the operation and what factor will it play in the 1988 presidential campaign? What influence did the operation have on U.S. foreign policy and credibility? Who judged the Iranian contacts to be "moderates" when, in fact, they apparently were not? Has the press been fair to the President or has it blown the story out of proportion?

For years, the Reagan administration assured the American public, "We will never deal with terrorists." But the revelations that have come out of the Iran-contra scandal have tainted that claim. *The Iran-Contra Arms Scandal: Foreign Policy Disaster* examines one of the most important stories of the decade and the challenges it poses for the Reagan administration in its final year.

January, 1988                                                    Oliver Trager

# Part I: The Story Breaks

For six years President Reagan seemed to be one of those rare politicians blessed with the ability to identify himself with the national purpose. However, the sudden revelations of the Iran-contra affair loosened the President's hold on the public and shook the presidency itself.

The confirmation of arms sales to Iran in apparent return for the release of U.S. hostages, the news that profits from the arms sales had been diverted to the contras, the emergence of Lt. Col. Oliver North as a key player in both operations and President Reagan's continued insistence that he knew nothing, shocked the American people. The administration's shifting stand on exactly what had taken place made matters more confusing. President Reagan said that the total amount of arms sent to Iran was less than a planeload, and that the arms had not altered the balance in the six-year war between Iran and Iraq. The President said that the "secret diplomatic initiative" had four goals: to renew a friendly relationship between the U.S. and Iran, to end the Iran-Iraq war, to eliminate state-sponsored terrorism, and—despite his denial of a deal—"to effect the safe return of all hostages." Although several laws required the President to notify Congress about arms shipments to Iran and about covert operations, Reagan denied that he had circumvented any laws, saying in a November 13, 1986 speech that all cabinet officials had been informed of the operations and that congressional committees "are being and will be fully informed."

When the White House revealed November 25, 1986 that profits of the arms sales had been secretly diverted to help the contras, President Reagan was left facing the most serious crisis of his presidency. As the revelations surrounding various aspects of the affair unfolded, it became apparent that the U.S. government's foreign policy apparatus had been seriously compromised.

# Nicaragua Downs U.S. Plane; Charges CIA Supply Operation

The Nicaraguan government October 7, 1986 charged that the United States Central Intelligence Agency (CIA) was responsible for a contra supply plane shot down over southern Nicaragua Oct. 5. A U.S. ex-Marine survived after parachuting from the plane and was captured Oct. 6. Two other Americans died when the plane was downed. The Reagan administration and the CIA denied any link to the plane, despite a claim by the survivor that the CIA had supervised the flight and previous supply operations. CIA aid to the contras had recently been restricted to the sharing of intelligence. The restrictions would be removed once the Congress gave final approval for $100 million in military and economic aid to the contras. Despite repeated denials of any official U.S. involvement with the downed plane or knowledge of who operated it, questions were raised as to whether the administration was revealing all it knew. Coming at a time when the administration was under attack for allegedly misleading the press in a disinformation campaign directed at Libya, the incident prompted new warnings that the administration's credibility was on the line. The downed aircraft was a C-123K cargo plane reportedly carrying Soviet-made ammunition, grenades and rifles intended for anti-Sandinista contras seeking to establish a front in southern Nicaragua. It was shot down some 18 miles north of San Carlos near the Costa Rican border. The two Americans who died were identified as William Cooper of Reno, Nev. and Wallace Blaine Sawyer, Jr. of Magnolia, Ark. Both were said to have worked for the CIA many years before.

At a brief press conference at which the surviving American was presented, the Nicaraguan government Oct. 7 gave details of alleged contra air supply operations using U.S., Filipino and other pilots based in El Salvador. On being captured, the survivor, Eugene Hasenfus, 45, of Marinette, Wis., identified himself as a U.S. military adviser serving in El Salvador. Salvadoran air force identity cards describing the three Americans as military advisers for the U.S. were found in the wreckage. Hasenfus told local journalists that the downed plane began its journey in Miami, picked him up in El Salvador and then stopped in Honduras, where a Nicaraguan boarded. It then flew into Nicaraguan airspace. Hasenfus, who served in the U.S. Marines from 1960-1965, elaborated on the supply operation at a second news conference Oct. 9. He maintained that the flights were directly supervised by CIA agents in El Salvador and were coordinated by two Cuban-Americans who worked for the CIA. He identified the two as Max Gomez and Ramon Medina. Hasenfus said that, along with Cooper and Sawyer, he worked for Corporate Air Services, which operated out of Ilopango air force base in El Salvador. He said Corporate Air was part of Southern Air Transport Co., an air cargo company based in Miami that was owned by the CIA from 1960 to 1975.

A volley of denials was issued by U.S. and Salvadoran officials Oct. 7-8. U.S. Secretary of State George Shultz asserted Oct. 7 that the flights were organized by private citizens. The CIA the same day denied that the downed plane had any direct link to the U.S. government. However, U.S. Vice President George Bush and one of his aides, Donald Gregg, Oct. 10 were linked to the supply operation to provide arms to anti-Sandinista contras in Nicaragua. The *San Francisco Examiner* had reported Oct. 10 that Vice President Bush, and not the CIA, was the Washington connection to the contra supply operation. Citing unidentified intelligence sources, the *Examiner* stated that Max Gomez had been assigned in 1984 to the Ilopango air force base in El Salvador by Gregg, national security adviser to Bush, on the vice president's instructions. Through a spokesman, Bush Oct. 12 acknowledged that Gregg had recommended Gomez for a job as a counterinsurgency specialist for the Salvadoran air force. The *Examiner* said Gomez was introduced to Bush by Robert Owen, identified in news reports as a former employee at the State Department's Nicaraguan Humanitarian Assistance Office (NHAO). The NHAO oversaw the supply of nonlethal aid to the contras. Bush, director of the CIA from 1976 to 1977, Oct. 11 denied "unequivovally" that he had played a role in directing the supply flights. He acknowledged that he had met Gomez on three occasions, but said they had not talked about Nicaragua, and described Gomez as "a patriot."

## Detroit Free Press

*Detroit, MI, October 9, 1986*

THERE IS NO absolute proof of CIA involvement in an aborted attempt by some Americans to deliver arms to rebel forces in Nicaragua. But the incident is suspicious enough that it ought to strengthen the hands of opponents of this country's wrongheaded policy of escalating aid to the contras.

The American-built cargo plane that was shot down over Nicaragua on Sunday was operated by a private group led by a retired United States Army major general, according to the administration. It reportedly had flown down to deliver ammunition and supplies to the Nicaraguan rebels.

Spokesmen for the administration, the State Department, the Central Intelligence Agency and the Department of Defense all denied any government connection to the flight. Somehow their denials were not enough to silence the troubling questions spawned by the incident.

One official said that the company set up by Gen. John K. Singlaub in El Salvador had been used by the CIA in the past, but claimed that this particular flight was not a CIA operation. That is a very fine distinction to try to make. Moreover, the plane was a C123, a turbo-prop formerly used by the Air Force to carry cargo and paratroopers. Only a few remain in service, and one would not expect them to be readily available to private groups.

Congressional prohibitions against military aid to the contras remain in effect, with $100 million in new aid awaiting final approval in Congress before new supplies and training can be offered legally to the insurgents. What this incident suggests is that the Reagan administration remains committed to finding ways to funnel covert military aid to the contras at all costs.

If it can be shown that the administration has been working through private groups to circumvent the prohibitions on contra aid — along with disregarding the War Powers Act and the Constitution — that ought to galvanize Congress into voting down any new aid for the rebels.

Already, there is disturbing evidence of misuse of the $27 million in so-called humanitarian aid that the United States has sent to the contras, with nearly two-thirds of the money going to Central American suppliers whom the U.S. government cannot control. There is still no answer, either, for this question: What will we have won if we succeed in toppling the Sandinista government and installing the contras — either for the long-suffering Nicaragua people or for U.S. interests in the region? The cargo plane incident makes it all the more compelling that we find the answer.

# The Hartford Courant

*Hartford, CT, October 8, 1986*

**W**ho is responsible for the military cargo plane shot down in Nicaragua Sunday, with four crewmen aboard who apparently were Americans?

Nicaraguan officials were quick to point fingers at the CIA and at the U.S. military advisers' mission in El Salvador. The CIA denied involvement, and Secretary of State George P. Shultz said the plane had been hired by private American citizens who have no connection to the U.S. government.

The accusations from Managua and the denials from Washington were all predictable, but they mean little and there's a need to clear the air.

What seems to be beyond dispute is this: A large cargo plane was brought down southeast of Managua by a surface-to-air missile fired by Nicaraguan troops. The plane contained ammunition, rifles and other supplies presumably meant for the contra rebels who are fighting the Sandinista government. Three crewmen, thought to be Americans, were killed and a fourth American was captured.

There's a good chance the Americans were breaking U.S. law, whether they were acting as private citizens or working for the CIA. For the past two years, during which Congress denied President Reagan's requests for military aid to the contras, some American citizens — in defiance of congressional intent — have been working behind the scenes to help the contras overthrow the Nicaraguan government.

The efforts apparently have had the tacit approval of the White House and have been under the unofficial direction of the CIA. Both the House and the Senate have passed bills providing the contras with $100 million in military and non-lethal aid for this fiscal year, but there has been no final action. The supplies in the downed plane were not part of the new aid program.

Moreover, the aid to the contras bill does not permit the involvement of U.S. personnel in the war through fighting on Nicaraguan soil or flying over Nicaragua.

Congress should look into the sub rosa efforts by Americans to aid the contras. It has an obligation to investigate the evidence of secret and illegal war-making. If it's found that U.S. officials have been involved, they should be held accountable.

# Los Angeles Times

*Los Angeles, CA, October 9, 1986*

It looks bad enough for the United States to have an airplane packed with arms for Nicaragua's rebels and flown by an American crew crash inside that country's borders. It makes it look unacceptably worse to have one of President Reagan's chief advisers on Latin America use the incident to encourage free-lance attacks a sovereign government with which we are officially at peace.

There will be more details in the days to come on the activities of Marine Corps veteran Eugene Hasenfus, the Wisconsin man who is the sole survivor of the four-man crew aboard the C-123 transport that Nicaraguan troops shot down Sunday near the Costa Rican border. Two other U.S. citizens, and a Nicaraguan, were killed when it crashed. Hasenfus has reportedly admitted his mission was to resupply anti-Sandinista *contra* rebels.

The U.S. government has disavowed any official connection with the airplane or its crew, but there can be little doubt the flight was part of a pattern of covert operations, either overseen directly or encouraged indirectly by the Central Intelligence Agency, in support of the contras, who Reagan considers freedom fighters. That an Administration irrationally obsessed with Nicaragua is linked to such activities is no surprise. What is amazing is how consistently U.S. officials, and their contra allies, botch up these operations and embarrass themselves before the world.

Take the way Assistant Secretary of State Elliot Abrams, the chief coordinator of Reagan Administration policy in Central America, praised the work of private U.S. groups that aid the contras, going so far as to call the downed plane's crew "heroes." They probably were brave men. But there are serious questions as to whether such activities are even legal under the Neutrality Act of 1972.

Quite apart from their legality, there are millions of Americans who consider such activities improper and unwise. Even the Republican chairman of the Senate Intelligence Committee, Minnesota's David Durenberger, is asking whether the CIA could bring free-lance contra aid operations under control if Congress were ever to allow it to go after Nicaragua unhindered. For Abrams to go out of his way to praise that kind of activity reflects profound arrogance.

But then, ignorance and a belief that we know better than the rest of the world what to do in Central America runs through all of the Administration's tactics and pronouncements with respect to Nicaragua. Reagan, Abrams and the rest are apparently determined to wage their war there regardless of what it costs in human lives or damaged U.S. prestige. The only way their campaign to overthrow the Sandinistas will be forced into a more constructive channel—like the Contadora negotiations suggested by our Latin American allies—will be if Congress flatly refuses to go along with it.

Congress should now delay final approval of the $100 million in contra aid it voted recently, until the Administration answers the many questions raised by the aircraft's downing. Congress must find out if the Administration is already using the contra aid money despite the fact it has not been finally approved, or whether the CIA is using its operating funds against Nicaragua, a strategy Congress specifically banned two years ago when it was revealed that CIA operatives had mined Nicaragua's harbors.

Congress must have a clear answer to those questions before allowing Reagan and his fellow adventurers to plunge deeper into the jungles of Central America.

# The Des Moines Register

*Des Moines, IA
October 10, 1986*

Private adventurers may have financed and flown the American-built cargo plane shot down over Nicaragua last Sunday, but Congress and the president are responsible for the undeclared, but no longer secret, United States war against Nicaragua.

The Constitution gives the president the authority to make foreign policy and Congress the right to declare war. But in Central America, the president seems to prefer CIA covert operations and private vigilantes rather than risk public debate by asking Congress to declare war.

Congress, for its part, has ducked its responsibility to debate whether this country should be at war by not declaring the war a war.

The Senate Foreign Relations Committee is now conducting an inquiry to determine if the U.S. government was directly or only indirectly behind the plane that was shot down. But it doesn't take much investigation to note that Congress itself endorsed the spirit and the financing of the secret war last August when it approved another $100 million in aid to U.S.-trained contras fighting to overthrow the Sandinista government.

Congress even failed to pass an amendment offered by Senator Tom Harkin of Iowa to limit the number of American advisers in Central America, so that now the administration can send 20 or 2,000 or 20,000 "advisers" and still not call it a war.

Last year, Congress contributed further to the secret war by refusing to approve a bill drafted by congressmen James Leach of Iowa and Mel Levine of California that would update the neutrality act to forbid private intervention in countries with which the United States is at peace. If the Leach-Levine bill had passed, two Americans might not have died last Sunday in Nicaragua.

•

But people die in wars. That is why the founding fathers gave Congress, and therefore the people, the responsibility to declare war. And in instances when Congress has tried to stifle public debate by fighting war without declaring war, such as in Vietnam, public outrage exploded when it became clear that Americans were killing and dying without having the chance to vote on whether they wanted to go to war.

If Congress and the administration approve of sending American money, equipment and citizens to support killing in Central America, they should at least have the courage to call it war and to stop pretending that such a policy can bring peace to Central America.

# The News and Courier

*Charleston, SC, October 12, 1986*

The brother of Eugene Hasenfus, the American veteran who is a "prisoner of war" in Nicaragua, has been complaining about the U.S. government. He says that his brother is a "political orphan" who has been deserted by his own country.

Since that complaint, however, Mr. Hasenfus has been claimed. The Nicaraguan Democratic Force (FDN), one of the groups of anti-Sandinista guerrillas known as the Contras, has announced that all four men aboard the plane shot down over southern Nicaragua have worked for the FDN since 1984.

It is in the interests of the Sandinistas to establish a CIA link with Mr. Hasenfus, the only man aboard the plane with a parachute and the only survivor. While there can be no doubt about CIA involvement with the Contras, there is also no reason to jump to the conclusion that the four men were hired by the agency. The FDN has private funding and can operate independently of the CIA.

If Mr. Hasenfus was working for the FDN, he cannot claim, nor should his relatives expect, the United States government to do any more for him than they would for any other U.S. citizen. Were he to be a CIA agent, he would know that he could not expect any special help in his present predicament. Whoever was his employer, Mr. Hasenfus must have read the job description and, given his background, would have known the terms of employment.

Mr. Hasenfus has not been deserted by his country or his government. A prominent member of the adminstration, Assistant Secretary of State Eliott Abrams, has described Americans who work for the Contras as heroes. It takes more to be a hero than parachute out of a crippled plane, but Mr. Hasenfus' courage will certainly be tested by the Sandinistas.

Not surprisingly, the Sandinistas are exploiting the downing of the plane, the deaths of three of its crew and the capture of Mr. Hasenfus, in their propaganda, which is stridently anti-American at the best of times. The delivery to the U.S. Embassy in Managua of the remains of two of the crewmen, and the unexplained retention of a third body, seem to be part of a campaign to keep this matter before the public eye. Although the description of the delivery of the coffins containing the remains of the two Americans as "ghoulish" may seem somewhat exaggerated, there can be no doubt that the Sandinistas are determined to picture the United States in the worst possible light. Because they are so insensitive themselves, the Sandinistas invariably end up by shooting themselves in the foot. That is precisely what they did when, instead of taking the bodies of the pilot William J. Cooper and co-pilot Wallace Blaine Sawyer Jr. to the embassy in the least conspicious way possible, they dumped two coffins containing their remains on a stretch of grass outside the embassy. The objective was to emphasize the symbolism of the delivery of two coffins to the embassy gates. It may not have been "ghoulish" exactly but it showed scant respect for the dead men, their families or their fellow citizens.

Regardless of Sandinista provocation, the U.S. response must be measured and decorous. President Reagan has never made any secret about his support for the Contras. He has called them "freedom fighters" from the start. The administration has no reason to be ashamed of CIA involvement with the Contras, or of private American citizens who work for them, as long as such activities are legal. The administration will, however, have to take some political heat because of the incident. President Reagan is likely to find himself in crossfire between the right and left extremes. He will be called upon by the former to adopt Mr. Hasenfus and by the latter to disown him. The right policy is to steer a centrist course, ignoring those who would like to see an invasion while turning a deaf ear to those who would like to see the United States abandon its support for democracy in Nicaragua.

## Wisconsin ▲ State Journal

*Madison, WI, October 10, 1986*

seeds of doubt planted by
ernment's alleged use of
rmation against Libyan
Moammar Gadhafi are
bitter fruit thousands of
ay in Nicaragua.

o plane loaded with arms
Marxist rebels has been
wn along Nicaragua's
border, leaving two
dead and a third, Eu-
nfus of Marinette, Wis.,
ds of gleeful Sandinista

ent Reagan says Hasen-
official connection with
government. Secretary of
eorge Shultz says the
et there are signs the ill-
ssion was connected with
ization headed by retired
en. John Singlaub, who
usiastically supported the
of the "Contras" through
means.

there are reports the two
Americans had links to
rn Air Transport, a Miami
once owned by the CIA and
edly still used by the intelli-
ce agency.

Coming when it did, at the
eight of an uproar over government disinformation in the case of
Libya, the mysterious circumstances surrounding the downing
of the C-123 cargo plane have
raised a host of questions.

Opponents of Reagan's pro-
Contra policy are asking — not

without good reason — whether
the administration is encouraging
private parties to carry out those
portions of the president's plan
which Congress has yet to approve. "It will bother me," said
Sen. Patrick Leahy, D-Vt., "if this
turns out to be connected with adjunct soldiers of fortune sent out
there with a wink and nod or a
shrug as a way of getting around
our foreign policy or the law."

Reagan insists that is not the
case, but adds: "We're in a free
country where private citizens
have a great many freedoms."
History suggests those freedoms
do include the right to get involved
in other people's wars, but only so
long as those individuals don't
drag the rest of us along.

The Senate Foreign Relations
committee, chaired by Sen. Richard Lugar, R-Ind., will conduct an
inquiry into whether or not the
cargo plane had ties with the Reagan administration.

Given Lugar's record for part-
ing company with the White House
when he believes necessary (the
Philippines and South Africa come
to mind) such a probe begins with
a strong measure of credibility.

Reagan is right — it's a free
country. But those freedoms do
not extend to private formulation
of foreign policy without the advice and consent of the president
and Congress.

## THE ASHEVILLE CITIZEN

*Asheville, NC, October 9, 1986*

The U.S. government should
render what aid it can in securing the release of Eugene Hasenfus from Nicaragua — and the return of the bodies of two Americans who were killed when his
cargo plane was shot down.

It isn't enough for U.S. officials simply to shrug and do the
"Who, me?" routine. Our government has an obligation to help
Hasenfus whether it was involved in the operation or not.

The official position is that
government agencies were not
involved. Yes, private mercenary
groups are active in supporting
the Nicaraguan rebels, but they
are working entirely on their
own. What they do is their business. If "patriotic Americans"
want to aid the cause of freedom
in Nicaragua, that's admirable —
but they have no connection to
the government.

President Reagan upheld the
official line Wednesday when he
spoke to reporters. "We're in a
free country where private citizens have a great many freedoms," said Reagan innocently.

The CIA is denying every-
thing it can: that the plane was a
government plane, that the
Americans involved worked either directly or indirectly for the
government, that the CIA had
any role in what they were
doing.

All of that may be true. The
CIA tries to maintain what it

calls "deniability" in operations
of the sort that American civilians are carrying out in Central
America.

Nonetheless, the private
groups active in the region work
with the encouragement, if not
the advice and support, of the
government. It was Miami-based
Southern Air Transport that serv-
iced the plane and issued identity
cards to the crew. Southern Air
was owned by the CIA until 1973
and still does contract work for
the agency.

As far as the fate of Hasenfus goes, CIA involvement in the
operation is irrelevant anyway —
or should be. The U.S. government tries to render assistance to
any American citizen who gets
into trouble abroad, whatever the
circumstances. Whether the trouble is his own doing or not, our
government is there, ready to
offer whatever aid is possible.

We should do no less with
Hasenfus. It would be unfortunate if U.S. officials abandoned
him simply to prove they have
clean hands.

They should try to get him
back — which may not be too difficult. After the Sandinistas parade Hasenfus around and milk
all the public relations they can
from his capture, they probably
would be willing to release him to
show their "humanitarian" concern.

## THE SACRAMENTO BEE

*Sacramento, CA, October 9, 1986*

Eugene Hasenfus and his fellow soldiers of
fortune are being portrayed by the
Reagan administration as private mercenaries. It contends that their free-lance gun-running mission into Nicaragua, in which an
American plane was shot down and all but
Hasenfus were killed, had no official connection with the U.S. government. So far there's
no reason to dispute that, but to argue that the
mission was not inspired and encouraged by
the administration's Central American policy
would be absurd.

Hasenfus (whose name, ironically, means
"rabbit's foot") and his companions were not
just solitary adventurers. Their mission, and
doubtless many others that don't end up on
the front pages, are part and parcel of the
Reagan administration's crusade to oust the
leftist regime in Managua by force.

For the most part, that crusade has had to
be waged surreptitiously and obliquely in recent years, through private organizations like
the one that sponsored Hasenfus' adventure,
because Congress forbade direct U.S. government involvement. That hasn't deterred the
administration from cheering on the mercenaries, however, a fact that was demonstrated again when a State Department official
praised men like Hasenfus as "very, very
brave people."

But Congress reversed course this year and
legitimized the war by approving $100 million
in direct aid to the Contras, who will now re-
sume the offensive against the Sandinista
government. Presumably private mercenaries will continue their work, too. But to what
end? The war against the Sandinistas is either
doomed to abject failure, because the effort
is too small, or destined to expand into a regional conflict on a far larger scale, with uncertain but certainly horrendous consequences.

How a tiny, impoverished nation of 2.5 million people threatens the United States is
hard to see. It ought not to be beyond the capacity of our policy-makers to devise a strategy of containment against this "threat" without getting into a shooting war with it. As long
as the administration continues on its present
course, there will be more mercenaries like
Eugene Hasenfus, more American deaths,
and a growing risk of wider war.

# Hostage Freed in Lebanon; U.S. Denies Policy Shift

David Jacobsen, an American held hostage in Lebanon for more than 17 months by Shiite Moslem extremists, was freed November 2, 1986 in Beirut. It was reported Nov. 3-6 that Jacobsen's release, along with the freeing of two other United States hostages over the previous year, had been linked to a secret deal involving the transfer of military parts by the U.S. to Iran via Israel. Jacobsen, 55, had been director of the American University Hospital when he was seized in May 1985. The purported secret agreement surprised observers. It appeared to violate the Reagan administration's vow never to negotiate with terrorists or with states that supported them, as well as the formal U.S. embargo on arms sales to Iran. American officials denied that the U.S. had changed its antiterrorist policies and warned that many of the details being reported in the press were based on speculation. But—by not issuing any specific, ironclad denials—high officials appeared to confirm the existence of the U.S.-Iranian deal. In addition to winning freedom for the hostages in Lebanon, the U.S. arms aid to Iran was reportedly intended to increase American influence in Teheran at a time when moderates and radicals were vying to shape the future course of the revolutionary Islamic government.

British Anglican Church lay official Terry Waite appeared in Beirut unexpectedly Oct. 31 and told reporters that "something might happen in the next day or two" regarding the American hostages. Waite had played an intermediary role in the earlier releases of two U.S. captives, Rev. Lawrence Jenco in July 1986 and Rev. Benjamin Weir in September 1985. Jacobsen, Jenco and Weir had been held by the Islamic Jihad (Holy War) organization, a Shiite group linked to Iran. With the release of Jacobsen, the group still held two other Americans: Associated Press correspondent Terry Anderson and American University of Beirut dean Thomas Sutherland. The fact that Waite was flown from Beirut in a U.S. military helicopter to Cyprus Oct. 31 and whisked away in a U.S. embassy limousine reinforced the impression that he was serving as an intermediary between the kidnappers and the U.S. government.

U.S. President Ronald Reagan hailed the freeing of Jacobsen Nov. 2 in a statement read by White House spokesman Larry Speakes. The release was "the logical conclusion" of U.S. efforts undertaken "through a number of sensitive channels for a very long time," Speakes said. He denied that the administration had made concessions to gain Jacobsen's freedom.

## The Miami Herald

*Miami, FL, November*

IF IT DIDN'T concern life a the Mideast hostage drama likened to a French farce. E a door opens onstage, another emerges with a twist to compl plot further. But when the p thing, the audience knows that end happily at the final curtain.

Not so in Beirut, where subplc around the center-stage action, Islamic Jihad's release this David Jacobsen. The story's a c ger, with Mr. Jacobsen happy to but concerned for the five Ar hostages still being held "in hell."

Snippets of dialogue confus subplots. The Islamic Jihad is kno hold at least two more American communique regarding their fate is on enigma: Their release could dep upon U.S. "approaches that could lead, continued, to a solution. ... " T official White House response is that th United States made "no concessions."

Despite the conjecture and terse official pronouncements, some of the story is clear. The Islamic Jihad wanted to exchange its hostages for the freedom of 17 convicted terrorists imprisoned in Kuwait. But the group obviously was tiring of its role as captor, so it nudged the U.S. Government after the Soviets released journalist Nicholas Daniloff last month. Washington reacted, but how or

through whom or on what terms is not yet known. The 17 in Kuwait remain jailed.

The Islamic Jihad is sympathetic to Iran, where factions interested in resuming friendly ties to the West are ascendant. One subplot therefore has Iran exerting influence with the Islamic Jihad to come to terms over the hostages' release in exchange for an end to a U.S. arms embargo.

Another subplot is that Syria, feeling the West's displeasure after Britain tied Damascus to a terrorist convicted of attempting to bomb an Israeli jetliner in London, helped in Mr. Jacobsen's release. Britain has called on Western nations to impose diplomatic and economic sanctions on Syria.

From the unconfirmed subplots, one thing that has long-term impact can be gleaned: Mideast countries, even the most isolated, appear to be discovering that they need the Western nations for economic, military, and technical purposes whether their rulers care to admit it publicly or not. Western diplomats must seize the moment to gain not just the remaining hostages' release but to connect with the more-reasonable forces within these troubled countries. It is imperative that the barbarians be moved off center stage in the Mideast drama.

## The Washington Post

*Washington, DC, November 4, 1986*

OF THE AMERICANS taken hostage in Lebanon, three—the latest being David Jacobsen—have now been released, and two are reported dead. That leaves five, of whom two were seized in the days of Lebanon's disintegration in 1985 and three this fall. The record affords scant cheer: American hostages have a not much better chance of being freed than of being killed. But in the circumstances it is not an altogether dismal record either.

The terrorists prefer underground ways—to cultivate a mystique, perhaps, and to reduce exposure to outside pressures. Yet it is clear they belong to Islamic factions seeking to destroy the existing Middle East order of which the United States is a part, and they act, under uncertain control, for regimes of the region, principally Iran and Syria. In seeking the hostages' safety and return, Washington has tried to make sure it would not incidentally serve the terrorists' or their sponsors' political aims, a difficult intention to fulfill, but a necessary one.

"No political goals are or will be achieved by resorting to terror and terrorism," President Reagan said in welcoming back David Jacobsen. The United States has sought, with some success, to draw the terrorists into an indirect dialogue on the American agenda, release of the hostages. (Only now, by the way, and responding in part to a clamor to match its public exertions for Nicholas Daniloff, does the White House call this dialogue a "negotiation," a word that it formerly rejected as tantamount to capitulation.) At the same time, the administration has rightly rejected the terrorists' call for talks on their agenda—a prisoner exchange for the 17 of their comrades, convicted terrorists all, whom Kuwait has held since 1983.

Caring as they do for their endangered fellow citizens, Americans feel the strain. Yet the terrorists are under strain too, and are plainly fazed by American constancy, by the feeling that has mounted against them internationally and, conceivably, by the apparent restlessness of the Syrians and Iranians, whose officials met just as the latest release took place. Islamic Holy War, announcing this release, reached for the moral high ground ("In the name of God . . .") in a way suggesting that the United States has successfully shifted the onus from its own regional role to the criminality of the terrorists themselves. We hope so. "In the name of God" they should stop threatening innocent lives.

## BUFFALO EVENING NEWS
*Buffalo, NY, November 4, 1986*

THE RELEASE of another American hostage held by Islamic terrorists in Beirut raises hopes for the eventual freeing of the 19 American and other hostages still missing in Lebanon.

How or why the American, David Jacobsen, was freed after 17 months in captivity is still shrouded in mystery. The White House, still seeking to obtain the release of others, could give few clues as to the process by which Jacobsen regained his freedom. But it was clear that, in some obscure way, contacts with the terrorists are being made.

Jacobsen himself appeared in good spirits and hopeful, but his joy at the end of his cruel incarceration was marred by the grim ordeal that is continuing for his fellow hostages. One of the six remaining American hostages is Terry Anderson, a former Batavia resident whose sister, Peggy Say, has carried on a tireless campaign to secure his release.

The freeing of Jacobsen comes three months after the similarly mysterious release of an American priest, the Rev. Lawrence Jenco, who was held by the same shadowy terrorist organization, Islamic Jihad, that held Jacobsen hostage. Father Jenco was hopeful last summer that further releases would be made. Since then, however, three more Americans have been kidnapped in Lebanon, but not necessarily by Islamic Jihad.

An American official gave much credit in the freeing of Jacobsen to Terry Waite, the Anglican Church representative who has acted as a negotiator or mediator with the terrorists. Syria and Iran also have much influence in Lebanon, but an official said Syria had not been involved in freeing Jacobsen. He did not say who was.

Other contacts might have been made with Algerian or Lebanese officials.

The White House said only that the United States is working on the problem "through a number of channels" but gave no details. The administration has said in the past that it would talk with anyone to free the hostages but would make no deals. Donald Reagan, White House chief of staff, said that negotiations had been going on for months, but he stressed that the United States was not making concessions.

That, indeed, is important, since rewarding terrorism would only encourage the seizure of other American hostages around the world. Terrorism actually appears to have declined since the United States struck back at Libya last April for its role in a terrorist bombing in West Berlin.

One sign of movement in the present obscure hostage situation is the tone of the latest message from the terrorist Islamic Jihad group. In a statement made on freeing Jacobsen, it mentioned a further "opportunity" for the United States to "proceed with current approaches."

This also is obscure, but it sounds much more conciliatory than the message accompanying Father Jenco's release in July. At that time, Islamic Jihad said the release was a "final good will gesture" and demanded the release of 17 terrorists imprisoned for atrocities in Kuwait. This time, Islamic Jihad made no mention of Kuwait.

Thus, there is evidence that something is going on that might bring an end to the long stalemate concerning the hostages, but information is necessarily limited. All the United States can do is to continue its policy of seeking a way through the labyrinthine maze of Middle Eastern political rivalry and terrorism.

# THE LINCOLN STAR
*Lincoln, NE, November 8, 1986*

Watching developments surrounding the remaining hostages in Lebanon, one can only feel a great uneasiness. Something appears to be afoot relating to release of the hostages, but not without troublesome details.

A persistent report has the United States supplying Iran with vital military equipment in exchange for its intervention on behalf of U.S. citizens remaining in the hands of Shiite terrorists in Lebanon. Confirmation of that has not yet become firm, but efforts to find the truth have produced circumstantial evidence supporting the report.

Release of the three American hostages and those from France would be cause for celebration, without a question. But there is a limit to the price the American people would pay for this.

Iran is a nation we have shunned, and rightly so, since the 1979 U.S. Embassy hostage situation there. From that, Iran has gone on to become one of the leading exporters of terrorism in the Middle East.

Reportedly, Iran is now having second thoughts and is beginning to seek a way out of its extremist isolation from most of the rest of the world. While the United States certainly should consider any overtures from Iran for a return to normalcy, to forge a relationship with U.S. hostages as the pawns would be widely condemned in this country.

President Reagan has expressed dissatisfaction with media efforts to force an explanation of this situation, maintaining publicity only makes release of the hostages a more difficult matter. Thus is the media on the horns of a dilemma.

To kill with publicity an honorable release of the hostages would be a tragedy. But to condone with silence a clandestine accord with such an uncivilized and unprincipled country as Iran would be an insult to democratic values.

And that is to say nothing of the credibility loss we would suffer as a supplier of military hardware to Iran while we support with our good will and our arms Iran's enemy in war, Iraq. That would constitute an intrigue bereft of honor.

It is a delicate situation we hope is soon resolved.

## THE ARIZONA REPUBLIC
*Phoenix, AZ, November 4, 1986*

THE West has shown itself to be a toothless tiger in the face of the threat of international state-sponsored terrorism. It has adopted the novel approach of treating humiliation as if it were victory.

It began with the release of the Iran hostages, and has become the standard response, especially of the United States, to the kidnapping and humiliation of citizens.

American civilians are taken off the streets of Beirut and subjected to barbaric treatment; U.S. airliners are seized and passengers are killed; and when the innocents are finally released the nation treats the settlement as a victory.

On a purely personal level, the release of David Jacobsen, who had been held hostage in Beirut for 17 months, is cause for rejoicing. On a policy level, however, his imprisonment by Islamic Jihad, a pro-Iranian Shiite terrorist group which enjoys the backing of Syria, was yet another humiliation for the United States.

When American citizens can be treated in this fashion with virtual impunity, it can be nothing less than a humiliation, and to regard it as anything else is national self-delusion.

The weak and irresolute response of the West to terrorism — typified by the failure of Western Europe to take any effective action against Syria in the face of irrefutable evidence that Damascus plotted to blow up a civilian airliner with 378 people on board — only inspires and emboldens the murderers to commit ever more heinous crimes.

Islamic Jihad operates in the Syrian-controlled sector of Lebanon where it runs terrorist training bases with the active support of Damascus. So does the Abu Nidal faction of the Palestine Liberation Organization, which hijacked the *Achille Lauro*.

Whether or not the five remaining American hostages in Lebanon are *directly* under Damascus' control, the United States should make it clear it holds Syria responsible for their safety since the terrorists holding the hostages enjoy Syrian patronage.

Until such a time as the West begins to hold governments such as Syria — which make the survival of international terrorism possible — responsible for their actions, there will be more bombings and kidnappings.

The release of David Jacobsen should not be the occasion of national celebration, but of renewed national resolve.

# U.S.-Iran Arms Furor; McFarlane Teheran Trip Reported

The news of covert contacts between Washington and Teheran was broken November 3, 1986 in the pro-Syrian Beirut magazine *Al Shiraa*, which quoted senior Iranian sources. It reported that former United States national security adviser Robert McFarlane had secretly visited Teheran in the previous month to discuss a cessation of Iranian support for terrorist groups and security guarantees for the Arab states of the Persian Gulf in exchange for the provision of U.S. military spare parts. The revelation embarrassed both the U.S. and Iranian governments and apparently prevented—at least temporarily—any more U.S. hostages in Lebanon from being freed. Some analysts suggested Syria had publicized the secret U.S.-Iranian contacts in order to prove that Damascus could not be excluded from a central role in Mideast affairs. The White House had insisted that Syria had played virtually no part in Jacobsen's release.

The *New York Times* and *Washington Post* Nov. 5-6 cited informed U.S. intelligence sources in reporting that the McFarlane visit to Teheran was part of a series of secret talks between U.S. and Iranian officials that had been taking place for more than a year both in Iran and in European cities. McFarlane allegedly worked with Adm. John Poindexter, his successor as White House national security adviser, and Col. Oliver North, a shadowy staff member of the National Security Council (NSC), who had played a key role in coordinating aid to the anti-Sandinista contra rebels fighting the Nicaraguan government. The secret Iranian contacts were handled by a select group of NSC officials, rather than by the Central Intelligence Agency, allegedly to avoid the possibility of a leak from the congressional intelligence committees. According to these accounts, in the wake of the hijacking of a Trans World Airlines jet in 1985, the administration became convinced that Iran, rather than Syria, held the key to the release of the U.S. hostages in Lebanon. Meanwhile Iran, engaged in a six-year-old war with Iraq, had become desperate for military parts, particularly for its U.S.-made fighter planes and radar systems. Some American officials said that, in return for Iran pushing the Islamic Jihad (Holy War) terrorist group to free the hostages, the U.S. promised only to "look the other way" while Iran bought the necessary equipment on the international market. Previously, the U.S. had prosecuted arms dealers who sought to circumvent the embargo against Iran. Other sources cited in news accounts said the U.S. had actually made direct shipments of American spare parts to Iran, and had persuaded third-party nations—particularly Israel—to do the same. The release of Rev. Benjamin Weir in 1985 and Rev. Lawrence Jenco in July 1986 was reportedly preceded by the delivery of U.S. military cargo to Iran. Sources in the press Nov. 6 asserted that Secretary of State George Shultz and those of his aides who were aware of the top-secret program had protested to President Reagan about it. They reportedly said that the operation compromised U.S. antiterrorist policy and would encourage the kidnapping of more Americans.

The Honolulu Advertiser
*Honolulu, HI*
*November 7, 1986*

Behind the various stories of intrigue, denials, White House silence and pleas for media discretion, this seems to be the story:

Months of talks between Iran and White House envoys and secret arms shipments to Iran, some via Israel, led to the release of the latest three American hostages in Lebanon.

Whether former national security adviser Robert McFarlane was arrested in Tehran for entering Iran illegally may be uncertain. But he apparently was involved in the months of talks.

In fact, there are several interlocking aspects in this story: One is the economic crisis and internal split in Iran, which could be important in hopes for moderation there. A second is its war with Iraq, where Iran is suffering from lack of spare parts and certain arms. A third is the plight of our hostages in Lebanon.

No doubt the White House reasoned it was worth the price of breaking its embargo and otherwise dealing with Iran to win freedom for the long-suffering Americans, and doubly so if that could help wean Iran away from backing Mideast terrorism and otherwise encourage more moderate policies.

Most Americans will agree. But there are those with other views. They fear that breaking our self-imposed quarantine of Iran has destroyed our arguments for tougher action against terrorism with France and other "soft" European countries. It's charged that leaders of Persian Gulf states fearful of Iran may also wonder about our reliability as an ally if a crisis comes.

For now it seems the rash of revelations from Iran and elsewhere has stalled efforts to free more Americans. That is grim for the hostages and otherwise unfortunate because the Reagan administration may now face the consequences of its secret dealings without getting the full benefits.

# Chicago Tribune

*Chicago, IL, November 11, 1986*

One thing that would be helpful in this unfolding fiasco over arms-for-hostages would be for White House Spokesman Larry Speakes to keep in mind just what his job is, what it is not and who pays him to do it.

Mr. Speakes is not editor-in-chief of America. Neither is he the nation's censor-in-chief.

He is the President's deputy press secretary, and his job is to dispense the truth about what is going on at the White House to the taxpayers who sign his checks.

Mr. Speakes, however, seems to be laboring under the delusion that it is, rather, his job to blow smoke over the facts, deliver lectures about media responsibility and issue threats to anyone who challenges his evasions.

Both Mr. Speakes and his boss, President Reagan, have taken the position that they just cannot answer questions about the Iran enterprise without endangering the American hostages in Lebanon and have appeared to suggest that no one should even be asking questions.

They seem to have forgotten that it was Middle East media that broke the story of the administration's secret dealings with Iran in the first place. It was the speaker of Iran's parliament who declared in a speech that the U.S. was now trying to "beg" Iran for help and spoke of the "defeat of America."

If Mr. Speakes—and Mr. Reagan, for that matter—think Americans are not entitled to ask questions on so profound and stunning a reversal of U.S. foreign policy as this one, they don't have a very sound idea of how this country works.

And instead of throwing tantrums and threatening to lop off the heads of reporters who ask questions that don't suit his distorted notions of propriety, Mr. Speakes might more usefully employ himself by dispensing some straight answers.

## THE PLAIN DEALER
*Cleveland, OH, November 7, 1986*

It's easier to believe that Robert C. McFarlane, the president's former national security adviser, actually traveled to Iran than to explain why he did so. According to reports that haven't been officially denied, McFarlane last visited Tehran in September. His alleged purpose was to enlist Iran's support in efforts to free American hostages in Lebanon. In exchange, the stories go, the United States would stop disrupting the supply of military equipment and spare parts to Iran, which is fighting a war of attrition and slaughter against Iraq.

Did McFarlane go to Tehran? A variety of shadowy "sources" confirm the allegation in a variety of shadowy ways. Still, the story has a credibility problem. It's hard to imagine McFarlane traveling in mechanic's overalls, carrying an Irish passport, and bearing a Bible signed by President Reagan and a cake shaped like a key. Not exactly inconspicuous . . . the cake would have been a dead giveaway had it not been eaten by hungry security men.

More troubling than breaches of discretion and subtlety, however, is the idea that the White House privately has been violating two major policy positions that it has steadfastly maintained in public. The first is the insistence, by the White House, that it will not negotiate with, or concede to, terrorists. The second is that as long as Iran insists on exporting terrorism (as it does without the barest shadow of a doubt) the United States will embargo arms shipments to it and attempt to halt the flow from other nations. There might be countless reasons why the Reagan administration should mislead the State Department and the public on those matters, but they have yet to be convincingly detailed.

What might those reasons be? How about the release of American hostages? Gaining their freedom has tremendous appeal and great worth. But better yet, from the regional and global view at least, is the argument that now is the moment to seek new connections with Tehran's fundamentalist leaders. Iran is on the brink of economic and political self-destruction, a fact that could threaten regional stability and, with it, an irreplaceable source of energy for the industrialized West.

Both ambitions have pitfalls, naturally. Is it wise to imply that hostage-taking does have rewards for terrorists? Should the United States get too deeply entwined in the Iran-Iraq war? Should it become too closely associated with one of Tehran's contending factions? And how about the administration? Should it practice policies that are marked by duplicity without trying to explain them?

White House officials won't comment on McFarlane's trip, nor on the process that led to the release of American hostage David P. Jacobsen, nor on the possibility that other Americans might soon be freed. To do so, they claim, might inhibit or destroy extant regional endeavors. That's a familiar and sometimes credible rejection of accountability. But it wears thin in light of such consistent allegations and back-alley confirmations. If the White House has changed its policy toward the Persian Gulf war or toward terrorism, now is the time to say so, and to explain why.

## The Times-Picayune
### The States-Item
*New Orleans, LA, November 12, 1986*

President Reagan's back-room diplomacy with Iran seems to have been a reasonable, well intentioned operation that succumbed to extraordinarily poor judgment.

Presidents have often run secret operations from the White House. Congress should not piously grandstand and clamor for restrictions on a president's power to do so. A president, on whose shoulders fall exceptional responsibilities for foreign affairs and national security, must have flexibility to deal with exceptional situations.

But the Iranian business didn't work out and should not have been allowed to take the turn it did. The original plan was apparently to explore relationships with a seemingly receptive moderate Iranian faction. The purpose was twofold: to try to moderate current Iranian policy and to prepare for the day when the intransigent Ayatollah Khomeini departs and new leaders take over.

One may doubt whether there was much room for successful maneuvering in the present situation in Iran. The political infighting has brought little clarity to the factional struggles; indeed, a group of Reagan emissaries, including former National Security Adviser Robert McFarlane (credited with initiating the operation), apparently got caught in the crossfire in Tehran and risked becoming hostages themselves.

A collateral operation to persuade the Iranians to have their Lebanese clients free American hostages seems to have been part of the original plan but to have virtually replaced it. It is here where things went bad, and the operation should have been suspended.

The Iranian demands required that President Reagan reverse in private positions he continued to espouse in public. Although he was dealing with a faction of the Iranian government, for all practical purposes, he was negotiating with terrorists. In agreeing to supply Iran with weapons, despite an American embargo, he was paying ransom.

He also compromised his efforts to pressure allies to take a common tough stand against terrorism. Those efforts call for not negotiating directly with terrorists and isolating nations proven to support terrorists or to act as terrorists themselves. Iran is high among such governments, even though administration officials assert that Iranian terrorism has been quiet for about a year. But that may be because Iran has its hands full with other matters — the internal struggles and the continuing war with Iraq.

That war makes provision of arms to Iran a particularly wrong move. Iraq is no rose, but the U.S. interest is that the war end as a negotiated stalemate that would block fanatical Iranian expansionism.

The plight of hostages held by terrorists in the Middle East is of deep human concern to the American government and people. But we are, in effect, at war with the terrorist groups and with some governments, and in a war there will be civilian casualties.

All acceptable efforts to free the hostages should be pursued. But we cannot yield to extortion and compromise the national interest. That would not only make us even more vulnerable to extortion but make it more difficult for us to assemble the multinational counterterrorism front that is the ultimate solution.

## Detroit Free Press
*Detroit, MI*
*November 11, 1986*

THE U.S. GOVERNMENT is obliged to try every reasonable means — overt or covert, direct or indirect, diplomatic and economic — to win the freedom of U.S. citizens held hostage in Lebanon. However, arranging the secret delivery of arms to Iran's fanatical, terrorism-sponsoring regime goes far beyond the reasonable: It is damaging to our vital political interests, foolish and morally disgraceful.

The evidence suggests that President ("Terrorists, be on notice: You can run but you cannot hide") Reagan approved the secret plan to bribe the regime of the Ayatollah Khomeini with military spare parts. The operation to ship hardware to Iran through an Israeli intermediary apparently began at the time when the United States was stepping up its official efforts to forge a unified anti-terrorist front with European allies. Secretary of State George Shultz was commuting to European capitals advocating a total ban on arms sales to Iran — a move that was supposed to bring the Tehran regime to its senses by denying it the supplies it needed to continue the war with Iraq.

Now, the whole world knows that the U.S. government was speaking with a forked tongue to both foe and ally. Why would the United States compromise itself as the leader in the crusade against terrorism? A semi-official leak from the White House has it that the president has been overwhelmed by a "deeply felt desire" to free the American hostages lately. But let's look at the results.

Over the last 1½ years, three Americans — the Rev. Benjamin Weir, the Rev. Lawrence Jenco and David Jacobsen — have been freed by Shiite Muslim groups that reportedly are Iran's proxies in Lebanon. Three others, however — Frank Reed, Joseph Cicippio and Edward Tracy — have been kidnapped in West Beirut in the past two months. So much for U.S. gains.

As to the losses, they are so staggering that one doesn't even know where to begin the count. They include the embarrassment for the United States — so bad that Mr. Shultz, one of the administration's biggest assets, a skilled diplomat and a man of integrity, is hard-pressed not to resign. They also include the inevitable collapse of efforts to prosecute individuals breaking the laws that prohibit selling arms to enemies of the United States. One such case involves an Israeli general and a dozen others accused of conspiring to sell Iran $2 billion worth of U.S. arms; the trial, now unlikely, was scheduled to begin next year in New York.

The Reagan administration has won nothing in its sleazy game with the Middle East's hostage-takers; the Iranians have only been given more reasons to believe that terrorism pays off. The administration's bungling has made the policies of the ailing Ayatollah Khomeini appear successful right at the moment when Iran is bracing itself for the era after his death. It is hard to imagine a more complete blunder.

## The Miami Herald
### Miami, FL, November 9, 1986

**PRESIDENT CARTER** in 1980 expanded his executive order freezing Iranian assets in the United States to void pre-1979 contracts involving "the sale, supply, or other transfer" by U.S. citizens of "items, commodities, or products" to Iran. It was essentially an arms embargo.

That U.S. policy has never been rescinded publicly. In fact, it was expanded by the Reagan Administration, which has repeatedly said that the U.S. Government won't deal with a government that sponsors terrorism.

Hostage-taking is a favored tactic of Iranian-backed terrorists. After all, it worked well for the Ayatollah Khomeini's henchmen when they ensnared 52 Americans in the U.S. Embassy in Tehran in 1979. That act triggered the arms embargo. And Ronald Reagan campaigned in that long autumn of the hostage drama on how he'd handle terrorists. Mr. Reagan said that once the U.S. Government has identified terrorists, it should move swiftly against them — with armed force if necessary.

The Reagan White House knows that the Islamic Jihad, the group holding two of the five Americans still hostage in Lebanon, is backed by Iran. Administration sources have admitted that the White House knows this because during the last year it secretly shipped to Tehran U.S.-made military parts contracted to Iran before 1979. In exchange, three U.S. hostages in Lebanon were freed.

It is gratifying for these men and their families that they are home. But the means aren't justified by the end, which is nowhere in sight. Giving in to terrorists once means only that they will strike again and again. And so they have: Three other Americans were taken hostage in Beirut in October.

Even beyond that threat, the consequences of U.S. appeasement of Iran and its jackals are appalling to contemplate. The United States is officially neutral on the Iran-Iraq war. Victory by an ayatollah-ruled Iran would increase the fanatical Islamic foment in the Mideast and leave control of a crucial portion of the West's oil supply in unreasonable hands. No wonder that Secretary of State George Shultz and Defense Secretary Caspar Weinberger opposed this deal. It contradicts sound U.S. policy on every count.

The White House refuses to explain this contradiction. Instead, it accuses the media of jeopardizing the release of the other hostages. It says that technically the arms embargo wasn't violated. That's splitting hairs, since the order does not specifically list military parts but does say U.S. "products."

When the President tells the world that his Administration is doing all in its power to free the remaining hostages, this should mean that the Republic's guiding principles will not be trampled in secret. The American people, along with U.S. allies whom this Administration urges to punish terrorist sponsors, deserve a full, immediate accounting from the President. Against the advice of his Secretaries of State and Defense, he has placed the United States's credibility and security against further terrorist acts at terrible risk.

## The Washington Times
### Washington, DC, November 6, 1986

Robert McFarlane's pilgrimage to Tehran, as bizarre as it was secretive, suggests a new low in the non-war against terrorism. U.S. intelligence sources have confirmed the McFarlane visit two months ago, and the speaker of the Iranian Parliament alleges that President Reagan's former national security adviser brought a Bible signed by Mr. Reagan and a cake in the shape of a key. The revolutionary guards promptly devoured the cake. What was done with the Bible we are not told, which perhaps is just as well.

The apparent purpose of this mysterious mission was to "open a dialogue" with what passes for a government in the merry old land of the ayatollah. In return for the cake and a compromise of the U.S. arms embargo, the ayatollah was supposed to keep his terrorists down on the ranch and free some more of the hostages his hatchet-men have sequestered.

The experiment in appeasement was a miserable and humiliating failure. The imam kept Mr. McFarlane and his party under house arrest for five days and then gave them an unceremonious boot. What do you do when even the tyrants you want to appease won't cooperate?

The mullahs that reign in Tehran are religious fanatics. They believe that the terrorism they have raised to a science is a duty laid on them by Allah, who speaks through the ayatollah. The Reagan administration should know better than to try to bargain with these worthies. Whatever the McFarlane approach might have accomplished, it was not worth the embarrassment that ensued.

Last week the Western world was in high but inconsequential dudgeon over Syrian complicity in international terrorism. This week, it transpires, we have been fiddling with Syria's ally in Tehran. What we will do for an encore in the "war against terrorism" is anyone's guess.

## The Record
### Hackensack, NJ, November 6, 1986

The word in Iran these days is beware of Americans bearing gifts — specifically Colt pistols, a key-shaped cake, and a Bible autographed by President Reagan.

Those were some of the items that former national-security adviser Robert McFarlane and four other Americans are said to have brought along when they flew secretly into Tehran in September. Their goal was to enlist the Islamic republic's aid in freeing a handful of American hostages held by Shiite Moslems in southern Lebanon.

Details of the mission are still emerging, but on balance it appears to have failed. The Iranians informed the envoys that the United States would first have to lift its ban on the sale of military equipment and spare parts; unfreeze Iran's bank holdings in this country; and turn over $3.5 billion in property accumulated by the late shah. Some progress may have been made before the talks were caught short, possibly due to protests from more militant, anti-American quarters.

We may never know exactly what went on in Iran. But in this country, the McFarlane mission has raised some provocative questions. Specifically, what ever became of President Reagan's promise never to negotiate with terrorists? Shiite Moslems who kidnap American civilians in southern Lebanon surely fit his definition of terrorists, even if U.S.-armed contras who kidnap Nicaraguan civilians do not. Yet here was Robert McFarlane negotiating with the terrorists' masters in Tehran itself. Does this mean that not all terrorists are equal? Are some more approachable than others?

•

Despite the apparent failure of the McFarlane mission, one hostage, David P. Jacobsen, was released this week. This welcome news may signify some even more welcome changes in the Islamic republic. When pro-Iranian elements in Lebanon released the Rev. Lawrence Jenco, another American, in July, they made clear that it was because of his pressing medical problems. When they released Mr. Jacobsen, they were conspicuously silent. This could be a sign that Iran's attitude toward the remaining hostages is softening — along with its implacable hostility toward all things Western.

And there are other signs. In Tehran, the police have arrested Mehdi Hashemi, a high official in charge of promoting and exporting Iran's fundamentalist revolution. In August, Mr. Hashemi was said to have tried to smuggle guns into Saudi Arabia via a planeload of pilgrims; to Iran's embarrassment, the weapons were discovered and several pilgrims arrested. Then, just last month, Mr. Hashemi's gunmen reportedly kidnapped the Syrian chargé d'affaires whose offense was to have pushed too hard for the Shiite-held hostages' release. The envoy was released a few hours later and the affair hushed up, but Iran was embarrassed once more. As Iran's sole Arab ally in the war with Iraq, Syria is one country it cannot afford to anger.

Is Mr. Hashemi's arrest an indication that the revolutionary government has begun curbing its most militant extremists? Is Mr. Jacobsen's release an indication that pro-Iranian elements in Lebanon are also getting the message? If so, the implications could be dramatic. A more moderate and pragmatic Iran might be in a position to reach an accommodation with Saudi Arabia and Kuwait, its conservative neighbors across the Persian Gulf. It might conclude a peace with Iraq, thereby ending six years of mass carnage. By reining in its followers in southern Lebanon, it might allow that shattered nation to pick up the pieces in its 11-year civil war. It might even lighten the burden of the Iranians themselves, who are suffering under the triple load of clerical oppression, never-ending war, and the collapse of the oil boom.

Of course, nothing of the sort might happen. In 1934, Hitler was supposed to have curbed the Nazi Party's "extremist" wing when he crushed his rival Ernst Rohm. Yet it is unlikely the world was any better off for it.

## St. Paul Pioneer Press & Dispatch

*St. Paul, MN, November 8, 1986*

The United States has bitter non-relations with a number of other countries. Is it a good idea for Washington to make overtures toward them occasionally? The answer is yes.

In the same way that reasonably friendly ties with China seemed inconceivable not long ago, envisioning the United States and Iran ever getting along again is awfully difficult. But only those who are strategically ignorant fail to recognize shared interests between the two countries, and only those who are shortsighted assume that Iran (much less the world) will remain the same.

Yet, has it been right for the Reagan administration to send military spare parts to Iran for use in its war with Iraq? It sure does not look like it, and only vagueness about White House actions and purpose softens the criticism.

If the primary aim has been to trade for hostages, it has been a mistake, as cruel as it sounds. The West simply cannot capitulate that way. Nor, more specifically, can Washington expect other capitals to take seriously its appeals for unbending toughness against terrorists.

If, however, the principal goal has been to strengthen more moderate elements in Iran, then the Reagan administration would be on slightly better footing.

Even then, however, the president still would be obligated to show how a marginally less radical regime in Tehran would pose a substantially smaller threat to the entire Middle East and elsewhere. Because unless the administration knows something secret about the infighting in the Iranian leadership, it is hard to believe that Iran will get and stay moderate enough soon.

## The Union Leader

*Manchester, NH, November 12, 1986*

The truth about the alleged U.S.-Iranian deal is that we don't know the truth, but that hasn't kept wolf-pack journalists and politicians from presuming President Reagan guilty until proven otherwise.

The leftist press and TV network media have seldom let responsible news-gathering get in the way of going after Ronald Reagan and this case seems no exception, even if innocent people get hurt in the process.

The usual "unnamed senior officials" and "anonymous spokesmen" have now been mixed in with Iranian officials (always a trustworthy lot!) to paint an all-black picture, one which the Democrats, newly-fattened by their election successes, are quick to exploit.

This newspaper isn't reluctant to pass judgment on the facts, but we won't do so until the facts are known.

In the meantime, we think former hostage David Jacobsen could have saved his breath when he pleaded with the news media last week, "In the name of God, will you please just be responsible and back off."

When it comes to Ronald Reagan, the liberal news media are stone deaf.

# ▎ran Arms Shipments Confirmed; ▎Deal for Hostage Releases Denied

President Reagan November 13, 1986 publicly acknowledged for the first time that the U.S. had secretly sent "defensive weapons and spare parts" to Iran but denied that the shipments were part of a deal for the release of American hostages held by Moslem extremists in Lebanon. In a nationally broadcast speech, Reagan said that he had sought to improve relations with Iran because of its strategic importance to the U.S., and that he had sent arms "to convince Teheran that our negotiators were acting with my authority." Various reports about shipments of arms to Iran had emerged since the release Nov. 2 of David Jacobsen, an American held hostage by the Islamic Jihad (Holy War), a Shiite group in Lebanon linked to the Iranian regime. Reagan and his former national security adviser Robert McFarlane confirmed that McFarlane had travelled to Iran with a planeload of military hardware in the spring of 1986 but provided no details about the mission except that the U.S. delegation stayed for four days and was treated civilly. Of other stories that had emerged, involving ships of Danish registry and ports in Spain and Italy, Reagan said, "As far as we're concerned, not one of them is true." Reagan said that the total amount of arms sent to Iran was less than a planeload, and that the arms had not altered the military balance in the six-year war between Iran and Iraq. The President said that the "secret diplomatic initiative" had four goals: to renew a friendly relationship between the U.S. and Iran, to end the Iran-Iraq war, to eliminate state-sponsored terrorism, and—despite his denial of a deal—"to effect the safe return of all hostages." Reagan did not mention widespread reports that Israel had been a conduit for American arms shipments to Iran. Many reports indicated that the U.S. had not shipped arms directly to Iran, but replenished supplies that Israel, with U.S. consent, had sent to Iran.

In his speech, Reagan insisted that he had not reversed the administration policy of making no concessions to terrorists. "Those who think that we have 'gone soft' on terrorism should take up the question with [Libyan leader] Col. [Muammer el-] Qaddafi," Reagan said, referring to the April 1986 bombing of Libyan cities. To back up his denial that he had reversed his policy of never negotiating with terrorists, Reagan said that "since U.S. government contact began with Iran, there's been no evidence of Iranian government complicity in acts of terrorism against the U.S."

## The Hutchinson News

*Hutchinson, KS*
*November 15, 1986*

Give Mr. Reagan credit for trying. But not much credit.

He did try for 18 months to reestablish official contact with the Iranian government, and do what diplomacy is supposed to do: Encourage them to do what we want them to do.

Then he blew it. Massively.

His failure is so miserable that it overshadows the scant credit he earns for beginning negotiations in the first place.

As he confessed publicly Thursday evening on national television, his 18 months of negotiations led his nation to send arms to Iran. He did this at the very moment the United States was demanding that our allies stop coddling terrorists.

His startling decision also came in the wake of his own repeated promises never to do it, thereby compounding an error of judgment with blue smoke, mirrors, and blatant lies.

If this were the first such wretched decision, it would be merely unfortunate.

However, the outrageous series of secret Iranian lies and policy reversals is part of an unfolding pattern of deceit, stupidity, and theatrical bumbling. While his deceit in Iran is being revealed, his administration's flauting of the law over Nicaragua also is being dangled before the world.

And all that comes with the backdrop of the "disinformation" scheme of only a few weeks ago, the transparency of a hostage trade with the Russians, and the astonishing imprecision resulting from a summit meeting in Iceland.

"Feel good politics" has its limitations. Everyone is getting a good dose of those limitations now, though the dismal prospect is that more of the same blue smoke, mirrors, lies and theatrical stupidity lies ahead.

## Richmond Times-Dispatch

*Richmond, VA, November 15, 1986*

President Reagan has now presented a spirited, almost indignant defense: By sending emissaries and a single planeload of defensive weapons to Iran, his administration did not breach its policies of no concessions to terrorists, no deals with terrorist states and no weapons to the state that won't compromise to end the Gulf war. His intentions, he insists, were honorable: to encourage moderation of Iran's abhorrent behavior at home and abroad.

Responsible critics will grant the president his good intentions. Iran is important. It is also in flux, and U.S. assistance for certain factions there could be mutually beneficial. But good intentions don't always amount to good answers. Mr Reagan and his inner circle decided that the hope of achieving a worthy goal outweighed the risk of appearing to contradict his own stated policies. They decided that utmost secrecy would minimize the risk. They decided wrong.

Would it have made a difference had President Reagan widened his consultations before acting? Many of his critics, on both sides of congressional aisles, say that had they been told of the plan they would have warned him off it. They say so, however, with the benefit of hindsight. And there is the probability, almost the certainty, that the more persons apprised of the plan, the more likely a pre-emptory leak, whether or not the majority of congressional or State Department representatives approved.

There seems also, after Mr. Reagan's speech Thursday night, the probability that he would have taken this initiative regardless of advice to the contrary. As president, he is the chief executor of foreign policy; as such, he takes the decisions, takes the chances — and takes the flak or the credit as it comes.

This time, he reaps flak, deservedly, though he's hardly the first or the last politician to argue that a slight deviation from principle ought not imperil his principled status. Certainly critics abroad who have themselves delivered pious public pronouncements and (large) private ransoms can hardly smirk at Mr. Reagan's claim to be only a little bit pregnant. But the quarrel is over means, not ends. The goals regarding Iran remain worthy. The president and his critics must realize that the nation's interest, and ultimately their own, lie more in finding ways to share credit for achieving them than dispensing blame for the failures so far.

## The Pittsburgh PRESS

*Pittsburgh, PA, November 14, 1986*

A government desiring respect and credibility at home and abroad should follow, among others, three clear rules: Do as you say. Admit mistakes as a first step to correcting them. Speak truthfully.

Sadly, the Reagan administration is violating those guidelines, as demonstrated by the embarrassing, harmful arms-for-hostages deals with Iran, deals that President Reagan insisted last night are not deals.

Since 1979, U.S. policy has been to deny weapons to the ayatollahs. Washington vociferously urged allies to join the embargo. It bolstered its words with sound geopolitical arguments: A victory by Iran in its six-year-old war with Iraq would destabilize the region and threaten such friends as Saudi Arabia.

In addition, the administration had a firm, principled policy on international terrorism:

"The U.S. government will make no concessions to terrorists. It will not pay ransoms, release prisoners, change its policies or agree to other acts that might encourage additional terrorism." Allies that strayed from that hard line were derided as wimps.

For two years, however, the White House has been secretly negotiating with Iran, arranging for arms shipments in return for the release of three hostages by pro-Iranian terrorists in Lebanon.

Incredibly, the administration thought it could say one thing, even to its own secretary of state, and do another. It learned otherwise when its covert action was made public by one Iranian faction.

The damage is incalculable. The administration had pressed Britain not to send Iran parts for Chieftain tanks. Meanwhile, it had been furnishing parts for lethal F-4 Phantom jets.

It had leaned on West Germany and Holland not to service Iran's civilian aircraft, which could fly supplies to Tehran. Meanwhile, it sent parts to keep C-130 military transports flying.

The Europeans are using words like "hypocrisy." The Iranians now know the great value President Reagan puts on each hostage and are busy marking up their merchandise.

An Iranian victory in the war would threaten stability throughout the Middle East by spreading Islamic fundamentalism and revolution throughout the region.

Saudi Arabia, Kuwait, Jordan and Egypt believe an Iranian victory over Iraq would, one Egyptian newspaper said, "sow the seeds of future conflict" and have a negative impact on their relations with the United States.

While most friendly Arab governments have remained publicly silent to this point because the hostages' lives are at stake, private mumblings of "double-cross" undoubtedly are being heard throughout the region.

Secretary of State George P. Shultz probably has mumbled the same word to himself a few times in the last week. Still the loyalist, though, he has reined in his pride to this point, probably waiting for the heat to cool before he resigns to preserve whatever dignity and credibility he still can muster. The guess here is that he will leave by the end of the year.

Who can blame him?

A sensible government — and more and more it appears that ours no longer is — would acknowledge its blunder and sit down with both political parties at home and with the allies abroad and seek to repair the shambles, to arrive at a unified, workable policy, if possible.

That policy might include working toward opening doors to Iran, not an unthinkable action if done aboveboard with an eye to laying some foundation of trust with the ailing Khomeini's potential successor.

Instead, Mr. Reagan said last night, the " 'no-concessions policy' remains in force," that weapons were not traded for hostages, that the 18-month initiative was an "evenhanded" attempt to settle the Iran-Iraq war.

In recent months, Mr. Reagan has had a non-summit summit and now explains he has made non-deal deals.

That's a non-explanation explanation.

### The Salt Lake Tribune

*Salt Lake City, UT*
*November 14, 1986*

Money has long been recognized as the "root of all evil," an observation that seems increasingly applicable to the current controversy involving American arms shipments to Iran and their possible linkage with the release of American and French hostages in Lebanon.

On the same day two Frenchmen were released after being taken to Damascus from Beirut, French Foreign Minister Jean-Bernard Raimond announced his government and Iran would soon sign an agreement under which Paris would make an initial $330 million payment on a $1 billion claim by Iran. The claim represents a loan extended by Iran in 1974.

A day later, the Iranian chief delegate to the United Nations, Said Rajaie-Khorassani, in confirming Iran had received some arms shipments from U.S. sources, said his country would consider it a positive step if the United States returned Iranian funds frozen following the seizure of the American embassy in Tehran in 1979, along with delivering arms Iran has already paid for.

He also dangled another plum, the prospect of better U.S.-Iranian relations: "Of course, the fulfillment of the United States obligation would be interpreted by us and the Moslem people of the region as a positive step toward the abandonment of its hostilities toward the Moslems of the region and would consequently ease up the anti-American sentiments in the region," he said.

His statement was, essentially, reiteration of the position taken some days earlier by the speaker of the Iranian Parliament, Hojatolislam Hashemi Rafsanjani. He said Tehran was prepared to mediate with the kidnappers of American and French hostages in Lebanon if Washington agreed to release the goods and money it had held since the time of the 1979 hostage crisis.

In short, it is becoming progressively obvious that if the right amount of silver crosses the right number of Iranian palms the likelihood rises proportionately that American and French hostages and maybe some others, held in Lebanon by Tehran's surrogates in Lebanon like Islamic Jihad and the Revolutionary Justice Organization, will be released.

## Minneapolis Star and Tribune

*Minneapolis, MN, November 14, 1986*

President Reagan has thrown a bucket of water on the firestorm kindled by his dealings with Iran. A bucket might have helped earlier, but Thursday night it fizzled. His brief television speech will not dampen bipartisan criticism, nor should it. The president can expect mild appreciation for saying more about what has gone on. He can expect strong challenges to his conduct of U.S. policy — conduct that shows every sign of ineptness.

The president said he had tried to send Iran a signal that the United States wanted to replace U.S.-Iranian animosity with a "new relationship." The goal is admirable. One sign of Iranian willingness to move in that direction, he said, would be helping to secure the release of hostages in Lebanon. So far, so good. But evidently the president decided that shipping "a small amount" of military supplies to Iran would be a sign of U.S. reciprocity. Last night he ridiculed the notion that the United States had "swapped boatloads or planeloads of American weapons for the return of American hostages." The United States had sent less than a planeload, he said, and only of "defensive weapons and spare parts for defensive systems." He did not make clear whether other shipments had gone through quasi-official channels with tacit U.S. approval, as Iranians and others have suggested.

Nothing is inherently wrong with furnishing military equipment to another country. But there is plenty wrong with sending it to a country that the president and his top aides have accused in the past of state-supported terrorism. There is plenty wrong with asserting that the United States would make no concessions to hostage holders when it has done so with those influencing, if not directing, the groups in Lebanon responsible. And there is plenty wrong with pious words about U.S. efforts to "bring an end to the Persian Gulf war" when the administration appears preoccupied with hostages. Reagan is right to pursue an opening to Iran. He is wrong to do so at the cost of U.S. credibility and good will in the Middle East and beyond.

## Detroit Free Press

*Detroit, MI  November 15, 1986*

SORRY, Mr. President, but we don't quite buy your geo-strategic explanation of why you sent your former national security adviser to Iran. Why don't you just admit that you have glimpsed the end of your remarkable presidency just around the corner and don't want to go out as your much-maligned predecessor did: as one unable to to do very much about releasing U.S. hostages?

Certainly it makes sense for the United States to try to keep some line of communication open to the ayatollahs and mullahs who are running Iran — but by giving them arms? The demise of Khomeini won't come close to ending the rule of the fanatic brand of Islamic fundamentalists who ousted and succeeded the late shah.

Certainly, though, if such a sage, well-thought-out strategy were the basis for an approach to Iran, we feel certain that your eminent secretary of state, George Shultz, would not only have known about and approved it, but would have been one of its architects. Mr. McFarlane and the mysterious Col. Oliver North were not the best choices for even the bizarre Bible-and-cake mission.

You really tried, though, Mr. President. Your charm and skill as the great communicator they say you are came through. It was a good speech. We are reminded, though, of another maker of good presidential speeches, who once said that "you may fool all of the people some of time; you can even fool some of the people all of the time; but you can't fool all of the people all of the time."

## The News and Courier
### CHARLESTON EVENING POST

*Charleston, SC, November 15, 1986*

When President Reagan announced that he would speak to the nation to answer allegations that the White House has been sending arms to Iran to secure the release of American hostages, he said that he could not recall another instance in which so much misinformation had been disseminated.

It is a pity that in his actual address the president did not remind his listeners how the tangled web of misinformation got started. Al Shiraa (The Mast), a Moslem magazine published in West Beirut, began spinning the first threads of half truths and outright lies in a story about the McFarlane mission to Tehran. The story that President Reagan's former national security adviser, Robert McFarlane, had negotiated a hostages-for-arms deal was planted with malicious aforethought, either by Syria or by Iranian hardliners. The objective was to rupture the new relationship the United States was attempting to establish with Iran by means of secret diplomacy.

Hojatolislam Akbar Hashemi Rafsanjani, speaker of Iran's Parliament and a leader of the moderate faction in the power struggle to succeed Ayatollah Ruhollah Khomeini, was forced to cover his back. Unable to deny that the McFarlane mission had taken place, he came up with a new version of what happened. He claimed that instead of being welcomed, as the Al Shiraa story had claimed, Mr. McFarlane was detained at his hotel and later sent away. It was Mr. Rafsanjani who introduced a ludicrous note into the story, describing a clown-like McFarlane bearing gifts — a Bible signed by President Reagan and a cake baked in the shape of a key.

Given a choice between the two versions of the McFarlane mission put out by the Iranians and/or Syrians and Mr. Reagan's account of what has been going on, it would seem reasonable to accept the president's word. Although bereft of any Arabian Nights color, the president's description of Mr. McFarlane' mission and his explanation of the initiative to improve relations with Iran was convincing. It would also be reasonable to assume that President Reagan's decision to sound out moderate elements in the Iranian regime, to sweeten them with a token shipment of defensive weapons and spare parts, and hope that these overtures would help in securing the release of American hostages held in Beirut, would be applauded by the Democrats. Mr. Reagan, after all, has merely been doing secretly, quietly and in miniature what many of his critics have been demanding.

It would not have been surprising if the admission of secret diplomacy with Iran, the relaxing of the arms ban and the bid to secure the hostages release through the good offices of Tehran had brought a heap of trouble on President Reagan's head from his own hardline purists; but for the Democrats to castigate the president for seeking solutions by negotiation is pure hypocrisy.

If the opening to Iran has been carried out in the prudent and modest way described by the president — and there is no reason to doubt his veracity — he has been given a bum rap, not only by his political foes but also by his in-house critics.

It is not only entirely ethical for the administration to seek normal relations with Iran — as was done successfully with Communist China and unsuccessfully with Cuba — it is necessary to establish contacts with the people who will rule in Tehran when the aged and ailing Ayatolloh Khomeini dies. It is not only ethical but necessary to try use U.S. influence to secure the release of U.S. hostages.

So many facts have been lost in all the story-telling. If, as a by-product, the release of three Americans held in Beirut by Islamic Jihad fanatics was secured by shipping a small consignment of arms, then the president's pledge not to give in to ransom demands by terrorists has not been violated. From the start the kidnappers in Beirut have been calling for the release of a group of 17 of their comrades who were convicted of terrorism and are imprisoned in Kuwait. They have not got what they wanted. But three Americans, who might be dead today, are free men.

A price was paid for the release of Nicholas Daniloff. It is not at all clear whether any price at all was paid for the release of Benjamin Weir, Lawrence Jenco and David Jacobsen. It would be naive to imagine that there would have been any diminution of terrorism if Mr. Daniloff had been abandoned in his KGB cell or if the three men released by the Islamic Jihad had been left to rot in Beirut. Dealing with terrorists is inevitable. They lose when they do not achieve their demands. We lose even if they do not achieve their demands but they kill their hostages. The murder of helpless prisoners is one of the worst forms of terrorism. Anything that can be done, short of giving in to terrorist demands, must be done.

Despite the howls from the media wolfpack, the barking of conservative columnists who rarely leave their kennels for the real world and the finger-pointing of hypocritical political opponents, we do not believe that President Reagan has betrayed his principles. When culpability is clear, as it was in the case of Moammar Gadhafi, you hit hard. When the evidence is shrouded in fog and the terrorist group is as enigmatic as the Islamic Jihad, you get as close to the enemy as possible before you strike.

As a result of all the hue and cry, Mr. Reagan has been caught in the glare of a searchlight. We are inclined to echo the words of hostage David Jacobsen and say to everyone: "In the name of God, will you just please be responsible and back off!"

ARMS FOR IRAN

# The Kansas City Times

*Kansas City, MO, November 15, 1986*

Faced with the unveiling of what Sen. Barry Goldwater calls "probably one of the major mistakes the United States has ever made in foreign policy," Mr. Reagan went on television Thursday night to offer a chaotic array of absurd arguments, half-baked excuses and informational tidbits billed as "the facts."

None of the president's explanations and excuses for sending military supplies to Iran makes sense. Some are more ridiculous than others. But all support the conclusion that common sense took a holiday every time the president sat down to consider Iran and the hostages in Lebanon.

Mr. Reagan went out of his way to deny specific details of certain press reports. But he confirmed a crucial and, until a few days ago, almost unimaginable charge: that he sent military supplies to a regime that once held American diplomats hostage, continues to denounce the U.S. in strident terms, supports international terrorism, and refuses to end a war in which Iranian children are used as human mine detectors.

Why? "My purpose was to convince Tehran that our negotiators were acting with my authority," Mr. Reagan said. The American people are supposed to sit in front of their television sets and believe the only way the president's representatives can get a hearing with Iranian officials of dubious authority is to buy it with the most humiliating currency the ayatollah could have demanded: military hardware.

It wasn't a lot of hardware, the president was quick to explain. Only "modest deliveries" that, piled together, "could easily fit into a single cargo plane." Even if this is true, it fails to address the charge that Israel, at the request of the U.S. and in return for American arms, sent more weapons to Iran. The Israeli role is central to the entire debate that Mr. Reagan sought to quell. He did not even mention Israel. The president noted that the shipments consisted partly of "defensive weapons," whatever that means.

Mr. Reagan insists that his stated policy of not dealing with terrorists remains intact. To say that, he also had to claim that Iran gave up terrorism a year and a half ago. He forgot to mention this to the State Department, which has been telling the world otherwise.

The taking of American hostages in Lebanon by pro-Iranian groups clearly constitutes terrorism. Mr. Reagan argues that the Iranian government cannot be held responsible. That is dubious. It becomes absurd when Mr. Reagan himself explicitly links the terrorists with Iran: "Hostages have come home — and we welcome the efforts that the government of Iran has taken in the past and is currently undertaking."

What more can a terrorist government want? Mr. Reagan holds it blameless when hostages are taken, and heaps praise upon it when hostages — the very same hostages, in fact — are released.

The president berates his critics for drawing logical conclusions when we send arms to Iran and — reportedly within days, if not hours — pro-Iranian groups release a hostage. Not once, not twice, but three times.

Mr. Reagan's central defense seems to be his own state of mind: He did not embark on his Iranian adventure with a deal in mind, and he still doesn't consider it a deal.

Even if this were true, it makes absolutely no difference in terms of the danger in which he has placed Americans around the world, and the harm he does to the logic of American foreign policy. No matter what he says, the conclusions that have been drawn by congressmen, academics, diplomats and the American people will also be drawn by terrorists and by our allies. Those conclusions are that Mr. Reagan will do virtually anything to win back American hostages, and that the national interest is not seen in terms of clear consistency and reason.

# The Salt Lake Tribune

*Salt Lake City, UT*
*November 15, 1986*

There seems to be considerable hair-splitting emanating from the White House over whether the weapons shipments to Iran played any role in the release of American hostages held in Lebanon. President Reagan told the American public Thursday night that such assertions were "utterly false."

tages must have been pretty high on the agenda during those 18 months of secret talks with Iranian "moderates." The president, after all, said one objective was "to effect the safe return of all hostages."

Also, a senior administration official who briefed reporters before Mr. Reagan's speech told them, "We got an agreement from the elements that we were dealing with that there would be no more hostage-taking or terrorism conducted against the United States by Iran or by any groups supported by Iran." Ordinarily, such an agreement would have to entail getting something in return, like arms shipments.

Then on Friday, about the same time the president was reiterating that the United States "does not pay tribute to terrorists," his national security adviser, Vice Adm. John Poindexter, said dialogue will continue with Iran in the hope that "we can make further progress and get the rest of the hostages home."

These statements make it clear that the administration, with the deserving and unfettered support of the American public, rates freeing the hostages as a prime target in its talks with the Iranians. Assertions by the president and his aides that their freedom was not contingent on the arms shipments become suspect when assessed against apparently accurate reports that the hostages' releases came coincidental with the several shipments of arms and spare parts to Tehran.

Adding substance to suspicions that some sort of "deal" was worked out involving hostage releases is the revelation by the Treasury Department that American and Iranian financial officials met two weeks ago in The Hague to discuss the return of nearly $500 million of impounded assets to the Tehran government. While no such transaction has taken place, logic dictates that some sort of quid pro quo would be demanded during such talks in order to consummate such a transaction; like the freeing of American hostages.

Mr. Reagan, in the strictest technical sense, may not have paid "tribute to terrorists." At least not directly. But his own utterances, and those of his aides, leave the impression that his administration has little aversion to dealing with the terrorists' sponsors, like those "moderates" in Tehran. It is a mighty fine distinction, one that borders on the untrue.

# THE COMMERCIAL APPEAL

*Memphis, TN, November 15, 1986*

A GOVERNMENT desiring respect and credibility at home and abroad should follow at least three clear rules: Do as you say. Admit mistakes as a first step to correcting them. Speak truthfully.

Sadly, the Reagan administration, in its sixth year in office, is violating those guidelines in the arms deals with Iran.

The President's defense Thursday night relied more on an appeal for trust than on facts and arguments.

Although he confirmed the secret arms shipments, he denied they were a trade for hostages. What did he mean, then, when he said that U.S. officials emphasized to their Iranian contacts that the "most significant step Iran could take would be to use its influence in Lebanon to secure the release of all hostages held there"?

In the simple language by which citizens of the world communicate with each other, that translates to "arms for hostages." Euphemisms don't change the cause-and-effect relationship.

The President also belittled the shipments, saying, "These modest deliveries . . . could easily fit into a single cargo plane."

So could a nuclear bomb.

But laying aside the possibility of high technology and advanced weaponry — he did not say what had been shipped — the President laid out a scenario of wishful thinking and artlessness.

The United States wanted to help Iranian moderates in their struggle to succeed the elderly and infirm Ayatollah Khomeini. The arms were intended to let those Iranians know that the President had authorized such contact.

The secret diplomacy, the President said, had four reasons: to renew relations with Iran, to bring an "honorable end" to the Iran-Iraq war, to reduce terrorism and to rescue the hostages.

Several factors intrude on the means chosen to achieve those admirable goals:

• Iran's rulers — those the United States wants to be ousted — had to know about the shipments and the visits of negotiators. Some of those officials decided to make the talks public, either to embarrass the United States — a favorite sport — or to protect their flanks — a condition of survival in Iranian politics. It was inevitable, and yet the administration had no rational, fall-back position, raising the suspicion that its double-talk is proportional to its blunder.

• Arms shipments don't bring stalemated wars to honorable ends. They give one side or the other that much more reason to continue fighting.

• Similarly, arms tend to strengthen a government that rules by force, as Iran's does, rather than a political opposition.

Listen to a "senior administration official" try to talk his way out of this diplomatic sinkhole: "If we reveal actually what (arms) went in — amount, dates, specifics — then the factions that are not operating in our interest in Iran will use that information against those factions that are more moderate and that are trying to help."

Iran is a police state. The hostile factions round up, torture and execute their opponents right and left. It is inconceivable that they were unaware of the fact or the content of the arms shipments.

The real background against which these events have taken place indicts the President's Iranian diplomacy as being foolish and self-destructive.

Since 1979, U.S. policy has been to deny weapons to the ayatollahs. Washington vociferously urged allies to join the embargo. It argued that a victory by Iran in its grinding war with Iraq would destabilize the region and threaten such friends as Saudi Arabia.

In addition, the administration had a firm, principled policy on international terrorism: No concessions to terrorists; no ransom to hostage-takers. Allies that strayed from that hard line were derided as wimps.

For two years, however, the White House has been negotiating secretly with Iran. It said one thing and did another.

The Europeans are using words like "hypocrisy." The Arabs, who had been assured of Washington's neutrality in the Gulf war, are using words like "doublecross." Secretary of State George Shultz, who opposed the arms shipments, has had his credibility around the world undermined.

Reagan's denials don't change reality. His diplomacy is a shambles.

# The Hartford Courant

*Hartford, CT, November 14, 1986*

The National Security Council's staff members have been used for sensitive diplomatic missions with good results in the past. National Security Adviser Henry A. Kissinger's secret negotiations with Chinese officials, leading to President Richard M. Nixon's historic trip to Peking in 1972, is an example. Mr. Kissinger didn't break any law or undermine U.S. foreign policy in setting up the U.S.-China rapprochement.

But under President Reagan, the council's staff has taken on the shape of a government within a government, apparently shaping new policy and acting on it without the approval of appropriate Cabinet members or the knowledge of Congress.

It is a deeply troubling development, despite the president's assurances in his speech Thursday night, and one that begs for the inquiry promised by members of Congress.

Mr. Reagan has used the council to circumvent established U.S. policy, and, probably, the law, in at least two instances. They are the recently disclosed shipment of military spare parts to Iran, and advising and coordinating the distribution of supplies to the Nicaraguan rebels during the time Congress had forbidden such activity.

Several congressional committees are interested in an investigation for good reason: The operations of the National Security Council and its staff are exempt from Congress' oversight. Appointment of the national security adviser and his top deputies does not require confirmation by the Senate.

Administration officials note that agents working for the NSC, rather than the CIA, were used to negotiate with Iran for a return of hostages in exchange for arms because Congress must be notified of the CIA's covert operations.

It doesn't take much imagination to think of what dangerous mischief an unaccountable agency could get into. The arms shipments to Iran suggest what could happen. The exchange probably violates several laws and does violate the U.S. policy of official neutrality in the Iran-Iraq war and the policy against negotiating with states that support terrorists.

White House cooperation in an inquiry is probably too much to hope for, considering the inclination of every administration to claim executive privilege. But Congress will have to act to protect the government — and the integrity of its laws and policies — from the trouble a runaway agency could cause. Limits have to be placed on what the NSC's staff can do. That could mean establishing oversight over such staff, and conditioning appointment of the national security adviser on approval by the Senate.

# St. Louis Review

*St. Louis, MO
November 14, 1986*

For centuries, diplomatic relations with the nations of the Middle East have been a political quagmire which no foreign nation has successfully dealt with over an extended period of time. Although there is a certain commonality of interest among the Islamic nations of that region, there is also fierce competition for leadership. This is complicated by the mutual hostility between Shiite and Zuni factions of Islam. Since 1948, the presence of the new nation of Israel and the plight of Palestinian refugees has stimulated a certain level of political cohesion among its Islamic neighbors. The military strength of Israel, tested in four major confrontations, has discouraged a united effort to destroy it. In addition, the consistent friendship of the United States and its massive arms support has been a major element in Israeli security which has also engendered the bitter hostility of Moslem extremists against the U.S.

Because of the rivalries and hostilities in the entire region, no nation has been able to establish a consistent foreign policy. While trying to foster the overall stability of the region, U.S. policy has also been directed to maintaining good relations with as many countries as possible without sacrificing its support for Israel.

This enabled the U.S. to persuade the late Shah of Iran to supply Israel with oil when the Arabic nations of the Middle East attempted a boycott.

Terrorism has at times been a major complicating factor in foreign and domestic politics. When American hostages are taken, the major concern of most Americans is their safe return. Secondarily, we would like to see terrorism discouraged and terrorists punished. Nevertheless, we tend to forget that the return of American hostages arranged by President Carter involved the release of more than $900 million in Iranian assets frozen in the U.S. Recent efforts to encourage the establishment of U.S. relations with more moderate factions in Iran and to persuade these factions to work for the release of American hostages in Lebanon has been exploited by extremists in Iran and politicians in the U.S.

Against the tangled web of competing interests in the Middle East, it is heartening to realize that every American administration has undertaken strenuous efforts on behalf of the lives and safe return of American citizens at risk.

# THE SUN

*Baltimore, MD, November 15, 1986*

Even if President Reagan's labored explanation of the Iran affair is taken at face value, it falls of its own illogic.

Two of his stated objectives in authorizing the secret shipment of arms to Tehran were to "eliminate state-sponsored terrorism and subversion and to effect the safe return of all hostages." Yet he utterly misconstrues the nature of state-sponsored terrorism. It does not consist solely of unleashing mobs to capture a foreign embassy or of sending hit-squads on assassination or hijacking missions. The essence of state-supported terrorism is to encourage clandestine groups to do dirty work for the sponsoring power.

Nothing in the administration's sad tale of its dealings with Iran contradicts this hard truth. By sending arms to encourage Iran to pressure its terrorist friends in Lebanon to release American hostages, Mr. Reagan was doing what he insists he was not doing — offering ransom, if only indirectly. Nor was he successful in ending the hostage-taking scourge. During the very period when he was obtaining the release of three kidnapped Americans, three more were grabbed off the streets of Beirut, a net gain of zero.

Perhaps one of the president's problems was one of Jimmy Carter's problems, too. He became too emotionally consumed by the plight of the hostages. Such compassion may be admirable, but in bargaining with unscrupulous fanatics, it merely makes a president prone to manipulation.

Mr. Reagan also tried to justify his actions by saying he sought "to renew a relationship with the nation of Iran [and] to bring an honorable end to the bloody six-year war between Iran and Iraq." His first point is well taken. Iran is of such large strategic importance that American interests would be served by better relations honorably arrived at.

Lamentably, Mr. Reagan's attempt to tie his maneuvers to the Iran-Iraq war made no sense at all. Iran currently holds the military initiative, so U.S. arms will hardly promote the stalemated settlement Washington has long sought. The president cannot have it both ways. He cannot persuasively contend the U.S. arms shipments were too small to make a difference and then pretend their delivery might help end the war.

Because the president found himself arguing an untenable position, there were obvious gaps in his Thursday night speech. He ignored Israel's large intermediary role in shipping arms to Iran. He said nothing about consternation among moderate Arab nations and our European allies, all of which received U.S. lectures on not paying ransom to terrorists. And he was silent about how some of his own top advisers were bypassed or ignored. They were as seriously compromised by this imbroglio as the White House operatives who actually carried it out.

# Reagan Defends Iran Policy, Ends Arms Sales; Shultz to Stay

President Reagan November 19, 1986 strongly defended his administration's recently disclosed weapons sales to Iran but said that no further arms would be sent. His remarks came in a nationally broadcast news conference, his first since August 12, 1986, which was almost exclusively devoted to questions about the U.S.-Iranian dealings. In an opening statement, Reagan admitted that his decision to provide Iran with arms was "deeply controversial" and that some of his top advisers had strongly opposed it. "The responsibility for the decision is mine, and mine alone," he said. He reiterated that his goals had been to open a channel to moderate elements in the Iranian government, to bring a peaceful end to the Iran-Iraq war, to end Teheran's support for terrorism and to gain the release of American hostages held by pro-Iranian groups in Lebanon. "These are the causes that justify taking risks," he said. "However, to eliminate the widespread and mistaken perception that we have been exchanging arms for hostages," Reagan said, "I have directed that no further sales of arms of any kind be sent to Iran. I have further directed that all information relating to our initiative be provided to appropriate members of Congress."

The news conference that followed was viewed by observers as one of the toughest faced by Reagan to date, with reporters sharply challenging him on a variety of points. He appeared unsure about some of the details of his Iran arms policy. Reagan repeatedly claimed that he had acted legally and properly in authorizing the covert Iranian initiative while not notifying Congress. He said that though it was a "high-risk gamble," the policy was not a "mistake" nor "a fiasco or a great failure of any kind." He denied having engaged in "duplicity," and vowed to continue to work on improving U.S.-Iranian contacts, despite the end to arms supplies. The President acknowledged that the U.S. had sold Iran 1,000 TOW antitank missiles and spare parts for Hawk antiaircraft missile batteries, but insisted that all such supplies were "defensive," could be fit in a single cargo plane and had in no way altered the military balance of the Persian Gulf war. While denying an arms-for-hostages swap, Reagan cited the release of three American captives over the previous year as evidence that his Iranian initiative had been partly successful. Other administration officials had made similarly contradictory remarks in defending the policy. Reagan also asserted that two other U.S. hostages in Lebanon would have been freed recently if it had not been for critical press reports about secret arms deals. He was then forced to acknowledge that the story had first been leaked by hostile elements in the Iranian government.

Reagan was asked about the admission by White House chief of staff Donald Regan that the U.S. had approved an Israeli arms shipment to Iran in September 1985, shortly before the release of one of the hostages. "I never heard Mr. Regan say that," the President replied. He claimed that the U.S. had not condoned "the shipment of arms by other countries" to Iran. He also asserted that the U.S. had only sent arms following the secret January 17, 1986 intelligence finding that he signed in order to authorize specific exceptions to the Iranian arms embargo. However, in an unusual move, Reagan issued a statement correcting his remarks shortly after the news conference ended. While not specifically mentioning Israel, the statement said: "There was a third country involved in our secret project with Iran."

Reagan denied rumors that U.S. Secretary of State George Shultz was considering resigning over his opposition to the Iranian arms shipments. He also denied reports that Shultz had agreed to stay only in the condition that no further arms be sent. Besides Shultz, it had been rumored that Defense Secretary Caspar Weinberger had also opposed the Iran arms shipments. But, distancing himself from Shultz's more open criticism, Weinberger Nov. 19 said that "any attempt" to try to moderate Iran's "extremely destructive" policies "can be well justified."

Both Democratic and Republican lawmakers Nov. 19 appeared to find Reagan's news conference comments confusing and misleading. Sen. Sam Nunn (D, Ga.) said: "I counted at least seven major contradictions from what I previously had been informed by top officials...We have a foreign policy that's in serious disarray now." Sen. John Chafee (R, R.I.) said, "We've really got a credibility problem here."

The Grand Rapids Press
*Grand Rapids, MI, November 23, 1986*

If President Reagan insists on salting his wounds with evasions and misinformation, the Iran debacle will not soon be put to rest. His best course is to admit the error of secret arms dealings to Iran, dismiss some of the cloak-and-dagger Inspector Clouseaus who roam the basement of the White House and return sanity and clear-headedness to U.S. foreign policy.

Mr. Reagan did none of the those things in his press conference last week. His intent, as it always is, was to accentuate the positive — in this case, the wooing of moderates in Iran, the desire to end the long Iran-Irag war, the safe return of several hostages.

The trouble is that while he was talking about shiny apples, the press and nation wanted to know about the rotten oranges — the sale, by the United States and Israel, of weapons to potential terrorists; the hypocrisy of publicly condemning arms shipments to terrorist countries while doing it ourselves; and the folly of acting unilaterally — with the Congress, State Department and Defense Department knowing nothing or very little.

The president should know that this is no small brushfire he can extinguish with a bit of charm and soothing talk. Increasingly, he and the White House he supervises are isolated from the other essential policy-making institutions in Washington. Congress is in an uproar and while much of fury is partisan at heart, loyal Republicans like Sen. Richard Lugar are disturbed by Mr. Reagan's disregard for the legislative branch. Secretary of State George Shultz and Defense Secretary Caspar Weinberger cannot disguise their contempt for this renegade policy.

Clearly, the national security adviser, Admiral John Poindexter, should resign, and Mr. Reagan should dismantle the little nest of undercover operatives built by Mr. Poindexter and Chief of Staff Donald Regan. Mr. Regan, too, should be called on the carpet and informed that he was hired to help the president, not sandbag him.

That this is done, and quickly, is important because two vital aspects of U.S. foreign policy are at risk as long as this trouble persists. They are the global war against terrorism, and Iran's relations with the West. Our success in persuading Europe to move the fight against state-sponsored terrorism away from rhetoric and into trade and diplomacy has been middling at best; the Iran caper has damaged that effort greatly. It is less important that we show Europe that we are above clandestine arms dealings than that we demonstrate that our foreign-policy apparatus is consistent and smooth and well-considered.

As to Iran, there is room to maneuver in the Khomeini state, if we step carefully. Iran wants to work with the West; trade under Khomeini has been greater with the West than under the shah. Moreover, as much as Iran dislikes United States, it has an even greater aversion for the Soviet Union, which is the antithesis of an Iran-style theocracy. Iran is not as monolithic as some believe; while the ayatollah's authority is unquestioned, there remain in business and government people less radical and more inclined to Western values. These are potential leaders worth cultivating.

Then, too, the Iran-Iraq war is a murderous tragedy that must be ended. The United States has a moral responsibility to stop the bloodshed if it can. But before that, President Reagan must patch his own roof. He cannot do that by pretending the holes aren't there.

# DAYTON DAILY NEWS
*Dayton, OH, November 25, 1986*

Because of the ways of Washington (don't ask what that means), President Reagan is being advised by his wife and others to fire those members of his staff who helped him do want he wanted to do on Iran *and* one member who fought him.

What's really strange is that this advice makes some sense.

Chief of Staff Donald Regan and National Security adviser John Poindexter should be replaced. Mr. Regan lacks the political sophistication and temperament to deal with a Democratic Congress

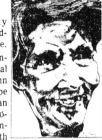

Nancy Reagan

and has tense relations with other administration people. And the fact is that Mr. Reagan did not get in this kind of trouble when James Baker was running the White House. As for Mr. Poindexter, he is apparently the architect of the bizarre Iran gambit. President Reagan simply needs wiser heads around him.

And it is not difficult to see why the people

in Mr. Reagan's kitchen cabinet" are mad at Secretary of State George Shultz. Lately Mr. Shultz has been displaying a degree of team spirit that any president would be justified in finding insufficient.

However, look at it from Mr. Shultz's point-of-view: Could *you* work with that White House bunch?

It is entirely possible that under normal circumstances, George Shultz could be a perfectly good team player, as he has been in the past.

However, dumping Mr. Poindexter (as suggested by some) for former U.N. Ambassador Jeane Kirkpatrick — while keeping Mr. Shultz — wouldn't work, because all of Washington knows that Jeane Kirkpatrick and George Shultz dislike each other with great enthusiasm.

Ultimately, the big question is this: What if the President accepts the advice of his "kitchen cabinet" — Nancy Reagan, Ed Meese, Holmes Tuttle, William Casey, et al — and fires his entire foreign policy apparatus and his chief of staff and then the whole thing doesn't work out? Does Mrs. Reagan have resign?

---

# The Atlanta Journal
## THE ATLANTA CONSTITUTION
*Atlanta, GA, November 21, 1986*

President Reagan's press-conference reckoning with the Iran arms deal was distressing to watch. No American, no matter how partisan, should enjoy seeing any president so humbled; the nation, too, is diminished.

Never a master of detail, President Reagan was astonishingly ill-equipped to meet with the media Wednesday night, requiring not one but *two* post-news conference "clarifications."

The worst of it is that he has yet to realize how dead-wrong he was to sell military materiel to Iran. He makes no apologies for a move that George Shultz vehemently opposed, that Caspar Weinberger labeled "absurd" and that Reagan's own agent in this sorry affair, Bud McFarlane, claims to have maintained throughout was a mistake.

Nobody seriously questions Reagan's professed intention to open communications channels with sane and sensible elements within Iran. One can legitimately wonder, though, if that was indeed his objective after he referred three times Wednesday night to retrieving three American hostages from their Iranian-connected captors as if that were proof of the wisdom of his policy.

Contradictions abound in the president's account, and more may surface when congressional panels yank at its myriad tangles. They are piling up to produce a staggering loss in confidence in this president and his administration. Consider:

• How can terrorists, Tehran-directed or otherwise, fail to note that arms were shipped to Iran on three occasions "to estab-

lish our bona fides" with the expectation that "moderates" there would establish theirs by seeing to the liberation of captured Americans? What does that say about our supposed abhorrence of paying ransom? Does that not encourage more kidnappings?

•How can Iraq possibly believe U.S. expressions of neutrality, especially after its aerial bombardment of Iran's main economic asset, the Kharg Island refinery complex, has stopped because Iraqi jets encountered for the first time sophisticated Phoenix anti-aircraft missiles, available presumably only through U.S. government channels?

• How can our European allies or Israel be expected to forswear munitions shipments to Iran — or to any other nation supporting terrorism — on this administration's say-so when it has been exposed as a long-time player in this dubious trade?

• Finally, don't the president's lapses and stumbles and what even loyal supporters charitably call his misunderstandings of the law suggest that he desperately needs to be rid of his mediocre inner circle?

One of the president's most vigorous and knowledgeable critics, Sen. Sam Nunn (D-Ga.) has urged Reagan to augment his White House advisers with wise old heads from past administrations: familiar names like Kissinger, Brzezinski, Scowcroft, Schlesinger. Certainly, if American foreign policy is to be set aright from its recent misdirection and continuing disorientation, the president must at the very least choose an experienced, thoughtful person of national stature to take the reins of his runaway National Security Council.

---

# The Forum
*Fargo, ND, November 23, 1986*

**R**eagan bashing is "in" these days, even by conservative columnists and Republican senators.

Much of it is thoughtful, reasoned. We've lent our own criticism to the attack, objecting to an "imperial presidency" and pointing out what seems obvious, that when weapons are sent to Iran and American hostages are released by Iran-leaning Shiite Moslems in Lebanon, there has been an exchange of favors that is difficult to minimize as incidental.

President Reagan has not helped his cause by his television appearances, first in a report to the nation, and then in a news conference in which hard-eyed, tough correspondents asked for precise answers which the president wasn't about to give.

He said he wanted to protect moderates in Iran with whom the U.S. had been working. He did not want to blow their cover.

He said national security is involved, that the weapons were of an insignificant character and number, and that additional hostages may have been released by this time but for the unfortunate publicity and accusations about trading weapons for hostages.

Polls have shown that the majority of people in this country do not believe the president on this issue, but that they still believe he is doing a good job.

The president is like a ballplayer who is in a run-down after being caught off base.

Congress will be conducting hearings on the presidential action. People in the administration will be questioned, and national security discussions will be behind closed doors.

The value of the attempted rapprochement with Iran will be examined. The necessity for secrecy and the waiving of an arms embargo will be evaluated.

The possibilities of peace in the Persian Gulf will be discussed. Congress will get some answers that the president could not or would not give at his news conference.

It is too early to be calling this "Irangate," an allusion to Watergate. The two cannot be compared.

Watergate was the result of dirty political tricks that President Nixon tried to hide. The dealings with Iran, while they may have been stupid, were not for selfish motives.

President Reagan, if we read him right, has a heartfelt concern for the hostages and their families. He has been getting tremendous pressure to retrieve them.

If he could do this as a part of the rapprochement, he reasoned, why not do it?

The president probably has been encouraged by foreign policy escapades which have been applauded by the American public: The

Grenada invasion, the bombing of Libya, the grounding of the plane carrying the terrorists who held the Italian liner hostage and killed one American, the release of hostages from Lebanon.

These things came as a result of measured actions, taken to accomplish a good end while not bringing the U.S. to the brink of war.

The president has not been apologetic for the Iranian intrigue. It remains to be seen if he will ever feel the need to admit a mistake was made.

We believe he did make a mistake, and we are holding him to the high standards our democracy demands.

If he were an Iron Curtain dictator, he would have no problems on his home ground. But this is the United States, and executive privilege has its bounds.

# THE ⬛ SUN

Baltimore, MD,
November 21, 1986

Does President Reagan have full intellectual command over his foreign policy agenda? Does he fully grasp the details and implications involved in arms control negotiations with the Soviet Union or weapons deals with terrorist Iran? Such disquieting questions arise as the president wrestles with the gravest challenges of his career.

Mr. Reagan's press conference Wednesday night did nothing to dispel concern. Washington often plunges into disputes over the substance of actions affecting national security. Credibility, too, is a constant issue, given the inherent conflict between the professed openness of our system and a White House instinct for secrecy. But Mr. Reagan's handling of the Reykjavik summit and the Iran caper pushes matters into another dimension — that of competency.

Our chief executive has never been a detail man. But when a president goes to the bargaining table with the likes of Soviet party chief Mikhail S. Gorbachev or starts dickering with fanatics in Tehran he had better be up to speed. And in both instances, Mr. Reagan was not — and is not.

During his press conference, the president misstated the American position at the Iceland summit. He said "there was an agreement reached on the desirability of eliminating all strategic nuclear missiles in a five year period" when, in fact, there had been no such accord. It would be one thing if this issue had lain dormant in the five weeks since Reykjavik. But only last weekend, Prime Minister Margaret Thatcher went to Camp David to dissuade Mr. Reagan from further consideration of a zero-missile option that would deprive Western Europe of its protective nuclear umbrella. Mr. Reagan's press conference remarks, therefore, reinforce the impression that he does not fully comprehend crucial arms control issues.

On the arms-to-Iran deal, Mr. Reagan had to issue an embarrassing written retraction 25 minutes after thrice stating that his administration had not condoned Israel's acting as a conduit in arms shipments to Tehran. The president's assertions that the weapons were "defensive," that they were not sold in exchange for hostages and that a 10-month failure to notify Congress did not violate the law were widely scorned.

Mr. Reagan even wound up scrambling some history he himself had made when he said "we went into Grenada without prior notice." In fact, congressional leaders were informed the night before the invasion.

The president conceded he went along with the Iran deal even though some of his top advisers, principally Secretary of State George P. Shultz, cautioned against it. His compassion for hostages, like his vision at Reykjavik of a world free of nuclear weapons, caused him to pursue serious actions whose particulars and consequences he has not fully mastered to this moment.

# The Honolulu Advertiser

Honolulu, HI, November 18, 1986

President Reagan should be glad for the headline attention the story on the fate of North Korea's Kim Il Sung is creating as a diversion from the American leader's troubles.

The question remains as to how much both his popular image and his effectiveness in Washington have been hurt by the hostage flap.

Not only was he revealed making an unseemly arms-for-hostages deal with Iran, he went on TV in what came across as a cover-up speech to the American people, making statements that were not only contradicted by the facts but by his own aides in following days.

Reagan is a man of compassion, and he obviously acted out of deep concern for the hostages. But, if he gets credit for that, he also looks both inept in foreign policy and sharply at odds with his hard-line image in dealing with terrorism.

On another level, the Iran fiasco underscores another serious point: The Reagan administration lacks a foreign-policy heavyweight in the White House, and that is where some important issues are being handled, often with Rambo-like insensitivity.

The total result of the Iran situation is still to be seen. Probably Reagan will remain a president popular with the public. But with Congress and perhaps with many foreign allies, he will be seen more and more as a lame-duck leader.

"IT'S THEIR FAULT..."

# The Record

Hackensack, NJ, November 21, 1986

President Reagan's press conference on the arms-for-hostages deal with Iran was a reminder that no one, not even presidents, can go on defying reality forever. Mr. Reagan has been able to get away with it longer than most, but it now appears that reality has caught up with him. The consequences Wednesday night were embarrassing. He contradicted himself, evaded questions, told outright falsehoods, and seemed increasingly uncomfortable as the session wore on. Caught on the horns of his own inconsistent foreign policy, Mr. Reagan strove to set things straight, yet succeeded only in bollixing them up further.

Four times he insisted emphatically that the United States had not sanctioned an Israeli arms shipment to Iran in September 1985. "We did not condone and do not condone the shipment of arms from other countries," he told one reporter. To another, he replied: "We, as I say, have nothing to do with other countries or their shipments of arms." Yet just a few days earlier, John Poindexter, his national-security adviser, and Donald Regan, his chief of staff, acknowledged that this was just what the administration had done. After the press conference, the president's handlers went to the extraordinary length of issuing a statement in his name confirming that "there was a third country involved in our secret project with Iran."

On the crucial question of whether Iran sponsors terrorism, President Reagan indicated that he was satisfied when the Iranians "gave us information that they did not." Yet a few minutes later he acknowledged that "Iran officially is still on our list of nations that have been supporting terrorism." He denied that he had exchanged arms for hostages, but then launched into an elaborate circumlocution that left no doubt that he had. All his emissaries had suggested, he said, was that if Iran was sincere in renouncing terrorism, it might wish to arrange the release of certain hostages in Lebanon "to verify that . . . th.. . the wa; you feel."

If this is not swapping ar.ns for hostage., what is? In fact, the United States has shipped arms to Iran three times over the last 14 months, and each time pro-Iranian elements in Lebanon have responded by releasing one American hostage no more than three or four weeks later. Meanwhile, terrorists continue to hold two other Americans in Lebanon and have since kidnapped three others (not to mention two more Frenchmen). Clearly the president *was* bargaining for hostages, and getting the worse of the bargain.

The inconsistencies, contradictions, and inaccuracies went on. Mr. Reagan summed up the state of U.S.-Soviet arms talks by saying the two sides had agreed "on the desirability of eliminating all strategic nuclear missiles in a five-year period," when in fact the topic of discussion at Reykjavik was a Soviet proposal to halve strategic nuclear weapons over five years and eliminate all strategic weapons (not just missiles) over 10. On Lebanon, he declared that "Iran does not own or have authority over the Hezbollah." This will be news to Ayatollah Khomeini, whose picture the fundamentalist-Shiite party is forever sporting. On Nicaragua, he said that "the contras have never proposed overthrowing the government," when it is obvious to all that this has been their intention from the start. For the umpteenth time, he called Nicaragua "a totalitarian Communist state," a statement no less spurious than his various pronouncements on Lebanon and Iran.

The Ronald Reagan who appeared before the American people Wednesday was poorly informed, illogical, unconcerned about the facts, and unaware of the various things his own administration is up to. It was a dismaying spectacle — a cruel unmasking of the Hollywood illusion that the White House media experts have succeeded in foisting on the American people these past half-dozen years.

# The Miami Herald

Miami, FL, November 25, 1986

THE IRANIAN arms deal, by far the worst crisis of his Presidency, threatens to make Ronald Reagan into something infinitely more vulnerable than a lame duck. It threatens to make him a clay-pigeon President. He is under so much fire that his capacity to rebuild his credibility and to lead the nation is imperiled.

There's only one way for the President to spike these guns: He must admit that he made a mistake. That done, his next step — accepting the resignations of the scheme's architects — would follow as a matter of course.

Mr. Reagan is fighting, and losing, a war on two fronts. Domestically, he is under fire both from Democrats and from some Republicans for acting on bad advice from a tiny White House cabal and then refusing to admit his mistake. From abroad, shrapnel rains down upon him from U.S. allies and from Iran alike. The allies feel betrayed because the President countenanced the arms shipments even as his Administration was assuring friend and foe alike that it never would pay ransom for American hostages. Iran gloats that it has humiliated America — "the Great Satan" — and that it's uninterested in *rapprochement*.

More is at stake here than the Reagan Administration's anti-terrorism policy. Indeed, that now-shattered policy must be put back together again, shard by shard. The glue for its reconstruction is credibility. And credibility, in this and in all his other policy initiatives, is what Mr. Reagan must re-create.

The re-creation can begin only when the President concedes his error. In so doing, he should replace Chief of Staff Donald Regan and National Security Adviser John Poindexter, who led him down this garden path.

Secretary of State George Shultz, who advised against the arms sale, has distanced himself from it since it became public. Mr. Shultz may have breached irreparably the cardinal rule that a President's advisers must defend his policies publicly whatever their privately expressed reservations. Mr. Shultz is not culpable, but his distancing may have made him expendable too.

The President's choice of policy makers is far less important than his ability to make and implement credible policy. That ability is in mortal peril. Only the President can redeem it, and himself. He must do so forthwith.

# The Boston Globe

Boston, MA, November 21, 1986

It is hard to tell whether President Reagan believes some of the things he has said about his secret dealings with Iran – or whether he is trying to carry off a damage-control operation.

Defying logic during his Wednesday press conference, Reagan persisted in his contention that his representatives "were dealing with individuals" in Iran – not with the government. He defended his decision to ship arms to Iran by asserting: "We weren't giving them to the Ayatollah Khomeini."

Yet, presumably, the president knows that the TOW and Hawk missiles he sent to Iran were fired at Iraqi tanks and planes by Khomeini's armed forces. If he believes the components for US F-4 jets delivered to Iran were destined for the use of unaffiliated individuals, then he has been the victim of very bad, or very incomplete, advice.

It seems more likely that Reagan's advisers wished him to present a brief of the kind a sharp lawyer might contrive, to win on technicalities a case that would seem lost on its merits. That Reagan was negotiating with Khomeini's regime, and was ransoming American hostages for arms, cannot be disguised under any linguistic fig leaf.

In his opening statement, the president spoke of "a secret initiative to the Islamic Republic of Iran." The Islamic Republic is the regime of Ayatollah Khomeini – of sadists who have tortured tens of thousands of men, women and children in their prisons.

Reagan's efforts to pretend he was not dealing with that regime, or to placate the implacable Khomeini by acknowledging his revolution as a fact of history, were of no avail. Hours after the president's press conference, Khomeini mocked him.

"Today they come whining and want to establish relations and ask pardon, but our nation does not accept," Khomeini said on Iranian radio. "The American president should go into mourning because of this disgrace, and the White House should change [its name] to the Black House, though it was always that."

The amateur White House strategists who tried to help Khomeini wage his insane war against Iraq made a blatant mistake. That mistake should be admitted and rectified.

# Wisconsin State Journal

Madison, WI
November 17, 1986

In his nationally televised speech on his dealings with the Ayatollah's Iran, President Reagan came off much like the Queen of Hearts in "Alice of Wonderland," who insisted: "A word is exactly what I mean it to say, no more, no less."

Only if one accepts the queen's lexicology is a swap not a swap, and are secret U.S. shipments of weapons to Iran not linked to Iranian string-pulling to release American hostages.

In short, the usually believable Reagan fell off the credibility chart when he took to the airwaves to deny he swapped guns for hostages. There was no doubting the president's sincere concern for the captured Americans, but his insistence that trade accusations were "utterly false" simply did not add up.

Reagan's luck is famous, but it seems no coincidence that each time someone shipped a planeload of war gear to Iran — breaking his own arms ban and neutrality vow — he got one hostage home.

On Sept. 14, 1985, an Israeli plane flew U.S. arms to Iran — the same day hostage Rev. Benjamin Weir was freed by zealots in Lebanon. Two other shipments set loose Rev. Lawrence Jenco in July and David Jacobsen on Nov. 2.

Reagan is semi-mythical in his ability to face a crowd or a television camera or a radio microphone and convert the non-believers. This time, he left even the believers scratching their heads.

The Great Communicator did not acquire that nickname by being the Fabulous Fantasizer. Let's see more genuine communication and less fact-stretching.

# The Chattanooga Times

Chattanooga, TN, November 21, 1986

On the defensive about secret U.S. arms deals with Iran, President Reagan left the clear impression during a press conference Wednesday night that he heads an administration in disarray on a vital foreign policy issue.

Following the 40-minute press conference, Sen. Sam Nunn, D- Ga., said the president "contradicted all the information put out by his aides in the past week. I counted at least seven contradictions from what I have been told by his top aides." That's an average of one contradiction every five minutes. The most dramatic of these concerned Israeli involvement in the Iranian connection.

Mr. Reagan repeatedly denied Israeli involvement in the arms deals. "We did not condone and do not condone the shipment of arms from other countries," he said, disavowing statements by his own chief of staff, Donald Regan. But after the press conference he issued a written statement of "clarification" acknowledging "There was a third country involved in our secret project with Iran" — an obvious reference to Israel. It is too much to believe the president temporarily forgot about the Israeli role in the undertaking.

Mr. Reagan continued to ask the American public to believe the unbelievable — that there was no arms-for-hostages swap. He contended Iran arranged release of the hostages simply to demonstrate that it was backing away from terrorism and implied that it was merely coincidental that U.S. hostages were released on three separate occasions just after Iran received arms shipments.

Asked whether the Iranian arms deal sent the very message Mr. Reagan has said should not be sent — that terrorists or their state sponsors can gain from hostage-taking — Mr. Reagan said he couldn't see that the hostage-takers gained anything. He sidestepped the fact that their state sponsor, Iran, did indeed realize gain.

Asked whether he thought "the American people would ever support weapons to the Ayatollah Khomeini," Mr. Reagan said, "We weren't giving them to the Ayatollah Khomeini." The disingenuousness of the statement is obvious. While the United States did not negotiate directly with the ayatollah on the arms shipments, the arms delivered to Iran will be used by the ayatollah's army. The president attempts to make a distinction where there is no difference.

Mr. Reagan also refused to face up to the inherently deceptive policy of undertaking secret arms deals with Iran while publicly urging our allies to block arms shipments to that country. The president flatly denied any duplicity, but the undisputed facts of the matter suggests otherwise.

Although most of the press conference focused on Iran, presidential denial of the facts was not limited to that issue. Mr. Reagan again maintained that the deal made to swap U.S. newsman Nicholas Daniloff for a Soviet spy was not a swap. He asserted that U.S.-backed contra rebels in Nicaragua have never had the goal of overthrowing the Sandinista government, although the contras themselves have acknowledged that goal. He contended that "all the agreements or the apparent places where we agreed at Reykjavik are on the table now with our arms negotiators in Geneva" although the head of his Arms Control and Disarmament Agency said Wedesnday the United States is backing away from a proposal to eliminate nuclear ballistic missiles that Mr. Reagan put forward in negotiations with Soviet leader Mikhail Gorbachev at Reykjavik.

The only obvious consistency in Mr. Reagan's meeting with the press on Wednesday was one of misrepresentation. And while the president said he is not on the defensive and does not see that his administration's credibility has been damaged by the Iranian affair, these too are facts that cannot be erased by denials.

# THE TAMPA TRIBUNE
*Tampa, FL, November 21, 1986*

His secret dealings with Iran have tied the tongue of the Great Communicator. President Reagan is losing his credibility.

His has been called the "Teflon presidency" because even when a majority of the nation's people disapproved of his policies, they continued to approve of *him*. Whatever went wrong, the Mr. Nice Guy in the White House was able to deflect the blame.

Since his Nov. 14 television address and his Wednesday night press conference, both of which focused on the dealings with Iran to obtain the freedom of U.S. hostages held by Shi'ite Moslems in Lebanon, the Teflon has eroded.

A Wall Street Journal poll early this week found his overall approval rating dipping to 57 percent, down 4 points in a month, and approval of his foreign policy only 38 percent, down 13 points. And a mere 10 percent approved his arms deliveries to Iran, while 84 percent disapproved.

A Los Angeles Times poll taken about the same time dealt directly with Mr. Reagan's credibility — and the results were harsh. Only 14 percent of 1,464 adults polled nationwide believe his declaration he did not swap arms for the hostages "essentially true." More than five times as many, 79 percent, said they believed his statement was essentially untrue or only technically true. By a margin of almost 3-1 they rejected his contention that the United States does not negotiate with terrorists, and only 20 percent said the president acted lawfully in his dealings with Iran. Eighty percent said the United States should not pay ransom of any kind to free hostages.

Wednesday night's press conference is unlikely to change what those polls found, because the president, declaring he has no reason to apologize and no mistake to admit, said basically what he had said the previous Thursday.

He made two clear errors — one of which the White House press office corrected 25 minutes after the event. He said there had been no third parties involved in the arms transfer; the White House conceded later that Israel had been involved. And he described the 1,000 TOW anti-tank missiles sent to Iran as shoulder-fired defense weapons; actually they are fired from either a tripod-held ground mount or from vehicles — including tanks.

Too often at other times he was splitting hairs or was self-contradictory:

• While whatever arms were delivered went to "individuals in the government," and were sent "to let them know ... they were dealing with the head of government over here," the weapons were not sent to the Ayatollah Khomeini.

• While the unidentified Iranians in the negotiations "gave us information that they did not (support terrorism) and ... that there had been a lessening of this on the part of Khomeini and the government" Iran "is officially still on our list of nations that have been supporting terrorism."

• While he repeatedly denied exchanging weapons directly for hostages, after he provided the arms as evidence of U.S. sincerity, he declared: "I said to them that there was something they could do to show ... if they really meant it that they were not in favor of backing terrorists, they could begin by releasing our hostages." Then, "Iran does not own or have authority over the Hezbollah (terrorists) ... but they can sometimes persuade or pressure the Hezbollah into doing what they did in this instance."

Congressional reaction did little to sustain the president's credibility. Of his contention that the law permits him to withhold information on the arms deal from Congress, Sen. Richard Lugar, R-Ind., outgoing chairman of the Senate Foreign Relations Committee, said, "I suspect the president does not understand the law with regard to informing Congress on these things." Another GOP senator, Rhode Island's John Chaffee, said the president's tarnished credibility has him "in a difficult spot, and we (Senate Republicans) really have a credibility problem."

Among Democrats, Georgia Sen. Sam Nunn said that during the press conference he counted "at least seven major contradictions" in what the president said and what administration officials had said earlier. "We have a foreign policy that is in serious disarray," Nunn added. Ohio's John Glenn said, "He can't continue deceiving the American people and expect us to trust him." Colorado's Gary Hart, said, "He's hurt pretty badly." Then he added the unkindest cut of all: "But no one expects him to know what's going on. That's a pretty low standard. This president has gotten away with not knowing very much."

What concerns the American people, however, is not the legalities. They just flat think it is wrong to ransom hostages, and that is what they think President Reagan did in sending arms to Iran. How many, and whether they are offensive or defensive is to them beside the point. Whatever stakes he was after — he said Nov. 14 the ultimate goal was to keep the Soviet Union out of Iran — they don't think the prize was worth encouraging more terrorists to kidnap more Americans.

For President Reagan, who heretofore has seemed to possess an almost magical ability to read the public mind, the deal with the Iranians was a massive and unfathomably stupid blunder.

# The Star-Ledger
*Newark, NJ, November 21, 1986*

It was clearly evident, right from the outset of his televised news conference, that the President was in for a rugged time trying to defend his controversial clandestine arms deal with Iran.

This was not the facile communicator who has established himself as one of the nation's most popular presidents, and one who enjoyed the positive political asset of great credibility.

This was not vintage Ronald Reagan, the President who in the past was generally able to handle even the toughest questions from the White House press corps. This was, instead, a seemingly beleaguered President, a President who has found himself under siege, unable to make out a persuasive, let alone a convincing, case for approving secret arms shipments to the Khomeini government in Iran.

The sole purpose of the President's first televised press conference in three months was to stage a national forum as a means of trying to overcome an erosion of credibility in the Reagan Administration in the wake of the Iranian arms disclosure. There can be little doubt that Mr. Reagan fell palpably short of that goal.

The President was faced with the apparently insoluble dilemma of trying to justify his arms decision on a political basis, while at the same time disavowing the widely held public belief that it was, in fact, a quid pro quo arrangement for the release of American hostages in Lebanon.

\* \* \*

It was a case of Mr. Reagan trying to work both sides of the street. He was willing to take credit for the release of three U.S. hostages, but not to be held accountable for any culpability of an arrangement for an Iranian intercession with terrorists holding Americans captive.

But even if the arms shipment was untainted by linkage with ransom to obtain the release of the hostages, it was an egregious presidential decision in fundamental terms of foreign policy realism. It conceivably could have serious political ramifications in the volatile Middle East, critically tilting the sensitive balance of military power in that troubled region.

This affair is the latest example of problems in the Reagan White House's foreign policy. Unlike the President's effectiveness in the domestic sector, foreign policy has not been one of the strong suits of his Administration.

Ironically, the President had given foreign affairs a high priority for his second and final term, placing an arms accord high on that agenda.

# U.S. Profits From Iran Arms Deal Found Sent to Nicaraguan Contras

President Reagan November 25, 1986 said he had not been informed about an aspect of his Iranian policy and as a consequence had accepted the resignation of national security adviser Vice Adm. John Poindexter and fired a key National Security Council aide, Lt. Col. Oliver North. This was followed by the disclosure that $10 million to $30 million in profits from the Israeli-brokered sale of American arms to Iran had been secretly diverted to help the contra rebels fighting Nicaragua's Sandinista government. The revelation of the contra connections, following a week of unprecedented public bickering among top administration officials over who was to blame, left Reagan facing the most serious crisis of his presidency.

Both Republican and Democratic leaders on Capital Hill expressed shock at the news and promised full-scale and wide-ranging congressional investigations. They noted that a number of laws might have been broken by the diversion of funds at a time when United States aid to the contras had been banned by Congress. Some lawmakers described Reagan's foreign policy as being in "total disarray." They viewed the claim that a major covert operation had been run out of the White House without the President's knowledge as having raised damaging questions about his competence and credibility.

Reagan made a brief statement to reporters. He said that the previous week he had directed U.S. Attorney General Edwin Meese 3rd to review the Iranian arms-supply policy, which had been aimed chiefly at establishing links with Teheran and winning the freedom of U.S. hostages in Lebanon. He said a preliminary report of Meese's findings had "led me to conclude that I was not fully informed on the nature of one of the activities undertaken with the initiative." He said, "This action raises some serious questions of propriety." Reagan said he would "appoint a special review board to conduct a comprehensive review of the National Security Council (NSC) staff in the conduct of foreign and national security policy." The NSC, which was created as a policy coordinating and advisory body, had run the Iran arms operation—skirting Congress, as well as the State and Defense departments in the process. Reagan said further actions would wait until after he had received the reports from the Justice Department and the special review board. "I am deeply troubled that the implementation of a policy aimed at resolving a truly tragic situation in the Middle East has resulted in such a controversy," Reagan continued. "As I've stated previously, I believe our policy goals toward Iran were well founded." But in one respect, the policy's implementation "was seriously flawed," he said.

According to Meese, a preliminary investigation by the Justice Department had established the following outline of what happened: Between January and September of 1986 the Central Intelligence Agency (CIA), under NSC direction, sent $12 million in Defense Department weapons stocks to Israel, which had agreed to broker the covert U.S.-Iranian contacts. "Representatives of Israel," not necessarily in the Israeli government, sold the arms to Iran with a premium of $10 million to $30 million added on top of their cost. The Israelis gave $12 million, plus transport costs, of the Iranian payment to the CIA, which in turn reimbursed the Pentagon. Either the Israelis or the Iranian representatives, acting with the knowledge of North, then transferred the extra funds to Swiss bank accounts controlled by "the forces in Central America that are opposing the Sandinista government there." Meese said that none of the other members of the NSC—including CIA Director William Casey, Secretary of State George Shultz and Defense Secretary Caspar Weinberger—had known about the Nicaraguan aspect. Meese said President Reagan had known nothing until the day before.

Some U.S. officials Nov. 25 noted that the disclosure of the skimming off of Iranian arms profits for the contras could partly explain how the rebels had been able to finance their resupply operation over the previous two years, when U.S. aid had been cut off. It was suggested that, at least since early 1986, the Iranian funds had paid for a large part of the resupply effort, which involved hundreds of covert drops over Nicaragua. The rebels, along with Lt. Col. Oliver North and other administration officials, had maintained that the money needed to keep the aid flowing came from anonymous private donors in the U.S. and abroad. Meanwhile, Adolfo Calero, political leader of the largest contra force, Nov. 25 in Miami denied that his group had received any of the Iranian money. He said the rebels "have no access" to any Swiss bank accounts of the type described by Meese.

The Grand Rapids Press

*Grand Rapids, MI, November 26, 1986*

Yesterday's revelations about the link between the Iran arms sale and covert aid to the Nicaragua contras are shocking and sad. They point to an arrogance of power in the Reagan White House and a foreign policy in tatters. To clear the air and to restore order, an independent inquiry with prosecutorial authority should be initiated.

This is no Watergate, not yet at least. President Reagan's best move in this whole sordid affair was to put Attorney General Edwin Meese before the television cameras yesterday and this morning to answer questions about his fledgling investigation. The president apparently is doing what Richard Nixon never did: Face the crisis squarely and in public view.

But Mr. Meese should not be the point man on this investigation. He is simply too closely allied to the president and his aides. His best efforts at impartiality will be colored by his affiliation with the president. Even if his probe is totally honest and thorough, the public might, because of Mr. Meese's relationship to Mr. Reagan, harbor lingering suspicions.

The attorney general gave credence to this view during yesterday's press conference, when he said that those in the administration should "stand shoulder to shoulder" with the president or resign. If those of Mr. Reagan's aides who have information about the Iran-contra dealings take Mr. Meese's advice, they would never come forward.

There are many questions for an independent prosecutor, and the appropriate congressional committees, to examine. Who knew that money received by Israel from the Iran arms sales was going to the contras? Did it stop with Lt. Col. Oliver North, who was fired yesterday, and his boss, Rear Adm. John Poindexter, who resigned?

Experience tells that this sort of operation is rarely done without tacit approval, if not authorization, from a higher level. We'd like to believe the president knew nothing of this arrangement, which seems to skirt the intent, if not the letter, of the law, but only the most scrutinizing and objective investigation will tell us for sure.

Also, how long has this multi-pronged network of arms and military aid been in operation? There have been reports that Israel has been involved with arms sales to Iran several times in the past; moreover, Israel has been linked with arms deals in Central America.

Has Israel, one of our closest allies, been acting as the Reagan administration's agent in bypassing the strictures of Congress and normal diplomacy to aid anti-communists such as the contras or to free the hostages?

There is much to examine and work must begin immediately. If nothing else, we know now the effects of ideological fervor — comparing the contras to "freedom fighters" and the American founding fathers — have on functionaries like Mr. North and Adm. Poindexter.

These men seemed to believe that their ends justified some very questionable means. And they might not have been the only ones. A full-fledged probe carried out in the public eye will, one hopes, resolve that question.

## The Register

Santa Ana, CA, November 27, 1986

During Attorney General Edwin Meese's press briefing on the latest development in the arms-to-Iran-and-money-to-the-Contras debacle, one reporter asked a question that provided an unintentional insight into modern attitudes about the presidency. *How could the president not have known,* he asked almost plaintively, about something so important?

Meese answered briskly that the president didn't know because nobody told him. That was a reasonable answer as far as it goes. The president is only human, and he can't be expected to know everything. But the unspoken assumption behind the question deserves some thought from time to time.

Many Americans have come to expect our presidents to be some sort of superhuman demigods, fully in charge of every aspect of every activity performed by the thousands of toilers in the bureaucratic vineyards. At some subconscious level there may be some necessity to want to believe such impossibilities, because we have acquiesced in the government taking over micro-management of so many aspects of our daily lives. We know that only a superhuman power can perform the tasks assigned to government with any degree of competence.

At the same time, perhaps on some other level of consciousness, most of us are secretly or openly delighted when a president fails to meet the superhuman specifications. We gripe that Jimmy Carter immersed himself too deeply in the day-to-day minutiae of the job and complain that Ronald Reagan makes gaffes and is a hands-off manager, letting subordinates make important decisions while having only the loosest grasp on what is being done in his name. There is justification in both criticisms. What we expect of presidents is clearly impossible for any mortal. Our subtle psychological expectations are even more absurd.

We routinely respond to poll questions like "How is the president managing the economy?" or "Has the president restored national dignity?" with little appreciation for their inherent absurdity. The president (thank goodness) can't really manage the economy, although his policies can affect it. Dignity is an attribute of individual Americans, not of some abstract entity we choose to call a nation-state.

Once the dust from the present flap has settled, perhaps there will be time to reflect on just how much we have asked the government to do — urged on by government officials at every step, of course — in recent years. It has demonstrated that, being populated by imperfect human beings, it can't eliminate poverty, usher in perfect peace, provide meaning and fulfillment to our individual lives and assure undisturbed tranquility.

Perhaps it's time to demand that the government stop trying to do so much, to take back from government agents full responsibility for our own lives and decisions, along with the freedom to make them ourselves. If those populating the government are only human too, why have we given them so much control over our lives?

## THE SAGINAW NEWS

Saginaw, MI, November 26, 1986

Somewhere in the basement of the White House, people other than the president have been running their own government of the United States while the president slept upstairs.

Ronald Reagan has been known for tending to let his aides fight out policies and even personalities, as long as, ultimately, he was the boss.

It seems some of his staff figured that what he didn't know wouldn't hurt him. This time, though, Reagan woke up.

So Vice Adm. John Poindexter, the national security adviser, is out. So is Lt. Col. Oliver North.

Oliver who? As chief aide to Poindexter, North apparently felt no obligation to advise the president, and perhaps even his direct boss, about certain transactions involving transfer of millions of dollars from the Iranian arms sale to some folks in Central America. The *president* was forced to admit that "I was not fully informed" about the arrangement.

Well, what the heck, it only affected a couple of sideshow wars in unimportant parts of the world. Why tell the Prez anything?

There is a breathtaking, dangerous arrogance about this that Reagan must eliminate, for the good of the nation and his presidency. He should probe not only the National Security Council, but his own hands-off attitudes.

The nation again needs someone to say, "I am in control here..." But this time it had better be Reagan.

## St. Petersburg Times

St. Petersburg, FL, November 26, 1986

Are Americans being asked to believe that a mere lieutenant colonel on the White House staff in 1985 authorized an illegal shipment of U.S. arms to the terrorist nation of Iran without the knowledge of the President? Or that the same Lt. Col. Oliver North on his own arranged for up to $30-million of money paid by Iran for those arms to be diverted to the *contra* rebels fighting to overthrow the government of Nicaragua? Or that North's boss, Vice Adm. John M. Poindexter, another well-trained military man, knew about the diversion of funds but failed to inform the President or his chief of staff?

"Ollie North is too good a soldier to have done that on his own," Florida's senior U.S. senator, Lawton Chiles, said Tuesday in St. Petersburg. "He's a soldier's soldier. If he is ordered to go through that wall, he'll go through it. But I don't see him doing something like this on his own."

Chiles' reaction illustrated the President's problem after Tuesday's extremely serious disclosures.

The facts according to Ed Meese just don't add up.

Congress won't believe the administration's version of what happened. Allied governments won't believe it. More important, the American people won't believe it, and until they do the President and his administration will be crippled. That is bad for the country.

This is not another case of confusion, ignorance or misstatement. What is at stake here is the integrity of the U.S. government and its adherence to the rule of law. Weigh these words spoken Tuesday by Mr. Reagan:

"While I cannot reverse what has happened, I'm initiating steps, including those I've announced today, to assure that the implementation of all future, foreign and national security policy initiatives will proceed only in accordance with my authorization."

When in the past has an American President found it necessary to make such a promise?

Who has been in charge of the United States government?

The serious questions about the operation of the Reagan White House are self-evident. Beyond those are several apparent violations of the law. According to Meese, the first in the series of arms shipments to Iran took place in August or September of 1985. At that time, it was undisputably a violation of U.S. law to sell arms to Iran. President Reagan did not sign the secret intelligence order purportedly legalizing such arms sales to Iran until January of this year. Also, the diversion of funds to the *contra* rebels appears to have occurred at a time when Congress had made it illegal for any U.S. government official to help the Nicaraguan rebels.

President Reagan proposed a small commission to examine the role of the National Security Council. That's appropriate.

Meese insisted Tuesday that his own Justice Department investigate any possible violations of the law. That carries the heavy odor of a coverup.

An administration, any administration, investigating itself on questions this serious will convince no one of its objectivity.

Needed immediately is a tough and independent investigator and prosecutor who enjoys the confidence of the American people. Until such an investigation is initiated, this administration will wallow in a sea of doubt and disbelief.

Like Sen. Chiles, not many Americans will be persuaded that Ollie North did all this on his own.

# The Charlotte Observer

Charlotte, NC, November 26, 1986

Struggling to regain his credibility and reputation, President Reagan has now jettisoned some, but not all, of the people who so poorly served him and the country in the Iranian arms fiasco. There may be more to come even as we write, but the departure of mid-level operatives cannot alone repair errors made at a far higher level.

The damage has been wide and serious. The country — the world — has been treated to the shocking spectacle of a top State Department official essentially disavowing the policy of the president in public testimony before Congress. The secretary of state has distanced himself from the affair to the point of disloyalty. The disclosure yesterday that millions of dollars generated in the arms trade ended up in Swiss bank accounts controlled by the Nicaraguan contras apparently shocked even the president.

The resignation of National Security Adviser John Poindexter and the firing of aide Oliver North — the central player in the financial dealings — are a start. The president's pledge to appoint a board to conduct a thorough review of the operations of the National Security Council staff is likewise welcome. Taken together, all that speaks to the concern over the competence of the NSC staff and the propriety of its free-lance operations, though it still fails to address the equally suspect role of White House Chief of Staff Donald Regan.

But even Mr. Regan's departure would not speak to the fundamental error, which was the president's. By all appearances to date, he embarked on a high-risk policy against the advice and without the professional assistance of his secretaries of state and defense. He seriously misjudged not only putative Iranian moderates, but his own competence as a policymaker and a manager.

That cannot be fixed simply by juggling the staff of the National Security Council. The president needs to commission a high-level look at the entire foreign-policy management of his administration. The departments of state and defense must be brought back into the picture. The president must find people and structures to protect him and the country he leads from his manifest shortcomings in matters of policy, detail and management. And he must also find the courage to speak the simple truth, to stop insisting that swaps aren't swaps, that deals aren't deals, that the departures of aides are not firings.

He must do it urgently — not to try to recoup the losses of the Iran deal, but to restore confidence and home and abroad in an administration that is engaged in fundamental negotiations about nuclear arms, missile defenses and the security of the world.

# Pittsburgh Post-Gazette

Pittsburg, PA, November 26, 1986

The one consolation for President Reagan in the uproar over his secret arms deal with Iran — and his inept efforts to rationalize it — was that things couldn't get worse. Now they have, with yesterday's revelation that up to $30 million of the funds paid by Iran for armaments were diverted to the U.S.-supported Contra rebels in Nicaragua.

It isn't just that the new developments prolong the crisis of credibility in the White House. They also provide Mr. Reagan's critics with something heretofore missing in the controversy over the Iran fiasco: a connection between Iran, where even Democrats concede bewilderment about how to advance American interests, and a foreign-policy adventure much closer to home and the president's heart, aid to the Contras.

Because the entire Iran operation was illegally kept from Congress, Democrats and Republicans alike on Capitol Hill had expressed no opinion on the idea of using weapons to foster a new relationship with "moderates" in Tehran (and perhaps the release of American hostages held by Iranian sympathizers in Lebanon). By contrast, opposition in Congress to Contra aid has been overt and vociferous.

Until yesterday, the president's Iranian adventure could be viewed as an operation unto itself, albeit one that seriously distorted the foreign policy-making process. A Contra connection guarantees a respectful audience for the contention that more was rotten in the Reagan White House than a chancy overture to ayatollahs. And it provides an impetus for the housecleaning at the National Security Council that even some of Mr. Reagan's political supporters have been demanding.

A new national security adviser is a certainty with yesterday's departure of Adm. John Poindexter, an architect of the Iran operation, and his chief operative, Lt. Col. Oliver North. It was Col. North, according to Attorney General Edwin Meese, who oversaw the diversion of funds to the Contras. More than personalities need to be changed, however. The NSC staff, including the security adviser, must be made more responsive to those with a mandate from the electorate or Congress to make foreign policy — the president and the secretaries of state and defense.

This isn't the first administration in which the NSC and the security adviser have vied with the secretaries of state and defense for influence, but there is an important difference between John Poindexter and predecessors like Henry Kissinger and Zbigniew Brzezinski. Those men worked for presidents who took a personal and informed interest in foreign policy. After last week's press conference and his admission yesterday that "I was not fully informed" about the Contra connection, it is clear that Ronald Reagan is a very different sort of president.

# THE ARIZONA REPUBLIC

Phoenix, AZ, November 29, 1986

S IX substantive years of the Reagan Revolution are in jeopardy of being sucked into a black hole, the president's accomplishments lost in space and his administration irrevocably tarnished over secret arms sales to Iran.

The American people are witnessing a disturbing array of disclosures and allegations on a daily basis: the dismissal of Lt. Col. Oliver North who was in charge of Central American policy for the National Security Council; the resignation of national security adviser Vice Adm. John Poindexter; the alleged shredding of documents by North before his firing; allegations and then denials from White House chief of staff Donald Regan that he knew of the plot to divert Iranian payments for U.S. weapons to the *contras* fighting the Nicaragua Sandinista regime; and now Friday's report that Reagan was informed regularly on a private pipeline of aid to Nicaraguan rebels, but may not have been aware of the source of the money.

The administration is under siege. The prestige and credibility of President Reagan are on the line. The administration's policy-making process is called into question with cries of who's in charge. The president's ability to govern is threatened.

Reagan could salvage a great deal by naming a special prosecutor with full subpoena power immediately. Thus far, he has chosen not to, unwisely relying on a probe being conducted by the Justice Department and his naming of a three-member special commission to look into National Security Council operations.

Attorney General Edwin Meese III, a Reagan confidant, may very well conduct a thorough and exemplary probe of the sale of U.S. weapons and spare parts to Iran, and the skimming of up to $30 million in Iranian payments to the anti-Sandinista rebels. But his relationship to Reagan and the administration gives the perception that a totally unbiased inquiry is impossible.

Reagan's selection of former Texas Sen. John Tower to head a bipartisan commission that includes former Secretary of State and Maine Sen. Edmund Muskie, and Brent Scowcroft, a former national security adviser, is good as far as it goes. But the commission's task to study the NSC and examine the council's role "in the development, coordination, oversight and conduct of foreign and national security policy" equally is unlikely to quell the uproar.

Democrats, now in full control of Congress, will want to get into the act, too. They must not appear too sanctimonious or too prosecutorial in any inquiry into the Iranian affair. Reagan still is a personally popular president. It would not be in their best interests to go for the jugular, but to participate positively to unearth details of this embarrassing saga.

Reagan's presidency is in danger of unraveling, as did those of former presidents Lyndon B. Johnson over Vietnam, Richard M. Nixon over Watergate and Jimmy Carter over Iran.

The appointment of a special prosecutor would be a major first step in controlling the damage, and restoring the credibility in what is Reagan's most serious crisis.

The good news is not one of us knew what was going on 'round here all this time...

## FORT WORTH STAR-TELEGRAM
*Fort Worth, TX, November 26, 1986*

The startling revelation that money from the sale of U.S. arms to Iran was diverted into Swiss bank accounts for the contra insurgents in Nicaragua delivers another seriously damaging blow to the credibility of the Reagan administration's foreign policy.

Congress and the American public have not yet received satisfactory explanations for the basic foreign policy blunder of sending arms to Iran in exchange for that country's assistance in obtaining freedom for Americans held hostage by terrorists in Lebanon.

That mistake, which President Reagan still refuses to acknowledge for what it is, had generated a general impression of a foreign policy-making network in disarray. The National Security Council, with the president's consent, appeared to be operating a miniature Central Intelligence Agency from the White House with members of the Cabinet, whose responsibilities include diplomacy and defense, being kept in the dark.

And now this. Attorney General Edward Meese has informed the world that in the course of his investigation into the Iranian arms deal, he discovered that funds from some of the arms sales were diverted to the contras at the same time Congress was refusing to authorize further assistance to the U.S.-backed insurgency in Nicaragua.

Meese said those diverted funds amounted to between $20 million and $30 million. He said the wholesale value of the arms was about $12 million, and that price was raised to the Iranians either by the Israelis or other middlemen in the deals. The excess, he said, was transferred to the contras after the U.S. government was paid the basic cost of the arms.

According to Meese, Reagan knew nothing of those goings-on. The attorney general said that as far as his investigation had determined, only Marine Corps Lt. Col. Oliver North, who was assigned to the NSC, and possibly Rear Adm. John M. Poindexter, national security chief, and former national security chief Robert McFarlane knew about it.

McFarlane supposedly learned about it early this year, after he had left office, and Poindexter may have had some general knowledge about it. The impression left by Meese is that North was the person in the know and in control. That's hard to believe.

Indeed, the possibility that a field-grade officer would have the leeway to control such a matter without the knowledge of someone in a policy-making position is extremely remote. Is it really possible that a lieutenant colonel could, in effect, make foreign policy for this nation in defiance of the will of Congress?

If the president knew about this, he must be held accountable. If he did not, it is almost as bad. It is becoming clear that the president is not nearly as informed as he should be on too many matters.

Both North and Poindexter have requested and have been granted reassignment back to the military. Of course, the matter will not end there. A thorough investigation must be conducted to determine if any criminal offenses have been committed.

This latest embellishment of the Iran arms sale debacle raises more doubts about the president's ability to govern effectively during the remainer of his term. Somehow, the president must find a way to defuse the furor over this matter before Congress reconvenes next year.

It will be difficult enough for the administration to get anything done with both the Senate and the House being controlled by the Democrats. And, if this controversy is not laid to rest soon, the president could become the lamest of lame ducks.

Reagan has decided to appoint a commission to make recommendations on how the NSC should function within the foreign policy-making machinery. That, however, is only cosmetology. Everyone already knows it is supposed to be primarily an advisory body and not a surrogate CIA.

If the president is to be effective, he must demonstrate some leadership. And that must involve some truth-telling and some major reshuffling in his administration.

## Birmingham Post-Herald
*Birmingham, AL*
*November 28, 1986*

The late French President Charles de Gaulle, who knew how to be ruthless in advancing the national interest, once described governments as "cold monsters."

Those chilling words come to mind as the Reagan White House seeks to distance itself from Marine Corps Lt. Col. Oliver North and to make him the scapegoat for the diversion of funds to the contra rebels in Nicaragua.

The purpose here is not to defend the president's secret arms sales to Iran or the funding of the anti-Sandinista guerrillas in an end-run around Congress. Rather, the purpose is to argue that a 43-year-old officer should not take the rap for his higher-ups.

Since he came to the National Security Council staff in August 1981, North tirelessly and loyally worked to carry out the president's objectives, especially in lining up private and foreign aid for the contras.

He was the White House's key player in the 1983 liberation of Grenada from communist thugs. He suggested last year's interception of the aircraft carrying the hijackers of the cruise ship Achille Lauro who had murdered an American.

Reagan was pleased to take the bows for those anti-terrorist actions and was personally close to the NSC aide. Now, amid fierce criticism of slipping Iranian arms money to the contras, his attitude seems to be: Who's North?

Trying to extricate the administration from the scandal, Attorney General Edwin Meese made it sound as though North conceived and operated the money-diversion scheme himself, national security adviser Vice Adm. John Poindexter knew a bit about it and everybody else was ignorant.

What politely can one say about that tale? Tell it to the Marines?

Anyone who ever was a GI was not surprised by what happened after the egg hit the fan. The admiral was reassigned, the lieutenant colonel got fired.

North, who earned the Silver Star and two Purple Hearts in Vietnam, is on his own. The Marines don't want him back because he stepped on high-ranking toes to get things done for the president. He faces lacerating congressional probes and possible criminal charges.

Oliver North deserves better. De Gaulle was right.

## The Hutchinson News

Hutchison, KS
November 29, 1986

The U.S.-Iran arms deal is un-raveling like an onion, each new pungent layer more acrid than the last.

Official denials are being pro-duced with the frequency of birth-ing rabbits.

The question Americans want answered is a historical refrain that may dog President Reagan for the rest of his tenure and perhaps for the rest of his life: What did he know, and when did he know it?

He denies knowing about the arms sale to Israel and the sub-sequent movement of arms to Iran and money to the Contras.

The labyrinthine complexity of this scheme would dull the senses of Rubik.

When organizations work within an old boy network, such frame-works oftentimes operate without direct orders. They often operate through nods, blinks and winks.

When an administration sets a tone and a mission, underlings are not always wont to seek direct or-ders to carry out objectives. In the current administration, the objec-tives float in the air like a bad odor.

What Reagan knew and when he knew it is a mere subplot in this epic scheme.

If the Reagan objective is to aid the Contra effort in Nicaragua at all costs — and it is — then the objective was met. The Reagan administration was able to cir-cumvent congressional restrictions and place as much as $30 million in Contra hands. $30 million more than the $100 million approved by Congress.

If an American hostage was re-leased in the bargain, it was icing on the cake.

Funding the Contra effort is a White House objective and that objective has been met.

With the inflammatory rhetoric used by the White House, the "I am a Contra" news conferences, efforts at disinformation for political pur-poses, and the sword-rattling movement of naval vessels around the world, this latest episode should not surprise the doting American electorate one bit.

Said Reagan shortly after the scheme came to light: "I'm not go-ing to lie … . I didn't make a mistake."

Exactly.

The president simply did it his way.

# THE PLAIN DEALER

Cleveland, OH, November 30, 1986

Was Israel dragged into the U.S.-Iranian arms deals or did it initiate the idea of such machinations with White House officials? That such a question should arise is staggering. It is easy to accept that Israel helped a friend close a sensitive deal or two; much more difficult to envision the United States' dancing to Israel's tune.

Nonetheless, reports have surfaced in the U.S. press that allege it was the Israelis, pursuing their geopolitical aims, who first proposed that they themselves sell arms to Iran. Nor were they neces-sarily interested in finding "moderates" to deal with, as President Reagan said he did. They were willing to do business with the regime of Ayatollah Ruhollah Khomeini.

If the same reports are to be believed, White House aides balked at dealing with Khomeini. Later, however, the Americans began to be influenced by Israeli interpretations of the Iranian political situation and of the best way to exploit it.

Whatever the truth, Israel's top leaders are on the defensive in their own parliament just as the Reagan administration is under increasing attack in Congress. While it is true that the government has the votes to nullify the criticism of minority party members, there is great concern in the coun-try about potential damage to Israel's good rela-tions with Congress. Without prejudging the extent of Israel's official involvement, such apprehension is justified.

It is, of course, plausible that Israel could have been sucked into a White House-sponsored scheme involving Iran and, perhaps unknowingly, the Nica-raguan contras, and that Israeli officials would have felt constrained to maintain secrecy to pro-tect the United States as much as Israel. It is not necessarily humbug for Foreign Minister Shimon Peres to suggest that, if asked, Israel has an obliga-tion to help the United States, its biggest benefac-tor; yet would Israel blindly cooperate in a scheme that, if publicized, was bound to plunge participants into dangerous controversy?

Inexorably, given the Israeli connection with the Iran negotiations, Peres and other Israeli leaders now find themselves in the same position as Rea-gan and his closest aides. No matter what they say, in the absence of independent investigation ques-tions will persist about their own understanding of what was going on, their own roles and their wil-lingness to sanction schemes that required great secrecy, not only because they were political dyna-mite, but also because they involved deceiving other branches of government in both countries.

## Arkansas Gazette

Little Rock, AR, November 26, 1986

A new and even more intriguing chapter of *l'affaire Iran* was revealed Tuesday in Presi-dent Reagan's dramatic announcement that his national security adviser had resigned and a key figure on the National Security Council staff who handled secret arms sales to the ter-rorist nation had been fired. Vice Admiral John M. Poindexter, the NSC chief, will return to the Navy and the fired adviser, Lt. Col. Oliver North, apparently will return to or re-tire from the Marine Corps.

Their leaving is not especially surprising, given the way things work. The Iranian matter had clearly exceeded Mr. Reagan's grasp, and even now he refuses to concede that he made a mistake during the 18 months of secret deal-ings with Iranians. Someone had to take some of the flak and somehow it is not surprising that even without the new findings Attorney General Edwin Meese says he offered the pres-ident on Monday the most likely candidates were in the White House, not the State Depart-ment.

The sense of drama and intrigue is height-ened by the sketchy outline — the agenda for congressional investigators grows longer by the day — of arms and money transfers pre-sumably presided over by Colonel North that was offered by the attorney general. What President Reagan knew and when he knew it frame questions that demand detailed answers unless Mr. Reagan is still wedded to the idea that no mistake was made and that stonewal-ling on his own role in the secret dealings is the best policy.

Now we have the Contra Connection, shaped during a time when Congress had prohibited direct American aid to the contras — Mr. Rea-gan's "freedom fighters" — battling the Sandi-nista government in Managua. This, in summary, is the tangled web in Mr. Meese's preliminary report:

The initial arms sale, with Israel the inter-mediary and Colonel North apparently acting without the president's knowledge, took place in 1985, but was approved after the fact by Mr. Reagan. Additional transfers of U.S. arms, pro-vided by the Defense Department and sent through Israel, have occurred since January under presidential approval. This timing should be of interest to the intelligence com-mittees of Congress that, not having been given prior notice, were to have been informed "in a timely fashion" under the Intelligence Oversight Act.

The money transfers are even more interest-ing and certainly legally questionable given the ban against American military aid to the contras in Nicaragua. Meese says that $10 mil-lion to $30 million collected from the Iranians for the arms was transferred through Israeli middlemen to bank accounts set up by the con-tras. The money, says Meese, was not due the United States government because the Central Intelligence Agency collected either from Ira-nians or Israeli middlemen and gave to the Pentagon the $12 million the United States is said to have been owed for the weapons.

So what began earlier this month as reve-lations of secret arms dealings with Iran, a na-tion that remains on the administration's list of terrorist nations, now expands to secret ar-rangements to funnel money for weapons to the contras seeking to overthrow the govern-ment of Nicaragua.

It is hard to tell whether American foreign policy under President Reagan is adrift or mis-guided or shattered, but, if the latter is the case, the time has arrived for someone to put Humpty-Dumpty back together again.

# DAILY NEWS

New York, NY, November 24, 1986

THE REAL DAMAGE, THE WISE always note, does not come from the mistake. It comes from mis-handling the aftermath. A third-rate burglary became a massive defiance of the law and Constitution.

Now, Ronald Reagan is in the most vulnerable position of his public career. There's little time to lose if he is to save his presidency from two waning years of—well—waning. The credibility of his administration, his capacity to lead, is threatened with catastrophe.

The details of the crisis range between shocking and unbelievable. The free-lance wheeling and arms-dealing, the layers of deception, the failures of communication—and worse. They ring more of a Peter Sellers production than of Rambo. The dangers defy exaggeration.

Reagan's done right on a few things: John Poindexter and the spooky Oliver North are well out of the National Security Council, the White House and the government. The study commission Reagan established under John Tower is a good idea; it has a serious job to do.

Still, watching small heads roll and a high commission convene are not going to convince the American people that Reagan is in charge of the nation's destiny or its government—or even the White House. Donald Regan must be held accountable: As a powerful chief of staff, he has served the President badly in this crisis.

All in all, Reagan's firmest chance of recovering the moral and political force of his presidency seems today to lie in fashioning what would amount, almost, to a new presidency.

Reagan must make a full, convincing report to the people. It must overcome his misleading statements of the last week and more. Reagan has got to clean his own slate—his personal trustworthiness is the core of his popularity and moral force. And then he has got to convince the public—and Washington's professional skeptics—that he's in charge.

# TULSA WORLD

Tulsa, OK, November 27, 1986

WASHINGTON hasn't been in such a state of high dudgeon since Watergate. But the Iranian crisis, for all its obvious damage to the country, is not the same as Watergate.

On the basis of what was known publicly on the eve of Thanksgiving, the Iranian affair was shaping up as a crisis of judgment and management at the top. Watergate was a revelation of illegal and immoral conduct. There is a difference.

It may yet develop that there has been lying, cover-up and the misappropriation of large sums of money at the highest level. But none of that has been proved.

The principals in this affair, including the president, cannot escape a judgment that they made serious mistakes. Sending arms to Iran with the hope of freeing hostages was a bummer from the start. The charge that some of the money involved in the arms deal went to the Nicaraguan contras made it much worse. It raised questions not only of judgment, but of flagrant violations of the law.

Still, the president himself revealed the contra connection and is taking sensible steps to get the full facts.

Members of Congress, the media and the public have a right to ask tough questions and to demand straight answers. Thorough investigations on several fronts are inevitable.

But these things can be accomplished with some restraint and with the understanding that the sooner it can cleared up the better.

There is a fine line between trying to repair the damage of past mistakes and simply making political hay. It will be big mistake, for example, if Democrats in Congress use the Iranian affair to wreck the president's policy in Latin America and turn it into a victory for the communist government of Nicaragua.

The president is not the only politician being tested by this crisis. His critics and opponents in Congress will also be judged on they handle their responsibility.

## RAPID CITY *JOURNAL*—

*Rapid City, SD, November 30, 1986*

Something good may result from the Iran-Nicaragua arms debacle. The apparently illegal action of diverting profits from the Iran arms deal to fund anti-Nicaraguan government Contras may result in Congress and the president adopting a sane policy towards Nicaragua's communist government.

Nicaragua is a major and immediate foreign policy problem, but fighting it with plots so bizarre they'd be rejected as too implausible for a Doonesbury comic strip is not the way to fight communism in Central America.

The U.S. has a lot of choices in Nicaragua. Unfortunately, it has pursued a policy which disgraces the very democratic ideals which our government insists that Nicaragua adopt. The U.S. has chosen to conduct an undeclared war using hired Nicaraguan thugs who mine roads, terrorize, murder and kidnap civilians and steal from the U.S. taxpayer.

If the United States is going to oppose terrorism anywhere in the world, it cannot sponsor it anywhere in the world. Doing so destroys the legitimate moral grounds on which terrorism can be opposed. Further, nobody except blind optimists expect the Contras to overthrow the communist regime settling into power in Nicaragua. The Contras' methods seem more likely to unite the nation behind despot Daniel Ortega than overthrow his regime.

Nicaragua's communist government is a serious problem that won't be overthrown by theater-of-the-absurd plots. There is no question that Nicaragua is a Soviet client-state or that Ortega and his henchmen are villains. The nation has established the largest army in Central America. It is involved in supplying arms to communist movements in other Central American nations. There is no doubt the Cubans and Soviets view it as a staging ground for the spread of communism in this hemisphere. There is no question that this must be opposed. The question is how.

The U.S. has intervened militarily in Nicaragua seven times in this century because we disapproved of how the nation was conducting its affairs. Only in the most recent case has communism been the excuse.

The way to counter communism is to help make Central American nations secure and stable enough so that communist movements can't succeed. We failed to do that in Cuba. We failed to do that in Nicaragua. In both cases, we supported a non-communist dictator who made communism seem attractive by comparison.

This will change only when we truly deal with other nations on a basis of democratic idealism — when we worry about the welfare of the people, rather than what deals we can make with the despots who plunder both their own people and the American taxpayer.

Congress should disenfranchise the Contras, who are certain to drive a wedge between the Nicaraguan people and the U.S. The Contras will harm U.S. long-range interests more than they will help them.

We should instead direct and increase efforts towards stopping the flow of weapons from Nicaragua to communist movements in other nations and bolster the determination of other countries to remain independent. If we are to use military force against Nicaragua, then that force should be open and directed against the Nicaraguan government and military — not against peasants in a truck driving down a farm road.

## Sunday Boston Herald

*Boston, MA, November 30, 1986*

A Democratic official recently remarked that the Iranian arms scandal may ultimately backfire on his own party, if certain Democrats continue behaving "like so many apprentice Torquemadas." We hope Senator John F. Kerry is listening to this sage advice.

Our junior senator has had to be dragged before the television cameras (at every available opportunity) to huff and puff about the crisis — demanding to know who knew what, when. A die-hard opponent of Contra aid from day one, Kerry now informs us he will use the fiasco to repeal the assistance measure passed earlier this year.

We too are eager for full disclosure in the matter. Such certainly will be forthcoming, from the president's non-partisan, blue-ribbon panel.

Acting in his accustomed role as the best senator Nicaragua ever had, Kerry has been looking for an excuse to kill Contra aid since the Democrats regained control of the Senate. To maintain that because certain administration officials abused their authority we therefore must abandon the Contras is illogical to the point of idiocy.

As Rep. Les Aspin (D-Wis.), a Democrat who supports Contra aid put it: "The issues should be separable. The vote should be on whether it is right or not right to aid the Contras, not on the basis of whether Ollie North was diverting money from Iran."

Right on. Concerning the reality of the Sandinista/Soviet menace in Central America, the North operation changes nothing. Nicaragua is still ruled by a i increasingly oppressive communist clique. An independent human rights group in the nation reports Sandinista repression now exceeds that of deposed dictator Somoza.

Moscow continues to arm Ortega & Co. to the teeth. Nicaragua remains a base for Soviet subversion in the Western hemisphere, an imminent threat to our national security.

To abandon the Nicaraguan freedom fighters because of the misfeasance of certain administration officials, would be to punish both the captive people of that land and ourselves in the long run.

## The Des Moines Register

*Des Moines, IA, November 26, 1986*

Ousting two top White House officials, John Poindexter and Oliver North, is a first step in dealing with the secret arms deal with Iran and the even more secret diversion of the profits to the Nicaraguan contras. But it does not answer the key question: Who is in charge of making foreign policy?

Evidently, not the State Department. Testimony before Congress by John C. Whitehead, the No. 2 man at State, suggests that department has been cut out of the process. Whitehead expressed embarrassment that the "Department of State doesn't have the basic information, two weeks after the fact."

The White House, in turn, is putting out mixed signals about who is in charge. Last week, President Reagan said he was solely responsible for approving the deal. But the departure of North and Poindexter suggests that the White House is now trying to put the blame on Reagan's advisers.

•

A staff shakeup alone will not solve the problem.

The deal has created a credibility problem between the United States and its allies in Europe and the Middle East. Just days before the secret arms shipment became public, Secretary of State George Shultz told the European allies that the United States would tolerate no dealings with terrorist nations.

Whitehead testified that the reaction among U.S. allies in the Middle East was "uniformly negative" and that the decision to ship arms secretly will make it more difficult to persuade other nations not to do so.

At home, a tremendous gap of mistrust has been created between the White House and the State Department over what role, if any, the secretary of state has in making and implementing foreign policy in this administration.

Whitehead's testimony, which apologized for the Reagan administration policy and disassociated the State Department from White House behavior, signals a deterioration in the relationship between the two foreign-policy-making branches of government.

The president very much needs to take constructive steps to heal the rift.

He should reaffirm his confidence in his secretary of state, or appoint a new secretary, so that U.S. diplomats, citizens and foreign leaders know who is responsible for American foreign policy. Anything short of a positive plan to undo the damage will perpetuate growing fears that no one in Washington is really in charge.

# Richmond Times-Dispatch

*Richmond, VA, November 26, 1986*

**Reagan**

Now President Reagan's fiercest foes no doubt believe they have what they have been seeking for six long years: a weapon sharp enough to pierce his Teflon coating and destroy his presidency. The president's announcement yesterday that a subordinate had improperly diverted funds from the Iranian arms sale to the *contras* of Nicaragua has added a bizarre and disturbing element to the Iranian controversy and prompted speculation about a Reagan Watergate. Congress will investigate the affair, and it is almost certain that some Democratic members will attempt to prove that the president is the chief culprit.

At this point, however, there is no justification whatever for equating the current controversy with Watergate. The principal presidential offense in that sordid affair was obstruction of justice. President Richard Nixon and some of his aides sought to protect wrongdoers and to conceal information and evidence. They lied and equivocated. But so far, Mr. Reagan has shown no inclination to engage in such obstructionist conduct.

To the contrary, the president has briefed congressional leaders several times on the Iranian arms sale and he has ordered members of his administration to cooperate with Congress as it investigates the matter. He has appeared before reporters at least three times, once in a full-scale nationally televised press conference, in the past week. He promptly removed his national security adviser, Vice Admiral John Poindexter, and the adviser's top assistant, Lt. Col. Oliver North, upon learning of the diversion of funds. Finally, he will appoint a commission to assess the role of the National Security Council, which some critics say has usurped foreign policy responsibilities that should be borne by the State Department. These are not the actions of a man who intends to cover up his administration's mistakes and to "stonewall" against corrective action.

The president's major mistake appears to have been his choice of men for key positions on his White House staff. Several of them have proved to be inefficient, and some have turned out to be untrustworthy. They did not keep him fully or timely informed on the plan to sell arms to Iran, a scheme designed primarily to establish credibility with elements in that country that might prove to be helpful in a post-Khomeini era but incidentally to obtain the release of American hostages held by Moslem terrorists in Lebanon. His advisers did not foresee the damage that might result to Mr. Reagan's credibility at home and with the United States' allies from a misunderstanding of the objectives of the Iranian arms sales. Finally, Attorney General Edwin Meese says the president was totally in the dark about the diversion of funds until Mr. Meese's investigation — which Mr. Reagan had requested — of the whole Iranian affair uncovered it.

The attorney general says that "the only person who precisely knew about this [the diversion] was Col. North." Admiral Poindexter was generally familiar with the colonel's actions, says Mr. Meese, but not in detail. The attorney general will continue his investigation to determine whether "there was any criminality involved."

That a lower-level aide like Col. North could engage in such a transaction without the detailed knowledge and specific approval of his immediate superior, Admiral Poindexter, is incredible. That White House Chief of Staff Donald Regan was ignorant of the colonel's activities is astonishing. And that the president's staff could serve him so ineptly and so callously is profoundly distressing.

But the buck stops in the Oval Office, and the president must bear the consequences of his staff's inefficiency. His task now is to regain the strength and credibility his administration will need to operate effectively for the two remaining years of his term. Removing the top men at the National Security Council was the first step on the road back. Replacing Donald Regan might not be a bad idea. As advisers, the president needs men and women of exceptional ability and certain loyalty.

•

**Shultz**

There are problems at the State Department, too. Though we have been among the admirers of Secretary of State George Shultz, we are becoming disillusioned. He has been less than candid about his own role in the Iranian affair, saying at first that he knew practically nothing about it but admitting later that he participated in at least two major meetings on the plan. His decision to send Deputy Secretary of State John C. Whitehead to the House Foreign Affairs Committee to testify disparagingly about the president's Iranian operation seemed to emphasize the secretary's contempt for the president's decision.

That Mr. Shultz and his associates resent the NSC's prominent intrusion into areas of foreign policy they consider to be the State Department's domain is understandable. The White House agency has gone too far, and the president is right to curtail its operations. But the State Department is part of the administration, and its objective should be to help the president recover from the Iranian debacle rather than to make matters worse by publicly sniping at him.

It is undeniable that the Iranian exercise was mishandled. No congressional investigation is needed to determine that. The president has acknowledged as much and is acting to repair the damage. But if there is to be a congressional inquiry, the nation will suffer if the president's critics strain to hype this situation into another Watergate. That would be a debilitating experience that the country, which faces so many other pressing problems, could not afford to undergo.

# Wisconsin State Journal

*Madison, WI*
*November 27, 1986*

If it were a John LeCarre spy novel, or the script of a Hollywood movie, few people would find this plot believable:

A "lone wolf" on the staff of the National Security Council, working out of the White House basement but without the advice and consent of the president of the United States, arranges to sell U.S. arms to Iran via Israel with the excess cash — a mere $30 million or so — funneled to Nicaraguan rebels through secret Swiss bank accounts.

Not only is the president in the dark, according to this bizarre story line, but so are the other members of the National Security Council: the vice president, the Central Intelligence Agency director, the secretary of Defense and the chairman of the Joint Chiefs of Staff.

The president's national security adviser knows something — but he decides not to look into it further and doesn't seem to suspect (or care) that a law or two might have been broken.

In fact, the only people who know, according to the attorney general of the United States, are a few "consultants" and some others who operate on the fringe of government. Even the Nicaraguan rebels claim ignorance — or, at least, can't explain what happened to the money.

That scenario would require a lot of imagination in print or on the silver screen — it takes even more in real life.

If President Reagan and others at the top did not know about this bizarre chain of events, that's appalling. If they did, that's even worse because of the disrespect for law and process.

Reagan is clearly facing the most trying episode of his presidency. If he mishandles events from this point forth, the enormous accomplishments of his first six years will be overshadowed and he will become a "lame duck" executive months before his time.

The nation cannot afford a powerless president who appears out of touch with his own administration. With both houses of Congress under Democratic control, arms-control talks with the Soviet Union continuing and severe budgetary problems demanding attention, the nation needs a leader who is capable of leading.

In short, all national business will remain on hold until the Reagan White House clears its decks and sets a fresh and law-abiding course.

Reagan must swallow his pride and consent to the fullest possible airing of the Iran fiasco. He should also not be afraid of cutting loose other close advisers if it turns out that Adm. John Poindexter and Lt. Col. Oliver North were not the only officials who knew.

If that leads to the offices nearest his own, so be it.

# Former President Nixon Consulted as Watergate Comparisons Abound

Former President Richard Nixon December 9, 1986 told a meeting of Republican governors that he had advised President Ronald Reagan several times about the unfolding Iran arms scandal, but said, "It is not going to be another Watergate." Nixon said that the Watergate scandal had been handled "abysmally" but that Reagan was handling the current crisis "expeditiously." Nixon drew on his conversation with Reagan, reporting that Reagan "just wasn't involved in the details. He has told me so." Nixon said that in executing legitimate goals, former national security adviser Robert McFarlane had "screwed it up."

In his weekly radio address Dec. 6, Reagan conceded that the "execution" of his Iran policies had been "flawed, and mistakes were made." In acknowledging mistakes in the execution of legitimate policy goals, Reagan stopped short of admitting that the policy of providing arms to Iran was a mistake, as several advisers had reportedly urged him to do. Reagan said that he regretted that the Iran affair had "caused such concern and consternation. But I pledge to you, I will set things right."

Reagan also rejected the advice of political allies that he call in two former National Security Council officials and ask them to tell him the facts about the diversion of funds from Iranian arms sales to the Nicaraguan contras, it was reported Dec. 8. Unidentified officials said that Reagan had declined to call in the officials, Lt. Col. Oliver North and Vice Adm. John Poindexter, because he said he did not want to act as "judge and jury." White House legal officials said that if North and Poindexter revealed details to Reagan while declining to answer questions from congressional committees on Fifth Amendment grounds, it could put Reagan in an ambiguous legal position. Earlier, Reagan had promised "to get all the facts out" about the arms sales and the diversion of funds.

A New York Times/CBS News poll reported Dec. 10 showed that 47% of the American people thought Reagan had been lying when he said he did not know that funds had been sent to the contras. Fewer, 37%, said they thought he had been telling the truth.

# THE BLADE

*Toledo, OH, December 18, 1986*

BASED on his comments on President Reagan's current travail over the Iranian-contra mess, former President Richard Nixon seems to have learned very little from the Watergate scandal that ousted him from the Oval Office in disgrace 12 years ago.

The thrust of his remarks recently to a meeting of Republican governors was for critics to "get off his (President Reagan's) back" and let him get on with the "quest for peace" with the Soviet Union. Not one word about coming clean with the facts behind all the controversy and confusion that surrounds the arms deal with Iran and sending of the profits to the Nicaraguan contras.

"We must instead look at the main ring," he counseled, "which is the larger question of Soviet-American relations and peace in the world." Those relations are important, of course, but this is precisely the blind spot that Mr. Nixon exhibited in failing to recognize that the cover-up of the Watergate break-in was worse for his administration than the actual deed itself.

The former president was right in commenting that one of the worst things (from the Reagan administration's viewpoint) that could result from the current furor is that the President's ability to conduct foreign policy would be restricted. But that is almost a foregone conclusion if Mr. Reagan persists in stonewalling, as Mr. Nixon did for so long, and protecting his closest aides, thus practically insuring that the investigating and the criticism will go on for another two years.

Despite repeated pledges of cooperation with investigating congressional committees, White House officials have refused to provide key documents dealing with the Iran-contra situation. Unless this kind of information is forthcoming soon, the perception that a cover-up of illegal actions is taking place will become fixed firmly in the public mind.

Mr. Nixon was right about another matter. Watergate, as he concedes now, "was handled abysmally." President Reagan can still learn a lesson from that even though Mr. Nixon obviously has not.

If the President has any real hope of salvaging his final two years in the White House and putting Iranagua behind him, he will ignore advice from an unindicted Watergate co-conspirator, clean up his official house, order his subordinates to cooperate with the investigations, and come clean with everything he knows about the issues.

# The Dispatch

*Columbus, OH, December 5, 1986*

Those who are calling the Iran-Nicaragua crisis President Reagan's Watergate are missing an important, indeed crucial, point.

In the Watergate turmoil it was the president, Richard Nixon, who stonewalled, using all his power to attempt to keep the truth from being revealed. Just about the opposite is true with Reagan, who seems genuinely committed to seeing that the facts are put before the American people. Thus his call for the appointment of a special counsel.

But if Nixon was finally undone by hiding what he knew, Reagan's problem is that he did not know what he should have known. Not being in control of the National Security Council operating in his own White House has cost him dearly, with a fresh poll showing his standing with the public has dropped precipitously.

There is no question that he must move not only to give the impression of being in command, but also to really reassert his supreme authority, to make it known that underlings cannot go off wandering around like loose cannons. The appointment of Frank Carlucci to head the National Security Counicl is a good first step, as we have said.

Some trusted voices within his own party are urging the president to make some changes in his White House staff. However, Reagan should carefully evaluate the performances of his key personnel before making a judgment on whether anything should be done in this regard. These people work for the president and are responsible for performing their duties as he wants them done.

Reagan's six years in office have seen some remarkable successes, and he has been astonishingly popular with the American people. He would like to finish his time in office with a flourish of accomplishments, and he can still do so. The American people will rally behind him, but first they will want to be sure that the president's hands are firmly on the wheel. That's the challenge that faces Reagan at this most critical time in his presidency.

## The Washington Times

*Washington, DC, December 3, 1986*

Those who supposed that, smarting over criticism of the Iranian fiasco, a resentful Ronald Reagan was going to hunker down and cover up, repeating all the stupidities of the Watergate scandal, will have to suppose again. Yesterday the president, seizing control of the growing imbroglio, asked for an independent counsel and a select congressional committee to sift the evidence and promised his complete cooperation.

"I recognize fully the interest of Congress in this matter," the president said, striking just the right note, "and the fact that in performing its important oversight and legislative role, Congress will need to inquire into what has occurred."

Mr. Reagan has done what needed to be done, and he has done it, not grudgingly, but in the proper spirit, eschewing rancor and pledging candor. During a picture-taking session yesterday morning, he went out of his way to underscore his commitment, lest there be any lingering doubt.

"I am determined to get all of the facts out and take whatever action is necessary," he said. Later in the day, responding to press inquiries about his knowledge of the surreptitious "contra"-skim, he authorized White House spokesman Larry Speakes to "tell them flat out that I had no knowledge whatsoever of it until Ed Meese briefed me on it Monday afternoon."

In view of the president's actions, making plain at last that his administration is committed unambiguously to full knowledge and disclosure, it is astonishing to find Sen. Richard Lugar, one of the Republican leaders in the Senate, in such unseemly haste to stick his thumb in the president's eye. The administration waited too long to seek an independent counsel, the senator declared on television. "They should not have fooled around for two or three days."

Few will disagree that, but for yesterday's prudent course change, the administration probably would have beached itself. But the lookout has been heard. Spurning flattery for the grim advice he needed to hear, the president has enunciated a policy calculated to satisfy legitimate demands for an impartial accounting. Now the air can be cleared and, within a reasonable time, the essential business of government resumed.

Throughout this crisis, Democratic leaders by and large have behaved with responsibility and restraint. Sen. Lugar might profit by their example. Especially in time of crisis, the national interest is scarcely served by having responsible members of the president's own party suggest that, because it has procrastinated, the administration is doomed.

## St. Petersburg Times

*St. Petersburg, FL, December 6, 1986*

President Reagan's radio broadcast Saturday, in which he pleaded with Americans "not (to) forget there are many other issues that concern us," brings to mind the effort of another president to control his own worst crisis.

The image is of Richard Nixon, at a press conference in August 1973, insisting "we must move on from Watergate to the business of the people . . . continuing with initiatives we began in the first administration."

There are other eerie similarities. Mr. Reagan, in telling *Time* magazine that "this whole thing boils down to a great irresponsibility on the part of the press," might have been Mr. Nixon blaming the press for Watergate. His description of Lt. Col. Oliver North as "a national hero" recalls Mr. Nixon's hasty praise of John Ehrlichman and Robert Haldeman as "two of the finest servants it has been my privilege to know."

All Americans — whether Democrats or Republicans, liberals or conservatives — can only hope the Watergate analogy ends there. It is in no one's best interest to have another fallen presidency, another government crippled for two years by scandal and ongoing investigation. Even Mr. Reagan's severest critics want to believe he did not know that money from the sale of arms to Iran had been diverted, with apparent gross illegality, to the support of Nicaraguan rebels.

But if Mr. Reagan had read the record of Watergate, he would know that he cannot avoid a paralyzed presidency unless there is immediate action to purge his own staff, appoint an independent counsel to conduct the criminal probe and establish a single bipartisan congressional investigation. When loyal Republicans such as Senate Majority Leader Robert Dole and Foreign Relations Chairman Richard Lugar are telling him that, it behooves the President to listen. Dole especially has been there before; he remembers Nixon aide Bryce Harlow promising him that Watergate would be "a three-day story."

Mr. Reagan has been saying the right things about wanting the truth out but has been showing himself glacially slow to act. On Monday, for example, he said he's thinking about the special session of Congress that Dole recommended and said also that he would "welcome" the appointment of an independent counsel if the Justice Department recommended it. That appointment is now more than a week overdue, and if Mr. Reagan were as concerned as he should be he would ask Ed Meese why North and North's boss, former National Security Council director John M. Poindexter, the only two men at the White House who were said to know about the *contra* connection, were allowed to have access to their files for two days after they had

> It is in no one's best interest to have another fallen presidency, another government crippled for two years by scandal and ongoing investigation.

come under suspicion. He might even ask Meese how he could have been so certain that Donald Regan, the White House chief of staff, was blameless in the affair when the FBI hadn't even been called into the case at that point.

If one thing is clear so far, it is that Mr. Reagan has been getting truly bad advice from many of those closest to him, such as Regan, who have failed to persuade him (or even, it would seem, to try) that it is a constitutional crisis of the first magnitude when the White House deliberately flouts laws enacted by Congress, whether or not the President himself knew. What kind of "national hero" gets a President into trouble like that? What kind of staff encourages him to stonewall?

## EVENING EXPRESS

*Portland, ME*
*December 6, 1986*

A question repeatedly raised during the congressional inquiry into the Watergate affair 13 years ago was this: "What did the president know and when did he first know it?"

Although parallels between Watergate and the scandal currently plaguing the Reagan administration ought not to be too glibly drawn — the cases are only superficially comparable — the same question is decidedly relevant today.

What President Reagan did or did not know about the diversion of profits from secret arms sales to Iran goes to the heart of White House responsibility and accountability in its conduct of foreign affairs.

The president admits that he knew about — indeed, that he authorized — the sale of arms to potentially friendly elements within the Khomeini government. It was a move which apparently violated not only the president's own oft-repeated vow never to pay ransom for hostages but also the official U.S. posture of neutrality in the Iran-Iraq war.

That's bad enough. But the president says he was wholly unaware of the arrangement whereby profits from the sale of arms to Iran were diverted to the Contras in Nicaragua.

What the president knew and when he knew it takes on considerable significance, therefore.

If he actually *did* know about the Contra connection, then he has deliberately misled the American people by denying it.

On the other hand, if he *did not* know about it, as he insists, it means that the most reckless sorts of foreign policy activities were able to be carried out in the very shadow of the Oval Office over a period of several months without the knowledge of the president.

Did the chief executive know or didn't he? Either way, it doesn't say much for the Reagan presidency.

## The Chattanooga Times
### Chattanooga, TN, December 10, 1986

In a *Newsweek* article last week, John Ehrlichman, who was a top adviser to then President Richard Nixon during the Watergate affair, suggested that President Reagan hold daily press conferences to answer any and all questions on the Iranian arms sales controversy. It's an interesting idea, particularly since President Reagan's tenure has been notable for the infrequency of his meetings with the press.

Mr. Ehrlichman's logic is that daily press conferences would "permit the nation to see a president who is fully engaged, demonstrably concerned with his problems, seeking results." Moreover, he said, it would steal the thunder of a Congress primed for lengthy investigations. "If we saw the president every day for a month, attacking the Iran-Nicaragua issue with candor and vig-

or, what would be left for the Joe Bidens to pick over in January?" he asked.

We will only know the answer to that if Mr. Reagan takes Mr. Ehrlichman's advice, which is hardly expected. The president is not at his best in non-scripted give-and-take with reporters.

Mr. Reagan has already fallen into another trap the former Nixon aide cautioned against. "There may be a tendency to believe that the current farrago is a 'Washington story' of interest only to people 'inside the beltway'," Mr. Ehrlichman said, warning from experience that such an assumption does not reflect reality and will backfire. But just last week, in an interview with *Time*, Mr. Reagan described the current controversy as a "beltway bloodletting." It will be to his detriment if he continues to underestimate its seriousness.

## The Record
### Hackensack, NJ
### December 11, 1986

Apparently determined to make the worst of a bad situation, the nation's Republican governors have sought some unlikely counsel on the Iran-contra arms fiasco. At their gathering in Parsippany this week, they heard words of wisdom from, of all people, Richard Nixon. Mr. Nixon delivered his remarks behind closed doors; according to an associate, he told the governors that the scandal was nothing more than "a sideshow in Washington" that could "weaken" President Reagan in his dealings with Moscow.

"We must look instead at the main ring, which is the larger question of Soviet-American relations and peace in the world," Mr. Nixon reportedly said. "It is time to get off his back so that the president does not lose two precious years in his quest for peace." He revealed that he has talked with the president three times over the last three weeks and advised him to get all the information out as soon as possible: "There is not going to be another Watergate as long as you keep ahead of the curve." President Reagan, for his part, assured his predecessor that he had known nothing about the diversion of arms-sales profits to the Nicaraguan contras. "And I believe him," Mr. Nixon said.

The Republican governors, their spouses, and their aides rose in applause and crowded around to have their picture taken with the former president. They then flew to Washington for an audience with the *current* president, who told them that the Iran-contra furor was "weird" but that he was doing his best to put the story out. "I just had a feeling of a man who totally wants to get to the bottom of this," Governor Kean said afterward. Asked if he believes him, he replied: "Yes, absolutely."

The American people are not quite so sure. The next day, pollsters for The New York Times and CBS News reported that only 37 percent of the public think President Reagan is telling the truth about Iran and Nicaragua; 47 percent think he is lying. While the Republican governors place stock in a man who resigned the presidency in disgrace for his role in the Watergate cover-up, a plurality of Americans choose instead to trust their own eyes and ears — which tell them that an arms conspiracy so massive must have been known to others in the White House besides a couple of underlings named Poindexter and North.

## The Hartford Courant
### Hartford, CT, December 3, 1986

Congressional leaders have all but decided to appoint a select committee to investigate allegations of wrongdoing by top White House officials. ... The U.S. attorney general asks federal judges to appoint a special counsel to look into possible criminal conduct in the White House. ... The president charges the news media with irresponsibility and calls his critics sharks. ... He stoutly defends an aide he fired. ... The president's popularity drops dramatically. ... A majority of Americans believe he's not telling the truth and that his administration is engaged in a cover-up.

Is this 1973 revisited? Is this a Watergate rerun?

No sensible person would want to relive the nightmare of 1973, when Richard M. Nixon, on the verge of being impeached, resigned from the presidency. A generation of Americans was turned off by government. Public service became a pursuit to be avoided.

Yet here we are again agonizing over another presidential crisis that could bring down the house of Ronald Reagan.

The lesson of Watergate has not gone entirely unlearned, however. President Reagan has acted more swiftly than Mr. Nixon did.

Two of Mr. Reagan's key subordinates on the National Security Council have been let go. He has called on Congress to form a select committee to investigate the odious U.S. arms sale to Iran and the even more odious use of profit from such sales to fund the overthrow of the government of Nicaragua. He has authorized his attorney general to request the appointment of an independent counsel, otherwise known as a special prosecutor, to probe the criminal aspects of the imbroglio. He has formed a blue-ribbon task force to review the operations of his national security apparatus.

Meanwhile, the National Security Council is prohibited by presidential directive from engaging in any covert operations. Foreign policy will be conducted from the State Department, not the basement of the White

House, Mr. Reagan has pledged.

All of this Mr. Reagan has done in the two weeks since the reports of the Iranian and contra deals first surfaced.

To be sure, the president did not respond to the reports willingly. But he could have resisted, as Mr. Nixon did, until paralysis set in at the White House.

It isn't over yet, of course. In fact, the agony has just begun. Mr. Reagan could minimize the pain for his administration and the nation by raising the shades at the White House and letting the sun shine in. It's not enough to call for a congressional investigation and for the appointment of a special counsel. Will he order his staff to cooperate fully or will he stonewall? Will he invoke executive privilege too often? Will he hide behind the veil of national security?

He promises full cooperation, and we shall see if the promise is kept when the probes begin.

If there's one overriding lesson from Watergate, it's that you'd better tell all. Once the revolting basic story is out, the only way to minimize the damage is to hide nothing from the American people. Mr. Reagan will lose badly if the public winds up with the impression that he's hiding something.

Even now, before the investigations begin, his chances of recovery will be greatly enhanced if he admits what his supporters are saying, privately and publicly: The deal to sell arms to a government that supports terrorism was wrong. His willingness to swap weapons for the American hostages in Lebanon was foolish. His subordinates' misuse of profits from the Iranian deal was an abuse of public trust. His failure to mind the store was a dereliction of responsibility.

Americans will look kindly at a leader who levels with them, and who tells them that although he meant well, his decisions, in retrospect, were unwise. Two words — "I'm sorry" — will go a long way in restoring public trust in Mr. Reagan, if they are genuinely uttered.

BillDay Detroit Free Press

'THIS IS DEJA VU ALL OVER AGAIN'
(FAMOUS SPORTS PROVERB)

# Chicago Tribune

*Chicago, IL, November 27, 1986*

How easily Washington slips back into the Watergate mode: What did he know and when did he know it? Demands for a special prosecutor. Predictions of another wrecked presidency.

Granted the Iran arms deal was a botched operation. And the use of money from it to provide support for the contras that Congress had been unwilling to give was imprudent.

But what is this scandal all about?

Taking the President at his word, he was betrayed by zealots on the National Security Council staff in the White House who took his pronouncement, "I am a contra," as an order to do anything and everything to support the cause.

Perhaps this demonstrates that he is inattentive to the details of the White House operation, which everyone had assumed all along. But the cause was not corrupt. He has made no secret that he will go to great lengths to resist the spread of Soviet influence, and this was the reason both for deciding to try to do business, however mistakenly, with certain elements in Iran's government and for his continued effort to put pressure on Nicaragua.

These are both controversial. A lot of people who are ordinarily willing to follow his lead dropped out of the parade when it turned out that it led back to the terrorist regime in Tehran. And he has had trouble getting Congress to back him up on the contras, though eventually it did come around, approving the very sort of aid that is at the heart of this latest mess.

At worst, President Reagan will turn out to have authorized an arms-for-hostages deal and then authorized sending the money to the anticommunist guerrillas in Central America. But nobody has suggested that he violated Americans' individual rights or used the power of the presidency to subvert an election. And so far there are no indications that national security interests are being invoked to excuse acts of political self-interest.

The movement of money to the contras may have violated American law, but that is a complicated issue involving more than simply the meaning of the restrictions passed by Congress. The Constitution grants presidents considerable power to set and implement foreign policy, and the scope of that power is unclear.

The most significant features of this episode, as it now appears, do not involve criminal conspiracy or mean-spiritedness. The administration, frustrated with its inability to keep secrets and the difficulty of dealing with a Congress that wants to control foreign policy, simply made a common mistake. It attempted to mount a delicate secret operation itself.

This cut out of the discussion people of good judgment and experience who might have warned of the dangers of selling arms to a terrorist regime and using the money to sustain a secret war. And the operation became dependent on a few misguided romantics who like to think of themselves as hardnosed realists ready to work in the lawless world of international intrigue. It is not the first time that the self-styled realists have turned out to be totally out of touch with reality, gravely underestimating the possibility that the mission would be compromised and misjudging the political consequences once the cover was blown.

The worst thing the President could do now is to hunker down and try to get out of the situation by deceit. The candor option is the best one he has, and if he takes it, his presidency and his foreign policy will survive. His adversaries would be making a mistake if they try to use this affair to destroy him two years before the end of his term. He is still an extraordinarily popular figure, and Americans have become tired of the spectacle of the nation ruining its leaders.

## ARGUS-LEADER
*Sioux Falls, SD*
*December 5, 1986*

More details are trickling out about the Reagan administration's secret sale of arms to Iran, reinforcing the haunting echo of a scandal that rocked the United States more than a decade ago: Watergate.

Indignant members of Congress, **Editorial** scheduling hearing after hearing, are trying to find out what happened and how it happened.

So are the national media, which, caught by surprise, belatedly unleashed their troops to help unravel the story.

The list of heroes and villains will be incomplete for a while, but there is a comforting message buried in the discomfort and uncertainly surrounding the arms sales and diversion of profits to rebels fighting in Nicaragua.

That message is noted in the current issue of *Time* magazine: The United States has a government of laws run by officials who can be held accountable.

That is our nation's fundamental strength. The moral principle underlying it overrides the talents and weaknesses of officeholders who come and go.

The resiliency of the government's backbone was demonstrated during the Watergate scandal. It is holding up under the arms scandal, which paints the portrait of a president dangerously detached from his own administration.

It's hard to take comfort in the thought that, unlike Watergate, the present scandal apparently was designed to further the cause of a nation, not an individual. A handful of idealistic zealots cannot devise and implement a nation's foreign policy. But at least President Reagan stepped forward to break news of the scandal on his own and is taking at least token efforts to uproot the truth.

Reagan is trying to calm the uproar with characteristic optimism. "The machinery is in place to seek answers to the questions that are being asked — to fix what needs fixing and to restore complete confidence to the conduct of our foreign policy," he says.

Restoring public confidence in general presidential leadership will be just as big a job, but the nation has survived such crises before. Remembering our government's fundamental strength will help.

# Reagan Blames Press For Scandal's Damage

*Time* magazine published a frank interview with President Reagan November 30, 1986. In it, the President expressed his bitterness toward the news media for its coverage of the Iran-contra affair. "There is bitter bile in my throat these days," he said. "I've never seen the sharks circling like they now are with blood in the water. What is driving me up the wall is that [the sale of arms to Iran] wasn't a failure until the press got a tip from that rag in Beirut and began to play it up. I told them that publicity could destroy this, that it could get people killed. They then went right on." Reagan continued: "This whole thing boils down to a great irresponsibility on the part of the press."

On the question of whether his presidency had been damaged, he implied that criticism of his policy was limited to the nation's capital. "This is a Beltway bloodletting," he said, referring to the highway that encircled Washington, D.C. "...I'm not going to crawl into a hole."

A CBS News/*New York Times* poll conducted Nov. 30 and reported December 2, 1986 found that Reagan's overall public approval rating had dived to 46% from 67% a month before. It was the lowest rating for Reagan since 1983, and the sharpest one-month drop in approval of a president's job performance ever recorded. The poll also found that 56% of Americans disapproved of Reagan's conduct of foreign policy, 75% opposed selling arms to Iran and 58% were against aiding the Nicaraguan contras. Asked to choose who they trusted more to make correct foreign policy decisions, respondents chose Congress over Reagan 61% to 27%. Although 53% of those polled believed that Reagan had known in advance of the Iran-contra connection, 59% still believed he had "more honesty and integrity than most people in public life." In addition, 47% believed that the crisis was "as serious for the country as Watergate was," with an additional 10% believing that it was even more serious.

## The Philadelphia Inquirer

*Philadelphia, PA, December 3, 1986*

President Reagan changed his tone yesterday — promising cooperation in getting to the bottom of the Iran-contra mess — but there was no hint he's about to change his tune. The tune is that the media have done him in. "This whole thing," he told Time magazine, "boils down to a great irresponsibility on the part of the press."

He didn't stop there. He implied that publicity alone put his Iran initiative into a tailspin and endangered the lives of remaining U.S. hostages. He's got a point — but only a piece of a point.

Publicity in fact *has* doomed his under-the-table arms deals with Iran and, perhaps, imperiled the hostages. But that publicity was not the result of nosy reporters prying the lid off sensitive negotiations. It came about because Iranian officials revealed the deals to serve their own political ends.

Such disclosure should have been anticipated and, in fact, more cautious members of the President's circle argued that a deal this big was impossible to keep quiet. If there was reckless irresponsibility involved, it lay in the White House's eagerness to pursue the policy, heedless of warnings.

This is not to say that the press is above reproach in either the scandal at hand or coverage of foreign policy in general. There's a case made by press critics that the media are far too compliant, superficial and crisis-oriented in reporting on foreign affairs.

One of those critics is William A. Dorman, who recently co-wrote a book on the U.S. press and Iran. He argues that the question shouldn't be whether the press *should* serve as a watchdog, but "how well the press is performing that function."

Too often, he contends, the media rely on administration definitions of world problems, reinforcing, rather than challenging, official assumptions. Only when "tactics come into question; when contradictions in rhetoric or policy become overwhelmingly obvious" does the press play hardball, and then it's "too late to correct damage."

There's a well-aimed *ping* of truth there — whether you accept Mr. Dorman's whole thesis or not. As criticisms go, it's a lot closer to the mark than the President's shameless, over-the-shoulder Parthian shot.

## Houston Chronicle

*Houston, TX, December 24, 1986*

Writers to the Houston Chronicle's Viewpoints column are frequently critical of the role the media are playing in the Iran-contra affair.

Those who support President Reagan are prone to accuse the press of being sharks, of lacking respect for the presidency and of having a liberal bias.

A few letter writers say the media are doing their job and are helping to bring out the facts.

The use of unidentified sources is frequently criticized, and that's not an easy matter to address.

Government practices contribute to the use of unidentified sources. Many agencies routinely brief reporters "on background," which means no names. The State Department puts up signs to let the press know the ground rules. The purpose is to make information available to the public without making a formal policy statement. The press goes along in order to get information from a responsible source.

Reporters frequently talk to people very high in government who agree to provide information if their names are not used. The reporter knows these individuals to be trustworthy, but also knows that if the request for anonymity is not respected, no further information will be forthcoming.

A secretary of state might talk very frankly with reporters on a flight between foreign capitals, but only on condition that what he says be attributed to "a highly placed source." That lets the American public know what is going on and lessens the possibility of an international incident over what is said.

This use of sources that cannot be identified poses a difficult problem for the media. Washington is like a colander, constantly leaking. And those doing the leaking have various motivations. Reporters and editors can and do use their best judgment, honed by years of experience.

Media carrying only official, on-the-record press releases would become a voice of government, just like Soviet publications. Dictatorships are neat: You are told what to believe and you had better not ask questions. Democracy, and the role of the news media in a democracy, is messy and full of tough questions, but it works.

# The Dispatch

*Columbus, OH, November 14, 1986*

The media are in the middle of the griddle of the White House/Iran/Hostage story and this points up the precarious position the press must occupy when such a complicated set of events develops.

The media serve, among other things, to report to the public about governmental actions. Some of the reports are routine; some are unusual, and some are of considerable interest.

The story of the fate of American hostages in Lebanon — including governmental action to gain their release — is one of great public interest. Much interest also is engendered when a hostage is released, just as speculation about the possible release of other hostages draws attention to the news. Public attention is further aroused when details of alleged government dealings with Iran are reported. When these dealings are reported to include arms sales in direct contravention of expressed U.S. policy, the interest becomes intense.

Members of the media work feverishly to present all the details, the complete picture, the full story to audiences around the globe. Their task is to find the truth, and the road to truth is often through the fog of speculative report, rumor and allegation.

It was in the midst of the journey that a just-released hostage, David Jacobsen, issued an impassioned plea to the media: "In the name of God, back off," arguing that media speculation was at best prolonging the captivity of the remaining hostages and at the worst endangering their lives.

Reagan administration officials followed up on this plea by maintaining that speculative media coverage of hostage-release efforts had "dashed our hopes" for their release. But just beneath the surface of these statements is a hint that another agenda would be served by silencing the press, that decisions have been made and actions taken to advance U.S. policy which, if revealed, would be politically embarrassing to some.

What are the media to do? Professionally, journalists have a responsibility to report the news without concern of consequence. They serve as non-commital conduits of information providing the public with the raw material of understanding. Humanly, they struggle with the idea that their actions could increase the hardship of the long-suffering captives. They hear the pleas of people such as Jacobsen, but worry about the self-serving, news-corrupting influences others can exert. They work and they wonder.

They know that the dilemma can never be resolved, that the needs of society and the needs of the individual will not always coincide and that there are no easy answers to the tough questions of ethics and fairness they sometimes cannot avoid. They toil on, trusting in their instincts and in the system they serve.

Mostly, they trust that the people they write for and the people they write about will understand.

*Washington, DC, December 8, 1986*

Once more a president faces a crippling credibility crisis, this time over arms shipments to Iran, and once more the press is criticized as the villain.

The president blames the news media. He says reporters ruined attempts to free more hostages from Lebanon.

The president's defenders blame the news media, too. They say that the "liberal" Washington press corps wants to create another Watergate and drive the president from office. They believe that secrecy must be the first order of any presidency. To them, it is perfectly legitimate to run rogue covert operations out of the White House basement.

So, they insist, it's nobody's business that the USA put arms in the hands of the fanatical government run by the Ayatollah Khomeini. So, it's nobody's business that millions of dollars from that arms sale helped fund "contra" rebels in Nicaragua in defiance of the will of Congress.

It's nobody's business, they say, that while the president was insisting that we would never pay ransom for hostages to terrorists, his White House staff was shaking down rich private citizens to raise money to do just that.

This business was so sensitive, so sacred, so secret that nobody could be trusted except a handful of White House intimates. The media couldn't be trusted. The Congress couldn't be trusted. And the people couldn't be trusted.

That is a distorted and dangerous view of democracy. It profanes the ideal of government by the people.

Sometimes, secrecy in government is crucial so that our enemies won't know what our government is doing. But the people are not the enemy. Neither is the Congress.

And neither — despite the media bashers now on the attack — is the news media.

Sure, the media can be rude, abrasive, abusive, and arrogant. But, those traits have not characterized the media's relationship with President Reagan. It is patently false to suggest that journalists covering the White House hate Reagan or want to drive him from the Oval Office.

Sure, some press critics are liberals. But voices now most critical of the president include many conservatives.

The news media deserve criticism in the current crisis.

For months, the media failed to find out that our government was freeing hostages by sending arms to Iran and that millions in Iranian dollars were smuggled into a Swiss bank account and diverted to the contras.

For months, the media failed to find out that we would, indeed, arrange ransom money for hostages; that laws of Congress were ignored; that our stated position of neutrality in the Iran-Iraq conflict was subverted; that our foreign policy was undermined.

The media have acted, not like a swarm of killer sharks — as Reagan suggests — but like a school of jellyfish.

The president admitted Saturday what has been obvious for weeks: His administration made grave mistakes. But the nature of many of those mistakes remains a secret today.

The media should be criticized not because it exposed those mistakes, but because it failed for so long to do so.

## THE SPOKESMAN-REVIEW
*Spokane, WA, December 7, 1986*

Each day, each hour practically, a new twist shows up in the troublesome controversy swirling around the White House. It is far too complex to go by any single name unless you have an abundance of hyphens with which to link the various facets together, as in arms-to-Iran-via-Israel-and-cash-to-Contras.

It was so much simpler a week ago, at least in President Reagan's eyes.

"This whole thing boils down to a great irresponsibility on the part of the press," he said in a widely quoted interview with Time magazine's Hugh Sidey.

Such words are coming back to haunt the president. Not because the nation's news media are above reproach. But because daily disclosures by Reagan's closest allies — and many of the president's own words — make it abundantly clear that there is far more here than the handiwork of rapacious reporters whom the president likened in the Time interview to sharks circling in bloody water.

Vice President George Bush has said that, "Clearly, mistakes were made."

Defense Secretary Caspar Weinberger has said that the escapade was "wrong" and that although the president was acting in good faith he was being steered by bad advice.

Secretary of State George Shultz, whose foreign-policy domain was battered by the loose cannons in the National Security Council, was among the first from within the White House intersanctum to offer criticism.

From left and right, the president has been hearing cries for the resignation of White House Chief of Staff Donald Regan.

And Lt. Col. Oliver North, the Security Council aide to whom administration officials attribute not only the idea for the scheme but also responsibility for its implementation, is dangling hints of trading what he knows (thus implying he knows something not yet disclosed) for immunity from prosecution.

Can all this, and more, really be nothing more than the creative manipulation of a hungry press corps as Reagan implied before the situation began to snowball?

Let's look at it another way. If the American news media had ignored the initial report in a Beirut magazine of the arms deal (which then was seen as a scheme to spring American hostages, was explained by Reagan as an attempt to develop relations with moderate forces in Iran, and since has been acknowledged as, at least in part, a ruse for putting money in the Nicaraguan Contras' pockets), when, if ever, would the subsequent disclosures have been made?

Are reporters never guilty of excesses? At times, certainly, and not only excessively zealous but excessively timid as well. One of the most frequently forgotten revelations of the Watergate scandal was that when Richard Nixon said some of his dubious practices were common tactics among his predecessors, further digging often showed he was generally correct.

Not that that provided justification, but it made the national press corps sit up and take notice that they might not have been looking at the highest institutions of government as closely, or as critically, as they should.

In a perfect world, reporters covering the government wouldn't have to be sharklike. The officials who explained government policies and government actions would be open and forthright, and the president of the United States wouldn't have to complain, after reading embarrassing disclosures in news reports, that "I wasn't told everything."

"YOU WILL EACH TAKE TEN PACES...TURN...AND COMMENCE SHOOTING."

## THE BLADE
*Toledo, OH, December 2, 1986*

IT IS ironic that President Reagan, a man who has often manipulated the press of this country to his own advantage, can still pretend to be blind to the essential role of the fourth estate in the functioning of a democratic form of government. But his denunciation of the press for what Mr. Reagan called its irresponsibility in reporting the Iranian arms-for-hostages deal makes it clear that the blind spot exists.

If the President remains convinced that there was nothing wrong in months of secret operations to run American weapons and other military equipment into Iran, a country dominated by as anti-American a ruling clique as exists in the world today, and use the profits to finance military aid to Nicaraguan contras, that is nothing short of incredible.

Thus the original sin — which was to ship arms illegally to a country linked to terrorism and to send the money, also illegally at the time, to the Nicaraguan rebels — is compounded by a continuing attempt at a cover-up and a refusal to acknowledge any culpability in the face of almost universal condemnation.

What the President is saying in effect is that secrecy is preferable to openness in carrying out foreign policies, no matter what the consequences of those actions might be. A degree of secrecy for a limited time and for good reason is understandable, but the Iranian-contra deals went far beyond that for as long as 18 months.

When Mr. Reagan says that "the whole thing boils down to a great irresponsibility on the part of the press," he is really conceding that the activities of his administration cannot stand the light of day. As columnist David Broder put it, the only sustainable policy in a nation like ours is one that can be articulated and defended in open debate.

The President was quoted in an interview last week as saying that "I've never seen the sharks circling like they now are with blood in the water." There is indeed blood in the water and the sharks are not likely to stop circling until the facts about this entire matter are laid out for responsible public scrutiny. Mr. Reagan will ignore that responsibility at his peril, and blaming the national press will not resolve the issue.

# The Augusta Chronicle

*Augusta, GA, December 12, 1986*

Several weeks ago, before the Iran arms sales story broke, media types were scurrying around getting petitions signed protesting that President Reagan wasn't doing enough to negotiate the release of Associated Press reporter Terry Anderson, a captive of Khomeini terrorists in Lebanon.

Since then, of course, it's been learned that the president was so concerned about Anderson and the other kidnap victims held in Beirut that he broke his own ban on selling arms to terrorist states, partly in expectation of getting all the American captives back.

He succeeded in getting only three out. But we haven't heard a word from the activist journalists who blamed him for Anderson's plight.

They're probably busy writing stories denouncing Mr. Reagan for negotiating with terrorists.

# The Register

*Santa Ana, CA, December 21, 1986*

Among the many paradoxes of the Iranian-contra affair is this exquisite one: Should the Reagan presidency collapse in scandal, such a turn of events — devoutly wished by its enemies in government and the media — could bring about the realization of Ronald Reagan's most fervent anti-government rhetoric. Just as the Nixon administration's fall a dozen years ago was accompanied by condemnations of "the imperial presidency" by liberal advocates of central government, so could the downfall of the Reagan administration depopularize the executive branch as the favored engine of liberalism.

To which the predictable response of those of us of the libertarian persuasion would be three cheers. But should it? For within the celebrated demise of the executive would be the seeds of a reassertive Congress. How would libertarians look upon the revolting development of, say, an emboldened Rep. Jim Wright, wielding more *de facto* power over foreign policy than the president of the 50 states?

Our answer, if you'll forgive the acrobatics, is that the free society could be better served by a presidency with both manueverability in foreign affairs and answerability. The primary reason for what *The New Republic* has dubbed "Iragua" is that Congress through the post-Vietnam years has been treading clumsily into foreign policy-making, which is where the framers of the Constitution were leary of placing the irresolute folks from Capitol Hill.

Libertarians have generally found the congressionally mandated restraints agreeable, if constitutionally dubious, imagining that they discouraged presidents from global adventuring. Alas, those restraints actually have encouraged global adventuring from the White House. All the "micro-management" from Congress, especially a Congress which in the space of a few months can first scorn and then wed the contras, amounts to is an embossed invitation to rogue National Security Council staffers to plot their extra-legal schemes; *voila!*, Ollie North.

Can a serious libertarian deny that "Iragua" (well, it's better than *Iran-* or *Contra-gate*) represents government at its duplicitous worst? Wouldn't it be better if the president were empowered to launch his foreign initiatives in the manner the framers intended? In these pages former National Security Adviser Zbigniew Brzezinski, surely a strange bedfellow for any libertarian, offers a prescription for the recovery of the presidency.

The framers did not envision a popularly elected president. But the paradox libertarians must face is that a president acting under his original constitutional authority necessarily follows a powerful restraint, *i.e.* a fully informed body politic, whereas a presidency of diffused bureaucratic power begins to operate out of control, leading to a final internment of the Constitution and dictatorship.

These reflections have nothing to do with a sentimental attachment to Ronald Reagan, who can be hanged before we would sacrifice our commitment to the principles of a free society. But if through this crucible of "Iragua," presidential activity can be brought more into the open, defiant of those who would bureaucratize it, then we say godspeed to the 39th heir of George Washington. We simply do not share the bloodlust evidenced by so many of our brethren in the Fourth Estate.

# The Washington Times

*Washington, DC, December 2, 1986*

After some rest and recuperation over the Thanksgiving weekend, President Reagan came out swinging in an interview in *Time* magazine. The personality that was revealed was not exactly what we are used to from Everybody's Uncle Charlie, and it doesn't fit Mr. Reagan very well.

The president called the critics of his secret policy with Iran "sharks" and blamed the press for "sabotaging" it. The policy was working fine, Mr. Reagan said, "until the press got a tip from that rag in Beirut and began to play it up." Among other insights, the president opined that Lt. Col. Oliver North was "a national hero," despite the colonel's enforced defenestration from the National Security Council.

The fact is that the president's policy was flawed from the beginning. It was based on false or unverifiable assumptions and was bound to fail, regardless of which "rag" leaked what or followed up the story afterward. Eighteen months of shadowy and perhaps illegal arms deals with Lord knows who in Tehran have wrecked our foreign policy. No "moderates" hold power there, none appear on the verge of coming to power, and Iran's support for terrorism seems to be as enthusiastic as ever.

It was inevitable that the unreliable intriguers with whom the White House was dealing would divulge something sooner or later. It also was inevitable that an inquisitive and adversarial American press would exploit the story and that, as night follows day, the president's political adversaries would extract maximum advantage from the multiplicity of leaks, miscalculations, finger-pointing, and pratfalls.

As for Col. North, he certainly has his virtues — loyalty and patriotism evidently among them — but this is hardly the time for the president to dwell on them. The colonel himself is not saying anything to anybody except his lawyer, and he better hope he has a good one.

Nor is it the time for the president to indict the motives of those who question his negotiations with the Iranians and who are trying to discover what and who were involved. Too many mistakes and gross miscalculations already are established for Mr. Reagan, a good man with a flawed policy, to try to shift the blame to his critics.

# Bush Concedes 'Mistakes' While Distancing Himself From Morass

Vice President George Bush, in his first detailed public comment on the Iran-Nicaragua affair, December 3, 1986 gave a carefully worded speech in which he voiced support for President Reagan while at the same time trying to distance himself from the scandal. His remarks, before the American Enterprise Institute, were televised nationally. Bush had been on vacation and virtually invisible for the previous several weeks. Analysts suggested that no matter what he did, the Iran crisis would have a negative impact on his undeclared candidacy for the 1988 presidential election.

Bush said that "in the hearts of the American people" there existed "an understandable animosity, a hatred really" of the Iran of Ayatollah Ruhollah Khomeini. "I feel that way myself, to be very honest with you." But he went on to make a detailed justification for the attempt to improve relations with Teheran because of its geopolitical importance. Speaking of the U.S. arms shipments that were meant to open a channel to moderates in the Iranian regime, Bush said: "Call it leadership. Given 20-20 hindsight, call it a mistaken tactic if you want to. It was risky, but potentially of long-term value."

Referring to the widespread perception that the U.S. had sold the arms to Iran in effect as ransom for American hostages in Lebanon, Bush said carefully: "I can tell you the President is absolutely convinced that he did not swap arms for hostages." He went on to admit that "clearly mistakes were made." But he praised Reagan for moving quickly to authorize investigations into the affair. "We gotta take our lumps and move ahead," he said.

Speaking of his own role, Bush said "I was not aware of and I oppose any diversion of funds, any ransom payments or any circumvention of the will of the Congress or the law." He went on to assert that U.S. support for the Nicaraguan rebels "should not, must not, be held hostage to actions unrelated to them."

## The Hutchinson News

*Hutchinson, KS*
*December 6, 1986*

Vice President George Bush has spoken out in character on the Iranian arms fiasco.

The character is a wimp.

He went before a private study group, the American Enterprise Institute, in Washington on Wednesday to declare that "mistakes were made" in the Iranian effort, though the effort itself was "potentially of long term value."

"The president hoped that we could open a channel that would serve the interests of the U. S. and our allies in a variety of ways," he said. "Call it leadership; give 20-20 hindsight and call it a mistaken tactic; call it whatever you want - it was risky, but potentially of long term value," he said.

Only a true wimp could find such redeeming value and such a trivial admission of error in this calamity.

Though Mr. Bush and the president, no doubt, would like the nation to focus on the manner in which the operation was conducted, the nation must keep looking at the basic decisions that led to the operation itself.

It isn't a "mistaken tactic" that is the calamity.

The calamity is the basic notion that a secret mission trading tons of armaments for hostages, escalating an existing war, and in contravention of our own laws and policies, is proper.

The tactics really worked very well. For 18 months, the Reagan crowd kept their secret operation secret. Their tactics did strengthen the crazy Iranians and tip the war balance against the Iraqis. Their tactics did lead to the return of an American hostage (though, of course, unknown numbers of non-Americans were slaughtered by the weapons they sent to Iran).

The "tactics" in the disaster are not overly important.

Keep your focus on the basic decision that set the operation in motion, no matter what the wimps such as George Bush may try to do.

## The Boston Globe

*Boston, MA, December 23, 1986*

Vice President George Bush did not offer the voters of Iowa a profile in courage – or clarity – when he addressed the graduating class of the Iowa Law Enforcement Academy. In his talk, Bush urged Adm. John Poindexter and Lt. Col. Oliver North to "make a great sacrifice" and stop invoking their Fifth Amendment right against self-incrimination.

When asked whether he meant that the two former officials of the National Security Council should testify to congressional committees about the arms-to-Iran deal, regardless of whether they are granted immunity against possible criminal prosecution, Bush replied: "I don't know. I'm not a lawyer. I can't make a judgment. All I want is for the American people to know the truth."

Bush himself may have important testimony to offer about the covert program to ship arms to the anti-Sandinista rebels in Nicaragua, a program apparently financed in part with money derived from the sale of weapons to Iran.

Felix Rodriguez, a Cuban native, is believed to be the coordinator of these arms shipments in Central America. A chronology released by Bush's office last week showed that Bush met with Rodriguez three times in the last two years. Donald P. Gregg, the vice president's na-

tional security adviser, met with Rodriguez 10 times in the same period.

When asked about his talks with Rodriguez, Bush said they only discussed helping the El Salvador army resist rebels in that country.

When asked whether he would follow his advice to North and Poindexter and disclose his own conversations with President Reagan on arms for Iran and for Central America, Bush rejected the analogy. "I never discuss what I advise the president," he said.

It is hard to see how these rambling remarks advance Bush's political prospects in the 1988 Iowa caucuses or do anything to enlighten the public about the Iranian affair.

No sitting vice president has been elected to succeed directly the president under whom he served since Martin Van Buren succeeded Andrew Jackson in 1837. Bush is not doing much to change that 150-year-old record.

He sounds more as if he is vindicating the wisdom of Finley Peter Dunne's Mr. Dooley, who explained: 'Th' prisidincy is th' highest office in th' gift iv th' people. The' vice-prisidincy is th' next highest an' th' lowest. It isn't a crime exactly. Ye can't be sint to jail fr it, but it's a kind iv a disgrace. It's like writing' anonymous letters."

# The Hartford Courant

*Hartford, CT, December 4, 1986*

Untrue, unfair and totally wrong.

Vice President George Bush used these words Wednesday in responding to allegations that he was involved in the private U.S. efforts to fuel the civil war in Nicaragua.

Yes, he met the Cuban-American Max Gomez three times, but they didn't discuss aid to the contras, Mr. Bush said. They discussed what Mr. Gomez was doing "in terms of the counterinsurgency in El Salvador," according to the vice president.

Mr. Gomez is said to have been the intelligence officer in charge of running the supply operation from military bases in El Salvador to the contras in Nicaragua. He may also have been involved in fighting the guerrillas in El Salvador, but that effort has long been superseded by the U.S. drive to overthrow the Sandinista government in Nicaragua.

Perhaps Mr. Gomez never brought up the contra operation during his three meetings with the vice president. Perhaps Mr. Bush didn't even bother to ask him how the war against the Sandinistas was going.

If that's difficult to believe, so is the vice president's claim that he was unaware that the profits made from the U.S. sale of arms to Iran were being illicitly transferred to the contras. Mr. Bush said he knew "of our Iran initiative and I supported the president's decision" to sell arms to a government that has

been branded by the administration as a supporter of terrorism.

We are baffled: In the White House discussions on the sale of such arms, didn't it occur to Mr. Bush or anyone else involved to ask about money. Didn't anyone ask if the arms were to be sold at cost or for a profit? Didn't anyone bring up the subject of where the profits will go? Didn't anyone wonder aloud how the transaction was to be recorded in the federal government's account books?

The notion that President Reagan and his vice president agreed to sell the arms but left it up to subordinates to do whatever they pleased with the revenue is farfetched. It seems highly unlikely that the top staff members at the National Security Council didn't ask their White House superiors what should be done with the $10 million to $30 million in profits.

Mr. Bush was on the mark when he said the American people are confused about, among other things, "how the administration could violate its own policy of not selling arms to Iran." But his remarks Wednesday did not clear up the confusion. It's now more obvious than ever that the only way to get straight answers is for congressional investigators and the soon-to-be appointed independent counsel to ask tough questions of the principals under oath.

# The Kansas City Times

*Kansas City, MO, December 5, 1986*

Just when things threatened to get too serious in Washington, along came George Bush. "When the flak gets heavy out there, the wingman doesn't go peeling off and pull away from the flight leader, especially when the flight leader is known to the wingman to have total ability and a good record," he told *Time* magazine.

The vice president has a gift for making himself sound mildly foolish in more than one way in a single sentence. Other people could have come up with an inappropriate metaphor, trying to elevate political expediency to the level of valor in combat. But it wouldn't be the same.

For one thing, who else would dilute this declaration of loyalty by hinting that perhaps he would desert a flight leader who didn't have the right stuff? And who else, having long been teased for trying to fit an Ivy League personality into a John Wayne mold, would introduce all this by pointing out: "I had a little combat experience in a world war"?

Despite all the cries for the vice president to speak out on the Iran fiasco, there really wasn't much for him to say. What could he say? "I'm happy that the president on whom I've staked my political future decided to deal with terrorists"? "I'm delighted that our national security staff knows how to use modern technology to avoid getting bogged down in a lot of paperwork"?

All the usual disadvantages of being a vice president apply to this situation; they are simply larger because of the size of the crisis.

So it is hardly surprising that the vice president's speech this week to the American Enterprise Institute followed the basic administration line. As usual, George Bush echoed Ronald Reagan. What else can a vice president do? Hubert Humphrey knew all about it.

"I'm sorry I didn't bring a map . . . " Bush told his audience, prefacing the little geography lesson that has become a standard part of the administration's defense. That's OK, Mr. Vice President; by now we all know that Iran isn't far from the Soviet Union. We all recognize that Iran is a big country in an important region. But some of us also realize that the regime there is founded on hatred of the United States and aggression against its neighbors.

Bush said he knew and approved of the dealings with Iran but did not know and did not approve of the diversion of money to the contras. The vice president did a better job than Reagan of acknowledging the legitimacy of public concern about the Iran affair, and for that he is already getting grief from some of the president's most steadfast supporters.

He obviously spent a lot of time trying to figure out how to hint his way out of heavy responsibility for the arms-for-hostages swap: "I can tell you the president is absolutely convinced in his own mind he did not swap arms for hostages." His audience before him, he thought that line in his prepared speech was still too strong. The phrase "in his own mind" said something that he shouldn't say about Reagan's mind. Bush decided to omit it. Such are the tough decisions that vice presidents must make.

# The Philadelphia Inquirer

*Philadelphia, PA*
*December 5, 1986*

Vice President Bush played it smart. When the Iran scandal broke three weeks ago, he kept his mouth shut. It would have been unseemly in those early days to undercut President Reagan and, as a presidential aspirant himself, pure folly for him to play cheerleader for a policy that was so clearly disastrous.

So Mr. Bush waited. He waited until things got so bad that even the President has begun to sound contrite. He waited until the moment was right to support the President's leadership, but to distance himself from the policy.

Mr. Bush's speech at the American Enterprise Institute Wednesday was a masterful piece of political craftsmanship. This is not surprising. The speech reportedly was drafted by a private communications consultant with input from, among others, the chairman of Mr. Bush's political action committee and his pollster. This is what it takes for a man of conscience to speak his mind these days.

Mr. Bush said he was aware of "our Iran initiative" and supported "the President's decision." He did not say it was his decision as well. He said that "the President is absolutely convinced that he did not swap arms for hostages." He did not say whether the vice president is also convinced.

In fact, Mr. Bush said very little about his role in any of this — other than to assert he knew nothing of the diversion of funds to the contras or any other effort to circumvent the Congress or break the law.

What Mr. Bush did do was use the word *mistake*, a word that sticks in the President's throat, but that the administration is no doubt glad to see in the public domain at this point.

"Given 20-20 hindsight, call it a mistaken tactic, if you like," Bush said of the arms-for-hostages dealings. "Clearly mistakes were made," he said of the National Security Council staff's shadowy dealings.

Mr. Bush is not out of the woods (or, more appropriate, jungle) yet. Congressional and legal investigations will determine what role he and members of his own staff played in this scandal. There have been allegations — categorically denied by Mr. Bush — that his office was running the secret supply missions to the contras that included Eugene Hasenfus' ill-fated flight into Nicaragua.

No matter how deftly he maneuvers now, the outcome of those inquiries and their impact on the administration's final two years will largely determine whether Mr. Bush has a political future beyond 1988.

# THE TENNESSEAN

*Nashville, TN, December 4, 1986*

THESE are also trying times for Vice President George Bush, who has presidential ambitions in 1988, and can't distance himself from President Reagan or the arms to Iran deal.

Mr. Bush has kept a fairly low profile since the disclosure of the Iran dealings and the diverting of funds to the contras. But in his first major speech — to the American Enterprise Institute — he said he was aware of the Iran initiative and said the attempt was "legitimate and arguable."

But he said he was not aware of and opposes any diversion of funds, any ransom payments, or any circumvention of the will of Congress. Referring to "rumors" and "false charges," the vice president said, "There is this insidious suggestion that I was conducting an operation. It's untrue, unfair and totally wrong."

When an American-manned contra supply plane was shot down in Nicaragua, it was disclosed that Cuban-American Max Gomez, who was running the supply operation out of El Salvador, had ties to Mr. Bush. "I met Max Gomez three times and never discussed Nicaragua with him," the vice president said. "What I did discuss was what he was doing in terms of the counterinsurgency in El Salvador."

In his address, Mr. Bush commented, "Still the question remains of how the administration could violate its own policy of not selling arms to Iran." He answered it by adding, "Simple human hope explains it better than anything else."

Simple human hope is not much of an explanation of why the administration waded into the Iran fiasco without serious discussion of what the consequences would be if it came to light, not only at home but within the alliance. Somebody surely must have known it would ultimately be disclosed.

Mr. Bush likened himself to a wingman when a squadron of military planes comes under fire, saying the "wingman doesn't go peeling off and pull away from the flight leader." So he has taken the best available choice, drawing closer to Mr. Reagan. But the greater his loyalty, the greater the damage if and when the full story comes to light.

Even Mr. Bush must know that his political future is damaged by the current storm over the Iran-contra affair. ■

# The Salt Lake Tribune

*Salt Lake City, UT, December 6, 1986*

If the predictions he indulged Wednesday are fulfilled, then political prospects for Vice President George Bush will surely improve. If not, his chances to become the Republican Party's 1988 presidential candidate diminish.

In his first extended, public comment on the Iran arms sale furor engulfing the White House, Mr. Bush said during an address Wednesday that when all the facts are known, the American public would fully understand why President Reagan authorized these peculiar, dismaying transactions. Moreover, he said, the president also would be forgiven any apparent misdeed. Predictions, perforce, loaded with fervent hope.

As Mr. Reagan's second and last term in office reaches the mid-point, the vice president has been positioning himself to become the GOP's heir-designate. Those Republicans who would contest him can't help but see some advantage for themselves in the Bush connection to an administration now flinching under looming scandal. The vice president's Wednesday comments illustrated his dilemma.

Obliged to defend and support Mr. Reagan, the vice president, if he is to be a convincing presidential candidate, must also distance himself from the worst implications of the Iran arms deal. He initiated the process in conceding Wednesday that "mistakes were made."

By acknowledging as much, he becomes one of the first White House, non-Cabinet people to do so. President Reagan compelled one National Security Council adviser to resign, replacing him with another. He fired the NSC deputy and appointed an ad hoc committee to fully examine the agency's past and future purposes.

A presidentially-mobilized Justice Department investigation divulged that Iran arms sale money was diverted to Nicaraguan counter-revolutionaries, in evident violation of Congressional prohibition, and Mr. Reagan has now authorized further probing by an independent counsel. But he has not confessed to making any serious "mistakes."

Vice President Bush, then, seems to disagree. That would signal a contention that, as president, he would have handled the matter differently, at least as far as secretly diverting money is concerned. He was quick to deny any knowledge of the Contra funding scheme while praising attempted contacts with possibly "moderate" elements in Iran. He naturally liked freedom for American hostages that the arms sales may have helped achieve.

Mr. Bush, then, associates himself with all the "good" found in the Iran arms deal, while ducking the "bad." That's politically understandable. But if the bad manages to ultimately overwhelm the Reagan administration, there probably won't be enough good left to carry the vice president triumphantly through the 1988 Republican convention, no matter how much he may try to appear a loyal, yet reluctant, and, therefore, wiser soldier.

# The Union Leader

*Manchester, NH, December 8, 1986*

One essential fact emerges from Vice President George Bush's rationalizations and tergiversations concerning questions that revolve

**VICE PRESIDENT BUSH**

about the administration's arms deal with Iran and its so-called Nicaragua connection. And Bush himself stated that key fact during his speech last Wednesday to the American Enterprise Institute in Washington when he said in full view of AEI members and guests and citizens across the land who were tuned in to Cable News Network coverage:

*"I was aware of our Iran initiative and I support the President's decision."*

It is that statement, we submit, that could crack the broad but thin layer of popular support that Bush enjoyed, crack it because the American people, however they may regard the diversion of funds from the arms deal to the anti-Communist freedom fighters in Nicaragua, emphatically reject the arms deal itself —and especially as it relates to the payment of ransom for Americans held hostage by the Ayatollah Khomeini.

Aware of this public perception, Bush posed the question during his AEI address: *"How can the United States government have a policy against countries sending arms to Iran and then turn around and itself send arms? I understand. I know the American people simply don't understand this."*

And, having by now digested his remarks of last Wednesday, they may understand it even less.

Entirely aside from the question of whether it was realistic to work recently with "pragmatic elements within Iran (that) were beginning to appreciate certain sobering realities" — e.g., the 115,000 Soviet troops in Afghanistan, the 26 Soviet divisions on Iran's northern border, the war with Iraq and Iran's teetering economy — and entirely aside also from the President's "human hope" that "we could open a channel that would serve the interests of the United States and of our allies in a variety of ways," the fact remains that the arms deal was, even by

Bush's own charitable definition, "risky."

"Given 20-20 hindsight, call it a mistaken tactic if you want to," he said. But millions of Americans endowed with common sense need no hindsight to regard it as a *tragic blunder* to send arms to Iran to try to assure Iranians "who were taking enormous risks by just talking to us" and "felt they needed a signal that their risks were worth it."

Granted, the policy of conducting a dialogue with Iran was, as Bush said, "legitimate and arguable." What was improper was to sacrifice the nation's integrity and credibility by warning other nations against sending arms to Iran and assuring the American people that "we will not deal with terrorists" while all the while the Reagan administration was doing both.

"Clearly mistakes were made," said Bush of "certain activities of the National Security Council staff." True, but more important is that the original policy itself was fatally flawed if for no other reason than that there was no reason to suppose that it could be kept secret.

Nor could Bush have satisfied many citizens when he said, "I can tell you that the President is absolutely convinced that he did not swap arms for hostages." Show us someone who believes there was no such swap and we'll show you someone who probably believes that one lieutenant colonel in the Marine Corps masterminded the diversion of funds that Bush told the gathering he was not aware of and opposed!

Bush strains credulity when he suggests that the release of the Reverend Benjamin Weir after the September 1985 shipment of two planeloads of arms was coincidental. He puts his own motivation in doubt when he asks the American people to believe that the release of Father Lawrence Jenco on July 26th of this year was not related to yet another planeload of arms that arrived in Iran on, of all days, the Fourth of July. And, in view of these two "coincidences," Bush loses all credibility when he suggests that there was no swap of arms for hostages when David Jacobson was freed early last month —freed only two weeks after a Danish freighter delivered Israeli-made military equipment to Iran in a deal reportedly approved by U.S. officials.

We offer one bit of kindly advice for George Bush as he prepares to traverse rural New Hampshire during his imminent bid for the presidency: *Mr. Vice President, please be careful not to step in the bushwah!*

## THE ⚓ SUN

*Baltimore, MD, December 5, 1986*

Vice President George Bush could be the principal political casualty of the Iran-Contra scandal. He has been the leading candidate for the Grand Old Party's presidential nomination in 1988, largely because he was regarded as the president's choice as heir apparent. Now President Reagan's popularity has plummeted. If Mr. Reagan stays down in the polls, he will likely take Mr. Bush with him. Mr. Bush could distance himself from the president — as he did by an inch or two in a speech Wednesday, calling the decision to deal with Iran a mistake — but that risks diluting his strong point, his loyalty.

He can't stay too close and he can't stray too far. And there may not be anything in between. It looks like a mission impossible. (This analysis assumes the vice president was not involved in the "contras" part of the deal. Some Republicans have suggested he might have been. If he was and that comes out, he would be finished politically. It also assumes he will not become president or acting president between now and 1988.)

If Mr. Bush loses, who wins? There are several possibilities. Rep. Jack Kemp could inherit Reaganites from the Bush camp. On economic matters, he has long been the sentimental favorite of the right. Many conservatives are suspicious of all other leading Republican choices.

Sen. Robert Dole has been and will continue to be on television a lot, as the Republican leader of the Senate. Publicity helps. The senator has already begun to talk publicly about the party's needs, as contrasted to the president's needs, in a time of peril. If the crisis approaches Watergate depths, he might be regarded as just the strong, experienced, skilled partisan the party needs to rally around at a dark moment.

Of course, some now little known Republican senator or representative may emerge from the congressional investigations of the crisis and capture the nation's imagination and the party's highest honor. Or the former co-star of the Watergate Committee, Howard Baker, may find his talents more appreciated now than before. Or GOP voters may just become disgusted with everything Washington and turn to a fresh candidate whose association is with some other venue. Examples: former Delaware Gov. Pete DuPont, or Pat Robertson.

# Part II: The Investigations Begin

After the broad outlines of the Iran-contra scandal were disclosed, bits and pieces of the story continued to leak out. The disclosures became the focus of public attention as the secret arms transfers appeared to run directly counter to declared United States policies. The U.S. had repeatedly claimed it would never pay ransom to hostage-takers. The Reagan administration unsuccessfully tried to minimize the damage of the burgeoning affair and inevitably it had to bow to investigations.

The Senate Intelligence Committee questioned many of the players after the scandal broke, and later two select committees of Congress began investigations that they subsequently merged. For his part, President Reagan had Larence Walsh appointed special prosecutor in the case, and the President charged a special review board—the Tower commission named after its chairman, former Senator John Tower (R, Texas)—with studying what went wrong with the National Security Council.

In an interview published in the November 30, 1986 edition of Time magazine, Reagan claimed that the U.S. arms shipments began after "the Iranians came to us first." That contradicted virtually all other accounts, which indicated that the idea had been developed by both American and Israeli officials. Reagan also said, "It wasn't us funneling money to [the contras]. This was another country"—apparently a reference to Israel. Israeli officials were reported to have been deeply disturbed by the remark, viewing it as a hint that they might be made a scapegoat in the scandal.

When President Reagan met with the Tower commission December 1, 1986, he denied "flat out" that he had any knowledge "whatsoever" of the contra fund transfer until November 24, 1986, the day before it was revealed to the nation. He told the review board that he "wanted all the facts to come out" in its probe of the NSC. He said he had directed the NSC not to engage in any active operations pending completion of the study.

Many more questions were raised than were answered when the Senate Intelligence Committee interviewed members and former members of the administration in mid-December 1986. White House chief of staff Donald Regan, in testimony before the committee, described Reagan as the victim of bad advice from aides who supported the arms sales to Iran. Attorney General Edwin Meese 3rd tesified that no evidence had emerged to make him think that anyone other than Lt. Col. Oliver North and former national security adviser John Poindexter had known of the diversion. But North and Poindexter both invoked their Fifth Amendment right to remain silent and the truth remained elusive.

# Administration in Turmoil as White House Attempts to Control Damage

President Reagan, facing the worst crisis of his presidency in the Iran arms scandal, found himself under growing pressure December 6-12, 1986 to replace top administration officials or take more decisive action on the crisis. Several of Reagan's closest advisers, including his wife, Nancy, and longtime political allies Michael Deaver and Stuart Spencer, were reportedly urging Reagan to remove Donald Regan as White House chief of staff. Reagan was reported to have firmly resisted pressure to remove Regan. With Regan present, a group of Republican senators met with the President Dec. 5 and urged him to remove the chief of staff, according to Sen. John Chafee (R, R.I.), who attended the meeting. Reagan replied that "he wasn't going to throw anybody to the wolves," Chafee said.

A former White House aide, quoted in the *New York Times*, said that "Regan would never have got in this trouble if he hadn't gone around telling everyone that he ran everything and knew everything. It turned out that he didn't know about some very important things, by his own admission, and a lot of the people he cut out of the loop are gunning for him."

It was also reported that key Reagan advisers sought the removal of William Casey as director of central intelligence. Sen. Paul Laxalt (R, Nev.), however, was known to support Casey. "The only unanimity is that Regan needs to go," according to an unidentified source cited by the *Washington Post*. Deaver had arranged for Reagan to seek advice from elder statesmen of both parties, according to the *Post* Dec. 12. Among those invited to the White House were former Democratic National Chairman Robert Strauss and former Secretary of State William Rogers. Former Senate Republican leader Howard Baker Jr. had met with Vice President Bush to discuss the crisis.

## Los Angeles Times
*Los Angeles, CA, December 3, 1986*

With his credibility wounded and the effectiveness of his remaining two years in office at stake, President Reagan has moved to rebuild the congressional and public confidence that disclosures of his Administration's arms deals with Iran have so gravely eroded. He has endorsed the appointment of a Watergate-style independent counsel to conduct an investigation of the scandal that will be free from political taint. He has not sought to claim executive privilege to block testimony by former subordinates before congressional committees. And he has brought Frank Carlucci, an experienced public servant, into the White House as his new national-security adviser. To these necessary steps one more must now be added. The President should fire his chief of staff, Donald T. Regan.

Regan must go because, by either commission or omission, he bears a central responsibility for the ill-conceived plan that made a shambles of America's anti-terrorism policy and a mockery of congressional intent. Time will determine how much Regan knew of the arms-for-hostages deal with Iran and the diversion of funds to Nicaraguan *contras* and perhaps rebel forces elsewhere. What is clear already is that Regan, who has always insisted on controlling whatever goes on in the White House, at a minimum *should* have known what the national-security apparatus was up to, and should have had the sense to stop it.

The three Administration officials who have so far been identified as White House participants in the Iran arms deal—Adm. John M. Poindexter, Robert C. McFarlane and Lt. Col. Oliver L. North —are all active or former military officers who have spent their adult lives carrying out the orders of their superiors. It is not inconceivable that, alone or in combination, they might have initiated actions whose consequences would bring dishonor to their government and embarrassment or worse to themselves. It is, though, extremely unlikely. What they did almost certainly was done with the approval of higher authority. In the Reagan White House the chain of command in such matters is a short one. It goes to the President, and it passes through his chief of staff. Donald Regan, a zealous acquirer of power, made sure of that.

The President says that he will cooperate fully in revealing and punishing any illegal activities that have occurred, and there is no reason to doubt that pledge. But if he is content to define the problem that he and his Administration face only as one of exposing crime and meting out punishment, then he is, not untypically, reducing it to its simplest and least consequential dimensions. In doing that he is wholly missing the point of what got him into this mess.

The wrongdoing that has taken place is not so much the product of a faulty process as of a fundamentally flawed cast of mind. The real problem that the President faces is one of judgment, of a view of the world and its affairs that too often fails to perceive how events and actions can sometimes explosively interrelate. It is an attitude that is prepared to ignore what Congress has explicitly required or what the public will support. It is the problem of a mind-set that sees public relations as the means to transform failures into triumphs, and that regards public deception as a fair and even preferable tool for furthering a cause.

It is in the nation's interest no less than the President's that confidence be restored in his Administration. Bringing out the full truth in the Iran arms scandal is only a beginning. It will be a beginning of only limited significance if the President does not use this opportunity to enlist some new advisers, to listen to what the wisest and most experienced among them have to say.

LEXINGTON HERALD-LEADER
*Lexington, KY*
*December 4, 1986*

President Reagan has taken two big steps toward quelling the crisis over arms sales to Iran.

The first step was instructing Attorney General Edwin Meese to seek a special prosecutor to handle the investigation of those arms sales. The president thus took the investigation out of the hands of Meese, one of his closest political advisers, and put it into the hands of a court-appointed independent prosecutor.

That will alleviate doubts about Meese's ability to conduct an unbiased investigation. It will also allow the investigation to proceed in an orderly and sensible fashion, without unnecessary controversy over who is conducting it.

The president's second useful step was naming Frank Carlucci as his new national security adviser. Carlucci has earned wide respect in Washington for his service to both Republican and Democratic presidents. He will bring to the job some important qualities that his predecessor, Adm. John Poindexter, lacked: a wide experience in government, a vision of the broad objectives of U.S. foreign policy, a preference for teamwork and planning over adventurism and cloak-and-dagger operations.

With these two decisions, the president has done a lot to overcome the notion that he had become politically paralyzed by the controversy over the arms sales. With the special prosecutor's appointment under way and a respected national security adviser in place, he has cleared the way for his administration to get back to the federal deficit, arms control negotiations and other pressing problems at hand.

The strange saga of arms sales to Iran will not go away, but now it can unfold without preoccupying the White House. That's good news for the president and for the country.

## The Dallas Morning News

*Dallas, TX, December 3, 1986*

President Reagan acted appropriately Tuesday to set a dual system in place to determine who in his administration may have violated laws in the once-secret but now-scandalous shipment of arms to Iran.

In his brief, almost perfunctory address to the nation, Reagan announced that Attorney General Edwin Meese would ask a circuit court panel to name an independent counsel to investigate whether criminal charges should be brought in connection with the arms deal. That investigation would proceed independent of the study by a blue-ribbon panel of the role of the National Security Council in the clandestine arms sale.

It was significant and sensible that Reagan also pledged to cooperate fully with Congress and named Frank Carlucci to serve as his new national security adviser. Carlucci should prove an apt choice because of his considerable experience as a deputy defense secretary and deputy director of the Central Intelligence Agency. He's known to be tough and capable, just what's needed to help mop up the mess in the national security apparatus.

The next step should be for congressional leaders to agree on a method for a third track for the investigation — a bipartisan, bicameral committee to consolidate the congressional inquiries into the arms imbroglio. Such an inquiry would help air the broader policy implications and other questions that may not be included in the more narrow mandates presented to the independent prosecutor or the blue-ribbon panel.

Although Democratic leaders would rather wait until after the new Congress convenes in January so they will have a majority in both houses, it would be in the best interests of the country to start as soon as possible to address the serious questions facing the office of the presidency and our country. A delay would mean a month of trial by leak. A delay could lead to the public perception that the trail is getting cold while collection of evidence is being bungled. What's more, the arms affair is sure to preoccupy and virtually paralyze the top White House staff, not a welcome prospect in today's hair-trigger world.

Congress should move now to set up a special session to begin its inquiry — and should hold the president to his pledge to cooperate by insisting his highest advisers must be available for testimony and should not hide behind the screen of executive privilege.

The goal for all concerned should be to make the system work. That would reinforce the crucial point that we are a nation of laws after all.

## THE SACRAMENTO BEE

*Sacramento, CA, December 4, 1986*

President Reagan has at last grasped that the furor over his secret Iran-Contra dealings is not a one-week media wonder but a genuine crisis of confidence that threatens his presidency.

By agreeing to name an independent counsel to investigate whether criminal conduct was involved in the diversion of funds to the Contras and by pledging to "cooperate fully" in congressional inquiries into the Iranian debacle, the president has taken the necessary first step toward restoring public and congressional confidence in the White House. "You're entitled to have your questions answered," he told the nation. By his actions, that full accounting of the facts becomes more likely.

The crisis will not end there, however. At base, the furor is not about a broken law here, a misjudgment there. It is about a presidency on automatic pilot. By the administration's own account of the Iranian affair, the president is detached from the basic flow of government, inattentive to details, isolated from conflicting points of view, and too dependent on a White House staff of dubious wisdom and character. Until Congress, including some of the president's closest Republican allies, are assured of the quality of advisers and advice the president is getting, the White House will be viewed with suspicion and the investigation into the Iran dealings will be a threat to the president's ability to act and lead.

The nation cannot afford two years with a crippled presidency. That is why the president must not wait — possibly for months — until an independent counsel or a congressional committee spells out what most of Washington already knows: that the presidency and the country have been badly served by aides such as Donald Regan, White House chief of staff, and William Casey, director of the Central Intelligence Agency.

The reputation and credibility of a president inclined to delegate so much of his job rests largely on the quality of those around him: on their pragmatism; on their commitment to the processes of democratic government, and on their willingness to harness the president's instincts with facts and protect him from freebooters who would operate under his authority. Whether Regan and Casey knew of the Iran-Contra connection or simply were negligent, they failed that test. Their continued presence at the president's side can only prolong this crisis.

By naming Frank Carlucci, a veteran servant of presidents both Democratic and Republican, as his new national security adviser, the president has begun to clean up his mess. The sooner Carlucci is joined in the White House by other respected officials capable of being not just the president's men, but the presidency's men, the better it will be for Reagan and the nation.

## Birmingham Post-Herald

*Birmingham, AL*
*December 3, 1986*

Anyone who lived through the long agony of Watergate knows that Ronald Reagan, if his presidency is to survive its present crisis, will have to do the following:

1. Have a special prosecutor appointed to investigate the White House's Iranian arms deal whose profits were diverted to the anti-Marxist rebels in Nicaragua.

2. Cause the formation of a Watergate-style Senate-House select committee to look into the matter, and thus prevent about eight separate committees from prolonging the scandal and nibbling the administration to death.

3. Get rid of Donald Regan, who failed to protect the president from crippling blunders, and replace him with a White House chief of staff capable of restoring Reagan's credibility and ability to govern.

The president will have to do these things sooner or later. Sooner is better, in that it may end the damage before it is irreversible.

Attorney General Edwin Meese now heads the investigation. He has the closest ties to the White House and advised Reagan that supplying arms to Iran was legal. We do not question Meese's integrity when we say few will have confidence in his findings or accept them as impartial.

Reagan's request yesterday that an independent counsel be appointed was a wise move. That is far better than having one imposed on you.

In the meantime, Reagan could help his cause by making fewer implausible claims. In his Time magazine interview, he said, "It wasn't us funneling money to them (the contras). This was another country."

The other country was Israel. But how did Israelis know to divert the arms money to the Nicaraguan guerrillas and not to American-backed rebels in, say, Afghanistan or Angola? Easy. White House officials told them.

The president also described Lt. Col. Oliver North, the dismissed National Security Council aide who got the money to the contras, as "a national hero." That raises an interesting question: Why fire a national hero?

## Rockford Register Star

*Rockford, IL, December 5, 1986*

President Reagan finally has turned around and taken the bull by the horns, after letting it chase him around the pasture for several weeks. He had no choice, really, as the "bull" — the Iranian arms deal and the Contra connection — was gaining speed and threatening to cripple the final two years of his administration.

Regardless of why the president chose to act, he made a wise decision in calling for the appointment of a special counsel to investigate the diversion of Iranian arms sale profits to the Nicaraguan Contras. Let us hope that the investigation also will look at the propriety of selling arms to Iran in the first place, in apparent contradiction of a ban on such deals.

In addition, the president put in place the first building block toward restructuring the nation's foreign policy. Reagan appointed a highly respected individual, Frank Carlucci, one-time deputy CIA director and deputy secretary of defense, to replace Vice Adm. John M. Poindexter as national security adviser. Poindexter resigned under fire last week after the Contra link was disclosed. If Carlucci recognizes that the National Security Council is not above the law and the mandates of Congress, he can be a successful presidential aide.

The president also urged the U.S. House and Senate to consolidate all their potential investigations into a single, joint effort. Congress should heed this logical advice and get on with the investigation — now.

It is extremely important that Congress move immediately, because no other national business of importance can be accomplished until the Iran Affair is history. As a country, we cannot afford to wallow in this crisis for very long.

This situation is serious, but there is no need for it to develop into a Watergate. It seems that the president has at last recognized the explosive potential of the circumstances and is responding appropriately to try to avoid a scandal of the magnitude that ended the Nixon presidency. All it would take for a repeat of that sad state of affairs would be for the president to stonewall and refuse to cooperate with Congress.

President Reagan is not doing that, although he obviously wishes the problem would just disappear. We are encouraged by his apparent openness and by his order to White House staff members to cooperate fully with Congress and the independent counsel. We are encouraged by his verbal promises to "get to the bottom of this matter." And we are convinced that the truth will come out about who knew what, when — and who, if anyone, violated the law.

And when the truth is known, the appropriate heads should roll, and roll quickly.

In the meantime, the president's damage control work is not finished. He might do well to take a lesson from Philippines President Corazon Aquino who demanded the resignations of her entire cabinet, and then chose which ones she wanted to retain and which one she needed to boot. The calls for Chief of Staff Donald Regan's resignation are becoming deafening, and they are coming from Republican and Democrat alike. Regan has become a real liability to his boss, and friendship or no friendship, he probably should be let go. Likewise, CIA Director William Casey's credibility is shot, and the president may find it impossible to justify retaining him. In both cases, they either are guilty of participating in the Iran-Contra Affair, or of failing in their responsibilities to the president and the nation by not knowing about it.

President Reagan has made a good start on getting the situation under control and now he simply must assert continued leadership if he is to put the Iran arms deal behind him. It can be done. It must be done. And soon.

## THE TENNESSEAN

*Nashville, TN, December 3, 1986*

UNDER intense pressure from his own party and from Congress to deal quickly with the Iran arms sales controversy, President Ronald Reagan has approved the appointment of an independent counsel to look into the whole affair. At least he recognized the need to act quickly.

The President also appointed Mr. Frank Carlucci, a former high-ranking official of the Pentagon and CIA, as his new national security adviser.

Earlier the Justice Department had said it found no grounds for asking for a special prosecutor. But in a televised address from the Oval Office Mr. Reagan said an administration review had turned up "reasonable grounds" to seek such an appointment.

Attorney General Edwin Meese had been under some criticism for conducting his own investigation of an administration that appointed him.

The law provides that the attorney general can conduct a preliminary probe when he gets information that high government officials may have committed a federal crime. He must then ask a three-judge panel to appoint a special prosecutor, known as "independent counsel" who will then look for criminal violations.

Mr. Meese, citing the law, said he was "not at liberty to discuss the specific grounds for the application, the statutes that may have been violated" or the individuals involved. But in taking the step there is strong presumption that violations of the law occurred.

The scope of the independent counsel's probe would include the secret arms sales to Iran as well as the diversion of arms profits to the contra revolutionaries. There will be plenty to investigate. Both the Congress and the public found unbelievable Mr. Meese's revelations that a small band of administration underlings arranged a covert sale of arms to Iran, not only to free U.S. hostages but to generate funding for the Nicarguan contras.

President Reagan has repeatedly said that he knew nothing of the "contra connection" until he was briefed on it by Mr. Meese. Somebody within the higher echelons of the administration had to know, and further, had to give some kind of approval. Lt. Col. Oliver North, the alleged mastermind within the NSC, couldn't have commanded that sort of influence without a "charter," or operating orders.

In the meanwhile, the Senate Intelligence Committee is conducting its own closed-door hearings, trying to find out who did what under whose directions.

Mr. Reagan seems sincere enough in insisting that, "no area will be immune from review...that if illegal acts were undertaken, those who did so will be brought to justice." But still, the damage may reach at least indirectly to his own Cainet and staff. The unraveling of the tale of intrigue will undoubtedly provide more shocks as the probing goes on.

Mr. Reagan will survive the whirlwind, but it may well strip away the trust in his judgment and in his relaxed and even detached style of leadership. That can be a costly loss to a leader who will find it more difficult to lead. ■

### SYRACUSE
## HERALD-JOURNAL

*Syacuse, NY, December 4, 1986*

President Reagan announces a three-man, blue-ribbon panel to get to the bottom of the Iran question. That's a good start. He announces publicly that he has ordered staffers and others to hold nothing back from investigators. That's better yet.

He fires Poindexter and North, hires Carlucci as his new national security adviser. Outstanding! Hey, the president's on a roll. In no time at all, he'll be out of the woods on this one.

But wait. What's this? First North, then Poindexter clam up in front of the Senate Intelligence Committee, claiming protection under the Fifth Amendment to the Constitution. Then we see Regan, Casey, Weinberger — Hear No Evil, See No Evil, Speak No Evil — continuing in their jobs, as if by pretending their stories of non-involvement were true, they could make them so.

We, like most other folks in the country, don't really know the full extent of their involvement, but in this instance there is enough circumstantial evidence to make the case that at the very least all three should look into their retirement prospects. Meese, at Justice, is another.

We're not talking here about guilt by association, or "guilty until proven innocent." We're talking about the government of the United States of America getting its act back together in the only way it can ... by cleaning house so we can get on the with the more important business at hand.

If that means treating such employees as Regan, Meese, Casey and Weinberger harshly, we know they, of all people, will understand. Otherwise, the president is going to have to live with this mess for the rest of his time in the White House. And things probably will get worse before they get better. We simply cannot afford a two-year preoccupation with bumbled foreign policy when we could soften the impact somewhat by putting as many of the bumblers as possible out to pasture.

If the president wants to tell us Regan and the others are "national heroes" at the same time he's handing them their walking papers, that's his option.

As for the president himself, he is coming perilously close to destroying his own credibility for the balance of his tenure, if he hasn't done it already. That means the only hope of salvaging what's left, if anything, is to bring in the best people available — the Carlucci appointment was a step in that direction — and tell them that from here on out, the government is operating in the sunlight.

Even then, we fear some things, such as arms control negotiations, will be put on hold until 1989, when the White House will be under new management.

# THE DENVER POST

*Denver, CO, December 3, 1986*

THE DAMAGED Reagan administration appears to have regained some equilibrium and gotten back on the track, hopefully headed toward recovery from the worst crisis of its six-year history and the worst U.S. foreign policy fiasco in recent memory.

President Reagan has recommended appointment of an independent counsel to probe the ever-enlarging mystery and potential criminality of arms shipments to Iran, trades for hostages and funneling of profits from arms sales to the Nicaraguan contras.

The president also has named Frank Carlucci, a seasoned veteran of top-level bureaucratic service in several administrations, to be the new chief of the White House National Security Council. In one other piece of White House positioning, the president pledged cooperation with congressional investigators and urged that Congress consolidate its Iran/contra probes under one panel.

Together with his appointment last week of a distinguished three-member board to review the work and direction of the NSC, President Reagan's actions Tuesday show he has at last faced the hard reality of the White House debacle and the need to restore order and public confidence.

The president still can't admit to any mistakes in White House handling of the startling and implausible events still unfolding. But even if the Reagan hubris won't permit it, his actions in seeking to mend a crippled administration are acknowledgment enough that mistakes have been made and have to be set right. Request for appointment of an independent counsel — expected to be granted by a three-judge federal panel — is a sound presidential decision. It eliminates the obvious problem of conflict of interest where Attorney General Edwin Meese III, a long-time and trusted Reagan adviser, would be investigating the White House to which he is so closely attached.

As for the congressional investigations of the White House imbroglio, there is widening agreement — which we join — with the suggestion from the president and others that a single "select committee" be given jurisdiction to investigate the affair. A bipartisan Senate-House panel, put to work in January soon after the convening of the 100th Congress and provided with the fruits of several congressional investigations already under way, might offer a clear picture of what has gone wrong and why and put forth recommendations for correcting legislation, if necessary. That's more than could be said for a 10-ring circus of committees and subcommittees that would — and still might — be leaping at the Iran/contras scandal to grab pieces of it in raw competition for publicity on Capitol Hill.

At least one other matter — the dismissal of White House Chief of Staff Donald Regan — still needs consideration by the president. In any way of looking at this tragedy of misgovernment, the president was badly served by his staff — whatever he knew about it or didn't know and whatever advice was given or withheld.

It's Donald Regan's job to prevent that kind of thing from happening. He didn't. The president, the office of the presidency and the nation have suffered. It ought to be clear that Regan's period of useful service is at an end.

## THE LINCOLN STAR

*Lincoln, NE, December 4, 1986*

With support of an independent counsel to investigate U.S. relations with Iran, President Reagan presumably has ended his stonewalling in the matter. His support is no admission of guilt of any kind, but neither is it an affirmation of innocence.

At this point, Reagan stands as a neutral amid the intrigue of secret arms sales to Iran and the laundering of funds for diversion to the Contra rebels of Nicaragua. Thus, the president has calmed the storm of controversy that he had fed with a continuing defense of his administration.

Now the administration will be independently judged on the merits of the Iran case and that should be sufficient for the moment. Those who believe, however, that Reagan is off the hook are badly mistaken.

Observers now contemplate which of two possibilities is the worse — whether Reagan knew or did not know about the extent of arms sales to Iran and the use of those revenues in support of the Contras.

In either case, the president suffers a serious blow.

Meanwhile the international ramifications of the case will continue to mount. The integrity and wisdom of U.S. foreign policy has been significantly damaged and our country will be weakened from that in such vital areas of concern as nuclear arms controls, foreign trade and world peace.

As a leader of the Western family of nations we have suffered a denigration of honor and a loss of confidence in our role. Our recovery will not be quick or easy. In the Middle East and in Latin America, an entirely new set of circumstances has been presented and they will demand a high level of statesmanship from the United States.

As the investigations into this series of events unfolds, it behooves the American people to examine also the workings of our democratic system of elections. We need to think twice about a system or a commanding national attitude that tends to push to the forefront individuals of great form but little substance.

# Birmingham Post-Herald

*Birmingham, AL, December 2, 1986*

President Reagan is getting some sound bipartisan advice on what should be done to clear up the Iran arms deal flap to prevent further damage to his presidency and to U.S. foreign policy.

At no time in his six years in office has this personally popular president faced a greater test of his sagacity and decision-making abilities.

He must act immediately or the nation itself will suffer from the political fallout which could paralyze the executive branch during the remaining two years of the Reagan presidency and frustrate the conduct of a rational approach to foreign affairs.

It is patently obvious that executive action must go beyond last week's naming of a three-man review board, headed by former Sen. John Tower of Texas, to analyze the National Security Council's role, the resignation of Reagan's national security adviser, Vice Admiral John Poindexter, and the dismissal of his aide, Marine Lt. Col. Oliver North. Politically, it should be equally obvious that a probe by the Justice Department and FBI of any wrongdoing in the Iran-Nicaraguan-Contras link will be suspect because of Attorney General Edwin Meese's close ties to Reagan.

Neither does blaming the press for seeking to get at the truth of a policy gone sour add to the president's stature.

Reagan can — no, must — avail himself of all the facts and come clean with the public, no matter whose political career is damaged. It is no time to stonewall.

The truth will out, if not willingly then by the damaging process of congressional inquiries. The Senate Intelligence Committee hearings are only the beginning of that process.

The president would do well to heed the advice of such prominent Republicans as Senate Majority Leader Bob Dole and Sen. Richard Lugar, outgoing chairman of the Senate Foreign Relations Committee, who both called for the appointment of a special counsel, independent of White House control, and the naming by Congress of a select investigating committee — advice echoed by Sen. Robert Byrd of West Virginia, who will be majority leader in the Democrat-controlled 100th Congress.

It would be helpful if a select committee could begin its work before the Congress convenes in January, though that would require the call of a special session this month.

If the president is the victim of bad advice, he should clean his executive house and bring in new advisers whose integrity and perspecuity command respect. No one is buying the suggestion that Poindexter and North were well-intentioned but loose cannon operating without the knowledge of political higher ups.

White House Chief of Staff Donald Regan, who has alienated Congress with his heavy handedness and sparked in-fighting over access to the president, is a logical candidate to get the axe. Other political careers may be on the line also.

The buck, of course, stops with the president.

He can stand tall by reporting openly and honestly to the nation what did occur and who was responsible for what decisions, even if the trail of evidence leads to Ronald Reagan himself.

# Reagan Names Carlucci National Security Adviser

President Reagan December 2, 1986 named Frank Carlucci to be his new national security adviser, replacing Vice Adm. John Poindexter, who had resigned over his role in the Iran-contra scandal. Carlucci became Reagan's fifth national security adviser in six years. He was lauded by both Democratic and Republican lawmakers, not only because of his long experience in intelligence, defense and diplomatic affairs, but also because of his political savvy and knowledge of Congress. His selection was widely seen as having weakened the position of White House chief of staff Donald Regan, who reportedly had backed outgoing NATO Ambassador David Abshire for the job. Carlucci was supported by Defense Secretary Caspar Weinberger, Secretary of State George Shultz and Central Intelligence Agency (CIA) Director William Casey. Carlucci was said to have accepted the post only on the condition that his access to the President would not be controlled by Regan. Analysts expected him to be the administration's most influential and powerful national security adviser to date. Carlucci had served as the number-two man in the Defense Department in the early days of the Reagan administration and as the deputy director of the CIA in the Carter administration. He had also held a number of Foreign Service posts over the years, including a controversial post as political officer in charge of Congolese affairs from 1962 to 1964 and a key stint as ambassador to Portugal in the mid-1970s.

## Pittsburgh Post-Gazette

*Pittsburgh, PA, December 4, 1986*

After weeks of fumbling in the Iran/Contra imbroglio, during which his standing plummeted, President Reagan finally is moving to regain his composure and has taken sensible steps which could salvage his presidency.

The president did well to name Frank Carlucci as his new national security adviser. Smart, tough-minded and experienced, Mr. Carlucci will not let lieutenant colonels on the National Security Council staff hare around the world conducting covert schemes.

Mr. Carlucci has been a foreign service officer, deputy secretary of defense, deputy CIA director and ambassador to Portugal. In the latter post — after Secretary of State Henry Kissinger had despaired of saving Portugal from communism — Mr. Carlucci persevered and helped steer that country to democracy.

In short, Mr. Carlucci knows the national security turf and can shield the president from costly errors, if Mr. Reagan listens to him.

The president also made a judicious move in calling for the appointment of a special prosecutor to investigate possible breaches of the law in the clandestine sale of arms to Iran and the diversion of the proceeds to the Nicaraguan rebels.

Now a panel of three federal judges will appoint a distinguished lawyer to lead the probe, which will have more credibility than if it were conducted by Mr. Reagan's friend and adviser, Attorney General Edwin Meese.

But in the case of Donald Regan, the president has not shown a willingness to make an absolutely necessary move. In his Tuesday broadcast, Mr. Reagan should have announced a replacement for the White House chief of staff.

Mr. Regan either knew or should have known what his protege, ousted national security adviser John Poindexter, and Lt. Col. Oliver North were up to in the Iran/Contra caper. If the president is to have a new start, Mr. Regan will have to go.

And if this country is to recover from the Iran/Contra affair during the remaining two years of Mr. Regan's administration, Congress must heed Mr. Reagan's plea that it form a single special committee to investigate the mess.

As it is now, nearly a dozen committees want parts of the case — and the attendant publicity. If they all get in the act, Congress will be preoccupied with the probe and unable to conduct other necessary business, especially if the media feeds on, rather than covers, the story.

Indeed, the presidency and the entire country could be held captive for however long it would take for the various committees to wind up their roles.

The president's moves came none too early. A New York Times/CBS News poll shows his job-approval rating had plunged to 46 percent, a drop of nearly one-third from 67 percent a month ago. The Gallup Organization said it was the sharpest such decline since approval polling began in 1936.

The poll demonstrates the public's good sense. A president cannot embargo arms to Iran and send them, proclaim no deals with terrorists and deal with them, and then evade blame with sophist arguments.

For his own good and for the good of the country, Mr. Reagan must regain the public trust he once had. Without it, the next two years will be hell.

## Wisconsin ▲ State Journal

*Madison, WI, December 4, 1986*

President Reagan has taken three important steps toward the rebuilding of his administration's credibility: naming Frank Carlucci as his fifth national security adviser, urging the appointment of an independent counsel to investigate the arms-to-Iran, cash-to-Contras fiasco, and vowing to cooperate with a consolidated congressional probe of that frightening and clandestine deal.

Three steps does not a marathon make, but Reagan is at least out of the starting blocks.

Carlucci is the kind of national security adviser the president should have had from the start. He is a seasoned foreign service officer with experience in two key federal agencies, Central Intelligence and Defense. He was the No. 2 man in the CIA during the Carter years and was the deputy to Defense Secretary Caspar Weinberger early in Reagan's first term.

Carlucci receives high marks as a manager and is known for his ability to work with Democrats as well as Republicans — no small consideration when the 100th Congress convenes in January.

By urging the appointment of a special counsel, Reagan has recognized the value of one of the most important Watergate-era reforms — the Independent Counsel Act — and guaranteed the American public that allegations of criminal behavior will be fully investigated by someone who is not named by the president and cannot be fired by the president.

Finally, Reagan has conceded that Congress has the right to mount its own political investigation. That seemed to be missing in Reagan's earlier, highly defensive pronouncements, which left the impression that he believed an in-house probe by Attorney General Ed Meese and the Justice Department — no matter how carefully carried out — would past the test of credibility.

Reagan's only advice to Congress is sound: Consolidate the probe into a Watergate-style select committee. A chorus of congressional committees (up to nine could claim jurisdiction) isn't needed; a single, clear voice would better inform and serve the public.

The president's long walk back through the thicket of arrogance and illegality planted by his aides was late starting, but at least he's moving down the path. Only through independent probes will the American people eventually learn the truth about who knew — or should have known — what was going on.

## THE SAGINAW NEWS
*Saginaw, MI, December 5, 1986*

When the White House looked for a new national security adviser to succeed the resigned John Poindexter, it found Frank Carlucci.

He is known as a strong supporter of President Reagan's foreign policy, and you would hardly expect otherwise. But what else is he?

Carlucci has been a diplomat in Africa, Europe and South America. He has held high posts with the Office of Economic Opportunity, the Department of Health, Education and Welfare — and with the CIA and Pentagon. He is described as a first-class manager who can separate politics from the job. A record of service under Republican Presidents Nixon, Ford and Reagan and Democrats Kennedy and Carter seems to confirm that reputation.

Nor was Carlucci the only respected candidate for the job.

The question is, with talented people like that around, why would this or any administration wind up in such hot water?

Too many, evidently, don't get appointed to posts that put them close to the seat of power and the president's ear. It's not too late to start finding and appointing more of them.

## THE TENNESSEAN
*Memphis, TN, December 5, 1986*

IN the beginning, the National Security Council was supposed to advise the president on foreign policy after pulling together the views of the various other leaders of an administration.

Under President Reagan it has strayed afield, becoming an operations center for covert activities such as the secret arms transfer to Iran and the funneling of money to Nicaraguan guerrillas. What else it has been up to isn't readily known. But its role has become a focal point of controversy that cost the jobs of NSC adviser John Poindexter and his aide, Lt. Col. Oliver North.

In fairly quick order, President Reagan named a three-member commission to investigate the agency's role, and a new adviser, Mr. Frank Carlucci, who is a former top-ranking CIA official and one-time deputy secretary of defense.

The review board is headed by former Republican Sen. John Tower of Texas. The other members are Mr. Edmund Muskie, a former Democratic senator and one-time secretary of State, and Mr. Brent Scowcroft, who was national security adviser in the Ford administration.

They have a fairly challenging task. It is not to seek out criminal wrongdoing, but to study the role and procedures of the council. In short their task is to find out what went wrong at the NSC, why it went wrong, and how to prevent it happening again.

The council was set up in 1947 and forced on a reluctant President Harry Truman as a helpful adjunct to the presidency. Its job was to sift through and condense the various conflicting advice from the various Cabinet departments involved in relations with other countries, namely State, Defense and Commerce.

The council evolved into an indispensable arm of the White House and a means of increasing presidential control over foreign policy. Various presidents used it differently. The previous high for the council's role was in the Nixon administration when Mr. Henry Kissinger, who ran it in Mr. Nixon's first term, used it as a channel for back stream diplomacy, such as the opening of relations with China.

Mr. Reagan at first downgraded the NSC, giving primacy in foreign affairs to the State Department. But somewhere along the line, the NSC went far beyond advice and minor diplomacy; it became an operational part of foreign policy, unwatched by the Congress, press, public and, if Mr. Reagan is right, the President.

The review panel is already aware of what went wrong. Why it went wrong may be more difficult. Some of the statutory members have pled ignorance of what was going on. Those members are President Reagan, Vice President George Bush, Secretary of State George Shultz and Defense Secretary Caspar Weinberger. If four major members of the NSC didn't know what it was doing, how could it operate on its own?

There are various ideas on how it can be fixed. Sen. Robert Byrd, D-W. Va., who will become Senate majority leader in January, suggested that the NSC adviser be confirmed by the Senate. Such confirmation wouldn't stop an adviser from doing exactly what has been done if he had the president's blessing.

Perhaps a better way would be to bring it, like the CIA, under the oversight of the intelligence committees insofar as covert operations are concerned. Even better, maybe Congress should do away with it. Let the President sift through conflicting advice from his advisers and make his own decision. That's what he was elected to do. ▪

## The Boston Globe
*Boston, MA, December 7, 1986*

Frank Carlucci, President Reagan's new national security adviser, reportedly owes his appointment to last-minute lobbying by CIA Director William Casey.

It is entirely appropriate for senior members of the administration to push their choices for such a sensitive position, and Carlucci brings to the job an impressively varied background, having served in diplomatic posts, as Caspar Weinberger's No. 2 man at the Defense Department, and as the former deputy director of the CIA during the Carter administration.

The appointment of Carlucci, who replaces Adm. John Poindexter, has been praised from many quarters, including former Vice President Walter Mondale. Legislators from both sides of the aisle, Cabinet members and former colleagues vouchsafe his integrity and his political and administrative skills.

Nonetheless, there is reason to suspect that Casey wanted Carlucci as national security adviser not merely for his skills, but also because his record suggests he can be counted on to protect the kinds of covert operations, and operatives, that caused the current crisis.

Maj. Gen. Richard Secord, the former Pentagon official implicated in the funneling of funds from the Iranian arms sale to the contras, was investigated by the Justice Department four years ago for participating with Edwin Wilson, the convicted former CIA officer, in EATSCO, an arms-dealing company that siphoned off government funds.

Secord had been suspended from his post pending a polygraph test; Carlucci intervened to reinstate him. When Carlucci left the Pentagon, he went to work at a subsidiary of Sears, Roebuck & Co., where he hired Erich von Marbod, a partner in EATSCO with Wilson, Secord and two former CIA officials.

Until now, the national security adviser has not had to be confirmed by the Senate. But as Congress traces the doings of dummy corporations, clandestine operators, arms dealers and drug runners, it will have to make sure that a new fox has not been installed in the old chicken coop.

# The Washington Post

Washington, DC, December 3, 1986

FRANK CARLUCCI knows his way around the neighborhood. He has had his successes and misadventures in all the principal agencies of government whose work the president's national security adviser is meant to coordinate. "Coordinate" is a key word here, suggesting, as it does, a rather modest mandate. The job to which Mr. Carlucci was named by the president yesterday has ballooned in importance over the years but without a corresponding growth of accountability. It has fitfully generated delusions of grandeur, conspiracies and bureaucratic gridlock, none of which was in the original plan. Sometimes it has become the seat of an alternative secretary of state, sort of like the time when you had a pope and an anti-pope. Reams of political science, most of it terminally boring, have been written about what the proper function of this White House office should be. It should be to help the president dig out from under the rock slide of advice he is getting from his Cabinet departments on national security affairs, to understand their disputes and monitor their actions and, above all, to understand his own choices.

Probably the office has gotten too big. At least that's what people say who think it has begun to regard itself as a Cabinet department of its own. For a time it was adulated on precisely the opposite ground: i.e., that it was small and secret enough to be a locus of some action and energy in a government of gluey, protocol-bound bureaucracy. Presidents have habitually been tempted by its protected status (outside the reach of congressional inquiry) to use it to get things done quietly, quickly, decisively and without a lot of foot-dragging from the Foreign Service or the military hierarchy. Just as habitually this instinct has come to grief. Mr. Reagan shouldn't need any schooling in that these days, and neither, we suspect, does Mr. Carlucci.

Mr. Carlucci, savvy and well-schooled in the substantive issues a national security adviser must deal with, has experience as well in dealing with the men who are President Reagan's principal foreign policy and defense advisers. Presumably he was acceptable to them; but that does not mean he is of some junior or servile status. We would guess that he comes as close as anyone could to being the right choice in that he a) would not aspire to being a substitute Cabinet officer himself but b) is also a man of some self-confidence and standing who would not gladly let himself or a president get shoved around. We hope the new appointment works. We also hope that Mr. Carlucci has arranged to report directly to the president.

## DESERET NEWS

Salt Lake City, UT, December 5, 1986

The quickest way to uncover someone's personal history, it's said, is to nominate them for public office.

Frank Carlucci must feel that way after being named as President Reagan's new national security adviser. Already he is coming in for a variety of accusations about his background.

Nicaragua's ruling Sandinista Front, for example, has accused him of being a specialist in Third World "dirty work and coup attempts" during the 1960s. Carlucci, claims a Marxist spokesman, planned Patrice Lumumba's assassination in 1961 "under orders from President Eisenhower."

More serious is a criticism from the General Accounting Office. The GAO claims that Carlucci knew of an illegal lobbying attempt in 1982 by Lockheed to gain Congress' approval for purchase of 50 C-5B planes. Carlucci in 1982 vigorously defended the legality of the lobbying effort. Since this attack didn't get anywhere four years ago, it's in poor grace for the GAO to raise the same tired charges now.

Carlucci has made a name for himself both as a dedicated foreign service officer and as an efficient public administrator. He served as No. 2 man at four major agencies — at the Office of Management and Budget; at Health, Education, and Welfare; and at the Defense Department; and at the Central Intelligence Agency. No one accumulates such an impressive record without outstanding administrative ability.

As the Iranian arms deal has demonstrated, administrative ability isn't always enough. A most critical need is judgment. It will be on this count that Carlucci either makes or breaks himself by what kind of advice he gives the president.

One encouraging indication is Carlucci's staunch stand, when he was ambassador to Portugal, for close U.S. ties to that nation as long as a semblance of democracy was present. That stance was opposed by Secretary of State Henry Kissinger. But when the communists lost miserably in Portugal's election in 1975, Carlucci's minority view was vindicated.

## THE RICHMOND NEWS LEADER

Richmond, VA, December 9, 1986

President Reagan's choice of Frank Carlucci as national security adviser has received wide applause, much of it no doubt justified. He plainly has more political sagacity than Adm. John Poindexter, his predecessor, and he has thick credentials.

In service to presidents of both parties, Carlucci has been director of the Office of Economic Opportunity, ambassador to Portugal, assistant director of the CIA and the No. 2 official in the Pentagon. He's a skilled survivor.

Sen. Jesse Helms all but filibustered Reagan's nomination of Carlucci as top aide to Defense Secretary Caspar Weinberger in 1981. That sally marked one of the senator's early moves to sidetrack Reagan appointees. The president finally got Carlucci confirmed. But, in the process, Helms wangled the No. 3 Pentagon job for an old Nixonian arms negotiator, Fred Ikle.

During Carlucci's term in the Pentagon, 25 high officials, including the chairman of the Joint Chiefs of Staff, agreed to be hooked up to lie-detector machines — simply because of a leak to the press. It was reliably reported that Carlucci touched off this spectacle of what the late Sen. Sam Ervin called "20th century witchcraft," volunteering for the first polygraph test and challenging the other 24 to follow.

And what was all this terrible security leak about? The press had quoted an undersecretary of defense who said that the United States would have to spend $750 billion more than the $1.5 trillion the Reagan administration had figured for its military projects over the following five years. The White House and Pentagon got embarrassed. Some security leak!

Most Americans surely hope Carlucci does an outstanding national security job — without ever subverting the will of Congress, without transgressing any laws and without lying. But most citizens will understand, in view of conditions under which Carlucci got his new job, that he hasn't made a lot of noise about asking folks to take lie detector tests. Nor has the fellow who chose him volunteered for the first hook-up.

# The Birmingham News

*Birmingham, AL, December 17, 1986*

When Frank Carlucci took over the reins of the National Security Council in the midst of revelations about the Iranian arms fiasco, President Reagan said he wanted someone who would take charge and whip the agency back into the kind of effective foreign policy oversight panel it was designed to be.

Carlucci is doing just that. According to reports this week, he plans not only a wholesale personnel shake-up, but also a change in the scope of the council's efforts which will have it doing only concentrated analysis work in a few critical areas of foreign policy.

Good for him. The NSC was never meant to be a rival State Department or a spawning ground for clandestine conduct of foreign affairs.

President Harry Truman set up the panel in 1947 to review the various foreign policy proposals about critical issues coming in from the State Department, the military, the CIA and other federal agencies and to mesh them into an effective, coordinated policy for the president.

The Iranian arms affair disclosed that the NSC had taken on a new, more cloak-and-dagger role in the last few years. At the same time, according to remarks made by former National Security Advisers Henry Kissinger and Zbigniew Brzezinski, the NSC has been doing only a mediocre job in its primary role of analysis.

Why did higher-ups in the NSC believe there actually were "moderate" elements in Iran willing to deal with them in secrecy? How would helping Iran, a radical state which already had the upper hand in its war with Iraq, help stabilize conditions in the Mideast?

Both men believe the Reykjavik summit, too, showed signs of an NSC staff not up to snuff. How did we get maneuvered into serious negotiations that might change 30 years of strategic planning without being adequately prepared for the substantive nature of the talks? Why did we proceed without consulting our allies?

Carlucci is right to upgrade the NSC staff and better focus its activities. The NSC can't outspy the CIA. It can't outnegotiate the State Department. But it can and should be the agency that makes sure the president considers all the angles.

# San Francisco Chronicle

*San Francisco, CA, December 17, 1986*

THE FIRST GOOD news to come out of the Iranian arms debacle is word that the new director of the National Security Council, Frank Carlucci, plans a thorough house cleaning. It's an understatement to say that application of a big broom there is long overdue.

The Council was set up in 1947 for a primarily "advise and review" role on matters dealing with this nation's security, particularly foreign policy. Its visibility was low and its members managed to keep out of turf wars and power struggles with other agencies. But ever since the Kennedy administration and the palmy days of Henry Kissinger, the Council has grown in influence. With the Reagan administration, it has played a key role not only in coordinating policy, but in molding it.

Carlucci hasn't actually taken over the Council's reins yet, but he is making the right noises about what should be done. An official close to him says the new director seeks "an entirely new approach, much closer to what they have had in the past. He sees the Council's mandate as coordinator of foreign policy amongst the government's many departments, not as an advocate of certain actions."

THIS IS A REASONABLE and temperate approach. Much of the current mess stems from the Council's new activist role. In the prevalent "gung ho" atmosphere, the boys in the White House basement evidently felt they had authority to carry out their own misguided agenda.

# Reagan Asks Independent Counsel to Probe Iran Affair

President Reagan December 2, 1986 asked for the appointment of an independent counsel to investigate charges of illegality in his administration's sale of arms to Iran and the diversion of profits to the Nicaraguan contra rebels. Congressional leaders of both parties welcomed the President's move but stressed that Congress would press ahead with its own inquiries despite the plan for an independent counsel. It was Reagan's fourth public effort in recent weeks to deal with the Iran affair, which had burgeoned into the worst crisis of his presidency. Earlier, on November 26, as he left for a Thanksgiving vacation at his California ranch, Reagan appointed three members to a National Security Council review board: John Tower, a former Republican senator from Texas; Edmund Muskie, a former Democratic senator from Maine and secretary of state in the Carter administration; and Brent Scowcroft, a former national security deputy and adviser in the Nixon and Ford administrations.

In a brief Dec. 2 speech, Reagan said Attorney General Edwin Meese 3rd had advised him that the Justice Department had "turned up reasonable grounds to believe that further investigation by an independent counsel would be appropriate. Accordingly, consistent with his responsibilities under the Independent Counsel Act," Reagan said, "I immediately urged him to apply" to a special three-judge panel of the U.S. Court of Appeals in Washington for the necessary appointment. The mechanism for appointing independent counsels—formerly known as special prosecutors—to probe misdeeds by high-level government officials was originally contained in the 1978 Ethics in Government Act and amended in a 1982 law. Six prosecutors had been named since 1978; two of them were still active. To date, not one had brought any criminal charges.

Meese said that his own department's investigation into the Iran affair had to give way to an independent counsel because he had "an apparent conflict of interest" due to his previous involvement in the case. Meese's involvement in the affair had been criticized by lawmakers because of his closeness to Reagan, because he had given oral advice to the White House in January justifying the Iranian arms policy and because of the informal inquiry he had carried out Nov. 22-23 that had uncovered the contra connection.

## THE ARIZONA REPUBLIC
### Phoenix, AZ, December 4, 1986

THE selection by President Reagan of John Tower, former Republican senator of Texas, to head the special three-man commission appointed to examine the nature and role of the National Security Council staff, might turn out to be unexpectedly fortuitous.

Tower may be in a unique position to understand the high-risk, high-stakes game the NSC staff ran out of the White House basement under the direction of Lt. Col. Oliver North with the shadowy involvement of private Israeli arms merchants, Iranian middlemen and Saudi Arabian oil financiers.

The twilight world of international arms merchants, numbered Swiss bank accounts and third-party cut-outs might be less of a mystery to Tower. Tower's big advantage is that his brother-in-law, Sam Cummings, is the biggest private arms dealer in the world. Cummings, the creator and guiding genius behind the London and Monte Carlo-based Interarms Corp., is a legend in the business of international arms trading.

There is no reason why Tower's familial connection with Cummings and Interarms would necessarily disqualify him from heading the NSC commission, nor does the relationship in any way call into question his integrity. But his relationship with the world's most successful private arms merchant, who has past connections with the CIA and on-going relationships with several countries in the Mideast, should have at least raised a few eyebrows. Although the relationship is not yet a matter of public discussion, it has the potential of at least creating the appearance of impropriety.

It is cause to wonder if the White House knew of Tower's relationship with Cummings. Is this yet another example of a bad presidential decision? Is the president being poorly served by an incompetent staff?

Tower is qualified by his past personal experience to do the job on the NSC commission, but someone in the White House should have run up some warning flags when his name was first broached.

## ST. LOUIS POST-DISPATCH
### St. Louis, MO, December 3, 1986

President Reagan and Attorney General Meese have done the right thing in deciding to seek the appointment of a special prosecutor to investigate the arms sales to Iran and the diversion of money from those sales to the Contras and perhaps others. The special prosecutor's investigation, assuming his appointment is approved by a panel of the U.S. Court of Appeals in Washington, will replace one headed by Mr. Meese. That investigation was bound to lack credibility because it amounted to the administration investigating itself.

Though the parallels with Watergate are superficial, the memory of that scandal is too recent and too painful not to have made the president and his advisers aware that nothing less than a no-holds-barred inquiry is acceptable. The special prosecutor, whose official title was changed to independent counsel in 1982 in an amendment to the 1978 Ethics in Government Act, will have the power of subpoena and will operate independently of the executive branch and Congress.

The area of investigation will be defined in the attorney general's filing with the appeals court, but the prosecutor's writ can reach as far as the appeals court wants it to, depending on where the investigation points. Present indications are that it will be limited to the particulars of the secret contacts with Iran and the disposition of the money from the arms sales.

In addition to assenting to a special prosecutor, Mr. Reagan called on Congress to establish a single Senate-House committee to investigate the Iran caper, and he named Frank Carlucci, former deputy secretary of defense, deputy director of the CIA and an experienced Foreign Service officer, as his new national security adviser. Whether Mr. Reagan will heed the advice of Republicans on Capitol Hill to conduct a major shake-up at the top level of his administration remains to be seen.

In any case, the most recent developments suggest that at last the president has grasped the seriousness of the situation for both the government and his party. Neither the nation nor the GOP can afford to let the matter drag on. If details are allowed to emerge in piecemeal fashion over a period of many months that could stretch into a year, the administration's attention and resources would be diverted from important national and international issues.

Up to now, though, Mr. Reagan seems to have regarded the whole business as a tempest in a teapot. Perhaps the most recent public opinion poll, which showed his approval rating dropping from 67 percent a month ago to 46 percent, convinced him (if his fellow Republicans couldn't) that he has a full-blown scandal on his hands.

For the special prosecutor, the issues are whether any laws were violated and, if so, who violated them. For Mr. Reagan, the issues are his personal integrity and his ability to govern. The most recent opinion poll, conducted for CBS and The New York Times, reveals that most people believe he is covering up. If, on the other hand, the president's version of events is truthful and accurate, which is to say that he didn't know what was going on, then he has confessed to a level of negligence that approaches incompetence.

# The Union Leader

*Manchester, NH, December 3, 1986*

While one cannot condone the Reagan administration's irrational policy of paying ransom, in the form of variously estimated amounts of armaments, to Iran to get back American hostages or the bizarre derivative of that policy, the so-called Nicaragua connection, it must be conceded at this writing that President Reagan is living up to his pledge to ascertain how the lat ter happened and how it can be prevented in the future. It is difficult to fault his recent actions.

• He appointed a Special Review Board, headed by former Texas Senator John Tower and composed also of former Secretary of State Edmund Muskie and former National Security Adviser Brent Scowcroft.

• He directed that board to study the operations of the National Security Council, whose top staff members, Vice Admiral John Poindexter and his aide, Lieutenant Colonel Oliver North, have been relieved of their duties because of "serious questions of impropriety."

• Pending completion of the panel's probe, which according to Tower would probably include questioning of the President himself, Reagan directed NSC employees to desist from any other operations.

• He promised to make "a full and complete airing of all the facts."

• He gave Attorney General Edwin Meese a "blank check" to look into the dealings with Iran and, indirectly, the Contra freedom fighters.

• Yesterday he endorsed the appointment of a special counsel to determine if any laws have been violated and by whom.

• He left the door open to Senate Republican Leader Robert Dole's proposal that he call Congress into special session this month to form a Watergate-style special committee the better to get the facts and avoid the circus of dozens of duplicative committee hearings by every committee with a conceivable (or even inconceivable) interest.

Understandably, for political reasons, Senate Democrats — from Minority Leader Robert Byrd and House Majority Leader Jim Wright to Senate Intelligence Committee Vice Chairman Patrick Leahy and Senator David Boren, who will replace Republican David Durenberger as committee chairman when the Democrats take control of the Senate leadership next year — are opposed to the special session idea. Even as they prepare to milk the issue of its full political value as the Republicans surely would do under similar circumstances, they contend that a special session now, which incidentally would enable Republicans to set the course of the special committee, would be an "overreaction" that would create an "aura of crisis."

Meanwhile, the President has denied — "flat out" — that he had any knowledge of the diversion of profits from the arms sales to Iran. And, in the absence of any evidence to the contrary, we believe him — just as we believe that the real story behind the arms trade with the Ayatollah Khomeini is that it was initiated without Reagan's consent and subsequently approved by him on the basis of exceedingly bad, save-face advice.

**But the biggest crisis the President faces, we submit, is to be found outside the Washington Beltline, away from the synthetic, media-charged atmosphere in the nation's capital. Tragically, that crisis, a crisis of confidence, exists in the very same American heartland where this President has been the most admired national chief executive in recent times. While we don't place too much confidence in the accuracy of public opinion polls, it seems likely that a Harris Poll finding is at least generally true —i.e., that, *even before* revelation of the Nicaragua connection, the people's confidence in Reagan and their job rating of him both dropped sharply.**

That occurred in the wake of the Daniloff-Zakharov spy swap that was not a swap (See Union Leader editorial "Lies, Lies, Lies" of October 2nd) and the arms-for-hostages deal that was not a deal (See editorial "Credibility Lost" in our November 17th editon).

*Nevertheless, in his recent actions, President Reagan has given encouraging evidence that he intends to retrieve the temporarily lost mantel of leadership and wear it with more confidence and zest than ever before. Moreover, we believe he could restore the complete confidence the people placed in him over the past half-dozen years by going public and drawing a clear distinction between his goal of fashioning some kind of post-Khomeini relationship with Iran out of geo-political considerations, most assuredly a worthy goal, and the paying of hostage ransom to Iran, an ignoble act that almost guarantees that other hostages will be taken in the future.*

## The Times-Picayune
### The States-Item

*New Orleans, LA, December 5, 1986*

President Reagan on Tuesday bit the first bullet in responding to the increasing furor over the covert Iran-contras-et al operation by calling for a special prosecutor. That will perhaps make somewhat easier biting other bullets that this case will surely produce and may repair, at least for the moment, his sudden drop in public confidence.

The president announced that his personal investigator, Attorney General Edwin Meese III, had informed him that he had found "reasonable grounds" for requesting an independent counsel to direct a full-scale investigation. Said the president: "If illegal acts were undertaken, those who did so will be brought to justice. If actions in implementing my policy were taken without my authorization, knowledge or concurrence, this would be exposed and appropriate corrective steps will be implemented."

These two aspects constitute the nub of the case: Were laws broken? Was the president fully involved in the operation and aware of all its details?

The position of special counsel and the procedures for appointing one were established by law following the Nixon Watergate scandal. But comparisons of this case to that carry more political than real freight.

Watergate involved low-level criminal activity and high-level coverup in pursuit of a president's personal political interests. This case involves a covert White House operation in pursuit of legitimate national interests. It may have been ill advised and certainly was bungled, but there is no law against stupidity.

Still, the truth must out. Any violations of law must be dealt with appropriately. Lack of high-level candor about even the legal aspects of the operation will surely also have its consequences.

We also support the president's request that Congress consolidate its own investigative activities. More than nine congressional committees have announced their intent to investigate.

This would mean a circus performance with a dizzying carousel of witnesses wheeling from committee hearing to committee hearing, bits and pieces of "revelations" and daily headlines for grandstanding members of Congress.

For consolidation, another Watergate precedent is at hand — a select committee with full powers to investigate. We urge House and Senate leaders to arrange such a committee quickly.

# Arkansas Gazette

Little Rock, AR, December 3, 1986

President Reagan's decision to seek appointment of a Watergate-style independent counsel to investigate the clandestine arms deal with Iran and diversion of as much as $30 million in profits to Nicaraguan rebels is prudent and appropriate given the allegations and evidence that already have come to the attention of the American people. Certainly the scandal has deepened in a relatively short time since the first inkling of the arms deal rose to the surface less than a month ago.

"Independent counsel" means essentially the same thing as the designation "special prosecutor" that became familiar during the Watergate scandal of the mid-1970s. There has to be some belief by Attorney General Edwin Meese that some unspecified laws may have been violated as a condition for appointing an independent counsel, who would operate in secrecy and look into only possible criminal violations.

This means that Congress should also continue its vigorous probing into what took place and who participated, from both a legal and public policy point of view. It is Congress that can assure that Americans are kept fully informed of the machinations so that the rule of accountability can be honored more fully than would be the case should the matter be left entirely to an independent counsel and the three-man inquiry into the workings of the National Security Council that also has been commissioned by Mr. Reagan.

In addition to his announcement that a request will be made for appointment of an independent counsel, Mr. Reagan also appointed Frank Carlucci, a former deputy director of the CIA, as his new national security adviser, succeeding the departed Vice Admiral John Poindexter. Mr. Carlucci presumably will be advising the president during the time the commissioned inquiry proceeds into the way the NSC has been operating in the immediate past, and in this role we would wish the new man good luck in overcoming the distractions.

Virtually no one at this point is prepared to believe that only Admiral Poindexter and an NSC deputy, Marine Lt. Col. Oliver North, knew anything about the funneling of proceeds from the arms sales to the contras or about many other aspects of this burgeoning scandal that apparently was centered in the White House basement but not necessarily limited to it.

Unfortunately, business as usual will be impossible either at the White House or on Capitol Hill until all the facts are known and laid bare before the American people. An independent counsel, as welcome as his appointment will be, can do only part of the job and his work cannot begin too soon or be too thorough and forthcoming. It is uncomfortable to think of the White House as being in such an apparent state of disarray although it surely will be viewed in this way until the whole scandal is laid to rest.

---

# ALBUQUERQUE JOURNAL

Albuquerque, NM, December 3, 1986

President Reagan, showing some of the engaging self-confidence that earned him the sobriquet The Great Communicator, made a decisive move to get back on top of events in the Iran-Nicaragua affair, promising full administration cooperation and seeking the appointment of an independent counsel to probe allegations of criminal misconduct.

Taken at face value, Reagan's pledge of complete cooperation and his promise to present all the facts to the American people leave little that could be asked of the president.

This all is in marked contrast to the stonewalling and obstructionist tactics of former President Richard Nixon when Watergate began to unfold.

Events of the next few days or weeks will show whether the performance will be as good as the promise. But Reagan has mapped the right course.

The best way to deal with the ramifications of the clandestine arms affair is first to thoroughly air its details.

Reagan's support for an independent counsel-directed criminal probe and a congressional committee investigation point the path to that end.

---

# THE SPOKESMAN-REVIEW

Spokane, WA, December 2, 1986

When President Reagan announced he would welcome a special prosecutor in the scandal over covert aid to Iran and the Nicaraguan Contras he showed better judgment than he showed when he declared that all was well until the news media blew the whistle.

Unfortunately, determining what happened in the secret arms deals is, at present, more difficult than determining which of the above remarks spoke for the real Ronald Reagan.

Only third-party investigators, with no ties to the Reagan administration, stand much chance of fulfilling the president's claim that he wants "all the facts to come out." The best approach would be the one used in the Watergate scandal, which likewise involved abuses of power within the executive branch: a special prosecutor and a congressionally appointed committee empowered to issue subpoenas and take sworn, public testimony.

But it's unlikely that such an investigation could commence or get much done until after the holidays. To call Congress into special session, as some have proposed, would achieve little. Time is short and the Republican Senate probably would deadlock with the Democratic House over how much power investigators should have over the Republican White House.

Meanwhile, it's not clear that Reagan really does want the public to know "all the facts."

Already, the White House has brought up the right of executive privilege in discussion of whether officials may testify to conversations they had with the president. Should that right be pursued, it would hinder and prolong the investigative process. But, as the Watergate saga showed, it also would magnify public suspicion and ultimately would not prevent the public from finding out what happened.

In addition, Reagan seems utterly unrepentant about the arms deal, insists there is nothing he would have done differently and says his only complaint is that the "national hero" who did the dirty work didn't keep him fully informed.

Although circumstances evidently have made it necessary for him to favor disclosure, some of his remarks indicate he would have been happier if he could have gone on deceiving the American public and U.S. allies.

In an interview with Time magazine, Reagan complained that "this wasn't a failure" until the news media noticed the first account, published by a Lebanese magazine, of the arms deal and "began to play it up." Reagan claimed the press is responsible for the fact two American hostages were not released. That, of course, is speculative.

The terrorists already knew the United States was willing to pay ransom for hostages and they made the most of it, on one occasion refusing a planeload of Hawk antiaircraft missiles and insisting, successfully, on delivery of a more advanced version of the missile. To hope that something known in terrorist circles and in the Mideast (as shown by the Lebanese magazine report) could be concealed from the Western world is ridiculous.

Furthermore, many of the recent disclosures about the arms deal have come from leaks by members of the president's own administration, who have commenced an undignified display of ducking, back-stabbing and finger-pointing.

There's always someone willing to spill the beans. For the president to suggest that the press should have helped him conceal a hypocritical, possibly illegal foreign policy is absurd.

Responsibility for the damage to U.S. credibility among our allies and our enemies alike rests upon the administration that chose to deceive, not upon the news media which did their job in reporting the deception.

# AUGUSTA HERALD

*Augusta, GA, December 3, 1986*

A president engaged in a cover-up would not do what Ronald Reagan did yesterday in 1) asking Congress to form a select committee to investigate the Iran-Contra arms deals and 2) requesting a special counsel be named to ferret out any wrongdoing by National Security Council and White House staffers.

If Richard Nixon had taken such forthright action at a comparable period in the Watergate scandal, he might well have served out his second term.

Mr. Reagan's primary contribution has been to restore public confidence in the office of the presidency — a confidence which polls show has plummeted dramatically in recent days.

It's clear the president knows now that that confidence must be restored again, and that cooperating with Congress and calling for an independent counsel are the most he can do under the circumstances.

We believe when the last chapter of this sordid tale is told, the public will be convinced that the president never lied, though he did show poor judgment. Poor judgment can be forgiven. It will not destroy his presidency.

In time, and with a renewal of a little Reagan luck, he might even be able to win back much of the public confidence this scandal has cost him. Incidentally, wouldn't former Atty. Gen. Griffin Bell, a centrist Democrat with an impeccable reputation for fairness and integrity, be an excellent choice for special counsel?

# DESERET NEWS

*Salt Lake City, UT, December 3/4, 1986*

Aside from firing a few more top aides, it's hard to say what else President Reagan could do about the growing scandal over the secret arms deal with Iran.

On Tuesday, he called for the appointment of an independent counsel or special prosecutor, suggested that Congress impanel a special select investigating committee as was done with Watergate, and named Frank Carlucci as his new National Security Adviser.

The call for a special prosecutor should lay to rest suspicions about a coverup or conflict of interest that would persist as long as the administration was in the position of investigating itself.

The suggestion that Congress set up a select committee is not self-serving even though it comes from the White House. Without some such consolidated investigating by the lawmakers, there could be at least three different congressional panels — each in danger of tripping over the other.

As for Carlucci, he brings to his sensitive new assignment some impressive credentials as a long-time government troubleshooter, including those as deputy defense secretary in the Reagan administration and deputy CIA director during the Carter years.

Earlier, President Reagan named a special blue-ribbon committee to examine the role of the NSC staff in planning and executing the Iranian arms deal. And he ordered the NSC staff to stop conducting diplomatic, military, or intelligence operations while that review is underway.

That touches just about all the bases. With a variety of investigations in the works, surely someone can be trusted to flush out the complete truth about who's responsible for this fiasco and whether or not any laws were broken.

One other possibility would be for President Reagan to call Congress back into session immediately, as some have suggested. That move is unnecessary and could just generate confusion. Some inquiries by Congress are already underway. Besides, control of the Senate will switch from the Republicans to the Democrats next month. That means a GOP-controlled probe started now might merely be dismantled later by Senate Democrats.

Even so, there is one other useful step the president could take: He should stop trying to blame the press for his current problems. The arms deals with Iran were so widely known in both Washington and Tehran that the secret was bound to leak out eventually. Besides, the Iranians started breaking their word on releasing hostages long before the press let the public in on the arms deals.

One final point: Whatever the special prosecutor and other probers may eventually turn up, there's no justification for weakening U.S. policy toward Nicaragua just because money from the Iranian arms deals was used to help the Contra rebels. Even the worst possible disclosure about the arms deals won't turn the Nicaraguan government from a Marxist cabal into a collection of freedom-loving good neighbors. It won't transform the Soviet helicopters and machine guns in Nicaragua into food packages. Nor will it make life safer for the peasants that the Nicaraguan government persecutes, or for the neighboring governments that Nicaragua seeks to overthrow.

By all means, the Iranian arms deal was a colossal blunder and investigators must get to the bottom of it. But it won't be nearly as big a mistake as the one Congress will make it if it uses the current scandal in Washington as an excuse to completely turn its back on the anti-communist rebels in Nicaragua.

# Winnipeg Free Press

*Winnipeg, Man., December 5, 1986*

U.S. President Ronald Reagan's tardy decision to call for the appointment of an independent prosecutor to investigate the Iran arms deal may help to shore up the credibility he has lost by his handling of an affair that involves lawlessness, lack of control and lack of accountability.

These are issues surrounding intelligence operations that have surfaced before in the United States and Canada. They now have surfaced in Great Britain.

In 1975, a committee of the U.S. Senate issued a report showing that the Central Intelligence Agency had broken the law by operating domestically, that it often seemed to operate beyond political control and that some of its senior executives seemed to regard themselves as accountable to no one. Measures were taken to bring the CIA back into line, especially during the presidency of Jimmy Carter. An important step was the requirement that the CIA report to intelligence oversight committees of both houses of Congress.

Canada faced problems of lawlessness, lack of control and lack of accountability in connection with the Security Service of the Royal Canadian Mounted Police. After a royal commission revealed the extent, a civilian counter-espionage agency was created and the RCMP security branch was abolished. The Canadian Security Intelligence Service was required by law to submit to oversight by privy councillors of the three major parties who would report annually to Parliament.

A legal and political row now going on in Britain and Australia concerns attempts by a former member of the British counter-intelligence service, called MI5, to publish in Australia a book that alleges lawlessness, lack of control and lack of accountability in MI5 in very recent times. It also claims that MI5's own boss between 1956 and 1965, Roger Hollis, was a Soviet agent.

The British government spent large amounts of money trying to persuade Australian courts to forbid publication, although many of the allegations were published five years ago in a book written by a British journalist based partly on information supplied to him by the former MI5 man.

The new book describes MI5 espionage operations against former Labor prime minister Harold Wilson, which broke the law, which may have been done without the permission of those running MI5 and which went undiscovered and unpunished because MI5 is nominally accountable to the Home Secretary and prime minister but to no one else. Conservative Prime Minister Margaret Thatcher apparently has failed to see the problem because she rejected this week a sensible proposal to establish a joint Lords-Commons oversight committee to which MI5 would report.

The law-breaking in the Iran affair includes the clandestine transfer to Nicaraguan rebels through Swiss bank accounts of profits from Mr. Reagan's gun-running. Mr. Reagan claims lack of knowledge of this, implicitly claims that he had no control over two National Security Council employees said to have done it all themselves and implicitly claims that they did not behave as if they were accountable to him.

This suggests a serious oversight gap in what is supposed to be simply an analysis centre to help a president develop policy options from the shoal of advice he gets from line departments. If Mr. Reagan's claims are true then yet another example is presented of the political and diplomatic danger to states that do not adequately oversee their covert diplomatic and intelligence operations.

# nquiries into Arms Scandal Widen; Administration Officials Testify

Officials of the Reagan administration testified before several committees of Congress December 5-11, 1986 on United States arms sales to Iran and the diversion of funds from the sales to the Nicaraguan contra rebels. Although several leading figures in the growing scandal declined to answer questions or testified in secret, Secretary of State George Shultz revealed Dec. 8 that the White House, without informing him, had opened secret communications with the U.S. ambassador to Lebanon, seeking the ambassador's cooperation in the Iranian arms shipments. Shultz told the House Foreign Affairs Committee that he was, "to put it mildly, shocked" to find out that the envoy, John Kelly, had known more about the sale of arms to Iran for the release of hostages than had the secretary of state. Kelly, a career Foreign Service officer, returned to Washington Dec. 9 for questioning about his role. According to a message from Kelly that Shultz read to the committee, the ambassador in early November had held "numerous conversations" with Lt. Col. Oliver North, the National Security Council staffer who was fired November 25, and with retired Air Force Maj. Gen. Richard Secord about the hostage releases. Secord was widely regarded as a key figure in the affair, but Shultz was the first administration official to acknowledge publicly that Secord had played a role.

Following Shultz's testimony, former national security adviser Robert McFarlane told the committee that North had informed him in May 1986, while the two were on a secret mission to Iran together, that "the U.S. government had applied part of the proceeds" of the arms sales to the contras fighting to overthrow the Sandinista government in Nicaragua. McFarlane testified that if he had been in office at the time, he would have pursued the matter further, but because he had resigned in December 1985, he let it drop. McFarlane said that he had assumed that North and then national security adviser Vice Adm. John Poindexter had received "higher authority" to divert funds to the contras, but he backed off from saying such authority necessarily would have come from the President. McFarlane's testimony contradicted early indications by President Reagan and Attorney General Edwin Meese 3rd that no Americans had been directly involved in the fund diversion. McFarlane also contradicted Meese's assertion that Reagan had known about the arms shipments "probably after the fact." McFarlane said that Reagan had given oral approval to Israeli shipments of U.S.-made arms to Iran in August 1985, before the first shipment occurred. He said that the White House had considered Reagan's spoken approval to have the same legal authority as a written intelligence "finding," the legal procedure for initiating a covert operation. Such a finding was not issued until January 1986, after the first shipments of weapons.

North and Poindexter, who resigned Nov. 25, declined Dec. 9 to answer the committee's questions, citing their Fifth Amendment rights against self-incrimination. Poindexter promised to cooperate "at an appropriate time," and North, appearing anguished, told a questioner, "I don't think there is another person in America who wants to tell his story as much as I do, sir." North and Poindexter took the Fifth on the advice of their lawyers, who denied that they were actively seeking immunity from criminal prosecution for their clients.

William Casey, the director of the Central Intelligence Agency (CIA), testified before the House Foreign Affairs Committee in a closed session Dec. 10-11. Casey reportedly said that "serious errors of judgment" had been committed by senior CIA officials who allowed North to use the agency's resources for the arms shipments. Casey was said to have testified that Reagan, in signing the finding January 17, 1986, had ordered him not to tell congressional intelligence committees about the program to ship arms to Iran. Casey Dec. 10 reportedly said that he had first heard hints that some of the funds were being diverted to the contras October 7, when a former legal client called him. The former client was Roy Furmark, a New York energy consultant who had reportedly worked with Adnan Khashoggi, a Saudi arms dealer said to have been a major figure in the sales.

## The Birmingham News

*Birmingham, AL, December 7, 1986*

Clearly it does not improve the climate of suspicion that has grown up around the Iranian arms fiasco for the two men who probably know the most about the affair to refuse to give testimony to congressional investigators.

But the decision last week by former National Security Adviser John Poindexter and his aide, Lt. Col. Oliver North, to plead their Fifth Amendment rights as they confronted members of the Senate Intelligence Committee doesn't mean that they are guilty of any crime, nor that the president is stonewalling nor that the investigation will be frustrated.

There is a great deal of debate over just what kind of crime, if any, might have been involved in the Iranian matter. Some veteran court observers believe it would be virtually impossible to sustain any criminal charges against Poindexter and North.

Still, as for any American citizen, it is within their rights to refuse to incriminate themselves through their own testimony. That is a right not even the president of the United States, even if he desperately wants his associates to cooperate in the Iranian probe, can force them to give up.

Poindexter and North do not have a duty to convict themselves nor to help investigators hunt for a suitable criminal charge to file against them. They do, as former public officials, have a duty to provide information about any illegal acts or inappropriate conduct of others involved in public service —

including their former boss, the president — if they can do so without giving up their own constitutional protections.

That can be arranged. The Watergate scandal provided a good legal method for letting witnesses testify without having their testimony used against them, while not completely letting them off the hook.

According to Henry Ruth, the third of four special prosecutors in the Watergate affair, the method was used for the testimony of John Dean.

The day before Dean testified, prosecutors filed a package with court officials saying, "This is everything we know about John Dean, so that when he testifies tomorrow we can truthfully say this is what we knew before and we didn't derive this from his testimony."

Dean testified without pleading the Fifth Amendment. He was later convicted and spent four months in jail for obstruction of justice.

That same method could be used on Poindexter and North if the special counsel who will be named in the Iran matter deems it necessary.

We need to get to the bottom of this matter, to correct any problems in policy and procedure that are apparent from it, and then move on to other matters. We can collect the information to do that without trampling on anybody's constitutional rights.

# The Record

Hackensack, NJ, December 15, 1986

Imagine that you're a police commissioner whose department is facing a federal anti-corruption probe. One of your lieutenants, called before a grand jury to testify about his knowledge of bribes in the department, repeatedly pleads the Fifth Amendment, refusing to give answers that might incriminate him. What should you do?

If you want to restore public confidence in the police force, you have little choice. You must make it known that any cop who refuses to cooperate with the federal probe will be removed. The lieutenant has a right not to incriminate himself. But in refusing to help root out corruption, he has no right to complain if his boss no longer trusts him to root it out himself.

This is why Sen. David Durenberger of Minnesota, the outgoing chairman of the Senate Intelligence Committee, was right on target last week when he called on John M. Poindexter and Oliver L. North to "either take off their uniforms or . . . take off their Fifth Amendments." Following their resignation from the National Security Council, both men have refused to testify before the intelligence committee on what they know concerning the growing Iran-contra arms scandal. They have a right not to incriminate themselves. Yet both are now back on active duty in the military, Mr. Poindexter as a vice-admiral in the Navy and Mr. North as a lieutenant-colonel in the Marines, where they give orders, receive them, and supposedly execute the will of Congress and the president.

Yet their ability to do so is hopelessly compromised. When pressed by Congress for information concerning the gravest issue of national security, they balked. This is bad enough under ordinary circumstances. But now Congress, like the beleaguered police commissioner, is struggling to reassert control over an intelligence and military apparatus that insists on setting its own foreign policy and financing its own guerrilla wars whether Congress likes it or not. It can no more afford to have two openly uncooperative officers in high-ranking positions than the police commissioner can allow the reluctant lieutenant to carry out *his* assignment.

Senator Durenberger is correct. Admiral Poindexter and Colonel North must be given an unequivocal choice: testify or resign.

●

What of the right against self-incrimination? Wouldn't firing John Poindexter and Oliver North mean penalizing them for exercising their constitutional guarantees — a 1980's reincarnation of 1950's McCarthyism?

The answer is no. When the Hollywood Ten were called before the House Un-American Activities Committee, they were asked about their membership in a legal political organization, one whose activities had no immediate relevance to their jobs in the film industry. They refused and pleaded the Fifth (although many legal authorities believed they would have been on firmer ground if they had cited their First Amendment right to freedom of association). Admiral Poindexter and Colonel North, by contrast, have been asked about illegal activities that bear directly on their positions. If democracy is to be served, they must tell what they know or concede that they can no longer function as U.S. military officers.

# The Miami Herald

Miami, FL, December 5, 1986

NO CHESS player would risk his entire position to capture a pawn. Congressional leaders ought to keep that in mind as they consider whether to offer immunity from prosecution to any participant in the Iranscam scandal in exchange for his full testimony about who knew and did what when.

Lt. Col. Oliver North, evidently the scheme's architect, invoked the Fifth Amendment's protection against self-incrimination before the Senate Intelligence Committee on Tuesday. His boss, Vice Adm. John Poindexter, who resigned as national-security director when President Reagan fired Colonel North on Nov. 25, "took the Fifth" on Wednesday. Frustrated, some congressional leaders urged granting both men immunity from prosecution for any compelled testimony before Congress.

That would be both premature and unwise for at least six reasons:

First, so many congressional committees could become involved as to wreck future prosecution by proliferating immunized testimony.

Second, Congress should name a Watergate-style select joint committee, along the bipartisan lines of the Senate committee named yesterday, to investigate Iranscam. If anyone is to be granted immunity, that joint committee alone should grant it.

Third, Attorney General Edwin Meese III will ask a special Federal-court panel to appoint a special prosecutor. It'll take a week to 10 days for the court to issue its expected assent.

Fourth, the FBI and Justice Department Criminal Division investigations continue apace. Their findings will be turned over to the independent counsel if one is named.

Fifth, hasty immunization of Messrs. Poindexter and North could impede the special prosecutor's inquiry. It also might taint evidence that the FBI or Criminal Division already is pursuing.

Sixth, whether or not Messrs. Poindexter and North are prosecuted is secondary, or even tertiary, to the nation's overriding interest in knowing all that can be learned about Iranscam. That overriding interest demands that the public know who else in the White House was involved, and when, and how. It demands as well that the Reagan Administration's procedures — beginning with its enamor with secrecy and the President's too-loose grip on his aides' reins — be examined and corrected where appropriate.

Where appropriate: That should be the operative phrase in deciding whether and when to grant immunity in exchange for any compelled testimony about Iranscam. It may be appropriate to grant it later to obtain evidence unobtainable otherwise. Later — not now.

# the Charleston Gazette

Charleston, WV, December 5, 1986

ADM. John Poindexter and Lt. Col. Oliver North took oaths promising to uphold the Constitution and obey all laws.

Anyone who honors these pledges needn't take the Fifth Amendment.

North — called "a national hero." by President Reagan — and Poindexter refuse to answer congressional questions about their White House covert acts on grounds it would incriminate them.

This infuriating development is evidence that they violated their oaths, thus they should be stripped of benefits and removed from the services.

More infuriatingly, the president Thursday gave his blessing to any Cabinet officer who takes the Fifth — contradicting his promise that the administration would cooperate fully with investigations.

Such stonewalling is futile, because probes won't cease until Americans know the whole truth of the secret delivery of weapons to a terrorist state and illicit funneling of money to guerrillas.

The Iran-contras scandal is producing non-stop allegations smacking of criminality. Revelations this week:

▲ A CIA Swiss bank account was used to funnel Iran weapons profits to the contra killers in Nicaragua during a period when it was illegal for the CIA or any federal agency to support the contras.

▲ CIA Director William Casey approved weapons shipments to Iran two months before President Reagan signed a top-secret memo approving the scheme. Sending U.S. arms to Iran is a crime — as convicted or indicted Americans have learned.

▲ North arranged for Texas billionaire H. Ross Perot to send $2 million in cash to Cyprus for a "ship-to-ship" exchange for American hostages. The money was sent, and Perot's courier waited on Cyprus five days, but the ransom scheme fizzled. (Thank heaven. Otherwise, any terrorist with an I.Q. of 50 would get the obvious message: Want $2 million? Grab five Americans off a foreign street and wait for White House offers.)

No matter how many officials take the Fifth, delving mustn't end until the dirty affair has been brought fully to light and to justice.

## THE SACRAMENTO BEE
### Sacramento, CA, December 11, 1986

"Poindexter, North," said the headlines, "Again Invoke 5th; Refuse to Answer Questions From House Panel on Roles in Iran Deal."

And so they did, this time before a televised hearing of the House Foreign Affairs Committee. But it should also be clear that under the Constitution they have every right to do so without anyone suggesting that they are trying to impede the legitimate and necessary investigation of this affair. Yesterday one member of the committee, Democrat Michael Barnes of Maryland, went so far as to propose that former National Security Council Director Poindexter waive his constitutional rights since the worst thing that could happen is that he would be found guilty "and probably (get) a very short, probably suspended sentence."

That kind of suggestion, for which Barnes subsequently apologized, is dangerous for any number of reasons. First, for its inference that a person exercising his constitutional right against self-incrimination must be guilty. Second, and as important, because the posturing that some members of Congress have engaged in puts the focus not on the damaging policy mistakes of the Iran arms deal but on the investigation itself.

If that conduct continues, it's almost certain not only to generate divisive backlash, particularly when the immediate targets are military officers who have served their country with distinction, but to risk diversion into marginal questions about investigative techniques and legal processes that can only trivialize the more urgent issues.

Crimes may well have been committed by people in powerful positions; they must be investigated, as they undoubtedly will, by the special prosecutor. More important, foreign policy — at Reykjavik, in Central America, in the Middle East — has been dreadfully mismanaged, raising serious questions about whether there is any effective leadership in the White House of any sort. The examination of those issues requires determined pursuit in Congress. But such determination also requires the planning, the preliminary interviews, the collection of documents and, above all, the decorum and restraint that keep the focus on the main questions.

Were the president more energetic and involved in getting the facts — for himself and for the country — some of this might have been unnecessary. But so far, there's no sign that he's interested in doing that. What's certain now is that Congress and the court-appointed independent counsel have to do the job, and do it in such a way that it's the substantive issues, and not the process of answering questions, on which attention rests.

## DESERET NEWS
### Salt Lake City, UT
### December 5, 1986

Though President Reagan promised Congress full cooperation in trying to get to the bottom of the Iran arms scandal, two ex-White House aides who could provide some answers are not talking.

Or, at least they're not talking to the Senate Intelligence Committee, which is now thinking of granting immunity from prosecution to former national security adviser John Poindexter and his key aide, Lt. Col. Oliver North.

While immunity is often granted to lesser figures in a case in return for their testimony about the more important targets of an investigation, it's much too soon for Congress to start granting immunity now in the Iran arms-Contra aid affair.

It isn't clear yet exactly which laws, if any, may have been violated. As many as dozen could be involved. The possible violations range from from making fraudulent and misuse of public money to conspiracy to defraud the government. Any immunity granted now could turn out to be more sweeping that Congress might care for later.

Moreover, even though Poindexter and North declined to talk to the Senate committee on grounds of possible self-incrimination, both indicated they would be willing to cooperate with a special prosecutor.

Suppose the special prosecutor, who has yet to be named, developed enough evidence to warrant an indictment but the Senate committee has granted immunity to Poindexter and North. It could be hard to prove that evidence was not derived from immunized testimony.

Just ask Arthur H. Christy, who was the nation's first special prosecutor. He strongly advises that key congressmen wait until a new independent counsel is named, then consult with him before deciding about immunity.

The point is well-taken. If Poindexter and North won't talk to the special prosecutor, they could still be granted immunity if there's no other way of getting the truth.

Besides, the law authorizing the selection of a special prosecutor is designed to let Congress and the prosecutor work together, not as adversaries. In investigating the Iran arms scandal, let's strive to make that law work as intended.

## St. Petersburg Times
### St. Petersburg, FL, December 14, 1986

Within hours of CIA Director William Casey's "secret" testimony this past week before the House Foreign Affairs Committee, many of the details of that testimony were available to anybody who reads the newspaper or watches television. Although those leaks didn't compromise any important national secrets, they were evidence of Congress' chronic inability to keep some kinds of information to itself. It's an institutional failing that eventually frustrates every presidential administration.

Some administrations become so frustrated that, in the name of national security, they begin to circumvent their constitutional obligations to inform appropriate congressional committees of their actions. That concern for secrecy obviously helps to explain the Reagan administration's conduct of foreign policy related to the Iran-*contra* affair.

It helps to explain it, but it doesn't justify it. For one thing, where does the secrecy end? In this case, the President defends his decision not to inform *any* members of Congress of the secret decision to sell weapons to Iran. But it also turns out that the secretary of state, the Joint Chiefs of Staff and perhaps even the director of the CIA were unaware of the diversion of funds to the *contras*. After all, the State Department and other offices of the executive branch have been known to leak, too. Did one arm of the White House have legitimate reason to keep secrets from the other — even when it was at the same time trusting international arms merchants and members of the Iranian government to keep those same secrets?

Presidents also play a dangerous game when they begin justifying unconstitutional secrecy on national security grounds. Defenders of the White House point out that President Roosevelt secretly violated the Neutrality Act by coming to Britain's aid prior to our official involvement in World War II. But are we really to equate the nature and scope of Nicaragua's threat to our security in 1986 to the threat posed by Nazi Germany in 1940?

On the same day that William Casey's "secret" testimony became common knowledge, the Soviet Union announced the death of 48-year-old Anatoly Marchenko, who had spent most of his adult life in prison or exile on charges of "anti-Soviet agitation and propaganda." At the same time, the government of South Africa was announcing a new series of restrictions on news coverage of racial unrest in that country. The Soviets and South Africans justify these and other instances of secrecy and repression on grounds of national security. Few leaks emanate from Moscow or Pretoria. Are those closed societies consequently more secure than ours?

In times of true national emergency, our Congress and our press have shown their ability to keep a secret. More often, though, our sometimes messy system of checks and balances helps to keep our political disputes from turning into national emergencies in the first place.

## San Francisco Chronicle

*San Francisco, CA, December 7, 1986*

**THERE MUST BE** a better way to get to the bottom of the Iran arms deal than the water torture currently being inflicted on the nation.

Drop by drop, information drips from open hearings, leaks from closed hearings, and trickles from informed sources. It is practically a full-time job to plow through all the news articles and catch all the radio and TV reports and news talk shows in order to glean a new fact or two each day.

But there is a better way. By granting some form of immunity to the two key players in the dirty business of secretly selling arms to terrorist Iran, and then sending some of the funds covertly, and presumably illegally, to the Contras in Central America, we vastly increase our chances of finding out right away what happened and who was involved.

As one member of Congress has pointed out, if Vice Adm. John Poindexter, the ousted national security adviser who oversaw the arms deal, and Marine Lt. Col. Oliver North, the White House aide who carried out the operation, can be convinced to tell what they know, "you'd be surprised how close we would be to concluding this investigation."

**UP UNTIL NOW**, both men have invoked, quite understandably, their constitutional rights to refuse to tell Congress, and the American people, what they did and whose orders they were following. If, in exchange for some form of immunity from prosecution, they will tell all, it seems to us quite a reasonable trade.

The nation may give up the chance of putting on trial two military officers whose careers and reputations are now tainted by controversy anyway, but it will find out what happened and who was responsible. And it will find out right away, instead of dragging out the sluggish process which has nearly paralyzed all other activity in Washington.

## DESERET NEWS

*Des Moines, IA, December 5, 1986*

"We want the truth. The president wants it. I want it. The American people have a fundamental right to it."

At the very time Vice President George Bush said that, former National Security Adviser John Poindexter was invoking his constitutional right to remain silent rather than testify before a congressional investigating committee.

Poindexter and his onetime assistant Oliver North have both invoked the Fifth Amendment allowing them to refuse to answer any questions on grounds of possible self-incrimination. That is their right, but their use of it is profoundly disappointing.

So, too, is an emerging pattern of contradiction between White House promises of full disclosure and the lack of cooperation with investigations of covert military-financing operations.

Just last week, Reagan told the American people that "you will be the final arbiters of this controversy. You will have all the facts and will be able to judge for yourselves."

Despite these promises, however, the president has been less than forthcoming with consistent information on covert White House activities. On Nov. 19, for example, Reagan said the United States initiated contact with Iran, then one week later contradicted that statement by insisting the Iranians approached the White House.

The administration has not revealed the names on the Swiss bank accounts through which the Iranian payments for U.S. weapons were laundered. Both the Israelis and the Nicaraguan contras insist they have not touched the money.

Far more is known inside the White House than has been revealed. Even if no other White House officials were involved in the secret deal, the Justice Department inquiry panel did interview Poindexter and North, causing Attorney General Edwin Meese to call for a special prosecutor to investigate what he determined to be potential criminal wrongdoing.

Rather than make full disclosure, however, the White House has tried to shift blame for the deal away from the administration. Last weekend, Reagan praised North as a national hero, blamed the Israelis for overcharging the Iranians (a charge denied by the Israeli government) and attacked the press for reporting the story.

The administration is not obliged to tell the public everything it knows about the deal. Nor is it required to cooperate with a congressional investigation.

But if the president and vice president chose the path of nondisclosure, they should admit it and stop pretending to be telling the whole truth.

## The Salt Lake Tribune

*Salt Lake City, UT,
December 15, 1986*

Contrary to the impression many of us acquired while serving in this country's armed forces, Americans don't surrender their civil rights when they enter the service.

So, Vice Adm. John Poindexter, the former national security director, Marine Lt. Col. Oliver North, one of the admiral's deputies who was fired from his National Security Council staff job by President Reagan, and Marine Lt. Col. Robert Earl, an assistant to Col. North at the NSC, were utilizing, as any American may, their consitutionally-endowed rights when they refused to testify before the Senate Intelligence Committee.

Nevertheless, the anger expressed by the committee chairman, Sen. Dave Durenberger, R-Minn., because of the three officers' refusals, can be readily appreciated by many Americans.

There is something almost irrational about these career military men's disinclination to share their knowledge of the Iran-Contra affair when it is recognized the three have voluntarily committed themselves to surrendering their lives for their country.

For that matter, Col. North has already lost considerable of his blood on behalf of his country; he was twice awarded the Purple Heart for wounds received during service in the Vietnam war. Possibly, Adm. Poindexter and Col. Earl have been similarly decorated. The public record is not clear on that point. They are all brave and dedicated men; their military records attest to that.

However, their actions before the intelligence panel are such that they naturally, and probably rightfully, trigger the anger of someone like Sen. Durenberger.

"Today [Friday] I'm angered by the fact that the third member of the military services of this nation has refused to give testimony on his role in this matter," Sen. Durenberger said.

"These guys are being praised as national heroes around this country because of what they did for their country in this Iran case . . . If they're such heroes, then why are they deserting their country when they are finally being put to the true test of their commitment to this country? . . . A national hero doesn't come in here and stiff the whole country."

The senator is likely to find considerable concurrence among many Americans. There is something unseemly about the trio's withholding testimony, given their willingness to surrender their lives in defense of their country, but are clearly reluctant to help clarify a situation that has the potential of letting the United States appear before its allies and the world as duplicitous and without honor.

## Herald News

*Fall River, MA, December 11, 1986*

Rear Adniral Poindexter and Colonel North have "taken the Fifth" and refused to answer questions of the House Foreign Affairs Committee about the transfer of Iranian payments for American weapons to the Nicaraguan Contras.

Their decision not to answer was taken on the advice of their counsel and is perfectly legal. They, like every other American, have a right to refuse to incriminate themselves.

All the same, as they cannot help but be aware, their refusal makes it difficult, if not impossible, for the House committee to find out what really did happen to the money the Iranians paid for the weapons.

It has been suggested that President Reagan should question Poindexter and North about their activities, and then disclose the facts to the country.

The President has reportedly refused to do this, preferring to let the various committing probing the Iranian affair proceed without interference from him.

Presumably Poindexter and North will also refuse to answer the Senate committee investigating the controversial affair.

That will leave the real probe to the special counsel the Department of Justice wants to appoint.

That counsel would have subpoena powers, and what is perhaps as important, would be independent of Congress.

If he discovers evidence of illegality, he would then turn the matter over to the courts.

The reason why counsel for Poindexter and North has advised them to "take the Fifth" is not yet clear. It may be they are waiting for the committee to grant them immunity, or they may feel that political motivations will affect the attitudes the congressional committee would take to their testimony.

Meanwhile, there is anger and frustration among the members of the House committee because they cannot get to the bottom of the affair.

Among the unpleasant repercussions from the arms dealing with Iran is the growing alienation of the administration from Congress.

It now appears unlikely that the President will do much, if anything, to help either the House or Senate committee probe the unfortunate episode.

And that in turn almost guarantees that the episode will drag on until it is settled in the courts. Meanwhile it will do almost unlimited damage to the administration's relations with Congress with repercussions on every aspect of the government's business.

The widening gulf between the White House and Capitol Hill may well turn out to be the most dangerous effect of the entire Iranian affair.

## Richmond Times-Dispatch

*Richmond, VA, December 10, 1986*

So far, the congressional hearings into "Iragua" have demonstrated only that ensuring against leaks is more easily said than done, and engaging in leaks is no sooner said than done.

Not only has Congress become a sieve; its leaks flow only one way: against the White House. On the Senate Select Committee on Intelligence are many senators and staffers who do their jobs scrupulously. There are also senators and staffers who profess horror at what they presume is law-breaking by administration officials but who seem not at all bothered by anonymous, piecemeal disclosure of what is supposed to be confidential testimony before the committee. In acknowledgment of the public's right to know, but in practice perhaps a reason for witnesses to take the Fifth, committee rules provide for the authorized disclosure of testimony given behind closed doors "after a determination by said committee that the public interest would be served by such disclosure." Has any such determination been made in the current hearings?

The Reagan administration, its critics insist, has selected those laws it wishes to obey and has ignored, circumvented or bent those it does not. In their zest to prove that, have unnamed congressional sources themselves selected whose testimony, and which parts of it, shall remain confidential? If Col. Oliver North broke any laws — and it is not known that he did — he did so out of a conviction that the value of what he was doing superseded the validity of legislative constraints. Do those anonymous sources, as eager to besmirch his name as to protect their own, make the same claim?

President Reagan's critics risk setting a precedent they themselves may greatly regret: that members of Congress and their staffs, if against presidential policy, may forget the rules and, at least in their own minds, suspend the law. Never mind the presumption of innocence, that cornerstone of American justice. Never mind the Fifth Amendment, a load-bearer in the judicial edifice. Never mind congressional rules of confidentiality. Breaking, bending, skirting — do congressional and other Reagan critics who consider these tactics despicable when used by Col. North consider them permissible, even admirable when used against him?

## THE SAGINAW NEWS
### *Saginaw, MI, December 10, 1986*

Finally, in his radio talk last Saturday, President Reagan admitted that mistakes were made with the Iranian-Contra arms and money connection. There sure were. He promised to "set it right." He should start with his own ideas of the role of the secretary of state.

In this affair, evidently, the insiders, from Reagan on down to relative minions such as a Mideast ambassador, didn't even consider the existence of a fellow named George Shultz.

No doubt Shultz was happy to testify, on the record, that he knew almost nothing of what was going on, and played no part in it. So in terms of culpability, he ought to be home free.

But it also had to be deeply embarrassing for a Cabinet officer of the highest rank, a man who is supposed to be the nation's top foreign-affairs specialist, to confess ignorance about a matter of enormous international import.

Yet there was Shultz, telling Congress and the country that:

He didn't know that the ambassador to Lebanon was working with Lt. Col. Oliver North on the hostage/arms arrangement.

He didn't know about the arms deal, period, until last month's disclosures.

He knew nothing of the fund diversion to the Nicaraguan Contra rebels.

Despite learning "bits and pieces" of the story, he did not feel compelled to seek out the whole truth.

It is an appalling tale, instructive as to why the administration went so wrong. No one asked the counsel of the official who is supposed to be the president's chief adviser on these things. Considering that Shultz labeled the money-laundering scheme illegal, there is little doubt that he might have saved the administration from this spot of trouble.

Any other secretary of state who had been deliberately cut out of a major operation in his own bailiwick would have quit by now. Shultz may yet do so, unless his president convinces him that he will be part of the setting-right process.

The one who really should be embarrassed is Ronald Reagan. Either he purposely withheld information from the secretary of state, or he did not realize that Shultz was not in on the deal. Either way, as Henry Kissinger understated during a visit to Port Huron, "that would not be a good way of running the government."

The latest fallout underscores the real scandal — the question of who, in fact, has been running the government. Ignorance in various degrees has been professed by Reagan himself, the secretary of defense and now the secretary of state. If Donald Regan files his own disclaimers, then perhaps Oliver North should not have been so quickly dismissed. He may be the only one who knows the combination to the White House safe.

## The Charlotte Observer
### *Charlotte, NC, December 7, 1986*

Lt. Col. Oliver North appears well on his way to earning his niche in American infamy — right up there with the John Deans and Gordon Liddys and others who became so swollen with the arrogance of power that they could no longer distinguish between right and wrong.

In some twisted way, the colonel may be a patriotic man. But his role in the illegalities of the Iranian arms deal, his attempt to get private ransom money for hostage-takers in Lebanon, and reports that he shredded National Security Council documents that may be incriminating to himself or others, all raise questions about how such a man came to wield the influence he did.

Col. North seemed to believe that if the *form* of the policy was macho and

brazen — if it was secret and illegal and sufficiently cloak-and-dagger — the *substance* of it could be downright craven: paying terrorists, for example, for the release of Americans held hostage.

The questions here are not only legal, though it seems very clear that laws were broken. It is also important to know which high-ranking officials, up through and including President Reagan, countenanced the kind of cloak-and-dagger cowardice that Lt. Col. North came to represent.

Illegalities aside, the attempt to pay ransom to international terrorists and the actual bribery of an outlaw nation infamous for crimes against the United States represent a pitiful low point in our diplomatic history.

## The Chattanooga Times
### *Chattanooga, TN, December 11, 1986*

Testifying before the House Foreign Affairs Committee on Monday, Secretary of State George Shultz confirmed that his department had solicited funds for the contra rebels in Nicaragua from the Sultan of Brunei. He described at length the legal foundation for the solicitation but sidestepped a vital part of the question put to him by Rep. William S. Broomfield, R-Mich.

Rep. Broomfield asked about the secret Swiss bank account into which the funds from Brunei were deposited and, specifically, who controls this fund. Mr. Shultz did not respond to those parts of the question, choosing instead to read the committee a lengthy report from the embassy in Nicaragua about the Soviet-style celebration of the November anniversary of the Sandinista revolution. It is unfortunate the secretary was not called on the evasion; the answer to Mr. Broomfield's question is of great significance.

When the story of contra support solicited from Brunei broke over last weekend, it was reported that the payments from the oil-rich Southeast Asian country went into a Swiss bank account managed by Lt. Col. Oliver North, the former National Security Council staff member dismissed over the diversion of payments from Iranian arms sales to the contras' war effort.

Unnamed administration officials quoted by *The New York Times* conceded that once payments were made into that account the State Department had no way of monitoring how the money was used. This is crucial because the foundation Secretary Shultz outlined Monday for the legality of the solicitation of funds relates specifically to their use for "humanitarian" assistance. It would in no way legitimize State Department solicitation of funds for military support to the contras.

As Mr. Shultz reminded the House committee, the 1985 legislation authorizing $27 million in humanitarian or non-lethal aid to the contras specifically did not preclude "activities of the Department of State to solicit such *humanitarian* assistance for the Nicaraguan democratic resistance" (emphasis added). On the basis of that Mr. Shultz insisted not only that there was "nothing illegal" about the Brunei solicitation but that it constituted "the policy of the United States, put into place by congressional action."

However, that congressionally enacted U.S. policy dealt not only with State Department requests for funds from other countries but also with how the solicited funds would be used. That's where Mr. Shultz's problem arises. If, indeed, the State Department failed to exercise control over how the contributed funds were used, it failed, and miserably, to comply with the dictates of Congress.

Col. North had served the administration as coordinator of "private" funding for military aid to the contras during the time when Congress prohibited the use of U.S. funds for military purposes. If the Brunei payments were made into the secret Swiss bank account managed by Col. North, which Mr. Shultz did not deny, the State Department would have had every reason to believe they might well be funneled to the purchase of armaments — a use clearly outside the realm of congressional approval.

Mr. Shultz effectively evaded Rep. Broomfield's question on Monday. But the question still stands: Who controlled the expenditure of the several million dollars donated by Brunei to the contra cause and how were the funds used? The secretary of state owes the nation and the Congress an answer.

## St. Paul Pioneer Press & Dispatch

*St. Paul, MN, December 11, 1986*

You're a federal official who may have done something that can get yourself thrown in jail. You're not necessarily ashamed of what you've done; in fact, you may be quite proud. Better than that, you actually may be eager to let the world know why you've done what you've done, as much of the world thinks you've acted stupidly. Nonetheless, you're not exactly enthusiastic about risking conviction for the pleasure of telling your side right away.

Enter your lawyer, who says there is a method of eventually revealing everything you wish to reveal, while simultaneously limiting (perhaps precluding) the possibility of imprisonment. That perfectly legal method entails invoking the Fifth Amendment during congressional hearings while seeking at least partial immunity from criminal prosecution. Given such options, what would you do?

Chances are you would do exactly what Vice Adm. John Poindexter and Lt. Col. Oliver North did in recent appearances before congressional panels: refuse to risk incriminating yourself, just as the Constitution assures.

Would investigation of the unacceptable Iranian-contra connection be further along if Mr. Poindexter and Mr. North bared all this week? Sure. But that does not mean their silence is permanent. Nor, more importantly, does it mean they acted dishonorably by availing themselves of the Constitution. Protection against the possibility of self-incrimination, after all, is integral to freedom; self-preservation is simply human.

But, the charge is made, didn't President Reagan promise to get to the bottom of this mess without delay? Yes, he did. And yes, he and the rest of his administration are so obligated. But Mr. Reagan has no authority to prevent anyone from pleading the Fifth Amendment. Nor should he.

In line, a wider point needs to be made.

Even if everyone involved in the Iranian arms affair dug and came clean at record speed, the various investigations would run for months. An independent counsel, lest one forget, has not even been named yet. More specifically, the very nature of the work at hand is complicated and time-consuming, meaning the country runs the risk of misinterpreting that fact for high-level intransigence. Or, in other words, while heat needs to be kept on the White House, it cannot be blamed for every real and imagined stall in the road.

## The Oregonian

*Portland, OR, December 5, 1986*

The idea of granting immunity from prosecution to secure testimony from former National Security Adviser Vice Adm. John M. Poindexter and his former staff member Lt. Col. Oliver L. North should be placed on indefinite hold — at least until a special prosecutor has investigated what laws they may have violated. That doesn't mean, however, that Cabinet members should blithely resort to the same privilege against self-incrimination when they testify.

Poindexter and North reportedly indicated they desired immunity when they refused on Fifth Amendment grounds to testify before the Senate Intelligence Committee about the sale of U.S. arms to Iran and funding of the Nicaraguan Contras. While their testimony might be of interest to the committee, there should be no rush to secure it by granting immunity at this early stage of proceedings.

Most certainly, the committee should not pre-empt the authority of the special prosecutor even before that prosecutor is on board, especially regarding the two figures most implicated in the suspect activities. Fortunately, there is no need in this case for emergency legislation or for immediate disclosure of facts on which to base that legislation. Congress can wait a bit, the same reasons that no special session needs to be called this month.

What for Poindexter and North is a constitutional privilege — not to testify on the grounds of possible self-incrimination — would be a serious mistake for Cabinet members when they go before the committee. President Reagan has said he will leave it up to those Cabinet members whether to follow his former staff members' example. For them to do so, however, would be disastrous. How could a Cabinet member retain credibility after admitting that he was likely to be incriminating himself if he testified?

The Senate should await the advice of a special prosecutor regarding immunity for North and Poindexter. But Reagan should reverse himself and make it clear that any Cabinet member refusing to fully disclose matters of proper interest to Congress will be replaced.

The Fifth Amendment is an appropriate shield for those facing the prospect of prosecution. It is totally inappropriate for a government official discussing matters relating to the conduct of his office.

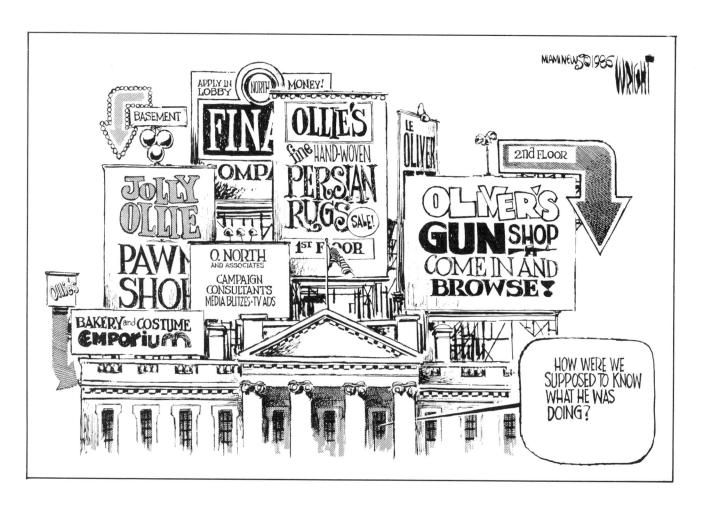

# Wisconsin State Journal

*Madison, WI, December 11, 1986*

It was an unusual day in the history of the republic.

Marine Lt. Col. Oliver North, in full uniform with his Presidential Service Badge prominent on his chest, refused to answer questions Tuesday from Congress, citing his Fifth Amendment right to remain silent.

On the advice of his lawyer, North said, he would "respectfully and regretfully" decline to testify before the House Foreign Affairs Committee.

Preceding him to the witness stand and taking the same position was Vice Admiral John Poindexter, former national security adviser.

As the key figures in the growing scandal of arms to Iran and cash to Contras, these men need to be heard.

Their positions, while not surprising in light of their earlier silence before a closed-door intelligence panel, leave Congress and the country still searching for answers.

Their silence also raises the question of whether they should be granted immunity from criminal prosecution.

Congress has the power to obtain a court order of immunity and force unwilling witnesses to testify. Refusal could result in 18-month jail terms for contempt of Congress.

North and Poindexter "took the Fifth," invoking the constitutional guarantee that no person "shall be compelled in any criminal case to be a witness against himself."

This right to remain silent was included in the Bill of Rights by Founding Fathers mindful of the abuses of England's Star Chamber hearings, where witnesses who refused to testify faced torture.

The Fifth Amendment was invoked by college professors during the McCarthy era. It was expanded in 1966 by the U.S. Supreme Court in its controversial Miranda decision giving suspects the right to refuse to answer police questions.

It is common for lawyers to advise clients to remain silent if there is any possibility they will face charges. It is equally common for prosecutors to grant immunity for testimony against those "higher up" or "more guilty" in a criminal scheme.

Nevertheless, smart prosecutors don't rush to protect the first witnesses they find. Nor should Congress act hastily to get answers from North and Poindexter.

The investigation is proceeding on several fronts: by the Justice Department, by Congress and by a soon-to-be-named independent counsel.

It is too soon to award immunity to anyone. A better route will be careful investigation, including subpoenas to anyone with any knowledge of the transactions.

It is worrisome to see the president's men invoking the Fifth Amendment. Despite the legal concept that it does not suggest guilt, we cannot help but wonder what North and Poindexter might have done for which they need immunity.

Still, we cannot accept the argument that high-ranking government officials have any less claim to their constitutional rights than the average burglar.

Rep. Michael Barnes, D-Md., told Poindexter his personal legal situation is less important than his responsibility to his country. He speculated that Poindexter might be convicted and put on probation someday, but should answer questions now.

That's unfair. No one knows yet if criminal laws were violated and, if so, by whom.

Only after as much information as possible is gathered should immunity be considered for any witnesses.

# THE ASHEVILLE CITIZEN

*Ashville, NC, December 6, 1986*

Vice Adm. John M. Poindexter and Marine Lt. Col. Oliver North were exercising an undeniable Constitutional right when they pleaded the Fifth Amendment in testimony before the Senate Intelligence Committee this week.

The Fifth Amendment to the Constitution gives every citizen of this country the right to refuse to incriminate himself. It is one of the cornerstones of our American freedoms.

So there can be no quarrel about the actions of North and Poindexter based on rights.

But it is a pathetic spectacle, nevertheless.

Poindexter and North are both high-ranking military officers. Both swore an oath to serve this country to the best of their abilities. In both of them this nation confided a special trust and reliance. And this nation expected of them a higher standard of personal conduct.

It is one thing to watch a Mafia chieftan plead the protection of the Fifth Amendment under questioning by a Congressional Committee. It is another thing to see two men in whom this country placed special trust and reliance do the same.

Up to now, both Poindexter and North appeared to have served the nation honorably and well. Both men have enjoyed distinguished military careers.

It is difficult, at this juncture, to determine with any accuracy where the investigations into the Iranian arms deal will go or who will be shown to be culpable.

But one thing is certain: there already are two casualties.

Their names are John Poindexter and Oliver North.

# THE INDIANAPOLIS STAR

*Indianapolis, IN, December 13, 1986*

After a week of congressional hearings on the secret Iran arms deals, there were no clear winners or losers. But to many Americans besides President Reagan, Marine Lt. Col. Oliver L. North had emerged as a hero.

North fought the communists in Vietnam. He was wounded and left for dead. He has a Silver Star for Valor and two Purple Hearts to show for his combat time.

He was waiting on the Turkish border hoping to help Americans escape from Iran during the ill-fated attempt to rescue hostages being held in the embassy at Tehran. He helped plan the successful invasion of Grenada. He masterminded the hijacking of the plane carrying the Achille Lauro terrorists.

He worked out a complex plan to free Americans kidnapped in Lebanon by Shiite terrorists. Three of the hostages were released.

But as questions grew about that and the diversion of money to the Contras in Nicaragua from the sale of U.S. arms to Iran, North was fired as an aide with the National Security Council.

The pieces may still take months to put together. At hearings of the Senate Intelligence Committee and later the House Intelligence Committee and the House Foreign Affairs Committee, Col. North and Vice Adm. John M. Poindexter, former National Security Council adviser, declined to answer questions, on advice of counsel, under the Fifth Amendment right against self-incrimination.

Both Poindexter, who had resigned under fire, and North said that they want to give the details in public at the appropriate time.

North said, "I don't think there's another person in America who wants to tell their story as much as I do."

In the packed House hearing, as TV cameras caught the moment, Rep. Tom Lantos, D-Calif., passed the hat as he noted that North's classmates at the U.S. Naval Academy at Annapolis, Md., are collecting for an Oliver North Defense Fund. Lantos said, "It is my privilege to contribute to that fund as hundreds of thousands of Americans will want to do."

Rep. Robert F. Dornan, R-Calif., improvised a rhyme based on Rudyard Kipling's *Tommy Atkins*, substituting "Ollie" for "Tommy," which, as Kipling readers know, is slang for a British soldier. Dornan's adaptation goes:

"Oh, he's Ollie this, he's Ollie that;
Get 'im out of here, the brute;
But he's the 'savior of his country.'
When the guns begin to shoot."

When North heard the line about "the brute," he lowered his eyebrows. When he heard the rest, he smiled. The rhyme was appropriate.

Some Americans are grateful for those who fight for freedom.

# Reagan Urges Congress to Grant Immunity to Former NSC Aides

President Reagan December 16, 1986 proposed that the Senate Intelligence Committee give limited immunity to two former National Security Council officials to induce them to testify about the Iran arms affair. The two, former national security adviser Vice Adm. John Poindexter and Lt. Col. Oliver North, had declined to answer questions before the intelligence panel and the House Foreign Affairs Committee, citing the Fifth Amendment right against self-incrimination.

A statement by Reagan said, "It is my desire to have the full story about Iran come out now." He asked the panel to allow North and Poindexter to testify in full "without depriving them of their constitutional rights," by granting what was known as "use immunity." Under use immunity, their testimony could not be used against them in a criminal case. Reagan said that such use immunity "does not prevent those responsible for any wrongdoing from being brought back to justice."

Sen. Patrick Leahy (D, Vt.) and Sen. David Boren (D, Okla.) described Reagan's request as "premature." The chairman of the intelligence panel, Sen. David Durenberger (R, Minn.), said that most of the committee opposed granting immediate immunity, and suggested that if Reagan wanted the full story of Iran, he should talk to North and Poindexter himself, a course of action the President rejected.

## The San Diego Union

*San Diego, CA, December 18, 1986*

The silver lining in the dark thunderhead of illegalities, hypocrisy, addlebrained schemes, and deception hanging over the White House is that Americans can be confident the truth will out, sooner or later.

Unlike the protracted Watergate scandal, the Iran-*contra* affair is being promptly scrutinized by an independent special prosecutor and select committees of the Senate and House. For all of their aggressive sleuthing, the American news media have unearthed relatively few scoops to date. The most important disclosures have come from a Syrian newspaper, the Justice Department, congressional testimony, and other official sources.

With all of this investigative machinery in place, a thorough probe cannot be doubted. Accordingly, this is not the time to short-circuit the investigative process by granting immunity from prosecution to the principals in the case in exchange for their early testimony. President Reagan's proposal, now rebuffed, for the Senate Intelligence Committee to give immunity to former national security adviser John Poindexter and his impetuous deputy, Lt. Col. Oliver North, is premature at best and probably unwise under any circumstances.

The key unanswered question at this stage is whether the diversion of profits from secret Iranian weapons sales to the Nicaraguan *contras* was a free-lance operation, executed solely by Mr. North, or was authorized by higher officials in the White House, namely Chief of Staff Donald Regan, CIA Director William Casey, or the President. Mr. Reagan appears to believe that his two former aides, if granted immunity, would corroborate his assertion that he knew nothing about the illegal *contra* link until he was informed by Attorney General Edwin Meese in late November.

By eliciting such public testimony from Mr. North and Mr. Poindexter, the White House hoped, as presidential spokesman Larry Speakes put it, to "get on with the business at hand and put this behind us." But closing the Iran-*contra* chapter of the Reagan presidency cannot be so easily accomplished.

There are two big unresolved issues: Whether the President is telling the truth and what happened to money generated by the Iranian arms transactions. These overriding concerns can be laid to rest only by an exhaustive criminal probe conducted by the special prosecutor. Granting immunity before the special pro-

secutor even is named would, for all intents and purposes, foreclose his investigation. That's because any information provided by the witnesses in their congressional testimony could not be used against them or others in court. The appropriate time to consider whether grants of immunity would facilitate justice is only after the special prosecutor has gathered enough evidence to gauge the depth of wrongdoing and assess who participated in it.

A very wide net must be cast before all of the facts can be made available to the American people. This includes a thorough review by the newly appointed select congressional committees of the policy implications of Mr. Reagan's secret Iranian policy. Broader questions about the proper role and oversight of the NSC staff in the conduct of U.S. foreign policy also must be examined by the special panels.

Despite the skepticism of the American people reflected in the opinion polls, there is no evidence yet of a White House cover-up intended to obstruct the unfolding investigations. But there are no shortcuts to the truth. The American people — and the President — will have to await the outcome of a deliberate probe that could be months in the making.

## EVENING EXPRESS

*Portland, ME, December 26, 1986*

Questions about if and when to grant limited immunity from prosecution to two former National Security Counsel officers implicated in secret arms dealings with Iran are not questions that stand alone.

What Vice Admiral John Poindexter may have known and when he knew it, what Lt. Col. Oliver North may have done and when he did it are part of a larger picture: accountability in the executive branch.

As is their right under the Constitution, Poindexter and North have refused to answer questions, invoking their Fifth Amendment protection against self-incrimination. Eager to put the scandal behind him, President Reagan last week asked Congress to give the two men limited immunity from prosecution. His purpose, he said, was to get the story out.

Congress, however, rightly declined. A special counsel, Lawrence E. Walsh, has been appointed by the courts. His disinterested investigation into the arms dealings is about to start. Granting immunity to Poindexter and North at this point could jeopardize Walsh's inquiries. For that reason, no immunity should be granted until we see what Walsh turns up.

Those who favor granting immunity immediately say that the Iran-Contra scandal is pre-occupying the Reagan administration and paralyzing U.S. foreign affairs. If that's the case, who better to address it than the president himself? Yet he has declined to grant Poindexter and North executive pardons.

The narrow focus upon the two men and their vulnerability to prosecution threatens to obscure the larger issues. Walsh and his team should move ahead, looking into what happened and, in Vice President George Bush's words, letting "the chips fall where they may."

Until that's done, talk of immunity is premature.

*Los Angeles, December 18, 1986*

Senate Intelligence Committee leaders were right to turn down President Reagan's request that limited immunity be offered to former National Security Adviser John Poindexter and Lt. Col. Oliver North, the two Iranscam figures who are stalling by taking the Fifth Amendment. Giving these men immunity now to get them to tell what they know could jeopardize the chances for their criminal prosecution later.

Immunity severely inhibits such prosecution because it bars the use of an individual's testimony against himself and it forfeits any evidence that might be linked to that testimony. A criminal conviction isn't impossible after these safeguards have been granted: John Dean, for example, was convicted for his role in Watergate after he was given immunity. But such a result is unlikely, and the legal procedure is made all the more complicated.

Moreover, offering Poindexter and North that protection at this point would be absurd, because the bodies that will have the major responsibility for probing the matter — the independent counsel and the special Senate and House investigating committees — haven't even begun their work.

It's only after they've completed their job that immunity should be offered, either because it will allow the investigators to go after bigger fish, or because prosecutors have determined it's unlikely that Poindexter and North could be convicted on their future testimony.

But granting immunity before the probes begin would make it difficult to know what investigators will get in return for their offer. And it's quite possible that once the investigations start, they'll turn up their own "Deep Throat" to blow the case open without Poindexter's and North's cooperation.

Meanwhile, however, both men could make these proceedings go far more smoothly if they simply agreed to testify without immunity. As their commander-in-chief, President Reagan should call on them to do so.

## Minneapolis Star and Tribune

*Minneapolis, MN. December 18, 1986*

In urging limited immunity for former National Security Advisor John Poindexter and Lt. Col. Oliver North, President Reagan argued that such a guarantee was essential to get at the truth about the brewing arms-sale scandal. In rejecting the request Wednesday, the Senate Intelligence Committee recognized that granting immediate immunity could have other, less salutary effects. It could protect suspected wrongdoers from deserved prosecution, and it could foreclose an inquiry just about to begin.

Congressional committees seeking details about the secret sale of arms to Iran are understandably frustrated by North's and Poindexter's decision to invoke their Fifth Amendment right against self-incrimination. Lawmakers have a legal way around that obstacle — if they want to use it. They can force witnesses to tell everything they know in return for a promise that none of the testimony will be used against them in any later criminal proceeding. A prosecutor would be required to build a case from information gathered independently; nothing that could be traced to the congressional testimony would be admissible in court.

Reagan said he favored such immunity for North and Poindexter to expedite the inquiry. But as Intelligence Committee Chairman Dave Durenberger observed, speed should not be the first concern; fairness and thoroughness matter more. The president's request came as the sun sets on the 99th Congress — and during the same week that the Senate and House established special committees to conduct full investigations.

Granting immunity to North and Poindexter at this early date would deprive the 100th Congress of its rightful investigative role. Worse, it would tie the hands of the yet-to-be-appointed independent counsel, who faces the daunting challenge of taking over the criminal investigation from the Justice Department. Despite White House assertions to the contrary, a promise of immunity might also make it impossible to prosecute North and Poindexter — not a small consideration in such a far-reaching scandal.

Granting immunity is still an option, but it should be a last resort. The American people are entitled to know all that this administration has done in their name. They are more likely to find out through a careful investigation than through hasty and ill-considered promises of immunity.

## The Charlotte Observer

*Charlotte, NC, December 21, 1986*

At the moment, it is still premature to grant immunity as a way of speeding the investigation into the Iran-Contra affair. The special Senate and House committees have only just been appointed; their investigations, like that of the special prosecutor, have not yet begun. But all that will quickly change. When the investigations come up to speed after the first of the year, Congress should not shy from grants of immunity even to such central figures as departed National Security Council officials John Poindexter and Oliver North.

We say that because the serious issue in this affair is not narrow criminality — certainly not the possible criminality of White House underlings. If they deserve censure beyond their dismissal from the White House — and their decision to invoke the Fifth Amendment protection against self-incrimination suggests strongly that they do — then punishment should lie primarily in public censure and military discharge rather than the courtroom.

But nothing that anybody can do to Oliver North and John Poindexter — not jail, not military discharge — will quiet the alarm about larger issues. Congress and the allies are not alarmed simply because somebody diverted money to the contras. The issues, rather, are U.S. foreign policy and responsibility for its conduct.

That is partly a narrow matter of personnel and structure. The first task is to fix the defects that made the National Security Council an unsafe vehicle for presidential policy and to restore the proper functioning of the entire foreign-policy apparatus. That housecleaning has begun, and a blue-ribbon panel is taking a longer view. In launching all that, the president shows that he, too, recognizes that something was seriously wrong in the NSC.

But the NSC staff, to a great extent, was simply doing what the president told it to do. And even the diversion of funds, which the president says he did not order and did not know about, was consonant with the administration's policy of aiding the contras by means that were creative to the point of illegality.

The trail inescapably leads to the president and his broader policy. The question is not just what did he know and when — did he order or knowingly condone the illegal diversion of funds to the contras, did he try to cover up illegality — but what does he understand even now? Although the questions of honesty and integrity are obviously important, the questions of competence are equally urgent.

That is far more important than possible criminal prosecution of Oliver North and John Poindexter. If their testimony is needed, and cannot be obtained without coercion, Congress should not hesitate to grant immunity. The country can afford to let Mr. North and Mr. Poindexter escape criminal punishment. It cannot afford to have foreign policy held hostage to the maneuverings of prosecutors and defense attorneys. Congress must put the nation first.

## RAPID CITY JOURNAL—

*Rapid City, SD, December 5, 1986*

It would be wrong to grant immunity from prosecution to Lt. Col. Oliver North and Vice Adm. John Poindexter in exchange for their testimony on the Iran-Nicaragua arms deal.

Both Oliver and Poindexter, identified by Attorney General Edwin Meese last week as the only two men who knew anything about the arrangements behind the arms scandal, refused to testify before the Senate Intelligence Committee earlier this week. Both invoked their Fifth Amendment right not to incriminate themselves.

North, who appeared Monday, reportedly is seeking a grant of immunity from prosecution before he testifies. Poindexter was advised by his attorney not to testify Wednesday.

Both have an absolute constitutional right not to incriminate themselves. There is nothing improper about their use of the Fifth Amendment.

However, since the administration has claimed they are the only two persons who knew about the Iran-Nicaragua deal, the lack of testimony is helping create the crisis of confidence rocking the Reagan presidency. The seriousness of Reagan's situation is demonstrated by an ABC News Poll released Wednesday that indicates 48 percent of Americans believe Reagan should resign if he lied about his knowledge of funds from the Iranian arms deal going to fund Nicaraguan Contras. That's stunning, considering Reagan's seemingly invincible past popularity.

Reagan's ability to lead is eroding. It may be destroyed if the situation isn't resolved quickly. That's against the best interests of the nation. So doesn't it make sense to grant immunity to Poindexter and North to clear up the confusion?

No.

First, Reagan has the ability to call his staff together and find out precisely what happened, when it happened, who knew about it and then make those findings public. The excuse that the administration can't discover these facts grows thinner every day. If true, it indicates Reagan is completely out of control of his staff.

Second, it seems clear that laws were broken. Those responsible should pay for thwarting the Constitution. Just Wednesday Vice President George Bush said the truth should come out and "let the chips fall where they may." We agree.

Third, lack of testimony from North and Poindexter won't cripple the investigation unless you buy the Brooklyn Bridge proposition: Only they knew about the arms deal and Contra funding. During the Watergate investigation, John Dean refused to testify unless granted immunity. His testimony was considered crucial, but immunity was not granted. The truth about Watergate came out and Dean ultimately served four months for obstruction of justice.

Fourth, both North and Poindexter took a mighty oath when they joined the military. They swore to protect the Constitution against all enemies "foreign and domestic." That Constitution will give them a legal protection which exists nowhere else in the world. If they violated the nation's laws in their zeal to do the commander-in-chief's bidding, they should pay the price for violating those laws and their oaths. If they acted at Reagan's behest, Reagan can pardon them if they are ever found guilty.

The current crisis — and it is a crisis — is not Watergate. It is worse. Watergate was an unnecessary political blunder. The attempt to hide Richard Nixon's advance knowledge of the matter brought down his presidency, where full disclosure immediately would have saved it. The Iran Arms deal potentially involves graver violations of law and indicates a lack of leadership at the highest levels of the government.

The truth must out. If laws were violated, those who acted against American democracy should pay for their actions.

*Washington, DC, December 18, 1986*

Finally, our president has made a decisive move toward getting the full story of the Iranian arms scandal in the open and putting it behind him.

On Tuesday, the White House put forward a plan designed to shift the burden of getting the whole story out from the White House to the Congress: The president asked the Senate intelligence committee to grant limited immunity to Adm. John Poindexter and Lt. Col. Oliver North.

But the committee members have grave reservations about letting the buck pass from the president to them. The chairman implied that the president could pardon the former national security officers of all their crimes and get them to tell all they know. The senators made it clear they didn't want to carry the burden.

The president apparently does not want to carry the burden, either.

But those who suggest that he was trying to dump the duty of disclosure on Congress ignore the mountain of pressure on the White House — pressure that has virtually paralyzed the government for more than a month. The president's credibility is mangled at home and battered abroad.

Some of our friends abroad are shocked that we sent arms to the Ayatollah Khomeini's government and because we apparently were willing to encourage ransom for hostages. Some of our enemies abroad are laughing because we provided intelligence to Iran's enemy, Iraq, while we were selling arms to Iran. Friend and foe alike are astounded to learn that we diverted funds from the arms sales to the Nicaraguan "contras."

And our citizens are disturbed to hear that some of the money from those sales may have been filtered into the political process here at home. No wonder President Reagan wants to get the full story out and behind him.

But he must understand that limited immunity would produce only a piece of the story. That might be a small step in the right direction, but, considering the possible crimes involved, nobody should be surprised that the Senate intelligence committee is unwilling to rush to judgment when the White House doesn't want to.

President Reagan is right not to pardon Poindexter and North. That would mock justice, put the White House seal of approval on covert operations by rogue security agents, give license to any super militant in government to engage in any hare-brained scheme that suited his own idea of what the government should be about, and label as "heroes" those who defy the laws of the land.

So it appears there won't be a quick answer to the Iranian arms scandal. Instead there will be a sometimes tedious process of committees, panels, and special counsel pursuing the whole story. Those separate investigations must proceed, even though it will make governance difficult. We all bear the burden of democratic government.

When the ordeal of disclosure is over, though, we will know not only what happened and why, but, more importantly, we will know that the system works.

## The Birmingham News

*Birmingham, AL, December 18, 1986*

If crimes were committed in the Iranian arms sales or the diversion of funds to the Contras, nobody involved should get off scot free. But there is also a compelling national need to get to the bottom of this mess.

President Reagan's request to the Senate Intelligence Committee probing the Iran debacle that a special kind of immunity from prosecution be given two key players in the affair to force them to testify might be a good way to satisfy both needs. But not right away.

Reagan Monday asked the committee to give "use immunity" to former National Security Adviser John Poindexter and his aide Lt. Col. Oliver North. Both have refused to testify to congressional investigators, citing their Fifth Amendment right to avoid self-incrimination.

"Use immunity" would mean that any testimony they gave could not be used against them later. But they could still be tried if prosecutors discovered, independently of their remarks, evidence that they broke the law.

Such immunity might become necessary, but investigators don't need to make a decision about it immediately. As Alabama Sen. Howell Heflin, a member of the special Senate panel named this week to investigate the probe, says, it should be used only as a last resort.

Too, any decision to give North and Poindexter limited immunity should wait until the independent counsel expected to be named shortly for the Justice Department's probe is on the job. He is the one who ultimately may decide if the two former National Security Council officials should be taken to court, and he should have a say about any arrangement affecting courtroom evidence.

# The Hartford Courant

*Hartford, CT, December 18, 1986*

President Reagan would like nothing better than for the Senate Intelligence Committee to agree to his request that the two central figures in the Iran-contra arms scandal be given limited immunity. Suspicions of a cover-up would be allayed, public attention would shift from the White House to the Capitol and the entire controversy would be speeded toward resolution.

To some members of Congress, especially the frustrated senators on the intelligence panel, who know that Vice Adm. John M. Poindexter and Lt. Col. Oliver L. North can illuminate the murky arms-and-aid scam, immunity must also be tempting.

The committee could partially immunize Mr. Reagan's former aides, but, to borrow an expression from former President Richard M. Nixon, it would be wrong. Immunity may be needed at some point, but using it now would be premature.

Immunity, if granted anytime soon, would hamstring the independent counsel, or special prosecutor, who will be looking for criminal wrongdoing. Nothing revealed by a witnesses who has been granted what is called use immunity can be used in any effort to prosecute him.

As its drastic nature suggests, immunity is appropriate only when every other avenue to the truth is blocked. And it shouldn't be used in a case like this one without the full concurrence of the special prosecutor. Yet the special prosecutor hasn't been appointed,

let alone begun looking down avenues.

It's understandable that a crippled president would want a speedy cure, and granting partial immunity to his former aides might hasten the investigative process. But the way in which the facts are assembled is more important than how quickly the job is done. Immunization would bring rushed hearings, and could leave important areas unexplored.

Granting immunity also would very likely let wrongdoing go unpunished. Sometimes that's unavoidable in criminal investigations, but there's no reason yet to think so in this case. President Reagan's aides may be guilty of some of the worst crimes ever committed by persons in such high office; if so, unnecessarily letting them escape justice would be unthinkable.

If Mr. Reagan is as interested in getting the Iran-contra story out as he says he is, there's a step he can take besides seeking legal shields for Vice Adm. Poindexter and Lt. Col. North. He can interview them, and anyone else who knows how the mess got started, then go on national television with the full truth.

Absent that, and assuming the intelligence committee won't grant immunity, Americans will just have to wait for the special prosecutor and the select committees to finish their work — unless, of course, the two military officers decide to serve their country by testifying without protection and accepting the consequences.

# FORT WORTH STAR-TELEGRAM

*Fort Worth, TX, December 26, 1986*

It doesn't really matter who suggested it or raised the possibility or seemed to urge it or considered doing it.

The idea of presidential pardons for Lt. Col. Oliver North, Adm. John Poindexter or any other Iran-contra scandal principals was a bad idea.

Upon reconsideration, House Speaker-elect Jim Wright clarified his seeming call for such pardons, emphasizing that pardons would amount to a prejudging of criminal culpability.

To President Reagan's credit, he rejected the idea within his own White House counsels. He may have rejected it for political reasons, since President Gerald Ford's pardon of Richard Nixon was costly to Ford, but he was right to say "no."

The political drawbacks to a presidential pardon would still be there if North or Poindexter were eventually convicted of criminal activity. But at least in that case there would be something to pardon.

It may have raised some congressional hackles, but North and Poindexter were quite within their rights to shield themselves behind the Fifth Amendment protection against self-incrimina-

tion during early appearances before House and Senate investigators.

It is as important to follow the law of the land — to stay within the American system of justice and maintain the presumption of innocence that is every American's birthright — in ferreting out the details of Irangate as it is to eventually spell out those details.

There is a natural frustration, within Congress and among most Americans, with the slowness of the process and its openness to speculation while awaiting the truth. Some form of immunity yet may have to be negotiated to obtain crucial testimony from North and Poindexter. If so, immunity granted by congressional committees or even by a special prosecutor is less unseemly than a pardon "in advance" from the president.

But there is time. Investigations into the Iran-contra mess, and particularly the special counsel's probe into possible criminal liability for any individuals, have barely begun. It would not be right to pre-empt these efforts before they have a chance to succeed.

The truth will out. The questions and answers will be coming for some time.

There need be no hurry for immunity and certainly not for offers of pardon.

# The Salt Lake Tribune

*Salt Lake City, UT*
*December 18, 1986*

Precisely because Vice Adm. John Poindexter and Marine Lt. Col. Oliver North remain central figures in investigations of the money-for-Contras-diverted-from-Iran-arms-sales escapade, they should not now be granted immunity for public testimony.

President Reagan is absolutely correct when he says the country deserves to get this bizarre matter behind it with full disclosure of the facts. But his preference for immunity granted Vice Adm. Poindexter and Lt. Col. North indulges too much anxiety

It may be that the situation accords with what many other high-level administration officials claim — that former National Security Adviser Poindexter, and the now-fired deputy NSC director North know more than anyone how some money from military hardware sold to Iran reached Swiss bank accounts for Nicaraguan counter-revolutionary use. But holding them responsible for their involvement in this and other capers could be as important as hearing what they might immediately divulge.

Since the two have already used the Fifth Amendment to withhold information from the Senate Intelligence Committee's probe of the Iran-Contra matter, granting them immunity from any possible prosecution is definitely tempting. Perhaps this would be the way to quickly wrap up an ordeal that harmfully afflicts the country the longer it lasts. Yet an important distinction needs to be considered.

No one knows for sure just how deeply implicated Vice Adm. Poindexter and Lt. Col. North are. Normally, immunity for testimony is granted after investigators and prosecutors acquire enough evidence on which to act, not before.

A special counsel is preparing to fully investigate the Iran-Contra connection, as is a select committee of Congress. Conceivably, either or both could find evidence requiring criminal charges. If so, justice would require such charges be filed.

Why, then, start granting immunity to people who might need to be prosecuted? Merely to "get this all behind us?" That's a strange way to run a country founded on laws rather than political expediency.

Even granted immunity, witnesses can still tailor whatever they say to fit their own purposes. Lacking previously obtained information about wrongdoing, investigators, whether congressmen, special counsel or Justice Department prosecutors, would be at a serious disadvantage in assuring all the facts are actually revealed if impaired from the beginning by generous dispensations of immunity.

It's a shame Vice Adm. Poindexter and Lt. Col. North cling to the Fifth Amendment when their country needs better cooperation from them. One more reason not to offer them premature exoneration in exchange for that cooperation.

# Buchanan Stirs Controversy by Lauding Lt. Col. North

White House communications director Patrick Buchanan stirred up some controversy with his outspoken defense of Lt. Col. Oliver North and former national security adviser Rear Adm. John Poindexter. In the *Washington Post* December 8, 1986, Buchanan, a former columnist, published an opinion article sharply attacking "the Republican Party establishment" for abandoning Reagan since the scandal broke. Buchanan said that North might have broken some laws but compared him to those who broke laws in organizing the Underground Railroad to take escaped slaves to Canada. Later Dec. 8, Buchanan told a mostly Cuban-American audience in Miami that "if Colonel North ripped off the Ayatollah Ruhollah Khomeini and took some $30 million to give to the contras, God bless Colonel North." Presidential spokesman Larry Speakes Dec. 9 said that Buchanan had not been speaking for President Ronald Reagan.

Col. North helped a political action committee mount a campaign in the autumn of 1986 to defeat congressional opponents of military aid to the contras, according to reports Dec. 15. The *New York Times* reported, but could not confirm, a charge in a small Massachusetts newspaper that funds from the Iran arms deal had been diverted to the political fund. The *Lowell Sun* said that North and other White House officials knew that about $5 million in Iranian funds had been used to subsidize commercials linking congressional liberals with communist leaders such as Fidel Castro of Cuba as well as Iran's leader, Ayatollah Khomeini. The Federal Bureau of Investigation said that it would look into the charges. Although the *Times* was not able to confirm that Iranian funds were involved, it said that North had helped to generate publicity for the little-known group, the National Endowment for the Preservation of Liberty. The group's organizer, Carl R. Spitz Channel, said that the group and several spinoffs had spent about $4 million trying to win backing in the United States for the contras. He said that his donors were "the usual 75-year-old Americans" who contributed to conservative causes. He vehemently denied having ever received any money that originated abroad. According to a report in the *Miami Herald*, White House communications director Patrick Buchanan had joined North and Channel in several meetings in 1986.

## THE ⬛ SUN

*Baltimore, MD, December 11, 1986*

Pat Buchanan is at it again. The pugnacious White House speech writer spoke to a Cuban-American group in Miami Monday, defending President Reagan against criticism of his handling of the Iranian arms deal. In it he made this statement: "All newsmen should remember that they are Americans first and newsmen second." This and subsequent attacks on journalists brought shouts of "traitors!" from the audience.

If there are any journalists who need to be reminded of the obligations of American citizenship, the last person they would look to for an explanation of those obligations would be a zealot like Mr. Buchanan. As a journalist-turned-propagandist, he has long made it clear that his ultra-rightist idea of Americanism is so narrow and exclusive (not to mention mean-spirited and wrong) that it mocks true patriotism. He needs to be reminded – - frequently — that he has an obligation to be an American first and an ideologue second.

Samuel Johnson said "patriotism is the last refuge of a scoundrel." Patriotism has been the first refuge of Mr. Buchanan so often that it raises a question as to what he's up to. Probably the answer is one given by TV commentator Eric Sevar-

eid years ago when speech writer Buchanan was putting words in Spiro Agnew's mouth. Mr. Sevareid said the vice president was "using patriotism as a club to try to silence his critics." That's clearly what's going on now. With President Reagan's foreign policy and management skill under attack from all sides (conservative Republicans as well as liberal Democrats, office holders as well as journalists), Mr. Buchanan has grabbed for his club.

This speech apparently was not cleared by other White House officials before it was delivered. Neither was an article Mr. Buchanan wrote for the *Washington Post* this week, a scathing attack on Republican senators for, ironically, putting loyalty to country ahead of loyalty to the president in the current foreign policy crisis. This is another example of Mr. Buchanan's grotesque idea of patriotism. In the speech and the article Mr. Buchanan made it perfectly clear he supported the very illegal acts by Col. Oliver L. North that caused the president to fire him. Yet the White House press spokesman says that is *not* Mr. Reagan's policy.

We hope it's not unpatriotic to ask this question: Can't the president control anybody on his staff anymore?

## The Honolulu Advertiser

*Honolulu, HI, December 20, 1986*

The fate of White House communications director Patrick Buchanan is not central to the outcome of Irangate and the crisis around President Reagan.

But Buchanan made himself the center of a secondary controversy with a Washington Post article and other comments attacking fellow Republicans for expressing justified questions about the policy of the beleaguered president. That minor flap was enough to merit an entire op edit page of columns about Buchanan in the Post.

Buried amid such comments was a news report that the State Department had vetoed a Buchanan bid to be U.S. ambassador to the North Atlantic Treaty Organization.

That may be the only bit of good news to come out so far in the Irangate controversy. Reagan has inflicted enough misery on our European allies and U.S. interests there without sending them an outspoken idealogue like Buchanan.

In fact, Buchanan's rightwing zealotry would be welcome in few countries. One might be South Africa, but that would cause a firestorm of criticism over his record on racial matters at home.

For, while he praised Lt. Colonel Oliver North in the context of others who practiced civil disobedience, recent news stories told how Buchanan wrote a 1969 memo to Richard Nixon.

The memo advised Nixon not to visit Coretta Scotta King on the first anniversary of her husband's assassination, saying it would "outrage many, many people who believe Dr. King was a fraud and demogogue and perhaps worse. . . . Others consider him the Devil incarnate."

Buchanan has a viewpoint that can and perhaps should be heard, although it can't be said he helped Reagan any more than he did Nixon. No doubt he will make much money in the media again. Few would argue with that.

But he is a problem that should be kept at home.

## The Kansas City Times

*Kansas City, MO, December 12, 1986*

The administration seems intent on self-destruction. A presidency that long infuriated enemies with its public relations skills has undergone a transformation. Now it cannot take even the most rudimentary steps to halt a sickening slide into anomie.

For many Americans, concern over the chaos in the White House has overshadowed worries over both the stupidity of trading weapons for hostages and the illegal diversion of money to Nicaraguan rebels. The latest *New York Times*/CBS poll found that most people considered the administration's handling of the facts the worst aspect of the Iran controversy. Yet administration officials cannot even bring themselves to take the crisis seriously.

Robert McFarlane, the president's former national security adviser, has testified under oath that Reagan approved sending arms to Iran in 1985, an apparent violation of U.S. law. Asked whether the president remembered giving such approval, White House spokesman Larry Speakes asked a reporter whether he could remember what he had for lunch on Sept. 1, 1985. Illegal arms shipments to a terrorist regime, roast beef and mashed potatoes — it's all the same as far as Speakes is concerned.

Then there's Patrick J. Buchanan, the president's director of communications. Instead of helping the president communicate the coherent explanation for which lawmakers of both parties are begging, Buchanan is out bellowing at conservative Republicans to man the ramparts. In an article published this week, Buchanan wrote that "when a mob shows up in the yard, howling that the head of the household be produced, the sons do not force the Old Man to sit down at a table and write up a list of his 'mistakes.' You start firing from the upper floors."

Buchanan cites history to imply that worthy goals can justify a decision by government officials to break federal law. This is a dangerous argument that, in normal times, would constitute sufficient grounds for Buchanan's dismissal from government service.

Buchanan also told a Miami audience this week that "All newsmen should remember that they're Americans first and newsmen second." The White House still hasn't given up the ludicrous proposition that American journalists — not the Iranians — announced the U.S. dealings with Iran.

The most damaging news stories have come not from anonymous sources and journalistic speculation. They are the straightforward accounts of events and on-the-record statements. What is the public supposed to think when the State Department publicly disputes the president's claim that Iran no longer practices terrorism? What are we to think when Reagan promises the country he will get to the bottom of all this, then turns around and says he won't ask the only aides who supposedly know what happened?

Lee Hamilton, chairman of the House Intelligence Committee and a lawmaker not known for public tantrums, said recently that his panel had received little of the information and cooperation promised by Reagan. "What they've told us does not approach a full disclosure . . . ," Hamilton said. "We can't answer basic questions like, 'Whose idea was this?', 'How many goods were shipped through Israel to Iran?' or 'Who knew about this?' "

In a typical response, a White House official blamed any lack of information on the same two former presidential aides who are supposed to take the rap for everything else. Meanwhile, Reagan is consulting with none other than Richard Nixon. The former president, in turn, went before a group of Republican governors this week to discuss their conversations, dismiss the controversy as a "sideshow in Washington" and personally vouch for Reagan's honesty. That's all he needs.

Through all of this, the White House has stuck to the sketchy story originally outlined more than two weeks ago by Attorney General Edwin Meese. It was a ridiculous account that was immediately challenged by the Israeli government, the contras and former high officials who have had experience with the agencies in question. Lawmakers in both parties dismissed it.

The administration claims that the president has already put everything on the table, done everything he can do. In fact, he has done nothing of the sort. The longer he waits, the more damage he does himself and his office.

## The Des Moines Register

*Des Moines, IA
December 17, 1986*

Despite the friendly, accommodating sounds that emanate from the White House when they have Pat Buchanan securely muzzled and leashed, stone-wall appears to be the operative Reagan policy.

If the president has made any effort to find out what John Poindexter, Lt. Col. Oliver North and Gen. Richard Secord did in his name, he has not made any discernible effort to keep his promise to tell the American people all about it.

Instead, there has been a clear effort, executed primarily by Buchanan, to politicize the Iranian-contra arms money deal. If you love Ronald Reagan, this scheme would have you think, then you don't care what someone might have done to further his policies.

Reagan has aided the effort by trying to change the subject. "We cannot, and we will not, let this stop us from getting on with the business of governing," he said the other day. It harmonizes perfectly with "I will not wallow in Watergate," as Reagan and his men should endeavor to recognize.

Candor, splendid candor, is the only lubricant that will allow anyone to get on with anything.

They're not dealing with an issue that gives itself over to politics, and if Reagan's uncritical lovers think so, they'll put him into the hands of his unloving critics.

So they ought to declare the present policy inoperative. In its place, have the president go back on the tube and tell in detail what he thinks the story to be, and support it with briefing papers and documents.

## Chicago Tribune

*Chicago, IL, December 16, 1986*

With his tirades against any and all critics of President Reagan, White House communications director Patrick Buchanan has been focusing fascinated attention on himself. Mr. Buchanan's voice seems to get shriller every day; you wonder when it will pass beyond human hearing range and start bothering dogs.

He is now denouncing as "a tribe of pygmies" all members of Congress who say they want to know more about Mr. Reagan's role in the secret arms deal with Iran. As Mr. Buchanan sees it, Congress already has the only information that matters: The President thought it was a good idea. What more could Congress or the public need to know?

Even without his talents as a scold, Mr. Buchanan would invite attention. He seems to be the last absolutist in government, the only person in public life who believes in presidential infallibility. In his view, if Mr. Reagan let presidential authority collapse into a gooey mess, that must have been the right thing to do, and it is the duty of all patriots to applaud.

Mr. Buchanan cannot contain his rage at those who do not applaud. But then rage is his specialty. His scolding, congested style is easily recognized; Mr. Buchanan may be the only person who can write the way a Pekingese barks.

His silly performance in the White House does the administration no good and Mr. Reagan no doubt would be wise to get rid of him. But meantime it's rather fun to see how high his voice can get.

# The Record

*Hackensack, NJ, December 10, 1986*

## THE KANSAS CITY STAR

*Kansas City, MO*
*December 16, 1986*

Patrick J. Buchanan, White House communications director, says a lot of things that communicate nothing but right-wing flights of fancy. Some soar higher than others. In a speech last week, Buchanan declared that if Lt. Col. Oliver North "ripped off the ayatollah and took $30 million and gave it to the contras, then God bless Col. North."

Wait a minute. Although the White House hasn't been consistent about much lately, up until now the story has always been that the president was dealing with moderates in Iran. The more we hear about these moderates, the more they seem just as loathsome as everyone else in the ayatollah's regime.

But the White House can't have it both ways. Reagan can't tell the country he was only sending weapons to moderates, then turn around and send Pat Buchanan down to a sympathetic audience in Miami to brag about ripping off the ayatollah himself on those same weapons.

How does overcharging the Iranian government—*and then boasting about it*—fit into the president's contention that this country desperately needs a better relationship with a country of such geopolitical importance as Iran?

Even more absurd is the notion that overcharging Iran meant we walked out of the Oriental bazaar ahead of the befuddled merchants. The administration's main goal was the release of hostages. Only three were freed, and they have been replaced by three more. Pro-Iranian terrorists hold five Americans, killed one this year and tortured another to death last year. Then, after receiving repeated shipments of military goods, the Iranian government told the world about its dealings with the United States. This humiliated the U.S., handed Reagan the worst crisis of his presidency, and allowed Iran to buy arms on the world market without restraint.

All this makes the suggestion that we outfoxed the ayatollah so preposterous that it hurts to hear it from a high government official, even a known buffoon like Patrick Buchanan. A high school student presenting such a feeble-minded analysis would be laughed out of Current Events class. But it apparently wins an "A" at the White House.

Not content to defend his boss's indefensible conduct in the Iran-contra arms affair, White House Communications Director Patrick Buchanan has gone on the offensive — attacking not just President Reagan's critics but the democratic system itself. Mr. Buchanan's remarks — before a group of Cuban exiles in Miami Monday and in an op-ed article in The Washington Post — scale new peaks of arrogance and demagoguery. Coming from a high-ranking government official, they are frightening and dangerous.

The arms affair, Mr. Buchanan told the 3,000 cheering Cuban exiles, is not about "whether some technical laws were broken, but whether we would stop communism in Central America." Lt. Col. Oliver L. North, the national-security official who ran the Iran-contra arms pipeline, may have made "some questionable judgments." But "if Colonel North ripped off the ayatollah and took the $30 million and gave it to the contras, then God bless Colonel North."

For the Post's supposedly more high-toned audience, Mr. Buchanan compared Colonel North to the abolitionists who broke the law by spiriting runaway slaves to safety; to the Zionists who ran guns to Palestine when it was still under British rule; and to Franklin Roosevelt, who, without informing Congress or the public, ordered American destroyers to track German submarines in 1940-41 and relay the information to the British fleet. All these people broke the law, he said, yet today are considered heroes. Similarly, whether or not Oliver North broke the law — Mr. Buchanan isn't saying — he is a hero nonetheless. He is "the Billy Mitchell of his generation, a man who saw further than others and took risks to his own career because he knew that in helping that peasant

army in Nicaragua, he was buying time for his own distracted and indifferent countrymen — [holding] 'the fort alone, till those who are half blind are half ready.' "

Mr. Buchanan is saying that laws, the will of Congress, and such are merely impediments on the road to victory over communism. Only lesser mortals are deterred by them — not heroes like Colonel North. If the press gets in the way by "gleefully" divulging sensitive information to the Soviets, smash it to bits. If Congress gets in the way, smash it too.

●

But if Mr. Buchanan thinks this affair is about communism, he is seriously mistaken. It is about law, the Constitution, and respect for democratic institutions, of which he clearly has none. Congress can no more ignore a presidential adviser who flouts its instructions than it could ignore the arrest of one of its members for criticizing the White House. Yet, through the use of inflammatory and quite outrageous rhetoric, this is just what the president's chief speech writer is trying to frighten it into doing.

It is unclear whether Mr. Buchanan is speaking for the president or just for himself. On Monday, a White House spokesman told United Press International that he had gone to Miami on his own; later in the day Mr. Buchanan told his audience that President Reagan himself had asked him to deliver the speech. But there is one simple way to remove the ambiguity. To let the world know how he feels about advisers who hold law and democracy in contempt, the president should fire his director of communications. People like Pat Buchanan are too dangerous to have around.

## AKRON BEACON JOURNAL

### Akron, OH, December 10, 1986

PRESIDENT Reagan's pit bull, Pat Buchanan, has now weighed in with his view of Mr. Reagan's current problems, and predictably has suggested that nothing would be wrong if all Republicans rallied to Mr. Reagan's defense like the good lapdogs they ought to be.

The sobering aspect of Mr. Buchanan's shrill column in the Washington Post attempting to rally the faithful is the fact that he is currently director of communications in the White House. That means that he is not only in close proximity to the President but even gets to speak to him and share his thoughts.

The Buchanan view, expressed in the Post column, is that the Republican Party "owes all it has and all it is" to Mr. Reagan. Clearly Ronald Reagan has been a popular political figure, but to suggest that his party would be in complete extinction without him is a bit much. There were at least a few Republicans, including some in these parts, who won office last month without the benefit of the regal coattails Pat Buchanan seems to see.

In addition, the Great Communicator's pit bull suggested that the country overlook any violation of law in the Iranian arms deal, that had profits secretly flowing to Nicaraguan rebels, because the cause was just.

The President's communications director is, of course, entitled to his opinion, but the U.S. is more likely to get in trouble than not when White House aides, whether Col. Oliver North, Adm. John Poindexter or others, decide a cause is so just that laws can be broken. Secretary of State George Shultz clearly understood that Monday when he testified that there had been illegal acts.

In short, Pat Buchanan's shrill musings sound similar to the sort of stonewalling, man-the-ramparts stuff that used to emanate from the Nixon administration during Watergate. But then he served in the Nixon White House, too.

## THE BLADE

### Toledo, OH, December 23, 1986

SECRETARY of State George Shultz has been getting his share of headlines lately, mostly favorable, but he has performed one inconspicuous service that should endear him to the American public: Reports are that he prevented White House communications director Patrick Buchanan from becoming U.S. ambassador to NATO.

That was the job that Mr. Buchanan — well known as the Administration's right-wing hatchet man — apparently wanted. But Mr. Shultz's logic was impeccable; he apparently believed that Mr. Buchanan was too controversial, would not be accepted by allied leaders, and would have trouble winning Senate confirmation. 'Nuff said.

One can easily imagine the endless turmoil that NATO affairs would be in if the vitriolic Mr. Buchanan applied his usual shotgun rhetoric to the defense of the western world as a representative of the No. 1 member of the organization. The American public can be thankful to Secretary Shultz for having squelched this incipient disaster in the bud.

## BUFFALO EVENING NEWS

### Buffalo, NY, December 12, 1986

PATRICK BUCHANAN, director of communications for the White House, is paid to defend the president and to put forward the strongest arguments in the president's behalf. But Buchanan's recent broadsides against Republicans in Congress, the press and critics of Lt. Col. Oliver North are more controversial than convincing.

Apparently, Buchanan thinks GOP leaders should rally around the president, whatever their honest views about the Iran-contra connection, and give him advice only in private while failing to share it with the constituents who elected them.

Buchanan scolds critics for prejudging North's actions as illegal when no charges have been brought. Yet he does his own prejudging by pronouncing North a hero.

Indeed, he compares North — whom President Reagan fired from the National Security Council — to Americans who took part in the underground railway to free slaves during the Civil War.

Yet the situations are hardly analogous. Moreover, a president takes a solemn oath to "faithfully execute the office of president" and to "preserve, protect and defend the Constitution," and that clearly applies to those serving under him. Their option is to try to change the law to which they object, not violate it.

And indeed, in response to Buchanan, the White House — to its credit — quickly said that the "president does not agree or condone the breaking of the law by any individual" and does not believe that any president "is above the law and has the right to pick and choose what laws may or may not be broken."

Buchanan reserved some of his toughest rhetoric for the press, blasting its coverage of the crisis as "frenzied, unbalanced and loaded with innuendoes . . . (a) windfall for the Soviets."

We don't necessarily defend every story published or broadcast anywhere in the country. But on the whole Buchanan's attack on the press is patently unjust. Even more so is his nasty implication of disloyalty to the nation by journalists. "All newsmen — and I was once a newsman — should remember that we are Americans first and journalists second," he lectured.

In the first place, the story of the U.S.-Iranian arms deal was broken by a Lebanese publication and an Iranian official, not American newsmen. And the diversion of profits to the contras was first disclosed by President Reagan himself and Attorney General Edwin Meese III. Would Buchanan have the American press ignore or hush up these stories? And what is more American than a press — its freedom expressly guaranteed by the Founding Fathers — that digs into an important news development in order to inform the public and push the government to get out all the facts?

It is not the American press, either, of course, that has been taking the Fifth Amendment before investigating committees on Capitol Hill.

Again, Buchanan's job is to defend the White House and explain its policies. But the problem here does not lie with the press, Republican congressional leaders or critics of the Iranian arms sales, including Secretary of State George Shultz.

The problem, rather, is with a policy decision by the administration and what the president himself admits were mistakes in its execution. Regrettably, Buchanan makes matters worse with his flawed defense of that confused policy.

## THE INDIANAPOLIS STAR

### Indianapolis, IN, December 29, 1986

The most disgraceful phase in the current Washington fuming and fussing is not the "liberals'" scalping party — that was to be expected — but desertion under fire by many of the president's conservative friends.

These summer soldiers and sunshine patriots caught a verbal barrage from Patrick J. Buchanan, the White House communications director, in the Washington Post.

"Is this how they repay the leader who has done more for the Republican Party than any American since Theodore Roosevelt, who brought us back from Watergate to become the party of vision and opportunity, the party of Middle America and the young — when all the pundits were saying we were finished for a generation?" wrote the gritty Buchanan.

"If elemental loyalty cannot convince these Republicans to stand up and speak for Ronald Reagan, what about basic self-interest?

"Do these Republicans truly think the investigative engines of a hostile Congress and the artillery of an Adversary Press are all being wheeled again into position — simply to 'get at the truth'? Do they seriously believe these pious declamations from the Democratic left that 'we must not have another failed presidency'?

"Do they not recognize that the target here is not Donald Regan, but Ronald Reagan — that what liberalism and the left have in mind is the second ruination of a Republican presidency within a generation? . . .

"In recent years, Republican candidates have taken to prattling at election time about their devotion to 'family values.' But among the first of those values is family loyalty. And when a mob shows up in the yard, howling that the head of the household be produced, the sons do not force the Old Man to sit down at a table and write up a list of his 'mistakes.' You fire from the upper floors.''

Buchanan's barrage ought to blow the blockages away from the field of vision of many conservatives' moral outposts.

# White House Names Abshire Investigation Liaison

The White House announced December 26, 1986 that it was creating a special group to coordinate the Reagan administration's responses and strategies in the Iran-contra arms scandal. The group would be headed by David Abshire, who was stepping down as United States ambassador to the North Atlantic Treaty Organization. Abshire would not have any role in investigating the arms sales to Iran or the diversion of funds to the contra rebels in Nicaragua. He would coordinate "responses to congressional and other requests for information in a timely manner," according to the announcement of Abshire's appointment.

Abshire's working group would consist of White House staffers detached from other offices, such as the press, legal and congressional relations offices, officials said. It was not clear how large the group would be. Abshire would have cabinet rank, but his position, special counselor, would not require confirmation by the Senate. White House chief of staff Donald Regan had reportedly advocated the creation of a special full-time position to coordinate the White House response to inquiries. Although other officials had opposed the move, Regan was said to have argued that it would allow the White House to focus on other business and avoid becoming preoccupied with the scandal.

## The Dallas Morning News

*Dallas, TX, December 30, 1986*

By naming David Abshire his special counselor in the Iran-*contra* arms affair, President Reagan may be able to keep his administration from coming to a full stop. The appointment is expected to relieve the sense of crisis that some observers feared might paralyze the White House's handling of other business.

Abshire, who recently resigned as the U.S. ambassador to NATO, has been given high marks by people within and outside the administration for his thorough knowledge of foreign policy issues and his ability to work well with Congress. Both skills should prove very useful in his role as the president's point man.

Abshire's weighty assignment will be to coordinate the White House's responses and strategy in the Iran-*contra* arms affair. He, and a staff of assistants to be drawn from elsewhere in the administration, will deal with the many questions raised by lawmakers and others investigating the matter.

Chief of staff Donald Regan and other senior White House aides ordinarily would be the ones expected to attend to such business. But the naming of a special counselor who will work independently of those high-ranking administration officials makes good sense for a couple of reasons:

■ Abshire's appointment will allow the rest of the White House staff to focus its attention on the normal business of government. There simply was no way that administration officials could immerse themselves in all the details of the Iran-*contra* deal and still concentrate on their other responsibilities.

The opening of the 100th Congress will place many new demands on the president and his staff, and there were fears that the administration would become so distracted by the Iran-*contra* matter that it no longer could give other pressing issues — like the 1987-88 budget — the attention they deserved.

■ The naming of a special counselor also lets the White House avoid even the appearance of a conflict of interest in any investigations. The importance of that should not be underestimated, for how the administration responds to this crisis may prove just as critical as what initially took place.

Abshire had no role in the secret arms deal with Iran or the diversion of funds to the Nicaraguan *contras*. He assumes his new job with no vested interest in protecting either himself or others. Consequently, there is no possibility of his wanting to try to conceal wrongdoing.

Abshire's appointment gives credence to the president's promise of ferreting out the truth in the Iran-*contra* affair and getting on with other business. It was a deft move that should be welcomed by all who want the president to stay on top of this controversy until it has been resolved

## The Augusta Chronicle

*Augusta, GA, December 30, 1986*

President Reagan's appointment of NATO Ambassador David Abshire to coordinate handling questions arising from the Iran-Contra affair represents an acknowledgment that this episode is not going away any time soon.

A Democratic-controlled Congress will milk the foreign policy embarrassment for all its worth during the lengthy special hearings due next month. When public interest in the fiasco begins to flag, watch for immunity to finally be granted to the two principals in the case, Adm. John Poindexter and Lt. Col. Oliver North.

Abshire's job will be to isolate the case from other important government business — to prevent it from crippling the administration's ability to move ahead on other issues, such as the budget proposals, legislative priorities and other key areas of foreign and domestic policy; in short, to keep the Reagan agenda alive.

In this, most Americans must hope Abshire is successful. To be sure, many Democrats will go about the investigations in a responsible fashion. We were impressed that the vast majority of Democrats picked to look into the affair come from the party's center, rather than its left-most fringes.

But there is no denying — as White House Communications Director Pat Buchanan has so eloquently pointed out — that there are powerful minority elements of the party (and the Big Media) which hope to use the hearings as a means to undo the presidential election mandates of 1980 and 1984.

That would be a catastrophe, not only for Reagan's presidency, but the nation. The system can only stand so many shocks. Voters are sure to lose confidence in a system which twice in 15 years sees a man they overwhelmingly elected president discredited.

If it weren't for the earlier Watergate experience, we doubt the Iran-Contra affair would amount to much of a scandal. But unfortunately, there are just enough surface similarities to the two incidents to whet the appetite of those who seek revenge instead of justice.

Part of Abshire's job will be to help keep this scandal in proper perspective. He has his work cut out for him.

## The Salt Lake Tribune
*Salt Lake City, UT, December 28, 1986*

It's the sort of stuff destined to trigger speculation: The appointment of David Abshire, the U.S. ambassador to NATO, as special counselor to President Reagan to coordinate responses to congressional and other investigations involving the Iran-arms, Contra-profits controversy.

Mr. Abshire will have cabinet rank and ". . . will head a team that will coordinate White House activities in all aspects of the Iran matter," the White House announcement said.

Nevertheless: Is the way being greased for White House Chief of Staff Donald Regan to slip easily out the door?

Ostensibly, Mr. Abshire was preparing to leave the NATO job to return to Georgetown University's Center for Strategic and International Studies, where he had been president before assuming the NATO assignment.

In fact, it looked like a rather routine change for the Brussels assignment: a successor, Alton Keel, the acting national security adviser, had been selected and Mr. Abshire had made public his intention of returning to academia. Then comes this rather surprising appointment to further

government service, virtually at the right hand of the president.

Further bolstering speculation that Mr. Abshire might be the heir-apparent to Mr. Regan are a series of facts and events, among them that Mr. Abshire was considered a candidate just after the 1980 elections for the job of national security adviser. That appointment, however, went to Richard V. Allen.

Later, Mr. Abshire was mentioned as a successor to Vice Adm. John Poindexter when he stepped down Nov. 25, at the same time National Security Council staffer Marine Lt. Col. Oliver North was fired.

That was not to be. Instead Frank Carlucci, a former high level official in the Defense Department and the CIA, has been named to take over that post in January.

Considering the enormous pressure that has been steadily and heavily exerted on Mr. Reagan to dismiss his chief of staff, the unanticipated appointment of Mr. Abshire to a cabinet-level, close-to-the-president job, makes it not inappropriate to wonder out loud whether Donald Regan's days of ready access to the Oval Office haven't been precisely numbered.

## The TENNESSEAN
*Nashville, TN, December 30, 1986*

THE new Cabinet-level post to coordinate handling of the Iran controversy would appear to serve two goals at the White House: coordinating its responses to investigations and freeing up senior members for other duties.

Senate Republican leader Robert Dole and others had suggested the appointment of a special counselor to deal with the Iran-contra affair. So the President went outside the White House and selected NATO Ambassador David Abshire, a Tennessee native, to be the point man.

Mr. Abshire won't be an investigator. His job will be that of overseeing the White House responses to the various investigations. That will require some heavy homework on the ambassador's part, since he will be expected to know who said what already and what went on as best he can reconstruct it.

Mr. Patrick Buchanan said, "It really is a detail job and the rest of the White House staff, which was not involved in the controversy, has got to get on with the budget, has got to get on with the State of the Union."

Although Mr. Abshire's background is varied, his reputation is not that of a detail man but one who sees the larger picture. He is a West Point graduate and combat veteran of the Korean war. He served from 1970 to 1972 as President Nixon's assistant secretary of state for congressional affairs. He is credited with developing the Georgetown University Center for Strategic and International Studies, a think-tank he co-founded in 1962.

His past experience with the Congress may be as relevant as anything in this particular matter. Both the House and Senate have named select committees to focus on the affair when the 100th Congress convenes next week. As Sen. Patrick Leahy, D-Vt., the vice chairman of the Intelligence Committee, noted, "This appointment will save them from asking committees in Congress for a report which will tell them what they have in the White House."

Some on the White House staff have already testified before congressional committees and there are conflicts in the testimony that Mr. Abshire might be able to clear up. At the same time he may enable the President to gain some management control over the crisis, since he will report directly to the Oval Office and not to Mr. Donald Regan, the chief of staff, or someone else.

Mr. Abshire could be most helpful, perhaps, if he can pull together a more complete report and chronology of what happened. The White House did put together a report and chronology shortly after the scandal broke, but that account was largely flawed in that it contradicts some of the sworn testimony of some participants, omits some critical parts of the story and, according to congressional investigators, may contain errors in fact.

A candid and accurate report from the White House as soon as possible would help the select committees and the public as well. ∎

## THE ARIZONA REPUBLIC
*Phoenix, AZ, December 28, 1986*

THE appointment of the respected and experienced David Abshire as the White House point man on the Iran arms-sale scandal can only be greeted with widespread approval.

The move shows again that despite the continuing sniping of his detractors, President Reagan is determined to cooperate fully with Congress and the independent counsel's office in getting to the bottom of the affair.

The White House has desperately needed someone to coordinate its handling of the two-month-old Iran affair.

The Reagan administration was in near disarray in its initial dealings with the scandal, with officials contradicting one another and mutinous departments attacking each other in public.

Abshire leaves his post as U.S. ambassador to NATO to assume the Cabinet-level position in the White House.

His name has been mentioned periodically for top administration posts, including that of national security adviser, and he is highly regarded in Washington for his foreign policy acumen.

Meanwhile, it appears that incapacitated CIA head William Casey has been selected as the designated administration scapegoat. Casey, who is recovering from brain surgery for a malignant cancer, is in no condition to defend himself.

This is not inconvenient for those who want to make the intelligence chief the administration fall guy.

Since the founding of the CIA after World War II, there hasn't been a director of central intelligence who hasn't created an army of enemies in Washington, and Casey has more than his share who are only too happy for the opportunity to exploit the Iran affair to his disadvantage.

Fortuitous leaks from anonymous administration sources have been making a concerted effort to link Casey with Lt. Col. Oliver North, the former National Security Council staffer who allegedly masterminded the sale of arms to Iran and the diversion of profits to the anti-Sandinista *contras* in Nicaragua.

There are plenty of grounds on which to fault Casey's running of the CIA, and many critics inside and outside the Reagan administration have long thought he should be removed, but the current chorus of leaks smacks of a contrived campaign, and is just a bit too convenient.

With North not talking on the basis of the Fifth Amendment, and with Casey hospitalized with an illness of indeterminate seriousness, it could be some time before the rumor mill grinds to a halt and hard facts begin to emerge about the two men's respective roles in the fiasco.

# Special Prosecutor Named to Probe Iran-Contra Arms Scandal

A special panel of three federal judges December 19, 1986 selected Lawrence Walsh as the independent counsel in the Iran-contra arms scandal. Walsh was a former prosecutor, judge and deputy United States attorney general. He had also served as president of the American Bar Association and as a corporate lawyer.

The panel of judges asked Walsh to investigate support given to the Nicaraguan contra rebels since 1984 by anyone in or out of government, as well as the government's sale of arms to Iran and the disposition of proceeds from the sale. Walsh's mandate went far beyond that suggested by Attorney General Edwin Meese 3rd, who had proposed that the prosecutor look into just the diversion of funds from the Iranian arms deal to the contras. Meese had also suggested that the period to be investigated begin a year later, in 1985. Walsh would take over any investigations currently being conducted by the Justice Department that fell under his broad jurisdiction.

## AKRON BEACON JOURNAL
### Akron, OH, December 28, 1986

AFTER A month of the drip, drip, drip of news leaks and much presidential fumbling, the Iran-Contra scandal has come down to four investigations:

• The Tower commission. Headed by former Republican Sen. John Tower of Texas, the panel was appointed by Mr. Reagan to study the role of the National Security Council in the conduct of foreign policy.

Its members include Brent Scowcroft, President Ford's national security adviser, and former Sen. Edmund Muskie of Maine, a Democrat who served as Jimmy Carter's secretary of state. This experienced trio offers the potential for a thoughtful look at an NSC, which, in recent years, has accumulated power far beyond its original mandate.

• The congressional investigations. Both the House and Senate have formed special select committees to look into the scandal. Their separate investigations will begin in January when Congress reconvenes.

The responsibilities of the panels will be broad. Not only will they be searching for the facts of the affair, but they will also examine the need for new legislation to define more clearly the way foreign policy should be conducted.

• The independent counsel. The choice of Lawrence Walsh as the independent counsel — more commonly known as the special prosecutor — struck many as wise. Those who have watched him in his long career in government and the law were quick to call him honorable, determined and intelligent. As a Republican, he will offer the administration little room to complain about partisanship.

The judicial panel that appointed Mr. Walsh rightly gave him a mandate much wider than Edwin Meese, the attorney general, requested. But the essence of his job is unchanged: He will be looking to see whether laws were violated. What's plain is that Mr. Walsh faces a huge job. Don't expect an early end to his investigation.

No one should underestimate the importance of determining whether laws were broken in the scandal. Still, the most important question involves how the policy was conceived of selling arms to Iran and using the profits to fund the Nicaraguan Contras. Did it begin, as many in the White House claim, as a well-intentioned attempt to open doors to moderates in Iran, only to fall apart as bargaining for the American hostages in Lebanon intensified and zealots on the NSC staff arrived at a way to evade the congressional ban on aid to the Contras?

What did the President know, and when did he know it is the familiar and apt refrain. Two top aides disagree over whether Mr. Reagan authorized Israel to sell arms to Iran in August of last year. According to the New York Times, a 1985 memo written by William Casey, the CIA director, established that the original purpose of the arms sales was to obtain the release of the hostages, and the political opening to Iran a mere cover if the operation should be exposed.

The questions are many: How much did the President and other top officials know about the methods Adm. John Poindexter, the national security adviser, and Lt. Col. Oliver North were using to obtain the hostages' release? Whose idea was it to divert funds to the Contras? Who knew about it? Did the money get to the rebels? Was the whole mess a reflection of a secret White House operation involved in covert operations and the conduct of foreign policy?

All these questions need answers. What's at stake is not just the future of the Reagan presidency. Indeed, already it seems Mr. Reagan has spent much of his enormous influence on a foolish policy that is, as yet, incompletely defined. The largest stakes in the scandal involve public trust in government. The task of the four investigations is to begin the job of restoring it.

## ST. LOUIS POST-DISPATCH
### St. Louis, MO, December 21, 1986

In naming Lawrence E. Walsh of Oklahoma City as special prosecutor in the Iran arms scandal, a special panel of the U.S. Court of Appeals in Washington broadened the prosecutor's mandate from that sought initially by Attorney General Edwin Meese. This ought to assure that the administration's program to circumvent the congressional ban on military aid to the Contras is thoroughly investigated.

In their charge to Mr. Walsh, the special panel said his investigation should go back to 1984 and include the "provision or coordination of support" for the Contras, the U.S.-financed rebel group that is seeking to overthrow the leftist government of Nicaragua. Mr. Meese's request for a special prosecutor had spoken of events going back to Jan. 1, 1985. By pushing the starting point into 1984, the judges ensured that the entire period of the congressional ban on military aid would fall within the purview of the inquiry. Additionally, the Meese request had not specifically mentioned the Contra aid operation, though the language could have been interpreted to include it. Now there can be no ambiguity.

Both the Iran arms deal and the Contra aid project are egregious examples of the imperial presidency at work. In both cases, the president decided that his objectives — the release of American hostages in one case and the overthrow of a leftist government in the other — were so important and so worthy that they justified placing himself above the law.

Of the two mistaken initiatives, the Contra aid project is probably the more serious. It required a calculated decision to find a way around the ban on military aid. To this end, the president privatized U.S. foreign policy, as Rep. Dante Fascell, chairman of the House Foreign Affairs committee, has observed.

Mr. Reagan had already started his administration down that road by organizing and financing a guerrilla army as surrogates to overthrow the Nicaraguan government. When Congress sought to force the president to use peaceful means to seek stability in Central America by prohibiting him from supplying the Contras with weapons, the White House organized a private network to continue supplying them.

It was a distinction without a difference. High-ranking officials in the White House, the State Department, the CIA and the office of Vice President George Bush were involved. The State Department went around the world with a tin cup asking for donations from wealthy governments, secret bank accounts were established, the CIA's old cargo airline was put at the disposal of the gun-runners and arms merchants in various countries were brought in to arrange the clandestine purchase of weapons. In the White House basement, Lt. Col. Oliver North oversaw the operation.

The president may be able to escape culpability in some aspects of the Iranian arms deal and in the diversion of funds from the arms sales to the Contra project, but he cannot claim he did not know that the resources of the government were deployed to do through private, clandestine channels what he had been told not to do.

## DAYTON DAILY NEWS
*Dayton, OH, December 17, 1986*

The independent counsel's investigation into the Iran-contra connection should be broadened to include all possibly illegal efforts to aid the contras. Attorney General Ed Meese has only asked the counsel to explore the diversion of Iranian money to Nicaragua.

Mr. Meese has said that the general question of illegal aid to the contras is being handled by a Justice Department investigation that began weeks ago. That investigation was prompted by congressional insistence after the crash of the contra-aid airplane to Nicaragua that was carrying Eugene Hasenfus and other Americans.

Whatever the reasons for the current arrangement, the whole contra question is entirely too sensitive for one part of the investigation to be handled by a department run by a man who has unsurpassed loyalty to Ronald Reagan — that is, Mr. Meese.

Moreover, there may be no sense in splitting up the contra-aid matter into two investigations if the whole effort was run by the same people.

Mr. Meese has acknowledged that the independent counsel's effort can still be broadened, upon the request of the independent counsel.

It is a move that should obviously be taken.

## THE PLAIN DEALER
*Cleveland, OH, December 23, 1986*

Fortunately, the mandate for Lawrence E. Walsh, who has been appointed special counsel to investigate the Iran crisis, is broader than the Justice Department had recommended. Walsh isn't limited to investigating just the arms-hostages-profits-contras fiasco. Instead, his brief has been widened to include probes into the organization and provision of aid "for persons or entities engaged as military insurgents in armed conflicts with the government of Nicaragua since 1984." That means *any* assistance to the contras, not just the cash generated by the Iran scheme.

The incentive to expand Walsh's authority came from congressional Democrats, who feared that the Justice Department request was too narrow. But just as congressional Democrats were winning that skirmish, they were losing another—the appointment itself. As special counsel, Walsh is charged with seeking (and if necessary, prosecuting) criminal violations. In the swampy world of Persian Gulf and Central American policy, however, he inevitably will be forced to make judgment calls about the validity of a criminal charge. Thus, there is a legitimate concern that, in close calls, the counsel's evident conservatism might make him more sensitive to the letter of the law than its spirit.

A liberal appointee would evoke similar concerns, of course. Instead of adhering too closely to the letter of the law, such a prosecutor might try to stretch the point of criminality too thin. Either way, the answer is the same: Let the counsel begin work and trust in the congressional committees that are pursuing similar probes to help restrain legal interpretations based on ideology.

Even that doesn't entirely vindicate Walsh's selection. Some ethical questions about his career haven't been adequately resolved. For example, Walsh led the legal team that defended Merrill Dow Pharmaceuticals against charges that one of its products caused birth defects. During the trial, Walsh failed to disclose that he had endorsed the trial's presiding judge while on the screening panel of the American Bar Association. Also, lawyers under his direction co-opted a secretary working for the plaintiff's team, providing financial support in exchange for testimony that ultimately led to the disqualification of two plaintiff lawyers.

Walsh has been described as "ruthless" and "meticulous." Critics charge that his handling of the Merrill Dow case was "deplorable." Regardless of who is correct, Walsh obviously is a lawyer of considerable controversy. Is that what an independent counsel should be? Probably not. Walsh will have to move quickly to gain the confidence of the Congress and the nation. If he doesn't, his tenure is likely to be more memorable for the skepticism it inspires than the answers it produces.

## The Boston Globe
*Boston, MA, December 16, 1986*

Lawrence E. Walsh is reportedly the choice of a panel of three senior judges to become the independent counsel to investigate the Iran-contra arms deal. It is a less than inspiring selection.

Under the Ethics in Government Act of 1978, the judges choose a special prosecutor when requested to do so by the attorney general in cases where a top federal official may have committed a crime. One would have expected the judges to seek an experienced lawyer who is at the height of his or her professional powers. Walsh, who will turn 75 next month, is simply too old to take on a task of this magnitude.

Walsh retired five years ago from the New York law firm of Davis, Polk & Wardwell. An insider in the city's legal and political establishments for decades, he was legal counsel to Gov. Thomas E. Dewey, served as a US district judge from 1954 to 1957 and then became President Eisenhower's deputy attorney general, a post in which he cleared the appointments of judges, marshals and US attorneys.

In 1969, Walsh was the Nixon administration's ambassador to the stalled Vietnam peace talks in Paris. A past president of the New York and American bar associations, Walsh is better remembered from the Nixon days for his service on the ABA committee that cleared the Supreme Court nominations of Clement F. Haynsworth and G. Harrold Carswell. Both were rejected by the Senate.

In the Justice Department, Walsh served under Attorney General William Rogers. Earlier this year, Rogers was chairman of the Reagan-appointed commission to investigate the Challenger disaster. The commission focused public attention on the weaknesses of the O-rings but skirted any aspects of the disaster that would embarrass the White House.

Rogers reportedly recommended Walsh to be independent counsel. What grounds are there for believing that Walsh's inquiries into the arms scandal will be any more thorough than Rogers' bland Challenger performance?

## THE TENNESSEAN
*Nashville, TN*
*December 24, 1986*

MR. Lawrence E. Walsh, appointed by the court to be the special prosecutor — officially the independent counsel — has a long record of service and generally seems to have all the desired qualifications to delve into the Iran arms sale, contra fund diversion scandal.

Attorney General Edwin Meese set some qualifications in asking for an independent counsel, saying the one chosen would have to deal with matters of "unusual sensitivity, complexity and importance to the nation." Mr. Meese said the person would have to be experienced in national security and defense, intelligence, counter-terrorism, foreign aid and foreign policy.

Mr. Walsh, who is close to his 75th birthday, has a career that goes back to helping crimebuster Mr. Thomas Dewere wage war on gangsters in the 1930's. At various times in his career, he has worked as a state prosecutor, a governor's counselor, a federal judge, a deputy U.S. attorney general, a Vietnam peace negotiator and a partner in a large Wall Street law firm.

He was appointed by President Dwight D. Eisenhower as a federal judge in 1954, and could have kept that job for a lifetime. But in 1957 he left to become the No. 2 man in the Justice Department. Mr. Leon Silverman, a New York attorney and a former special prosecutor, described Mr. Walsh as an "unflappable, extraordinary person" who is "enormously intelligent; a person who sees the forest as well as the trees."

Mr. Walsh has also been described as somewhat reserved, but a well-organized lawyer who doesn't "suffer fools gladly" and is not taken in by superficial arguments or pleadings.

Mr. Walsh does have an awesome task ahead in probing the labyrinthine paths and channels that the Iran arms affair seems to have taken before its existence was made public and then mushroomed into scandal. But by all accounts, Mr. Walsh is a very, very capable man who isn't awed by challenge. He seems to be a remarkably good choice. ■

# Part III: The Administration Under Fire

The President's Special Review Board, commonly known as the Tower commission, after its chairman, former Senator John Tower (R, Texas), released its report February 27, 1987. The report presented the first official look at the Iran-contra arms scandal. Underlining its significance was the fact that President Reagan himself had requested its compilation. It was given weight by the men who signed it: former Senator John Tower, former Senator and Secretary of State Edmund Muskie (D, Maine) and Brent Scowcroft, a retired Air Force general who served under several Republican presidents as a key foreign policy adviser.

The report faulted key members of the the administration, collectively and individually. It criticized the men Reagan chose and on whom he relied, and it questioned the loose style of management Reagan employed, first as governor California and then in Washington. Very few top administration officials escaped the criticism of the commission: Former national security adviser Robert McFarlane, Rear Admiral John Poindexter, Lt. Col. Oliver North, Secretary of State George Shultz, White House chief of staff Donald Regan, Defense Secretary Caspar Weinberger and Director of Central Intelligence William Casey were all specifically singled out. The report accused these men of giving Reagan bad advice, saying they had failed to grasp "the serious political and legal risks" involved in the whole undertaking.

Perhaps the most devastating aspect of the Tower commission report was the picture it painted of President Reagan, one that was different than what most of the world had become accustomed to see in his six years as president. The confidence and control that had characterized Reagan were replaced by a sense of a man so distracted, confused and so remote that he failed to understand the implications of implementing an initiative that would free American hostages and reestablish American influence in Iran.

The political fallout from the release of the Tower commission report was swift. Donald Regan was immediately replaced as White House chief of staff with former Senator Howard H. Baker Jr. Although Shultz, Weinberger and Meese held on to their positions, the administration seemed to be weakened as the congressional hearings on the Iran-contra scandal commenced in May.

# New Senate Report Aired; Reagan's Claims Disputed

The Senate Intelligence Committee January 29, 1987 made public a 65-page report based on its investigations in 1986 of United States shipments of arms to Iran and the diversion of funds from the arms sales to the Nicaraguan contra rebels. The report provided a chronology of the arms sales that it described as "necessarily incomplete," because of the refusal of key figures in the affair to discuss their roles. The report was addressed to Sen. Daniel Inouye (D, Hawaii), chairman of the Senate Select Committee on Secret Military Assistance to Iran and the Nicaraguan Opposition. The report was intended as a starting point for the Inouye special committee's probe.

The Iranian initiative originated in "the confluence of several factors," according to the report, including a reappraisal in the National Security Council of overall policy toward Iran, concern over U.S. hostages in Lebanon, pressure from Israel to participate in its contacts with Iran, and pressure from "private parties, including international arms dealers." The report examined closely the roles of Israel and private citizens.

The report cited evidence disputing President Reagan's assertion that the main purpose of the arms deals was to establish relationships with moderates in Iran. Attorney General Edwin Meese 3rd had told the committee that Lt. Col Oliver North said that whenever North discussed Iranian moderates with Reagan, the President returned to the issue of U.S. hostages held in Lebanon. The report described Meese as saying that North had told him that "it was a terrible mistake to say that the President wanted a strategic relationship, because the President wanted the hostages." The report concluded with 14 "unresolved issues" for Inouye's committee to look into. The most important of these was the role of private individuals in conducting U.S. foreign policy.

## Newsday

*Long Island, NY, February 3, 1987*

The president is out of touch. The National Security Council and the Central Intelligence Agency are operating without proper controls, without adequate information and probably outside the law. The highest officials in the land are lying to each other and to the American people.

This is the picture drawn in the Senate Intelligence Committee's preliminary report on the Iran-contra scandal. While it doesn't unveil dramatic new facts, the report, by putting together everything known thus far, portrays an administration both inept and deceitful.

At the very least there was a serious breakdown of the administration's national security decision-making apparatus. At worst, crimes were committed by some of the nation's senior officials — and one more president ignored the rule of law and lied to the American people. Throughout the report there is no sense that anybody in the administration was making a careful calculation about the feasibility of the plan to sell arms to Iran, the consequences of the undertaking or the effects on other aspects of American foreign policy.

And this is just a preliminary report. Testimony from key officials is missing. There are contradictions and gaps in the chronology. Overall, more questions have been raised than answered.

Critical among the questions is President Ronald Reagan's role. The White House's zeal to claim that the preliminary report proves Reagan didn't know about the diversion of funds to the contras is troubling, if not suspicious. The report only says that there is no evidence yet to link the president with that part of the mess. It does not exonerate him on this critical point. But how could it when most of the central figures have refused to testify?

Indeed, the gaps and inconsistencies in the report argue strongly for Reagan to share with the American people everything he knows about the affair. Yesterday's offer to reveal excerpts from his personal notes that bear on the affair is a welcome beginning.

The report is also disturbing because it leaves no doubt that the CIA had a much more active role in the whole matter than its officials have been willing to admit. The agency initiated the idea of contacts with Iran in May of 1985, and CIA Director William Casey was the most consistent and vociferous backer of the plan. The report shows that Casey deceived the committee about the agency's role.

Another critical unanswered question has to do with the arms-sale money that was diverted to the contras. It has not been accounted for. Now there are reports that as much as $40 million was involved. Who got the money?

The committee's report is valuable because it gives us all a sense of how much we still don't know about the entire affair. While it's not possible to come to conclusions based on this evidence, the report does provide powerful justification for the investigations that are being launched by committees in the House and Senate and by a special prosecutor.

## St. Petersburg Times

*St. Petersburg, FL, February 4, 1987*

Harry Truman's motto, "The buck stops here," would be out of place on Ronald Reagan's desk top, where the buck seems never to arrive, much less to stop. His administration out of control, the President found himself in a foreign policy crisis serious enough to have toppled almost any other democratic government. His defense? He didn't know.

Weak as it is, that defense applies only to the second half of the Iran-Contra connection, the allegation that profits from the arms sales were diverted illegally to the aid of Nicaraguan rebels if not also to certain private bank accounts. The original catastrophic error — that of selling arms to Iran under any circumstances — remains Mr. Reagan's admitted responsibility, even as he continues to try to rationalize it.

For example, the White House took last week's official report of the Senate Intelligence Committee to be "consistent" with Mr. Reagan's belief that the decision to sell the arms was well founded. It says the report confirms his claim that he did not authorize or know about the illegal diversion of profits to the Contras. By such remarkable reasoning, the San Francisco earthquake might have been called an urban renewal project.

In fact, the committee report describes an administration hopelessly tangled in its own web of deceit, with senior officials involved in the arms sales regularly lying to each other and to Congress, and disagreeing to this day about what happened at certain critical junctures.

The report also contradicts the President on a most important point: Whether his motive in selling the arms was only to establish strategic relations with "moderate" elements in Iran, or whether it was to ransom hostages. If the former, why did Lt. Col. Oliver North, the cashiered national security aide, complain to Attorney General Edwin Meese that whenever the subject of the moderates came up, the President insisted on talking about hostages?

The only comfort in that report for the President is that the committee did not find any evidence that he knew of the illegal Contra aid. The committee could not have been expected to settle that question, given the refusal of such key witnesses as

North and former National Security Adviser John M. Poindexter to testify without immunity. Indeed, the matters of who knew what when are among the 14 "unresolved questions" cited by the committee for the benefit of the special Senate and House committees that will continue the investigation.

Yet the preliminary report was conclusive in another way. As Chairman David Boren pointed out, it established "a picture of making foreign policy that was in real disarray." Robert McFarlane, a former national security adviser, apparently felt free to open discussions with Israel pertaining to the potential Iranian deal without notifying the Department of State. When Secretary of State George Shultz protested, McFarlane misled him, saying that McFarlane's emissary had been acting "on his own hook" and promising that he was "turning it (the Iran initiative) off entirely." The President apparently never learned of Shultz's early warning that Israel's interest in dealing with Iran "is not the same as ours." Policies were being made — or broken — in half a dozen different places, none accountable to the others or to the President, the Congress and the public.

Subsequent to the publication of the Senate report, the *New York Times* has alleged that Pentagon intelligence officials knew of and tolerated illegal private attempts to sell Iran 39 American fighter planes and many other weapons, hoping to get intelligence information in return.

The "disarray," as Boren put it, is an inevitable result of Mr. Reagan's disdain for details and his excessive reliance on subordinates, especially Chief of Staff Donald Regan. As Boren points out, "Key people, advisers to the President, who could have given him expert advice, were closed out — the secretary of state, the chairman of the Joint Chiefs. What was the chief of staff doing closing out people like that but letting in very low-echelon people?" Bringing his President to the point of ruin, that's what.

The damage to our foreign policy has been disastrous and there is no time to waste in undertaking to repair it. The world is waiting for some sign that Mr. Reagan knows the trouble he's in. He could give that sign by following Boren's advice to get himself a new chief of staff.

## Detroit Free Press

*Detroit, MI, February 2, 1987*

A NEW, MORE detailed version of a Senate Intelligence Committee report on the Iran-contra affair (an earlier version was stopped by the committee's new Democratic majority earlier this month) has finally been released to the public. The report breaks little new ground, but it sheds a lot of light on the procedures, formal and informal, that are actually followed by the administration. It may be, then, a good starting point for more extensive investigations of the affair to be conducted this year by special committees in both the House and the Senate.

The committee's findings appear to exculpate the president at least as far as the narrow question of the illegal funding of the Nicaraguan contras is concerned. No evidence has been found that President Reagan knew that some of the proceeds from the arms sales to Iran were diverted to Central America. The report, however, doesn't clear the Reagan administration in the way Senate Republicans earlier suggested, by putting the whole controversy behind it.

The president and his aides, it turns out, were less than candid when they publicly insisted that the main purpose of the secret sales of U.S. missiles was to make contact with "moderate elements" in Iran. All that Mr. Reagan really wanted in return, the report suggests, was to free the hostages. His top officers tried to deliver; and in their zeal to please the president, they disregarded elementary foreign policy interests of the United States.

The cynicism, shortsightedness and incompetence displayed by top U.S. officials in their dealings with Iran — reconstructed in the report in painstaking detail — is truly worrisome. The Senate report confirms our earlier suspicions that the nation's foreign policy-making process is a shambles. That's bad news, especially since we see no real proof that Mr. Reagan has learned from the Iranian experience and intends to do anything to fix the problem. Most likely, we are afraid, he doesn't even recognize it.

## The Sunday Record

*Hackensack, NJ, February 1, 1987*

The new Senate Intelligence Committee report on the Iran-contra arms scandal removes the lid from the Reagan White House and reveals a most astonishing combination of ineptitude and double dealing. According to the report: Free-lance arms dealer Manucher Ghorbanifar misled Oliver North; Colonel North misled George Shultz; Elliot Abrams, the State Department's point man on Latin America, misled the intelligence committee; while off in Israel former Prime Minister Shimon Peres and his director-general of the foreign ministry, David Kimche, expertly manipulated just about everyone else. But if there's a moral to this sorry affair, it is that in fooling each other, these men only succeeded in fooling themselves.

Despite its differences with the Khomeini regime, for instance, Israel has been secretly selling Iran arms since 1981. This was widely reported in the press at the time. Yet when Mr. Peres and CIA Director William Casey personally assured National Security Adviser Robert McFarlane that the stories weren't true, Mr. McFarlane, according to the report, believed them both.

Whether Mr. Casey was duplicitous or just plain ignorant is impossible to determine, but Mr. Peres's reasons for reportedly misleading his ally are fairly clear. A U.S.-Iran alliance would serve as a counterweight to Washington's ties with such "moderate" (although bitterly anti-Israel) Arab regimes as Saudi Arabia and Kuwait, and would therefore take some of the pressure off the Israelis.

The United States had its own reasons for improving relations with Iran as well. In May 1985, the Intelligence Committee report goes on, memos prepared by the CIA and the National Security Council staff noted that Iran was "increasingly unstable and threatened by Soviet regional aims" and proposed that U.S. arms sales were "one alternative means of establishing Western influence so as to offset growing Soviet inroads." Secretary of State George Shultz rejected the idea as "perverse," Secretary of Defense Caspar Weinberger dismissed it as "absurd," yet the fact remained that it dovetailed perfectly with Israel's desires for an alliance with a non-Arab state in the Middle East.

Thus, despite the objections, the deal soon acquired a momentum of its own. George Shultz cautioned that Israeli interests were not entirely consonant with U.S. interests, but he was ignored. Mr. Ghorbanifar, the arms dealer, acted as a go-between. While the CIA was suspicious of him, describing him at one point as a "talented fabricator," both Robert McFarlane and Oliver North clung to Israeli assurances that he was on the up and up.

But he wasn't. Mr. Ghorbanifar's influence with the Iranian government was more limited than he let on. When a delegation headed by Mr. McFarlane (the one bearing the key-shaped cake and the Bible inscribed by President Reagan), prepared to leave for Tehran, he assured them that they would be met by Iran's three top political officials. They weren't. And as the talks dragged on, it soon became apparent that the top leadership, including the Ayatollah Khomeini himself, had not been apprised of the negotiations. The Americans gave up and went home. Nonetheless, the arms deliveries resumed a few months later.

Meanwhile, as the arms-for-hostages deal was shaping up, the report states, Mr. Shultz complained that the would-be James Bonds of the National Security Council were bypassing his department, while Colonel North instructed the CIA not to share top-secret intelligence on the deal with the secretary of state. Mr. McFarlane told the committee that President Reagan approved the initial Israeli shipment of U.S.-supplied TOW antitank missiles, while White House Chief of Staff Donald Regan told it that the president did not.

Elliot Abrams initially testified before the Senate Intelligence Committee that the administration solicited no third-country aid for the contras. But he later apologized, saying it had indeed solicited such aid from the Southeast Asian nation of Brunei, among others. CIA Director Casey failed to inform the committee of the contra arms diversion when he came before it in November (before the scandal become public) even though, as the report makes clear, he already had material indicating that the diversion had taken place.

Thus, deceptions and self-deceptions in this tragicomic affair multiply like grains of sand in the Iranian desert. As for Mr. Reagan, he hovers above the scandal like a great gray void. Mr. McFarlane's assertions that the president authorized the initial Israel shipment seem plausible. And even though the president denies it, it appears clear that an arms-for-hostage swap was one of the things that he had in mind. Whether he knew of the contra arms diversion is as yet unknown. But despite Mr. Reagan's notoriously short attention span, it seems increasingly likely that he did.

## ST. LOUIS POST-DISPATCH

*St. Louis, MO, February 1, 1987*

The revised report on the Iran-Contras arms scandal released by the Senate Intelligence Committee does not differ substantially from the report the committee had originally voted not to disclose but that was leaked. The Intelligence Committee reported that it did not find any evidence that President Ronald Reagan either authorized or was aware of the diversion to the Contras of funds from the sale of arms to Iran. Given Mr. Reagan's indifference to detail and his lack of intellectual curiosity, it is entirely plausible that he did not know money from one illegal enterprise was being diverted to another.

But that excuses neither the decision to ransom American hostages in Lebanon with military weapons nor the decision to continue supplying arms to the Contras when such activity was forbidden by Congress. In the former case, the president knowingly contravened his own foreign policy of not making deals with terrorist states, his own executive order prohibiting arms sales to Iran and a congressional injunction against arms sales to Iran. In the latter case, Mr. Reagan sanctioned a scheme, carried out from the White House, to evade a congressional ban on military assistance to the Contras by organizing and directing a private, clandestine weapons supply network.

It is true that if Mr. Reagan had respected the law and followed prescribed procedures, none of this would have happened. Yet it would be a mistake to see that as the only lesson of this shameful episode. The more important lesson is that the extensive apparatus of secrecy and deceit that has been established in the name of protecting freedom is by its very existence an invitation to lawlessness. If that lesson is not grasped and acted on, there will be more Iran-Contras scandals.

## TULSA WORLD

*Tulsa, OK, February 2, 1987*

THE Senate Intelligence Committee's formal report on the Iran-Contra affair contains few surprises. Its greatest value may be that it ends one phase of the investigation and puts the government and the American people a step closer to a final resolution of the scandal.

The damage from this affair is done. Many details are missing, but the basic facts are clear: President Reagan attempted to swap arms to Iran for American hostages in Lebanon; some of the money from the arms sales was apparently diverted to the Nicaraguan Contras.

The investigation is subject to the law of diminishing returns. At some point the value of new information that might be uncovered will be more than offset by the harm done by the investigative process.

Sen. David Boren, new chairman of the Intelligence Committee, and his colleagues have done a good job, considering the only witnesses who can answer the key questions have taken the Fifth Amendment.

The matter now goes before a special Senate committee for a more extensive probe. The House also will be conducting an investigation. A special prosecutor has been appointed. So the affair will be around for at least several more months.

The Iran deal has soured U.S. relations with some of our most valuable allies and has hurt American credibility worldwide. But that's done.

The next question: How long do we want to extend the damage in an effort to clear up the last interesting details? There surely must come a time when the Congress and the public can say: "Enough. Let's get on with other important business."

## The Oregonian

*Portland, OR, February 3, 1987*

The White House claims that the preliminary report of the Senate Intelligence Committee is a vindication of President Reagan. After all, although it reveals administration officials lying to Congress and to each other, although it depicts what Sen. David Boren, D-Okla., calls "a foreign policy in disarray," although it describes private arms dealers guiding the actions of the U.S. government, the report does not demonstrate that the president knew that the arms-sale money was being redirected to the Contras.

To the White House, that's vindication.

The kind of outlook that could see things that way was vividly illustrated earlier last week, when White House spokesman Larry Speakes finally admitted that, yes, Reagan had written a message in a Bible and sent it to Iran with his negotiators.

The detail had first appeared at the time the story broke, and for months the White House had dismissed or ignored it. Nov. 13, Reagan said on television, "Don't believe all these wild stories."

Last week, the speaker of Iran's parliament, Hojatolislam Hashemi Rafsanjani, displayed the Bible to reporters, with the inscription in Reagan's handwriting. At that point, the White House admitted the story.

The administration's attitude here is revealing. For almost three months, the White House disparaged the story that the president had sought to move the Iranians with an autographed Bible, all the while knowing that the Iranians had it in their possession and could embarrass the president anytime they tired of the game.

Even the idea to send the Bible is hard to understand. The thought that the Shiite mullahs who lead Iran, who have made it clear at every point that they regard Westerners as infidels, could be stirred by an allusion to the common roots of Islam, Christianity and Judaism could not have survived analysis by anyone who knew anything of Iran. We now know it never received any.

The naivete and ineptness of the individuals risking the credibility of the United States in this covert operation are breathtaking. It is the same outlook that now claims to see in the Senate Intelligence Committee report a vindication.

## The Des Moines Register

*Des Moines, IA, February 9, 1987*

In the scramble to cover their tracks, those mired in the Iran-contra mess have created countless layers of deception and lying: to Congress, the people and each other. The Senate Intelligence Committee's report details a maze of testimony that suggests more people knew much more than has been publicly admitted.

The report shows a chaotic and divided White House, in which top officials' accounts are in contradiction and those opposed to the arms sales were kept in the dark. The report also suggests that the president may have known far more than has been stated. It outlines a close association between top administration officials, the CIA and the military-aid network for the contras during the two-year congressional ban on such assistance.

Even the State Department and Pentagon were not entirely free of deception. High Pentagon intelligence officials learned more than a year ago that private arms dealers were trying illegally to ship U.S. weapons to Iran.

Assistant Secretary of State Elliot Abrams last month withheld from the committee the information that he had solicited contra money from foreign countries.

As deception multiplies, administration officials running from the truth will find themselves increasingly stumbling over one another's evasions as two congressional committees gear up for more investigations.

## BUFFALO EVENING NEWS

*Buffalo, NY, February 2, 1987*

THE REPORT on the Iran-contra scandal by the Senate Intelligence Committee is necessarily incomplete, since its investigation was frustrated in part by the refusal of key Reagan administration figures to testify.

But the findings offer a dismaying commentary on the administration's formulation of foreign policy. As the committee chairman, Senator David Boren, D-Okla., said, the report gave "a picture of making foreign policy that was in real disarray."

So far as the panel was able to discover, the blundering arms deals were hatched by lower-level White House aides and their foreign contacts, often without the knowledge of the State Department, the Joint Chiefs of Staff or the Central Intelligence Agency.

The evidence also suggests that President Reagan, who has said repeatedly he would make no deals with terrorists, was primarily interested in the hostage aspects of the negotiations. This conflicts with his insistence that the overture to Iran was made mainly for strategic reasons and that the freeing of the hostages was secondary.

Administration officials in general appeared to have a similar preoccupation. The report said that to many officials the idea of forming contacts with "moderates" in Iran was little more than a "cover story" to be used if the story ever was made public.

Commenting on the report, the White House said that the events "could be interpreted as a trade of arms for hostages," but that the administration had broader goals. The committee uncovered no evidence that the president knew about or directed the diversion of arms-sales profits to the Nicaragua contras.

Symptomatic of the disarray within the administration was the report's finding that key officials deceived each other and members of Congress about the affair. It said CIA Director William Casey had been less than frank with Robert McFarlane, who undertook a mission to Iran.

Assistant Secretary of State Elliott Abrams told the committee that money for the contras had not been solicited from other countries. Later he apologized to the committee.

The picture pieced together by the committee is not a pretty one. It shows a zealous White House aide, Lt. Col. Oliver North, acting on an important foreign policy matter without the participation of the secretary of state. It includes mysterious, secret bank accounts in Switzerland and elsewhere, set up to funnel funds from Iran and possibly to evade the law concerning aid to the contras.

At the time, Congress had specifically barred the United States from "directly or indirectly" providing military assistance to the Nicaraguan rebels. To circumvent this ban, the administration called for private contributions to the contras, and North was actively engaged in organizing such efforts.

The committee's report noted that many key questions remain unanswered, including the role of the White House staff and other nations and the degree to which U.S. foreign policy had been turned over to private individuals accountable to no one.

These questions remain for investigation by the House and Senate special committees, the independent counsel and the presidential panel that is also examining the affair.

## FORT WORTH STAR-TELEGRAM

*Fort Worth, TX, February 11, 1987*

Spending billions for national defense and then implementing shamefully slipshod procedures for safeguarding secrets vital to that defense defies logic, yet that apparently is what the United States is doing and has been doing for far too long.

A report by the Senate Intelligence Committee several months ago should have raised the necessary alarm flags about the shaky condition of this country's security systems. Apparently, it did not.

A newly released report by the House Intelligence Committee reiterates the warnings issued by the earlier Senate findings, but in much stronger terms, and properly urges remedial action by U.S. intelligence-gathering organizations if there is to be any hope of keeping this nation's defense secrets secret.

The report said the House panel found "a litany of disaster" while investigating American intelligence agencies and called for a major overhaul in the way they conduct their business.

Shortcomings the committee found included:

● Carelessness in hiring people for sensitive intelligence positions. A case specifically cited was that of Edward Howard, whom the CIA hired despite "an extensive history of using hard drugs." Howard subsequently defected to the Soviet Union and turned many secrets over to the Russians.

● Failure to take seriously the implications of the arrests of 27 U.S. citizens for spying from 1984 to 1986.

● A relaxation of strictures that should govern the most highly classified information.

● Relatively indiscriminate issuance of security clearances. Of 200,000 applications for top secret status in 1984, only 1 percent were denied, which indicates a lax screening process.

Because most of the shortcomings uncovered by House investigators are the same ones the Senate panel found months ago, it is safe to assume that few corrective steps were taken by the responsible agencies in response to the Senate investigation. That being the case, it is incumbent upon Congress to apply whatever pressure is necessary upon the entire intelligence structure to bring about needed changes.

This country's secrets can be just as important to national defense as are ships, tanks and planes and should be guarded every bit as zealously.

# Reagan Notes at Issue; Position Reversed

White House officials February 1, 1987 confirmed that President Reagan had periodically made notes that contained references to the administration's decision to ship arms to Iran. A controversy arose after the *Washington Post* reported Feb. 1 that White House chief of staff Donald Regan had told the Senate Intelligence Committee about the notes in closed testimony. Asked whether Reagan took notes for his memoirs, Regan reportedly told the committee "of course," but took offense at the suggestion that the notes might be made available to the investigators seeking to find out what actions Reagan authorized and when he did so.

White House officials first said they would not release the notes because they were private. The refusal raised for the first time in the scandal the issue of executive privilege, which had been central in President Richard Nixon's attempt to withhold notes and tapes from a criminal investigation of the Watergate scandal. Although executive privilege was considered one of the most ambiguous of constitutional issues, legal scholars agreed that the Supreme Court's 1974 ruling ordering Nixon to turn over the materials from his office set a firm precedent that a president could not withhold subpoenaed evidence. Although the precedent would certainly apply to a criminal probe, it was not clear whether it would apply to a general investigation by a congressional committee.

Reagan had decided to share "relavent excerpts" of his notes with congressional investigators, White House spokesman Marlin Fitzwater said Feb. 2, reversing the administration's stand on the issue. Fitzwater said that the administration had not anticipated that the notes would be needed by the committees. Reagan was said to have used the notes in preparing for a recent interview with the special commission chaired by former Sen. John Tower, appointed to study the National Security Council's involvement in the Iran-contra arms scandal.

# THE DENVER POST

*Denver, CO, February 12, 1987*

ONLY ONE OF the many contradictions in President Reagan's handling of the Iran-contra affair is between his repeated promise to get all the facts before the American people and his repeated failure — or refusal — to make sure that it's done.

The president has even declined — as he did again Tuesday — to require that his own close aides, past and present, inform him of what they know of the arms sales to Iran and the skimming of profits to the Nicaraguan contras or wherever else.

In response to a specific request from the special board he appointed to review operations of the National Security Council, the president refused to order Vice Adm. John Poindexter and Marine Lt. Col. Oliver North to submit to questioning by the board.

Poindexter, the former chief of the NSC, and North, a former principal aide, were at the heart of the Iran-contra machinations, and both men are still on active military duty — in the pay of the people. By refusing to order Poindexter and North to cooperate, the president blocks the success of his own inquiry and places the American people even further from what he's promised time and again.

The special review board, headed by former Sen. John Tower of Texas, is not a formally constituted judicial or legislative body with criminal or contempt powers. It will report to the president himself. It's therefore a lame explanation when President Reagan says he can't give an "unlawful" order that Poindexter and North "testify against themselves."

Beginning with his televised speech from the Oval Office Nov. 13 and in other appearances since then, the president has been insistent that the American people should "hear the facts" about the Iran-contra scandal and that he would help in that process.

It is a continuing disappointment and aggravation that President Reagan won't help get the facts out to the public and even refuses to find them out for himself.

# The Washington Post

*Washington, DC, February 3, 1987*

IT IS POSSIBLE to be a zealous seeker after the relevant facts—all of them—in the Iran-contra investigation and yet to be made uneasy by the prospect of the search's being extended to the president's handwritten diary notes and information acquired by his biographer, Edmund Morris. These questions as to some necessary residue of privilege and privacy even in the great affairs of government arose over the weekend when some senators said they were contemplating a request for material in the notes and also testimony from Mr. Morris that might bear on the investigation. The prospect that a confrontation would come about was diminished yesterday when the White House agreed to make relevant material available—though it is still not clear who determines which notes are relevant.

The question of Mr. Morris' knowledge and material is different from the issues concerning the president. Mr. Morris has been given special access to the president in order to facilitate his work. He is not a government official or employee; his notes, drafts and even his final work product—a book—are not government documents but private property. He can assert no claim of executive privilege, but like a reporter gathering information, he is collecting material for future publication and that kind of activity has been protected to a certain extent when balanced against the need for information in legal proceedings.

In the matter of the president's notes, there are different considerations. One set is legal. There are major differences between the current investigation and that surrounding the Watergate scandal, and even in light of that precedent it is not at all clear that the courts would sustain a subpoena from Capitol Hill for Mr. Reagan's notes.

But no matter what the legal possibilities are,

other questions arise. Sens. Boren and Cohen, who are deeply engaged in the inquiry, have both given evidence that they are sensitive to issues of privacy, confidentiality and executive privilege that hover around this undertaking. "Any individual including the president of the United States is entitled to have confidentiality of personal comments which have no bearing on public policy," as Sen. Boren put it yesterday. What about material that does have a bearing on public policy but that has a personal, private character? Is there any such thing? Should everyone, even a president, be able to write his private thoughts secure in the knowledge that they are for his eyes alone? When every fleeting impression, every word revealing discouragement, uncertainty or overconfidence must be weighed with an eye toward future publication, a large portion of personal freedom is lost.

The competing claim here is a powerful one: getting at the truth in the Iran-contra affair. And it is thought that some particular entries in the president's notes may dispose of some conflict over who met with whom and when. This is the information that the Senate needs to elicit; with luck it will be provided under the set-up agreed to by the White House yesterday. It is good that these efforts at avoiding a confrontation are being undertaken, because important values are in conflict here. The time may come in this case when it becomes clear that criminal acts have been committed and will be prosecuted. A court may rule, at such a time, that even in the face of adamant presidential resistance, very personal papers must be produced. But that time has not come, and if Congress and the White House take care to make the investigation proceed in a rigorous, intelligent way, it may never come.

# Richmond Times-Dispatch

*Richmond, VA, February 6, 1987*

The most public of people are entitled to some privacy. Even the president of the United States. Neither the Constitution nor common sense requires Ronald Reagan to reveal to Congress and the nation his midnight meditations on Iran, the arms negotiations or any other issue.

But does the situation change if he jots those thoughts down on a piece of paper intended for his own eyes only? This is not an idle question. It goes to the very heart of congressional plans to peek into the president's diary to search for new information on the Iran-*contra* controversy. In his residence at the end of his official schedule, the president usually records memories and impressions of the day's activities, possibly making highly personal references to associates and members of his family in the process. Some congressmen believe his notes may also include revealing information about the Iran-*contra* affair. There have been hints of court action to force Mr. Reagan to open his diary if he refuses to do so voluntarily.

But the president, as another sign of his eagerness to learn the truth about the Iran-*contra* affair, has said he would be "glad" to allow Congress to read relevant parts of his diary. Exactly who would determine which entries to be relevant has yet to be settled, so there remains the possibility of an ugly and potentially damaging constitutional struggle between the president and Congress on this whole issue.

Our hope is that Congress will show the same conciliatory spirit the president has displayed and back off. He would have had considerable legal and public support had he chosen to fight to keep his entire diary under lock and key but he

obviously concluded that it would be in the nation's interest to compromise. Congress should reciprocate by abandoning any thought of insisting on seeing the diary in its entirety, unedited.

The president's notes, it is important to emphasize, are not official documents. They are not part of the official record of his administration. Nor are they in the category of Richard Nixon's tapes, which did capture official conversations between him and other public officials in the president's office. The fact that the courts ultimately ordered the Nixon tapes released does not necessarily mean they would direct President Reagan to allow Congress to rummage through his personal diary.

Were they to do so they would be saying in effect that a president is entitled to no privacy at all, that his thoughts become public property the very minute they are transmitted to paper. How would this affect the quality of administration? To be able to reflect frankly on past events, or to contemplate impending matters, can be an important part of the decision-making process. The search for truth often requires the consideration of exploratory ideas that turn out to be dumb, but how willing to explore is a president likely to be if he knows that his tentative musings can be forced into public view at almost any time?

A bruising constitutional battle on this issue should be avoided. With the information Mr. Reagan has promised and the information obtainable from other sources, Congress and the court-appointed special counsel should be able to learn the truth about the Iran-*contra* affair.

# ST. LOUIS POST-DISPATCH

*St. Louis, MO*
*February 14, 1987*

Compelling circumstantial evidence has long existed of direct White House involvement in the private network established to supply the Contras with weapons. Now the special White House commission created after the Iran-Contras scandal broke is said to have uncovered documentary evidence that removes the last shred of doubt. If so, the news comes as no surprise. The surprise is that President Ronald Reagan has passively waited all these months for the commission to develop information he was in a position to make public, and act on, months ago.

The mission of the special three-member commission, which was established by Mr. Reagan and is headed by former Republican Sen. John Tower of Texas, is not to conduct a criminal investigation but to examine the operations of the National Security Council. It was the NSC that instigated the illegal arms sales to Iran and organized and directed the gun running on behalf of the Contras at a time when the government was prohibited from providing them with military aid. The NSC, it should be added, is the president's personal intelligence agency and reports directly to him.

When he established the commission, Mr. Reagan promised his full cooperation and that of his entire staff. But when the commission sought to review the notes he had made on meetings with aides about the Iranian arms deal, his cooperation did not match his promises. What the commission was allowed to see were excerpts from the notes. Even these the commission was allowed only to read; it was prevented from keeping them or making copies.

And the president declined once again to direct Vice Adm. Poindexter, the resigned head of the NSC staff, and Lt. Col. North, the fired NSC deputy, to talk to the commission. Earlier, they had invoked their Fifth Amendment right against self-incrimination in appearances before congressional committees. When they refused also to talk to the commission, Mr. Reagan said he would not order them to do so. It is proper that he did not, but it is not proper for the president to persist in the fiction that he and his staff are cooperating fully.

The commission is expected to issue its report Feb. 27. No doubt it will find that the NSC staff was transformed from an intelligence analysis team into a rogue elephant. What the commission will say as to the president's part in the NSC's covert dealings with Iran and its covert operations on behalf of the Contras remains to be seen.

If the Tower commission simply recommends procedures or laws to safeguard against future misuse of the NSC, however, it will have failed the American people. It ought to consider a more fundamental question: whether the president should have at his command a large, secret bureaucracy insulated from congressional review and not accountable — even, Mr. Reagan would like America to believe, to the president himself.

# Roanoke Times & World-News

*Roanoke, VA, February 3, 1987*

RONALD REAGAN has offered to go through his private notes and to make available to a Senate committee those excerpts that deal with the arms-for-hostages deal with Iran and the diversion of profits to the Nicaraguan Contras.

This could help congressional investigators find their way through the labyrinth of lies and distortions that got the president the nation into this mess.

At the end of the day, in the privacy of the White House residential quarters, Reagan makes personal notes on his private and official actions.

Members of the Senate committee investigating the arms scandal would like to review the notes. The president says he's willing to release excerpts that would be pertinent to the investigation. Some members of Congress prefer to let a special intermediary review the notes and determine what is pertinent.

This takes the president and Congress into a delicate area of interbranch relations. Richard Nixon defied congressional efforts at getting to his tape recordings of Watergate-related conversations. He cited executive privilege. The president eventually had to yield the tapes.

But this is not Watergate and Ronald Reagan is not Richard Nixon. No one is yet accusing Reagan of breaking the law or committing an impeachable offense.

The president's notes may help, if he actually recorded the substance of conversations involving the deal with Iran. But is the Senate entitled to peer into what amounts to the president's private diary? Does someone from the legislative branch have the right to fish for damning evidence among the presi-

dent's notes about his aching prostate, his private opinion of Bob Dole or his pillow talk with his wife?

This is the type of dilemma that should yield to compromise. Congress should not have the power to subpoena the president's notes absent probable cause for an impeachable offense. But Reagan could voluntarily make them available. He could winnow from his notes anything of a delicate personal nature that would prove embarrassing if made public. But this would leave skeptics wondering whether the president had held back certain details that might reflect unfavorably on him or his administration.

Surely there is a third party to whom the president could entrust the excerpting — a party who enjoys the respect of the president and of the Senate. Nixon was willing to trust Sen. John Stennis, D-Miss., to go through his tapes to extract pertinent material. The circumstances, and motives, were far different from those pertinent to the Reagan notes. We are not, apparently, dealing with a cynical president trying to hide the truth, but rather with a confused president trying to identify the facts. A friendly third party could resolve the impasse.

It's unfortunate that we have a president who can't recall clearly or recount candidly what he discussed with his top aides. Reagan's fuzzy memory and penchant for obfuscation make it all the harder to get at the truth. It is encouraging to know that he is willing to cull his notes and make them available to the Senate. His information would be much more credible if someone else were doing the culling.

**BillDay** Detroit Free Press Tribune Media

# THE PRESIDENT RELEASES HIS PERSONAL NOTES TO CONGRESS:

WED. NOV. 19, 1986

Slept late. Nan fixed my favorite breakfast. Staff read me the Washington Post. Heard a funny joke from Don Regan—says Ollie North told him. That North is a very funny guy. Took a nap.

THUR. NOV. 20, 1986

Woke up early. Got a call from Patty—started the day off mad. Staff read me the Washington Post. What a bunch of jerks. Don Regan tells me a funny joke he heard from Poindexter. He's the guy in the basement. I should go down there some day. Took a nap.

FRI. NOV. 21, 1986

Got an early call from Meese. He tells me a great joke about black people! Staff read me the Washington Post—up yours too, Bradlee! Meese calls again—something about Iran. I tell him a great joke about the Ayatollah! Took a nap.

MON. NOV. 24, 1986

Meese calls. Tells me money from arms sales to Iran went to contras. I thought it was a joke. Meese never could tell a good joke. Took a nap.

TUE. NOV. 25, 1986

We go public. Took a nap.

---

## THE CHRISTIAN SCIENCE MONITOR

*Boston, MA, February 5, 1987*

PRESIDENT Reagan's offer to disclose his personal notes taken during the Iran-arms decision period, at least those pertinent to Congress's ~quiries, was generous enough at this time. If it is established that crimes were committed, it may be necessary to ask for the larger body of handwritten daily notes Mr. Reagan has been taking for an eventual book. If Congress wants more, there will be time enough later to consider confrontation over disclosure, such as had occurred during the Nixon period over the Watergate tapes.

Notes taken by Reagan biographer Edmund Morris, who talks with the President regularly, should also be exempt from congressional impounding.

The privacy, privilege, and confidentiality issues of the two sets of notes differ. But they share a common base: There should be some initial work stage where thoughts and doubts, and conversations, can be put down without fear of disclosure. Unless some compelling legal matter argues otherwise, this should be true for public persons no less than private.

## The Birmingham News

*Birmingham, AL, February 5, 1987*

President Reagan was right to agree to release excerpts of his personal notes pertaining to the Iran-Contra controversy. We hope his openness will prevent further comparisons to the stonewalling that occurred in the Nixon administration during the Watergate scandal.

Reagan vowed in his State of the Union address to get to the bottom of this mess, which saw U.S. arms sold to Iran and the proceeds designated for the Contra rebels fighting Nicaragua's Marxist government. The president also has talked, and has had Chief of Staff Donald Regan talk, to a panel investigating the possibility of illegal acts.

If the president had then decided to be less than candid about his knowledge of events leading up to revelation of the arms deal, his administration would have lost considerable credibility.

White House staff members initially indicated the president would not release any part of his notes on the grounds that such would violate his right to privacy as an individual. But as pointed out by Sen. Howell Heflin, a former Alabama chief justice, that argument has no legal standing. A citizen's personal privacy does not prevent investigating authorities from legally obtaining documents from that person.

Reagan could have invoked the right of executive privilege to keep the notes from being reviewed by Congress. But although the Supreme Court has ruled a president has such a right, it also ruled Richard Nixon could not use it to keep secret his memos. So, there would be no guarantee that Reagan would have been any more successful.

We're glad he didn't attempt to go that route. More than likely, it would only have led to a court battle initiated by partisan congressmen who relish every chance they get to make the president look bad.

The public still has confidence in Mr. Reagan. His decision to release his personal notes on the Iran-Conta affair bolsters that confidence and allows the president to get on with other matters.

## THE SAGINAW NEWS

*Saginaw, MI, February 6, 1987*

President Reagan needs to pay closer attention to the rules of the hunt. When the hounds smell it, they just won't let go. Word that Reagan kept notes on the Iran-Contra affair raised a yelp just like they were — well, tapes.

So Reagan had no choice but to offer to turn over "relevant" parts of his diary. What he still doesn't understand is that he no longer is the judge of what's relevant. All he can do now is make sure he doesn't have to explain an 18-word gap.

## Los Angeles Times

*Los Angeles, CA, February 9, 1987*

Throughout his political career, Ronald Reagan has had a special financial safety net under him, held by the close group of wealthy friends and advisers who first promoted him for governor of California and then for President of the United States. The safety net is at work again.

When the Reagans fled the Victorian mansion that used to serve as California's executive residence, this group bought a stately home on Sacramento's 45th Street for the governor to use. They organized a campaign to buy land in a fashionable suburb to build a new governor's mansion. Members of the group helped Reagan invest in a Riverside area ranch, and then assisted him in selling that ranch and buying the Reagans' present property near Santa Barbara.

The suggestion all along was that Reagan's time was too important to the state and nation to have to worry about financial details and where to live.

Now it has been disclosed that about 20 of the President's California friends have chipped in, through a holding company, to buy a $2.5-million home on 1¼ acres of land in old Bel-Air just in case that is where the Reagans choose to retire. There

is no obligation, should they elect to buy another home. And, of course, it was emphasized, the First Family still will have to pay for the Bel-Air house if they decide that they like it.

Those close to Reagan point out that his finances are in a blind trust while he is President, although that would not seem to preclude administrators of the trust from using some of the money for the house. There never has been any serious allegation of conflict of interest about these comfortable financial arrangements. Other Presidents have had wealthy friends do similar favors, but not usually without tinges of scandal or questions of impropriety—and certainly not so often or so faithfully over such a long period.

The Reagan charm and innocence have shielded him from such. "Never look a gift house in the mouth," Reagan quipped when his friends bought the Sacramento home for his use. This is not the time to begrudge the President's having wealthy friends who are concerned about his welfare. But when the President talks about the needs of the needy in America, it is well to remember that there are safety nets—and then there are safety nets.

## The Evening Gazette

*Worcester, MA, FEbruary 6, 1987*

It was one of those delicious coincidences that crop up in politics from time to time. While President Reagan was offering investigators a peek at his private notes on the Iran-Contra affair the other day, former President Nixon was pledging an all-out fight to prevent the scheduled May release of more Watergate tapes and papers.

Although the two actions seem diametrically opposed, they may not be as contradictory as they first appear.

Nixon, as an aspiring elder statesman consigned to the political sidelines, can afford the luxury of standing on principle. Still smarting from the public disclosure of embarrassing Watergate-related tapes and papers, Nixon sees himself as protector of the right of future presidents to maintain the privacy of personal records.

So far, Nixon has successfully delayed the release of much of the material from his White House years, but his principle of "presidential privilege" has fared poorly. Congress ordered release of countless documents and tape recordings 12 years ago, and the Supreme Court has

refused to recognize any absolute presidential privilege to withhold information in all circumstances.

By contrast, Reagan's apparent openness stems from very practical considerations concerning a very practical incumbent president. Faced with crumbling credibility and beset with allegations of wrongdoing or incompetence, Reagan must make it a priority to establish the credibility of his repeated vow to "get to the bottom" of the arms-for-hostages deal.

Furthermore, Reagan's offer may not be all that it seems. The White House was careful to promise "relevant excerpts" from the president's private notes, not the papers themselves. Presumably, decisions on what is relevant will be made by the White House.

Still, the irony of the timing of the two announcements was inescapable. Perhaps neither man will ultimately allow us a meaningful peek into his private papers. But their very different reactions already have given us a revealing glimpse into the character of our leaders and into the political process itself.

The Honolulu Advertiser
*Honolulu, HI*
*February 4, 1987*

President Reagan deserves credit for good sense in deciding to share with Congress at least some of his personal notes relating to the Iran-contra scandal.

Initial indications from the White House were that the notes would be kept private under the executive privilege of confidentiality. A spokesman said there was concern about "invasion of the president's privacy and the privacy of others" if the notes were released.

There is part of a point in that position. But the much larger point is that refusing to release the notes could have meant both embarrassment and political damage for Reagan.

It would undermine the position stated in his State of the Union address that he is determined "to get to the bottom of this" and would cooperate fully with investigations.

Moreover, even the appearance of stonewalling could damage his residual personal affection from the American people. That is now based in part on his statements that he didn't know what was going on but wants to find out.

Behind everything else are memories of the Watergate era when the Supreme Court rejected former President Nixon's claim of executive privilege and he was ordered to surrender White House tapes and memos he had dictated.

Whether Monday's offer to make available "relevant excerpts" from Reagan's personal notes will satisfy everyone is uncertain. But for now it avoids a fight and a shadow on his position.

## Iran Contacts Called Radicals

Contradictng White House assertions that the Iran arms deal had been part of an effort to reach moderate elements in that country, an aide to Vice President George Bush February 7, 1987 asserted that an Israeli official had told him in July 1986 that "we are dealing with radical elements" in Iran. The Bush aide, Donald Gregg, said that the United States had turned to the anti-Western radicals because contacts with moderates had failed.

The White House Feb. 9 confirmed the essence of Gregg's remarks, but spokesman Marlin Fitzwater called the distinction between radicals and moderates in Iran's government "a semantic difference." Fitzwater said that "moderate" was a term used broadly to describe Iranians "who would have some reason to be friendly to the United States."

The *Washington Post* Feb. 7 had published a memo, labeled "Top Secret," that outlined a meeting in Israel July 29, 1986 between Bush, Gregg, Bush aide George Fuller, and Amiram Nir, an Israeli emissary in the discussions between the U.S. and Iran. Nir had Bush that Israel had turned to the Iranian radicals "because we've learned that they can deliver and the moderates can't." Gregg later confirmed the authenticity of the memo.

## ST. LOUIS POST-DISPATCH
*St. Louis, MO*
*February 10, 1987*

President Ronald Reagan's repeated insistence that he authorized the Iran arms deal in order to influence moderate elements within the Iranian government has been revealed as a concoction. The story lacked plausibility from the beginning, but until a weekend disclosure by *The Washington Post* there was no documentary evidence to contradict him.

Now, *The Post* has disclosed that in July 1986 a key Israeli official told Vice President George Bush that "we are dealing with the most radical elements" in Iran because "they can deliver and the moderates can't." The person who conveyed this information to Mr. Bush was Amiram Nir, adviser to Shimon Peres when Peres was Israeli prime minister. At that time Mr. Nir was the principal Israeli on a team of Americans and Israelis negotiating an arms sale with the Iranians.

According to members of Mr. Bush's staff, Mr. Nir's remarks were passed on in a memo to Vice Adm. John Poindexter, who at that time was the president's national security adviser and a key figure in the arms deal, and other White House staff members. In addition, Mr. Bush met regularly with Col. Oliver North, a Poindexter deputy who was deeply involved in the arms deal, and with the president himself. It would be odd if he said nothing to them about his conversation with Mr. Nir unless, of course, he saw no need to tell them something he was sure they already knew.

If U.S. officials were aware they were dealing with the radicals who control the government, it follows that the sole purpose of selling them arms was to get them to intervene with the militant Moslems holding Americans hostage in Lebanon. Hence, the last vestige of doubt that the arms were offered as ransom for the hostages has been removed. To hold otherwise is to say that Mr. Reagan was lied to by all of those around him and, moreover, that he was so gullible he never suspected a thing. It won't wash.

The story about dealing with moderates was a cover story made necessary by a policy of deceit and illegality sanctioned by President Reagan himself. To conceal the effort to trade arms for hostages, Mr. Reagan disregarded a law forbidding arms sales to terrorist states, ignored a requirement that certain members of Congress be told of covert activities and deceived high-ranking members of his own administration. Finally, and not surprisingly, the illegal Iran initiative intersected with the illegal Contras aid initiative, which involved similar evasions and falsehoods. The result is that Mr. Reagan has brought disgrace on himself, damaged his ability to lead the country and weakened America's credibility in the world.

The shameful episode calls into question not just the adequacy of the safeguards established for covert operations but the compatibility of such undertakings with a democratic system. It may very well be that what the nation has witnessed was less an aberration than an inevitable outcome of allowing an apparatus of secrecy and deceit to function alongside a system of openness, accountability and consensus.

## THE PLAIN DEALER
*Cleveland, OH, February 11, 1987*

In its scramble to explain the Iran-contra scandal, the White House finally has crossed over from the deliberately sublime to the incredibly ridiculous. As long as the administration argued that it needed to deal with Iranian moderates to ransom American hostages, it could at least limit the scandal to a debate over whether that decision was wise. Now, however, The Washington Post has published a memo describing a meeting between Vice President George Bush and an Israeli official in Jerusalem. At that meeting Bush was told, "we are dealing with the most radical elements (in Iran)." In his response to the story, presidential spokesman Marlin Fitzwater said: "The question of moderates and radicals is a semantic difference." Oh.

The White House belatedly contends that, in Iran, the terms "moderate" and "radical" are indistinct and, thus, merely titles of convenience. Even if you accept that false proposition, though, it is impossible to ignore the pivotal role the word "moderate" has played in presidential efforts to explain the blundering and duplicity. If the terms are meaningless in Iran, then why has the president consistently used them? How could he possibly have been trying to open a channel to Tehran moderates, as he has claimed, if such moderates don't exist?

Of course, there's a difference between moderates and radicals, even in Iran. A radical might want to obliterate the United States, whereas a moderate might want only to overthrow it. Such a distinction is relative, to be sure, but it does exist, and in the scheme of the president's decision to ransom hostages, it is pivotal. As early as 1980, Reagan was rejecting any thought of concessions to terrorists or terrorist-minded governments like the

one in Tehran. That key policy—still the correct course—was an important factor in his election. That's why when Reagan came face to face with the intractability of terrorism, he chose to explain his arms deals in terms of contacts with the lesser of two evils. Now, even that unpleasant compromise seems to have been deliberate fiction.

In the wake of the Iran-contra scandal, Reagan's White House has been accused of being rudderless and inert—a partisan assessment that is given body when the administration resorts to laughable, semantical niggling. If Reagan wants to salvage the remainder of his term, his only choice is to force his minions to produce a full and honest accounting of the decisions that led to the hostage ransoms and the subsequent transfer of funds to rebel forces in Nicaragua. Failure to do so simply will aggravate the crisis of credibility that quickly is metastasizing from Reagan's foreign policies throughout his beseiged presidency.

□

As the hospitalization of former National Security Adviser Robert McFarlane illustrates, the Iran-contra scandal is exacting a mounting human toll. There's no conclusive evidence that McFarlane deliberately overdosed on Valium, but the question of attempted suicide is impossible to ignore. Reports indicate that since the crisis broke open, McFarlane has been suffering from severe depression. Stress is an inherent part of any vital White House post, but the administration's reluctance to admit its mistakes, accept its blame and get on with the business of guiding the nation compounds the problem and raises the potential of adding tragedy to incompetence. McFarlane has sent a signal that the White House must not ignore.

TIM MENEES © 1986 PITTSBURGH POST-GAZETTE

THIS ISN'T A KIDNAPPING--WE'RE JUST MODERATES LOOKING FOR SOME SUPPORT FROM MR. REAGAN!

Reagan: No hostage deal

SCREEE

# The Courier-Journal

*Louisville, KY, December 5, 1986*

WHAT kind of regime was the Reagan administration helping to keep in business when it shipped arms to Iran? It is one that, according to Amnesty International, is responsible for "large-scale execution of prisoners for both political and non-political offenses, following summary trials with no defense counsel and no right of appeal."

The Ayatollah Khomeini's Islamic republic also routinely resorts to the most grisly forms of torture to extract confessions. It persecutes such religious minorities as Bahais and Jews. It ruthlessly punishes men and teen-age boys who try to escape being sent to the front in Iran's six-year-old war with Iraq.

Many of these abuses have been cited by the U. S. State Department in its annual reports on the status of human rights around the world.

Nevertheless, some foreign policy experts in this country have endorsed President Reagan's overtures to Iran — if not the exchange of arms sales for American hostages — on grounds that the government in Tehran has begun to show more "moderation" in its dealings with other countries in the region.

Maybe so. But whether or not the Ayatollah's regime is still trying to export terror and subvert its Middle East neighbors, it is clearly guilty of terrorizing its own people. It also continues to wage a war with Iraq that is, in terms of casualties, the bloodiest conflict in the world.

America had no business keeping that war going by peddling weapons to one of the combatants. And to the extent that the arms sales contribute to the survival of the repressive regime in Tehran, the Reagan administration is indirectly responsible for the fate of that regime's domestic victims.

I DON'T KNOW, IMAM! IT WAS WORKING FINE ALL DAY YESTERDAY...

MacNELLY Chicago Tribune

# TULSA WORLD

*Tulsa, OK, December 5, 1986*

IN this country, opinion is still divided on the Iranian arms deal. President Reagan still refuses to admit it was a mistake.

In Iran, there is no disagreement. The arms-for-hostages trade — or as President Reagan calls it, the effort to establish ties with "Iranian moderates," — is a cause for celebration.

Parliament Speaker Hashemi Rafsanjani, presumably one of the moderates with whom the Reagan administration wished to establish rapport, had this to say Wednesday in a speech to 100,000 young conscripts on their way to the battle front:

"The greatest powers of the world and the most Satanic enemies of mankind thought they were undefeatable. ...

"They knelt before you ... held out their begging arms asking for your attention and ties. They hoped that you and your leaders would talk to them. This kind of victory is rare in history."

The draftees punctuated his speech with repeated shouts of "Death to America."

So much for the Iranian moderates.

A disquieting trend in the current crisis is that many in Congress and some of the President's most vocal critics have more or less forgotten the original sin — that the U.S. and Israel secretly provided arms to the most brutal regime on earth while publicly pretending to oppose terrorist governments. These critics are more alarmed by the fact that some of the profit from the arms deal was sent to the contras opposing the communist government of Nicaragua.

Part of the reason for this focus is that the gift to the contras appeared on its face to be a violation of the law whereas the arms sale to Iran technically might have been legal. So perhaps the critics are taking their best shot in a strictly legal sense.

But it is an interesting — and troubling — fact that many members of Congress can tolerate a cynical scheme to send guns to the Ayatollah Khomeini but are outraged because White House underlings may have bootlegged some money to a group trying to fight communism.

It's a crazy, mixed up world.

## The Chattanooga Times

*Chattanooga, TN, February 11, 1987*

Under fire for selling arms to the Ayatollah Khomeini, President Reagan has repeatedly stressed that the arms deals were an overture to "moderates" in Tehran, an effort to strengthen "moderate" elements of the government there. But now the White House has acknowledged that the United States was not dealing with "moderates" at all, but with perhaps the most radical elements of the governing elite.

From the beginning critics argued that the administration's "moderates" rationale was a cover story, designed to make the arms deals more palatable to the public and to disguise the purpose of ransoming American hostages in the Middle East. And from the beginning, logic was on the side of the critics.

To describe any powerful element of the radical regime in Iran as moderate is to pervert the meaning of that word. And, as White House spokesman Marlin M. Fitzwater has now admitted, the administration simply chose to describe as moderate anyone who would cooperate. "We were hoping for moderates in the sense of elements who were willing to work with us," Mr. Fitzwater said. " 'Moderate' was a term used to define those kinds of people." It was a convenient but meaningless definition. An Iranian government desperately in need of military equipment for its war with Iraq was willing to work with the United States not because of any moderate political philosophy but purely and simply in return for arms.

The idea that selling arms to supposed moderates would somehow strengthen them for the post-Khomeini era in Iran is equally contrived, given that the arms did not go to any so-called moderate element in the government but to the armed forces of the ayatollah.

Nevertheless, the administration clung to its "moderates" story until last weekend when it became known that Vice President Bush had been told last July by an Israeli official that "we were dealing with the most radical elements in Iran" because only they could be helpful in securing the freedom of American hostages. On Monday Mr. Fitzwater reluctantly conceded that what Mr. Bush had been told may have been true. The White House spokesman said he would not "rule in or out" any terms to describe the Iranians with whom the administration has been working.

It is just one more development that proves President Reagan's willingness to mislead the public in hopes of limiting the political damage from his wholly misguided initiative in Iran.

## THE KANSAS CITY STAR

*Kansas City, MO, February 10, 1987*

One of the few remaining parts of President Reagan's story about Iran has collapsed with the revelation of a memorandum written last year by Craig L. Fuller, chief of staff for Vice President George Bush. The memo makes clear that the administration was dealing not with Iranian "moderates" but with the very extremists Reagan claims he wanted to undermine.

The memo recounts a briefing that Bush received last July from Amiram Nir, an Israeli official who was negotiating with Iran on Reagan's behalf. It quoted Nir as telling Bush: "We are dealing with the most radical elements . . . They were called yesterday and thanked and today more phone calls. This is good because we've learned they can deliver and the moderates can't."

The White House has always maintained—indeed, continues to maintain—that Reagan dealt only with moderates. This story never seemed to fit well with the claim that these friends of ours in Tehran had power over the terrorists holding Americans hostage in Lebanon.

The memo further damages the administration's credibility on Iran. That credibility has already taken so many hits that officials have given up trying to repair the damage. Reagan has fallen silent, hiding behind claims that he cannot discuss matters under investigation as though he were involved in a criminal trial and must, on his attorney's advice, keep quiet.

The Fuller memo shoots down all the the administration's arguments about fostering moderation in Iran. It leaves the administration bare in facing the objections of foreign countries to our Iran policy. It makes it that much more ridiculous for the White House to claim it wasn't trading arms for hostages, or that it didn't abandon its own anti-terrorism policy.

We are back to a familiar question: Has the president knowingly deceived the public or is he simply so out of touch that he has no idea what his top aides are doing? Administration officials, intent on protecting the president's image, would have us believe he has just been out of touch.

Yet that claim begins to seem worse than the possibility that Reagan has simply lied to the public. It portrays a president who had no idea with whom he was dealing because other top government officials—including the vice president—deliberately kept him in the dark.

Bush aides are busy claiming that other officials knew what was going on, too. No matter who else knew, it seems hard to imagine that Bush would not have raised the subject with the president if Reagan didn't already know he was dealing with Iranian crazies.

Did he just forget? Or has he purposely misled the people for the last three months? If he has not intentionally deceived the country, does he plan to denounce Bush and fire a lot of top officials for doing so? We don't know. The president's not talking.

A RADICAL IRANIAN          A MODERATE IRANIAN

BE MY MODERATE!

@THE BOSTON GLOBE

## Arkansas Gazette

*Little Rock, AR, February 11, 1987*

The Reagan administration's credibility in the Iran arms-contra aid scandal continues to erode as time passes and as various inquiries quietly go their own ways. Take, for example, the dealings in the sale of arms to Iran, several versions of which keep dribbling from the White House.

When the sales of arms to Iran became public in November, the administration's explanation was that the sale was undertaken to establish some relationship with moderate elements in Iran because the country occupies such a strategic position in the Persian Gulf region. As time went along, there was a begrudging recognition that, yes, there was some hope that these contacts might also lead to the release of Americans held hostage in Lebanon because their kidnappers were known to have close contacts with Iran.

In a nationally televised speech on November 13, President Reagan said that "we did not — repeat — did not trade weapons or anything else for hostages nor will we."

Now, however, comes another bit of information, disclosed first in *The Washington Post* and verified subsequently by an aide to Vice President George Bush as being authentic. The memorandum cited in the report was by another aide to Bush and it was about a meeting Mr. Bush had last July with an Israeli official. The memo makes clear that the focus of the new relationship with Iran centered on the release of the hostages in Lebanon, and that the dealings were with the most radical elements in Iran because they were the ones who could deliver.

In responding to this news, White House spokesman Marlin Fitzwater has been practicing what some may call a little revisionism, dismissing the distinctions between "moderate" and "radical" factions in Iran as only a "semantic difference" of no significance. This may be true (Iran's rulers include no moderates), but it is the first time since the whole scandal reached public notice three months ago that the White House has backed off the theme that the administration was dealing with moderates.

The fact is, as it has been all along, that the American arms were funneled to Iran to help its radical government fight a war with neighboring Iraq and to win release of Americans held hostage in Lebanon. Thus the arms went to shore up a radical regime not only against outsiders but also against anyone — "moderates"? — who might rival the ayatollahs. Why the administration tried for so long to float the idea that it was dealing only with "moderates" and then dropped it with revelations of the memo on Mr. Bush's meeting last July only the administration knows right now.

Lest we forget, the sale of arms was made not to individuals but to a nation that remains on the United States' list of nations that support terrorism, and one that has links with terrorist groups in Lebanon that blew up a United States marine barracks and now hold American hostages. The various investigators, including the special counsel, have a great deal of work to do before these puzzles are put together and the result most likely will not be a pleasant sight.

## Roanoke Times & World-News

*Roanoke, VA, February 15, 1987*

'WHEN I USE a word," said Humpty-Dumpty in Lewis Carroll's "Through the Looking Glass," "it means just what I choose it to mean — no more and no less." The Reagan administration, hoist on its own petard in the Iran-Contra affair, has discovered the utility of flexible definitions.

Not much about the White House version of the arms deal with Iran has stayed the same since President Reagan first tried to explain it publicly. There have been too many conflicting versions from too many administration insiders.

One part of the story, however, remained fairly consistent: The United States had made its approach to Iran, and its offer of arms, as a way of wooing "moderate" elements in that regime.

The idea that any such elements have influence in Iran has always been suspect. But it has been put forward as the essential justification for the deal. Unless the White House could say that it was trying to open a dialogue with Iranian moderates, this was nothing more than a swap of arms for hostages — something that the president has sworn he never did and never will do.

But in recent days, a secret U.S. government memo has come to light that shatters this contention. The memo reports on a meeting of Vice President Bush with an Israeli official, Amiram Nir. Israel, remember, was an intermediary for the arms deal, and the United States relied on Israeli intelligence in setting up its contacts with Iran.

The memo says Nir told Bush last summer that "we are dealing with the most radical elements" in Iran because "we've learned they can deliver and the moderates can't." Whether Bush passed on this information to Reagan is unspecified. But the White House has not disputed the accuracy of the memo.

Instead, presidential spokesman Marlin Fitzwater now pooh-poohs the notion of trying to pin definitions on factions in Iran. It's a semantic question that could never be resolved in that country, he says: "We were hoping for moderates in the sense of elements who were willing to work with us. But you can define moderates and radicals in hundreds of different ways, particularly in I ."

Fitzwater is new in his job, . . . fast. At a White House press b . . . in Reagan's State of the Union address, the president had said that the risk he'd taken in Iran didn't work, but that he did not feel it was wrong to seek freedom for U.S. hostages in Lebanon. "Once you've said that," Fitzwater commented, "it doesn't matter whether you try to label it radicals, moderates, whatever." In other words, the president has rendered past definitions, and versions of his Iran-Contra story, inoperative. And the rest of us never knew it until now.

The press, ever pesky, wanted to know whether the administration would stop describing the Iranians it contacted as moderates. "I'm not going to rule in or out any terms," Fitzwater airily replied. "We'll probably use it and probably, maybe not use it."

And if you do, will the American people believe you? Probably, maybe not. The same goes for just about anything the White House has to say at this point.

# Former NSC Adviser McFarlane in Suicide Bid

Former national security adviser Robert McFarlane was hospitalized February 9, 1987 after taking an overdose of Valium, a tranquilizer. Although the estimated 20 to 30 pills that McFarlane took were not sufficient to kill him, police and doctors regarded the incident as an apparent attempt at suicide. McFarlane had been scheduled to meet later that day with the special commission appointed by President Reagan to study the workings of the National Security Council (NSC) with an eye to preventing incidents like the sale of arms to Iran. Although the meeting was to be lengthy, it was not expected to be confrontational. Two of the commission members, former Republican Senator John Tower of Texas and Brent Scowcroft, who had held the national adviser security post under President Gerald Ford, had been mentors to McFarlane in the early stages of his career.

Friends of McFarlane's were quoted as saying that he had been depressed recently because he felt that he had failed as national security adviser, not because he feared the investigations. Also, he was said to be concerned about finding an appropriate job. His career of government service had ended in December 1985 when he resigned from the NSC after losing a bureaucratic turf battle with White House chief of staff Donald Regan. McFarlane had then taken an academic post at the Georgetown Center for Strategic and International Affairs. McFarlane had also reportedly suffered from severe lower back pain, for which the Valium had been prescribed.

## The Virginian-Pilot

*Norfolk, VA, February 13, 1987*

However well-intentioned the White House attempt to develop an opening to Iranians who might come to power following the demise of the Ayatollah Khomeini, the way in which the administration pursued a connection to Iran was clumsy, the swap of arms for hostages held in Lebanon naive and the diversion of proceeds from the arms sale to the Nicaraguan Contras duplicitous.

That former National Security Adviser Robert McFarlane should be depressed by the mistaken course and costly failure of the Iranian venture is understandable. Few could wish Mr. McFarlane ill or, indeed, feel less than compassion for him in his struggle with the psychological pain that prompted his apparent suicide attempt.

Friends of the former presidential aide report that he reproaches himself for setting in motion the events that have severely damaged the Reagan presidency. But Mr. McFarlane should temper his harsh judgment on himself by recognizing that Mr. Reagan and his White House circle have demonstrated all along a preference for jury-rigged responses to a wide range of sensitive challenges, routinely ignoring conservative institutional procedures for the formation, disciplined review and execution of foreign and domestic policies.

No president and his staff have a corner on wisdom, but the Reagan presidency, even more than previous administrations, has been impervious to the advice of well-informed counselors. By going it alone on Iran, after scorning the objections of Secretary of State George Shultz and Defense Secretary Caspar Weinberger, Mr. Reagan was burned, badly.

In using his National Security Council for a series of covert adventures, Mr. Reagan abused the power provided by the Constitution to the executive branch. Although Henry Kissinger, as national security adviser to President Nixon, slipped off secretly to Peking to prepare the ground for rapprochement between the United States and China, his mission was a sharply limited one. In no administration other than Mr. Reagan's would the National Security Council have been encouraged to plunge into clandestine operations beyond its charter and competence. The sad result of those operations is not wholly Mr. McFarlane's fault.

## THE ARIZONA REPUBLIC

*Phoenix, AZ, February 11, 1987*

APPEARANCES often disguise how brittle people can be beneath a tough exterior. Robert C. McFarlane, we now know, was brittle, and he apparently broke under the strain of the Iran arms sale investigation.

This stoic ex-Marine lieutenant colonel and former head of the National Security Council hid behind a facade which often gave the impression of icy aloofness, of condescending superiority.

McFarlane's apparent suicide attempt, just hours before a scheduled appearance before the Tower commission investigating the role and procedures of the NSC, reveals how deeply the affair wounded him.

Sen. Gordon Humphrey, R-N.H., sounded a warning to congressional investigators and press critics, urging all "to have more regard" for the subjects of their criticism. It is not necessary, the senator said, to hound people, to exact every last pound of flesh out of some misguided sense of vindictiveness or partisan advantage.

Bud McFarlane was roundly, and deservedly, criticized for the Iran arms sale fiasco. It was a policy disaster. It was not, however, a "scandal" as some have conveniently labeled it. The word scandal connotes some kind of personal impropriety, corruption, moral transgression or monetary gain.

Whatever the shortcomings of his Iran policy, McFarlane acted as a patriotic and loyal American in what he believed to be the best interests of his country. The personal ridicule to which he has been subjected — criticism which should have been reserved for his policy not his person — has been unfair and undeserved.

While McFarlane's successor at the NSC, Adm. John Poindexter, and his assistant, Lt. Col. Oliver North, both have retreated behind the protection of their Fifth Amendment rights, McFarlane has testified whenever asked without benefit of access to his NSC files. Memory can be good, bad or convenient, and it should not be surprising that some of McFarlane's testimony is apparently self-contradictory or at odds with that of other administration officials. What had to hurt was the allegation that his memory was convenient, that he lied and deceived.

McFarlane was reported to be depressed and troubled in recent days over the ongoing problems he believed he was causing President Reagan. For a man possessed of his standards of integrity and loyalty, it must have been too much to bear, even for a Vietnam combat veteran. Perhaps the unfortunate incident will help restore a measure of mutual respect and civility to our public debate.

"IT'S NOT OUR FAULT! WE TOLD BUD TIME AND AGAIN TO 'JUST SAY NO'."

# THE
# KANSAS CITY STAR

*Kansas City, MO, February 12, 1987*

Seemingly alone among the figures in the Iran arms scandal, Robert McFarlane has tried to face the past. He has admitted personal errors that may cost the country dearly. In doing so, he has shown greater honesty—with himself and with the public—than has been shown by former colleagues or by the president he served.

McFarlane, Reagan's national security adviser until late 1985, played an important role at the start of the Iran deals. By the time he resigned he had serious doubts about the wisdom of those deals. By then, however, many other officials were involved. They wanted to continue playing Iran's game, and even brought McFarlane back into it several months later.

These other officials and former officials have spent the last three months scurrying for cover behind the Fifth Amendment, the prestige of the Oval Office, foggy memories, willful ignorance, absurd semantics, phony legal talk and outright lies.

McFarlane, meanwhile, did penance before congressional committees, presidential investigators, reporters and anyone else who wanted to know how the U.S. government could have been so stupid. "The irony is that the more information he gave, the more he became the target, because he was the only one furnishing information," said McFarlane's

attorney, Leonard Garment.

When the secret Iran deals became public, McFarlane quickly conceded that they had been a mistake. Contrary to statements by infuriated White House aides, McFarlane accepted the blame that was his.

"As a senior adviser to the president, I should have anticipated this potential outcome," McFarlane said in a Nov. 20 statement. "The failure to do so represents a serious error in judgment for which I accept full responsibility."

Although McFarlane botched his job as national security adviser, from all appearances he has served the country well in recent months. It was McFarlane, for example, who jogged memories at the White House about when Reagan first approved arms shipments to Iran.

He said Reagan approved arms shipments in August, 1985, long before the president signed an intelligence finding that made such shipments legal. Chief of Staff Don Regan has claimed that Reagan did not. The president himself says he can't recall. White House chronologies, according to a report by the Senate Select Committee on Intelligence, have offered "conflicting accounts" on this point.

A clear memory can be a troubling thing right now in Washington. Its value is increased by its rarity.

# THE LINCOLN STAR

*Lincoln, NE, February 12, 1987*

We would not expect former Reagan national security staffer Robert McFarlane to explain to the American people the facts surrounding his hospitalization this week for an overdose of a prescription tranquilizer. Police view the overdose as a suicide attempt, while McFarlane's attorney called that "the most irresponsible and obscene piece of sourcing and reporting I've heard of in my whole professional life."

Whatever the truth of the matter, McFarlane has obviously been taking medication for depression. That is a personal thing of no great consequence insofar as the general public is concerned but the reason for it could be significant.

Sen. Patrick J. Leahy, D-Vt., is vice chairman of the Senate Select Committee on Intelligence that is investigating the Iran-Contra issue in which McFarlane has had so prominent a part.

"I DON'T KNOW WHAT would have prompted this amount of strain," Leahy said of McFarlane's illness. "I think there are others who probably should have a lot more concern than Col. McFarlane does."

A decorated Marine officer and a man of high patriotic ideals, McFarlane might well be emotionally drained from his Iran-Contra

experience. He has been a key witness in Congress, his testimony even linking President Reagan to an early awareness of U.S. arms aid to Iran in exchange for U.S. hostages in Lebanon.

That testimony contradicts the public statements of the president.

So McFarlane could be suffering great stress simply from such a conflict. On the other hand, many other possibilities exist.

VICE ADM. JOHN M. Poindexter was superior to North, serving as Reagan's national security advisor. Poindexter has offered no public testimony.

Is it possible McFarlane is stressed by lack of higher testimony that would tend to improve his image? Is it possible that McFarlane may find himself in that most troubling position of all, unable to fully explain matters in deference to his allegiance to the president?

Does McFarlane, in short, see himself as a fall guy, after many years of meritorious service to his country? Hopefully, McFarlane will hang in there, as he offers one of a rather few possibilities for investigators to finally unravel the real story of our secret relations with Iran and their connection to Lebanon hostages and Contra rebels of Nicaragua.

# Tower Commission Blames Reagan, Aides for 'Chaos' in Scandal

President Reagan, confused and unaware, allowed himself to be misled by dishonest staff members who organized the trade of arms to Iran for hostages held in Lebanon and pursued a secret war against the Nicaraguan government, the Tower Commission concluded February 23, 1987. The Tower Commission was a special review board appointed to review the National Security Council (NSC). The 300-page document quoted dozens of secret communications among senior national security officials, showing how United States policy had evolved into "chaos" as "amateurish" staff members failed to subject their complex dealings with Iran, Israel, the contra rebels in Nicaragua and various arms dealers to a comprehensive policy review. The report charged that Reagan had failed to "insist upon accountability and performance review," allowing the NSC process to collapse.

While carefully wording its criticisms of Reagan's "personal management style," the report bluntly assailed numerous other top officials:

■ White House chief of staff Donald Regan "must bear responsibility for the chaos," the report said, charging that "more than almost any chief of staff of recent memory, he asserted personal control over the White House staff and sought to extend this control to the national security adviser."

■ Former national security adviser Robert McFarlane failed to fully inform cabinet members about the progress of the Iran initiative. His successor, Vice Adm. John Poindexter, "actively misled" cabinet members.

■ Secretary of State George Shultz and Defense Secretary Caspar Weinberger, while opposing the initiative, "actively distanced themselves from the march of events."

■ The former director of the Central Intelligence Agency (CIA), William Casey, allowed the CIA to lose control of the operation to the NSC and failed to tell Reagan or Congress about it.

The Tower Commission had been appointed to study the workings of the NSC and to make recomendations on ways to change the NSC process so that disasters like the Iran-contra operation would not recur. But the members of the panel went beyond its mandate, concluding that "NSC process did not fail; it simply was largely ignored." The panel recommended no major changes in the law authorizing the NSC but examined the Iran-contra affair in great detail as a "case study" of how the process was ignored.

The commission, known formally as the President's Special Review Board, had been appointed by Reagan in November 1986, following the administration's announcement that it had discovered that funds from the arms sales had been diverted to the contras. The panel's members were John Tower, a former Republican senator from Texas who chaired the Senate Armed Services Committee; Brent Scowcroft, a retired Air Force general who had served as national security adviser under President Gerald Ford; and Edmund Muskie, a former Democratic senator from Maine who had briefly been secretary of state under President Jimmy Carter.

The three members held a press conference to announce the release of the report. They were introduced to the press and a national television audience by Reagan, who had promised to "carefully study" the report and respond to it in a televised address in the coming week. At the press conference, the commission members were cautious in their criticisms and insistent that, despite their differing political views, they had not disagreed over the substance of their report. "The President did make mistakes," Tower asserted. He added that "every president made some mistakes from time to time, some of far greater consequence than the ones President Reagan has made." Tower said that Reagan had not been involved in an effort to cover-up the scandal. "We don't use the term cover-up," he said. But Tower asserted that "there was a deliberate effort to mislead" by those who prepared a chronology for Reagan in November 1986. In its account of the arms shipments, the report confirmed that the deal originated with two motives: President Reagan's emotional commitment to the release of the hostages held in Lebanon and a "latent and unresolved" geopolitical interest in better U.S. ties with Iran to prevent the Soviet Union from gaining a foothold in that strategically important nation. After the arms shipments began, however, the motives quickly evolved into a strict arms-for-hostages trade, the commission reported.

the **Charleston Gazette**

*Charleston, WV, March 5, 1987*

**H**IDDEN offenses committed in the White House in pursuit of President Reagan's secret war against Nicaragua and secret arming of Iran undoubtedly will continue surfacing for months, perhaps years.

Buried in the 350 pages of the Tower Commission report are many clues to wrongdoing. Examples:

▲ About $20 million received from Iran cannot be traced. The concealed, tangled, amateurish nature of the money-handling "invited kickbacks and payoffs," the report said. White House aide Oliver North funneled cash through banks in Switzerland, the Cayman Islands, Bermuda and Panama.

▲ Congress was deceived. In a confidential White House memo, North described how he had misinformed the House Intelligence Committee about his role in directing covert aid to the contra rebels. His boss, Vice Adm. John Poindexter, replied: "Well done."

▲ A diagram in North's safe outlined 23 organizations used as conduits for money and weapons for the contras. Three were right-wing committees run by Carl "Spitz" Channell from Elkins who brought aging, conservative donors to meet North and Reagan.

▲ Three North memos imply that the president knew of the secret money pipeline. On May 16, 1986, North told Poindexter: "I have no idea what Don Regan does or does not know re my private U.S. operation, but the President obviously knows why he has been meeting with several select people to thank them for their support for Democracy in CentAm [Central America]."

▲ North's operation, code-named Project Democracy, built a secret airfield in Costa Rica. North said in a memo that he threatened Costa Rican President Oscar Arias with a cutoff of U.S. foreign aid if he exposed the airstrip. North informed Poindexter he had gone "well beyond my charter in dealing w/a head of state this way and in making threat/offers that may be impossible to deliver." Poindexter replied: "You did the right thing, but let's try to keep it quiet."

▲ Israeli leaders who urged delivery of U.S. weapons to Iran wanted to prolong Arab-vs.-Arab warfare and to create markets for Israeli weapons — goals not benefiting America. Notes of White House discussions of the Israeli plan are missing — a situation called "appalling" and suspicious.

▲ The Israelis "pressed Mr. Ghorbanifar on the U.S.," the report said. Thus the White House utilized Iranian arms dealer Manucher Ghorbanifar, although the CIA previously labeled him "neither reliable nor trustworthy."

Step by step, a tower of evidence is growing in the scandal, just as it did in the Watergate affair a decade ago.

No matter what excuses are offered to absolve the president in this mess, he bears the primary guilt. When he set out to wage a clandestine war against Nicaragua and to conduct a furtive Iranian policy — both concealed from Congress and the American people — the course was set for calamity, like a Greek tragedy that proceeds inexorably to doom.

# The Washington Post

*Washington, DC, February 27, 1987*

FROM JOHN TOWER, Edmund Muskie and Brent Scowcroft comes an incisive and painstaking report that becomes the new base line for both an understanding of the Iran-contra affair and for addressing the astonishing lapses and derelictions in policy making that created this mess in the first place. It is devastating.

The report adds to the store of what was known about unorthodox funding, from various sources, including profits from the Iran arms sales, for the Nicaraguan contras. Its centerpiece, however, is the rich and freshly detailed picture it draws of what one of the rogues, Lt. Col. Oliver North, called at one point "the damndest operation I have ever seen."

The report is principally a catalogue of the human failings that no policy process, however deftly organized, run or even reformed, could altogether screen out. Adm. John Poindexter, at one time national security adviser, seems out of his depth, devious, furtive, negligently focused on narrow operational goals, forever concerned that the list of those in the know be shortened, that this one or that one be walled out. His aide, Col. North, inventing fantasies, bullying his way around, is absolutely off the wall, with an unfortunate talent for mesmerizing his superiors. Read Robert McFarlane's statement to him that "if the world only knew how many times you have kept a semblance of integrity and gumption to U.S. policy, they would make you Secretary of State." (That Col. North was not made secretary of state is one of the few blessings one can think of in reading this report.) On his own account, Mr.

McFarlane is at best confusing and at times disingenuous. George Shultz and Caspar Weinberger, though more right in tactical judgment where the national security cowboys were wrong, unaccountably failed to raise their strong dissents to the consistent hollers that alone might have awakened the president. Meanwhile, Donald Regan, chief of staff, was carrying on a monumental dereliction of duty to the president he ostensibly served.

President Reagan is reaping a measure of praise for opening himself to the Tower Commission's critique. The commission was inclined to believe, furthermore, that he was telling the truth. But it is chilling to see a president so utterly given to sentiment over the hostages, so incurious and uncritical about the events that were unfolding around him and so vulnerable to the weaknesses of character and lapses of judgment of the people in whom he had put his trust. His was an administration in the back seat of a car rolling down a hill with no one at the wheel.

The commission has some intelligent things to say about the possibilities and the limits of tinkering with the policy-making mechanism. As experienced Washington hands, however, the commission's members realize that no process can save a president from himself. This is where it places the principal responsibility for this affair. Mr. Reagan introduced the commission at the White House yesterday and, appearing somewhat shaken, at once left the stage. When he returns to it, next week, he will be under brutal pressure to show he has learned from this ordeal and has the strength to pass beyond it.

# The Hutchinson News

*Hutchinson, KS*
*February 27, 1987*

Moses did the job with 10 short commandments.

The Tower Commission decided it needed to write a book.

The Tower Commission was President Reagan's official investigator of the Iranian scandal. In its huge report Thursday, the commission gave the president the benefit of the doubt. It viewed him as merely ignorant and incompetent. It viewed his chief aides as liars and thieves of public property.

The Tower Commission's findings are consistent. Ronald Reagan is out of touch with reality, with his administration, and with the guiding principles of this nation as shown by his reliance on people like Regan, North, Poindexter, Casey, Watt, Burford, Deaver and Meese.

He has surrounded himself with incompetents whom he describes as heroes, in a frighteningly unreal world in which the rewriting of history and truth is embraced as readily as the writing of fiction and illusion.

And he still does not see it.

"I think it's possible to forget," he quipped on the eve of the report's release.

"Everybody that can remember what they were doing on Aug. 8, 1985, raise your hands," he said, trying idiotically to excuse his purported ignorance of approving one of the more calamitous decisions in the history of American foreign policy.

He had promised never to trade with terrorists. Yet he not only secretly agreed to trade with terrorists, he sent them arms even as they tortured to death a leading American foreign agent. Before the nation last fall, he went on national television to argue how small the shipments of arms to the thugs were, even as his aides were working feverishly to doctor the official records.

A greater authority will judge compliance with two of those Ten Commandments.

But a nation must instantly repudiate the lies, thefts, stupidity and incompetence of an administration that has wrecked foreign policy, created havoc in the nation's domestic heartland and holds a finger on the button that could unleash 30,000 nuclear warheads.

# Minneapolis Star and Tribune

*Minneapolis, MN, February 27, 1987*

The explosion you heard Wednesday was the Tower Commission delivering its report on National Security Council mismanagement of the Iran-contras affair. Everyone knew the impact would be greater than imagined at the commission's inception last fall, but the shock was stunning nonetheless. The commission pictures top White House advisers as inept or worse. It does not spare the secretaries of state and defense, who opposed the arms-for-hostage dealings but failed to exert their full influence. Nor does it spare the man at the top. President Reagan therefore will have much to account for when he addresses the nation on television next week.

But Reagan will do so without the same burden Richard Nixon carried as the dimensions of the Watergate scandal became known. This is more a case of presidential ineffectiveness than of venality. Public support for Reagan remains substantial despite public disapproval of much of what his administration has done. Concern for Reagan, even sympathy, are more evident than the antipathy so often exhibited toward Nixon.

In the commission's report the damning comment that sums up its critique of the president is this: He "did not seem to be aware of the way in which the (Iran arms sales) operation was implemented and the full consequences of U.S. participation." Commission chairman John Tower, a conservative Republican and a Reagan ally, offered his own

summing up in yesterday's press conference. The president was poorly advised, Tower said, and poorly served, and he should have monitored what his advisers were doing.

Those low-key comments were apt. So were several by the other panelists, former Secretary of State Edmund Muskie and former National Security Adviser Brent Scowcroft. But the report itself best conveys the flavor of a tangentially involved president nodding vague approval to advisers operating in duplicitous, unprofessional and perhaps illegal ways. For example:

". . . even if the president in some sense consented to or approved the transactions, a serious question of law remains . . . . The consent did not meet the conditions of the Arms Export Control Act" and "was never reduced to writing. It appears to have been conveyed to only one person. The president himself has no memory of it . . . the requirement for congressional notification was ignored."

Tower and his colleagues have produced a report that deals harshly and, it appears, fairly with the Reagan administration's national-security apparatus. The president's response yesterday was a promise to make the necessary reforms. We hope he realizes, finally, how grave were the mistakes he mentioned so casually in his State of the Union speech. The first test of recognition will come next week when he speaks to the nation.

## LEXINGTON HERALD-LEADER
*Lexington, KY, February 27, 1987*

The results of the first inquiry into the Iran-contra affair are now public. Those results are hardly flattering to President Reagan or his administration.

The report of the Tower Commission confirms many facts already reported. It says that the deal almost immediately turned into an arms-for-hostages swap. It points out the disastrous effects of this policy on the nation's credibility and on the president's efforts to fight terrorism.

The report is appropriately harsh in its judgments of several key government officials. Its criticism of White House chief of staff Donald Regan is blunt and well founded. So is the criticism of former National Security Adviser John Poindexter and former CIA Director William Casey. The criticism of the self-preserving attitudes of Secretary of State George Shultz and Defense Secretary Caspar Weinberger also is on target.

But for all its apparent thoughtfulness, the report is ultimately unsatisfying. It leaves unanswered the most important questions arising from this affair.

That should not be surprising, because the commission was not appointed to answer all questions. Its primary mission was to report to the president on the role of the National Security Council in the Iran-contra affair.

Understanding that agency's role is important, no doubt. It is also important to understand just how so misguided a policy as selling arms to Iran was put into action.

But there is now general agreement that the arms sales to Iran were a mistake. While it's important to understand how that mistake was made and to prevent similar ones, that understanding will not address the most important questions left unanswered.

One group of those questions concerns basic tenets of constitutional law. Profits from the arms sales were diverted to Nicaraguan rebels in direct contradiction of United States law. The diversion appears to have been directed by military officers. The diversion amounted to an effort to use public funds to finance a war. Congress had disapproved our financing of that war.

Who was responsible for these apparent violations of law and the Constitution? Under whose authority were military officers proceeding in this fashion? How could no one in the administration not see that this situation raised grave issues of legality and constitutionality?

The Tower Commission report sheds no light on these critical questions. The commission's chairman, former Sen. John Tower, told reporters yesterday that he did not believe the president knew of the diversion. But Tower offered no substantiation for the assertion.

The second set of questions is political but no less important. President Reagan has given conflicting accounts of this affair. As the Tower Commission report points out, Reagan seems to have had little understanding of the reality of his own policy or of its effects. The president apparently cannot recall key facts about this matter.

The question that arises is unpleasant but basic to the functioning of our democratic government: Is the president in control? The Tower Commission report leaves this key question unanswered.

As noted earlier, answering these questions was outside the scope of the Tower Commission. Its members — Tower, former Sen. Edmund Muskie and Gen. Brent Scowcroft — had a limited mission and appear to have discharged their responsibilities diligently. Now it falls to others to handle the remaining and more important questions.

The special prosecutor probing this affair will deal with matters of criminal misconduct. Special House and Senate committees will confront the constitutional issues and the question of the president's control of his administration.

Answers to those questions are probably months away. By the time these answers are known, the Tower Commission report is apt to appear little more than a footnote to this unhappy affair.

The Honolulu Advertiser

*Honolulu, HI, February 27, 1987*

Now that the Tower Commission Report is on the record, the essential question is what happens next in Washington with the Iran-contra situation.

President Reagan has to get rid of Chief of Staff Donald Regan, otherwise clean up the White House staff, and start working hard if he is to salvage what's left of his term in office. An analysis on the opposite page focuses on that aspect.

Beyond that, there will be more revelations to come from the special prosecutor and the House and Senate investigations. For there are still plenty of unanswered questions, including about the president's role.

Within its limited role of looking at the National Security Council, the Tower Commission seems to have done a credible job.

Although the report is highly critical of his administration, it may be the best the president could hope for. It says he personally didn't engage in a cover-up (although others did), that he was motivated by compassion for the hostages in Lebanon, and that he didn't know of the illegal diversion of profits from sales of arms to Iran to the Nicaraguan rebels.

But in a polite way it is also a damning portrait of an ill-informed, forgetful and inattentive president who was poorly served by aides who were both inept and authoritarian.

Moreover, the president himself must take the rap for approving flawed arms-for-hostages deals that not only didn't produce enough results but created an incentive for the seizure of more hostages.

Again, this report is not the end of the story, just another chapter. But the report's release to the public almost mandates the president to finally say he made mistakes, to regroup and reorganize, and to assure the American people he will be more attentive to his ultimate responsibilities in his final 23 months.

It may be the president's last opportunity to help clean up the largest blot on his administration's record.

## THE LINCOLN STAR

*Lincoln, NE, February 27, 1987*

The Tower Commission report on the U.S. overtures to Iran is a piece of work deserving of the careful attention of the American people. Without that, a substantial element of that report will be lost.

Clearly, the document is an indictment of the administration of President Ronald Reagan. Just as clearly, it is an indictment of the American people.

The American people elected Reagan, a man who simply lacks the intellectual capacity and the management skills to adequately handle his responsibilities. Reagan failed on two counts in his handling of this situation.

One, he was without sufficient world perspective to fully appreciate the ramifications of his dedication to the freedom of Americans held hostage in Lebanon. His emotional preoccupation with their freedom sent a message to subordinates that convinced them of the wisdom of trying to exchange arms with Iran for hostages in Lebanon.

**SUCH A DEVELOPMENT** is a natural consequence of Reagan's inclination to simplicity. That simplicity was demonstrated in his most recent reaction to skepticism about his stated inability to remember if he approved of arms shipments to Iran for exchange of the hostages.

At a meeting with business executives, Reagan asked of them: "Everybody that can remember what they were doing on Aug. 8, 1985, raise your hands."

No hands were raised. "I think it's possible to forget. Nobody's raised any hands," the president said as he chuckled.

In that exercise, Reagan trivialized what is the most significant foreign policy matter of his entire administration. Of course, people do not remember unimportant day to day events. They do not try to lodge within their memory an instant recall of the content of every single day of their lives.

Reagan's analogy is an insult to the intelligence of the American people and an indication of the shallowness of his own thinking.

**ALSO, THE** Tower Commission report paints a vivid picture of a presidential management style of fundamental weakness. He believed in and practiced the delegation of authority. But he went beyond delegation to the point of abdication of responsibility and that is a cardinal managerial sin.

In the Iran case, Reagan showed both intellectual and administrative inadequacy. The same two things have shown up consistently in his more than six years in the White House.

As the American people look to 1988 and the election of another president, they should find cause in Reagan's presidency to look for candidates with the skills demanded of the office. Reagan offered an engaging personality and a penchant for clever phrase-making, attributes far down the list of important credentials for a president.

The Wichita

## Eagle-Beacon

*Wichita, KS, February 28, 1987*

THE Tower Commission report on the Iran arms sale-hostage affair struck like a bolt from the heavens on Thursday, laying bare the failings of the Reagan presidency. Its central conclusion was that all that was planned, all that was done, and all that even was thought about was done in the name of one person: Ronald Reagan. Because of the president's management style of delegating everything he doesn't absolutely have to handle himself, then not monitoring the results to ensure proper performance, the management of the affairs of this country was in the hands of third- and fourth- and fifth-ranking aides during much of this whole tragic affair.

And "tragic" isn't too strong a word. The arms-for-hostage deals that Mr. Reagan's subordinates struck in his name undoubtedly were the reason other hostages then were taken, replenishing the terrorists' stock. The infusion of sophisticated American weaponry into the Iranian arsenal unquestionably has prolonged the terrible Iran-Iraq war, with recent Iraqi losses being attributed to the Iranians' new edge. Other nations, seeing the readiness with which the United States abandoned its embargo on arms sales to Iran, have had cause to be less circumspect in their own dealings.

Exceeding even the bizarre nature of such a foreign policy is the bizarre manner in which it was formulated: primarily by an aide to an aide to the president, a near-fanatical lieutenant colonel with former mental problems who operated, apparently, with almost unlimited, unquestioned powers. That Oliver North was doing Ronald Reagan's bidding he had no doubt, a perception that was heightened when the president called him a "national hero" even after it became evident what he had done.

The only way a president can manage the way Mr. Reagan has in the past is with first-rate people around him, people who don't just tell him what he wants to know, but will tell him when things are going wrong. Evidently the president did not have this kind of team in place; even his secretary of state, George Shultz, and his secretary of defense, Caspar Weinberger, were more interested in saving their own reputations than in insisting their president not flirt with terrorists in the skewed hope of getting the hostages back.

The Reagan administration's moment of truth comes next week, when the president goes before the people and tells them what he's going to do about this incredible failing in what had been one of the most successful American presidencies. Replacing his discredited chief of staff, Donald Regan, with the respected Howard Baker will help, but it's only a beginning. He still has to convince the once adoring public he indeed can govern, he remains in charge, and American foreign policy again will bring credit, instead of derision, to this nation. It will be the performance of the president's lifetime, with two years of continuing malaise being the awful price of failure.

THE FOG LIFTS AT FOGGY BOTTOM

## St. Paul Pioneer Press & Dispatch

*St. Paul, MN, March 1, 1987*

Correctly ripping the president and many of his men was not the only work of the Tower Commission — only its most riveting and best reported. Its investigation also makes sound, if unremarkable, recommendations about improving national security arrangements and procedures, both in current and succeeding administrations as well as in Congress.

For example, John Tower, Edmund Muskie and Brent Scowcroft recommend that "Congress consider replacing the existing intelligence committees of the respective houses with a new joint committee with a restricted staff to oversee the intelligence community, patterned after the Joint Committee on Atomic Energy that existed until the mid-1970s."

It is hard to envision any significant drawbacks to such a change, as it is hard to think of any productive reasons why administrations should be required to share twice that which they are inclined to share not at all.

Should administrations be legally bound to keep a small number of legislators informed of covert activities? Of course. Does such oversight serve presidents no less than Congress? Yes, again. And is not one of the reasons for Iranamok the fact that the Reagan team never gave anyone in Congress a chance to set them straight on their crazy ideas? Yes, a third time.

But the Reagan administration is neither the first nor will it be the last to chafe under congressional oversight obligations. Better to streamline those obligations, if safely possible, than to needlessly challenge what presidents and aides largely view as their own, constitutionally sanctioned business.

The Tower report also makes this obvious point: It is the responsibility of the national security adviser to ensure that "matters submitted for consideration by the [NSC] cover the full range of issues on which review is required; and that those issues are fully analyzed; that a full range of options is considered . . ."

Mr. Reagan entered office six years ago saying that his style was to encourage debate among colleagues and then make decisions based on those exchanges. The approach sounded fine. Yet one of the most disturbing points made by the Tower Commission and other reviews is that in the matter of Iranian arms, at least, internal debate was infrequent and lousy. Especially for this president, it's essential that the national security adviser recognize the value of intellectual agitation.

## Portland Press Herald

*Portland, ME, March 7, 1987*

In direct, plain language, the Tower commission charged that Secretary of State George P. Shultz and Defense Secretary Caspar W. Weinberger deliberately kept their distance from President Reagan's Iranian arms-for-hostages program at a time their advice was sorely needed.

"Their obligation," the board's report states, "was to give the president their full support and continued advice with respect to the program or, if they could not in conscience do that, to so inform the president. Instead they simply distanced themselves from the program. They protected the record as to their own positions on this issue. They were not energetic in attempting to protect the president from the consequences of his personal commitment to freeing the hostages."

Now the two Cabinet officials are distancing themselves again.

Shultz, traveling in Asia, maintains he did nothing wrong. In the climate of secrecy surrounding the arms dealing, he said, "I took the position that I wanted to know what I needed to know and the department should know what it needed to know to do our job." Not too bad.

Far worse is Weinberger's attempt to dismiss the Tower commission's findings, for, in the process, he all but dismisses the president, too.

Speaking Wednesday night, Reagan said the commission's "findings are honest, convincing and highly critical, and I accept them." In Boston a day later, Weinberger demurred. "The president didn't say anything at all about the part relating to George Shultz and me," he insisted. "Those aren't findings really; those are just conclusions and statements."

The irony is hard to miss. At a time when Reagan could use these two men to move forward, Shultz and Weinberger are busy protecting their rears.

Just what the Tower commission said they'd done in the first place.

## The Virginian-Pilot

*Norfolk, VA, March 2, 1987*

Among the Tower Commission's suggested remedies for the policy debacle it chronicled was creation of a new joint congressional committee to oversee U.S. intelligence matters. Excellent suggestion.

One of the key failures of the Reagan administration's formulation of arms-dealing with Iran and money-diversion to the Contras was that Congress was never notified. The administration's "obsession with secrecy" was the reason for this failure, the commission concluded.

The panel added, however, that some secrecy is justified, and the growth of intelligence committees in both the Senate and the House, each with large staffs, "provides cause for concern" — namely, Capitol Hill leaking sensitive intelligence.

That's a legitimate concern, although the White House deserves at least as much blame for leakage as the legislature. To control congressional leaks and to encourage more executive consultation with Congress, the Tower report recommended a merger of the two intelligence panels into one joint committee — with a restricted staff.

The model cited for this merger is the former Joint Atomic Energy Committee, which expired in 1977. The Joint Committee on Taxes, the congressional power behind last year's tax-reform law, is a current example of effective non-partisan joint legislating and oversight.

A joint intelligence oversight committee could streamline congressional procedure, limiting the number of people with access to sensitive information — thus limiting the potential for leaks.

There is no sure way of preventing the White House and the CIA from deceiving Congress in the name of "national security." But having a small, joint oversight committee would limit the rationale for such deception. The Iran-Contra affair points out the necessity of having congressional checks on the White House policy-making process, and any step that aids that oversight is a plus.

## Post-Tribune

*Gary, IN, March 1, 1987*

If the president's men who plotted the Iran arms caper were bank robbers or burglars, they could star in a movie. Their ineptness would make a great spoof.

But what they did to the country and to the presidency is no spoof. It is not funny.

**Our opinions**

What they did to President Ronald Reagan the man is not the important issue — he gave them authority and turned them loose, so he can pay the price of being inattentive. But they have damaged the office, and that is intolerable.

Reagan finally has been forced to start making changes. He had no choice. He can no longer just say, "Shucks, folks, everything is fine."

The Tower Commission report does not suggest that the president tried to mislead the country or to coverup the bungled arms deal. That may be true, but that conclusion is faint, dubious praise for a presidential performance. He did not know, probably did not understand, and obviously did not try to control what was happening. Deceit is bad, but the presidential weakness laid bare by this report may be just as bad.

There was a misguided trade of arms for hostages, a move that failed and made the hostage situation even worse. Reagan insisted that there would be no dealing with terrorists, but his escapade contradicted that proud, tough policy and embarrassed the country abroad.

The issue here is not so much an attempt to mislead, but a clear showing of a failure to lead at all.

Sending Chief of Staff Donald Regan on his way can't end the sorry story, even though replacing him with former Sen. Howard Baker brings some respectability to the White House. Regan served the president and the country poorly. But so did several others, when the president turned them loose on foreign policy.

The president is supposed to make foreign policy and oversee its conduct. Instead, some underlings wrote their own scripts and played games of intrigue and military adventure.

Rear Adm. John Poindexter was a misfit as national security adviser. The report said he "failed grievously."

Lt. Col. Oliver North has been revealed to be unstable, and a man who dreamed up so much fiction he may have believed his own stories.

When asked a question about criticism of him in the Tower report, North reminded news people of the Beatitude: "Blessed are those who are persecuted for righteousness' sake, for theirs is the kingdom of heaven." How touching.

He is the fellow who talked about God's promise to Abraham when he discussed the deal with the Iranians.

Of course, the deadly truth about the North and Poindexter operations is that they were supposed to be representing the best interests of the United States through policies created and directed by the president.

The president's image as a leader always has been built more on perceptions than on facts. Now the perceptions have changed and the facts still are lacking.

This is indeed a Looney Tunes scenario. Inside the White House circle, the actors are pointing at each other saying, "He did it."

The president has said he couldn't remember if he approved the first shipment of arms to Iran. He asked some visitors if they could remember what they were doing on a specific day. Some question. How could a president forget something so important?

The big question now is whether he remembers, or knows, how to govern.

## ST. LOUIS POST-DISPATCH

*St. Louis, MO, March 1, 1987*

The principal impression created by the Tower Commission report is one of a remote and confused president, one who did not even know what he had done about the Iran-Contra affair, or when.

Secondary to that is the finding of a "flawed process," in which contradictory policies were pursued and the implementation was unprofessional. Procedures were too informal and did not allow for a full hearing before the president or, at some point, notification of Congress. This finding, in effect, condemns the misuse of the National Security Council system.

We would not disagree with any of that, but it should be asked: What of the process itself, and what of the system?

The National Security Council is intended to give the chief executive advice and information. In this case, the NSC staff acted in a far different way. It ran its own covert operations. It became a hidden government. It sold arms to Iran and apparently diverted the proceeds to the Contras fighting in Nicaragua, part of this violating declared policy and part violating law.

Congress knew nothing about it until the press began to stumble upon some of the details. Administration officials developed cover stories that were not true and arranged for "plausible denials." Much of the secrecy and many of the lies were at least based on a more rational idea than the policies involved, for officials knew that the American people would be outraged if they learned their government was selling arms to a nation that inspired hostage-taking, with profits going to the Contras.

The Tower Commission is uncertain as to how much of this hidden government was concealed from President Reagan, considering his inattentiveness to it. In any event, he was responsible for it. But the portrait of the president and his hidden White House operation displays more than a flawed process. It demonstrates a disregard for the constitutional process.

This is the 200th anniversary of the Constitution, and it is fair to ask whether the Founding Fathers could ever remotely have imagined what has happened in the White House today. They established a series of checks and balances to prevent abuses of power at any level, and particularly at the level of the presidency.

It is often said that the president conducts foreign policy, but wait! He initiates treaties, with the consent of the Senate. He names ambassadors, with the consent of the Senate. He commands the armed forces, but Congress finances them. He may conduct war, but only if Congress declares it. At every step of the way, Congress is made a part of the process.

What is new to the process is the increasing efforts of presidents to develop covert operations short of war. Finally recognizing the dangers implicit in such executive actions, Congress passed a law requiring the president and the CIA to advise it of covert initiatives. In the Iran-Contra case, congressional intelligence committees were not advised; indeed, elaborate efforts were developed to hide the truth.

Thus Congress was not made part of the "flawed process" described by the Tower Commission. It was deliberately ignored in an assumption of arbitrary power. The process itself was not only flawed; it was wrong. It was an affront to the Constitution.

# Regan Ousted as Chief of Staff; Howard Baker Named Replacement

In a move that was dramatic even though it was widely expected, President Reagan February 27, 1987 accepted the resignation of White House chief of staff Donald Regan. He immediately named former Senate Majority Leader Howard Baker Jr. (R, Tenn.) as Regan's replacement. The moves came one day after the President received the report of the Tower Commission, the President's Special Review Board, chaired by former Sen. John Tower (R, Texas) that investigated the role of the National Security Council staff in the Iran-contra arms scandal. The report condemned Regan for the "chaos" in the White House that ensued after the Iran policy was disclosed. At a news conference, Baker stated that he would work to carry out the President's policies. "I will try to go forward with his programs as best as I know how," Baker said. "I do not expect any conflict. I am there to serve the President."

By all accounts, Regan had been living on borrowed time, politically speaking, for the last few weeks. Regan was widely blamed by Republicans for bungling the President's handling of the affair. Perhaps more significantly, he had alienated First Lady Nancy Reagan, who had reportedly opposed Regan's plan to push the President, who was still recovering from prostate surgery, to mount a vigorous counteroffensive.

Baker was offered the job (by his account for the second time) after former Sen. Paul Laxalt (R, Nev.) and former Transportation Secretary Drew Lewis reportedly turned it down. Upon hearing of the President's decision to replace him immediately, Regan submitted a terse, one sentence letter of resignation. There had been reports that Regan, at least, believed he had been promised a face-saving interval of a few days or weeks before his resignation would be required. Baker, who said he had "pretty much made up my mind" to run for president in 1988, declared he was now dropping out of the race. The replacement of Regan with Baker drew instant applause on Capitol Hill, with some members of Congress claiming that Baker had restored "instant credibility" to the White House.

## THE RICHMOND NEWS LEADER
*Richmond, VA, March 3, 1987*

The appointment of former Sen. Howard H. Baker as President Reagan's new chief of staff offers comfort that a savvy and Congress-wise veteran will be at the president's right hand, but it should not be seen as a cure-all for a White House run amok. To be sure, Baker enjoys considerably more respect on Capitol Hill than the stubborn Donald Regan, the man credited, or discredited, with guiding the president into the Iran-contra mess and shielding him not wisely, but too well.

But political acumen does not a White House administrator make. The new post will call on Baker to demonstrate some organizational skills untested to this point — even in his days as Senate majority leader. And Baker is only one new face. The old Reagan team remains in place at the departments of Justice, Defense and State. One crucial question facing the new chief of staff is how to operate as part of that team and at the same time try to shake the mud from the Iran-contra scandal and rescue the final two years of Ronald Reagan's presidency.

In addition to the problem of joining a team with more losses than wins lately, it is Baker's task to force the captain of that team to immerse himself in the tough, serious business of decision-making — a task that demands of Reagan more hard work and attention to detail than he previously has shown.

In the days and months and years ahead, the buck will not stop with Howard Baker. It stops — historically, inevitably and properly — in the Oval Office. And no matter whom President Reagan installs down the hall, only he can determine whether or not he will now have the stuff to measure up to that office.

## THE PLAIN DEALER
*Cleveland, OH, February 28, 1987*

Donald T. Regan's resignation is genuinely good news. As President Reagan's chief of staff, his arrogance and autocratic nature, combined with the president's own managerial diffidence, contributed greatly to the frequently disastrous policy initiatives of the past year. Certainly, Regan managed to shield the president from intrusive ideas, dissent and alternative viewpoints. But he also managed to encyst the president. The result was a string of failures in arms control, Soviet-American relations and foreign policy as well as increasing animosity in Congress, where Regan was disliked.

Regan's replacement, former Senate Republican Leader Howard Baker, is a completely different type of operator—respected in Congress, widely regarded as fair and knowledgeable and politically astute. Even those attributes might prove inadequate to the task of reviving the president's fading leadership. Most of the investigations into the Iran-contra scandal are far from complete, and the subject is sure to haunt both Reagan and Baker in the months to come. Accepting Regan's departure is the first crucial step in putting the Iran affair in the past. But the president cannot expect Baker's refreshing presence to complete the job alone. After all, Donald Regan was not entirely responsible for the Iran scandal, and replacing him is not the total remedy.

It is worth noting that Baker has made a huge sacrifice to take the position. The former senator has presidential ambitions, and although support has been slow to gel, it still is early. Almost surely, Baker will have to take a cut in income. He already has abandoned his candidacy. That he is willing to do so for the responsibility of managing the White House through its darkest hours is a testament to his commitment to public service.

President Reagan also deserves credit. He easily could have allowed Regan to stay on to coordinate his response to the sharp indictments of the Tower Commission report. And he easily could have found a less impressive, more compatible replacement. Baker harks from a different wing of the Republican Party and has been at odds with the president in the past. Although Baker downplays those differences, they seem sure to contribute to a more forthright presentation of alternatives in future White House planning and policy sessions. Reagan's promise of carte blanche to Baker also sends a signal that the president recognizes the need to make changes beyond his staff chief.

Again, Baker's appointment is only part of the remedy the Reagan presidency needs. But still, the timing and selection are noteworthy indications that a lesson has been learned. At a press conference Friday night, Baker was asked by a photographer to smile. Baker responded: "What's there to smile about?" His appointment, for one thing.

## The Times-Picayune
### The States-Item

*New Orleans, LA, March 10, 1987*

The departure of Donald Regan and the arrival of Howard Baker as White House chief of staff are widely seen as putting White House operations back on track. The moves also have important implications for the administration's economic policies and, therefore, for the national economy.

To begin with, Mr. Baker's arrival vastly improves the chances that Federal Reserve Chairman Paul Volcker will be asked to stay on for a third five-year term in July. Despite Mr. Volcker's widely acclaimed role in the dramatic lowering of inflation and interest rates, Mr. Regan reportedly was determined to get rid of him.

Mr. Baker, on the other hand, is a Volcker admirer. He also is a pragmatist and probably values Mr. Volcker's presence at the Fed as a stabilizing influence on the economy and the financial markets.

If Mr. Volcker is asked to stay and remains, the Fed can be expected to maintain its close watch on interest rates and inflation, tightening money at the first sign of inflation and loosening credit if the economy sags further and needs stimulating.

Because of his ability to work with Congress, Mr. Baker, Senate majority leader in Mr. Reagan's first term, is expected to bring President Reagan and congressional leaders into discussions on the budget-deficit prob-lem. The White House might even be more receptive to the discussion of small tax increases to help reduce the deficit.

In general, the White House is expected to be much less confrontational in its relations with Congress than it was when Mr. Regan was chief of staff.

Howard Baker's presence in the White House is also expected to enhance the power of another Baker — Treasury Secretary James Baker. The latter is already the administration's leader in negotiations on international monetary policy. Liked and respected by Howard Baker, he could also have a stronger role in the administration's overall economic policies.

While the nation is not likely to see any basic retrenchment in the policies that have become known as "Reaganomics," the White House undoubtedly will become more conciliatory in its approach to Congress on economic matters. Although the Democrats have regained control of both houses, neither Democrats nor Republicans have anything to gain from a continuous stalemate on budgetary matters.

The administration might be expected to work for compromises that will lead to meaningful reductions in the deficit, but Mr. Reagan can hardly be expected to do an about-face and support a major tax increase. That would go against everything that he has stood for to date.

## The Washington Post

*Washington, DC, March 1, 1987*

HOWARD BAKER and Frank Carlucci as the president's two principal White House assistants will be a vast improvement over Donald Regan and John Poindexter. You won't get an argument from practically anyone on that. Far from it, there is—oddly, given the fact that it has been only a matter of days since Disaster seemed to prevail—something akin to euphoria in the air. People who only hours before were sunk in bleakest fugues suddenly all seemed to be singing "Ding, dong, the witch is dead!" More than Howard Baker's popularity or Donald Regan's lack of it was responsible. Another element was surely the perception that people had been put in charge who know how to govern and care about governing, people who actually respect both the process and those who have chosen to involve themselves in it.

It is worth noting that we go through these things periodically in Washington, a kind of cathartic experience in which it is finally agreed by some stubborn president or other that it would be well for the White House to recognize that the other end of Pennsylvania Avenue exists and to put some people in place who not only have civil relations with the rest of the city, but also partake in the ancestral memory of how things get done here. We thought Mr. Carlucci fit this bill nicely when he was appointed, and we think the same of Sen. Baker. Mr. Baker is an honest, personable and extremely intelligent man. He is a man who likes other people and who likes governing, and he is a grown-up. As Senate Republican leader in President Reagan's earlier days, Mr. Baker rightly challenged him on fiscal policy. He will be a loyal assistant. But he is no yes man, so he will also be a valuable assistant.

But Howard Baker is not going to be president. It is Ronald Reagan who has the comeback to make. There has been a kind of drum roll for this comeback. You get the sense that the president is about to step back on stage in some new role, that he has been sustained and even invigorated by the closing of Republican ranks, the dramatic consultations, the suspense, the desperate calls upon him to reappear and demonstrate that he is not the somnambulant, unfocused figure who emerges from the pages of the Tower Commission Report. We suspect that he is about to do it. And we hope that he is, that the administration will not be immobilized into a final two years of drift by the exposure of the terrible Iran-contra folly.

But, importantly, more than cosmetic changes are required if the comeback is to have meaning. People need to know that Mr. Reagan has understood what went so wrong in his national security advisers' activities and that he has faced his own part in it. In the coming week the president will indicate, by his actions and in his appearances, whether he has done so. One other thing: the senators who are warning Mr. Reagan that he should withdraw his nomination of Robert Gates to be director of the CIA are right. Mr. Gates has undoubted qualities as an analyst and manager, but he has emerged from both his hearings and the Tower Commission Report as just not big enough or strong enough for the job. The president will be setting about to restore confidence in himself and his government after a very bad period. He will need to show he understands what went wrong and that he means things to be different now. Howard Baker is a right signal to send on that account. Robert Gates is no villain, but he is not a right signal or the right man either.

## Detroit Free Press

*Detroit, MI*
*February 28, 1987*

THE INEVITABLE came mercifully sooner than many had expected, and Donald Regan is now gone from the White House. His resignation came one day after the Tower Commission had laid on him much of the blame for President Reagan's faulty knowledge of the Iran arms deal and his failure to control the National Security Council. His departure from the administration ought to signal a thorough shake-up of the White House command structure.

The appointment of former Sen. Howard Baker as Mr. Regan's successor is an indication that such a new beginning is being made. It is, moreover, a fortunate appointment because Mr. Baker is a mainstream Republican who displays a perennially refreshing independence. That independence has earned him the respect and confidence of many on both sides of the aisle in Congress.

As majority leader of the Senate from 1981 until his retirement in 1984, he was known as a keen administrator who could make the legislative process work. That together with his experience in government and his political distance from the Reagan White House should help his credibility as chief of staff.

When Mr. Baker was the Senate majority leader, he made no secret of his doubts about some of the Reagan legislative program. Once he had made his point, he helped steer a modified program through Congress — but not until he had told President Reagan clearly of his own misgivings.

That is precisely what is needed in a White House chief of staff. As the Tower Commission said on Thursday, the chief of staff must make sure the president knows what is going on, and what the downside and consequences of any policy may be.

It is this characterization of a chief of staff that makes us confident that Howard Baker is the man for the job — especially now that it is abundantly clear that the White House needs order and process restored to its workings. Mr. Baker's long experience in government and the reputation of integrity and effectiveness he established will stand him and the president and, therefore, the country in good stead.

# The Star-Ledger

*Newark, NJ, March 3, 1987*

The President's choice for his new chief of staff was unexpected and dramatic, but an eminently correct choice for an urgently needed, overdue change to revive his flagging Administration. In tapping former Sen. Howard Baker Jr., Mr. Reagan has brought on board an able, respected, experienced Washington hand with proven credentials for a demanding key post.

Mr. Baker will bring to the beleaguered Reagan White House a sense of order and direction needed to get presidential operations back on track. But perhaps even more significant in a political sense, the new chief of staff has an estimable legislative record of long and productive service that will be invaluable for the Reagan presidency in beginning to restore a viable, working relationship with a Congress now in control of the opposition Democratic Party.

In a pragmatic perspective, Mr. Baker is the right man for the right job. The timing, however, would have been much better if the President had not agonized and procrastinated over removing a chief of staff who was a major factor in the Administration's current deeply troubled state.

With Mr. Baker as the President's right-hand man, the White House will be more open and accessible than it had been under the strained, restrictive, Marine-drill-sergeant atmosphere that was the political trademark of Donald Regan's powerful, abrasive stewardship.

Moreover, the Baker appointment should be a positive element in an all-important political sector: A vitally needed starting point to restore credibility to the shaken Reagan presidency critically diminished by its ill-advised involvement in the clandestine Iran-contra arms scandal, which was made even worse by the subsequent bumbling effort at a coverup involving Mr. Regan, former CIA Director William Casey, a National Security Council staff member and his aide, and the role of the President himself.

From a symbolic point, Mr. Reagan could not have done better than his choice of Mr. Baker to bring his presidency out of an executive and political torpor—a debilitating, besieged state. But much remains to be accomplished before the Reagan Administration will be able to recover from its current state of disarray.

Uppermost in importance is how the President reacts to the harshly critical findings of the Tower commission. He must be willing to assimilate and act in a positive, assertive manner, firmly addressing the executive failings disclosed by the independent panel.

He no longer can revert to a passive presidency and be content to delegate extensive powers and duties to aides. It is imperative that he become fully informed on major issues, domestic and foreign, and assume a decisive role in the decision-making process. An able, energetic chief of staff like Mr. Baker will be invaluable, of course, but the President must be prepared to have the final say when the buck reaches the Oval Office.

# The Hutchinson News

*Hutchinson, KS, March 6, 1987*

Don't underestimate the power of the Washington press or the importance of understanding that power.

President Reagan's appointment of former Sen. Howard Baker will prove a boon to the administration's failing image.

The fact is the press likes Baker. The fact is the press disliked former Chief of Staff Don Regan. It is hard to get excited about a dullard as bland as Regan. He was as tasty a subject as instant potatoes.

When the press talks about objectivity and cold, emotionless reporting, it is being lofty and altruistic. Such purpose is difficult to achieve when you're writing about a cold-blooded bureaucrat who had not the slightest idea how to romance the press into favoring him.

Howard Baker, on the other hand, is a reporter's dream. He'll tell you how it is, and he'll tell you only when he's ready to tell you. It's hard not to like him.

Regan came out of the nation's financial board rooms, where the press is as welcome as bacteria in a hospital; Baker, meanwhile, is an old hand at press management, having gone through numerous political campaigns and enduring the pressures of massive scrutiny when he was involved in the Watergate hearings. His experience required that the press be a constant appendage. Baker is neither mystified nor intimidated by the press, and that's his secret.

Already it is obvious that Reagan is profiting by Baker's presence. The ink in the nation's newspapers is already turning from violent blood red to silky lavender.

That says as much about the fickle Washington-based press corps as it does about the appeal and power of Howard Baker.

# THE TENNESSEAN

*Nashville, TN, March 3, 1987*

AFTER being appointed as President Reagan's chief of staff, former Sen. Howard Baker was asked by a photographer to smile for the cameras, and he asked, "What is there to smile about?" That sums up the enormity of Mr. Baker's task.

For Mr. Baker must somehow try to rescue a presidency mired down by the Iran arms-contra scandal and a President hit hard by the Tower Commission report that pictured him as an aloof chief executive, inattentive to governance, and inclined to delegate to others all the problem of dealing with nuts and bolts.

The President is lucky in being able to attract the Tennessean to the White House. Mr. Baker is a man of integrity and capability who has a legislative background that will be immensely helpful. The former Senate majority leader is the consummate politician who understands better than most how government works.

He is also a man who possesses good common sense and has a pragmatic view of the arts and skills of governing. There will be no more amateurs running amok from the White House basement. There will be no unthinking adventurism to drag the White House into such quagmires as the Iran arms sale and its link to contra aid.

Mr. Baker, who had been considering making a run for the presidency himself in 1988, has given up that opportunity. He said that when Mr. Reagan called him he found that he could not turn down a President "with significant problems."

It is doubtful that Mr. Baker, persuasive as he can be, will be able to transform Mr. Reagan into a hands-on chief executive. That has never been the President's style and it is not likely to become his style now. But Mr. Baker will at least be able to keep him informed of the pitfalls that lie in the road.

Mr. Baker will be a distinctly different chief of staff than was Mr. Donald Regan, who was something of a martinet who tried to keep all the lines of authority in his own hands. As the Tower Commission noted, Mr. Regan did not serve the President well. Mr. Regen did not get along smoothly with the Congress or, if reports are to be believed, with Mrs. Reagan, who is said to have speeded his exit.

The former majority leader is not a man who closes people out. Rather, he tries to include them in. He tries for a consensus, although he can be firm in dealing with the tasks that the White House will require.

Unless it is in the area of arms control, the foreign policy landscape doesn't present great hopes at this time for the White House. But there may be places where a revived administration could make gains.

Whether Mr. Baker can spark the revival is speculative. If he can't, probably no one else under consideration by the White House could. Much now depends on the President himself. He is slated to make a speech tomorrow night in response to the Tower Commission report. His old friends and advisers have counseled that he admit the Iran arms sales were flawed policy and instead of trying to justify the operation, simply say "It was a trip that shouldn't have been taken."

Only the President can say that, and only he can concede his own mistakes. If he does not, Mr. Baker's task is all the more formidable in taking on a rescue mission at the White House. ■

## The Kansas City Times

*Kansas City, MO, March 2, 1987*

Howard Baker needs to take charge immediately in the beleaguered White House. The time has come to forget about public relations perceptions and deal strictly in substance.

Late in the week the stunned remnants of the White House old guard were calling for the president to act firmly to demonstrate that he is in control. They were talking of "image," of the damage done by the Tower Commission. Horrors! The Tower report gave the impression that the president was not in control.

Aides were urging the president to act decisively in a show of firm purpose. What do they want him to do? Fire the first lady? Suspend the Constitution? Dissolve Congress? Drop the bomb?

The fanatical concern with image is the very superficiality that has landed the administration in this crisis of confidence. The obsession with polls, the concern with fleeting visions on the evening news, the acting out of a script, the great communicator theory of government, all have been substitutes for a design of policy and steady competence to carry out that design.

The facade began to crumble in public view at Reykjavik where chaos ensued in the president's one-on-one improvisations with Mikhail Gorbachev. The Soviets were well-prepared; the Americans were disorganized and confused. Departments of government and allies still are trying to repair the ruin. The knots of the Iceland Summit yet are unraveling.

The president has said he will read and digest the report and "think carefully about its findings and promptly act on its recommendations." In getting rid of Donald Regan and putting Howard Baker in command he has taken the necessary first step. What counts now is to truly govern. That means paying attention to Baker, to George Shultz and to Caspar Weinberger for starters, and then making decisions based on knowledge and calm judgment.

The speech expected this week is important in that it can present a recital of intentions. But it will only be a speech, not the reality of the acts that must follow. Government is not image, it is deliberate action after thoughtful preparation. If it is purposeful and successful, the American people and the world will know. If it is not, no slick presentation will change that.

## The Honolulu Advertiser

*Honolulu, HI*
*February 28, 1987*

It was a double dose of good news yesterday when White House Chief of Staff Donald Regan resigned and former Senate Republican leader Howard Baker was named as his replacement.

Regan's departure had been a foregone conclusion for weeks, except possibly to himself and President Reagan. But the fact the chief of staff went right after the Tower Commission report came out says something about the president's desire to clean house and move on quickly.

Baker brings many good and needed qualities to the White House job. Most important the former Senate majority and minority leader is known for his political skill, common sense and good judgment.

His experience with Congress should be a major help. So also should his service on the special Senate Watergate committee be valuable in dealing with the Iran-contra situation, which will be the subject of two sets of congressional hearings.

The new job means Baker, who has been a lawyer in private practice in Washington, will be too busy to run for the 1988 Republican presidential nomination, which he was considering. That is a boost for Senator Bob Dole, the current minority leader who is also a known as a competant centrist.

But there is much to do in the White House between now and the 1988 election. While Reagan himself must set the pace with more work and attention if he is to salvage the rest of his term from irrelevancy, there is no doubt that Baker will be a key figure there for the next 23 months.

His choice is a needed hopeful sign.

## Rockford Register Star

*Rockford, IL, March 4, 1987*

President Reagan, reading the handwriting on the wall as well as the scathing assessment of his leadership from the Tower Commission, has taken an essential first step toward salvaging his presidency by naming former Senate Majority Leader Howard Baker as White House chief of staff.

Appointing a respected and experienced government leader like Baker to replace Donald Regan was a brilliant piece of casting. We can only speculate now about the plot, which stars the president as the ultra-conservative leader and Baker as the more moderately-inclined supporting character who arrives on the scene to restore sense to a chaotic storyline.

How the two men's styles ultimately will mesh remains to be seen. How Baker will impose his more middle-of-the-road philosophical bent on a White House that has for six years been inhabited by individuals of decidedly very conservative leanings is something that only time will tell.

What we do know now is that Baker will serve well as chief of staff. He has the stature and established leadership skills to recapture for the battered administration the confidence of a suspicious Congress. We feel certain he will insist upon and help the president decide upon a consistent foreign policy that Congress and the American people can support.

Baker also has the necessary track record of candor to restore a skeptical public's confidence in those who sit in the highest seats of power.

On his first day on the job, Baker tried to persuade a group of reporters that President Reagan was in control of the White House by insisting that he is not "a hands-off" leader or "an AWOL president." As much as we would like to accept Baker's word on that score, we're going to have to see more evidence before concluding that all the White House problems have been solved.

But Baker's appointment was a good move by the president to reassert control over a staff of mavericks, who in recent months have served him poorly. We hope that hiring Baker is just the first of several essential decisions to get the government back on track.

## WINSTON-SALEM JOURNAL

*Winston-Salem, NC, March 1, 1987*

This was not the only newspaper in the country to voice doubt when Donald T. Regan became the White House chief of staff. But Howard Henry Baker Jr., the former senator from Tennessee, is nearly the best choice imaginable for that job and for this president at this (pardon the expression) point in time.

What complicated Regan's case was that he could not give the president bad news or unwelcome advice. He did not know how to listen to members of Congress. He couldn't sense when he had gone too far and needed to pull back.

Whatever his personal responsibility in the Iran affair, legal and otherwise, Donald Regan was about the worst possible man for that job under President Reagan. The administration's problems today are, after all, deeper than one incident. The current mess is an illustration of overall disarray. The Iceland summit is a similar and perhaps more important case study of an administration out of order.

Where Regan was a courtier, Baker is a politician, a man who had to get elected to come to Washington and then was chosen by his Republican peers in the Senate to lead them. He ran for president, and he was always one of the GOP's stock of talent for the vice presidential nomination.

All this gives him some standing and independence as well as knowledge. The Tower report makes it clear that Ronald Reagan needs more than toadying yes-men at his heels.

And since he is a politician and not a Marine, Baker has no intention of ending his political life, or even dirtying himself, for another. Beware the public man with the suicidal impulse. Baker will make everything he can of the last two years of Ronald Reagan's presidency for the sake of Baker's own reputation.

Where Regan was ignorant of the ways of Washington, Baker is the insider's insider. He spent 20 years mending fences in Congress, soothing egos, and finding the point of compromise and consensus. Before that, Baker sat at the knee of his father-in-law, Everett Dirksen, who in his day was the LBJ of his party. And both of Baker's parents were members of Congress.

No choice for chief of staff could please the present Congress more.

Many may wonder why Baker took the job. Clearly, he missed the action, even though he turned down an offer to become the head of the CIA a few weeks ago. His sense of his own limitations may be the key.

When Howard Baker came to Winston-Salem last year, he seemed then more suited to be a prime minister than a president. He appears to be a contented man; he is "not driven," says an associate. That's a welcome quality.

Baker is also not an issues man. He is short on vision, and his rhetoric is sparse. Examine his Watergate utterances — they are poli-babble. But Baker *is* the quintessential process man, and Ronald Reagan flunks process.

Now all the nonsense about the president "changing style" or resigning can be dropped.

Reagan and Howard Baker should make a good team. What a shame it didn't happen sooner.

# Herald ☆ News

Fall River, MA, March 4, 1987

The best thing about the appointment of former Senator Howard Baker to succeed Donald Regan as chief of the White House staff is that it was made.

The appointment has been greeted with universal applause, as it deserves.

Senator Baker was remarkably successful during the years when he was the Senate majority leader.

He did not run for reelection because he wished to concentrate his energies on a possible candidacy for president in 1988.

Those plans will be held in abeyance now, although it has been pointed out that if Baker is successful in restoring the Reagan administration's credibility and prestige, he may well find his new post a springboard to the presidency.

In any case his past experience in the Senate has won him many friends in both the Senate and House. He is in an excellent position to serve as a badly needed liaison between the administration and Congress.

But the most encouraging aspect of this excellent appointment is that the White House, in the midst of a shattering crisis, was capable of making it.

It is known that former Senator Paul Laxalt was approached to become chief of staff, but refused because of his possible presidential plans. It is widely reported that Drew Lewis was also approached and refused.

Instead of moving then toward the appointment of someone who, however able, would be lesser known, the administration moved ahead and came up with an appointee more widely known and admired than either Laxalt or Lewis.

This suggests that much of the verbiage about a floundering administration incapable of decisive action is no more than that, and that the capacity to act swiftly and effectively is still there.

The events leading up to an invitation being extended to Baker are not yet known, nor whose idea it was to ask him.

But whoever thought of it, it was a smart idea, and after so much confusion in the last couple of months, it is all the more welcome for that reason.

Senator Baker inspires confidence in Congress and the public. In his new position, he should be able to steer the administration toward other, similarly wise appointments and decisions.

He is now in charge at the White House, and with his coming, the rebuilding of confidence in the administration after this shattering winter has already begun.

It would be absurd to claim that his presence will make all the difference between reinvigoration and further drift to the Reagan administration, but it is certainly a major first step in the right direction.

## FORT WORTH STAR-TELEGRAM

Fort Worth, TX, March 3, 1987

Donald Regan is gone, to the relief of the nation.

Howard Baker is White House chief of staff, also to the relief of the nation.

Baker should prove to be an excellent choice. He is able. He is respected within the Congress, which is important at this stage of the Iran-wracked administration of President Reagan. Baker joins the president's staff untainted by previous service within the executive branch.

He has been a pragmatic politician all his public life, and the president needs political insight and pragmatism at his side.

The appointment of Baker, though, is merely Step 1 if the White House is to recover the credibility it has lost.

Damage control has become an important aspect of the chief of staff's job, and considering the damage done to the Reagan presidency, Baker has his work cut out for him.

In large part, Baker's success as chief of staff will hinge on Reagan himself, and on the way the president responds to last week's findings by the Tower Commission.

Reagan must discard form for substance, beginning with his speech to the American public Wednesday.

The president must demonstrate that he understands the nature of the Iran arms scandal and the fundamental flaws in the private policy that spawned it — not as he wishes it were but as it actually is. This he has not done.

The president must demonstrate that he understands the depth of the damage done to his administration, particularly to its foreign policy credibility, and that he is willing — and intellectually able — to handle matters differently in the future.

It won't be enough for Reagan to say the right things, to mouth the proper words, without understanding that the words must mean a greater degree of presidential leadership and awareness.

Howard Baker can help resurrect faith in the operation of the White House.

But the bottom line is that Ronald Reagan is president, and only the president, by his performance in the coming months, can re-establish public and international trust in the ability of his administration.

## THE DAILY OKLAHOMAN

Oklahoma City, OK
March 12, 1987

HOWARD BAKER'S actions as President Reagan's chief of staff are watched closely by conservatives, many of whom harbor distrust for him because of his past record.

After all, Baker pursued a moderate course as Republican leader of the Senate and veered into the wrong camp when he supported the Panama Canal treaties. His legislative career was characterized by compromise rather than controversy and he resisted efforts to advance a conservative social agenda.

Baker sought to allay concerns that he might use his new position of power to promote his own ideological views, stating flatly: "Ronald Reagan is president, and I am not."

His pledge not to be a "prime minister" running the government is bolstered by the fact that he was recommended by former Sen. Paul Laxalt, R-Nev., whose loyalty to Reagan and principles are unquestioned.

An initial volley of criticism of Baker's appointment by conservative activists has subsided, helped along by his selection of Kenneth Cribb as a member of his transition team. Cribb is a longtime Reaganite brought over from Attorney General Ed Meese's staff.

Baker will be judged by his future actions on personnel, as well as domestic and foreign policy issues. Will the pragmatic Tennesseean, for example, lean too far in seeking consensus on arms control, deficit reduction, catastrophic health insurance, trade legislation and other key initiatives?

A lot of Reagan followers are anxiously waiting to see.

# Webster, not Gates, to Head Central Intelligence Agency

Robert Gates withdrew March 2, 1987 as President Reagan's nominee to be the director of the Central Intelligence Agency. The President named a new nominee March 3—William Webster, director of the Federal Bureau of Investigation. In a letter to President Reagan, Gates said the Senate seemed bent on finishing its investigation of the Iran-contra arms scandal before acting on his nomination and "a prolonged period of uncertainty would be harmful to the Central Intelligence Agency, the intelligence community and potentially our national security." In his letter of reply, accepting the withdrawal, Reagan called Gates "remarkably talented and dedicated" and said he had shown "class" under "the enormous pressures of recent weeks." "At any other time, I am certain that he would have been confirmed without delay," Reagan said.

Gates had come under increasing criticism since his confirmation hearings before the Senate Select Committee on Intelligence. Concern had mounted within the administration that a drawn-out confirmation proceeding would keep the glare of publicity on the Iran-contra affair while the administration was trying to move away from it. Congressional investigators had indicated they were unsure about Gates's commitment to a course independent of White House political pressures, and they were concerned about the failure of the CIA, while he was deputy director of the agency, to keep Congress posted on the Iran-contra events. Some believed Congress had actually been misled. Much of the criticism stemmed from an appearance before the Senate committee in November 1986 by then CIA-Director William Casey, whose testimony about the matter, reportedly prepared with key input from Gates, bore little resemblance to the actual operation as known by the agency at the time.

The choice of Webster drew immediate praise from all quarters. Webster, 62, had headed the FBI since 1978. "A highly regarded professional who will bring much-needed credibility to the CIA," said Senate Majority Leader Robert Byrd (D, W. Va.). President Reagan's statement described Webster as "a man of honor and integrity, a man who is committed to the rule of law." Webster had no known direct involvement with the Iran-contra affair, although there were questions raised about the FBI's suspension of a criminal investigation of a Miami-based cargo airline suspected of shipping arms to both Iran and the Nicaraguan contra rebels.

## The Cincinnati Post

*Cincinnati, OH, March 6, 1987*

Particularly good presidential appointments are sometimes called "inspired." That description seems to fit the nomination of FBI Director William Webster to be head of the Central Intelligence Agency.

At once, the CIA gets a leader whose integrity and honesty is broadly heralded, and the Reagan administration takes another substantial step to remove the heavy burden of the Iran-Contra affair.

The CIA needs a director who can restore public and congressional confidence in it. Former director William Casey was credited with improving morale among agency employees after the battering the CIA took during Watergate investigations, but he was widely criticized for not leveling with Congress about the agency's covert operations and his own knowledge of arms dealings with Iran.

Some of the tarnish rubbed off on Deputy Director Robert Gates, whose nomination to succeed Casey was withdrawn when opposition developed in the Senate and it appeared that sticking with Gates would contribute to a protracted focus on the Iran scandal.

Webster has an excellent nine-year record at the FBI. He took over an agency in turmoil, and with a sure and steady hand has restored its reputation. He shifted the agency's focus from bank robberies and stolen cars to organized crime, white-collar misdeeds, corrupt unions and espionage.

A former federal judge, he is committed to the rule of law. He once said that the FBI under his direction was "doing the work the American people expect of us, and doing it the way the Constitution demands of us." That should be a prescription for success at the CIA, which has been faulted for not always hewing to the letter of the law.

## The Register-Guard

*Eugene, OR, March 5, 1987*

President Reagan did the right thing when he withdrew Robert Gates' nomination to succeed William Casey as director of the CIA. Gates, the No. 2 man at the agency, is unavoidably tainted by the CIA's involvement in the Iran-Contra affair. The CIA needs a qualified chief from outside the agency, someone unencumbered by an association with the debilitating scandal. FBI director William Webster, nominated by Reagan Tuesday, fits that description.

Gates may very well be telling the truth when he says he was not informed of the CIA's role in shipping arms to Iran. His claim that he was misled by the ubiquitous Lt. Col. Oliver North about the nature of the National Security Council's activities in support of the Contra rebels in Nicaragua is equally plausible. But Congress is properly skeptical of the notion that the CIA's deputy director could be uninvolved in such large and controversial operations. A battle in the Senate over Gates' confirmation would have consumed months and might have ended in rejection.

Beyond the immediate political obstacle in the Senate, the CIA has problems that demand the attention of someone who is not a part of the agency's status quo. CIA activities in Nicaragua such as the mining of harbors and distribution of an assassination manual are what led Congress to block aid to the Contras. The administration's attempts to evade aid restrictions make up a large part of the substance of the Iran-Contra affair. In that respect, the CIA's clumsiness and lack of restraint are responsible for many of Reagan's difficulties.

Webster, a 62-year-old former federal judge, is well prepared to curb the CIA's excesses and improve its credibility. He faced a similar challenge when he became head of the FBI in 1978. The bureau had been damaged by accusations of civil rights abuses and involvement in domestic surveillance. Webster restored the FBI's crime-fighting image, scoring notable successes against organized crime, drug rings, foreign spies and corrupt politicians. His record makes him a better choice than former Sen. John Tower, who was offered the CIA job but turned it down.

Webster is expected to win Senate confirmation easily. He can then begin the task of rehabilitating the CIA. The nation needs an effective intelligence agency. The tangle of covert activities, renegade operatives, secret dealings and private support networks that produced the Iran-Contra mess is evidence of ineffectiveness at best, and criminality at worst. Reagan correctly recognized that the situation is serious enough to require new leadership at the top.

# DESERET NEWS
*Salt Lake City, UT, March 4-5, 1987*

If there is anything the Reagan administration does not need, it is to keep generating controversy over the Iran arms deal longer than is really necessary.

Likewise, if there is anything the Central Intelligence Agency does not need, it is to be deprived of a director for many more weeks.

Under the circumstances, acting director Robert Gates, 43, did the right thing for the country as well as for himself this week in withdrawing his nomination to become full-fledged director of the CIA. If confirmed, he would have been the youngest CIA director ever.

Despite his consistent denials of any wrong-doing in the sale of U.S. arms to Iran and the scheme to divert profits to the Contra rebels in Nicaragua, Gates was unable to satisfy Senators who questioned whether he should have used his position as deputy CIA director to warn the administration of poor policy.

Though the nomination might have been forced through the Senate, it would have required a long and acrimonious fight that no one wants or needs.

By promptly replacing Gates' nomination with that of FBI Director William Webster to lead the CIA, President Reagan showed a discerning eye for talent and a desire to rebuild his administration as quickly as possible in the wake of last week's scathing report from the Tower Commission.

A 62-year-old former federal judge, Webster has run the FBI for 10 years, longer than anyone but J. Edgar Hoover. Webster took over when the FBI was still reeling from disclosures of civil rights and political abuses by its agents. During his tenure, Webster has rebuilt public confidence in the agency. He also has developed good relations with Congress. Under Webster, the FBI has pursued a stepped up counter-intelligence program that contributed to the series of unprecedented spy arrests the past two years. This background gives him credibility where the new CIA director will need it — on Capitol Hill and in the intelligence community.

As FBI director, Webster has warned that the U.S. faced threats by terrorists, but during his tenure acts of domestic terrorism declined. There were more than 100 terrorist acts in the U.S. in 1978, but the number fell steadily, reaching 13 two years ago.

If confirmed, Webster will be faced with the task of extricating the CIA from the Iran-Contra scandal. Both the Tower Commission and the Senate Intelligence Committee have reported deep CIA involvement in arranging the 1985-86 arms-for-hostages deal with Iran. The CIA is also under investigation by two special congressional committees and the independent counsel over the agency's apparent involvement in supplying the Nicaraguan Contras with arms in possible violation of U.S. law.

In any event, because Webster is so well known, the Senate should need little time to scrutinize his background and qualifications. Let's fill the vacancy at the CIA as quickly as possible and strive to keep the agency from being crippled by a long, bitter confirmation process.

# THE CHRISTIAN SCIENCE MONITOR
*Boston, MA, March 5, 1987*

FROM its inception back in the 1940s, the United States Central Intelligence Agency has more often than not found itself caught up in controversy. Unique power, after all, coupled with the broad mantle of secrecy so cultivated by the intelligence community, almost ensures that the CIA will be a government agency difficult to administer under the best of circumstances – let alone during a period of challenge, such as the moment.

Precisely for such reasons, President Reagan's nomination of William H. Webster as new director of central intelligence makes good sense. As noted by Senate majority leader Robert Byrd, Mr. Webster "is a highly regarded professional who will bring much-needed credibility to the CIA." Webster deserves special appreciation for rebuilding the Federal Bureau of Investigation. Given the equal importance of the CIA, it would seem in the best interest of the American people for the Senate to move on the Webster nomination as expeditiously as possible.

Fortunately, the CIA has been substantially improved in recent years, under former Director Stansfield Turner, during the Carter years, and, to an extent, under Mr. Reagan's first director, William Casey. Mr. Turner had stressed a rebuilding of the agency's technical intelligence-gathering side, as opposed to covert operations. Mr. Casey was not as averse to covert operations (such as the unfortunate mining of Nicaraguan harbors). But to his credit, he also sought to rebuild morale in the agency, and largely succeeded.

Webster's task will be to reconcile the two sides of the agency – intelligence gathering and operations. A former federal judge, Webster has repeatedly stressed the importance of working within the framework of the law. Such a scrupulous regard for law will be essential for the CIA in the months ahead, now that congressional committees as well as the special prosecutor are probing possible agency involvement in the Iran-contra affair.

In a democracy, public support for an intelligence agency is necessarily ambivalent. Moving Mr. Webster from the FBI to the CIA should help ease the public's legitimate concerns.

# The Star-Ledger
*Newark, NJ, March 5, 1987*

President Reagan has come up with the right choice to head the Central Intelligence Agency—FBI Director William Webster. Mr. Webster not only has a proven background in law enforcement experience, but he has shown an uncommon ability to handle what conceivably could be the crisis-management assignment of restoring the CIA's credibility.

It is highly likely that the President's new nominee will be faced with that kind of a formidable administrative task if his appointment is approved, as expected, by the Senate. In taking over the FBI directorship nine years ago, Mr. Webster had to deal with a crisis situation.

That he was able to do so in a highly creditable manner has been clearly established in the transformation he has achieved in his tenure, restoring the bureau to its present estimable high standing as a proficient, productive law enforcement agency.

Mr. Webster will be taking command of an agency that is under a cloud because of the dubious role of its former director, William Casey, in the Irangate scandal—the clandestine sale of arms to Iran and the diversion of some of the proceeds to the Nicaraguan rebels.

This was the decisive factor for the President's withdrawal of his first nominee, Robert Gates, a high-ranking CIA official. At another time, in a less stressful, more uncomplicated political climate, Mr. Gates likely would have been considered an excellent choice to head the intelligence agency.

Certainly, there would have been no question about his qualifications to fill that key post, for he had highly creditable credentials as a longtime career employee of the intelligence agency. The difficulty with the Gates nomination derived from the reportedly deep involvement of his boss, Mr. Casey, in the Iran-contra affair. Mr. Gates was questioned extensively by the Senate Intelligence Committee about his involvement. While he may not have been participant in policy decisions, he reportedly was aware of the agency's involvement.

In those uncertain, murky circumstances, the Gates nomination was treading troubled waters, a confrontation with the Senate that a shaken Reagan presidency could not afford. The President has more than enough problems trying to restore credibility in his Administration. But of even greater importance in picking a new CIA chief was the pressing need to make a break from the Casey era in the CIA, a transition that would be helpful in removing a residual concern about the agency's future operations.

The President made an excellent choice in selecting former Sen. Howard Baker to replace the imperious, controversial Donald Regan as his chief of staff. And he has made another eminently suitable choice in tapping FBI Director Webster to head the CIA. Mr. Webster not only is well qualified to assume this sensitive intelligence assignment, but he also offers another urgently needed element—a clean break from the past. This is of great importance for an agency that may come under heavy critical fire if probes of the Iran-contra scandal uncover a deep CIA involvement in this lamentable affair.

"If you need anything, just scream."

## ST. LOUIS POST-DISPATCH

St. Louis, MO, March 4, 1987

President Reagan has now made two sound appointments in an effort to pick up the pieces of the Iran-Contra affair. The first, of course, was his choice of former Sen. Howard H. Baker Jr. as White House chief of staff. The second is his nomination of FBI Director William H. Webster to direct the Central Intelligence Agency.

Mr. Webster is, of course, well known to St. Louis. He was born here, he was graduated from Washington University, and he served here both as U.S. district attorney and as a federal district judge. He also is well known to Congress, since he has had a good working relationship there and is respected by both Democrats and Republicans. He has a fine record as a public official and is known as a man of integrity and thoughtfulness. In that respect, Mr. Webster is the kind of director the CIA needs. He should have no problem being confirmed by the Senate.

The nominee was a good choice for the most obvious reason: unlike Mr. Reagan's first nominee, Robert M. Gates, who withdrew, Mr. Webster had no connection with the Iran arms deal and diversion of funds to the Nicaraguan rebels. But there is a better reason than that for the Webster nomination. Again unlike Mr. Gates, Mr. Webster is not a career CIA officer, and he has no ties to the CIA's record of covert actions and unaccountability. Mr. Webster ran a tight ship at the Federal Bureau of Investigation. Though his direction was not beyond criticism, Mr. Webster showed due respect for the law the FBI is meant to enforce and for the Constitution.

Mr. Webster offers the prospect of a director who can correct abuses in the CIA. But the Iran-Contra affair illustrated many other abuses, and the public will learn from an address tonight to what extent Mr. Reagan proposes to deal with them.

## THE SPOKESMAN-REVIEW

Spokane, WA, March 5, 1987

Assuming he is confirmed by the Senate, William Webster will take over the CIA under approximately the same circumstances that he assumed the helm of the FBI nine years ago.

Here's hoping he has the same success.

In 1978, when President Carter picked the St. Louis Republican as the FBI's third director since reorganization in 1934, 68 current or former agents were under investigation for domestic spying activities. The agency, coasting on the momentum of J. Edgar Hoover's influence, had trampled on the civil rights of American citizens whose political views were at odds with those of their government.

Wiretaps and domestic surveillance had been employed liberally in conjunction with investigations of anti-war activists. As such antics came to light, the FBI was being regarded suspiciously as an American Gestapo.

Webster, without overreacting, brought a welcome end to that era. He punished only a handful of the 68, letting the rest off the hook, but he charted a fresh course for the agency.

Under his guidance, the FBI abandoned its ideological bent and focused instead on white-collar crime, the mob, terrorism — matters that Webster rightly considered the agency's proper concern.

Now, with only a year before his 10-year FBI term ends, Webster is being summoned by President Reagan to take charge of the CIA. Like the FBI of a decade ago, the CIA has been directly involved in operations that have the nation concerned. not to mention a president in trouble.

The agency's involvement in Central American subterfuge equates in some ways with the FBI's dubious activities in the early 1970s. The CIA has subverted the express will of Congress, violated international law and interfered in the affairs of sovereign nations. This it has done not only without the knowledge or consent of Congress but also many times without the say-so of the White House.

Initial reaction in Congress to Webster's selection has been favorable, although that should not be seen as an assurance of smooth sailing. Congress is not in a mood to deal cursorily with confirmations just now, especially not confirmations in the foreign-policy arena.

Besides, after nine years in a sensitive public role, Webster has accumulated plenty of vulnerabilities to be probed. Webster and the FBI have been accused of being overly gentle with various Reagan administration figures — from former national security adviser Richard Allen and former Labor Secretary Raymond Donovan to Lt. Col. Oliver North — and the Senate is likely to pose some pointed questions along those lines.

Webster's reputation for forthright answers will be tested.

If he survives this process, as he did before another Democratic Senate in 1978, William Webster's demonstrated talent at taming a runaway agency could be artfully applied in the organization which the late Sen. Frank Church of Idaho once labeled a "rogue elephant," the CIA.

## Post-Tribune

*Gary, IN, March 5, 1987*

President Reagan has made two excellent choices for top spots in his administration. Howard Baker brings ability, political understanding and experience to the chief of staff office. William Webster is the right man to rescue the Central Intelligence Agency from mediocrity and fumbling.

Reagan needs people of that caliber in his period of trial resulting from incredible mistakes in his administration.

The president has tried to run the government with several lightweights, so it is encouraging to see him add a couple of heavyweights. Baker has replaced Donald Regan, a man of considerable ability in the business world who did not belong in a public position of such power. He lacked sensitivity and he could not control his ego. Regan was not a team player.

Baker will be a great improvement.

Picking Webster to head the CIA suggests that the president either has seen the light or is getting some very wise advice. Webster was a federal judge when President Jimmy Carter made him head of the FBI in 1977. He brought integrity and efficiency to the agency that was floundering. He will have no difficulty winning confirmation.

Under William Casey, who resigned because of illness, the CIA's involvement in the Iran arms deal and aid to the rebels in Nicaragua negated some of the positive aspects of his reign. It was the agency's involvement that doomed the comfirmation of Robert Gates, deputy director of the agency.

Baker and Webster were chosen because they will help the president regain some of his lost credibility, but that is secondary — they are competent. They were not chosen out of friendship or to repay a political debt. That's a switch.

## THE DENVER POST

*Denver, CO, March 2, 1987*

President Reagan's nomination of Robert Gates to become director of the Central Intelligence Agency has come under criticism and may be put on hold by the Senate.

That's a good idea.

While Gates is a career CIA man — a fact that we find appealing — there's accumulating evidence he's more a bureaucrat than he is a leader and, worse, a man willing to hide in the bureaucracy.

In confirmation hearings before the Senate Intelligence Committee, Gates' answers ranged from evasive to plain dumb.

He professed to know little about testimony he had actually helped prepare for his predecessor, William J. Casey, testimony that concerned the Iran-contra scandal and CIA involvement.

When questioned about secret — and likely illegal — payments reportedly made to the Nicaraguan contras, Gates displayed less curiosity and deductive instincts than the average elevator operator on Capitol Hill. His statements, if they were to be believed, amounted to a kind of studious ignorance.

Many senators now describe themselves as uneasy with, if not opposed to, the Gates confirmation.

He's serving as the acting CIA director, and he'll stay there. It would seem wise to postpone his confirmation until more of the facts of the Iran-contra mess are uncovered. Such disclosures might illuminate Gates' own case.

## Los Angeles Times

*Los Angeles, CA, March 4, 1987*

President Reagan's decision to name William H. Webster, director of the Federal Bureau of Investigation, to succeed William J. Casey as director of Central Intelligence is a wise move that should go far toward restoring the people's confidence in the integrity of the CIA. Webster's willingness to accept a messy and complicated challenge speaks of his honor and sense of duty as a public servant.

"Judge" Webster, as he is known from his previous service on the federal bench, is the kind of public official in whom the United States abounds but whose numbers have been conspicuously sparse recently at the top levels of the Reagan Administration. He is a straightforward man of integrity who, by all accounts, puts personal considerations aside in favor of his obligations to his public charge.

The CIA is in need of such a man. By its secretive nature naturally prey to the abuse of power, the CIA in Casey has had for the last six years a director who was as indifferent to constitutional restraints as he was enthusiastic about the use of secret means and covert wars.

The agency must give honest reports and untainted assessments to its master, the government; when the CIA acts, it must act in strict conformity to the demands of the Constitution and the requirements of Congress. Judge Webster's record in restoring the integrity of the FBI is testimony to his fitness for doing the same for the CIA.

Well, sweet can be the uses of adversity. After humiliating himself and his office and his country with the help of some of his top assistants, the President has replaced his headstrong chief of staff, Donald T. Regan, with the eminently sensible Howard H. Baker Jr., and now he has given us Webster for Casey. There is much more to do. This is a beginning, but it is a good beginning.

## THE BLADE

*Toledo, OH, March 5, 1987*

ANYONE who thinks the impact of the Irangate scandal is limited to the Oval Office should consider the case of Robert Gates, whose nomination to head the Central Intelligence Agency has been withdrawn by President Reagan. William Webster, FBI chief, has been nominated to head the agency.

When CIA Director William Casey resigned in December because of brain cancer, Mr. Gates became acting director and was nominated to succeed Mr. Casey. This seemed logical at the time because Mr. Gates had been Mr. Casey's deputy since last April.

But Mr. Gates found that the agency's work in the Iran-contra mess has become his tar baby, too. Several members of the Senate Intelligence Committee said Mr. Gates "was not forthcoming" about his role in the controversy.

With Irangate uppermost in Congress' mind, the nomination quickly became doomed. Mr. Reagan instead has chosen Mr. Webster, a highly qualified individual who is not implicated in Irangate. He has considerable experience in government work, including a federal judgeship. This experience will help give him the perspective needed to review the role that the CIA is supposed to play in the world today.

No one questions the use of the agency as the eyes and ears of the United States. But how active the CIA should be in covert activities is a matter that should be debated within the executive and legislative branches of government.

The agency must not again become an out-of-control entity that answers to virtually no one outside its walls, as seemingly was the case during the Iran-contra mess. But the CIA also cannot be the kind of totally accountable and accessible agency that some critics would like it to be.

Mr. Webster will undergo close scrutiny from Congress. That is necessary and desirable in order to determine if he is as capable as he appears to be to fill the CIA post.

## Reagan Admits 'Mistake' in Iran Arms-for-Hostages Trade

President Ronald Reagan March 4, 1987 acknowledged for the first time that his administration had swapped arms for hostages, and concluded that "it was a mistake." In a 13-minute, nationally televised speech, Reagan responded to the Tower Commission, which a week earlier had issued a report highly critical of the President for allowing his staff to engineer arms sales to Iran and private assistance to the Nicaraguan rebels. The report said that he accepted the Tower panel's "convincing" analysis of the scandal. Although he said he would take "full responsibility" for the actions of his administration, Reagan stopped short of apologizing or accepting personal blame for the scandal. He said that he was angry about "activities undertaken without my knowledge" but that he was accountable for those activities because, "as the Navy would say, this happened on my watch."

Acknowledging that he had earlier said that his administration had not traded arms for hostages, Reagan said, "My heart and my best intentions still tell me that is true, but the facts and the evidence tell me it is not." What had begun "as a strategic opening to Iran deteriorated in its implementation into trading arms for hostages," Reagan said, hewing closely to the Tower Commission's analysis. Reagan stated that he had inadvertently allowed the Iranian initiative to become an arms-for-hostages trade because "I asked so many questions about the hostages' welfare that I didn't ask enough about the specifics of the Iran plan." Reagan promised the families of the hostages held in Lebanon that he would "use every legitimate means to free your loved ones." He also warned that Americans remaining in "such dangerous areas" would be considered responsible for their own safety. On the diversion of funds from the arms sales to the contras, Reagan said that he had told the Tower board that he knew nothing about it. Reagan did not comment on the Tower report's extensive documentation of a private air network for the contras run from Lt. Col. Oliver North's National Security Council office.

## THE RICHMOND NEWS LEADER
*Richmond, VA, MArch 5, 1987*

Last night President Reagan faced the nation. He looked solemn and sounded contrite, but he spoke with undiminished authority. While admitting his administration made mistakes, he said he intends to move ahead with his agenda during the two final years of his presidency. His speech ranks among his finest hours.

Yet it may not prove enough. The Psalmist said, "For thou desirest no sacrifice, else would I give it thee; But thou delightest not in burnt offerings." Congress, however, is not so forgiving. It wants its pound of flesh. Because Mr. Reagan did not don sackcloth, commentators stressed that he did not "apologize." Thank Heaven for that.

Since the moment the Iran story broke, the critics have sought much more than just discovering what took place. They have sought the evisceration of a presidency whose legitimacy they never have accepted. Those complaining that the President is "not in charge" really don't *want* him in charge. Their criticisms are beside the point. If trading arms for hostages or channeling cash to the Contras were the issue, the story would have vanished faster than you could say Desert One or Bay of Pigs.

In the twilight struggle against Communism — which towers over all other foreign-policy concerns — Nicaragua is the immediate battleground. Mr. Reagan bravely stands by the Contras; Congress wants to cut and crawl. Indeed, congressional pusillanimity made the Contra connection inevitable. Had the administration let the Contras die while waiting for Congress to act, it would have abdicated its responsiblity to defend the nation against an alien ideology.

Ronald Reagan's vision remains clear. His magnificent performance last night suggested once again his essential goodness. He is a man at peace with himself — aware of his duties, confident of his powers. The speech should put the sorry episode to rest. Sadly, it will not. The demand for a burnt offering will continue. The day is far spent, and if the Iran controversy results in an end to Contra funding, then the whole point of the Reagan administration will be lost.

# THE SUN
*Baltimore, MD, March 6, 1987*

Ronald Reagan is now well-launched on a campaign to put the Iran-contra debacle behind him, to turn the nation's attention from what he described yesterday as "inside-Washington politics" to the fun things of the presidency — speeches to adoring audiences, trips to Venice and Berlin, maybe even an arms-agreement summit with Soviet leader Mikhail S. Gorbachev.

Though presidential events may proceed on schedule, inside-Washington will be marching to its own drummer. Two congressional committees and a special prosecutor selected by Mr. Reagan will be following up all those tantalizing leads in the Tower Commission report. Congress will be fighting, perhaps as early as next week, over aid to the Nicaraguan rebels while the money trail from Iran to the contras is still uncharted.

Just why Washington reality won't conform any longer to Reaganesque fantasies lies embedded in the artful formulations of the president's Wednesday night speech. On the surface it was good stuff — a mixture of contrition, folksiness and firm resolution to do better. "By the time you reach my age (76)," said the Communicator, ". . . you learn, you put things in perspective, you pull your energies together, you *change.*"

Alas, there was little internal evidence of change. Not once did he admit that the very idea of sending arms to terrorist Iran was wrong. He talked about poor record-keeping at the White House but not the shredding of some of those records or the drafting of false chronologies. His explanation for *three* months of presidential silence was bizarre. "I felt it was improper to come to you with sketchy reports or possibly even erroneous statements," the president told his fellow Americans, neglecting to remind them that he had done precisely that *four* months ago.

As for aid to the contras, in possible violation of laws prohibiting government assistance, Mr. Reagan merely repeated that he didn't know about any diversion of Iranian arms sale profits to the rebels. He made no mention of the private-aid network set up by former National Security Council aide Oliver North, or of Colonel North's memo alleging that "the president obviously knows why he has been meeting" with network contributors.

In defending his detached "management style," the president said it had "worked successfully" before only to go off track in the arms deals because of mistakes in "execution" by "free-lancing" aides. But had Mr. Reagan's aloofness, his inattention to detail really worked in the past? Former budget director David Stockman has written that Mr. Reagan simply didn't know — or want to know — that his huge 1981 tax cuts would create mountainous deficits. At the Reykjavik summit, an unprepared Mr. Reagan was "snookered" (in the word of the House Armed Services Committee) by the Russians.

Despite the omissions and circumlocutions that abounded in the president's Wednesday night speech, his acceptance of responsibility for what happened on his watch was reassuring. We are heartened by his pledge to put the recommendations of the Tower Commission into practice and his appointment of Howard Baker as White House chief of staff. Iran-contra has changed everything, much of it for the better, and Mr. Reagan's task is to prove he can really change with it.

# The Kansas City Times

*Kansas City, MO, March 6, 1987*

President Reagan's speech on the Iran-contra affair can be divided into two parts, one reviewing what has happened and the other looking to the future and a repaired foreign policy. The look back was inadequate, the look forward was promising.

Too much attention has been devoted to the question of a presidential apology, whatever that word means. Far more important than whether Reagan speaks the apologetic phrase he has studiously avoided is whether the president ever plans to explain certain things to the country.

On Wednesday Reagan was content to simply embrace the Tower Commission's report. Yet that report is incomplete in many areas and uncertain in others, a point that commission members have emphasized. They did not have all the information they wanted, nor did they have the time to analyze all that they had.

In addition, Reagan's statements did not exactly match the commission's findings. To take a conspicuous example, the president said that "what began as a strategic opening to Iran deteriorated in its implementation into trading arms for hostages." In fact, the commission found that such trades were the basis of the Iran deals "almost from the beginning" and quoted many administration documents to back up that conclusion.

A worthy policy did not simply deteriorate "in its implementation." The president himself signed an order early last year that sent arms and intelligence data to Iran with the intention of "furthering the release of the American hostages held in Beirut."

Reagan said Wednesday that he accepted full responsibility. Yet while saying "it was a mistake" to trade arms for hostages, he seemed to be trying to foist responsibility for this mistake on subordinates for faulty implementation. Later in the speech, the president noted that much of the professional staff of the National Security Council had been replaced. Were all these people replaced for following the president's written instructions of a year ago, or were they found to have played a role in the diversion of contra funds? Or was it something else?

There were many other issues that Reagan chose not to address. Is it wrong to send arms and intelligence to a hostile, aggressive regime if hostages are not involved? Did Vice President George Bush or anyone else ever tell him that we were dealing with Iranian radicals rather than "moderates"? Why did Reagan personally order the circumvention of Congress? With the facts he has now, how does the president view the shoddy Meese investigation last November? Will he reconsider his handling of Lt. Col. Oliver North and former national security adviser John Poindexter?

All of these questions have a bearing on the country's future, as well as whether the president can regain the trust of Americans who think he has lied to them.

On the positive side, the president called attention to important steps he has taken already and he promised further changes. As he indicated, men like Howard Baker, Frank Carlucci and William Webster could improve things dramatically.

The president said he had issued an order prohibiting the National Security Council staff from undertaking covert operations. This no-exceptions policy may prove to be too stringent, but right now it looks good compared to what we have had in the past.

The president said he was adopting the Tower Commission's model for the National Security Council staff, a model based on the most comprehensive study every conducted of the NSC. He ordered the staff to review all covert operations.

The president promised "greater sensitivity to matters of the law" and a fresh look at U.S. anti-terrorism policy. He offered a strong commitment to following correct procedures for consulting with Congress, "not only in letter but in spirit." Finally, he promised to report back to Congress on everything he had done in response to the Tower Commission's recommendations. All of this sounds good. We'll see.

# Los Angeles Times

*Los Angeles, CA, March 5, 1987*

Facing an unprecedented crisis of confidence in his ability to lead, President Reagan on Wednesday night tried to assure Americans that he will move to regain the trust that he lost when the grievous blunder of his Iran arms enterprise became known. For the first time, albeit reluctantly, Reagan acknowledged that his attempt to trade arms to Iran for hostages in Lebanon was "a mistake"—a fact that was witheringly documented by the Tower Commission in its report on the scandal.

Americans want to see their President succeed. Just as certainly, as the opinion polls starkly show, powerful doubts now exist about whether he can do so. In the wake of the Tower Commission's findings, popular respect for the President has given way to widespread disappointment, while affection has been diluted with pity. Reagan's casual approach to his job has never been a secret. Until now, however, few outside his inner circle had grasped how uncertain and detached from key issues he has been, or had known of the unwise profligacy with which he yielded power to others.

Reagan is said to have been shocked by the criticisms in the Tower Commission report. The American people were hit even harder by its revelations of presidential inattentiveness and managerial sloth. A speech can't wash this mood away. Lost confidence can be restored only if the President is seen clearly to be taking command of his job.

Such a change won't come easily, if it is even tried at all. It's not simply a matter of the President's age or his intellectual powers. The real problem may be that Ronald Reagan, after basing his entire political career on the notion that government is an enemy, is emotionally incapable of immersing himself in the necessary gritty details of the most vital government job of all. But paying attention to the burdens of the office, and not simply glorying in its pomp, is what Reagan committed himself to when he solemnly contracted to become President. The office is his for 22 more months. So is the weighty and unshiftable responsibility for proving that he can do the job. In his speech, steadily delivered, he discussed changes that he is making in both personnel and policy to prevent a repetition of the most grievous errors of the past. But it will take more than a speech to show whether he can master the task before him.

# The Dispatch

*Columbus, OH, March 8, 1987*

President Reagan's speech last week outlining his administration's mistakes in the Iran-contra affair and the steps he has taken to correct them was unique in the annals of the modern American presidency.

There was no stonewalling or deception. The president took responsibility for the errors and vowed they would not be repeated.

Indeed, he has moved aggressively in naming former Sen. Howard H. Baker Jr. as his new chief of staff and moving William Webster, the highly respected FBI director, to head the Central Intelligence Agency. The quality of these appointments underscores Reagan's commitment to a new beginning, one that can rekindle the enthusiasm the American people felt for his leadership prior to the Iran-contra disclosures.

Members of Congress will continue their investigations into that controversy. The investigations are important if the full scope of the government's role is to be determined, but should not rehash areas already dealt with effectively in the Tower Commission report.

Much other work remains. For openers, the federal deficit, trade policy and national defense issues, including a studied response to the latest Soviet disarmament initiative, demand careful attention. Already, there is ample evidence the American people would like the government's attention directed toward more substantive issues such as these.

Preoccupation with the Iran-contra affair does the nation and the presidency a disservice. The investigations under way should seek to remedy whatever problems existed and to punish wrongdoers. Any effort to exploit the situation for political gain, however, must be thwarted.

And the media share an important responsibility. But their coverage must be kept in perspective and their reporting in balance.

The people, too, share an important responsibility. They must demand proper behavior from officials and professional performance from journalists. Still, they must ensure that compassion is not sacrificed at the altar of efficiency, that good intentions are not condemned at the bar of justice.

"The people" always have been and always will be the strength of this nation. With the people's support and guidance, those involved in the problem-solving process can go forward while the vital role of the chief executive continues, undeterred, in the nation's best interests.

# The Burlington Free Press

March 6, 1987
Burlington, VT

President Reagan's third effort Wednesday to explain the Iran-Contra affair still failed to answer some crucial questions about the fiasco that has done serious damage to his administration.

Contrite as he appeared to be in the television address, he did not, however, tell the public what he knew about the Iranian arms sales and the Contra connection or when he knew it. Did he, for instance, know that money for weapons was being given to the Nicaraguan rebels in violation of a congressional ban on such aid? And why did he not carry out his duty as president by ordering it to stop?

Belatedly acknowledging that it was a "mistake" to send arms to Iran does not mitigate the gravity of the action, particularly in light of his vow to get tough with terrorists. To proclaim publicly that he would not negotiate with terrorists while doing so privately was the height of hypocrisy. Even after coming under sharp criticism from the Tower Commission for the arms-for hostages deal, he refused in Wednesday's speech to admit that it was an integral part of his policy from the outset. Instead, he said that "what began as a strategic opening to Iran deteriorated in its implementation into trading arms for hostages." But the commission quoted several White House documents to support its conclusion that release of the hostages was the principal purpose of the arms sales.

Serious as the Iranian transaction was, it pales in the face of the White House's defiance of Congress and U.S. laws in sending lethal aid to the Contras. Channeling money from the arms sales to the rebels clearly was a violation of the Boland amendment. If Reagan knew about it, he abrogated his pledge to uphold the laws of the nation.

While several congressmen contend that there are no parallels between the Iran-Contra affair and Watergate, neither the public nor Congress has sufficient information for drawing any conclusions on the matter.

It now appears that the people will have to wait for reports from congressional committees to get the complete facts about the situation.

# THE SACRAMENTO BEE

Sacramento, CA, March 6, 1987

Ronald Reagan has made a tentative start toward rehabilitating his presidency with a well-crafted speech whose tone was contrite but whose text carefully hedged the president's own degree of responsibility for the Iran-Contra fiasco. Whether that calculated balance augurs well or ill for the nation's business during the remaining 22 months of this administration depends on how faithfully Reagan keeps the commitments he made in his speech, on what continuing investigations uncover about the diversion of funds to the Nicaraguan Contras and what role, if any, the president played in it.

Reagan admitted that his administration's policy of trying to develop a dialogue with Iran "deteriorated in its implementation into trading arms for hostages" and that that (meaning the trade) "was a mistake." That's hardly the same as saying the policy itself was wrong. Indeed, the president's admission that "I didn't ask enough about the specifics of the total Iran plan" suggests that he still seeks to blame others for his own policy failures. The impression thus left is a confusing one: The president accepts responsibility without saying exactly what it is he's responsible for.

If his *mea culpa* was less than convincing, Reagan's commitments about the future conduct of national security policy were more explicit. He pledged that policy will henceforth reflect "the will of the Congress as well as the White House," that future covert activity will be "in support of clear policy objectives" and that the National Security Council staff will develop "proper procedures for consultation with the Congress . . ."

On the face of it, that's reassuring, as is the housecleaning operation the president has begun by replacing Donald Regan with Howard Baker as White House chief of staff and by nominating FBI Director William Webster to take over the Central Intelligence Agency. Yet the true depth of Reagan's commitment can be measured only by what other changes, in personnel and in policy, he makes; by how much the president becomes involved in overseeing policy implementation and, most important, by how willing he will be to work with Congress on major issues on which sharp disagreement remains.

The most crucial test may come over Central America. The president said nothing about that in his speech, yet it's indisputable that his own fervent pursuit of a military solution there, in defiance of congressional and public opinion, inspired Lt. Col. Oliver North and his associates to bypass accepted channels and mount the bizarre operation aimed at diverting arms-sale funds. The president's failure to acknowledge this link, whether inadvertent or not, is hardly confidence-inspiring.

By accepting at least some of the blame, and by naming Baker and Webster, Reagan has taken a crucial first step out of the morass in which his administration has been caught. If that reflects a genuine willingness to make and implement policies in partnership with Congress and a better understanding of what led to the current state of paralysis, the next 22 months may be less disastrous than now seems all but inevitable.

# The Boston Globe

Boston, MA, March 6, 1987

He has been both a creature of the medium and its master, which is why his internal struggles sometimes resemble that staple of television, professional wrestling. Even as he spoke convincingly and accepted blame Wednesday night, President Reagan was his own referee:

In this corner, the red-white-and-blue tag team, "my heart and my best intentions," doing battle against those black-garbed villains on a triumphant worldwide tour since November, "the facts and the evidence."

The truth has been elusive for the president since the arms-for-the-ayatollah scandal began. Occasionally he makes a lunge, as he did Wednesday night: "As the Navy would say, this happened on my watch." But he has trouble defining the problem, saying, "As the Tower board reported, what began as a strategic opening to Iran deteriorated . . . ."

"Strategic" is a not-so-folksy word designed to obscure the essence of the scandal: caving in to a terrorist nation that barbarously kidnaps diplomats, butchers its citizens, menaces is neighbors and ordered the truck-bomb slaughter of 241 US Marines.

The president admitted that "I let my personal concern for the hostages spill over into the geopolitical strategy of reaching out to Iran." Again, "geopolitical" is a highfalutin way to camouflage sending ransom to an outlaw regime.

Despite these excursions into obfuscation, the president did what most Americans and allies wanted him to do: own up and move on, while reaffirming "American values" and the rule of law. Reagan also took care not to diminish "the importance of continuing investigations."

"You know, by the time you reach my age, you've made plenty of mistakes," he said appealingly. He has finally fired some of these mistakes. At 76, he is not likely to become a sudden slave to detail, so his new team of Frank Carlucci, William Webster and Howard Baker (already on a good-will mission to Congress) can bring important changes in attitude – open-mindedness toward arms control and the Contadora peace plan in Central America.

If these men do what they are capable of, US foreign policy could be as refreshingly different as the president's promise on covert activity – "in support of clear policy objectives and in compliance with American values."

THINGS JUST SORT OF...DETERIORATED!

## The Seattle Times

*Seattle, WA, March 5, 1987*

THE picture of President Reagan that the American people saw on their television screens yesterday evening was one of a sympathetic but sadly ineffective leader.

Mistakes were made in the Iran/contra affair, he said, but he could not quite bring himself to apologize to the American people or to say, flat out, "I made mistakes."

No excuses, he said — and then proceeded to list a number of them as explanations for what went wrong.

Last November, he told the nation that he did not trade arms for hostages. But that was when he was following what his "heart and best intentions" were telling him. Later, "the facts and the evidence" told him otherwise.

With high-minded purpose, he undertook "a geopolitical strategy of reaching out to Iran." But that strategy was undermined by his concern for the American hostages.

The diversion of arms-sale profits to the contras? The Tower commission was unable to find out what happened to that money, so why should the president, who was in charge, have been expected to know a thing about it?

As Reagan explained things, every mistake was due either to his heart ruling his head, or a failed memory, or a lack of proper record-keeping or disappointing performances by subordinates.

Overall, the nation was asked to focus on the president's initial intentions — the one aspect of the entire scandal about which there has been no controversy. Of course he meant well.

But if Reagan was unable or unwilling to shed light on the past, he was able to address the future with a degree of confidence. He is taking action in three areas — personnel, policy and process.

Personnel: He was entitled to point with enthusiasm to the appointments of Howard Baker and Frank Carlucci and the nomination of William Webster to key posts affecting national security.

Policy: No more covert actions by the National Security Council staff, and no covert actions of any kind unless "if Americans saw it on the front page of their newspapers, they'd say, 'That makes sense.' "

Process: NSC workings are being redesigned in line with the Tower commission's recommendations.

Those steps provide a measure of hope that out of the wreckage of a largely unresolved crisis, the president can, in the concluding words of last night's speech, change and go forward.

## TULSA WORLD

*Tulsa, OK, March 6, 1987*

CRITICS and sympathizers alike recognize President Ronald Reagan's 12-minute apology for the Iran fiasco as the first step in restoring a presidency that has been crippled by the incident.

The president was, as usual, masterful in the brief address to the country.

He admitted to mistakes and assumed the responsibility for a National Security Council that clearly was out of control in his own White House.

While contending his original intent was to build contacts with Iranian moderates in that maniacal country, he admitted that his repeated questions about the effect on American hostages held in Lebanon probably shifted the initiative to a pure arms-for-hostages matter.

The president accepted the Tower Commission report in toto, vowing to not only enact its recommendations but go even farther in straightening up the security council. He promised to abide by not only the letter but the spirit of the law in informing Congress of such matters in the future.

It appears the president has taken the criticisms of the Iran matter to heart. He has appointed two men of stellar backgrounds in former Sen. Howard Baker as his new chief of staff and Frank Carlucci to head the NSC.

Nevertheless, there is little doubt Irangate will continue to dog the president in his relations with a Democratic Congress and with the American public.

He is, because of the ticking of the clock, a lame duck president, but a strong one. He still holds great power in dealing with Congress on such matters as the budget. He still holds the key — if there be one — in reaching an arms agreement with the Soviet Union.

In these important matters, we can only hope that his moves to restore order at the White House will lead to a stable presidency for the remainder of his term.

# Walsh Asks Delay on Immunity

Lawrence Walsh, the special prosecutor investigating the Iran-contra scandal, March 10, 1987 asked the congressional committees to put off for at least 90 days granting immunity to Lt. Col. Oliver North, Vice Adm. John Poindexter or retired Gen. Richard Secord. Poindexter was a former national security adviser and North had been on the staff of the National Security Council. Both men had previously refused to testify about their roles in the scandal, citing their Fifth Amendment protection from self-incrimination. Walsh had no power to prevent the committees from granting immunity to witnesses. He could, however, delay the process for up to 30 days.

At a news conference following his meeting with the committees, Walsh said, "There is inevitable jeopardy to the prosecution from a premature grant of immunity." Under use immunity, witnesses could be prosecuted, but only based on evidence obtained independently from their testimony. In practice, this meant that criminal investigators had to obtain sufficient evidence to prosecute before immunity was granted, in order to avoid claims that the evidence was provided in the testimony.

Leaders of the committees apparently made no specific commitment to follow Walsh's timetable on immunity. But Sen. Warren Rudman (R, N.H.) said that as a practical matter, immunity for the three would be delayed for at least 60 days—30 days to "prepare the witness for testimony" and the 30 days by which Walsh could legally delay the immunity grant while he assembled and sealed evidence for prosecution. Senators on the committee said that North, Poindexter and Secord were likely to be given immunity eventually if they continued to refuse to testify voluntarily. President Ronald Reagan in 1986 had urged that immunity be granted to North and Poindexter with the objective, he said, of getting all the facts out as soon as possible.

# The Washington Post

*Washington, DC, March 11, 1987*

THE SPECIAL House and Senate committees charged with investigating the Iran arms scandal are getting restless. The Tower Commission has made its report; the president has made his speech, and the guard has changed at the White House. Lawrence Walsh, the independent counsel appointed to look for possible criminal law violations, continues his investigation quietly and without publicity, and he may need a few more months before he files a report. Meanwhile, though, the special committees have been stymied because the principal witnesses in the case—Lt. Col. Oliver North and Admiral John Poindexter—refuse to talk. Without their testimony, it is said, the congressional investigation cannot go forward.

Some legislators have begun to clamor for immunity. They would compel witnesses now taking the Fifth Amendment to testify by promising that such testimony would not be used against the witnesses in court. This form of limited immunity would not preclude the prosecutor from bringing charges based on evidence obtained outside the congressional hearing room—John Dean, for example, was tried and convicted in spite of having been granted this kind of immunity—but it would make the prosecutor's job infinitely more difficult and might very well make it impossible to obtain a conviction. That's why Judge Walsh has been meeting with congressional leaders this week urging restraint. He's right.

Sen. Paul Trible argues, on the opposite page today, for a quick grant of immunity because it is "time for the government to move on." He blithely assures us that "if Lawrence Walsh has a case of conspiracy or obstruction of justice against Poindexter and North, it exists now, and it will not be jeopardized" by granting them limited immunity. More time, he asserts, "adds nothing to the independent counsel's probe." But how on earth can Sen. Trible justify his statements in light of the prosecutor's own arguments to the contrary?

Our own view is that Judge Walsh should be given the benefit of every doubt. There is no real emergency about congressional hearings. There is no urgent need to start with grants of immunity to the big fish instead of the little fish. And there is a real political risk, to the administration as well as to the congressional committees, in appearing to short-circuit possible criminal charges in the interest of winding up the investigation quickly. No one believes the prosecutor is dragging his feet. If he says he needs 90 days more to finish his work, he should have it.

BUFFALO EVENING NEWS
*Buffalo, NY, March 14, 1987*

THE HOUSE AND SENATE committees investigating the Iran-contra affair should cooperate with special prosecutor Lawrence E. Walsh on the issue of granting limited immunity from prosecution to witnesses scheduled to appear before those two panels on Capitol Hill.

Understandably, the two special committees are impatient to launch the public hearings in order to get out the full story about the secret sale of arms to Iran and the diversion of proceeds from the sales to the Nicaragua contras.

But Walsh, the independently appointed counsel given the responsibility of looking into the possible criminality of those involved, has asked the House and Senate panels to delay public hearings for up to 90 days.

Their decision to delay the public hearings for at least three weeks responds positively to that legitimate request, at least providing time for details and compromises to be worked out.

There is no question that it is important for Congress to explain the facts of this messy affair to the public as expeditiously as possible. But that process should not undermine the essential work of Walsh. And premature grants of immunity to two key witnesses — former White House aides John M. Poindexter and Oliver L. North — could jeopardize their prosecution if Walsh decides the evidence warrants their indictment.

Poindexter and North have refused to testify without immunity, invoking their Fifth Amendment rights against possible self-incrimination. Additional time will allow Walsh to assemble any evidence of criminality against them, seal it and file it with the court.

With that accomplished, as was done with several witnesses before the Senate Watergate Committee years ago, grants of carefully limited immunity by the congressional panels would not foreclose subsequent indictments based, not on what the immunized witnesses told the House and Senate panels, but on evidence independently gathered and filed before immunity was extended.

The findings and recommendations of Walsh, selected by the federal courts, are bound to carry impressive credibility with the American public. Nothing essential will be lost by accommodating his request for adequate time to do the job for which he was appointed. The full story can still come out fairly quickly.

Premature grants of immunity, on the other hand, could produce a most damaging consequence — discovering the truth, but being unable to bring persons suspected of criminal conduct to full account for their actions.

## The Register

*Santa Ana, CA, March 12, 1987*

Both the House and Senate Iranamok committees are considering granting immunity from prosecution to several of the key participants in the affair. Their lust for testimony, however, could render useless much of the evidence already developed by independent counsel Lawrence Walsh, raising the question: Is the cost of congressional testimony too high?

Walsh wants at least 90 days to develop evidence against several key participants in the affair, including former National Security Adviser John Poindexter and his sidekick, Lt. Col. Oliver North. The congressmen, on the other hand, want those two front and center before the cameras a.s.a.p.

The rush is on, the congressmen claim, because the American people need to know what really happened. Most Americans, however, probably aren't so much concerned with who tells them or when — a congressional committee now on the evening news or the independent counsel later in court — as what they are told.

If criminal activity was involved in the arms trading with Iran, most folks probably would just as soon let the independent counsel build the case — and take it to a grand jury — without congressional interference. That, however, would leave the congressmen without a handy vehicle for appearing on the evening news. Congress is, above all else, politically motivated, no matter how lofty the rhetoric of its members.

The very concept of congressional inquiry is likely to cause problems for Walsh. Even if he succeeds in getting the 90 days (which seems unlikely), withholding immunity for principals in the Iran affair until after grand jury proceedings are completed would raise a new issue of whether persons indicted for criminal misconduct could receive a fair trial if forced to appear in public hearings before Congress.

Clearly, there is little logical justification for both branches of Congress to be conducting simultaneous investigations. It's hard to see how the American people are in any way served by duplicate staffs turning up duplicate information. Throw in the independent counsel — appointed by Congress — and you have three staffs all pursuing the same information. Not to mention the Tower commission, which had a staff all its own.

Politicians have an ingrained need to have their fingers in every pie. It helps come election time. But the rest of the time their monkeying about generally causes more problems than it solves. That seems to be the case here.

Undoubtedly both committees will compromise with Walsh, granting immunity after only a small delay. But Congress should consider junking its investigations altogether. Certainly the members have enough else to keep themselves busy.

## LEXINGTON HERALD-LEADER

*Lexington, KY, March 15, 1987*

It has been a week of point and counterpoint maneuvering on the Iran-contra front, with Lt. Col. Oliver North the apparent loser in both instances.

First, independent counsel Lawrence Walsh asked Congress to wait 90 days before seeking immunity for three principals — among them North — in the Iran-contra case. Then a federal court threw out one of North's legal challenges to Walsh's investigation.

These procedural matters may not mean much after North and friends write the book, do the tour and fade into a well-padded obscurity. Now, however, the questions of immunity and the investigative powers of a special prosecutor may make a dramatic difference in what the nation ultimately learns about the Iran-contra affair. They also may make a dramatic difference in whether justice is done.

Granting immunity is a calculated gamble. There's no guarantee that the three principals who are up for immunity — North, former national security adviser Vice Adm. John M. Poindexter and retired Air Force Maj. Gen. Richard V. Secord — will tell all before Congress if they're granted immunity from prosecution for their testimony. And there's the risk that granting immunity may completely rule out prosecution for crimes that may have been committed in the Iran-contra affair.

Walsh isn't asking Congress to forgo the granting of immunity; he's simply begging more time to pursue his own investigation. This is a reasonable request. At this point, no one knows enough to say whether immunity is sensible or warranted.

It can be argued that Congress has an obligation to provide the public with testimony from the trio before summer's dog days. But that doesn't hold up very well next to Walsh's contention that an immediate grant of immunity will jeopardize his own investigation. No matter how much anyone might like to see the end of this protracted controversy, there is no compelling case for rushing to either judgment or immunity.

## Chicago Tribune

*Chicago, IL, March 12, 1987*

Politics and the law move at different gaits. The law proceeds slowly, deliberately—often with a painful limping kind of step. Politics needs to capture the fleeting interest, make its points and move on, and so it strides briskly, looking straight ahead.

This difference in pace is why certain members of Congress are at odds with the independent prosecutor investigating the Iran-contra affair. A group of senators has begun to put pressure on Lawrence Walsh to hurry up with his work so that two key figures in the affair can be given immunity soon and be compelled to testify before congressional committees.

Mr. Walsh doesn't want anybody getting immunity for anything right now, with good reason. A grant of immunity at this stage only can serve to complicate his efforts to determine whether anyone violated criminal law and to obtain indictments and convictions of the guilty parties.

Congress, naturally, is restless. It wants to turn on the klieg lights in the hearing rooms as soon as possible before public attention veers off in some new direction. It asserts, with some force, that the public deserves a full airing of the facts of this affair as soon as possible and that Rear Adm. John Poindexter, the President's former national security adviser, and Marine Lt. Col. Oliver North, a National Security Council staff member, possess key pieces of information.

Both of them have declined to testify, citing their constitutional privilege against self-incrimination, which is why immunity is an issue.

Of the two interests—Congress' desire to get the story out rapidly and Mr. Walsh's need to build a solid foundation of evidence upon which to decide whether anyone ought to be indicted—Mr. Walsh's has to be considered paramount. Once the awesome processes and powers of the criminal law are invoked, they must be allowed to operate in an orderly fashion.

The consequence might be delay, though if Mr. Walsh is prudent he will try to minimize it in order to avoid unnecessary friction with the legislative branch. But a little delay will not hurt so much. It could blunt the impact of Adm. Poindexter's and Col. North's evidence. But it is hard to believe that people's attention in this particular matter is so fickle that they will not have any interest when the time comes. After all, it is the public's revulsion at the arms sale that has given this scandal its real bite.

It may turn out that criminal law violations will be among the least significant aspects of the Iran-contra affair. It may end as it began, as a monumental foreign policy fumble. But even so, the last thing Congress ought to want to do is to bollix up the effort to bring to account anyone who actually broke the solemn laws it has enacted.

## TULSA WORLD
### Tulsa, OK, March 12, 1987

LAWRENCE E. Walsh, independent counsel in the Iran-Contra investigation, has urged Congress to wait at least 90 days before granting immunity to key witnesses in the affair.

Lawmakers should honor the request without argument.

Many lawmakers are eager to grant immunity to Col. Oliver North and former National Security Advisor John M. Poindexter. Their goal is admirable. They want to reveal the full facts of the Iranian arms deals and diversion of profits to the anti-communist forces in Nicaragua as soon as possible.

Walsh is interested in enforcing the law. He makes a convincing case that premature immunity for the principals will interfere with his job.

Archibald Cox, former Watergate special prosecutor, explained the risk of granting immunity too soon.

"The public will be shocked," Cox said, "if the principal players revealed thus far in the Iran-Contra affair escape prosecution solely because of undue haste by the select (congressional) committee."

The twin goals of full disclosure and prosecution of the guilty are not incompatible. The public is entitled to see the full truth. But the value of that revelation will be severely reduced if it comes at the cost of letting law-breakers off the hook.

Full disclosure is important. But so is the administration of justice.

## Portland Press Herald
### Portland, ME, March 12, 1987

It's understandable that many would want to get to the bottom of the Iran-Contra scandal as rapidly as possible. Nevertheless, the independent counsel investigating the mess is right in urging Congress not to grant limited immunity to key witnesses for at least three months.

Vice Adm. John M. Poindexter and Lt. Col. Oliver North, the two men with the most to tell, have taken the Fifth before Congress. Granting them limited immunity from prosecution would compel their testimony. But it could also jeopardize the efforts of Lawrence E. Walsh, the independent counsel, to determine whether they or anyone else have violated any laws.

Walsh wants three months to continue his investigation, time that would allow him to gather any evidence against Poindexter, the former national security adviser; his fired aide, North; or others and then seal it prior to their congressional testimony. While no testimony given by them could be used against them, sealed evidence that was gathered earlier could be used as a basis for prosecution.

Congressional investigating committees of the House and Senate, along with the rest of America, want to hear what Poindexter and North have to say. Their testimony is vital to getting to the bottom of the Iran arms sales and the diversion of money to the Contras. But there is no way to guarantee that those who testify under the shield of immunity from prosecution will testify truthfully.

What Walsh wants is time to see what he can turn up on his own without the aid of Poindexter and North. He's entitled to it. If any laws have been broken, justice demands that those who broke them ought to be punished.

## The State
### Columbia, SC, March 7, 1987

ONE CAN say they've got a lot of gall, audacity, chutzpah, or whatever for taking action under the circumstances, but Michael Deaver and Lt. Col. Oliver North do have grounds to challenge the independent counsel provision of the 1978 Ethics in Government Act.

Independent counsel Lawrence E. Walsh is investigating the Iran-Contra affair in which Colonel North had a major role. Whitney North Seymour Jr., also serving as an independent counsel (special prosecutor), has conducted an extensive probe of the lobbying and influence-peddling activities of former top Reagan aide Deaver. He was preparing to ask for an indictment on perjury charges the other day when Mr. Deaver's attorney got a temporary injunction blocking the move on constitutional grounds, even though Mr. Deaver had asked for such an investigation to clear his name.

Colonel North has mounted a similar challenge, even though he was the principal actor in a drama that is shaking the nation and urgently needs to be aired.

Mr. Deaver's attorney argued that the method of appointing independent counsels established under the Ethics in Government Act is a constitutional violation of the separation-of-powers doctrine. The act, a congressional response to the firing of a special Watergate prosecutor named by the attorney general, provided for the naming of special prosecutors by a standing panel of federal judges, appointed by the Chief Justice of the United States. It gives them "full power and independent authority to exercise all investigative and prosecutorial functions and powers of the Department of Justice."

It was an effort to get around the necessity of the executive branch investigating itself. There was substantial debate over the legality of the office at the time the bill was being considered. Normally, prosecution is a function of the executive branch and is carried out by the Justice Department. But trust-destroying conflict can arise when an Administration official is the object of investigation and possible prosecution.

The Constitution (Article II, Section 2) gives the President the authority to appoint federal officers. But it added that "Congress may by law vest the appointment of such inferior officers, as they think proper, in the President alone, in the courts of law, or in the heads of departments." It was under that last portion that Congress acted in establishing the office of special prosecutor as a judicial officer.

A federal judge in Washington will hear arguments this week on making the injunction permanent. Whatever his ruling, the loser will appeal and the question will eventually wind up before the Supreme Court. The nation can stand the delay and the uncertainty in the Deaver case, but a ruling invalidating the independent counsel law could also hold up Mr. Walsh's probe into the arms-for-hostages scandal, a far more pressing piece of business that is holding the Presidency itself hostage.

The independent counsel provision has become an important tool in investigating official wrong-doing, and we believe — hope — that it will stand constitutional muster.

But if it falls, these investigations would fall back into the hands of the Justice Department. Under normal circumstances, Attorney General Edwin Meese would have the duty of carrying on the case against Mr. Deaver, his old friend and White House colleague, as well as the Iran-Contra probe. That would not be a confidence-building prospect.

President Reagan, trying to reestablish credibility and trust, has said he wants all the facts out on the Iran affair. Thus the Administration acted promptly and wisely Thursday when it took out an "insurance policy" to make sure the investigation goes forward. Mr. Meese urged the court to dismiss Colonel North's suit. At the same time he gave Mr. Walsh a parallel appointment as a special prosecutor for the Justice Department and offered him the same guarantees of independence that he has under his judicial appointment.

That should keep the investigation on track even if the ethics act is shot down. It demonstrates the President's resolve to get this unhappy business behind him in a way that invites public confidence that justice will triumph.

## Roanoke Times & World-News

*Roanoke, VA, March 10, 1987*

ATTORNEY GENERAL Edwin Meese III has his own, sometimes idiosyncratic, readings of the law, and he can be slow on the uptake. But he appears to have acted both timely and soundly in defending the role of a special prosecutor in the Iran-Contra affair.

Lt. Col. Oliver North, former staff member of the National Security Council, is one of those under investigation by Lawrence Walsh. Walsh was named special prosecutor by a special judicial panel under a law that derives from the Watergate scandal. The purpose of that law is to avoid a conflict of interest that could arise if an attorney general were called upon to investigate and possibly prosecute colleagues or associates in the administration he serves.

North has avowed that only his lawyer's advice prevents his testifying about his role in the sale of arms to Iran and the reported diversion of its profits to the anti-Sandinista Contras in Nicaragua. Despite that, he has filed suit challenging the constitutionality of Walsh's appointment, asserting that it usurps power from the executive branch of government — of which the Justice Department is a part.

Meese — one of the defendants in North's suit — met with Walsh and agreed to seek dismissal of North's action. The attorney general went an important step further: To avoid any delay in Walsh's work, Meese named him to a special post within the Justice Department so that he can carry on his investigation even if the courts uphold the challenge.

Washington is full of suspicious people, and often there is ample reason for their attitude. Some see Meese's move as potentially devious: If he puts Walsh on his own staff, they contend, he could thereby claim the right to discharge him — just as Richard Nixon sought to fire Archibald Cox, the first special prosecutor during Watergate.

Anything's possible, but that seems unlikely. After he'd discovered evidence of the diversion of funds to the Contras, reportedly it took Meese a few days to decide that, yes, this might involve law-breaking. But since he and the president made this discovery public, both seem to have cooperated in making evidence available to both Walsh and the investigating committees of Congress. And Meese seems now to be supporting Walsh's role and his activities.

On its face, North's challenge lacks substance. Article II, Section 2 of the Constitution says that "Congress may by law vest the appointment of such inferior officers, as they think proper, in the president alone, in the courts of law, or in the heads of departments."

That looks like authority enough for the process by which special prosecutors are named. But a federal district judge last month referred to a grand jury a similar challenge by Michael K. Deaver, former White House deputy chief of staff. The judge said that Deaver "has raised substantial questions as to the constitutionality of the independent counsel provisions of the Ethics in Government Act."

So Deaver will get his hearing, as will North. It is interesting, however, to recall that last April — pressed by allegations that he had violated conflict-of-interest laws — Deaver himself said that "elementary due process and fairness to me and my family require appointment of an independent counsel. . . . This is the only way to resolve the issue fairly." When that special prosecutor, Whitney North Seymour, said an indictment would be sought against Deaver on four counts of perjury, the former White House aide decided that he'd made a mistake.

This maneuver amounts to legal pettifoggery. North may be playing for time in hopes that congressional investigators will grant him immunity. In any event, his and Deaver's reluctance to allow investigation and prosecution of their cases to go forward strongly suggests they feel their positions are weak. There's no hurry to dispose of Deaver's case. But as Meese recognizes, the administration — already on the spot — would look much worse if it gave any kind of comfort to Ollie North.

## The Miami Herald

*Miami, FL, March 14, 1987*

THUS FAR, independent counsel Lawrence E. Walsh's Iran-*contras* investigation has been twice jeopardized: in Federal court and by Congress. One barrier was struck down this week when U.S. District Judge Barrington D. Parker dismissed as premature Lt. Col. Oliver North's Constitutional challenge of the Walsh investigation.

This comes on the heels of Attorney General Edwin Meese's appointment of Mr. Walsh as special prosecutor by order of the Executive Branch. Mr. Meese acted to safeguard the investigation should a court later find that Mr. Walsh's Judicial Branch appointment was unconstitutional.

The Walsh investigation's second challenge is a congressional grant of immunity from prosecution to Colonel North and Rear Adm. John M. Poindexter in exchange for testimony. Mr. Walsh met with leaders of the Senate and House committees investigating the scandal last week after the panels gave immunity to Iranian-American arms dealer Albert Hakim. The independent counsel asked the committees to hold off considering immunity for two of the central figures in this mess — Colonel North and Admiral Poindexter — for 90 days to give him adequate time to finish his investigation.

Mr. Hakim will testify on his role in the financial transactions between Colonel North, the Iranians, and the *contras*. Colonel North's secretary, Fawn Hall, also was given immunity. The committees agreed to grant freedom from prosecution to peripheral characters in this sordid affair to get the truth that the key figures, including Richard V. Secord, a retired Air Force major general and Mr. Hakim's business partner, have refused to give under their Fifth Amendment right to avoid self-incrimination.

The investigative committees already accommodated Mr. Walsh by delaying their full hearings to mid-May; neither Colonel North nor Admiral Poindexter will be called until at least the end of May.

While it is important for this nation not to remain bogged down in th Iran-*contras* scandal, it is imperative t America's well-being that the whol truth be revealed. To that end, an decision on congressional immunity fo Messrs. North and Poindexter can wai until Mr. Walsh, without further hin drance, can unravel this tangled skein.

## Minneapolis Star and Tribune

*Minneapolis, MN, March 13, 1987*

Sensible people will not quibble with the decision of the Senate and House committees investigating the Iran arms affair to grant immunity to a few figures in the scandal. Only by shielding some suspected culprits from prosecution can lawmakers secure the testimony needed to get at the truth. But the two committees should not yet extend protection to two central players, Lt. Col. Oliver North and Vice Adm. John Poindexter. As special prosecutor Lawrence Walsh told both panels this week, granting immunity to those two figures now could foreclose prosecution of the operation's likely masterminds.

The committees last week approved immunity for several people on the sidelines of the case, including Fawn Hall, the secretary who said she helped North shred and alter important National Security Council documents. Wednesday lawmakers went further, voting to give immunity to Albert Hakim, who is said to have helped arrange the sale of arms to Iran and the secret diversion of funds to the Nicaraguan contras. Because of his apparent deep involvement in both efforts, Hakim could answer questions that so far have baffled investigators. Most important among those questions is where proceeds from the arms sales went after the money passed through secret Swiss bank accounts.

Unless those questions are answered, the investigating panels might never uncover the full scope of the scandal. Without help from Hakim, the answers might remain forever out of reach. The decision to promise immunity therefore represents a shrewd swap: limited protection for a key player in return for testimony that could open the case to full examination.

Some lawmakers now favor striking similar deals with North and Poindexter. Granting immunity to them, some insist, would assure quick exposure of the complete story. But as Walsh argued in meetings with both committees this week, doing so could also have the less wholesome consequence of jeopardizing prosecution of the scandal's two central figures. Were North and Poindexter to receive a promise of immunity at this point, Walsh would be forced to prove in court that his case against them was in no way built upon the congressional testimony — a daunting and perhaps impossible task.

To spare himself trouble and preserve the prosecution option, Walsh has asked both House and Senate panels to delay granting immunity to North and Poindexter for 90 days. That is a reasonable request. The committees should comply.

# Barbara Walters Carried Message

Barbara Walters of American Broadcasting Company (ABC) News delivered a memo from Iranian arms dealer Manucher Ghorbanifar to the White House following an interview with Ghorbanifar, it was reported March 16, 1987. ABC and the White House confirmed the report, with ABC noting that Walters' action "was in violation of a literal interpretation of network policy."

Walters had interviewed Ghorbanifar together with Saudi arms dealer Adnan Khashoggi in December 1986. After the interview, Ghorbanifar took Walters aside and asked her to convey some information to President Reagan. Walters gave the White House a typed, unsigned letter and her handwritten notes from the private conversation with Ghorbanifar. Walters told the *Wall Street Journal*, which first reported the story, that some of the material concerned payments from the Iran arms deal that were passed to a faction in Iran controlled by Ayatollah Hussein Ali Montazeri, the designated successor to Ayatollah Ruhollah Khomeini.

## The Hutchinson News

*Hutchinson, KS, March 17, 1987*

The U.S. Postal Service need not feel so bad about its high cost of delivering mail.

No matter how much the Postal Service begins to charge for its stamps, the service will never reach the new levels of mail delivery cost set by Barbara Walters. Ms. Walters, who is paid many millions of dollars each year for her journalistic-entertainment show on ABC, is also in the business on the side of delivering mail to the president.

She acted as an agent to deliver secret messages from an Iranian arms merchant to President Reagan shortly after the Iran arms-hostage scandal broke. Her role in the delivery of a private message from arms dealer Manucher Ghorbanifar to President Reagan last December was exposed Monday by the Wall Street Journal.

She carried messages from the key Iranian arms dealer to Reagan, who read them and months later turned the copies over to the Tower Commission, which investigated the scandal.

Whether or not the Iranian's secret messages helped Mr. Reagan, the delivery service most certainly does not help the news business.

Too many news reporters or high priced readers of news on TV are already perceived as being biased, with their own axes to grind, or with too much power for their own good.

Barbara Walters' mail service is a disservice to journalism, though whether or not TV news is journalism may be open to further discussion. Reporters should report news, not make it.

## SYRACUSE HERALD·JOURNAL

*Syracuse, NY, March 20, 1987*

Television interviewer Barbara Walters' admission that she passed secret messages from Iranian arms dealer Manucher Ghorbanifar to President Reagan, has caused a mild furor in the journalistic community.

At issue is whether Walters abused her role as a journalist by acting as a conduit for the White House and delivering two notes dealing with the Iranian arms sales.

Walters, who felt "terrible" about what she had done, had little to say, except that she believed the notes contained essential information. "So, I made sure it was delivered," she told the Wall Street Journal.

Some journalists felt differently. Comments ranged from "journalists, no matter how important they think they are ... should not become part of a story or act as an agent to anyone," to "her actions damaged the credibility of the entire American press."

But, the central issue here seems to be buried in the debate over how, specifically, Walters violated her journalistic responsibilities.

Instead, perhaps discussion should be aimed at defining Walter's true vocation. Only then can the depth of her transgressions — if any exist — be determined.

Is Walters a journalist? Or, is she a television celebrity who interviews other celebrities for a living?

What complicates the assessment is that Walters, like so many of her peers, has so successfully merged the roles of television journalist and television personality/host, it is difficult to distinquish one from the other.

If she is a journalist, then why at the height of the Philippine crisis did she fail to mention that subject when interviewing the president? Instead, she inquired about his movie-viewing habits, one newspaper editor observed.

Much of the lack of clarity of positions can be blamed on the television network executives. They are responsible for elevating newscasters to celebrity status with million-plus salaries and perks befitting rock stars. In the fight to win the ratings war, they have replaced journalists with personalities or allowed journalists to play both sides of the fence.

Even Dan Rather, with solid journalism credentials, evoked criticism after he wrote a passionate article in the New York Times Op/Ed section, bemoaning the cutbacks at CBS.

Critics pointed out the networks might be able to maintain journalistic standards if they didn't have to spend millions of dollars on salaries, elite hotel accommodations, limousine service, etc., for golden-newscasters.

ABC's comment on Walters' note-passing was an evasive statement, which surely would have been dismissed as a case of hiding behind corporate mumbo jumbo if another company or government agency had been the source.

It is apparent that since ABC considers Walters a journalist, she should adhere to the rules of journalism, particularly the one that calls for distance between a journalist and the story.

Perhaps the networks should clearly reaffirm to Walters and others like her exactly who they are supposed to be.

Obviously, Walters is confused, too.

"It is unimportant whether I delivered it (the notes) or somebody else did," she said.

The Editors
The Wall Stweet Journal

Sirs:
In weplying to the wecent scuwwilous attacks upon me
wegarding my actions in cawwying messages fwom Mr.
Ghorbanifar, the arms middleman, to Pwesident Weagan
during the Iwan Arms Cwisis, let me pwotest the
weckless diswegard some cowwespondents seem to have
for my woyal status in the pwess world. We all know
Mr. Ghorbanifar is a wuthless wogue, and I find it
extweemely embawwassing to my weputation to be winked
with him in this wegard. We of the multi-million dollar
pwess cannot be held to such wigid wules which would
pwevent us fwom serving our Pwesident and Countwy.
We are beyond this silly wecwimination and wepwoach.
Wemember, we too, are Amewicans!
I twust you will wemedy the situation and pwevent a
wecuwwence of this wuthless hounding of the Media
by the media.
　　　　　　　　Wespectfully yours,

　　　　　　　Barbara WaWa

P.S. I only hope my pubwic will understand.

HOW WUDE-
YOU MUST BE
FUWIOUS!

## The Grand Rapids Press

*Grand Rapids, MI, March 20, 1987*

Barbara Walters delivered a message from arms dealer Ghorbnifar to President Reagan. Sometimes it's hard to tell a celebrity journalist from a groupie.

George Bush delivered a message from a contra financier to Oliver North. Sometimes it's hard to tell a vice president from a celebrity journalist.

Food and Drug administrators delivered approval of the hair restorer Menoxydil. Sometimes it's hard to tell a food and drug administrator from a guy who uses his head as a government test site.

Massachusetts Gov. Michael Dukakis will run for president. Sometimes it's hard to tell a Dukakis from a Babbitt or a Gephardt — or a Stassen.

## The Seattle Times

*Seattle, WA, March 18, 1987*

CALL it Iwanscam. Baba Wawa, pwominent ABC television cowwespondent, wepowtedly agweed to cawwy secwet messages fwom an Iwanian awms mewchant to Pwesident Wonald Weagan.

Wawa was wwong. Wepowtews shouldn't sewve as intewmediawies. She has tawnished the weputation of the pwess.

While not a cwime, Wawa's act bwoke ABC news wegulations bawwing coopewwation with govewnment agencies, netwowk officials said. But Wawa, who has a multimillion-dollaw contwact, won't be webuked.

**Barbara Walters**    Bill Plympton

At least she could say: "I'm sowwy."

There's appawently no twuth to wumows that due to Wawa's tewwible fowesight, ABC's populaw pwogwam "Twenty/Twenty" will be wenamed "Twenty/Fowty" — or that Wawa may soon co-staw with fowmew ABC pewsonality Gewaldo Wivewa in "We Weopened Al Capone's Secwet Undewgwound Wumpus Woom."

# The Evening Gazette

*Worcester, MA, March 19, 1987*

Barbara Walters' gushy, simpering interviewing style grates on a lot of people, not the least other journalists. Her latest exploit — inserting herself into a story as a news source instead of a news reporter — has even raised the hackles of ABC News, which pays her multimillion-dollar salary.

After interviewing an Iranian arms dealer and a Saudi businessman for ABC's "20/20," Ms. Walters sent two private memos to the White House, passing on messages about the diversion of arms profits to the Nicaraguan Contras — including some information apparently not included in the televised interviews.

Some might venture that Ms. Walters performed some small service to the government in relaying the information, although the Tower Commission didn't consider the memos important enough to include in its report. But by becoming part of the action — perhaps in an attempt to cozy up to the White House — Ms. Walters violated ABC's own stricture against such actions.

Furthermore, by omitting some information from the broadcast, she also did a disservice to the public, which depends on journalists to report all the significant news — and she considered this important enough to pass on to the White House. Her viewers will be forgiven for wondering what other information is being withheld.

If only Ms. Walter's reputation were at stake, the issue would hardly be worth comment. But such lapses also besmirch the honest efforts of other journalists to maintain an objective, even adversarial stance — a role acknowledged by the Founding Fathers and protected by the Bill of Rights.

America's free press has survived worse than this unseemly incident, and no doubt it will survive this one, too. Still, we can't help but sympathize with the wag who suggested that ABC should air a one-liner before each of Ms. Walters' interviews: "I'm not a journalist, but I play one on TV."

# U.S. Senate Rejects Contra Aid Cutoff

By a narrow margin, 52-48, the United States Senate March 18, 1987 voted against a resolution that would block payment to the Nicaraguan contras of the $40 million in aid remaining from a $100 million package approved in 1986. The House of Representatives a week earlier had approved a resolution delaying further aid for six months and requiring President Reagan to provide an accounting of all funds disbursed to date.

Senate leaders characterized the March 18 vote as a signal to the Reagan administration that it faced problems gaining approval of its request for $105 million in contra aid for the 1988 fiscal year. Majority Leader Robert Byrd (D, W. Va.) said, "This vote is not a victory for the administration's course of action in Central America." He added, "it says the American people themselves have grave reservations about the administration's policy." Forty Democrats and eight Republicans voted to cut off the $40 million, while 38 Republicans and 14 Democrats voted against the cutoff measure. The resolution was sponsored by Republican Sen. Lowell Weicker (Conn.), who argued that the Reagan administration's policies in Central America had tarnished the image of the U.S. throughout the world. He called the contra program a "grubby, sleazy little operation."

Before the vote, Nicaraguan president Danield Ortega Saavedra expressed his concern. In an interview March 17, Nicaragua's president, Daniel Ortega Saavedra, said fundamental changes in attitudes of the Reagan administration were necessary before any regional peace plan could succeed. At the same time he offered concessions to satisfy U.S. security concerns in Central America. Ortega said Nicaragua was willing to sign an accord that would permit the U.S. to establish bases and conduct maneuvers in any country that invited American troops. The U.S. Senate, in a nonbinding vote March 12, had endorsed a peace plan for Central America proposed in January by the president of Costa Rica, Oscar Arias Sanchez that would offer an amnesty and cease-fire to rebels fighting the governments of these nations.

## THE ARIZONA REPUBLIC
### Phoenix, AZ, March 19, 1987

CONGRESSIONAL opponents of the Nicaraguan *contras* have been on a scavenger hunt, looking for excuses to cut off U.S. aid. The Iran arms sale affair has provided them just the pretense to attempt to suspend the final $40 million of the $100 million voted last year.

Although the Senate Wednesday turned back an attempt to renege on promises made to the *contras* on a 52-48 vote — a measure similar to one which passed the House — further congressional funding appears doubtful and the Reagan administration's whole Nicaragua policy is in jeopardy, but for erroneous reasons.

*Contra* opponents, such as Sen. Joe Biden, D-Del., have used the Irans arms affair as a pretext to assault the policy. Reports persist, without a shred of material evidence, that profits from the sale of arms to Iran were diverted to the *contras*. It now appears, however, that much of the money remained in the Mideast, paid to Iranian politicians and Mideast arms merchants.

According to reports in *The New York Times*, substantial bribes were paid to Hashemi Rafsanjani, speaker of the Iranian Parliament, and to the Global Islamic Movement. The latter is controlled by Ayatollah Hussein Ali Montazeri, who is responsible for Iran's international revolutionary groups.

Global Islamic Movement and Montazeri control thousands of Iranian Revolutionary Guards in Lebanon, as well as pro-Iranian terrorist groups in Beirut, such as Hezbollah, who are believed to hold some of the American hostages. Montazeri and Rafsanjani are political rivals and each aspires to succeed the Ayatollah Khomeini when the seemingly immortal mullah finally dies.

As much as $15 million of the arms sale profits reportedly was paid out to these Iranian parties as bribes and more probably ended up in the hands of Mideast arms dealers as commissions for their services. This leaves precious little for the *contras*.

What any of this Iranian lunacy has to do with Nicaragua or the *contras* is clear only to the likes of Biden, who embraces any excuse, no matter how absurd, to attack the Reagan administration's Central American policy. The idea of paying ransom to the kidnappers of American hostages is repulsive on the face of it, but it is utterly irrelevant to the merits of the *contra* policy.

Sen. Richard Lugar, R-Ind., ranking minority member of the Foreign Relations Committee, puts the case succinctly: Opponents of *contra* aid have no viable alternative policy to prevent Nicaragua from becoming another Soviet colony.

If Biden and other congressional naysayers are determined to abandon those fighting to return democracy to their homeland, it is incumbent upon them to bring forth an alternative policy. They haven't because they can't. For honesty's sake they should admit their opposition to the *contras* amounts to abandoning Nicaragua to the twilight zone of communist totalitarianism. For better or worse, the *contras* represent the only realistic hope of restoring freedom to Nicaragua.

## THE RICHMOND NEWS LEADER
### Richmond, VA, March 18, 1987

Does Jim Wright know anything about American history? His leadership in the House's vote to cut off aid to the Contras raises doubts.

Here's how the House "reasoned" — if that's the word for it: The Contras can't win and their leaders don't get along, so we should abandon them and try to negotiate with Nicaragua's Communists instead.

Thank goodness the French thought differently during the American Revolution. The U.S. would not have won Independence when it did (if at all) without French aid, and France supported the Americans despite their miserable won-lost record.

The Minutemen didn't win many big battles. They took Saratoga, Princeton, and several others, but the Redcoats won most of the major contests. The British held the big cities, controlled the crucial roads, and occupied the strategic forts.

Moreover, the American leaders did not always like each other. George Washington is the father of his country, but during the Revolution other officers challenged his custody rights. Some Americans "defected" to the British — Benedict Arnold, for one. The networks would have described the Continental leadership as being — at the very least — in "disarray."

Although the cause looked hopeless, the French came in on America's side. They provided "secret" aid before Rochambeau arrived in Virginia with 6,000 French troops. At Yorktown, the French stood side by side with the Americans; the French fleet kept the British navy at bay. If he had faced American forces alone, Cornwallis would not have surrendered.

Thus if France had treated the Patriots the way the House treats the Contras, we all would be singing, "God save the Queen." When other Central American countries fall to Communism — and the issue is no longer *if* but *when* — the remnant will not sing "God save Jim Wright and the Congress," but rather "God help us — and them."

## The Courier-Journal & TIMES
*Louisville, KY, March 20, 1987*

NICARAGUA'S *contra* rebels are being supplied with the plans for U.S.-built installations in that country. The idea is to make it easier for *contra* fighters to destroy dams, bridges, power stations and port installations and thus weaken the leftist Sandinista government.

Now, if the Sandinista regime should fall, we will get the bill for rebuilding them. Just another reason for the world to laugh at us.

## The State
*Columbia, SC, March 27, 1987*

OPPONENTS of the Contras, who are battling the Marxist-sponsored Sandinistas in Nicaragua, have reason to celebrate. The ragtag, loosely linked rebels are in trouble on at least three fronts — in their leadership, in the halls of Congress and on the battlefield.

The Contras' umbrella leadership is falling apart. Arturo Cruz, a respected former Sandinista, has resigned from the three-man directorate over the Contras in protest of the group's failure to move toward democracy and civilian rule.

Earlier, Cruz had indicated he would stay on the panel after another member of the directorate, Adolfo Calero, resigned. Calero was replaced by Fernando Chamorro. But Sunday, Chamorro said he was withdrawing his party, the Nicaraguan Democratic Union, and his troops from the United Nicaraguan Opposition. It should be pointed out that Cruz still supports aid to the Contras and that his criticism of the Contras could apply more so to the Sandinistas.

Meanwhile, President Reagan could take little comfort from a Senate decision to send the Contras a final allotment of $40 million in United States aid. The vote was only 52-48 and anti-Contra forces were still fighting final release of the money early this week. And, key Senate leaders warned the President to get back on the negotiating track with the Sandinistas.

The big strike against the Contras, particularly in Congress, stems from the indication that the Administration funneled illegal aid to the rebel group. If so, the Contras obviously and understandably accepted the money gleefully. But that has nothing to do with the merits of the case for or against the Contras or the Sandinista strong men.

Indeed, the broader issue is the motives and designs of the Sandinistas and their Marxist sponsors. The American people and their leadership seem to have seen the issue more clearly in distant Afghanistan, where aid has been more bounteous and the national security stakes are smaller.

A recent (March 23) article in *Newsweek* noted that serious questions are now being raised about U.S. aid to Afghanistan, which borders on the Soviet Union. The magazine, in an article headlined, "The U.S.-backed Rebels in Afghanistan are having almost as much trouble as the woebegone Contras," cited not only accusations of skimming and waste of aid to anti-government guerrillas, but questioned the conventional wisdom about how effective the rebel campaign really is.

*Newsweek* concluded: "The Soviets will have to bleed a lot more before they allow the rebels to win at the negotiating table a victory that is far beyond their reach on the battlefield."

Inducing the Sandinistas to engage in realistic negotiations that protect its neighbors and that avoid an armed Marxist camp in Central America is what aid to the Contras is all about. To us, negotiations are certainly more important in Nicaragua than in a nation that borders on the Soviet Union.

S.C. Sen. Ernest F. Hollings captured the point when he stressed, "It's time to gamble with our money now" by providing help to the Contras "or we'll have to gamble with our men later."

The issue is not only heading off another Cuba on the continent, but one dealing with a leadership that refutes its own pledges to democracy and strikes fear into the hearts of its beleaguered neighbors.

It seems myopic to rage about providing $100 million to the contras in Congress when, according to *Newsweek,* "the stalemate in Afghanistan has soaked up $1.35 billion covert U.S. aid since 1980" and, according to Senator Hollings, "the Soviets have put $2 billion into Nicaragua."

While the loss of Contra leadership will prolong the agony in Nicaragua, an anti-Sandinista force is inevitable, perhaps with diminishing hopes, as long as the Sandinistas hold sway. As those hopes diminish, so will aspirations for democracy in Nicaragua and security for its neighbors.

## The Grand Rapids Press
*Grand Rapids, MI, March 24, 1987*

As often happens, the U.S. Senate last week said one thing but meant another. Behind the narrow approval of $40 million for the Nicaraguan contras was a clear signal to President Reagan to stop fighting and start talking.

The message was appropriate and should be reiterated if the president, as expected, returns this summer with a request for $105 million more in military aid.

The contras are in tatters, a ragtag army that has yet to gain popular support in the nation it wishes to rescue. Still, the Reagan administration pushes the contras as the best alternative to the Soviet-dominated Sandinistas. Mr. Reagan's belief is that military pressure is the only way to force the Sandinistas to negotiate. Without it, the scenario goes, the Soviets will extend their beachhead from Managua to other vulnerable Central American countries.

Some of this analysis seems less far-fetched today that a year or two ago. The repressive Sandinista government is moving toward a Cuba-like relationship with the Soviets. While the Sandinistas' ability to promote their revolution is suspect, the United States has reason to fear such a firm Soviet foothold in this hemisphere.

But the contras are not the remedy. With the $40 million approved by the Senate, the contras will have received $100 million in official aid in the last year, most of its going to the war effort. Moreover, the extent of private support and covert assistance by the Central Intelligence Agency has been considerable.

Yet the contras continue to lose ground. They have never won a major victory against the Sandinistas and, more important, they have utterly failed to gain the hearts and minds of the rural Nicaraguans, many of whom see the contras as a reincarnation of the brutal, pre-Sandinista oligarchy.

The contras will not succeed unless the U.S. joins forces with them on the battlefield — and that is a course the American people time and again have said they do not want to take. The Reagan administration must move away from the dead-end contras and find another way to keep the Sandinistas in check.

That was what the Senate, despite its yes vote, and the House are trying to impress on Mr. Reagan. If he needs individual testimony, the president could speak with Rep. Paul Henry, R-Grand Rapids Township, who last year supported the contras and this year voted against them.

Mr. Henry is no Sandinista sympathizer; he simply wants negotiations with Nicaragua's neighbors to find regional solutions to the political crises in Central America.

The opportunity for such solutions is excellent now, given the recent peace proposal of Costa Rican president Oscar Arias Sanchez. The plan hinges on a ceasefire and a cutoff of aid to the rebels — a moratorium, in effect, to see if a full-fledged try at negotiation might work.

Mr. Reagan has yet to endorse the proposal and seems committed to a military solution. He should listen more carefully to the Congress and American people. They are telling him his Central American policy is on a one-way track to nowhere.

## The Washington Times

*Washington, DC, March 19, 1987*

They barked and snarled, but when it came time to bite, the Democratic Senate spared the Nicaraguan resistance. By declining to stop the final $40 million installment of previously approved aid, the Senate acted as if had some principles left, which in fact it may have.

Despite the antics of Oliver North and the resulting temptation to embarrass the administration, the Democrats seem reluctant to accept the blame for surrendering Nicaragua to unchallenged Soviet control. They may prate about the promise of Contadora, but only the most naive believe it will work. A sober look at the evidence leads to one conclusion: if Washington abandons the resistance, it had better be prepared to finish the job on its own.

Sensing that Congress would dump the "contras" if he consented to be nice, Daniel Ortega now promises to lift restrictions on personal liberty once the war is called off. Of course. But if his revolution were as popular as he asserts, such restrictions would be unnecessary and Nicaraguans would flock to the regime's defense.

Instead, they flee in numbers or take up arms against the regime. As for a totalitarian regime with a Bill of Rights, it is not to be expected. The Sandinistas will promise anything to induce Washington to call off the "contra" threat. They promised free elections once they came to power, on the strength of which promise they extracted more than $118 million from the U.S.

If the present ruse works and the "contras" are abandoned, the Iranamok affair will be regarded as no more than a blip by comparison. The major crime of the decade will be seen as unsteady congressional support for the forces of democracy in this hemisphere. Yesterday's Senate vote suggests that more than a few Democrats have come to realize as much.

## The Record

*Hackensack, NJ, March 24, 1987*

Last week the Senate defeated, 52 to 48, a proposal to freeze $40 million in military aid for the Nicaraguan contras. The vote was followed particularly closely in New Jersey, for there were hopes that Sen. Bill Bradley would renounce his earlier support for the contras.

He didn't. The senior senator joined with 38 Republicans and 13 of his fellow Democrats — all but one from the Deep South — to defeat the proposed moratorium, which had earlier been passed in the House.

Those who know Mr. Bradley know that he dislikes abandoning a position once he adopts it. Still, the vote was dismaying. His first pro-contra vote came a year ago, with what he described as "misgivings and reservations," in support of the Reagan administration's $100-million military-assistance package. Since then, the contras have gone from bad to worse.

Reports of human-rights abuses have continued to multiply. Two weeks ago, The New York Times ran a grisly account of the murder of civilians by rebels in the village of El Nispero: Contras shot two men as they were running for their houses, killed two elderly women after making them lie down on a dirt floor, shot a pregnant woman in the stomach, and stabbed to death a 9-month-old infant with bayonets. Meanwhile, Arturo Cruz, the token liberal on the rebels' three-man directorate, has resigned, saying he no longer has any hope of transforming the contras into a democratic force. Recent polls show that public support for the administration's contra policy has fallen as low as 22 percent. Amid continuing revelations of a vast, illegal White House supply operation to keep the contras afloat, congressional support is crumbling.

In a letter to constituents last December, Mr. Bradley accused the Nicaraguan government of subverting its neighbors and intensifying political repression at home — as if abuses by Nicaragua's left-wing government justified the far bloodier abuses by the U.S.-backed contras. Last week, in explaining his vote to release the final $40 million in contra military aid, the senator was equally unsatisfactory. "My support for the contras is not a blank check," he said. "There will come a time for reappraisal of U.S. policy toward Central America."

If so, when? The Reagan administration's Central American policy already stands exposed as a fraud. The contras may still be able to wreak havoc thanks to a generous supply of U.S. weaponry, but as a political force their capital is spent. They have nothing to offer the average Nicaraguan except a return to the corrupt, right-wing dictatorship from which the country emerged in 1979. Costa Rica, Nicaragua's neighbor to the south, has cracked down on contras seeking to use it as a base of operations; in the border regions of Honduras, to the north, popular resentment of the rebels is growing.

Meanwhile, people are dying. The $40 million in military aid that Senator Bradley helped approve means that more peasants will be killed, more rural cooperatives burned, more land mines planted along country roads. Already, according to the Nicaraguan government, 16,000 people have lost their lives to the contras, which is proportionately greater than U.S. losses in World War iI. People in wheelchairs, on crutches, or with war wounds have become common in the streets of Managua. Thanks to misguided members of Congress like Bill Bradley, their numbers will grow.

# THE TENNESSEAN
*Nashville, TN, March 19, 1987*

THERE is a new regional peace plan for Central America being discussed in Washington these days and it seems to have more than a little appeal, especially to Democrats who would like a new policy option.

The Contadora process, launched by Mexico, Venezuela, Colombia and Panama had been an alternative to military aid in the region. But that process has flagged, largely because the Reagan administration has been indifferent to it.

So there is a new initiative — a regional peace plan proposed by Costa Rican President Oscar Arias Sanchez to the presidents of Guatemala, Honduras and El Salvador.

Under the Arias plan, all Central American countries would guarantee full observance of civil rights and pluralistic and democratic processes. Free elections would be overseen by foreign teams, after each president now in office completes his term. All foreign funding of rebel groups would cease. All governments facing armed rebellion would declare cease fires and within 60 days, amnesties. And, a Central American parliament would be revived, with elections of representatives from each nation scheduled for early next year.

The Arias plan is short on specifics, but one of the keys it holds is internal reforms. And, negotiations would move from the hands of outside countries to the Central American countries themselves. So there would be a shift of power from the Contadora nations to those in the immediate region.

The Reagan administration is under considerable pressure to make some strides on the diplomatic front. Further, there is growing doubt that the Congress will be amenable to voting another $100 million or so for contra aid in the future.

The contra policy of the administration has been damaged by the recent resignation of Mr. Arturo Cruz, a moderate contra leader, and by some disarray within the leadership of the rebels generally. So the Arias plan does seem to be a candidate for a two-pronged approach to the Nicaraguan problem.

For the Democrats in Congress that plan offers a policy option. Recently the Senate Foreign Relations Committee passed a resolution backing the initiative by a 19 to 0 vote.

A key question, of course, is what Nicaragua's view will be. Initially, it condemned the plan, but later voiced a guarded support. There will be a meeting of Central American presidents in Guatemala in May, including Nicaraguan President Daniel Ortega, presumably to fill in details and to try to iron out differences that may arise.

Nicaragua is somewhat worried about U.S. influence on the other Central American countries in hammering out an agreement on a peace plan.

In any event the Arias plan does present an option for pursuing peace in the region as long as it is not watered down to the point of being almost meaningless. The military option hasn't worked, and won't work. The contras lack the strength to bring down the Nicaraguan government. At best they can be an irritation to the Sandinistas and a threat to the people whose support they would desperately need for any real success. ■

# Pittsburgh Post-Gazette
*Pittsburgh, PA, March 20, 1987*

If the U.S. Senate, in narrowly rejecting a cutoff of aid to Nicaragua's Contras Wednesday, was sounding "an alarm bell" — as Majority Leader Robert C. Byrd characterized the vote — the Reagan administration apparently isn't ready to respond.

While some senators were warning that no further financial support will be forthcoming unless the administration more actively explores diplomatic solutions to the six-year war, it was disclosed that the Central Intelligence Agency has begun providing the Contras with detailed plans to launch an economic war.

Having failed thus far to achieve battlefield victory, the rebels now are reportedly mounting a spring campaign aimed at the destruction of dams, bridges, power plants and other non-military facilities, many of which had been erected by the U.S. Army Corps of Engineers in pre-Sandinista days.

It is questionable what wreaking this sort of havoc on the civilian population will achieve beyond further alienating the people from the Contras. And by supplying engineering data as a lethal weapon, this country would assume a new "technical advisor" role and move another step closer to direct military involvement.

Nicaraguan leaders recently reiterated their willingness to negotiate non-aggression pacts with verification provisions. Nora Astorga, the country's United Nations ambassador, catalogued here in Pittsburgh on Tuesday the economic damage the war has done to her country of 3.3 million people. She also promised active Nicaraguan participation in the regional summit meeting that President Oscar Arias Sanchez of Costa Rica is arranging in Guatemala in May to discuss his peace plan.

Managua's motives are suspect; its interests are not America's. But unless Washington is willing to plunge in further militarily, it must push harder for a diplomatic solution. To advise the Contras in the meantime on how to flood the countryside and disrupt electric power promises only to produce the same kind of unified resolve as did the bombings of Hanoi and Haiphong. The United States has been down that road before.

# The Miami Herald
*Miami, FL, March 26, 1987*

THANKS to help approved by Congress last year, before Iranscam became public, the CIA-led *contras* are poised for a make-or-break spring offensive against the Sandinistas. Only if the *contras* achieve notable military gains, inside Nicaragua, is there any chance for them to win renewed congressional support. So, better armed and trained than ever, they have been moving back into Nicaragua.

What *kind* of action can waiting Americans — and Nicaraguans — expect? That remains to be seen. The ugly ghost of the CIA's 1984 mining of Nicaraguan harbors looms in many minds.

But if winning U.S. political support is an immediate goal of the expected sabotage and infiltration, as *contra* backers assert, then targets must be selected with the utmost care. A chilling *Herald* report on the plans this week noted that CIA advisers are urging the *contras* to hit fewer "soft" targets, such as medical clinics, and concentrate on "harder" objectives such as military roads.

*Fewer* clinics? *None* is more like it. And no power stations that serve health facilities and other primarily civilian needs. The *contras* cannot win the support of the oppressed Nicaraguan people by making their lives harder or more dangerous. Neither can they win support in Congress with such tactics. Instruments of Sandinista coercion abound as targets for an able and courageous guerrilla movement: Military installations and prisons that house political dissenters are among them. Attacks on such facilities would be true blows against Marxist repression. As such, they might win sympathy both inside and outside the country.

Sabotage of ordinary public works has the opposite effect. Bombs set at civilian power stations, common roads and bridges, and especially at medical and school facilities can only raise the accusation of "terrorism" and undermine assertions that past *contra* human-rights abuses have been corrected.

The risk to the *contras* of winning this spring-offense battle but losing the war by choosing inappropriate, too-easy targets is high. If U.S. support for an anti-Sandinista military force is to survive, that pitfall must be avoided.

# Reagan Fields Questions on Iran-Contra Arms Scandal

President Reagan March 19, 1987 defended his decision to sell arms to Iran but assured reporters that he "would not go down that road again." The President fielded reporters' questions on the Iran-contra arms scandal and other topics in his first nationally broadcast news conference in four months. Reagan had last held a news conference on November 19, 1986 at which it was widely believed that his answers had added to his difficulties over the Iran-contra affair. Mounting pressure to meet the press again had intensified after the release of the Tower Commission report, which criticized Reagan for confusion and a hands-off style of management. The latest press conference had been portrayed as important to Reagan's hopes of reclaiming political leadership. Viewed as performance, the event got favorable reviews from many commentators, as the President fielded questions with poise and avoided major blunders or misstatements. But he offered little new information and on occasion contradicted the findings of the Tower Commission.

Among his statements about the Iran-contra scandal:

▪ Reagan apparently drew a distinction between his motivations when arms sales to Iran began and his feelings now. "If I hadn't thought it was right in the beginning" to sell arms to Iran, he said, "we never would have started it."

▪ Asked about the previous news conference, when he had asserted repeatedly that Israel had not been involved in the Iran arms shipments, Reagan said he "did not know that I had said it in such a way as to seemingly deny Israel's participation. And when they told me this, and when I finished bumping my head, I said to them, 'Quick! Write down a correction on this.'" (According to the Tower Commission, the original contacts had been initiated through Israel and approved by Reagan, and the United States had only later begun selling U.S. arms directly to Iran.)

▪ Reagan flatly denied that he might have forgotten authorizing diversion of Iran arms profits to the Nicaraguan contra rebels. "You would have heard from me, without opening the door to the office, if I had been told that at any time," he said.

▪ As the press conference broke up, Reagan appeared to reply to a shouted question that Vice President George Bush, unlike Secretary of State George Shultz and Defense Secretary Caspar Weinberger, had not counseled against the Iran arms sales.

## LOS ANGELES HERALD

*Los Angeles, CA, March 22, 1987*

President Reagan was back to his comfortably confident self in his half-hour news conference Thursday evening. Considering how well he handled the high-pressure, fast-paced affair, it's mystifying why he has held fewer, and kept them shorter, than any modern-day president.

He responded on sensitive topics and was clearly well-prepared on many issues. There were, however, key questions on the Iran-contra affair left unanswered, as well as other pressing concerns such as the deficit that went unaddressed.

By allowing reporters only 30 minutes or so for questions, he and his staff may believe they are setting the news conference agenda. But, in fact, the White House is forcing many reporters to be almost single-minded: They only have time to probe the most important issue, which currently is Iranscam.

Given the chance, most reporters would gladly delve into other areas. Indeed, if the president were to make himself more accessible, the agenda would naturally broaden, which would do more to bring Iranscam into perspective than all the administration's rationalizing. We have called for the president to have regular semi-monthly press conferences. His advisers should learn from last week's event and implement more frequent exchanges.

Of course, the presidential crisis has to be addressed adequately first. The American people still do not know how much money traded hands, exactly how it was used and the president's role.

The most important part of the Thursday conference was that he showed remorse. He didn't deliver an apology, but he did assure Americans that he won't go "down that path again." That's as close as Reagan's likely to get to saying he's sorry.

## Newsday

*Long Island, NY, March 20, 1987*

President Ronald Reagan seemed dull but not incompetent last night. For his purposes, that was enough. There were no blatant stumbles, no egregious misstatements of fact, no smoking words. If the president's purpose was to demonstrate that he is not senile or visibly incapable of performing his duties, he cannot be unhappy with his performance.

As a press conference, the 32-minute session — the first Reagan has held in four months — was a flop. It didn't really produce any news. From the president's point of view, of course, that was just fine. He went before the American people and responded to every question that was fired at him. The tone wasn't hostile and he wasn't overly defensive.

The only person who might have been hurt by the press conference was Vice President George Bush, who has said he expressed reservations about the policy of sending arms to Iran. Last night Reagan said Bush had not opposed it.

But if the president and his advisers can take comfort from the fact that he survived the ordeal of a press conference, the American people should not be satisfied with the quality of his answers. He gave the same muddled explanations that he offered last November for getting into the mess in the first place. He continued to maintain that he did not know of key facts, such as the diversion of profits from the Iran arms sale to the Nicaraguan contras, or remember key facts, such as when he approved of the plan for Israel to sell American-made weapons to Iran. And while he now says he "would not go down the same road again," he continues to defend the tortured logic that took him there.

One of the more disturbing aspects of the session was Reagan's lame explanation for denying at his Nov. 19 press conference that he had given approval for another country — Israel — to ship arms to Iran.

"I didn't realize I had given that impression," he said last night. "I did not know that I had said it in such a way as to deny Israel's participation. It was just a misstatement that I didn't realize I was making."

But on Nov. 19, Reagan's statement seemed to be more than a misunderstanding. At one point he said, "We did not condone, and do not condone, the shipment of arms from other countries."

If the press conference demonstrated anything last night, it was that the answers to the remaining questions about the Iran-contra affair will not come from the White House, no matter what the forum. Getting them is now the job of the congressional committees and the special prosecutor.

# The Burlington Free Press

*Burlington, VT, March 25, 1987*

Members of Congress do it! So do governors and many other elected officials!

Why shouldn't President Reagan do it too?

What Reagan does do is hold infrequent press conferences which often turn into shouting matches as the pack of Washington journalists tries to get answers to what it considers relevant questions.

Each time one of the sessions involving Reagan and reporters takes place, the media takes a beating.

Some critics say the correspondents are rude, even disrespectful of the office; other critics claim the press isn't tough enough, that some questions don't get asked and other questions don't get followed up.

When Reagan and the press squared off last week, it was Reagan's first press conference since Nov. 19.

That's part of the problem. Not since the disgraced presidency of Richard M. Nixon has a president done a better job of avoiding reporters' questions.

More frequent press conferences would help but there is a better solution; and that gets us back to the opening paragraph.

What members of Congress, governors and other political leaders do that Reagan doesn't do is appear regularly on television news programs to answer questions from small groups of reporters.

They also make themselves available to be interviewed by print media reporters.

Perhaps the format for President Reagan's press conferences is wrong, but that's not the fault of the media.

Perhaps, too, Reagan's advisors see an advantage in the present format.

How often does someone say, "I don't blame the president for avoiding the press. They treat him like they were a pack of wolves."

The result: some questions aren't asked; other questions aren't adequately answered, and a compassionate nation has been manipulated by the White House into offering sympathy to a president who continues to hide.

# The Philadelphia Inquirer

*Philadelphia, PA, March 22, 1987*

Ronald Reagan is not senile. He seems as up to being President as he ever was. The nation can now stop worrying about whether its President has lost all capacity to do the job and focus again on how well he is doing it.

Mr. Reagan began his press conference Thursday night by announcing for the umpteenth time that he opposes any tax increases and wants early action on a constitutional amendment to balance the budget. That kind of unrealistic and hypocritical statement from a President who presided over a doubling of the national debt should have invited all manner of questions. In fact, there were none.

Nor were there any questions on the trade deficit, his beleaguered Central America policy or his reaction to the latest moves by his Kremlin counterpart. It was the President's first press conference in four months, and the nation's entire agenda was virtually ignored.

There is little point in blaming the questioners. They were performing a useful service — the nation's first nationally televised senility test of a sitting President. If Mr. Reagan had bungled his answers on the Iran scandal as badly as he did at his last press conference on Nov. 19, his mental competence would have become a matter of open and heated speculation, dooming his political recovery. He rose to the challenge, as he has done so often in the past, and laid that issue to rest. Indeed, there was a forcefulness to his performance that was lacking in either his State of the Union address or the brief speech after the release of the Tower commission report.

Quibbling over Mr. Reagan's previous "misstatements" or the extent to which he now realizes that his policy was wrong no longer seems important. It is very important, however, that his current version of events hold up against the findings of congressional investigators and the special prosecutor. He was emphatic in saying that he knew nothing of Lt. Col. Oliver North's elaborate operation to provide covert, congressionally banned military aid to the Nicaraguan contras. If that proves untrue, he's a goner.

When Mr. Reagan finished talking, the reporters surged forward and began peppering him with questions. That spontaneous collective act underlined how invisible the President has been in recent months and how many questions remain unasked. He should follow Thursday night's make-or-break event with a series of opportunities for reporters to question him in real depth without a helicopter rotor whirring overhead. The Iran questions are bound to play out, and when they do the broader questions about where the nation is headed over the next 21 months are bound to come to the fore.

# The Chattanooga Times

*Chattanooga, TN, March 23, 1987*

The relationship between the press and the president, any president, is of necessity an adversarial one. For all politicians, desire to control the flow of information and have the news presented in ways most favorable to them. But reporters have a different mission: to discover the unvarnished facts and relay them to the public without any politician's "spin" on them. Though some people react negatively to the aggressiveness of reporters when questioning the president, that aggressiveness is essential to the functioning of a free press; and a free press is essential to our democracy.

The Reagan administration has, more than most, emphasized political "management" of the news. Reporters' access to the president has been drastically curtailed, and press conferences have become rare occasions. Last Thursday was the first time President Reagan had met the press since November.

Since the intervening months have been marked by startling revelations in the Iran-Contra affair, the question-and-answer session was dominated by that issue. Those who would fault reporters for hammering away at this subject to the virtual exclusion of others should recognize that if Mr. Reagan made himself available to answer questions more frequently there would be time and opportunity to explore with him a whole range of important issues — to the public's benefit. It is Mr. Reagan's policy of isolating himself from the media that sets up the type of single-issue conference witnessed last week.

Though long-awaited, however, the press conference shed little new light on the Iran-Contra scandal. Neither did Mr. Reagan take advantage of the opportunity it presented to set the record straight on some previous statements on the affair.

Take, for example, Mr. Reagan's repeated denials during his November press conference of Israel's involvement in the U.S. policy of shipping arms to Iran. When asked about them Thursday, the president said he had never intended to deny U.S. approval of Israel's role. Mr. Reagan's explanation only deepens concern about his lack of candor with the American people.

In response to four separate questions during the November press conference, Mr. Reagan unequivocally denied a U.S. role in early arms transfers to Iran from Israel: 1) "We did not condone, and do not condone, the shipment of arms from other countries." 2) "We . . . have nothing to do with other countries or their shipment of arms . . ." 3) Asked whether he was saying the U.S. role in arms shipments to Iran did not begin until January 1986, four months after Israel's first shipment of arms: "That's right." 4) Asked about then-chief of staff Donald Regan's statement that the United States had condoned that Israeli shipment: "I've never heard Mr. Regan say that. And I'll ask him about that . . ."

Yet, President Reagan apparently expects the American public to believe he left that press conference unaware he had denied knowledge of the Israeli role in this affair. He expects too much.

Asked Thursday whether he felt it was proper to mislead the public "for a higher diplomatic purpose," Mr. Reagan said, "I'm not going to tell falsehoods to the American people." But the question was a follow up to one about the president's false denial when the Iranian arms deals were first revealed in a newspaper in Beirut. He told U.S. reporters that the story, which he knew to be true, was without foundation.

Questions designed to clear up discrepancies in the president's statements on this affair are not malicious or unwarranted. It is the duty of reporters to seek the truth, and it is in the public interest that official lies be unmasked. For democratic government rests, in the final analysis, on public trust.

# The Star-Ledger

*Newark, NJ, March 21, 1987*

It wasn't so much what he said, it was the way that he said it. Or, perhaps even more important, it was the way that he didn't say it.

The contents of President Reagan's news conference, his first in exactly four months, produced little that was new. Once again, the President insisted he has told all he knows about the Iran contra scandal, upon which he was grilled closely.

Once again, he voiced some regrets about the direction the Iran arms sales led the country and said that "he would not go down that same road again." He also reiterated his belief that the nation ought to continue to look for ways to improve relations with Iran and "explore every legitimate means for getting our hostages back."

On the question that has been asked so often—what did the President know and when did he know it?—Mr. Reagan was firm. He did not know of the diversion of funds from the Iran arms sales to the Nicaraguan rebels when it happened. He only learned on Nov. 25, the time Attorney General Edwin Meese also informed the nation.

But what was most significant to many who viewed the news conference was the way the President handled himself. Since the Iran-contra scandals began, Mr. Reagan's critics have consistently tried to picture him as either a fool or a liar. At the news conference, he didn't look like either.

The perfomance may not have been vintage Reagan but it was still convincing. Mr. Reagan answered all questions and he answered them intelligently. He appeared convincing and he did not contradict himself or show a lack of awareness as to what was being asked.

In short, he gave such answers as he had on Irangate and he gave them in a plausible manner. He dispelled the all-too-prevalent assumption that he had been reduced to helplessness by the scandals.

Irangate is not over. There remains a criminal investigation to determine if there was illegal conduct by officials or others and a congressional probe with wider goals.

But the time when Irangate was able to overshadow all other affairs and weaken the effectiveness of the presidency seems to be coming to a close. And that is something virtually all Americans—as well as our friends abroad—deeply desire.

## AKRON BEACON JOURNAL

*Akron, OH, March 21, 1987*

PERHAPS Hugh Sidey, the Washington columnist for Time magazine, was right Thursday night in his reflections on ABC following President Reagan's press conference. Perhaps the presidential press conference has outlived its usefulness.

Whether it is a result of this president or the reporters, or both, is unclear, but what we saw and heard Thursday night struck us as pure show biz. And that's the way presidential press conferences have seemed for some time.

Mr. Reagan looked fine, seemed in command of himself and was obviously well-rehearsed. If the purpose of a press conference is to have a president *appear* presidential, he probably filled the bill.

But there was virtually no information imparted to the press or public that had not, in some way, been imparted before. At some point in the recent past, presidential press conferences ceased being events at which information was developed for the reading and viewing public and turned into something else.

Perhaps that is because of the style of this President, who seldom deals with fact and detail. It may also be because White House reporters are too busy posturing for the cameras. With only two exceptions the other night, the questions from the reporters covered ground already hashed and rehashed.

Watching the pre-press conference evening news shows, on which White House reporters interviewed each other on the White House lawn about what Mr. Reagan should or shouldn't say in the upcoming press conference, or what he needed to do, made us want to — well — throw up. Maybe we're just old-fashioned, but what we'd expect and hope for from White House reporters is digging, questions, news and information — not personal opinions. As Helen Thomas, UPI's White House correspondent, said: "The most important thing for us is to do our job, get the information out, and let the people decide."

We don't know what the answer is, but what we saw and heard Thursday night struck us as not very useful to the President, the press or the public. Maybe it's time for the White House and the press to consider different methods and settings for allowing reporters to question presidents and permitting presidents to impart information to the public in response to those questions.

# THE ARIZONA REPUBLIC

*Phoenix, AZ, March 20, 1987*

TWO weeks ago we had "the most important speech" of his presidency. Last night it was the "one of the most important press conferences." Presumably the "most important photo opportunity" still awaits.

President Reagan continues to help himself out of his self-made Iran arms sale quagmire. His sweeping staff changes, his formal set-piece speech March 4 and now a successful press conference has shown a chief executive on the rebound, in charge of the facts, in control of policy and, well, presidential.

There surely must have been sighs of relief in the White House after Reagan's confident performance Thursday night. In his last disastrous confrontation with the White House press corps Nov. 19, the president was befuddled, uninformed and misstated facts. Last night, however, a different Ronald Reagan faced a press corps obviously anxious to pose tough questions stored up during a frustrating hiatus of nearly four months.

With the advent of television, the importance of presidential press conferences probably has been artificially inflated. Nevertheless, as the White House deputy press secretary, Marlin Fitzwater, observes, the press conference usually conveys "the most honest record" of a president's physical, mental and political health. Style is generally more important than substance, and the adroitness with which the president fields questions is usually as significant as the information elicited.

The long-awaited and eagerly anticipated press conference free-for-all never developed. Reagan defused most of the bombs thrown at him, and the questioning, rather surprisingly, became progressively more tame as it proceeded. Like the month of March, the vaunted White House press corps came in like a lion and went out like a lamb. The president grew increasingly confident and even loosed a few of the ripostes for which he is well-known.

No new information about the Iran arms sale emerged — simply because there probably is little that isn't yet known about the affair — but Reagan did establish a record on the most important question still outstanding.

He stated unequivocally that he never approved, nor had any knowledge of, the diversion of profits from the arms sale to the Nicaraguan *contras*. It is doubtful anyone other than Lt. Col. Oliver North and Vice Adm. John Poindexter can fully answer that question.

Reagan could not have finally put the Iran affair behind him without holding a press conference. Now that he has — and in rather strong fashion — perhaps the nation's attention can turn to other more pressing concerns while the independent counsel and congressional committees complete their investigations.

# THE SACRAMENTO BEE

*Sacramento, CA, March 21, 1987*

It was probably inevitable that Thursday's presidential press conference would be more concerned with style and form — even cosmetics — than the substance of national policy. After four months of White House obfuscation about the Iran arms scandal and many more months of doubt about the president's health — his memory, his acuity — the air had to be cleared. In that sense, Thursday's exercise was itself a sign of the damage that the affair has done to the president and the country.

What we learned was that, with proper preparation, Ronald Reagan can still answer questions, even those — of which there were several — that fall into the "when are you going to stop beating your wife?" category. At the same time, the press, having had no chance to confront the president since November — when much of what he said about the Iran affair was flatly untrue — had to ask some of those questions. The president has never had great command of the complexities of national and international affairs, and he showed no more Thursday, but neither did he show any less.

But that's hardly enough. One wishes there had been some focus on real substance, even if most of it had to do with Iran. One wishes the president had publicly shown some of that anger about North, Poindexter, et al., that he has been reported to have shown privately. He has cleaned house, after all; why didn't he put some emphasis on — even celebrate — that important fact? Even more, one wishes that he had been confronted with broader and more basic issues: Do we have an anti-terrorist policy now, and what is it? How much damage was done to U.S. credibility, if any, both in the Middle East and in Europe as a result of the Iran arms sales? And what, other than dealing arms to Iran, is our Middle East policy?

The questions run on and on: about U.S.-Soviet disarmament talks; about trade policy; about a sluggish economy; about relations with the Democratic Congress. In his opening statement Thursday, the president issued some more platitudes about the need for a balanced budget amendment, and some more make-my-day tough-guy challenges about vetoing tax increases. If this is what he and his handlers believe represents a return to strong presidential leadership, spare us from it.

The wisest thing Reagan could do now would be to call another press conference soon, one in which it would be assumed that whatever questions he could or would answer about his own recollection and feelings about the Iran-Contra affair had been asked and, pending further disclosures, answered. Then maybe he could be forced to confront the substantive issues that face the nation. The answers to questions about those issues are, of course, important in their own right. But incidentally they'd also give a far better indication than we got the other night about whether Ronald Reagan has learned anything from his Iran debacle and whether he's really in command of his office.

## SYRACUSE HERALD-JOURNAL

*Syracuse, NY, March 22, 1987*

Not surprisingly, the president said the other night he would not "go down that road again," meaning if he had the opportunity, he would not attempt to swap arms for American hostages again.

He did not say, however, that he believed the policy was wrong. That bothers us a bit.

On the matter of channeling profits from the arms sales to the anti-government Contras in Nicaragua, he continues to maintain he knew nothing about that, so he's not going to talk about it. We're concerned about that, as well.

We're not surprised that he would not make the same mistake again because nobody enjoys taking the kind of abuse President Reagan has taken since the first week of November. Our unease about his assertions Thursday night comes about because that apparently is the only reason he would not do it again.

However, "I will keep my eyes open for any opportunity for improving relations (with Iran?)," he said. He also said, "If I would not have thought it was right in the beginning, I would not have started that."

In fact, the plan was wrong, wrongheaded, possibly illegal and most certainly counterproductive. It was wrong in the beginning, and at this point, it's becoming painfully obvious that President Reagan, Oliver North and a couple of others are the only ones who don't believe that. They still don't see, apparently, the dangers of paying ransom to terrorists, whether by direct payment or through third parties. The president, if we are to believe what he said Thursday night, doesn't see any connection between making payments to third parties and acceding to ransom demands directly.

If the national press did not pick up on any of that Thursday night, it probably is because they didn't choose to. It appears that commentators and reporters on the scene, themselves a bit battered by Reagan supporters who perceived them all as Reagan-haters, have put the kid gloves back on.

Nearly to a person, they characterized his performance as yes, lacking in substance ("no new ground"), but long on style and "command." The latter, they knew, was the result of several hours of "rehearsing," with the president fielding questions thrown by his aides. In their eyes, it was the "command" that counted. It's a matter of imagery, perception.

Imagery, the perception of "the great communicator" has been the centerpiece of the Reagan presidency. When the wrong image is presented, serious damage can result.

When substance is abandoned in the name of perception, when "looking good" becomes the most important thing, we might seriously consider nominating an inhabitant of Madame Toussaud's Wax Museum to be president. They never say the wrong thing.

## Congressional Committees Merged as Iran-Contra Hearings Approach

The special House and Senate committees investigating the Iran-contra arms scandal voted March 18, 1987 to hold joint hearings, merge their staffs and share evidence. Public hearings were set to begin May 5, 1987. The committees also set a timetable for granting immunity from prosecution to two key witnesses, Lt. Col. Oliver North and former national security adviser Vice Adm. John Poindexter. To accommodate a request by the special prosecutor in the affair, Lawrence Walsh, that he be given time to develop criminal cases against North and Poindexter before they received immunity, the committees agreed to delay public testimony by the two men until mid-June. Under the agreement, the committees could question Poindexter in closed sessions as early as May 2, "for planning purposes only," according to Rep. Lee Hamilton (D, Ind.), who chaired the House panel. A limited number of legislators and staff members would be present at the closed sessions, notes would be sealed, and no transcript would be made. This would allow Walsh to establish that any prosecution of Poindexter was not based on his comments to the committees. The committees decided to delay until June 4 a final decision on the timing of immunity for North, a former staff member of the National Security Council.

The agreement to join forces was regarded as a remarkable accomplishment in that senators and representatives were traditionally reluctant to cooperate with one another. But there was growing concern that two separate investigations would cause delays and conflicts over issues such as immunity. Legislators said the unusual agreement reflected the general respect in both chambers for the committees' chairmen Hamilton and Sen. Danial Inouye (D, Hawaii). Before the agreement the committees had planned to hold separate hearings during alternate weeks.

Hamilton and Inouye said that the hearings would proceed in three phases. In the first phase the committees would probe assistance to the contra rebels in Nicaragua, from private sources in the United States as well as from funds diverted from the arms sales to Iran. The second phase would be devoted to the actual arms sales, and in the third, according to Hamilton, the committees would concentrate on "assignment of responsibility."

## Newsday
*Long Island, NY, March 21, 1987*

In Congress, duplication or even triplication of effort isn't just an occasional failing; it's practically a way of life. Senate and House committees typically dig up the same turf in separate hearings on similar legislation. In each chamber, spending proposals are plowed through in budget resolutions, authorization bills and appropriations.

So it was noteworthy this week when the House and Senate committees investigating the Iran-contra connection decided to hold joint hearings and to have their staffs work together, not on parallel tracks. No less welcome was the committees' agreement with the independent counsel in the case on a schedule for granting two of its leading figures immunity from prosecution.

The congressional committees quite rightly want to get as much of the Iran-contra story on the record as they can from Lt. Col. Oliver North and his former chief at the National Security Council, Rear Adm. John Poindexter. But those two won't speak freely in congressional hearings if they might be convicted on the basis of their testimony. And independent counsel Lawrence Walsh needs time to gather, sift and seal any other evidence that could be used against them before the committees grant them limited immunity.

So on Wednesday the committee members agreed that they won't even take a vote on immunizing Poindexter until April 21 at the earliest. A vote on immunity for North will be postponed at least until June 4.

There's nothing wrong with putting the independent counsel under some time pressure on all this: The White House has been singularly uninformative about the Iran-contra affair, and the American people are entitled to some answers soon. But they don't want to let the guilty go unpunished because of public impatience. If this week's agreement still doesn't give Walsh the time he needs to make his case, he shouldn't be shy about asking the committees for a bit more.

## THE DENVER POST
*Denver, CO, March 23, 1987*

WHERE IT was once predicted that political rivalries would produce chaos, the Senate and House special committees probing the Iran-contra affair have quietly and efficiently worked out arrangements to unify a single major effort and responsibility.

In addition, the chairmen, Sen. Daniel Inouye of Hawaii and Rep. Lee Hamilton of Indiana, have come to an understanding with the Iran-contra special prosecutor, Lawrence Walsh, so committee actions can proceed but not hamper Walsh's investigation for criminal wrong-doing.

Walsh, concerned that witnesses called by the congressional committees might give evidence he'd then be barred from using in court, has been given most of the time he asked for before the committee grants immunity to several principals in the scandal, notably Rear Admiral John Poindexter, the former head of the White House National Security Council, and his former top aide, Lt. Col. Oliver North.

What Inouye and Hamilton have accomplished is a genuine congressional rarity — the effective merging of panels from both sides of the Capitol, including staff, investigative responsibilities and scheduling, even to holding joint hearings.

Their agreement also sets a timetable under which public hearings will begin in May, continue until August and produce final reports by October.

The prospect of two congressional committees fighting to occupy the TV spotlights and battling over witnesses and information had been a principal target of criticism and honest concern when plans were first announced for the congressional probe of the Iran-contra affair.

Now Inouye and Hamilton have come together to calm that criticism and quiet the partisan complaint that majority Democrats intended to stretch the business into the 1988 election year.

It is, as we've suggested, a rare occurrence on Capitol Hill that holds promise of efficiency. That, we submit, would be another rarity, one that all the leaders, members and staff of Congress might pay close attention.

## Rockford Register Star
*Rockford, IL, March 23, 1987*

Because of the importance of getting to the bottom of the Iran-Contra affair, the U.S. Congress is trying to shelve the natural competition between the two houses and keep a rein on the lawmakers' penchant for theatrics by combining their investigations.

Conducting one set of hearings instead of two is responsible and logical and it should lessen confusion when the hearings start May 5. In addition, the combined investigation involving both houses should reduce competition between the House and Senate over which one will "break the case," thereby increasing the possiblity of a more complete report when the information starts flowing.

The two houses also have reached agreement with the special prosecutor investigating the case on a schedule for granting limited immunity to some key individuals involved in the Iran arms sale and profit diversion to the Contras.

While the idea of immunity for possible lawbreakers still is hard to swallow, the current schedule would allow the prosecutor, Lawrence E. Walsh, the time he has requested to compile his case. Under the agreement, key witnesses could start testifying in secret to congressional investigators, while Walsh could continue gathering evidence independently to determine if criminal charges can be filed.

The impetus behind the immunity schedule and the combined hearings indicates lawmakers' recognition that the Iran-Contra affair must be dealt with thoroughly and expediently. Congress, just like President Reagan, would like to move forward, but the House and Senate know they cannot be productive until this unfinished business is resolved.

# The Charlotte Observer

*Charlotte, NC, March 26, 1987*

The decision of the Senate and House committees investigating the Iran-contra affair to combine forces and hold joint hearings — beginning in May — is welcome and appropriate. It should speed the investigation, avoid the technical complications of having two bodies tracking through the same evidence and minimize the potential for a circus atmosphere.

All that should make it easier for the committees — and the country — to focus on the enormously important matters of substance at issue. This case involves far more than mere political embarrassment, or a single failure of judgment in the White House. It raises disturbing questions about presidential competence and about the administration's use and misuse of private networks to carry out an unofficial foreign policy.

There will be an inevitable — if regrettable — tendency for opinion to divide politically. But the fundamental issues are not narrowly political and need to be faced honestly by Republicans and Democrats alike. By combining their investigations — reported to be the first such joint probe since the postwar inquiry into the attack on Pearl Harbor — the House and Senate committees have recognized the importance of their task and increased the chances of doing it properly.

# The State

*Columbia, SC, March 24, 1987*

AFTER circling each other for several days on the issue of granting immunity to the leading figures of the Iran-Contra affair, the congressional committees investigating the scandal and special prosecutor Lawrence E. Walsh have arrived at a reasonable agreement.

Judge Walsh wanted time to independently gather as much information as he can for possible use in criminal prosecutions before the congressional investigators grant limited immunity from prosecution based on testimony by key witnesses before Congress.

Among others, former National Security Adviser John M. Poindexter and NSC staffer Oliver L. North, considered the leading players in this tragic farce, have claimed their Fifth Amendment right against self-incrimination, and immunity is necessary to compel their essential testimony in this issue of critical national importance.

It is more important, in our view, to get the full story out expeditiously than it is to bring criminal charges against former Administration operatives and their associates, but the three investigative units have now agreed to a timetable that should accommodate both interests.

The timetable will not move things along as fast as some would like. The public learned the first bits of information on the arms-for-hostages deal with Iran early last November. The scandal has grown and festered ever since, and the questions still far out-number the answers. It's past time for some answers, but some things can't be rushed.

A welcome part of the congressional agreement last week was the one to have the select committees of the two houses hold joint hearings. They also agreed to merge the staffs of the two panels and share information. Other than turf protection, we could never see any reason to have two congressional investigations of this complicated affair in the first place.

Wyoming's Republican Rep. Dick Cheney, the ranking minority member of the House panel, called the decision to dovetail the probes "virtually an unprecedented agreement between the House and the Senate." It shows the members of the committees are serious about getting to the bottom of this business as rapidly as possible. Senate Chairman Daniel Inouye, D-Hawaii, said he also hopes the coordination of efforts will help avoid "theatrics." Well, maybe, but televised hearings on a subject of high interest do tend to bring out the ham on the Hill.

The timetable calls for the hearings to begin in early May, and some of the supporting players will be granted immunity by then to get things rolling. But the public testimony of Admiral Poindexter and Colonel North will be delayed until after June 15.

In the meantime, the probers are having trouble getting information out of the Israeli government on its involvement in the arms shipments, which is outrageous in view of our massive support of the Jewish State. And they are heading to court to seek a civil contempt citation against retired Air Force Maj. Gen. Richard Secord, who apparently had roles in the arms sales and the diversion of proceeds to the Nicaraguan Contras. He has refused to waive his rights under Switzerland's bank privacy laws to let the investigators trace money through Swiss accounts he supposedly controls.

All of this stonewalling suggests that a lot more than bad judgment, bad policy, and bad management is involved in this case. That increases the importance of the decision to give special prosecutor Walsh sufficient time to gather evidence independently of Congress so that he can use it if criminal charges are indicated.

While the pace is slower than one would wish, last week's agreement put the investigations on track. He may be acting, but President Reagan sounds like he is genuinely interested in learning what he forgot and what he wasn't told. Maybe his curiosity — and the nation's — will be satisfied before too long.

# Chicago Tribune

*Chicago, IL, March 23, 1987*

Awe, amazement and applause—definitely applause—are all in order for the Senate and House committees investigating the Iran-contras affair.

Against all the odds and virtually all precedent, the two committees have agreed to merge their efforts and hold joint public hearings into the affair that has wracked the nation and the Reagan administration. They also have agreed to share their evidence and operate on a specific timetable for granting limited immunity from prosecution to the two principal witnesses, Lt. Col. Oliver North and Adm. John Poindexter.

It never did make sense that two separate committees should hold separate investigations into the same issues, parading the same witnesses before the same TV cameras on alternate weeks, as was originally intended.

But grandstanding and limelight hogging have become standard ingredients of congressional investigations which are sure to command as much attention and deliver as much publicity as this one will. House members do not want to be seen as playing second fiddle to Senate members, who tend never to let anyone forget they belong to the "upper chamber," and no one in either chamber wants to forfeit time or prominence in the TV coverage.

That the two committees have forgone such selfish silliness, at least in part, this time makes their agreement a genuinely extraordinary achievement.

Sen. Daniel Inouye (D., Hawaii), chairman of the Senate panel, observed, "This is a serious and disturbing event in American history and it must be told without theatrics. Neither the Congress nor the American people would tolerate a circus-like atmosphere in which individual investigating committees compete for witnesses or for attention."

He's right.

# Part IV: The Hearings

The nation sat poised for the congressional hearings into the Iran-contra arms scandal in the spring of 1987. Although it was billed as a real-life political thriller built on sensational testimony with the climactic discovery of a presidential "smoking gun," the smoking gun turned out to be just smoke. The welter of contradictory testimony and memory lapses by key witnesses seemed to obfuscate the issues. There were dramatic moments: Lt. Col. Oliver North's testimony certainly captured the imagination of the nation, albeit temporarily, and the parade of government bureaucrats, intelligence personnel and shadowy arms merchants raised more than a few eyebrows as to the legality of the Iran initiative. But when the public segment of the hearings closed in early August, committee members were sent searching for explanations as to how and why things had gone wrong.

In sorting through the 250 hours of testimony and 200,000 documents, the committees had to reconcile dozens of contradictions and fill in dozens of gaps where witnesses said they could not remember what happened. For example, Rear Adm. John Poindexter—who as a Navy officer had been recommended for promotion on the basis of his "photographic memory" used the two phrases "I don't recall" and "I don't remember" 184 times in five days, according to a committee staffer. The conflicts ranged from minor matters, such as whether North ever told others that he was planning a "shredding party" to destroy key documents, to larger issues, such as whether North's actions on behalf of the contras were authorized. North said they were. Former national security adviser Robert McFarlane said they were not. After committee Republicans made the point that the so-called Boland Amendment limiting military aid to the contras did not explicitly refer to the NSC, the question had turned to whether the NSC believed it was restricted by the amendment. McFarlane said that he thought the NSC was bound by the amendment and tried to follow it; Poindexter said that he never heard such an interpretation of the law. "As the conflicts in testimony increase in number and importance," Sen. George Mitchell (D, Maine) said August 1, 1987, "at some point you move from the vagaries of memory to the conclusion that someone is not telling the truth."

The House and Senate committees issued their final report November 18, 1987. The 690-page document chronicled the many questions unanswered about the affair, but placed blame firmly on the shoulders of President Reagan for policies in Iran and Central America that hinged on "secrecy, deception and disdain for the law." The policies of selling arms to Iran and diverting funds from the arms sales to the contras were masterminded by a "cabal of zealots" in and out of the White House, the report concluded. "The Iran-contra affair was characterized by pervasive dishonesty and inordinate secrecy." But the charge that President Reagan's Iran overture had been handled outside established foreign policy channels caused no great surge for sweeping reforms. Though many realize that there is no quick fix, lawmakers will no doubt attempt to strengthen institutional checks and balances on the modus operandi of foreign policy. Though the Iran-contra scandal will apparently not force President Reagan from office, it has deeply affected relations between the United States and its friends as well as its enemies. Indeed, it wounded the Reagan presidency, at least temporarily, and forever changed the way the world would look at this President.

# Conservative Fund-Raiser Pleads Guilty on Aid to Contras

A fund raiser for conservative political causes, Carl R. "Spitz" Channell, April 29, 1987 pleaded guilty in Washington, D.C. to conspiracy to defraud the government for his role in funding Nicaraguan contra rebels. Channell's surprise plea marked the first criminal case in the Iran-contra arms scandal. Channell admitted illegally using his organization's tax-exempt status to fund the contras and to place political advertisements on the air for candidates who supported President Reagan's anticommunist policies in Central America. Asked by United States District Judge Stanley Harris to name his coconspirators, Channell named Lt. Col. Oliver North, formerly of the National Security Council staff, and Richard Miller, a former Reagan political aide, State Department staffer and president of International Business Communications (IBC), a public relations firm. Some of the money Channell raised was reportedly transferred through IBC and other firms before being placed in a Swiss bank account for the contras to which North had access. Miller had issued a statement denying that he had "conspired with Mr. Channell or anyone else for that purpose or any illegal purpose."

Many of the details of Channell's operation had previously been reported. The reports were based on revelations by a disillusioned former employee of Channell, Jane McLaughlin, and on an audit Channell had issued to dispel rumors that his National Endowment for the Preservation of Liberty (NEPL) had received funds diverted from the sale of arms to Iran.

White House spokesman Marlin Fitzwater said April 30 that President Reagan did not take part in the conspiracy cited by Channell. "In the legal view of the White House, the President is not part of the conspiracy."

In a progress report issued April 28, independent counsel Lawrence Walsh said that there was "ample basis" for a broad criminal investigation of the scandal. Walsh was responding in part to criticism from Sen. Warren Rudman (R, N.H.), who had accused him of moving too slowly in seeking to prove "some grand, wild conspiracy." Walsh also spoke out against additional grants of limited immunity from prosecution, saying that such grants would have "a devastating effect on possible prosecutions."

## Buffalo Evening News

*Buffalo, NY, May 5, 1987*

CARL R. CHANNELL'S admission that he conspired to defraud the government in fund-raising schemes to buy arms for the Nicaraguan contras demonstrates that the independent counsel's criminal investigation into the Iran-contra affair is making progress.

Channell, a fund-raiser for conservative causes, is the first person charged in the probe being conducted by Lawrence E. Walsh, who has been criticized by some in Congress for moving too slowly.

Channell's guilty plea also represents the first conviction obtained under the independent counsel law passed by Congress in 1978.

More significant, the guilty plea proves that law-breaking occurred in connection with contra aid and brings with it strong hints that additional violations lurk beneath the surface of what is publicly known so far.

Channell, who has agreed to cooperate with the investigators, named Marine Lt. Col. Oliver L. North as a co-conspirator in the scheme. North, a member of the White House's National Security Counsel at the time, was dismissed by President Reagan last November when the scandal broke.

Channell pleaded guilty to conspiring to defraud the Internal Revenue Service by collecting $2 million in tax-exempt donations and then using the money for non-deductible purposes — namely, purchasing "military and other types of non-humanitarian aid for the contras."

Regardless of who was involved or what laws may have been violated, the impetus for these actions appears to have been the unrestrained desire to substitute private funds for public funds to arm the contras during the two-year congressional ban on U.S. military aid to the Nicaraguan insurgents.

Breaking the law, even by those who act on the basis of what they consider noble purposes, cannot be tolerated in a democratic nation governed by the rule of law. The investiation by the special counsel, as well as the congressional probe, must be vigorously pursued.

If subsequent events show that members of the Reagan administration knowingly cooperated in these or other violations, including the alleged diversion to the contras of profits from the secret Iranian arms sales, that will be even more intolerable.

## St. Petersburg Times

*St. Petersburg, FL, May 1, 1987*

The first criminal charge — and conviction — in the Iran-Contra affair is a significant one. No after-the-fact obstruction of justice this time. Tax fraud is a substantive charge. Fund-raiser Carl R. "Spitz" Channell has admitted raising more than $2-million to arm the Contras in the guise of tax-exempt contributions to his National Endowment for the Preservation of Liberty. He has pleaded guilty to a tax-fraud conspiracy. Though it wasn't charged, it was also a cynical fraud against public policy as set by the U.S. Congress.

Another term for tax deduction is tax expenditure. Letting someone take a tax deduction is the same as writing a check on the treasury for the amount of tax that otherwise would have been paid. Congress has been generous with the blank checks; virtually any contribution for a religious, educational or charitable purpose can qualify. But Congress never authorized deductions for weapons to anyone, least of all the Contras in Nicaragua. As a matter of fact, Congress had voted at the time to bar any non-humanitarian assistance from the U.S. government. To provide the Contras with arms purchased with tax-deducted contributions took money from the treasury as surely as if Congress had voted it or it had been stolen at the point of a gun.

The *New York Times* had reported April 9 that the National Endowment had raised at least $2.28-million for a project nicknamed "Toys." A Channell spokesman said at the time that the funds were mainly for Christmas gifts for the children of Contra rebels. That much money? Some toys!

Channell's acknowledged diversion of tax-exempt contributions to the Contras brings to mind earlier allegations, still under investigation, that he or his associates had used tax-exempt money in the 1986 election to try to defeat members of Congress who opposed government aid to the Contras. Was

Lt. Col. Oliver North, Channell's alleged conspirator in the Contra aid, involved in that, too? Or will the net cast wider?

It is potentially a serious problem for President Reagan because of connections that have been established between Channell and former White House officials including not only North but David C. Fischer, a former special assistant to the President, who later became a consultant to Channell's National Foundation and apparently arranged an interview with the President last November for one of Channell's wealthiest conservative contributors. Of earlier such meetings with the President, North wrote in a memorandum last spring, "The President obviously knows why he has been meeting with several select people to thank them for their 'support for democracy' in CentAm." Just how much did Mr. Reagan know?

The fact that Channell named North as an co-conspirator does not mean North is guilty in the tax case, but it does appear to vindicate special prosecutor Lawrence E. Walsh's judgment when he urged the House and Senate investigating committees not to be hasty about conferring immunity on North.

What Channell has admitted was so brazen as to make one wonder how he ever thought it could be carried off. He may not have had reason to fear that Congress or the press would ever find out, but how could he forget that the Internal Revenue Service never sleeps?

Channell's organizations raised funds in the name of democracy and the cause of anti-communism. His guilty plea to tax fraud this week is yet another unfortunate reminder that good causes are not always what they seem. As always, the vast majority of charities that are honest will suffer because of the one that was not.

# The TENNESSEAN
*Nashville, TN, May 5, 1987*

TODAY the curtain will rise on the Iran arms-contra scandal hearings, likely to be the most absorbing show in Congress since the Watergate hearings, and one most certain to involve high administration officials.

One of the central questions has been whether federal criminal laws were broken. There is one answer to that already. Mr. Carl R. Channell, a conservative fund raiser pleaded guilty to charges of defrauding the government last week. He named Lt. Col. Oliver North, the former White House aide who oversaw the contra resupply network, as a co-conspirator.

One of Mr. Channell's organizations, the National Endowment for the Preservation of Liberty, collected more than $2 million from donors who were told they could deduct their contributions for tax-exempt educational purposes. But much of the donors' money was actually for the purchase of guns and ammunition for the contras.

The so-called Boland Amendment prohibited direct or indirect military aid from the U.S. government to the contras for two years, so a conspiracy to circumvent the amendment could be punishable by up to five years in prison.

And, the inquiry has drawn closer to the White House. Newly-revealed documents show that Mr. David C. Fisher, a presidential assistant who had a small office next to the Oval Office, received consulting fees from Mr. Channell of $20,000 a month and helped arrange meetings with Mr. Reagan and others. He kept his White House pass until 1986.

In another development, Mr. Lewis A. Tambs, who resigned as ambassador to Costa Rica in January amid reports he had improperly assisted the Nicaraguan rebels, said all his actions were taken on specific orders from senior administration officials in Washington. "Now the people who gave us the orders are trying to paint us as running amok," he said.

Mr. Tambs said his orders came from the Restricted Interagency Group, an informal organization of government officials. He said the men who gave him the orders were Mr. North; Mr. Alan Fiers, who helped make policy as head of the CIA Central American Task Force; and Mr. Elliott Abrams, an assistant secretary of state. Spokesmen for Mr. Abrams and the CIA denied the allegations.

There has been a lot of finger pointing at Colonel North, but those outside of government have been incredulous about the allegations that he actually ran the contra resupply show without the knowledge of the President or the orders of superiors in the government.

One of the key questions of the hearings will be how much President Reagan knew of the contra operation. He has said he knew nothing of the diversion of profits at the time. While acknowledging he met with some donors to a private foundation managed by Mr. Channell, he said he thought it was seeking money to pay for pro-contra television ads.

Sen. Daniel Inouye, D-Hawaii, the chairman of the Senate investigating committee, said Mr. Reagan "knew much more" about the affair than the White House is willing to admit.

Investigators have indicated that the labyrinthine searches for answers may have results more quickly than first assumed. A good many of the answers may come today when retired Maj. Gen. Richard V. Secord — who was involved in the secret network to supply the contras — takes the witness stand before the Congress. It is safe to say that land mines are going to start exploding shortly. ■

# ST. LOUIS POST-DISPATCH
*St. Louis, MO, May 1, 1987*

The guilty plea of fund-raiser Carl R. Channell is tantamount to a confirmation that the Reagan administration deliberately violated the law prohibiting the government from supplying arms to the Contras. Moreover, it is difficult to avoid the conclusion that President Reagan himself was not aware of the illegal gun-running. Given the president's forgetfulness and his casual approach toward his responsibilities as chief executive, however, the possibility that he was ignorant of what was going on must be conceded.

In admitting that he abused the tax-exempt status of one of his foundations by using the money it collected to purchase military supplies, Mr. Channell told a federal judge that Lt. Col. Oliver North was one of those who conspired with him in the deception. At the time, Lt. Col. North was a member of the National Security Council staff, which operates out of the White House. The other conspirator named by Mr. Channell was Richard R. Miller, the head of a public relations firm. *The New York Times* reported that prosecutors believe funds raised by Mr. Channell were routed through Mr. Miller's firm to a Swiss bank account.

Mr. Channell was well-connected in the White House, so much so that he was able to arrange for some of the contributors to be thanked personally by President Reagan. Did Mr. Reagan really believe he was thanking them for helping to buy $2.2 million worth of toys for Contras' families, the ostensible purpose of the fund raising? A decision to disregard a congressional mandate against supplying weapons to the Contras, which would require elaborate secrecy and coordination at numerous levels, could not go forward without the concurrence of officials of very high rank. Lt. Col. North doesn't fit that description.

# The Star-Ledger
*Newark, NJ, May 1, 1987*

The process of investigating the Iran-contra affair and determining precisely what was done, who did it and what, if anything, was against the law has finally reached the critical stage. Next week marks the start of joint Senate-House public hearings on the matter. Meanwhile, independent counsel Lawrence Walsh filed the first criminal complaint stemming from the investigation—and promptly got his first guilty plea.

For many Americans, the overriding consideration is to get the unpleasant matter over with. This reaction is understandable; we have too long been distracted from important public goals by something which is, in some ways, no more than a sideshow to the top policy issues.

Still, public confidence—and our national self-esteem—require that the matter be brought fully into the open, with no coverup and no political maneuvering. Openness and even-handed application of the law are the best ways to put this matter behind us once and for all.

The public hearings in Washington, to be chaired by Sen. Daniel Inouye (D-Hawaii), will begin with testimony by Maj. Gen. Richard V. Secord, a central figure in the Iran-contra affair who has never testified publicly about his role. Gen. Secord is expected to testify without a grant of immunity.

The defendant in the initial case brought by Mr. Walsh is Carl (Spitz) Channell, a conservative activist accused of defrauding the government by raising tax-exempt funds to arm Nicaraguan rebels. Mr. Channell, who is cooperating with the government, identified Lt. Col. Oliver North as a co-conspirator.

So far, the independent counsel and congressional investigators have been cooperating effectively in achieving their related but distinct goals. Congress has refrained in most instances from granting immunity to potential witnesses until the independent counsel's office has completed its investigation.

It is not impossible, however, that there may be some conflict in the period ahead. Congress wants testimony and the prosecutor wants to be able to indict when he feels he has established a case.

In cases of conflict, Congress ought in most instances to defer to the wishes of the independent counsel, for he has the more important task. Congress' investigation is largely informational. But the independent counsel is charged with upholding the law and punishing transgressors. This clearly deserves primacy.

# The Evening Gazette

*Worcester, MA, May 1, 1987*

Spitz Channell in some ways seems like small potatoes in the face of the Byzantine scandal that revolves around selling arms to Iran and using the profits to fund the Nicaraguan Contra rebels.

But his guilty plea and agreement to cooperate with the special prosecutor, Lawrence E. Walsh, are the important first cracks in the case. Channell has implicated Lt. Col. Oliver North publicly in court. The mysterious Maj. Gen. Richard V. Secord is to be the opening witness next week before the congressional committee. Little by little, the truth may emerge.

Evidently, Channell raised private funds for the Contras. He pleaded guilty to misrepresenting those contributions as being for charitable purposes and thus tax deductible.

Walsh succeeded where others before him failed: He secured in the Channell investigation the first conviction since the law allowing for independent counselors, or special prosecutors as they are commonly known, was passed in 1978.

But the real significance of Channell's decision to cooperate with the special prosecutor goes beyond one individual case. Now the public has a better chance of learning what transpired in the Iran-Contra scandal and what laws may have been broken. This small victory holds the promise that justice may be done and the whole mess laid to rest at last.

# The Des Moines Register

*Des Moines, IA, May 5, 1987*

Congressional hearings on the Irangate affair begin today, and evidence is already being uncovered to suggest that the scandal may be serious enough to support charges of criminal conspiracy.

Carl R. Channell, a prominent conservative fund-raiser, has pleaded guilty in federal court to charges of conspiring to defraud the government. He named former National Security Council staffer, Lt. Col. Oliver North, as his co-conspirator.

Channell and his cohorts at the National Endowment for the Preservation of Liberty collected more than $2 million from private donors, telling them they could deduct their gifts as tax-exempt educational contributions.

Some of the money was used to buy television ads promoting the Reagan administration's Central America policy, but much of it went to purchase guns and ammunition for the contras — clearly not tax-deductible.

These revelations pull the inquiry closer to the White House. There has even been a suggestion by Senator Daniel Inouye, head of the Senate's special Iran-contra investigating committee, that President Reagan knew about efforts to raise money to arm the contras.

From the beginning, the president and many of his closest advisers were implicated in the political offense of sending arms to Iran without congressional approval and trying to swap arms for hostages, despite public promises never to deal with terrorists. These actions may have damaged public trust, but weren't crimes.

Now, however, the prosecutor and several investigators are suggesting that top-level administration people may have committed criminal offenses as well. For example, a conspiracy to circumvent the Boland Amendment, which prohibited direct or indirect military aid from the U.S. government to the contras, could be punishable by up to five years' imprisonment.

Some of the evidence also suggests that the purpose of the illegal fund-raising may have been simple greed, rather than profound ideological commitment. Documents show, for example, that Channell paid David C. Fisher, a former presidential assistant, $20,000 each *month* for arranging meetings between Reagan and key donors. Fisher kept a White House pass until November 1986, while on Channell's payroll.

These and other allegations suggest that the investigation may blossom under the heat of a Washington summer and TV cameras into charges of criminal conspiracy at the highest levels.

## Rockford Register Star

*Rockford, IL, May 6, 1987*

When things go wrong in Washington, D.C., a fair guess would link the cause to money. Money to sponsor an undeclared war against Nicaragua landed Carl "Spitz" Channell in federal court the other day, the first of Irangate participants to face a court of justice — and subsequent punishment.

Channell, 41, pleaded guilty to a federal charge of conspiracy to defraud the government. U.S. District Judge Stanley Harris said the maximum penalty for such a crime is 10 years in prison and a $250,000 fine. However, the fact Channell has been cooperating with U.S. investigators and was released by Judge Harris on his own recognizance would indicate a more modest sentence.

Between April 1985 and May 1986, Channell solicited funds through a non-profit educational firm he heads, the National Endowment for the Preservation of Liberty, later funneling this money to the Contras fighting the communist regime in Nicaragua.

Channell supplied records indicating that Lt. Col. Oliver North, then on the National Security Agency (from which he was subsequently fired by President Reagan) persuaded donors to part with their money, advising them they could deduct their gifts from their income taxes.

Channell identified North as a co-conspirator.

In pleading guilty, Channell shared the spotlight with Independent Counsel Lawrence Walsh who is the first to hold this job created by Congress in 1978. Thus Walsh also is the first to get a guilty plea. The post was designed to allow for more aggressive pursuit of crime involving the executive branch.

Walsh has announced that Channell may face another charge of violating U.S. elections laws by using funds diverted from tax-free political action committees to promote Reagan's support for the Contras.

Get ready for bigger game. Independent Counsel Walsh has said his staff and FBI aides have pinpointed "extensive and specific" instances in which former federal officials misused their public offices.

# Portland Press Herald

*Portland, ME, May 1, 1987*

Special prosecutor Lawrence E. Walsh has bagged his first confessed lawbreaker in the Iran-Contra affair. And testimony Walsh has received from conservative fund-raiser Carl R. Channell suggests that Congress should reconsider any plans to grant immunity from prosecution to Lt. Col. Oliver North.

As of now, House and Senate Select Committees apparently plan to grant limited immunity to North next month in order to get him to tell what he knows. But Walsh is having pretty good luck on his own, uncovering testimony that suggests wrongdoing at high levels.

In pleading guilty to conspiracy to defraud the Internal Revenue Service of $2 million, Channell admitted he collected money that donors wrote off as tax-deductible contributions and used it illegally "to purchase military and other types of non-humanitarian aid for the Contras." U.S. District Judge Stanley S. Harris put the question to Channell: With whom did he conspire? "Col. North, an official of the National Security Council," he answered.

Channell's testimony, the first to be shaken loose by Walsh's investigation, goes to the heart of the matter: namely, any involvement by administration officials in an illegal aid network giving military support to the Contras in defiance of Congress. Who was involved? That's what Walsh and Congress need to find out in a way that enables prosecution of wrongdoers.

Walsh has put the entire Iran-Contra scandal on a track toward tough answers — and indictments. Good. It's up to the congressional investigatory committees — whose membership includes Sens. William S. Cohen and George J. Mitchell — to keep it there.

©1987 HERBLOCK

## THE COMMERCIAL APPEAL

*Memphis, TN, May 7, 1987*

CARL Channell is a relatively minor player in the Iran/contra affair, but his plea of guilty on a tax-fraud charge must be unsettling to the Reagan administration.

Channell was not accused of involvement in the sale of arms to Iran to make money for Nicaragua's anti-Communist rebels. But he was deeply engaged in raising private money in the United States to buy arms for the contras.

That in itself is not a violation of the law. Where Channell went awry was in funneling the money through a "tax-exempt" foundation, which meant contributors could deduct their contributions as charitable donations. According to one news account, a Channell organization collected at least $2.28 million for a project nicknamed "Toys", which ostensibly was to be used to buy Christmas gifts for children of contra fighters, when the money actually was intended for arms purchases.

Channell's activities were so clearly an illegal abuse of the tax laws that he did not wait for a formal indictment. He agreed with the special prosecutor investigating the Iran/contra affair to plead guilty and cooperate further with investigators, probably in exchange for a light sentence.

Whether Channell knows of any other illegal activities is uncertain. He did name Marine Lt. Col. Oliver North as a "co-conspirator" in the tax fraud, which doesn't bode well for the former White House aide who is at the middle of the Iran/contra investigation.

It also is evident that Channell had access to other White House figures, including President Reagan, who met with some of Channell's contributors. At a news conference in March, Reagan said he met with the donors "to thank them because they had raised money to put spot ads on television in favor of the contras."

This doesn't mean that Reagan knew anything about the tax fraud or that the money collected was for the purchase of arms for the rebels fighting Nicaragua's Sandinista regime.

But Channell's guilty plea in the criminal courts marks the first drawing of real blood in the Iran/contra investigation. There's no telling how much more will be on the floor before it's all over.

## The Chattanooga Times

*Chattanooga, TN, May 7, 1987*

By pleading guilty to abusing the tax-exempt status of one of his foundations, Carl R. Channell has in effect confirmed that the Reagan administration deliberately violated Congress' ban on supplying war materiel to the Nicaraguan Contras. Mr. Channell is only the first person in this scandal to take a fall, but the congressional hearings that began looking into the matter Tuesday are likely to identify others who are vulnerable to criminal prosecution. The testimony by retired Maj. Gen. Richard Secord to the committee made clear that persons higher on the command ladder were aware of the illegalities.

The key question that still remains is whether President Reagan was aware of the diversion of funds from the Iran arms sales to the Contras. The president insists he was not aware, and given his relaxed style of governing, his ignorance of the affair is certainly possible.

Mr. Channell admitted that money raised by one of his foundations, ostensibly to buy toys and medical equipment, was used instead for military equipment for the Contras. Who else was involved? Mr. Channell said in federal court that Lt. Col. Oliver North, then a member of the National Security Council based in the White House, was also part of the conspiracy. Another man, public relations expert Richard Miller, reportedly provided a Swiss bank account through which the funds were channeled.

Given Mr. Channell's tight connections in the White House, he was able to arrange for President Reagan to thank personally those who contributed funds to the project. It strains credulity to think that Mr. Reagan really believed he was thanking people for contributing $2.2 million to buy toys for the Contras' families.

To carry out this deceptive campaign, those involved had to flout a law passed by Congress that barred supplying any weapons to the Contras. The success of the campaign thus depended on elaborate secrecy, and on the type of intra-government coordination at several levels that made it resemble a military operation. Small wonder, then, that "good soldier" Secord really believed, as he told the committee Tuesday, that those involved were carrying out the president's wishes. That certainly implies that Gen. Secord was convinced Mr. Reagan knew what was going on. It goes without saying this scheme was not just the handiwork of a Marine lieutenant colonel.

Is Gen. Secord telling the truth? Will his testimony be corroborated by others? The answers will emerge over the next three months as others on the command ladder testify. And on that testimony rides, ultimately, the credibility of the Reagan presidency.

# William Casey, Former CIA Chief and Key Contragate Figure, Dies

William J. Casey, 74, director of the Central Intelligence Agency from 1981 until a stroke forced his resignation in January 1987, died May 6, 1987 of pneumonia and cancer in Glen Cove, New York. Casey was rewarded with the directorship of the CIA after managing President Reagan's successful 1980 presidential campaign. With the support of the Reagan administration he oversaw one of the biggest peacetime buildups in the American intelligence community. His last days as director were overshadowed by the burgeoning Iran-contra arms scandal and the question of the degree of his involvement in it.

Trained as a tax lawyer, Casey served in World War II as chief of secret intelligence in Europe for the Office of Strategic Services, the forerunner of the CIA. Later he became a multimillionaire in private life, first as a supplier of technical information for corporate customers and later mainly as a venture capitalist. He had been chairman of the Securities and Exchange Commission (1971-73), undersecretary of state for economic affairs (1973-74) and president of the Export-Import Bank (1974-75).

## THE TENNESSEAN
*Nashville, TN, May 8, 1987*

MR. William J. Casey, former CIA director and a central figure in the Iran arms sale scandal, died Wednesday of complications of brain cancer. He was 74 years old.

Although he was a highly successful tax attorney, Mr. Casey had spent much of his life in government and was best known to the public in that role. During World War II, he was European chief of the old intelligence agency, the Office of Strategic Services, and was noted for penetrating Nazi Germany with secret agents.

He served as chairman of the Securities and Exchange Commission in the Nixon and Ford administrations. He later served as undersecretary of state for economic affairs and president of the Export-Import Bank. He was named CIA chief by President Reagan in 1981 and served in that post until resigning last February after becoming ill.

His goal at the CIA was to rebuild the agency after it had become involved in controversy during the Nixon administration for activities ranging from surveillance of domestic political groups to alleged involvement in assassination plots against foreign leaders.

He succeeded in large part in the rebuilding effort, by coaxing money out of Congress and trying to lift some of the restrictions from the CIA's operations, but controversy continued to dog the agency and its director.

Congress and the people are always suspicious of any government agency that needs to operate in secrecy. And Mr. Casey himself, hardly ever a stranger to controversy, continued to furnish fuel for conflict. He was caught up in a whirlwind of criticism over his personal finances and also for a number of CIA actions such as the mining of Nicaragua's harbors and the preparation of a manual for use by Nicaraguan rebels to "neutralize" civilian officials by the "selective use of violence."

Mr. Casey had a unique style. His part in the Iran arms-contra affair may never be fully known. But whatever may be disclosed, those who have followed his career will not likely be surprised. He was a blunt, hard-driving public official who saw a particular role for himself in government and moved in direct fashion to fill it. Many have disagreed with his tactics. But few questioned his ability or his sincerity of purpose. ∎

## THE SACRAMENTO BEE
*Sacramento, CA, May 7, 1987*

William J. Casey, who died yesterday at the age of 74, leaves more questions than answers behind him. He helped reinvigorate the Central Intelligence Agency, which he headed through most of the Reagan presidency, from the demoralized state in which it found itself after a decade of accusations about its involvement in assassination plots abroad and the illegal surveillance of citizens at home. But Casey, who had himself been a World War II spy, and who was sometimes accused of trying to relive his wartime adventures, did no more to resolve the dilemmas raised by covert operations in a democracy than his more timid predecessors. His relations with Congress were abominable, his contempt for legal processes often unbounded.

We will probably never know how deeply Casey and his agency were involved in the diversion of funds and the illegal delivery of weapons to the Nicaraguan Contras. But that he was involved there's no doubt. A few hours before he died, one of the key players in the affair, retired Air Force Gen. Richard V. Secord, testified about the assistance he got from Casey in the Contra supply effort. It was Casey's CIA that mined the Nicaraguan harbors and printed terrorism manuals for its Contra clients; it was Casey's CIA that covertly — and counter to law — provided training for the Contras.

There's no doubt that along the way the cantankerous Casey made substantial improvements in the analytical capabilities of the agency, increasing the reliability of its reports and accurately predicting certain key events, among them the Israeli invasion of Lebanon. But Casey, a self-made millionaire — he was a tax lawyer — managed his own financial affairs with such disdain for possible conflicts of interest and expressed such contempt for both public and congressional sensibilities that Congress, after an investigation, gave him no more than a grudging clearance: "Not unfit to serve."

And yet Casey was a faithful executor of the policies of the president who appointed him and whose close friend he was. If someone was needed to skirt the restrictions of the law for an administration that chafed under them — in the Middle East, in Central America, in Angola — Casey was the man. And if he did little to help resolve the conflict between democratic government and covert foreign operations, neither did he create it. Casey represented one side of the national ambivalence about such operations. He was there to do it when it was wanted and to take the blame when it failed or the country changed its mind. Unfortunately, in his zeal and his contempt for democratic procedures, he not only helped bring on the Iran-Contra debacle but may have set the stage for still another wave of restrictions on the agency he worked so hard to invigorate.

## The Dallas Morning News
*Dallas, TX, May 8, 1987*

Like Othello, Bill Casey has done the state some service. And if, in the present controversy surrounding the Iran-contra hearings, they do not know it at the hour of his passing, it is fitting to remind them.

William J. Casey died Wednesday of pneumonia that he suffered as a result of cancer. Tax lawyer, multimillionaire, venture capitalist, pioneer leader in the establishment of the Office of Strategic Service and the Central Intelligence Agency, Casey was rich in years, honors and money when he returned to the political arena to manage Ronald Reagan's winning 1980 campaign. He could have capped an illustrious career with this spectacular finale and gone into retirement. But Casey was called upon for one more service to the state — and he heeded the call.

He took on the difficult new challenge of rebuilding his old team, the CIA, which was struggling in the wreckage and demoralization left over from the Watergate disaster. He succeeded because he was a skilled old pro at the sometimes disreputable but crucial business of gathering intelligence information. Spymasters may not be popular, but, in a dangerous world, they are necessary.

In the end, Casey's frustration with the new post-Watergate rules, the obstructionism he had to contend with and perhaps the limits imposed by his worsening health may have led him to serious mistakes — that question is one of those to be addressed by the current congressional hearings.

But when a veteran public servant dies, he deserves consideration of more than his final days. He deserves to have recalled to the public's memory all the days of his long service to the commonweal. So let it be with Bill Casey.

## Post-Tribune
*Gary, IN, May 9, 1987*

The death of William Casey ended a remarkable career of public service. It also may cheat history. Some essential questions about the Iran-Contra affair cannot be answered — he probably knew as much as anyone about it, except for Lt. Col. Oliver North.

If a full accounting of this bizarre episode is to be achieved, the road will be much longer without the testimony of Casey. He might have been able to help his long-time friend, President Reagan. Maybe not. But his testimony would have helped remove some of the tantalizing mystery about the operations.

The first witness at the congressional hearings, retired Maj. Gen. Richard Secord, has told the committee that Casey helped put the fund-raising efforts into motion when Congress had forbidden the administration to send military aid to the Contras in Nicaragua. The country will never know beyond reasonable doubt what Casey knew or what he may have told the president.

But there is no doubt that William Casey was an unusual patriot. He was a star in OSS operations in Europe and then made millions as a tax lawyer and on Wall Street. Before heading the CIA, he was chairman of the Securities and Exchange Commission. He was a political adviser to Reagan.

His role in the arms deal raises deep questions about his respect for working within the system — he did not like Congress and often proved it. But even his detractors must admit that Casey thought he was serving the country's best interests. That judgment must wait awhile.

He restored the CIA's image and morale after it had some bad years in the 1970s, and for that the nation should be grateful.

Sen. Patrick Leahy, a Democrat from Vermont, said Casey's death marked "the passing of an era." He's probably right.

## THE PLAIN DEALER
*Cleveland, OH, May 7, 1987*

The courage of William J. Casey, the former CIA director who died this week at age 74, was never questioned. But like most men who believe that their ends justify the use of questionable means, affection for Casey was confined within the narrow limits of those who thought as he did.

Part of Casey's cachet as CIA director was his exploits during World War II with the Office of Strategic Services. He served with distinction as chief of OSS secret intelligence for Europe and directed the planting of agents inside Nazi Germany. Of that rough-and-tumble experience, conducted in the shadowy and highly dangerous world of spying, Casey was to remember fondly that the work was "exciting, challenging, high-spirited and mysterious."

He sought—successfully—to instill that sense of exuberance within the CIA after being named director in 1981. Casey won large budget increases for the agency and worked actively to reduce the restrictions placed on CIA activities in earlier years, which involved domestic spying on political groups and reported involvement in assassination plots against foreign leaders.

Casey's efforts did boost CIA morale. But they also increased the apprehension of Congress, which was frustrated in its attempts to monitor the agency's intelligence activities. Casey had little tolerance for congressional oversight. As he told the Senate during his confirmation hearing, "rigid accountability . . . can impair performance."

That attitude is part and parcel to the Iran-contra arms deal that congressional committees now are investigating. Possibly no one in Washington—with the exception of Marine Lt. Col. Oliver North—knew more about the secret arms sale to Iran and the diversion of funds to the contras than Casey. Yet, the man who made it his business to know so much claimed to know little about the deal in which the CIA was so deeply involved. William Casey will be remembered not only as a man who went his own way, but also as one who led the CIA into a new round of questionable activities that may result in further restrictions on the agency.

## THE RICHMOND NEWS LEADER
*Richmond, VA, May 11, 1987*

Church is supposed to be a place of healing and understanding, of compassion and comfort. It is supposed to be large and all-embracing.

It emphatically is *not* supposed to be narrow, petty, and small. Its leaders are *not* supposed to be in the business of bearing grudges and getting the last word — particularly at funerals.

But things are different in too many churches these days — as demonstrated Saturday in St. Mary's Catholic Church in Roslyn Harbor, New York.

Many went to the church on that day to mourn William Casey, former Director of the CIA — to remember him fondly, as funeral-goers are wont to do. Among those attending were the President and Mrs. Reagan (seated in the front row), many Reagan administration officials, and former United Nations Ambassador Jeane Kirkpatrick.

In remarks to the congregation, Bishop John McGann had the bad taste to speak back-handedly of Mr. Casey, taking him to task (a) for his beliefs regarding Central America and (b) for not comprehending the bishop's views:

*[His] conviction about the fundamentally moral purpose of American actions [in support of the anti-Communist Nicaraguan Contras], I'm sure, made incomprehensible to him the ethical questions raised by me as his bishop about our nation's defense policies since the dawn of the nuclear age. . . . I'm equally sure that [he] must have thought us bishops blind to the potential for a Communist threat in this hemisphere as we opposed and continue to oppose the violence wrought in Central America by support of the Contras. . . . I cannot conceal nor disguise my fundamental disagreement on this matter.*

Perhaps in partial response to the bishop's insults, Mrs. Kirkpatrick said in her eulogy that recently Mr. Casey had been the target of many "mean-spirited and ill-informed comments." Mean-spirited, indeed.

But despite their possession of manners more commendable than the bishop's, perhaps those in attendance — led by President Reagan himself — should have walked out. Surely they would have been justified in this case, just as droves of mainline parishioners — offended by the offensive purveying of offensive political views by kook-Left clerics — are justified in staying home or playing golf instead of being proselytized in the pews.

## THE ARIZONA REPUBLIC

*Phoenix, AZ, July 9, 1987*

THE long-awaited testimony of Lt. Col. Oliver North is at the midway point. Up to now — to the surprise of no one — North has not made any startling revelations in his two days of appearances before the congressional Iran-*contra* committees.

North's answers to the barrage of questions fired at him have been a major disappointment to those who have been hoping for North to reveal a smoking gun in the White House. Nothing of the sort has appeared.

Instead, the former National Security Council aide has been emphatic in saying that he had no specific knowledge that the president had approved the diversion of Iran arms-sale profits to the Nicaraguan rebels. North said he "never carried out a single act" without authorization, but that no memorandum ever came back to him initialed by the president.

If anything, North's testimony has reaffirmed the notion that the more that's learned about the Iran-*contra* affair, the less likely it appears that the whole truth of the matter ever will be known. The answers to many of the questions posed seem to have been buried with CIA Director William Casey.

Take Wednesday's testimony, for example. North told Congress that the decision to divert money from the arms sales to the Nicaraguan rebels was enthusiastically approved by Casey, who also wanted to use the arms profits as a sort of slush fund for anti-communist operations throughout the world. North's testimony was a direct contradiction of earlier statements by Casey, who died May 6.

As for direct authorization, North said the diversion of funds was approved by his superior, former national security adviser John Poindexter, and that he simply assumed President Reagan OK'd the diversion. On the basis of what North has said so far, the president knew nothing of the operation.

Doubts have been raised about North's credibility. After all, he has defended the lies and deceptions in the Iran-*contra* affair as justified by the need to protect a covert operation he believed crucial to the United States and authorized by the president.

There are grounds for questioning North's answers. The whole point of the hearings is to get to the bottom of the Iran-*contra* affair.

The exercise, however, should not be limited to trying to pin something on the president — as has sometimes seemed to be the case over the last couple of days. Questioners blinded by that obsession lose sight of the overall objective.

# WORCESTER TELEGRAM

*Worcester, MA, May 8, 1987*

Life was either kind or cruel to William J. Casey, depending on how one looks at it.

It was kind because his death, the day after congressional hearings began on the Iran-Contra affair, spared him the agony of being constantly harassed by investigators. But it may have been unfair because his departure prevented the former director of the Central Intelligence Agency from setting the record straight on his involvement.

One thing is certain: Casey's contribution to the United States does not need posthumous vindication. He has done more for his country than most of his critics could do in several lifetimes.

He was a World War II hero and became chief of secret intelligence of the Office of Strategic Services, the CIA's forerunner. He directed clandestine operations to penetrate Nazi Germany with secret agents. Through law, teaching, writing, business acumen and public office, he distinguished himself in civilian life as well. He has been known for his "analytical mind, tenacious will and a capacity to generate high morale among his staff."

Those qualities played an important role when Casey set out to rejuvenate the badly dispirited CIA in 1981. To repair the damage of the Jimmy Carter years, he boosted funding, manpower and morale. He returned to a more realistic assessment of foreign threats to U.S. security and built a strong counterintelligence network that gave the KGB fits.

His commitment to preventing communist expansionism in small nations around the world may have persuaded him to quietly support covert private actions against such threats. The extent of his involvement in the Iran-Contra venture will remain a matter of speculation. The congressional testimony of retired Air Force Maj. Gen. Richard Secord revealed that the pro-Contra cause received more sympathy than material aid from the CIA.

It is sad that William Casey had to go out on a sour note. But his contribution must be judged in its entirety and not through recent suspicions. He deserves the nation's gratitude for services rendered.

YOU CAN TAKE IT WITH YOU!

# Chicago Tribune

*Chicago, IL, May 7, 1987*

On the last morning of his life there once again was the inimitable William Casey—in the headlines, all over the front pages and the TV news, smack in the middle of cloak and dagger mystery and controversy and questions that now may never be answered.

The former CIA director died at age 74 on the morning after congressional committees formally opened their public hearings into the Iran-contras scandal that has wracked the administration of his great friend, President Reagan.

Except possibly for Lt. Col. Oliver North, no one could better have supplied the answers to the questions the committees will be asking than Mr. Casey. The first witness at those hearings, retired Air Force Maj. Gen. Richard Secord, for instance, testified on opening day that Mr. Casey had helped orchestrate fundraising efforts for the Nicaraguan contras at a time when Congress had forbidden U.S. military aid to them.

It was none other than Mr. Casey, according to Gen. Secord, who suggested putting the arm on the Sultan of Brunei for a $10 million donation which apparently somehow has vanished.

And "now we'll never know" what Mr. Casey knew because, as Sen. Patrick Leahy (D., Vt.) observed, "He didn't really tell us much about it before he died."

That was Mr. Casey's way. He was an authentic American original. He was a heroically successful operative with the OSS in Europe and he never lost his zest for the cloak and dagger stuff. He made a fortune as a tax lawyer and in Wall Street. He was active for many years in Republican politics and he held several high government posts including, before taking command of the CIA, chairmanship of the Securities and Exchange Commission.

Always he did things his way. And never did he doubt that his way was the best way to serve America's interests. He was tough. He didn't have much use for questions, let alone anybody else's answers. He never seemed to care much for doing things by the book. He was no stranger to mystery or controversy. He made little effort to disguise his contempt for Congress and particularly its efforts to oversee the operations of the CIA.

He came under fire with some regularity—over his personal financial operations, over a campaign contribution by fugitive financier Robert Vesco to the Richard Nixon campaign, over allegations that he worked as a lawyer for Indonesia without registering as a foreign agent, over such CIA operations as mining Nicaraguan harbors during his stewardship of the spy agency.

But, as Mr. Casey once observed, "I've been confirmed by the Senate five times. Every now and then somebody tries to get something on me and nobody's ever succeeded."

He lived on the edge. And when he died he was on the edge again. His death marked the "passing of an era," as Sen. Leahy noted, and he was "sort of a larger than life" chief of the CIA.

# Honolulu Star-Bulletin

*Honolulu, HI, May 6, 1987*

The death of William Casey at age 74 adds a somber note at the outset of the Iran-Contra hearings. The former CIA director had been incapacitated for months and had thus been eliminated as a potential witness. Had he been able to testify, however, he might have contributed much important information.

Casey's long and colorful career in government and politics reached a controversial climax in his tenure at the CIA. A final judgment on his labors will no doubt be clouded by the attempt to finance the Nicaraguan rebels by unconventional and probably illegal means, including the Iran arms sales.

Casey appeared to have little patience with congressional attempts to rein in the CIA. In the end, his attempts to circumvent those restraints may overshadow his accomplishments in rejuvenating the intelligence agency.

# ALBUQUERQUE JOURNAL

*Albuquerque, NM, May 7, 1987*

The death of William J. Casey makes it unlikely that the full extent of his involvement in the Iran-contra affair will ever be known. Questions about his role and a lingering suspicion that one of President Reagan's top advisors was the moving force behind the initiative will go with him to the grave.

With the possible exception of Lt. Col. Oliver North, Casey was in a better position than anyone else to be knowledgeable about the entire affair.

Casey's name will be heard often in testimony during congressional hearings expected to continue into August. During the first day of testimony, the day before his death, Casey was named by a witness as one of the U.S. government officials who — in spite of a congressional prohibition against military aid to Nicaraguan rebels — helped in an operation to supply weapons to the contras. Casey had denied knowing specifically about either a secret arms deal with Iran or diversion of money to the contras.

Even before his death, Casey's ill health was expected to preclude his appearing before the congressional hearing. Nonetheless, the committee had been gathering evidence about his role and what role the Central Intelligence Agency might have played in the Iran-contra affair. That evidence may become public in due course.

While the true extent of Casey's role in the Iran-contra affair may never be fully known, there were solid accomplishments in his record. He should be remembered for rebuilding the U.S. intelligence capability from the sad state it had fallen into during the Carter years. In spite of differences with Congress in the areas of accountability and authority, Casey restored credibility and improved the morale of the CIA during his six years as its head.

Casey's associates describe him as having been a tough, single-minded super patriot. That is the man they will remember.

# The Birmingham News

*Birmingham, AL, May 7, 1987*

William J. Casey gave much more to his country than his shadowy involvement in the Iran-Contra arms deals. Unfortunately, his death Wednesday came at a time which makes it likely he may be most remembered for his role in that episode.

The former hard-nosed director of the Central Intelligence Agency died only a few hours after the first witness in the congressional probe of the Iran-Contra affair, retired Maj. Gen. Richard V. Secord, testified that Casey helped in the effort to supply the Nicaraguan rebels with arms, even after Congress had prohibited such aid.

It is virtually assured Mr. Casey's name will come up repeatedly as the congressional committee wends its way through the details of the arms double-dealings over the next few months.

Mr. Casey had a long and distinguished record of public service that deserves to be remembered also. During World War II, he served as chief of the Office of Strategic Services' section for European intelligence, with direct responsibility for penetrating Nazi Germany with secret agents.

In the Nixon and Ford administrations, he served as chairman of the Securities and Exchange Commission and president of the Export-Import Bank. In his post as CIA director, Mr. Casey was credited with skillfully restoring the agency's intelligence gathering capabilities which had been diminished in the aftermath of Watergate.

Congressional probers will and should continue their investigation of what role William Casey played in the Iran-Contra matter. It is extremely important to know if the head of the CIA contradicted the will of the elected representatives of the people. If he did, it is just as important for Congress to try to design a safeguard to prevent that kind of abuse of power in the future.

At the same time, Mr. Casey should be recalled also for his long years of dedicated, meritorious public service.

# Secord Testifies as Scandal Hearings Open

House and Senate committees investigating the Iran-contra arms scandal opened their joint public hearings May 5, 1987. The committees devoted the first week to the testimony of retired Air Force Maj. Gen. Richard Secord, who had agreed to testify voluntarily after earlier invoking his Fifth Amendment protection against self-incrimination. Secord, a skilled covert operator who had been involved in arms shipments to both Iran and the contras, was questioned at length about possible profits he took from the schemes. Much of the questioning concerned minor points in the investigation, and the first week of hearings brought no major revelations.

On the first day of public congressional hearings, Secord testified that about $3.5 of the $12 million in profits from the United States arms sales to Iran was diverted to the contra rebels fighting the Nicaraguan government. Questioning by John Nields Jr., chief counsel for the House committee, focused on establishing the trail of money from the arms sales. Secord alluded to several other covert operations that he had been involved in, but Nields declined to pursue them, sticking to the narrow question of where the money went and whether Secord had lined his own pockets from the arms sales. Secord testified that he had been recruited in 1984 by Lt. Col. Oliver North, then a member of the National Security Council staff, to organize air delivery of weapons to the contras. In 1985, he said, then-national security adviser Robert McFarlane asked him to become involved in the Iranian operation. The White House "knew of my conduct and approved it," Secord told the congressional panels.

In his opening statement, Secord expressed admiration for North and Rear Adm. John Poindexter, and lashed out at Attorney General Edwin Meese 3rd. Meese, he said, had committed a "particularly unforgiveable" act by revealing in November 1986 that profits from the Iran arms sales had been relayed to the contras. Secord explained his earlier refusal to testify by saying that Meese's announcement had left his organization "betrayed, abandoned and left to defend ourselves." His first reaction after Meese's announcement was to be "equally self-protective," but he had recently reconsidered, Secord said.

According to Secord, Iran deposited $30 million in the Swiss bank account that Secord's business partner, Albert Hakim, controlled in the name of Lake Resources Inc. Of that $30 million, $12.3 million went to the U.S. government to pay for the arms, and $3 million was expended to transport the weapons. The diversion to the contras totaled $3.5 million, Secord said, which included monthly stipends for two contra leaders, the construction of an airstrip and the purchase of five airplanes. About $1 million from the sales went to other projects, details of which Nields did not pursue. Secord said that $350,000 had gone to purchase a ship, at North's request, for a purpose not related to either Iran or Nicaragua. Secord said that, as a private citizen arranging the arms sales, he had been entitled to a share of the profits. He declined to take money from the operation, Secord said, because he hoped to return to government service. Secord had been a deputy assistant secretary of defense early in the Reagan administration, but had been suspended in 1982 and later retired amid questions about his involvement, with former Central Intelligence Agency agent Thomas Clines, in a scheme to overcharge the U.S. government on arms sales to Egypt.

On the second day of Secord's testimony, Nields continued to press Secord on whether he had profited from the arms deals. Secord said that he and North had decided how much to charge the Iranians for three major arms shipments in 1986. In deciding to charge more than twice as much as the U.S. government originally paid for the weapons, "there were a number of reasons and the contra was one of them," Secord said.

In the most notable testimony of the hearing, Secord said that North had told him that President Reagan had been told of the diversion of funds from the Iran arms sales to the contras. President Reagan, in a brief Rose Garden appearance May 7, called Secord "misinformed" about the extent of his knowledge of the fund diversion and aid to the contras. Reagan acknowledged having known that Secord "was engaged with other private citizens in trying to get aid to the contras, and so forth, and there's nothing against the law in that."

## Houston Chronicle

*Houston, TX, May 7, 1987*

It didn't take Richard V. Secord long to take a lot of the mystery out of the Iran-to-contra money transactions.

The retired general pointed a finger at the White House and Lt. Col. Oliver North, the former national security aide.

Secord said he was taking directions from Col. North and had occasional meetings with then-CIA Director William Casey.

"I also understood that this administration knew of my conduct and approved it," he said. But he did not produce a direct link to President Reagan.

Secord's testimony showed Col. North paid little attention to the legal provision that between October 1984 and October 1986 no U.S. agencies involved in intelligence activities were to spend money in support of the contras.

North and Secord had $18 million to work with after Iran paid for weapons in the hostage deal that fell through. Secord said $3.5 million went to the contras, $2.5 million is unaccounted for, $8 million is still in a Swiss bank account, $3 million was spent on expenses and $1 million on activities unrelated to Iran or Nicaragua. Whether these transactions broke any laws is something yet to be determined.

Those directing the Iran-to-contra funding operation considered themselves free agents, operating in a cavalier manner for a cause in which they believed. The question the congressional probers want answered is, was Reagan one of the cavaliers?

## Wisconsin ▲ State Journal
*Madison, WI, May 7, 1987*

It's something of a relief to hear that Lt. Col. Oliver North and former national security adviser John Poindexter weren't saving the world all by themselves.

Until retired Air Force Maj. Gen. Richard Secord took the stand as leadoff witness in congressional hearings on the Iran-Contra affair, most of the blame for this exercise in executive excess had been pinned on the omnipresent North and his boss, Poindexter.

Since this story broke in November 1986, North has been portrayed as a one-man commando unit, popping up around the world in connection with complicated and clandestine deals. In a perverse sort of way, accounts of his globe-trotting exploits were impressive.

We now know — courtesy of Secord — that while North and Poindexter may have been overworked, they did not shoulder this heavy burden alone.

Secord has testified under oath that former CIA director William Casey helped in the operation to funnel arms to Nicaraguan rebels after Congress had prohibited such aid, and that he believed he was acting with the full backing of the Reagan administration. Casey, who died Wednesday, had previously denied such involvement.

"We believed our conduct was in the furtherance of the president's policies," Secord said, speaking for himself and his colleagues in the assorted transactions. "I also understand that this administration knew of my conduct and approved it."

Officials of the CIA and State Department in Central America assisted his efforts to run guns to the Contras, Secord said, and he was told (but did not know firsthand) that Vice President George Bush was aware of the Contra-supply network. Bush has said repeatedly he was unaware of covert government efforts to arm the Contras.

On the other end of Secord's supply line were a variety of shadowy characters such as Iranian-born financier Albert Hakim, Iranian arms dealer Manucher Ghorbanifar, Israeli arms dealer Al Schwimmer and Felix Rodriguez, a former CIA operative who served as his liaison with the Contras.

Privatization of government services is a fine goal — but must we start with our foreign policy? And a covert foreign policy that defies the will of Congress, to boot?

It is too early to tell how far up the slope of command this trail of abuse will lead; the committee has yet to lay a glove on President Reagan himself. But with the congressional hearings only two days old, the nation has already heard *voluntary* testimony from a star witness who says high government officials worked outside normal channels to achieve a policy goal that had been rejected by Congress.

Secret diplomacy has always been an executive prerogative and should continue to be so, but the U.S. Constitution makes it clear that policy-making is a joint exercise that must involve the legislative branch. In this, the 200th anniversary of the Constitution, some government officials are getting a long overdue refresher course.

## The Hutchinson News
*Hutchison, KS, May 8, 1987*

The Iran-Contra hearings prove you need a guide to wade through the daily televised proceedings.

President Reagan, hearing that retired Maj. Gen. Richard Secord claimed Reagan was informed about the diversion of money to the Contras, denies the claim and alleges that Secord is "misinformed."

A claim, a denial. Who's right, who's wrong? Here we go again.

The claims and the players in this Iran-Contra arms deal will make your head spin.

"This is crazy," Secord told chief counsel Arthur Liman under questioning.

He's right.

The sentence may be the key footnote to the whole affair.

The early days of the hearings haven't provided much clarity. The findings thus far also compete for attention from the ongoing separate investigation and subsequent charges against other players in the Iran affair.

The pity of it all is that the hearings lack the drama of the televised Watergate hearings, which drew the interest of a great many Americans.

The maze of denials, contradictions and misinformation that continues to plague the scandal will determine its appeal to the American public.

As important as it is, it just doesn't have the clear-cut, good-guy, bad-guy elements that make it more palatable and understandable to a large segment of the public.

That will diminish the importance of these hearings in the American psyche.

That's too bad, since the hearings may eventually disclose more about the character of the Reagan administration than anything else it has encountered.

## ALBUQUERQUE JOURNAL
*Albuquerque, NM, May 13, 1987*

To hear retired Maj. Gen. Richard V. Secord tell it, he participated in the wheeling and dealing that has become known as the Iran-contra affair out of a sense of patriotism.

This despite President Reagan's disavowal of trade with terrorists and congressional prohibitions against commerce with terrorist states such as Iran and a bar against direct military aid to Nicaraguan rebels. And just how patriotic is it to substitute one's own judgment for the U.S. Constitution?

In the end, that is what the Iran-contra affair is all about — the disdain for constitutional checks and balances by men such as the former head of President Reagan's National Security Council, Admiral John M. Poindexter; his deputy, Lt. Col. Oliver North; the late William Casey, then director of the Central Intelligence Agency; Secord; and possibly, the president himself.

Secord seemed candid in telling a congressional hearing about his role as a key player in a private network created by Reagan administration officials to secretly sell arms to Iran, in the misguided belief the transactions could lead to freedom for American hostages.

Secord was much less candid about the antecedents and whereabouts of $8 million or more in Swiss bank accounts, coming mostly from profits from the sale of U.S. arms to Iran, and the distribution of part of that money to Nicaraguan rebels.

The former Air Force general asserted that the money belongs to the "enterprise" — his organization — and said perhaps it should go to a memorial to Casey. But whose money is it? Secord seems to consider the profit — from transactions of questionable legality that amounted to selling back to the United States assets the United States already had paid for — to be the private assets of his "organization."

Secord did say that the millions in Swiss bank accounts are controlled by his business partner, Albert Hakim; that there are still bills to be paid; and that no one knows how much will be left when the accounts are settled. Lacking Secord's cooperation, U.S. government requests of the Swiss to provide full records of the bank accounts involved in the Iranian and contra transactions have been unsuccessful.

"The money," Secord said at the hearing, "was a matter of little concern to me." If that's true, he should have no qualms about relinquishing his claim and providing a detailed accounting for the congressmen, senators and the American public.

The Iran-contra affair raises the specter of a dual American government, one public and constitutionally accountable, the other private and answerable only to those few who have extraordinary access to the inner circles and bountiful resources of the representative government. One way to curtail the activities of the latter would be to vigorously pursue the return of Secord's millions, and pursue all the remedies — and penalties — of law against those responsible for its diversion.

# THE DAILY HERALD

*Biloxi, MS, May 12, 1987*

Former Air Force Maj. Gen. Richard V. Secord shed more light on the disposition of the $30 million paid by Iran for the secret purchase of U.S. arms in opening testimony before a joint House-Senate hearing expected to last through the summer.

But the political gut issue, whether President Reagan knew of and acceded to a diversion of some of the proceeds to the Nicaraguan Contras in contravention of a congressionally-imposed ban on military aid, has yet to be documented.

Secord's statement that he "understood that this administration" knew what was going on and approved it was as close as he came to involving Reagan.

Reagan continues to maintain he did not know of any illegal fund raising or diversion of money to the Contras, although it is clear some of his top aides did. White House Chief of Staff Howard Baker said he believes Reagan is telling the truth.

Any disclosures which would place Reagan's veracity in doubt would be a devastating blow to his presidency. The issue will sit there, like a ticking time bomb, as the public hearings continue.

Marine Lt. Col. Oliver North, the fired White House national security aide who recruited Secord, and North's former boss, Vice Admiral John Poindexter, are other key witnesses who will testify under limited immunity. Both have intimate knowledge of the arms sale debacle but previously had claimed Fifth Amendment privileges against self-incrimination.

The death Wednesday of another prominent administration official, former CIA Director William Casey, precludes any further inquiry into his recollections. Secord said he discussed his activities on three occasions with Casey during the time period when a ban was in effect on military aide to the Contras.

Before surgery in December for a brain tumor which contributed to his death, Casey had told congressional committees he did not learn of diversions of arms sale profits to the Contras until October 1986 and not with certainty until a day before Attorney General Edwin Meese made a public disclosure on Nov. 4.

His testimony was greeted with considerable skepticism since Casey was known to be a passionate supporter of the Contra cause.

Secord's account of what happened to the $30 million paid for arms by Iran indicates very little, about $3.5 million, went to the Contras along with another $2 million raised by private contributions.

The U.S. was reimbursed the original $12 million value of the arms, $8 million remains in Swiss bank accounts more than $1 million was spent for efforts to secure the release of American hostages in Lebanon and other projects, and $2 million is yet unaccounted for, Secord said.

Interesting stuff, but comparatively ho-hum.

The prime target of the hearings is Reagan himself. Did he, or did he not, knowingly direct any illegal executive department operations to circumvent the will of Congress at a time the Contra's cause was in desperate need of aid to survive?

That question hangs there, yet unanswered save for Reagan's personal assurance that it is not true.

## The Philadelphia Inquirer

*Philadephia, PA, May 10, 1987*

At the start, his testimony was so cool and forthcoming that retired Maj. Gen. Richard V. Secord's self-portrayed role in the Iran-contra network seemed almost forgivable, the selfless service of an American patriot. But as the hearings have continued, the veil has slowly dropped.

Another picture has emerged — that of Secord as a "commercial" operative who made it his business to run arms to places where government feared to tread, a shadowy operative with contempt not only for the rule of law, a contempt apparently shared by the White House, but for the agencies empowered to safeguard national security.

"And you felt indeed that you could do a better job than the people who were in charge of covert operations?" asked Arthur L. Liman, the Senate counsel.

"I thought so," Mr. Secord replied.

It was the same kind of arrogance that drove CIA director William J. Casey to end-run the professionals of his agency, that led to the privatizing of foreign policy by the Reagan administration, and, finally, to the humiliating spectacle now under way in the Senate Caucus Room. It reflected the arrogance of an executive branch that considered legal checks and balances a congenital defect, not the strength, of American democracy, an arrogance that considered exposure its only enemy.

That was Mr. Secord's theme on Day Four. "In my opinion the whole world is laughing at us," he said, because the United States has been forced to "open up our guts to the rest of the world." But U.S. credibility has been damaged not by the hearings but by a President who said one thing and did another.

If the keystone of the President's anti-terrorism policy was refusal to do business with hostage-takers, was it sound to risk sending arms to Iran in contradiction of that policy?

If neither Congress nor the American people could be persuaded to fund the contras, was it wise to wing it, deepening American involvement in Nicaragua absent a mandate?

The time has come to pay the piper — to confront clandestine operations that, from their inception, could not stand the light of day or pass the test of good judgment. No, it is not pretty. But no one is laughing.

Three years ago, it was none other than Sen. Barry Goldwater, the conservative from Arizona, who upbraided Mr. Casey for failing to notify congressional intelligence committees about the mining of habors in Nicaragua. But the lecture didn't sink in. Mr. Casey continued, until felled by illness, to advise a White House that would sanction Mr. Secord's off-the-books "enterprise," a subversive activity dressed up as official business.

Incredibly, Mr. Secord now proposes turning over the $8 million left over from the Iran-contra operation to the William J. Casey Fund for the Nicaraguan Freedom Fighters — proof that zealotry excuses its excesses.

The only comfort, as this week's hearings concluded, was that the independent counsel was watching. The case for criminal conspiracy grows stronger by the day.

## Detroit Free Press

*Detroit, MI, May 7, 1987*

THE INITIAL testimony of Richard Secord before the joint congressional committee investigating the Iran-contra affair must have sent shock waves through the top levels of the Reagan administration. Despite repeated denials from President Reagan on down, the probe is focusing more and more on the White House and high administration officials.

Among Gen. Secord's disclosures were that the late William Casey, then director of the CIA, was directly involved in supplying weapons to the contras at a time when Congress had banned such aid. Moreover, Gen. Secord said, he believed that he was carrying out such covert and illegal operations with the blessing of the president and with full knowledge of Vice-President George Bush.

What is becoming more painfully clear with each

**Gen. Secord**

new revelation is that some people in power believed and perhaps still believe that they are above the law, that a congressional ban on covert aid is but a fly to be flicked off and forgotten about in the pursuit of an ideological cause.

The congressional inquiries should go a long way toward untangling the web that has been woven for the past three years and stretches from Iran, to Israel, to Nicaragua — and to the White House. The inquiry is a painful but necessary employment of the self-correction mechanism the Constitution provides in the separation of powers.

That the U.S. government is a government of laws, not individuals, is a lesson that evidently must be taught and learned again and again. The congressional hearings are teaching that lesson anew.

WHAT IT WAS WAS PATRIOTISM!

SECORD

©1987 MIAMI NEWS

# TULSA WORLD

*Tulsa, OK, May 10, 1987*

AFTER the first week of formal hearings by a joint Senate-House committee, the Iran-Contra affair is still a confusing mess. But the fog is beginning to lift, thanks in part to the work of Oklahoma's Sen. David Boren.

Boren's concise questioning of retired Maj. Gen. Richard Secord was the high moment of the opening rounds.

Boren caught some flak in some radio-tv call-in shows for boring in too hard on the confident general. But this is no time for soft questions and fear of stepping on toes. If the full truth is to emerge, it will come from relentless, orderly, lawyer-like questioning of witnesses, like Secord, who know the facts.

As an interrogator, Boren put the committee counsel and its other members to shame. He lucidly traced the more than $30 millions of complex financial transactions known to the committee and shed new light on what happened, or might have happened, to large sums as yet unaccounted for.

Boren also raised pertinent questions that went to the heart of the inquiry: the legality and propriety of important U.S. foreign policy adventures being carried out by private agencies instead of the government.

If Secord and his assorted private corporations were, in fact, in full control of the transfer of funds to the Contras, then the U.S. Government will have admitted that it abdicated responsibility for sensitive and controversial foreign policy operations to a bunch of freelancers.

If it turns out that the Reagan Administration officially sanctioned and controlled the Contra funding, then it raises the question of violating laws prohibiting government aid to the anti-Sandinista rebels.

There is, of course, a lot of gray in these questions. Lawyers will be poles apart on what constitutes a violation. The final answers are unlikely to be either clear-cut or unanimous.

But after Gen. Secord's first days of testimony, it looks as if the light will eventually shine through and the American people can pass a judgment based on sufficient facts.

# AKRON BEACON JOURNAL
*Akron, OH, May 10, 1987*

ONE QUESTION that surfaced frequently in the testimony of Richard Secord before the special congressional committees investigating the Iran-Contra affair was: Why did the retired Air Force major general get involved in a secret, and apparently illegal, operation to divert funds to the Nicaraguan Contras?

Mr. Secord's answer, in short, was that he *believed* in the cause. He believed in the Nicaraguan Contras and this country's need to support them. And the strength of his convictions permitted him to be, in the jargon of the legal community, "a good witness." Mr. Secord was credible when he told the committee that he never intended to profit from the venture. He saw himself as fulfilling his duty.

What upsets the Secord testimony, however, is the fundamental principle that a democracy functions on the rule of law, not a set of ideological beliefs. Frustrated with congressional reluctance to support their cause, officials in the Reagan administration organized an elaborate and secret program to aid the Contras. The law that banned aid to the rebels, the Boland amendment, might have been full of loopholes, as Mr. Secord claimed, but, at the very least, its spirit was unmistakable, and the result of much debate.

President Reagan's huge election victory in 1984 was impressive, but it was not an invitation for officials to ignore the checks and balances of the system. But that's what happened.

Mr. Secord added several fascinating details to the story, but most striking about his testimony was the description of how vast the covert operation was that he headed. Arms were sold to Iran; some of the profits transferred to the Contras; there were planes, code names, National Security Agency communications equipment, secret foreign bank accounts and secret sources of funding. An enormously complex arrangement was set up to cover the administration's involvement. The intention was to deceive, to circumvent congressional oversight.

Increasingly, it has become clear the Iran-Contra mission was not a rogue operation. President Reagan may not have known of the diversion of funds — as he repeated again last week — but higher ups in the administration were apparently deeply involved. Lewis Tambs, who resigned as ambassador to Costa Rica amid speculation that he gave improper military help to the Contras, insisted last week that he went through authorized channels.

Sen. Daniel Inouye, the chairman of the Senate investigating committee, remarked at the outset of the hearings that "the story is one . . . of covert foreign policy. Not secret diplomacy, which Congress has always accepted, but secret policymaking, which the Constitution has always rejected." He called it "sad and sordid," and from hearing Mr. Secord's testimony, he's right. In a democracy, one administration's beliefs cannot supplant the law.

# McFarlane Testifies in Iran-Contra Hearings

The House and Senate select committees investigating the Iran-contra arms affair held their second week of public hearings May 11-14, 1987. The main witness was Robert McFarlane, the White House national security adviser from 1983 to 1985. He testified voluntarily. Unlike retired Maj. Gen. Richard Secord, the previous week's witness, McFarlane had been in a position to judge the degree of President Reagan's involvement in various stages of the Iranian arms initiative and the effort to resupply the Nicaraguan contra rebels during the period such aid had been barred by Congress. However, a combination of incomplete or evasive answers by McFarlane and a lack of probing follow-up questions by lawmakers left specific details about Reagan's role still unclear. The major revelation concerned Reagan's personal involvement in the apparent solicitation of funds from Saudi Arabia to support the Nicaraguan insurgents. McFarlane's testimony seemed to put the White House on the defensive. After months of stressing that the President had known little of what his staff had been doing to aid the contras, administration officials began a new tack. They now suggested that the various laws passed by Congress restricting aid to the contras had not applied to the President in his capacity as chief architect of United States foreign policy.

McFarlane, in his opening statement to the committees, said that after Congress banned support for the Nicaraguan contra rebels, President Reagan "repeatedly made clear in public and in private that he did not intend to break faith with the contras." McFarlane went on to describe cases in which Reagan intervened personally to promote foreign contributions to the contras. In his statement McFarlane sought to portray U.S. support for the contras in geopolitical terms, arguing that covert support for the rebels was a mistake only because of the absence of "a fundamental government-wide analysis" of the rationale for the policy. McFarlane's first day before the joint committee included testimony concerning President Reagan's alleged personal solicitation of funds for the contras from King Fahd of Saudi Arabia in early 1985. Although throughout most of the hearings he spoke slowly in a melancholic monotone, McFarlane punctuated his testimony May 13 with sudden bursts of emotion.

On the fourth and final day of the week's testimony, Rep. Lee Hamilton (D, Ind.), chairman of the House select committee, summed up by saying that he admired McFarlane's often expressed willingness "to take the blame on yourself." But he added that President Reagan could not escape responsibility for his administration's secret aid to the contras.

## The Charlotte Observer

*Charlotte, NC, May 27, 1987*

The example of Robert McFarlane holds a lesson for all of us. In his recent testimony before the congressional committee investigating the Iran-contra affair, Mr. McFarlane defended many of the goals he and others pursued in the Iran-contra affair, but he acknowledged that in pursuing them through a quasi-governmental undercover operation, "we didn't choose the right instrument to do it. Succinctly put, where I went wrong was not having the guts to stand up and tell the president that."

**McFarlane**

And why didn't he stand up?

"To tell you the truth," he told the committee, "probably the reason I didn't is because if I'd done that, [former CIA director] Bill Casey, [former U.N. ambassador] Jeane Kirkpatrick and [Defense Secretary] Cap Weinberger would have said I was some kind of commie, you know."

It's sad to consider how often a similar statement could be made about recent scandals on Wall Street and in executive suites as well as in the White House basement. The problem is not so much that no one knew something was wrong, but that no one would speak out against it. Excuses are easy to come by: It's not my decision. They'll think I'm a coward. If I draw the line here, I won't be here to stop something worse from happening.

The essential commodity in shortest supply in America today is not oil or gold, it's moral courage — the backbone needed to speak out for what you think is right and against what you think is wrong. In the Reagan administration and elsewhere, there's too much macho bluster and too little moral courage.

## the Charleston Gazette

*Charleston, WV, May 20, 1987*

DELIBERATE lies to Congress and the U.S. public were utilized by the White House to hide the severity of President Reagan's secret war against Nicaragua.

In August 1985, Lt. Col. Oliver North told the House Intelligence Committee he had no role in arranging support for the contras — when, in truth, he was running a major support operation. The following day, National Security Council chief John Poindexter sent him a note saying "Well done."

In October 1985, former NSC director Robert McFarlane told the same committee "there is no official or unofficial relationship with any member of the NSC staff regarding fund-raising for the Nicaraguan democratic opposition" — a brazen falsehood.

In late 1986, again before the same committee, McFarlane was asked what he knew about contra fund-raising. He replied, "I have no idea of the extent of that or anything else." In fact, he had just helped obtain $32 million from Saudi Arabia for the contras.

Last week in the Contragate hearings, McFarlane admitted he previously testified "inappropriately . . . It wasn't a full account."

*Inappropriately?* It was pure perjury — and both McFarlane and North should go to jail for it.

Investigators have found a February 1985 memo from North to contra leader Adolfo Calero advising him that $20 million more was being deposited in "the usual account." The letter warned:

"We need to make sure that this new financing does NOT become known. The Congress must believe that there continues to be an urgent need for funding."

Thus North declared in writing an intent to deceive Congress members to induce them to vote money for the contras.

Other falsehoods: North, McFarlane and Poindexter wrote a false White House chronology of events to shield the president. They falsely listed Hawk missiles as "oil drilling equipment." They utilized false "end-user certificates" indicating that weapons were going to Guatemala when they were being passed on for use against Nicaragua.

Lies, lies, lies.

As McFarlane was leaving the witness stand last week, Rep. Lee Hamilton, D-Ind., asked him a final question: "How can our system of government work if the administration is not candid in its answers to Congress?"

McFarlane replied simply: "There is no rebuttal."

At least *that* answer wasn't perjured. The system can't work when White House leaders lie to America.

# Richmond Times-Dispatch

*Richmond, VA, May 16, 1987*

The really interesting question in the Iran-*contra* hearings so far is why it took Bud McFarlane three days to balk at the badgering, contemptuous, prosecutorial tones of his congressional questioners. Mr. McFarlane was determined to cooperate — and prepared to take his lumps — in a select committee inquiry into what and who went wrong and why, and how to prevent a recurrence. He found himself in the dock instead, his Democratic interrogators shedding any pretense at a non-partisan effort to comprehend this particular affair and to draw from it larger lessons for the nation. If — if — it should come to trials, the independent prosecutor is, as a combative Richard Secord pointed out to the panel, hard at work up the street.

The only enlightening revelations so far are the lack of a smoking gun or a hand in which to put it, and the trace of powder burns on Congress' pointing fingers. It seems that Congress itself agreed to exclude the National Security Council from designation as an intelligence agency, an exclusion that would exempt the NSC from the subsequent Boland amendment(s) proscription(s) on sort(s) of aid to the *contras*. It seems that Congress, which by its own vacillation has shown that it isn't sure but what the president's *contra* policy is right, may have provided itself deniability and the administration a loophole through which Ollie North and Richard Secord could fly *contra* supplies.

The Democrats' search for illegalities has uncovered only one: a shipping magnate in Geneva who kept $10 million intended for the *contras* but put erroneously in his Swiss account. So odds are they will continue to phrase and rephrase their questions, or restate not quite accurately an answer, to imply wrongdoing when a recalcitrant witness doesn't give the answer they want. They will act as though witnesses who say they were doing *their* job — and rather better — were villains operating in a vacuum, though their decisions were made in a context in which Congress' geeing and hawing was crucial.

We are, Democratic inquisitors will say, doing our job. But when their disputatiousness exhausts the patience and contrition of the so patient and contrite Bud McFarland, when their questions are far more self-serving and far less elucidating than the answers, they ought to worry about alienating whatever audience is still tuned in. They have spurned prime time in which to review and analyze, to discuss the foreign-policy tug of war between the executive and legislative branches, and to own up to and resolve Congress' own contribution to this mess.

Administration officials have their own owning up to do, the worst of which may be yet to come. But a word of caution to the committeemen who see these hearings as an occasion not for taking stock but for honing their own reputations. The details of the affair aren't easily retained, but the atmospherics of the hearing are. Questioners who persist in trying, and failing, to make administration officials look irredeemably bad will themselves look worse.

# The Des Moines Register

*Des Moines, IA, May 17, 1987*

*Truth will come to light; murder cannot be hid long.* — **William Shakespeare, "The Merchant of Venice."**

The Iran-contra affair is not murder, but the truth *will* come to light, a lesson that many people can't seem to learn, including President Reagan and his advisers.

Some of that truth has come to light in the painful and confused testimony of a deeply troubled Robert McFarlane, Reagan's former national-security adviser. As a result, the president's defense has been turned 180 degrees within these past few days.

First, it was being said that he knew nothing of the secret arms shipments to the contras.

Then, when testimony before Congress knocked out that defense, it was said that he knew about some private fund-raising efforts in behalf of the contras, but had no part in them.

Finally — or maybe it isn't finally — McFarlane made a convincing case that Reagan not only knew about, but took part in, some of that fund-raising.

So now the defense is that he did nothing unlawful. The White House legal staff is trying to build a case that the Boland Amendment, forbidding direct or indirect U.S. government aid to the contras, did not apply to the president.

What new evidence will bring what convoluted new story?

How tempting it is to try to keep the lid on the steaming kettle, in the hope that the truth won't boil over. Because the president failed to tell the whole truth at the outset, he now is being contradicted and refuted, bit by bit, forced to backtrack, left with hardly a shred of credibility. No matter what he may say now, few can believe him.

Slowly, inexorably, the truth *is* coming to light.

# THE BLADE

*Toledo, OH, May 21, 1987*

IT IS simply referred to by congressmen and newsmen as Iran-contra. It is not quite a scandal. It has not yet been called by the higher pundits a "crisis," constitutional or otherwise, and no one speaks of revelations, for while much is exposed little is revealed.

Consider Robert C. "Bud" McFarlane. A former marine corps officer who became Ronald Reagan's national security adviser, he was up to his ears in Iran-contra.

This fellow took to Iran a cake and a Bible inscribed by the president. In case he was kidnaped he took along drugs with which to take his own life. Later, back in America after the story broke Mr. McFarlane tried the same plan with the same drugs because he had let down his president.

Before the relevant committees last week, Mr. McFarlane admitted that he has, representing the president, lied to members of Congress about funding the contras, about arms for hostages, and possibly other things.

If any larger points have come through in the congressional hearings thus far, they are these two. First, paying ransom was not just one nasty error but practically a trend in this administration. That makes liars, in a really big way, out of most of the central foreign policy makers, gentlemen who used to talk mighty tough on terror.

The second point is that private aid to the contras was encourged if not solicited by the president's men and by the President himself. That's a violation of the spirit of the congressional intent, if not the letter.

But again to what end? Mr. McFarlane could not explain. Did the White House really believe this would make the difference in Central America or to our overall position in the world?

The current crowd is comparable to the Nixon cowboys in one respect. With so many important things going on around them they became obsessed with a sideshow. And to accomplish what they wanted they began to make secret covenants and form a secret, utterly incompetent apparatus.

The White House is now claiming that the war-making power is the president's, that he acted as commander in chief. But if he really thought it so important why didn't the President act as commander in chief openly? If the threat was so great, why not send all the Marines, not just Mr. McFarlane?

Mr. McFarlane said he knew the contra aid plans were dubious but feared to say so. He said he was frightened that Caspar Weinberger, Jeane Kirkpatrick, or William Casey might call him a communist. In the fast lanes of Washington, policy is born of group-think, and every conspicious patriot's deepest fear is that he won't be chosen for the team.

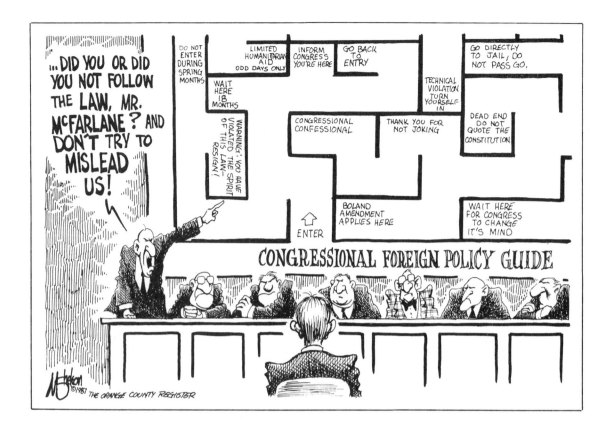

CONGRESSIONAL FOREIGN POLICY GUIDE

## News-Tribune & Herald

*Duluth, MN, May 16, 1987*

Let's find ways to evade the law without violating the law.

That is the essence of Robert McFarlane's testimony to Congress on the Reagan administration's ill-conceived Iran-contra policies. McFarlane, Ronald Reagan's former national security adviser, spent four days before a joint Senate-House investigations committee.

A major portion of McFarlane's testimony seemed intended to establish that, while he and others in the administration had previously been less than candid, less than honest, with Congress about Iran arms sales and Nicaraguan contra support efforts, the executive branch of our government *had not* violated laws passed by Congress. Of particular note was the Boland amendment, passed in October 1984 and now lapsed, which prohibited "direct or indirect" federal military assistance to the Nicaraguan rebels.

Congress clearly opposed the administration's desires of continuing military aid to the contras. The Boland amendment codified that opposition.

Presidential spokesman Marlin Fitzwater said late in the week that "there has been a great deal of confusion" over interpretation of that amendment. Yet the language of the law was certainly no more confusing than the wording of the oath of office Reagan took as president, swearing to uphold the Constitution and the laws of the United States.

Perhaps the letter of the law of the Boland amendment was not broken. But McFarlane's testimony clearly shows that the administration sought all avenues to bend and distort that legislation to serve its own purposes.

Such willful distortion by the top echelon of our government is disheartening. It fosters public distrust of our government and of its public policy processes.

## THE DAILY OKLAHOMAN

*Oklahoma City, OK, May 18, 1987*

IN an emotional moment, Robert McFarlane told congressional investigators of his frustration over dealing with terrorism and his admiration for the Israeli approach.

"Terrorists know that whenever they commit terrorism against Israel, something, somehow, somewhere is going to happen," he said.

McFarlane acknowledged that Israel's methods would not be acceptable in the United States. In case there is any doubt, consider the action taken by a California judge last week.

U.S. Immigration Judge Ingrid Hrycenko dismissed all charges against eight foreign nationals accused of being members of a Palestinian terrorist organization. She was miffed because a certain immigration official failed to appear at the deportation hearing.

Government attorneys may appeal the decision or refile the charges. Meanwhile, the eight suspected terrorists are free to do as they please.

The Justice Department has been hampered in its efforts to treat terrorists as criminals because of the "political exception" provisions of bilateral extradition treaties with other nations. In four separate cases during the past two years, U.S. courts ruled that Irish Republican Army terrorists could not be sent back to Great Britain to stand trial because of a claim that their motives were political. An agreement finally was reached to eliminate the exception for violent crimes.

Attorney General Edwin Meese signed a new treaty with Belgium last month which should diminish the availability of the political exception. In a speech in Brussels, Meese explained the underlying premise of these efforts. "Where there is democracy and a responsive judicial system, we do not, and we must not, accept violence as a legitimate method of achieving political change."

One sign of encouragement is that countries around the world are getting tougher on terrorists. In January, Italian authorities arrested a Lebanese terrorist as he tried to smuggle explosives through the Milan airport. The next day, German authorities seized another Lebanese terrorist wanted by the United States for the hijacking of TWA flight 847 two years ago, in which an American citizen was killed.

With such progress being made, it is disheartening to see an American judge undermine U.S. efforts to combat terrorism.

## St. Paul Pioneer Press & Dispatch

*St. Paul, MN, May 16, 1987*

Former National Security Adviser Robert McFarlane conceded Thursday that Reagan administration policy in Nicaragua was flawed from inception because the president and other officials never bothered to clearly and truthfully explain their actual intentions to the American people.

During his fourth and perhaps last day of testimony before a joint congressional investigative committee, Mr. McFarlane said that he should have had the "guts" to tell Mr. Reagan about the omission, but that he feared being labeled "some kind of commie."

He feared being called a *what*?

In fairness to Mr. McFarlane, he may have been satirically sticking it to ideological hard-liners (those who find softies in the strangest places). But even so, just his confession that he did not have the courage to tell Mr. Reagan that his Central American policy was seriously lacking says something terribly embarrassing about himself. It also says something uncomplimentary about the president's capacity for setting the right tone and his stomach for bad news.

Here, after all, was the man Mr. Reagan relied on hourly to provide sound counsel about the most dangerous issues facing the country. And he did not have enough self-confidence to tell his boss that a centerpiece policy had a giant hole dead in the middle? And that the climate in the White House was such that even ex-Marines who had fought in Vietnam had to worry about being thought pink? In fairness once more to the former national security chief, he has assumed more responsibility for Iranamok than ordinary honor requires, and one would like to think (for his sake) that his testimony this week has been truthful throughout. But Mr. McFarlane's testimony does accentuate the general point that senior governmental service is no place for anyone other than the strongest and best-equipped men and women, and (more specifically) that this administration has not been consistently stocked with them.

# ARGUS-LEADER

*Sioux Falls, SD, May 12, 1987*

As Gary Hart's social life and failed presidential campaign fade from the forefront of the news, the Iran-Contra hearing will attract more attention.

That's bad news for President Reagan.

The first week of the congressional inquiry did not reflect flatteringly on Reagan's claims of detached innocence. **Editorial**

The second week is soiling the president's image even more.

Members of Congress are looking into the Reagan administration's attempts to free U.S. hostages in Lebanon by selling arms to Iran. They also are examining administration aides' attempts to raise money for the Contra rebels fighting Nicaragua's leftist government.

So far, the second week of the hearing has not produced anything as odd as Richard Secord's suggestion that remaining arms sale profits be turned over to a new Contra fund established in the memory of the late William Casey, former director of the CIA. Secord, a retired Air Force major general, was the first and only witness to testify last week.

So far this week, the spotlight has been on Robert McFarlane, Reagan's former national security adviser. His testimony is filling in a lot of blanks in the Iran-Contra story.

McFarlane testified Monday that Reagan ordered him to help the Contra rebels "hold body and soul together" even though Congress had banned direct or indirect U.S. military aid to them. McFarlane felt he could not directly solicit contributions from private individuals but felt it was permissible to express concern about the Contras' shortage of money in conversations with potential donors, and express thanks if a pledge were made.

What's that, again?

We fail to see much difference in those fund-raising techniques. Whether the seeker is asking for money directly or indirectly, soliciting money is soliciting money.

That was not the only confusing statement that came out of Monday's session.

McFarlane testified at another point that he notified Reagan in writing of a foreign official's promise to donate $1 million a month to the Contras at a time when U.S. military aid was banned. The note was returned to McFarlane with a message that Reagan was pleased.

At the White House, presidential spokesman Marlin Fitzwater said that while Reagan had sought to rally support for the Contras, "Let no one believe that the president was involved in asking the staff or anyone else to provide illegal support for the freedom fighters."

What's that, again?

By week's end, Reagan may be hoping that Hart makes a comeback.

## Post-Tribune

*Gary, IN, May 18, 1987*

With another week of congressional hearings on the Iran-Contra affair over, the White House can't breathe a sigh of relief. As hard as Robert McFarlane tried to take the blame himself, his testimony kept bringing President Reagan into the picture, too.

The testimony definitely suggested that Reagan was more involved in aiding the Contras than has been acknowledged. It's no wonder that he embraced the Tower Commission's earlier report that his management style kept him out of touch with key aspects of his Iran and Contra policies. Better a bad management image than being implicated in shady activities.

**Our opinions**

Before the hearings, the White House kept attention directed to whether the president knew about the diversion of Iran arms profits to the Contras. The hearings are bringing the arms diversion into focus as only a part of an elaborate system for getting aid to the Contras during a period when it was forbidden by congressional action. And Reagan is coming across as someone who was aware of what was being done.

On top of McFarlane's testimony, the White House was further implemented when a former State Department consultant testified that Johnathan Miller, director of the White House office of administration, cashed traveler's checks from Oliver North for distribution to a Contra leader. Miller then resigned from his post.

So now the administration is trying to shift the debate to whether those congressional restrictions apply to the president and other White House officials.

McFarlane's testimony mirrored what seems to be an administration attitude putting the "cause" above both ethics and the law. He admitted that North exceeded his instructions, didn't keep his boss informed of what he was doing and probably broke the law more than once. Yet he described him as a great American and outstanding public servant.

With North and Rear Adm. John Poindexter yet to testify, the White House staff is going to have a hard time coming up with ways to absolve the president of responsibility. But the hearings probably won't change any minds.

Those who think the U.S. should be aiding the Contras are going to forgive those involved no matter what. Those who think Nicaragua should be left alone to resolve its own destiny will see a criminal conspiracy going all the way to the top.

One thing for sure, accountability is suffering.

# Reagan, in Reversal, Says Contra Fund Was 'My Idea'

After months of denying that he knew specifics about private efforts to aid the Nicaraguan contra rebels, President Reagan May 15, 1987 told a group of Southern journalists that he had been regularly briefed on contra aid because it was "my idea to begin with." Reagan made the statement straightforwardly, without indicating an awareness that it conflicted with his earlier statements that he had known about aid to the contras from private individuals and foreign countries but did not know the details.

Reagan's new statement came in response to a different topic, recent changes in the structure of the National Security Council. Reagan complained that "they've seemed to portray me as claiming to be uninformed about everything." With regard to the contras, he said, "Here there's no question about my being informed...I was kept briefed on that. As a matter of fact, I was definitely involved in the decisions about support to the freedom fighters." Reagan reiterated that he had not "directly ever engaged in soliciting from other countries," but claimed that such solicitation was not prohibited by the Boland Amendment ban on contra aid. Reagan further claimed that the Boland Amendment said that "we should encourage such support to the freedom fighters in Nicaragua." One of several versions of the amendment permitted a small amount of nonlethal assistance to the rebels.

Observers saw Reagan's statements as part of an overall White House effort to limit the political damage from continuing revelations about Reagan's involvement in the contra aid network. In the past week, the administration had begun to assert that the Boland Amendment did not apply to the President and that it did not apply to contributions from other countries.

## THE SACRAMENTO BEE
*Sacramento, CA, May 22, 1987*

After three years of dissembling and months of shifting defenses in the Iran-Contra affair, President Reagan has joined the issue: Yes, he knew about Ollie North's program of private aid to the Contras. "It was my idea." But the White House and its supporters deny Reagan violated the law forbidding U.S. aid to the Contras because the president's foreign policy authority cannot be restricted by Congress. In that expansive claim, neither the Constitution nor history supports the president.

Out of practical necessity, the executive branch of government is responsible for the development and execution of the nation's foreign affairs. But the Constitution makes no exclusive grant of foreign policy prerogative to the executive, such as Reagan claims.

All of the president's enumerated foreign responsibilities are shared with Congress. He makes treaties, but the Senate must ratify them. He names ambassadors, but the Senate must confirm them. He is commander-in-chief, but only Congress can declare war and raise the armed forces. There is nothing in the founding charter of government to suggest that the president "is the sole person to whom our Constitution gives the responsibility for conducting foreign relations," as Sen. Orrin Hatch incorrectly describes it. Precisely to deny the president such kingly prerogatives, the framers of the Constitution made the conduct of foreign affairs a "joint possession," as Alexander Hamilton put it, a system of shared power and checks and balances between the executive and legislative branches.

Where the letter of the Constitution fails them, the president's defenders cite historical parallels to Contra aid to prove their contention. Chief among them is Franklin D. Roosevelt's 1940 destroyers-for-bases deal with Great Britain. But Roosevelt consulted extensively with congressional leaders and his presidential opponent before going ahead with that deal. He did not, as Reagan has done, furtively defy a congressional ban on helping England. He did not launder money through Swiss bank accounts or hire soldiers of fortune or send young aides with code names to Chinese groceries in New York City to await secret cash drops. Roosevelt moved to executive action through consensus and consultation; Reagan and his men did so behind a curtain of lies and deceit. If their action was all legal and constitutional, why did they conceal it and contract it out to private freebooters, arms dealers and charity scam artists?

It was bad enough when the Tower Commission found that the president was negligently unaware and uninvolved as the zealots of his administration, in defiance of Congress, conducted their guerrilla war out of the back door of the White House. It is worse still when Reagan embraces such lawbreaking as a presidential prerogative. The argument pretends to raise this disaster to a highfalutin constitutional dispute. But at bottom it's a last-minute defense of the indefensible.

## AKRON BEACON JOURNAL
*Akron, OH, May 17, 1987*

REP. LEE Hamilton, the chairman of the House committee investigating the Iran-Contra affair, drew the only conclusion he could from the testimony of Robert McFarlane: Admirable as it was for Mr. McFarlane, a former national security adviser, to accept blame for deceiving Congress on the extent of clandestine White House support for the Nicaraguan Contras, the responsibility really lay with President Reagan.

If Mr. Reagan had been doing his job in 1985, he would have called in his top national security staffers and explained that the Boland amendment meant there could be no direct or indirect U.S. government funding of the Contras. He didn't do that; he didn't even come close. Instead, his administration pursued an elaborate and secret scheme to evade the congressional ban and aid the rebels.

The tone was set by the President, and after two weeks of testimony, it has become clear that he was, in the words of Sen. Daniel Inouye, "much more knowledgeable" about the affair than previously claimed by the White House. Mr. McFarlane told lawmakers that he briefed the President "frequently" on what his staff was doing to help the Contras. Mr. Reagan has admitted that he discussed Contra aid with King Fahd of Saudi Arabia several days before the Saudis doubled their donation to the rebels.

As yet, much still remains unknown about the President's role. But indications are the White House is jittery. No longer able to argue credibly that the President was out of touch on key details of the Contra policy, the administration has erected a new defense. Mr. Reagan, it's now said, did nothing illegal. Officials argue that the Boland amendment did not limit the President's "constitutional and historical power" to manage foreign policy.

It's easy to become mired in the details and doubletalk of the Iran-Contra affair. Remember: White House officials were deceiving each other. But at its core, the scandal is simple: Congress passed a law banning U.S. aid to the Contras, and the administration ignored it.

Perhaps Mr. Reagan didn't know about the diversion of funds from the Iranian arms sales to the Contras. But that was just one part of the effort to aid the rebels. The President made it clear that, in this case, his highest priority was the Contras. In terms of the Constitution, he made the wrong choice. It says the President "shall take care that the laws are faithfully executed." Mr. Reagan neglected his duty.

# THE TENNESSEAN

*Nashville, TN, May 20, 1987*

ON the theory that the best defense is a good offense, the White House has shifted its tactics from a position of careful denial that President Ronald Reagan may have violated the Boland Amendment to one that it didn't apply to him in any case.

The changing strategy became apparent when White House spokesmen began to say that there were several versions of the Boland Amendment, by which the Congress said no U.S. funds could be obligated or expended in support of the Nicaraguan contra rebels. It precisely banned the use of funds "available" to any government office involved in intelligence activities.

The use of available funds seems broad enough to apply even to funds that might have been channeled to the contras through third countries. White House attorneys argue that the Boland Amendment didn't purport to limit "the constitutional and historic powers of the President" to personally carry out foreign policy and conduct conversations with foreign leaders.

That was clearly in reference to Mr. Reagan's conversation with Saudi Arabia's King Fahd about that country's multi-million dollar contributions to the contras. Mr. Reagan said the king brought up the matter but he didn't solicit the funds.

What the congressional hearings have brought out already is that Mr. Reagan was far more involved in the contra affair than previously thought. The Tower Commission report pictured him as somewhat inattentive to what was going on, and he has pleaded memory lapses about what he knew or didn't know.

But according to former National Security Adviser Robert McFarlane, Mr. Reagan was briefed "dozens of times" about the Central American situation. Also, according to Mr. McFarlane, the President took a "more liberal interpretation" of the Boland Amendment and had reiterated often the U.S. tradition of helping "freedom fighters" — although, as Mr. McFarlane noted, he didn't urge or authorize anyone to undertake illegal activity.

There are now some clearer answers as to what the President knew and when he knew it. And the testimony of Maj. General Richard Secord and Mr. McFarlane just about demolishes the idea that Lt. Col. Oliver North was running amok in the basement while the upstairs White House was in the dark about what was going on. Mr. Secord said the White House "approved my conduct." Mr. McFarlane made it clear the President was kept informed at all times.

There is no evidence that Mr. Reagan knew of the fund diversion from the sale of the Iran arms. He has repeatedly denied that. But the sudden White House shift on the Boland Amendment would indicate that presidential aids may be bracing for more damaging things to come.

The focus has been sharp at times on how the White House interprets the law restricting aid to the rebels, especially as the law relates to solicitation of funds from third countries. There is one thing fairly clear: White House credibility is becoming a little frayed. ∎

# The Miami Herald

*Miami, FL, May 20, 1987*

AS THE searchlight of responsibility for the Iranscam scandal sweeps closer and closer to the Oval Office itself, President Reagan has invented a novel new weapon to negate anything it might reveal. He and Chief of Staff Howard Baker say that the Boland Amendment, which forbade lethal aid to the Nicaraguan *contras* for a time, doesn't apply to the President. Even if it did, they add, it would unconstitutionally constrain the President's powers.

Like Star Wars, this Executive Defense Initiative sounds good on paper — but it won't meet the test of reality.

The President has the same individual free-speech rights as anyone else, of course. He therefore has the right, in private conversation with a foreign official, to advocate policies — military aid to the *contras*, say — that Congress for a time forbade.

Advocacy and action aren't the same, however — and there's where this defense strategy fails. It is clear that some of the President's men broke the law in supplying military aid to the *contras* at a time — 1984 to last October — when Congress forbade it. The House-Senate investigating committee is trying to determine whether the President, in addition to *advocating* arming the *contras*, actively took part in the illegalities of Iranscam.

While the President's Iranscam role remains to be revealed, this pre-emptive effort to deny that the Boland Amendment applies to him won't wash. It's true, as Mr. Reagan and Mr. Baker contend, that the Constitution empowers the President to make and carry out foreign policy. Yet the Framers did not give the President an unfettered hand.

Fearing a President who thought himself king, the Framers checked his powers in several ways. They required that the Senate ratify treaties. They gave Congress alone the power to regulate foreign commerce, to raise and support armies, and to declare war. The power to tax and spend, necessary to sustain a war, also reposes with Congress alone.

Given those constraints, it is simply inconceivable that the Framers intended the President to be able to pursue a foreign military policy against Congress's express prohibition. To assume otherwise, as Mr. Reagan and Mr. Baker are doing, is to assume that the Framers would embrace what they in fact abhorred: a President above the law.

# The Idaho STATESMAN

*Boise, ID, May 18, 1987*

Those Reagan administration officials involved in the Iran-contra affair seem to have invented a perpetual motion blame machine. The revelations of the past two weeks suggest that everyone and no one merits blame.

It doesn't matter. Culpability rests not just in a theoretical sense, but also in a real and practical sense with the man in the Oval Office.

So far, we have heard Robert McFarlane, President Reagan's former national security adviser, say that if anyone is to blame for the whole mess, he is — but also saying that he had briefed the president "frequently" on his staff's contra activities.

We have heard retired Air Force Maj. Gen. Richard Secord alternately say that only he made important decisions — and that he was merely responding as any patriot would to the requests of his superiors.

Meanwhile, two other officials have pleaded guilty to Iran-contra-related charges. And the two big witnesses, Lt. Col. Oliver North and Rear Adm. John Poindexter, have yet to be heard — probably under conditions of at least limited immunity, which may yield some candor.

The American people probably never will know precisely who gave which orders. Some of the many contradictions in testimony and documents probably will remain. Some witnesses, immunized or not from legal action, probably will withhold some dirt. Information from other key sources – such as former CIA Director William Casey, who died May 6, his secrets intact – will never surface.

But the important points are clear.

The people can understand that if the president did not know what was happening in the White House, he should have. He is culpable, in the true sense, either way.

They should realize that even the incomplete information revealed so far has nailed down a pattern of White House arrogance, of a haughty indifference to federal law and even to the importance of our constitutional form of government. The extent of these feelings in the White House shows either a tolerance for, or an acceptance of, them by the president.

They ought to know that presidents can set events in motion, not only by direct orders but also by simply suggesting he would be pleased if the hostages in Lebanon were released, or if the contras in Nicaragua would prevail. An even moderately zealous aide would be quick to take the hint, allowing the president truthfully to say that no, he didn't issue an order.

While a long line of witnesses parades across our television screens in the weeks ahead, don't forget that this is the president's show.

## THE ANN ARBOR NEWS
### Ann Arbor, MI, May 29, 1987

The wide scope of presidential powers notwithstanding, no president is above the law. The experience of Watergate proved that conclusively.

President Nixon repeatedly invoked the concept of executive privilege to withhold from congressional investigators what proved to be damaging material. The Supreme Court unanimously ruled against Nixon.

The object lesson to the American people and to the rulers they elect to govern them was that the law is king and that the president must obey the law. Article I of the Constitution obligates the president to "take care that the laws be faithfully executed."

Is the president, then, free to pick and choose which laws he will faithfully execute? Can he and his advisers determine for themselves which are "bad" laws and which laws may be unconstitutional even before they have been found to be so by the judiciary?

These familiar questions have surfaced on Capitol Hill with the unfolding testimony in the Iran-Contra scandal. Once again, the president of the U.S. is laying claim to broad powers which is not justified by a close reading of the law.

President Reagan is claiming that the Boland amendment, passed by Congress to ban aid directly or indirectly to Nicaraguan Contras until Dec. 3, 1985, does not apply to him as president, to his national security adviser or to the National Security Council.

The basis for that claim is that the amendment allegedly placed only one restriction on the president: He could not use money available to the CIA, the Defense Department or any "entity of the U.S. involved in intelligence activities" to help the Contras. Otherwise, he was free to encourage private donations or contributions from other countries, for example.

Any other reading of the amendment, according to Reagan supporters, would unconstitutionally restrict the president's power to conduct foreign policy.

Lloyd Cutler, who served as counsel to President Jimmy Carter, is quoted in Time magazine as saying that "normally a statute that mentions other executive agencies but not the president explicitly is interpreted as not applying to him." The flaw in that argument, of course, is that it elevates the president above the law.

The author of the amendment in question, Rep. Edward Boland, D-Mass., said that if Reagan wanted to claim exemption from the amendment, he should have done so when it was discussed in Congress. Reagan signed the bill to which the Boland amendment was attached without public comment.

The distinguished constitutional scholar Laurence Tribe, professor of law at Harvard, writes: "Congress' control over the purse would be rendered a nullity if the president's pocket could conceal a slush fund dedicated to purposes and projects prohibited by the laws of the U.S."

The Boland amendment *did* go through several congressional rewrites (see article below). Some believe it is poorly drafted and ambiguous. It *may* even be foolish national policy to farm out the president's conduct of foreign policy to 535 members of the House and Senate.

But that really is beside the point. Boland was the law at the time of the Iran-Contra transactions. The Constitution limits the president in that it charges him to faithfully execute the laws without exception.

As Robert McFarlane has testified, administration higherups believed they were violating the spirit, if not the letter, of the Boland amendment when covert operations to aid the Contras were set into motion. A high state of secrecy was maintained in the White House. Congress and the public were misled.

It is the height of arrogance for anyone to assume that the Boland amendment was deliberately vague in not mentioning the chief executive. It is becoming increasingly clear that an unpopular law was intentionally circumvented and probably violated outright by Reagan's merry crew of government shredders and gumshoe cowboys. And once again, even if he wasn't aware of what was going on, the occupant of the Oval Office must take full responsibility. The law, indeed, reaches that far.

## THE LINCOLN STAR
### Lincoln, NE, May 20, 1987

As congressional hearings proceed in the Iran-Contra fiasco, the feeling grows that President Reagan knew more than he would like to admit regarding illegal funding of the Nicaraguan rebels. Did he take a direct part in any scheme for illegal arms aid to the Contra rebels?

Probably not. But swirling around him was a beehive of activity that may have been and very likely was illegal.

Is it logical to believe that the president knew nothing of any such activities? That question needs changing. What should now be asked is whether the president created a climate in which the desired aid for the Contras was obvious.

Further, is the president's lack of knowledge deliberate or happenstance? If the president knew that his aides were fully aware of his intentions and desires and would seek to go that route, then he would have every reason to distance himself from the matter.

In the case of a foreign government's aid to the Contras, Reagan said the donation was not solicited by him, even though he was apprised of it. But the foreign government involved knew full well that its donation would please the president. Reagan had no need to make the request.

By now, a large majority of Americans believe that Reagan "knew about the diversion of Iranian arms profits to Contras in Nicaragua when it was happening," according to the Harris Poll. That does not say the president sanctioned such diversion of funds, only that he was aware of them.

With testimony to date before the Senate and House committee, it is difficult to believe the president was as detached from the Iran-Contra affair as his denial of events would have you believe. He did not have to be aware of things, only sure by one way or another that events would unfold as he so desired.

# ARGUS-LEADER
*Sioux Falls, SD, May 23, 1987*

We spoke too soon.

And we may have been too easy on President Reagan.

After the Tower Commission released its report in February, we criticized Reagan for being dangerously out of touch with his own government.

The Tower Commission investigated the administration's attempts to free U.S. hostages in Lebanon by selling weapons to Iran and the diversion of profits to Contra rebels fighting in Nicaragua.

The portrait that emerged in the Tower report was that of a president who delegated so much responsibility that he did not know what overzealous aides were doing.

A different but equally distressing portrait is emerging now in the Iran-Contra hearings in Washington, D.C. Members of Congress are investigating the arms sale to Iran and unrelated efforts to help the Contras.

Reagan has not been linked to the diversion of arms sale profits to the Contras. But, according to witnesses' testimony, he has been deeply involved in efforts to raise money from private donors.

Thursday, wealthy private contributors testified that they were promised that Reagan would meet with $300,000 donors.

What is so troubling about this new image of Reagan is his apparent contempt of the spirit of U.S. law.

Congress passsed a law called the Boland Amendment, and it was in effect in 1984 and 1985. It said: "No funds available to the CIA, the Department of Defense or any other agency or entity of the U.S. involved in intelligence activities may be obligated or expended for the purpose or which would have the effect of supporting, directly or indirectly, military or paramilitary operations in Nicaragua by any nation, organization, movement or individual."

That seems clear to us. Congress was trying to put the administration's war against Nicaragua's Sandinista government on hold.

Operatives in the administration's Contra network, including retired Maj. Gen. Richard Secord, have excused themselves from the legal restriction by saying they acted as private individuals and therefore were not subject to the law.

Private citizens or not, government resources and officials were used to help raise money.

Five hundred and thirty-five members of Congress cannot conduct the nation's foreign policy. Nor should a network of private citizens and corporations decide and implement policy.

Reagan is in charge. But his policy should not run counter to legally expressed national desires.

We don't know which is worse: a detached president unaware of misdoing or a deeply involved president who ignores the law. Either way, the nation loses.

# The Honolulu Advertiser
*Honolulu, HI, May 16, 1987*

After two weeks of the Iran-Contra hearings, the White House seems to feel President Reagan will not be ruined, a view explained in an adjoining column.

But Reagan is taking his share of nicks and scratches, a process that is likely to continue and maybe increase in weeks ahead with appearances of former White House security aides Lt. Colonel Oliver North and Rear Admiral John Poindexter.

The president didn't look good again this past week. That was so even though his former national security adviser, Robert McFarlane, loyally tried to take responsibility himself for secret White House efforts to dodge the law Congress passed forbidding aid to the Contra rebels in Nicaragua.

Reagan, who still sometimes says he doesn't know what happened, this time resorted to word games and legalisms to dodge damaging revelations.

If one could feel sympathy for McFarlane for his personal ordeal, he was not convincing as the one saying he was responsible for what happened. Rather it seemed he sometimes didn't know what was going on. Even worse, he indicated he didn't speak out at the time against a doubtful policy out of fear of being denounced as a "commie" by Reagan administration hardliners.

# THE ATLANTA CONSTITUTION
*Atlanta, GA, May 30, 1987*

President Reagan, in interviews with foreign journalists, has complained that the news media are damaging his image. They are picturing him, he says, as having tried to get around a past congressional ban on U.S. military aid to the contra rebels fighting the Nicaraguan government.

The president is no doubt right that much of the reporting and commentary on the matter have made his 8-by-10 glossies curl up a bit at the edges. There is, however, a fairly defensible reason why Reagan has been portrayed as he has been.

The picture is simply true. Reagan may or may not have broken the law. (Probably not, though even if he did, no one is keen to hang him for it, just to bawl him out.) But a string of witnesses, and past statements and actions by Reagan himself, have made it plain that the president encouraged a number of artifices meant to keep the contras in the field and fighting.

Reagan is right that he has an image problem in this issue, but he created the image all by himself.

# Rockford Register Star
*Rockford, IL, May 22, 1987*

It is improper for the president of the United States to say that he is exempt from the law of the land.

As a growing number of fingers are pointing to the Oval Office to share the blame for the Iran-Contra debacle, the president continues to look for a defense.

In recent weeks he has claimed in turn that he was a.) exempt from the law; b.) unaware the law was being broken; c.) can't remember what he did.

Reagan's defense now is all of the above. Claiming that he is above the law is the least acceptable of his defenses.

At issue is the Boland Amendment, which prohibited direct or indirect government aid to the Contras during the period that funds from the Iran arms sale were being diverted to the so-called freedom fighters and during the time government officials apparently were carrying out private fund-raising efforts.

All of a sudden, the president's memory is crystal clear as he claims he never did anything to violate the Boland Amendment which, by the way, he says doesn't apply to him anyway, or to the National Security Council or the national security adviser.

How neatly that would tie up the legal loose ends surrounding the Iran-Contra hearings. We hope everything is not that cut-and-dried in this democracy.

House Majority Leader Rep. Thomas Foley, D-Wash., attacked the president's stance. "I reject the notion that the president can, by claiming some constitutional right to conduct foreign policy for himself, absolve the entire National Security staff from the reach of the Boland Amendment," he said.

As Foley pointed out, had the NSC staff truly believed they were exempt from the law, they would not have been sneaking around to launder money and keep their actions secret from Congress.

No, they knew their activities went counter to the letter of the law as well as the will of Congress and the American people as a whole.

It is just possible that those involved in this affair may yet discover a loophole in the amendment that allows them to escape with clean legal records. However, it is clear from the limited details that have been revealed so far that they won't escape with their integrity.

# Abrams Testifies, Claiming No 'Southern Front' Order

Congressional hearings into the Iran-contra arms scandal continued June 2-4, 1987 with testimony from Elliott Abrams, assistant secretary of state for Inter-American affairs. Abrams's testimony focused almost entirely on whether he had intentionally deceived the Senate Intelligence Committee November 25, 1986, just as the scandal broke.

Abrams was asked June 2 about the claim by Lewis Tambs, the former U.S. ambassador to Costa Rica, that he had been ordered to open a "southern front" against Nicaragua. Tambs, in testimony the previous week, had said that the order came from North but had originated with a three-man Restricted Interagency Group (RIG) consisting of Lt. Col. Oliver North, Director of the Central Intelligence Agency's Central American task force Alan Fiers and Abrams, who Tambs said chaired the RIG. Abrams retorted that Tambs "doesn't know what he's talking about." Abrams said that the RIG consisted of 15 to 20 people and "was not a decision-making or policy-making board—it was a coordinating body." Abrams denied any knowledge of the order to Tambs to open a southern front.

Abrams also contradicted testimony given by Maj. Gen. John Singlaub (ret.). Singlaub had told the committees May 20-21 that before traveling to Taiwan and South Korea to ask for contra aid, he had met with Abrams, who agreed to send messages to those countries giving the U.S. government's endorsement of Singlaub's request. Abrams said that he had not met with Singlaub before the general's trip to Asia. Confronted with a memo by Abrams's deputy that backed Singlaub's account of the episode, Abrams said, "The memorandum is in error."

Abrams also gave testimony about his November 1986 appearance before the Senate Intelligence Committee. Abrams admitted that he had left a misleading impression with the committee, but insisted that his statements had been technically correct and that he had not intentionally deceived the senators. At the hearing, Abrams had been asked whether any foreign governments had contributed to the contras. Although Abrams had personally solicited a $10 million contribution from Brunei a few months earlier, he had told the intelligence panel that "we're not, you know, in the fund-raising business."

## Herald News

*Fall River, MA, June 5, 1987*

Assistant Secretary of State Elliott Abrams is the State Department's man in charge of Latin American affairs.

As such, he presumably has been in charge of supervising government activities in behalf of the Contras.

His testimony before the Joint Congressional Committee investigating the Iran-Contras affair makes clear that in earlier statements to Congress he was deliberately misleading.

Abrams insists that he will remain in office and has the support of Secretary Shultz.

Several of the committee members, however, have made no effort to disguise their belief that the administration cannot rebuild the confidence of Congress in its activities if Abrams remains on the job.

It is certainly true that the current impasse over foreign policy between the administration and Congress will have to be resolved if the federal government is going to function normally once again.

The executive branch is responsible for formulating foreign policy and executing it, but Congress has the sole power to appropriate funds.

When it refused to sanction funds for the Contras except for strictly non-military purposes, it precipitated the activities on behalf of the Contras which are now being investigated.

Some of those activities, including the solicitation of funds from foreign governments, were apparently carried on clandestinely on high levels of the State Department. Others were mainly carried on through the National Security Council under the direction of Oliver North.

But either way, the administration was executing a foreign policy that Congress had refused to sanction by appropriating the funds for it.

The real issue is between the President and Congress, and it must be resolved for the good of the country.

But as the committee members pointed out to Abrams, it cannot be resolved if the administration retains persons who, for whatever reason, have forfeited the right to congressional trust.

## The Philadelphia Inquirer

*Philadelphia, PA, June 4, 1987*

On one point, Elliott Abrams, the "point man" for U.S. policy in Central America, got little argument from his Iran-contra panel inquisitors as he limply concluded two days of testimony yesterday. "There is such a thing," he acknowledged, "as being too clever." He was, of course, talking about himself and his slippery answers in the past about who was soliciting what money from whom to support the

contras — and why he had seemed inexplicably in the dark about the private Keystone Kops-style network operating all around him.

But as the hearings have been unfolding, he might as well have been talking about the entire secret Iran-contra enterprise, which in the end was so clever it often worked against itself, wrapped in layers of deception so thick that key operatives and departments lost track of the big picture.

Private benefactors were bypassing the State Department. National Security Council functionaries were in cahoots with parts of the CIA, but hiding activities from Mr. Abrams. Retired generals were dealing with ambassadors who were reporting not through, but around, the normal chain of command.

This, Mr. Abrams concluded, was a recipe not for coherent foreign policy, but "a formula for disaster." The tactics, not to mention Mr. Abrams' own "legalisms and word games ... impeded, if not defeated the policy," House Chairman Lee H. Hamilton (D., Ind.), observed.

Perhaps that's just as well. The policy was not a good one. But if there is to be an effort to reconstruct a new one and to reconstruct, too, a partnership between the White House and Congress, Mr. Abrams' too-cleverness remains an impediment.

He is a point man, today, who ought to be pointed in one direction — the exit.

## The Hartford Courant

*Hartford, CT, June 5, 1987*

The Iran-contra hearings often threaten to put even the most attentive listener to sleep, but occasionally the testimony deals with something so outrageous, preposterous or both that the mind snaps to attention.

Thus it was when Assistant Secretary of State Elliott Abrams described Lt. Col. Oliver L. North's bizarre plan to win American admiration for the Nicaraguan rebels, known as contras, and, with luck, to draw U.S. combat forces into the war.

According to Mr. Abrams, Lt. Col. North suggested at a meeting of U.S. officials that the contras seize a spot on Nicaragua's Atlantic coast and defend it to the last man. The idea, said Mr. Abrams, was "that one of two things would be bound to happen: Either, seeing these freedom fighters killed day by day, we would rescue them, or, seeing them fighting to the last man — kind of an Alamo-style fight — the public perception of their bravery would change."

The scheme was rejected out of hand by Defense Department and Central Intelligence Agency officials, Mr. Abrams said. It would be reassuring if the same could be said of him. Mr. Abrams recalled that his own first reaction was that the contra suicide mission was an "interesting proposal," but that he didn't know whether it could be done.

That speaks volumes about Mr. Abrams' approach to policy-making in Central America.

## Arkansas Gazette

*Little Rock, AR, June 8, 1987*

If the name had not been preempted by an earlier group, "Know-Nothings" could be applied quite appropriately to the assortment of characters who make up the Iran-contra apparatus. Since the original clan rose to prominence in the 1850 decade, the copyright (if any existed) on the name has elapsed and the term may still be useful.

Elliott Abrams, assistant secretary of State for Inter-American Affairs, exemplified the creed at the congressional hearings when he described his relationship with Lt. Col. Oliver L. North. "Most of us were careful not to ask North a lot of questions," he said.

The statement, in context, was an explanation of why he did not wish to know what Colonel North was doing in the area of soliciting funds from assorted sources to support the contras. He understood that it would have been illegal for officials, in any position, to gather money and if someone was doing it, he did not want to know the details. Representative Jack Brooks of Texas brought the matter into sharper focus when he remarked that most people take pride in their knowledge.

"You seem to be very proud of not knowing anything about the technical problems and the very sticky problems with which you are involved," Mr. Brooks said. "I believe you'd be a lot better informed if you'd been reading the daily newspapers and listening to the television and to radio."

Mr. Abrams must have known somewhat more than he admitted about the solicitation of funds. Questioning developed that he had put the arm on the Sultan of Brunei for $10 million — a fact he had managed to camouflage at earlier hearings — but the contras received no benefit. He sent the money to the "wrong" bank account.

Albert Hakim, an Iranian-born American citizen who is a part of the apparatus, apparently has not learned all the rules of Know-Nothingism. He revealed too much about the inside workings of the organization.

Mr. Hakim admitted, for example, that he was in the game for the best of all capitalistic reasons: The money. He claimed that, as a secondary consideration, he "hoped and understood that our efforts would assist the United States government."

The deal with Iran apparently netted out more than $9 million (his partner in the operation had claimed a larger figure) for Mr. Hakim and his associates in the gun-running operation. His cut was $6 million and the remainder went to Gen. Richard V. Secord, Thomas Clines, and some others. Mr. Hakim also had become so fond of Colonel North that he set aside $200,000 in a special account to supplement the income of the Marine officer. He wanted to make it $500,000 but General Secord explained that the lifestyle of a professional military man did not require half-a-mil. Besides, other testimony revealed Colonel North had access to funds from a different source.

In keeping with the high tradition of the Know-Nothings, Colonel North was not even aware of Mr. Hakim's generosity (according to the testimony). Even after arrangements were made for Mrs. North to travel to Philadelphia and work out details for the transfer of the cash, the witness insisted the Colonel had no knowledge of the developing payoff. So long as Colonel North was not aware of the fact that $200,000 had been appropriated for the benefit of him and his family, he could continue to be guided by his patriotism — as were all the others in the apparatus with the exception of Mr. Hakim. The strategy, to the highest level of government, was to know as little as possible.

Secretary of State George Shultz has professed virtually no knowledge of the events leading up to the scandal, despite the fact that his assistant secretary on the beat picked up $10 million from the Sultan of Brunei and had intimate dealings with the participants. Defense Secretary Caspar Weinberger, whose department supplied the arms for the initial sale, did not know what was happening. President Reagan initially adopted the stock answer of the original Know-Nothings: "You tell me what happened."

The knowledge possessed by some of the other key members of the apparatus has not been revealed. They have sought protection behind the Fifth Amendment.

## The Hutchinson News

*Hutchinson, KS, June 6, 1987*

Though the Iran-Contra hearings long ago showed most Americans the virtue of snoozing in front of the tube, a top U.S. official did his best this week to keep up with the afternoon game shows.

Elliott Abrams, senior State Department official for Central American policy, tried to explain the art of lying in government today.

"I was careful not to ask Colonel North questions I did not need to know the answers to," Abrams said.

If you don't see any evil, hear any evil, or speak any evil, you're clean (by Mr. Abrams' rules). Even so, he had to confess to the joint Senate-House investigators that he had, indeed, deceived Congress in earlier inquiries. Some of his statements last fall to Senate and House committees about aid to the Nicaraguan Contras had been "misleading," he testified.

Since Congress itself is one of the more dishonest collections of citizens in the country (it hasn't voted for an honest collection of taxes to pay for its spending in years), there is something of an ironic twist in its complaining about somebody being dishonest with it.

But why must public service be surrounded by lies?

Or even more to the point, why does the nation merely wink at such transgressions as openly admitted lies, misleading testimony, or public officials who know something fishy is going on but are more determined to protect their own fannies than their conscience?

Of course Abrams ought to be kicked out of office for his deceptions (or his minimal curiosity about Col. North's activities). But Congress should get no pity for its being lied to (until, of course, it shows that it has learned to tell the difference between honesty and dishonesty.

LOS ANGELES HERALD

*Los Angeles, CA, June 4, 1987*

In his first day of testimony before the Iranscam hearings this week, Elliott Abrams, the State Department's point-man on Central American policy, proved to be one of the worst friends the contras could have. For an administration so obviously committed to the cause of the Nicaraguan rebels, we can only wonder why they keep him around. Even more alarming is how Secretary of State George Shultz could allow such a subordinate to continue to undermine him.

Abrams twisted the truth repeatedly when he testified in front of three congressional committees last year about the government's efforts to skirt the Boland amendment restrictions on contra aid. Abrams himself insists that his previous statements were technically correct, though admittedly misleading. Such legalistic distinctions may suffice in some courtrooms, but they don't square with a public policy affecting millions of lives and America's reputation.

And now, in front of the Iran contra hearings in Congress, he has contradicted his own deputy's memo and sworn statements of two earlier witnesses, former ambassador to Costa Rica Lewis Tambs and retired Maj. Gen. John K. Singlaub. Both claim to have discussed with him their role in the contra aid operation run out of Lt. Col. Oliver North's hip pocket at the National Security Council, discussions he seems to have forgotten. Abrams just may be telling the truth, but there's good reason not to believe him.

Secretary of State Shultz has praised Abrams for his energy *and* integrity. But can Shultz, who's distanced himself from Ollie North's fantastic covert aid schemes, really afford to have someone like Abrams on his team?

Abrams can no longer be effective, as even administration defenders have told him. His duplicity only confirms the worst suspicions of those who challenge the basis for the whole contra program. That bodes ill for the administration's foreign-policy aspirations far beyond Central America.

Shultz's personal reputation may be unassailable. But the credibility of his State Department is now inextricably bound up with that of Elliott Abrams. That's reason enough for Abrams to get the boot.

The Charlotte Observer

*Charlotte, NC, June 4, 1987*

Elliott Abrams, the assistant secretary of state for inter-American affairs, acknowledges that he misled Congress by claiming that the Reagan administration had not solicited funds from foreign governments for the Nicaraguan contras — even though he himself had solicited $10 million from the sultan of Brunei.

Mr. Abrams acknowledges that Secretary of State George Shultz told him Col. Oliver North was a "loose cannon" and instructed Mr. Abrams to "monitor him." Yet Mr. Abrams says he didn't know what Col. North was up to because he was careful not to ask too many questions about the colonel's activities.

Secretary of State Shultz says Mr.

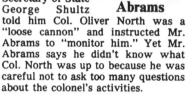

**Abrams**

Abrams should not resign his post because he did not violate any laws and merely made a "mistake."

That's a fine and loyal statement from the secretary of state, but the fact is that Mr. Abrams has raised the practices of skillful deception and willful ignorance to fine arts. Based on his testimony before the congressional panel investigating the Iran-contra affair, Mr. Abrams has about as much claim to being trustworthy as Jim and Tammy Bakker have to being thrifty.

Mr. Abrams has been the Reagan administration's chief spokesman in behalf of funding for the contras and other initiatives in Latin America. His testimony always has been impressive for its certainty and authority. Now Congress knows not to mistake his apparent certainty and authority for truth.

Mr. Abrams's artful dodging of his responsibility has ended usefulness as a policy advocate. He should seek other employment.

## THE SACRAMENTO BEE

*Sacramento, CA, June 5, 1987*

In testifying before Congress about his involvement in the Iran-Contra affair, Assistant Secretary of State Elliot Abrams revealed himself as someone who chose to know little and to tell even less.

Did he ask Oliver North, the White House paymaster for the guerrilla war in Nicaragua, about North's efforts on behalf of the Contras, of which Abrams says he was vaguely aware? No. Did he ask North about bank accounts used for the Contras? No. Did he worry about reports that North was soliciting funds for the Contras? Not after hearing assurances from Robert McFarlane, national security adviser, and North that they were not violating the law. Abrams' rule in such matters was simple: "I was careful not to ask Colonel North questions I did not need to know the answers to."

Abrams now professes to be surprised and sobered by what he says he did not know and did not bother to ask. The act is unconvincing. Like North, Abrams has cared passionately about the Contra war; unlike North, he was clever and cautious, a consummate bureaucrat careful about where he left his fingerprints in a messy business. The results of his behavior were the same: to evade Congress' clear direction, deceive the public and shave the law.

Abrams denies that, saying that he attempted to keep in mind both the letter and the spirit of the law. But such denials fail to square with other testimony given to the committee investigating the administration's rogue foreign policy. Lewis Tambs, former ambassador to Costa Rica, testified he received directives to assist the Contras from a group of which Abrams was a leading member and that Abrams had shown himself to be aware of North's activities. Retired Gen. John Singlaub testified that Abrams approved his efforts to solicit funds for the Contras from South Korea. Abrams says both are lying.

Who to believe? The Elliot Abrams who contradicts Tambs and Singlaub also testified to Congress last fall that no foreign nation had given money to the Contras and that the State Department was "not in the fund-raising business." In fact, Abrams had himself solicited money from the Sultan of Brunei. But Abrams now says his testimony was "literally correct" because the money sent by the sultan had been mistakenly deposited in the wrong bank account. And he says he simply ducked the question about fund-raising because the question had been about solicitations of Middle Eastern nations, and Brunei is in the Far East. Abrams may not wish to call such deceptions lies, but by any other name they stink just as much.

Throughout his testimony, Abrams displayed the same qualities that produced the White House secret foreign policy: arrogance about the rectitude of his course, contempt for Congress and the nation it represents and a willingness to cut words to serve a cause instead of the truth. A democracy cannot abide having in responsible policy positions officials who feign contrition at their misdeeds while they sneer at the processes that make self-rule possible. Abrams may be more suave than North or Adm. John Poindexter, but he shares responsibility with them for the conduct of the White House's illegal policy. That he is still in office dishonors the State Department and destroys credibility of anything it does in Central America.

# MILWAUKEE SENTINEL

*Milwaukee, WI, June 5, 1987*

In testimony before the House-Senate contra hearings this week, Elliot Abrams, assistant secretary of state for Latin American affairs, said he didn't lie last October when he said the Reagan administration "absolutely" was not involved in the ill-fated contra supply mission of Wisconsinite Eugene Hasenfus.

The problem, Abrams said, was that he simply had not received all the information himself. Nonetheless, Abrams was pretty sure of himself when he made the statement which he has now recanted.

And however he wants to characterize his corrections to the record, it appears that Abrams did a little soul-searching and decided to tell the truth in order to save a part of his anatomy.

In addition to the Hasenfus error, Abrams on Tuesday said he misled the Senate Intelligence Committee Nov. 25 when he didn't disclose his solicitation of the sultan of Brunei for a $10 million contribution to the contras because the sultan wanted it to be confidential.

Abrams also said he was not authorized to make such a disclosure at the time.

He made an apology in a follow-up appearance Dec. 8.

Abrams denies leading a three-man group to help the contras, as another witness alleged he did. Former US Ambassador to Costa Rica Lewis Tambs "doesn't know what he's talking about," Abrams said.

Abrams also reported to the committee that he had been assigned to monitor Lt. Col. Oliver North, alleged to have run the Iran-contra operation when he was with the National Security Council, but apparently took North's word that the Marine officer was doing nothing illegal.

Just to be on the safe side, the committee should consider calling Abrams again. On the basis of the record, it usually takes him a little time to get things right.

---

# The Chattanooga Times

*Chattanooga, TN, June 9, 1987*

In this democracy, where responsibility for the conduct of foreign affairs is shared by the president and the Congress, it is essential that representatives of the executive branch speak truthfully when they testify on Capitol Hill. Yet Elliott Abrams, assistant secretary of state for inter-American affairs, repeatedly lied in congressional testimony last year. He thus betrayed the public trust of his office and should be removed.

But far from exhibiting concern about Mr. Abrams' deliberate misleading of Congress, Secretary of State George Shultz continues to characterize Mr. Abrams as a "person of tremendous ... integrity." And through a spokesman last week, the secretary related that he thinks Mr. Abrams is doing "a sensational job." By thus condoning Mr. Abrams' misdeeds, Secretary Shultz becomes a party to them.

Mr. Abrams would argue with the characterization of his congressional testimony last year as lies. He maintained in a two-day appearance last week before the congressional committee investigating the Iran-Contra scandal that he always took pains to be "technically" truthful, even when his intent was to hide the truth from his congressional questioners. He makes a distinction where there is no difference.

Questioned repeatedly by congressional committees last year on whether the United States had solicited funds from foreign countries for the Contra rebels in Nicaragua, Mr. Abrams replied that funds had not been solicited. That was a lie, and he knew it since he himself had solicited a multi-million-dollar contribution from the sultan of Brunei. Mr. Abrams, however, argues that it wasn't a lie because when he denied having solicited funds, the contribution from Brunei had not yet been received. That tortured rationalization would be laughable were the subject of executive branch credibility with Congress not so serious.

Another example of Mr. Abrams' disdain for his responsibility to keep Congress accurately informed occurred during the period of time immediately following the downing of a Contra supply plane in Nicaragua last year and the capture of the American mercenary Eugene Hasenfus. Asked whether there was any U.S. government involvement in the "private" Contra resupply effort, Mr. Abrams offered categorical assurances, time and again, that there was no such involvement. That, of course, was not the truth. Now, Mr. Abrams explains his dissemination of false information by saying, "I was careful not to ask Col. (Oliver) North questions that I did not need to know the answers to."

So Mr. Abrams didn't think he needed answers from Col. North before offering unqualified assurances to Congress and the public that the U.S. government was not involved — even though he knew the then-National Security Council aide was deeply involved with private Contra-aid efforts. It is really quite remarkable that Mr. Abrams, obviously a bright man, expects us to believe his explanation. It seems much more likely that he didn't question Col. North because he didn't want to have confirmed what was generally suspected; he wanted to be able to disseminate false information and later, if necessary, to hide behind a claim of ignorance.

In his testimony last week, Mr. Abrams flatly contradicted the earlier testimony of former ambassador to Costa Rica, Lewis Tambs, who claimed Mr. Abrams was well aware of Mr. Tambs' instructions from Col. North to "open a southern front" for the Contras. He also flatly denied the testimony of former Gen. John Singlaub that Mr. Abrams agreed to make initial contacts with South Korea and Taiwan before the general followed up with solicitation of funds for the Contras. Confronted with a memorandum that made reference to that agreement, he simply said, "The memorandum is in error." There is no reason for Congress to believe Mr. Abrams' testimony on these matters. His history of lying to Congress has destroyed his credibility.

Secretary of State Shultz should re-evaluate his opinion that Mr. Abrams is a man of high integrity, for that is an attribute characterized by truthfulness. And he should remove Mr. Abrams from his position.

## North Refuses to Testify in Private

Lawyers for Lt. Col. Oliver North informed congressional investigators June 17, 1987 that the former National Security Council staffer would refuse to answer questions in private about his role in the Iran-contra arms scandal. North had been scheduled to meet that morning with the lawyers for the House and Senate committees probing the scandal. It was to have been his first testimony since he received a grant of limited immunity June 15. In all previous meetings with investigators, North had refused to testify, using his Fifth Amendment right against self-incrimination. Under the immunity agreement, which compelled North to testify but allowed only evidence obtained before the testimony began to be used against him, North was scheduled to begin public testimony in mid-July. Before that, the lawyers wanted to question him privately, as they usually do to lay the groundwork for a public appearance.

To compel North to testify, the committees would have to find him in contempt of Congress, a possibly lengthy procedure that would ultimately require the intervention of a judge. North's lawyer, Brendan Sullivan, supported his client's refusal to testify with a legal brief arguing that a private deposition would not be covered by the immunity statute. The brief also raised questions about "secrecy, access to documents and double questioning," according to Rep. Lee Hamilton (D, Ind.), who chaired the House panel investigating the scandal. Members of the committees met with North's lawyers June 18 to attempt to work out a compromise on his refusal to testify in private.

North's refusal to testify in private was only the latest in a series of legal gambits by which he had attempted to avoid questioning or prosecution. His other skirmishes had been with special prosecutor Lawrence Walsh, and occurred in closed court proceedings. Lawyers for the *Washington Post* and the *Wall Street Journal* June 12 asked two federal courts to lift the secrecy surrounding North's battle with Walsh. In particular, they protested an alteration of the docket sheets of the U.S. Court of Appeals for the District of Columbia that the newspapers said was intended "to prevent the public's knowing that Mr. North had filed a motion for bail." Papers in the case had been sealed since May 8. Sources cited in the *Post* said that on that day, U.S. District Court Judge Aubrey Robinson had found North in contempt of court for refusing to provide the grand jury convened by Walsh with a sample of his handwriting.

## Herald News

*Fall River, MA, June 26, 1987*

Lt. Colonel Oliver is now scheduled to testify about his role in the Iran-Contras affair on July 7.

The extraordinary negotiations tha have been going on between the joint Congressional Committee investigating the Iran-Contras affair and North's legal representatives came close to exhausting the patience of the committee members.

Either North or his lawyers were remarkably adroit in finding obstacles to put in the committee's way as it tried to interrogate him privately in advance of his scheduled public testimony.

He was equally reluctant to deposit documents with the congressional committee relating to his role in the affair.

In the end the committee was forced to threaten him with a contempt citation in order to get him to turn over the documents.

He will be questioned behind closed doors next week and will turn over the documents the committee sought.

The committee's patience with Colonel North has been exemplary, but there was always the danger it might backfire, since if North's tac-. tics succeeded in letting him stave off the testimony he seems so unwilling to give, then other reluctant witnesses would be likely to imitate him with deplorable results for the probe the committee is trying to conduct.

For this reason the congressional committee had to come out on top in its negotiations with North's lawyers.

The committee is being as uninquisitorial as, given the circumstances, it is possible for it to be.

This is admirable, but all along, it has been obvious that Colonel North is the person who knows most about what went on during the Iranian arms deals and the attempt to divert some of the profits from the deals to the Contras.

Rear Admiral Poindexter may have been privy to what went on, but judging by all that has been said so far in the congressional hearings, it was Colonel North who, more often than not, was the person on the spot.

Hence the negotiations with his lawyers, as well as what certainly seem to be delaying tactics on his part.

Congress has finally prevailed, and the Iran-Contras hearings should now move to their delayed climax.

## MILWAUKEE SENTINEL

*Milwaukee, WI, June 27, 1987*

After a lengthy joust over the terms on which the most controversial figure in the Iran-contra scam would give testimony, a congressional committee investigating the controversy has given Lt. Col. Oliver L. North almost everything he wanted and declared victory.

Indeed, North was negotiating his appearance before the lawmakers as though he were a sought-after actor wanted for the lead role in a television series with sagging ratings.

And why shouldn't he?

North, who had pleaded the Fifth Amendment to avoid testifying, was finally granted limited immunity by Congress because lawmakers felt his testimony was vital to their probe. The ending would have been flat without an appearance by a man who has been implicated by one witness after another.

The bargaining began after North surprised the committee by saying he would not give a private deposition to the panel's lawyers before testifying in open session, thus depriving them of preparing a script of sorts for developing the case in public.

The result is that North has agreed to testify after receiving written assurance that public questioning would be limited to four days and that private questioning would be limited to North's knowledge of President Reagan's role in the Iran-contra affair.

For gosh sakes, the man got everything but TV residuals.

Rep. Jack Brooks (D-Texas) aptly described the arrangement as "disastrous." He also was right when he said that instead of allowing North to tell them when, where and how long he would testify, the committee should have offered North the simple choice of answering its questions or going to jail.

# THE DENVER POST

*Denver, CO, June 25, 1987*

THE COUNTRY has had quite enough of Oliver North's haggling over what, if anything, he will tell and when, if ever, he'll tell it. President Reagan and Congress should give this evasive witness a simple if somewhat incongruous order: Shut up and talk.

The shut-up portion covers the dickering and bickering that North and his lawyer, Brendan Sullivan, have used to evade the questioning of Congress in the Iran-contra scandal.

Attempting to avoid an outright citation for contempt of Congress, North hasn't quite refused to testify. But he has refused to testify in private — which would make it impossible to probe portions of the scandal that touch on national security questions. Lieutenant Colonel North also has demanded that his public testimony be strictly limited and that Congress not be allowed to recall him as a witness if other witnesses later contradict his tales.

In short, North wants a little public relations podium from which he can flash a few medals at the cameras, mumble a few shibboleths about defending freedom and fade away without answering any serious questions.

Congress shouldn't buy it. North is a criminal suspect, not a hero. He should be given the same constitutional protections afforded any other suspect — but no more. And those rights do not include the right to rig the terms of his testimony.

Indeed, North can't legitimately hide behind the Fifth Amendment's safeguard against self-incrimination. He has already been granted limited immunity by independent counsel Lawrence Walsh. That specifies that nothing North tells committees can be used by Walsh against North in a possible future prosecution unless Walsh's office already had obtained the information from an independent source.

Under those terms, if North doesn't stop ducking questions and start answering them, he should be cited for contempt and thrown into the brig.

It's worth noting that North is still a Marine lieutenant colonel on active duty — and thus answerable to his commander-in-chief, President Reagan. Reagan promised full cooperation with the congressional probes.

It's long past time that Reagan backed up that promise with a direct order to his subordinate to stop shilly-shallying around and tell Congress everything he knows about the scandal. If the president refuses to take that step, the public can only conclude that Reagan is conniving in North's cover-up attempt.

## The Honolulu Advertiser

*Honolulu, HI, June 18, 1987*

Lt. Colonel Oliver North may or may not have the legal right to refuse to testify in private before appearing in public before the congressional committees in the Iran-Contra hearings. But his use of that tactic is also a statement in itself.

North is best remembered by TV audiences for his public statement in December before the House Foreign Affairs Committee. In his Marine uniform with a chest full of medals, he told the members:

"I don't think there's another person in America that wants to tell this story as much as I do."

His posture has changed since then, with legal challenges to the special prosecutor, refusal to turn over handwriting samples to the grand jury, and now this latest move.

Perhaps the easiest explanation is that this is an effort to gain the element of surprise before the national TV audience. It avoids the usual situation where committee members and their staffs can first study private testimony for possible false statements or other weaknesses to be explored in later public sessions.

If the intent is to let North make a strong first impression with an emotional appeal, the legal move is understandable. But the public should also understand that cross examination will be weakened or delayed. And that says something about North's desire to inform his fellow Americans.

A more disturbing prospect is that North, with stalling and other tactics, is seeking to avoid testimony. That possibility was raised yesterday by Senator Warren Rudman, the Republican vice chairman of the Senate select committee.

That would be damning for North. But it would be equally unfortunate for the American people because North's testimony seems so central to understanding our biggest Washington scandal since Watergate.

## The Idaho STATESMAN

*Boise, ID, June 20, 1987*

So, Lt. Col. Oliver North, kingpin of the Iran-contra scandal and a national hero to President Reagan, won't testify privately before Congress. String him up. Figuratively, of course.

The ever-smiling lieutenant colonel has been mentioned by nearly every witness who has appeared before the joint Senate-House investigating committee. Hearing what he has to say is crucial to finding out who was behind diverting profits from Iranian arm sales to the Nicaraguan contra rebels.

The public's patience for Lt. Col. North is wearing thin. First he refused to testify before congressional committees earlier this year, citing his constitutional Fifth Amendment right against self-incrimination. Then, two days after he was granted limited immunity from prosecution, Lt. Col. North refused Wednesday to testify privately.

This from a U.S. Marine and former National Security Council official who last year told Congress, "I don't think there is a person in America that wants to to tell this story as much as I do."

Lt. Col. North is playing games. By stonewalling committee members, he is baiting them into citing him for contempt of Congress – which he richly deserves. But if that happens, Lt. Col. North's lawyers could drag the citation through court for months, delaying and possibly precluding his public testimony scheduled for July.

The joint committee had agreed to wait for Lt. Col. North's public testimony so that independent counsel Lawrence Walsh could complete his criminal investigation of Lt. Col. North. If Mr. Walsh found grounds to indict the lieutenant colonel, then he would not be able to testify before Congress, which is trying to wrap up the hearings by Aug. 8.

It's all very cute, the kind of Machiavellian maneuvering one would expect from the orchestrator of Irangate. But it's a hell of a behavior from a man sworn to defend his country.

## Novice Wrote Legal Opinion

Bretton G. Sciaroni, the first witness to be called by Republican members of the joint congressional committees investigating the Iran-contra arms scandal, testified briefly June 8, 1987. Sciaroni was the counsel to the President's Intelligence Oversight Board who had written the legal opinion cited by White House officials, including President Reagan, to support their claim that the Boland amendment banning covert aid to the contras did not apply to the National Security Council. The little known Intelligence Oversight Board was established by President Gerald Ford to investigate allegations of illegal intelligence agency activities. As an investigative body, its paid staff of one (Sciaroni) was not prepared to originate legal opinions. Its investigative powers were also limited to information provided by the Central Intelligence Agency's inspector general.

Rather than legal issues, questions to Sciaroni focused on his qualifications as a lawyer and the thoroughness of his investigation of the Boland amendment. Sciaroni admitted that he had failed the California bar exam twice and the District of Columbia exam twice before passing the bar exam in Pennsylvania, where he had never lived or worked, which allowed him to be "waived in" to practice in Washington. Sciaroni also acknowledged that his 1985 legal opinion, which was his first such project as an attorney, was based on brief talks with North and NSC lawyer Cmdr. Paul Thompson, and on a quick review of documents that Thompson had said were sufficient. Nonetheless, Sciaroni said he would stand by his legal opinion, and called his examination "probably as thorough as the one that had been conducted by [Capitol] Hill."

Sciaroni was criticized for having sent North a draft of the legal opinion, with a note describing it as "the legal basis for covert action" in Central America. Sen. Paul Sarbanes (D, Md.) accused Sciaroni of writing the opinion as a legal "cover" for the NSC to aid the contras, a charge Sciaroni denied.

## The Philadelphia Inquirer

*Philadelphia, PA*
*June 9, 1987*

The duplicity that underlay the Reagan administration's Iran-contra fiasco stared congressional investigators in the face Monday in testimony by Bretton Sciaroni, legal adviser to the White House Intelligence Oversight Board, that was both amazing and pitiful.

Mr. Sciaroni, 35, testified that in the fall of 1985 he was the author of the secret legal opinion that the Boland amendment, cutting off military assistance to the Nicaraguan contras for 1984-86, did not apply to the National Security Council. His opinion was used by the administration as the legal cover for NSC staffer Lt. Col. Oliver L. North to spearhead the covert effort to sell arms to Iran in exchange for release of U.S. hostages held in Lebanon and to funnel millions of dollars raised from private contributors to the the contras.

It was the first legal opinion Mr. Sciaroni had written on a legislative act. He had never practiced law when he was hired as the Oversight Board's counsel in 1984. A condition of his getting the job, he said, was that he would be admitted to the bar.

The White House and some Republican members of the Iran-contra investigating committee have contended that the Boland amendment unconstitutionally infringed on the President's power to conduct foreign policy. And while courts eventually may rule that the amendment contained as large a loophole as the White House perceived, Mr. Sciaroni, by his own testimony, appeared to be a weak legal reed to rely upon. He said he did not consult any other legal authorities in the White House or the Department of Justice before writing his opinion. It was based on two brief interviews and an incomplete search of the files.

The only common sense conclusion that can be drawn from his testimony is that he was a foil used by the White House to circumvent the Boland amendment and that the Oversight Board, which is supposed to inform the President about any intelligence abuses, was hoodwinked.

## The Boston Globe

*Boston, MA, June 11, 1987*

The questioning of Bretton Sciaroni (the hapless lawyer who flunked four bar exams but still qualified as the top White House legal adviser on waging secret wars) revealed the dynamics of the Iran-contra hearings. Administration defenders cling to an agenda of sowing confusion to obscure responsibility. Administration critics often let themselves be drawn into circular semantic debates.

"We are in a morass of ambiguity," said Rep. Henry Hyde (R-Ill.), the chief administration apologist on the investigating committee, after he led Sciaroni through a string of softball questions. What the committee really was in was an exercise in deliberate confusion. Hyde uses the law the way a squid uses ink.

Administration defenders know their best chance is to exploit the inherent subtlety of orchestrating a secret war. Their strategy is to create an impression of overwhelming complexity. When they are pinned down in one untenable position, they change the terms of argument and duck away to another.

The most consistently applied ruse is the complaint about shifts in the wording of the Boland Amendment, as if those shifts from one year to the next show congressional vacillation about the basic issue of attacking Nicaragua. Actually, they signify Congress' attempt to catch up with administration efforts to squirm away from earlier laws.

Critics of the Iran-contra conspiracy must not be drawn into disputes about shifting definitions of the Boland Amendment and the impracticality of congressional "micro-management" of foreign policy. They must simplify and clarify the argument that Contragate was wrong. They must lock, like homing missiles, onto simpler questions: Can a president rightly take a democracy into an unwanted war by funneling money outside congressional systems of accountability?

Henry Hyde and other Contragate apologists must explain whether there is, in their model of total presidential authority in foreign policy, any difference between a democracy and a monarchy. Otherwise, they will continue to escape in swirls of obfuscatory ink.

THE CHICKEN IN THE FOX COOP

INTELLIGENCE OVERSIGHT BOARD

AUTH
THE PHILADELPHIA INQUIRER. 6/10/87
UNIVERSAL PRESS SYNDICATE.

## The Courier-Journal

*Louisville, KY, June 10, 1987*

IF THE White House selected physicians the way it selects lawyers, the Secret Service wouldn't let a doctor within five miles of President Reagan. That much is clear from the curious tale of Bretton Sciaroni, the young lawyer who testified Monday at the congressional Iran-*contra* hearings.

Though he flunked the bar exam twice in California and twice in Washington, D. C., before finally passing in Pennsylvania, Mr. Sciaroni was hired in 1984 as counsel for the President's Intelligence Oversight Board. In that capacity, and after a five-minute chat with Lt. Col. Oliver North, he wrote an opinion advising that congressional restrictions on aid to the *contras* didn't apply to the National Security Council, where Col. North was then a very busy staffer.

HERBLOCK IN THE WASHINGTON POST
**White House tour**

These restrictions, incorporated in several versions of the so-called 'Boland Amendment,'' were clearly aimed at preventing the administration from continuing its surrogate war in Nicaragua. But, as the nation has since learned, Col. North and his team of fund-raisers and free-lance arms merchants merrily ignored the law.

They would have done so, no doubt, even if Mr. Sciaroni hadn't been ready with a convenient rationale. But his opinion — the only one Mr. Sciaroni can recall ever writing in his brief professional career — enabled the administration to pretend that it had analyzed the Boland Amendment and found a legitimate loophole.

Had it been evaluated on its legal merits, this document would have been quickly consigned to a shredder in the White House basement. But Mr. Sciaroni told his bosses what they wanted to hear, and that's what counts in this Congress-be-damned administration.

## Newsday

*Long Island, NY, June 10, 1987*

This puts it all in perfect perspective: The White House lawyer who gave the legal opinion justifying Lt. Col. Oliver North's romps over, around and through the law had flunked four different bar exams and was issuing his very first analysis of legislation.

The lawyer, Bretton Sciaroni, was an apt counterpart to the other players in the Iran-contra affair: a bumbling novice. He failed bar examinations twice in California and twice in the District of Columbia. He finally passed in Pennsylvania, which allowed him to practice in Washington. Asked at Monday's hearing if he had taken "an easy way" to get admitted to the D.C. bar, he said, "Right."

Sciaroni admitted to the congressional committee on Iran-contra that he issued his opinion after only the most cursory review of the facts: a five-minute interview with North — a friend — and a half-hour discussion with the counsel to the National Security Council. In retrospect, he said, information had been withheld from him. Just small details, such as North's fund raising and coordination of military activities for the Nicaraguan rebels.

Sciaroni's opinion appears to be the only White House legal study of the congressional ban on aid to the contras. This wasn't a serious attempt to determine whether's North's activities were legal. It was a cynical maneuver designed to allow the White House to say it had sought the advice of counsel.

You wouldn't hire this guy to do a simple will, yet President Ronald Reagan appointed him as counsel to his Intelligence Oversight Board — just more evidence of this administration's disregard for the laws passed by Congress and of the need for greater oversight of intelligence activities.

# Hall's Testimony Closes Session

Congressional committees investigating the Iran-contra arms scandal ended the first of three phases June 9, 1987 after hearing two days of testimony from Fawn Hall, who had been Lt. Col. Oliver North's secretary at the National Security Council. Hall June 8-9 offered few new details about her role in the scandal, but because she was a blonde part-time model, her appearance drew more media attention than previous witnesses. The National Broadcasting Company (NBC), for example, preempted its regular daytime programming to broadcast Hall's testimony, something it had not done since the very beginning of the hearings. Throughout her testimony, Hall generally sought to describe herself as a loyal and hardworking secretary who was not a policy maker and not in a position to question her instructions.

Hall described altering four memos on November 21, 1986. All the memos, she said, had been addressed to former NSC chief Robert McFarlane from North, and had been written in 1985. One of the memos proposed that the Nicaraguan contras try to destroy a ship carrying weapons from Asia to the Nicaraguan government. North had Hall change the proposal to an innocuous recommendation that information about the ship be declassified. The other altered memos referred to Guatemalan, Saudi Arabian and private efforts to aid the contras. That evening North, Hall and North's deputy, Robert Earl, had shredded a large number of documents—enough so that the only documents Hall specifically remembered shredding were North's telephone logs. Hall revealed that after the scandal broke, she found in her desk copies of documents she deemed sensitive, including originals of the altered memos. She said she called North and then smuggled the documents out of the building in her boots and stuffed down her back. After removing the documents, Hall said she gave them to North in the car of Thomas Green, a lawyer, who at the time was representing North. She said Green asked her what she would say if she was asked about the shredding of the documents. Hall said she told Green that she would say, "We shred every day," and Green replied, "That's great."

Hall June 9 defended her actions in altering, shredding, and smuggling certain documents. "Sometimes you have to go above the written law," she said.

## The Atlanta Journal
### AND
### THE ATLANTA CONSTITUTION
#### Atlanta, GA, June 13, 1987

As in a well-constructed mystery tale, the first segment of Congress' inquiry into the Reagan administration's under-the-table dealings with Iran and the Nicaraguan contras ended on a dramatic note. Just before fade-out, investigators produced a smoking gun, with fingerprints no less.

Granted, Fawn Hall's testimony is privileged by grant of partial immunity. Still, her recounting of a "shredding party" in which she and Lt. Col. Oliver North destroyed a foot-and-a-half-tall stack of incriminating documents last November says plainly that laws were broken.

And not, as Hall put it, for the purpose of protecting vital secrets and the lives of U.S. hostages, either. By the time she and North were force-feeding the shredder, the intelligence services of Iran, the Soviet Union and Nicaragua all had a pretty fair idea of the cockeyed machinations this administration had set in motion. The only important players who were in the dark were the Congress and the American people.

No wonder North tried to shield his dual operations from public view. Revelations of the combined House and Senate panels recall feelings of turning over damp rocks and observing the wrigglings thus exposed.

We already knew President Reagan, who had vowed not to negotiate with terrorists, had authorized the secret payment of ransom to the kidnappers of American hostages. We also knew that after imploring our allies not to sell weapons to the implacably hostile mullahs of Iran, he had given the OK to do precisely that. We knew, too, that profits from this misbegotten enterprise had been funneled, somehow, to the contras, in apparent contravention of a congressional ban that bore the signature of the president.

What the investigators were not prepared for was the extent to which Reagan had turned his foreign-policy prerogatives over to third-level subordinates and rent-a-spooks. Congressmen of both parties are appalled, rightly so, that North could take upon himself the authority to make wild promises to the Iranians or that unscreened free-lancers would get access to supersecret U.S. codes, equipment and bank accounts.

Further, the panels confirmed that Congress had been deliberately misled when it tried to get answers about its suspicions of administration misadventures. Understandably, the lawmakers' level of trust for, say, Elliott Abrams hovers around zero.

And throughout the inquiry, one could hear strains of arrogance and venality, odd tunes indeed for this chorus of superpatriots.

When the questioning resumes, the tracking of this conspiracy will draw ever closer to the top. Congress and the public may yet be able to determine if President Reagan was or wasn't in charge when all this skulduggery was undertaken in his name. Either alternative is a bleak one.

## The Des Moines Register
#### Des Moines, IA, June 16, 1987

Fawn Hall is a good-looking young woman. Elliott Abrams is a good-looking man. But this latter circumstance has been called to the public's attention far less than the former; in fact, has it even been mentioned? Are good looks presumed to be Hall's only accomplishment?

She was advised by her attorney to dress in a certain way that he thought would make the most appropriate impression on the congressional questioners and their legal staff at the Iran-contra hearings last week. We're fairly sure that nobody told Abrams what to wear, or that it would have made much difference anyhow.

The given name, Fawn, kept apppearing in news stories. The name Elliott, after the first reference, disappeared. It was as though reporters wanted to keep reminding their readers that this "Hall" is a woman and please bear that in mind — and enjoy thinking about it — while you read her account of helping Oliver North break the law.

Yet, apart from the difference in their rank — Abrams is an assistant secretary of state; Hall is the kind of secretary who does typing — and the fact that one was giving orders and the other following them, why draw distinctions? Both were deeply involved in the contra-arms scam. Both are dedicated to the contras' cause. And both are pretty tough cookies.

Abrams sneered and insulted Congress. Hall sharply corrected a questioner who mentioned "cover-up"; no, she said, it was "protecting" an operation so patriotic and worthy as to justify breaking an unjustifed law.

The questioners, however, handled Hall more delicately than they handled Abrams. It was as if they feared causing her to burst out in tears before millions, making them appear ungentlemanly. Nonsense.

If a Marine corporal named Fred Hall had held Fawn Hall's job and done and said the same things she did, it would have been a far different spectacle in the hearing room, in the newspapers and magazines and on the flickering screen.

You've come a long way, baby, but unfortunately you still have a distance to go.

# DAYTON DAILY NEWS
*Dayton, OH, June 11, 1987*

Fawn Hall's loyalty to Lt. Col. Oliver North, was intense. Col. North's loyalty to the inspiration of his president was more so. Although she withdrew the statement immediately and then again later, Ms. Hall may have been speaking her heart — and her boss' — when she told Congress, "Sometimes you have to go above the written law."

Oh, how seductive and confusing the world of covert action is, especially when a high-level cabal becomes a government unto itself — setting national policy outside the law, conducting illegal operations, treating Congress as the enemy. But when contempt shines from on high, what else are subordinates expected to guide themselves by?

Ms. Hall — who as a secretary helped shred, forge and smuggle out documents in order to obstruct justice — no doubt regards herself as a victim now. She is, but not a victim of the outsiders she and her colleagues see as the threat. It was an inside job, where loyalty to a president can sometimes be confused with loyalty to the nation's principles and laws.

# THE ASHEVILLE CITIZEN
*Asheville, NC, June 12, 1987*

"Sometimes you have to go above the written law."

There it is in a nutshell — the mentality that characterizes the whole Iran-Contra affair.

The comment came from Fawn Hall — who was Lt. Col. Oliver North's secretary at the National Security Council — during her testimony before the joint House and Senate committees investigating the scandal that brought North's ouster and has shaken the nation's faith in the Reagan administration.

Hall made the comment while trying to justify her role in altering, shredding and removing sensitive documents in North's White House office after the Iran-Contra affair came to light.

Where do you suppose she came by her opinions about skirting the law? Was she a power behind the formulation of national security and foreign policies? No, she was merely parroting the line fed to her by her boss, Oliver North.

Hall later tried to retract the statement, but it was too late. The truth was out.

It is indeed unfortunate that government officials like North — and others — believe they are justified in winking at the law to accomplish what they see as a worthy goal.

We see in the Iran-Contra affair where such thinking can lead. One after another, various government officials have admitted during the hearings that they had covered up the truth and made efforts to mislead Congress about their activities in the covert sale of arms to Iran, the diversion of some of the arms-sale money to the Contra rebels in Nicaragua and the establishment of a secret supply network to aid the Contras.

As Rep. Lee Hamilton, D-Ind., chairman of the House committee, said, it is "a depressing story. It is a story of not telling the truth to the Congress and the American people."

There are, of course, certain government operations that must be conducted in secret in the interest of national security. The reference here is to covert operations that are within the law.

The use of government funds to support the Contras was in direct opposition to a congressional ban on such activities and, therefore, outside the law.

The United States is a nation of laws, not of men. It's a shame that some government officials can't accept that principle.

# Arkansas Gazette
*Little Rock, AR, June 12, 1987*

For a couple of centuries, one of the proudest boasts of patriots has been that the strength of the United States lay in the very concept of the Republic. The country grew and prospered because the functions of the political structure were clearly spelled out in a Constitution that provided for " a government of law and not of people."

It remained for Fawn Hall, the secretary who worked for Lt. Col. Oliver L. North, to reinterpret the concept. Appearing as the 18th witness in the six-weeks-old hearing into the Iran-contra scandal, Miss Hall proclaimed a startling interpretation of the high principles that obviously guided the privatized apparatus responsible for the Reagan administration's foreign policy.

"Sometimes," she said, "you have to go above the written law."

Several previous witnesses had confirmed the policy when they described the devious strategies designed to circumvent the law that President Reagan had signed. The so-called Boland Amendment was designed to prevent the United States from supplying arms to the contras in Nicaragua, either directly or indirectly, but a "shadow" foreign policy — operated by a strange mixture of people in and out of government — worked full time to collect funds and ferry supplies to the rag-tag rebels Mr. Reagan chose to call "Freedom Fighters." Rationalization for the action apparently rested on an informal "opinion" provided by Bretton G. Sciaroni, a novice lawyer who acknowledged having failed four bar examinations before he finally passed (in Pennsylvania) and was appointed counsel for the President's Intelligence Oversight Board.

Mr. Sciaroni graduated from the law school at the University of California at Los Angeles then failed twice to pass the bar examination in California and twice more at Washington. He took the Pennsylvania examination in July 1984 and went to work for the Board the next day, before he learned whether he had finally qualified as a lawyer.

After a five-minute interview with Colonel North, at which he received assurance that the National Security Council was planning nothing illegal, Mr. Sciaroni provided the "opinion" that the Iran-contra initiative violated no law. The study appears to be the only legal basis for the White House conclusion that the Boland Amendment did not really mean what it said. Even though the Sciaroni document may never rank among this country's landmark legal decisions, it formed the basis for Mr. Reagan's assertion last month that the National Security Council was not bound by the law.

In the context of related events, the work confirmed that Miss Hall was merely stating established policy when she asserted that "Sometimes you have to go above the written law." Obviously, if the policy calls for ignoring all legal constraints, there is no need to inquire too diligently into what the law really says.

The practice of allowing private citizens and lower-tier public officials to make and execute foreign policy can be downright dangerous. Colonel North, according to some witnesses, promised Iran the United States would "go to war" with the Soviet Union if the arms sales somehow created a crisis. He proposed a plan to sink an Asian ship that was headed for Nicaragua but, when the FBI closed in, he directed Miss Hall to alter the document. When federal officials were preparing to "secure" Colonel North's office, Miss Hall altered and shredded documents and carried secret papers past the guards in her clothing, then admitted, as a witness, that she knew the guards at the door did not represent the KGB.

The whole performance inspired Representative Lee A. Hamilton of Indiana to describe the hearings as the "most extraordinary testimony ever given to the United States Congress."

Mr. Hamilton seemed primarily disturbed by the absence of accountability, a little matter the Founding Fathers must have thought they covered in the Constitution.

"Accountability and responsibility have been absent," he said. "My concern is not simply the accountability of funds, but accountability for policy. Who supervised Colonel North? Who was responsible for funds earned from the sale of U.S. arms? Who asked whether the actions were lawful?"

The answer is that no one asked and no one was supposed to ask. When a privatized foreign policy "rises above the law" and seeks the pre-determined ends spelled out by the leader, without regard to the legality of the means, a nation ends up in a confusing and dangerous situation.

Moreover, the administration that leads a nation into the morass finds itself saddled with what may be the most serious scandal of the century that produced Teapot Dome and the Watergate.

# MILWAUKEE SENTINEL

*Milwaukee, WI, June 10, 1987*

The granting of immunity from prosecution to Fawn Hall for her testimony at the Iran-contra hearings was not a routine concession.

Without immunity, the former secretary on the National Security Council staff could have been knee-deep in trouble when she told a congressional investigating committee that she smuggled documents past security personnel at the White House by placing them in her boots and under her clothing.

Other questionable activities that Hall admitted to included participation with Lt. Col. Oliver L. North, her old boss at the NSC, in a hectic session of shredding and altering documents related to the Iran-contra affair after the inquiry on that controversy had begun.

Throughout her testimony, Hall tried to portray herself as the epitome of a loyal secretary carrying out the orders of a superior whom she admired and trusted. But, in fact, she was an accomplice in heretofore alleged activities of North that are, to say the least, subject to question.

For example, when she noticed a week later that some of the originals of altered documents had been overlooked, she called North and insisted he come back to the office even though he had been fired that same morning. And North and his attorney were with Hall when she cleared security, literally stuffed with evidence.

As Sen. William Cohen (D-Maine) put it: "It's clear she engaged in an obstruction of evidence, and I don't think it was unwitting."

Indeed, although Hall's idea of secretarial ethics may be suspect, she certainly had her wits about her when she accepted the immunity offer.

# THE TENNESSEAN

*Nashville, TN, June 11, 1987*

TO a packed chamber and live television, Ms. Fawn Hall, the former secretary to former NSC aid Lt. Col. Oliver North, told the Iran-contra hearings of a shredding party in which they destroyed hundreds of pages from his safe, so many that the shredder broke down.

There were also documents that were altered, somewhat clumsily. Of the shredding, she said she felt a bit of "uneasiness when he asked me to do it." But she said, "I believed in Colonel North and felt (he) must have a good reason. I did as I was told."

Ms. Hall was a loyal secretary and felt that her boss was any secretary's dream superior and that her job was most fulfilling although the hours were long and arduous.

So, it was on a Tuesday afternoon that she discovered she had forgotten to destroy some incriminating documents. What's a good secretary to do? She called Colonel North and insisted he come back to the White House. So he did.

Ms. Hall said, "I placed copies of the altered documents inside my boots." Then she ran to another official's office and stuffed some computer memos down her back.

"Do you see anything in my back?" she asked Mr. North. 'No," he answered.

Later when they were safely out of the Old Executive Office Building and into the car of Mr. Thomas Green, Colonel North's lawyer, she handed the documents over to Mr. North. It was a busy and emotional afternoon.

The shredding of official documents is certainly of iffy legality. But the surreptitious removal of official documents from the executive office building is clearly illegal. But then Ms. Hall doesn't have to worry too much. She testified under a grant of immunity. She couldn't shed light on how much the Oval Office might have known. But she certainly enlivened the hearings. ■

# Herald News

*Fall River, MA, June 11, 1987*

The first extended series of hearings by the Joint Congressional Committee investigating the Iran-Contras affair came to a theatrically effective climax with the testimony of Lt. Col. Oliver North's secretary, Fawn Hall.

Miss Hall testified under a grent of immunity and described shredding documents and memos under the direction of Col. North.

She resisted all efforts by the committee to join in criticism of North, however, and insisted that he was motivated exclusively by patriotism.

After hearing Miss Hall, the committee recessed. It has heard in bits and pieces a remarkable tale of the activities pursued by persons in and out of the government both in relation to the Iranian arms deals and the attempt to finance the Contras.

At the end of these sessions, however, neither Col. North nor his superior in the National Security Council, Rear Admiral Poindexter, has testified. They have both now been given immunity from prosecution and will appear before the joint committee in July.

Although there are still major gaps in the story of what went on before Congress and the public became aware of the Iranian arms deals and the unofficial efforts to finance the Contras, enough is already known to make clear that the refusal of Congress to appropriate funds for the fight against the Sandanistas led the administration to find unofficial ways of finding the money the Contras needed.

The direct participation of the President in the attempt to fund the Contras has not been demonstrated, although he was certainly aware in a general way of what was going on.

He did know and approve of the arms deals with the Iranians, but this has been open knowledge for some time. He has insisted that he did not know of the plan to divert some of the profits from those deals to the Contras, and nothing said so far contradicts his claim.

So, in spite of all that has been learned, and all that has been said and written about the affair, there is still more to be found out.

Meanwhile the special prosecutor appointed by the Department of Justice is still accumulating evidence of wrongdoing, and much of this evidence has still to be revealed.

So the joint committee's recess is merely a respite for its members and for the public. It is not a conclusion, if in fact a conclusion to this affair is ever to be reached.

Rather, the final ramifications of the Iran-Contras episode will only be known when it comes time to assess whether the damage to the relations between the administration and Congress are irreparable.

# EVOLUTION of the WASHINGTON SECRETARY

## ELIZABETH RAY
- Can't type

## FAWN HALL
- Knows steno
- Takes dictation
- Wordprocessor skills
- Shreds 60,000 words a minute

MARGULIES
©1987 HOUSTON POST

## THE RICHMOND NEWS LEADER

*Richmond, VA, June 11, 1987*

It took Oliver North's secretary, Fawn Hall, to put the first phase of the Iran/Contra hearings into proper perspective.

An exchange with Democratic Senator Sam Nunn of Georgia began when he asked if Miss Hall had any remorse for her deeds, particularly the shredding of papers.

Said she:

"Sir, I wished a lot of things could have been done differently. I wish that Congress had voted the money for the Contras, so this wouldn't have had to happen."

Said Nunn:

"In other words, you wouldn't have had to shred the documents if Congress had gone on and done its job, and voted aid?"

Perhaps sensing a trap, Miss Hall stumbled. Finally she said, "I have no comment."

Consider:

Had Congress been responsibly generous in its dealings with the anti-Communist Nicaraguan resistance — had Congress even been *consistent* in its dealings with the resistance — there would have been no need for the effort to supply it through a devious backstairs channel. Political damage would have been limited to the Iran overture.

Miss Hall was exact.

## THE SPOKESMAN-REVIEW

*Spokane, WA, June 10, 1987*

When does loyalty cease to be a virtue?

Never, Fawn Hall would say.

She still harbors a fierce loyalty to Lt. Col. Oliver North, describing him for her congressional interrogators this week as "every secretary's dream of a boss."

Too many bosses would describe Hall as a dream secretary.

But many secretaries, after watching this loyal but pathetic figure cross the stage of history this week, must be wondering what they would do if loyalty to the boss ever comes in conflict with loyalty to one's own conscience.

Thoughtful bosses must be wondering what they do to their subordinates — and themselves — if they ask them to deceive and cover up wrongdoing.

Hall would have us believe she acted out of sheer loyalty and obedience when she altered, shredded and smuggled government documents.

She also acted out of loyalty when she testified before Congress this week. She did as she was told; she answered the questions and told the truth. In the process, she implicated herself and her former boss in the obstruction of justice.

Thus can unquestioning loyalty come back to haunt those who seek to manipulate it.

However, Hall went beyond doing as she was told in her final days as secretary to the National Security Council aide who conducted renegade foreign-policy adventures out of the White House basement.

As the Justice Department, the FBI and the media closed in on the tangled web now referred to as "the Iran-Contra affair," Hall followed North's orders, retyping documents to delete information North deemed damaging to himself and others. In the final hours, she and North shredded the incriminating original documents.

But then, beneath the noses of Justice Department officials who were securing evidence in the National Security Council office, Hall discovered a six-inch stack of incriminating documents she had missed in the effort to rewrite history; she took it upon herself to stuff the documents into her boots and beneath her blouse and then marched out of the White House.

Those were the actions of a person protecting herself as well as her boss.

Nevertheless, Hall's self-described motives fit her origins as the bright daughter of a National Security Council secretary; she had set out to follow in her mother's footsteps from the day she launched her secretarial career in the Pentagon at age 16. Like many executive secretaries, she still enjoys a warm, loyal relationship with the boss's wife and children; North's kids recently sent her some cookies.

And Hall takes a professional pride in saying, "It was a policy of mine not to ask questions and just to follow instructions. I believed in Col. North and what he was doing. I had no right to question him."

With those words, Fawn Hall carved herself a place in history as the secretary who followed orders, even when that meant obstructing justice. Loyalty may be a strength, but it also can be misplaced, and when it is blind, it can place personal integrity at risk. No job is worth that.

# Justice Department Opposes Prosecutor Law

The United States Justice Department June 16, 1987 challenged the constitutionality of the Ethics in Government Act, under which special prosecutors were appointed to probe wrongdoing by government officials. The department recommended that President Reagan veto any extension of the act which expired in January 1988. Both Lt. Col. Oliver North, under investigation by a special prosecutor for his role in the Iran-contra arms scandal, and former White House aide Michael Deaver, under indictment for influence peddling, had challenged the law on constitutional grounds. Several other Reagan administration officials were currently under investigation by special prosecutors, including Attorney General Edwin Meese 3rd, whose role in the Wedtech Corp. scandal was currently under scrutiny.

In a letter to Congress released June 16, the department said that the 1978 law violated the Constitution because it put the special prosecutor under the control of the judicial branch, rather than the executive. The law had been passed in the wake of the Watergate scandal and was intended to prevent such abuses as President Richard Nixon's 1973 firing of prosecutor Archibald Cox.

In a public statement defending the department's position, John Bolton, assistant attorney general for legislative affairs, stressed the cost of special prosecutors over the constitutional issues. Bolton complained that Lawrence Walsh's probe of the Iran-contra arms scandal had spent $1.3 as of the end of May. Bolton lashed out specifically at Walsh's spending, alleging that Walsh had offices in a building that "charged within a dollar of the highest federal rent for any space in Washington." A member of Walsh's staff said that the office space, like most federal offices, had been chosen for them by the General Services Administration. Rep. Barney Frank (D, Mass.) said that Bolton's "attack on Walsh for spending too much money is an attack for too much investigating."

# The Honolulu Advertiser

Honolulu, HI, July 8, 1987

It's no surprise the Justice Department opposes congressional plans to extend the law under which independent counsels, or special prosecutors, are chosen to investigate top government officials.

Six special prosecutors are now investigating members of the Reagan administration, one of the more scandal-ridden in memory. They include the chief of the Justice Department, Attorney General Edwin Meese; two former White House advisors, Reagan-confidante Michael Deaver and politico Lyn Nofziger; and two ex-national security officials in the Iran-Contra case, Admiral John Poindexter and Lt. Colonel Oliver North.

The Justice Department says its objections are constitutional, that federal prosecutors should be part of the executive branch, accountable to the president. Under the 1978 law, a three-judge federal court appoints and supervises special prosecutors. Deaver and North are challenging the law's constitutionality, so the Supreme Court may eventually rule.

The department is on slightly firmer ground in criticizing the cost of special prosecutors, which might be better controlled. But top-notch legal work in complex cases is expensive. Nothing less will do.

The present law grew out of the nation's Watergate experience. When the inquiry into his administration's actions got too hot, former President Nixon was able to fire a special prosecutor, though the then-attorney general and his deputy resigned in protest.

The special-prosecutor law is an imperfect antidote to that "Saturday night massacre," but something like it is needed. The American people won't believe the results of in-house investigations of politically powerful top members of an administration. The law is a way to handle apparent conflicts of interest and help to keep government honest.

# The Dallas Morning News

Dallas, TX, June 19, 1987

President Reagan would be making a grave mistake if he followed the advice of some aides and vetoed legislation reauthorizing the appointment of independent counsels. The present law, one of the major responses to the Watergate scandal, has attempted to ensure that investigations of possible misconduct by high-level government officials are free of undue political interference.

Although the advisers' opposition to the independent counsel process is nothing new, their current attack on the law is more direct than previous criticisms. By their thinking, public pressure alone would be sufficient to guarantee that the president or other top administration officials would not interfere with the investigation of any alleged official wrongdoing.

They may be right. But they just as likely are wrong. And Congress wisely decided in the aftermath of Watergate not to leave such a matter to chance. By providing for the court appointment of independent counsels, the law guards against a real or perceived lack of investigative zeal in cases involving the associates, friends or superiors of Justice Department officials.

The president's aides also object to the huge amount of money that the independent counsels have spent over the years. But if there are problems with the way that the system works, they can be corrected. They should not be used as arguments for dismantling a mechanism that legal scholars generally believe has served the nation well the past nine years.

If the president's advisers are not careful, their attack on the independent counsel law is likely to be viewed as merely a self-serving attempt to discredit the current inquiries into the Iran-contra scandal and other possible wrongdoing by past and present administration officials.

## The Philadelphia Inquirer

*Philadelphia, PA, June 19, 1987*

It is easy — too easy — to be cynical about the Justice Department's denunciation of the law empowering special prosecutors as unconstitutional.

After all, prosecutors operating under that law are making life miserable for the Reagan administration. Six investigations by special prosecutors are probing alleged criminal wrongdoing by current or former senior administration officials — among them, Attorney General Edwin Meese 3d for the second time.

So it's easy to assume cynically that the Meese Justice Department wants to scuttle the law now because the nation's top law-enforcement officer's colleagues are more interested in taking the heat off of senior officials than in holding them accountable. Under circumstances prevailing today in Washington, such conclusions are difficult to resist.

Nevertheless, such presumptions may be unfair. Justice Department lawyers may believe themselves duty-bound to advise President Reagan to veto the special-prosecutor law if Congress renews it rather than letting it expire Dec. 31. They challenge the law because it puts the prosecutors under the authority of a special court. They say the Constitution's separation of powers requires all federal prosecutors to answer to the executive branch of government. They indeed may believe it. Justice lawyers voiced such reservations in 1983 — before Mr. Meese became attorney general, before he was investigated — though President Reagan signed a bill renewing it four more years anyhow.

Yet even if Justice's lawyers are acting in good faith, their position is unpersuasive. They complain that special prosecutors are spending too much money, and cite Lawrence E. Walsh. So far he has spent $1.3 million investigating the criminal implications of the Iran-contra fiasco. That is nothing less than alleged subversion of constitutional government. What price should be put on exacting justice for that?

Justice lawyers complain that special prosecutors answer to no authority, an equally specious objection. A special court appoints them only after the attorney general asks; he asks only when allegations of criminal conduct are leveled at administration officials so influential that public faith in the integrity of the investigation requires special sanitizing to rid any possible political taint. Ultimately special prosecutors answer to the rule of law, like all other prosecutors — they are just one step removed from Justice Department direction.

History dictates the necessity of that one step. Is that unconstitutional? Congress, in the wake of Watergate, didn't think so. The only two federal courts that have ruled so far on the question didn't think so. The American Bar Association doesn't think so.

Anyone who thinks so should consider this: Seven senior officials of the Reagan administration have been indicted. That has shaken public faith in the integrity of government, so essential if democracy is to work, and by this stand the Justice Department shakes it more. Shoring up that shaken faith is the justification for special prosecutors, and it is compelling. If the Reagan administration's experience does not prove the need for them, nothing can.

## The Miami Herald

*Miami, FL, June 23, 1987*

UNDER THE circumstances, the Justice Department's grousing about the expenses of special prosecutors appointed under the 1978 Ethics in Government Act is specious. Citing costs and alleging that it violates the Executive Branch's Constitutional power to prosecute, Justice recommends that the President veto a renewal of the special-prosecutor law. It expires in January.

That law resulted from Watergate, in which the Executive tried to thwart investigations into its illegal activities. Nixon Administration Attorney General John Mitchell went to prison for obstructing justice.

Independent counsels currently are investigating former Reagan Administration figures involved in Iranscam, *and* Attorney General Edwin Meese's alleged connection with illegal bidding for Government contracts in the Wedtech affair, *and* charges of influence-peddling against former White House aides Michael Deaver and Lynn Nofziger.

The Justice Department hasn't always held this law in disregard. Mr. Meese twice has requested independent investigations of allegations against him. He said that appointment of a special prosecutor was "essential" when questions of financial improprieties arose after his nomination. He was cleared of wrong-doing. When he was linked to the Wedtech scandal this year, Mr. Meese again sought a special prosecutor. He recused himself from the decision on the independent-counsel law.

The Constitutionality of the current provision is in question. The Supreme Court likely will rule on that issue in challenges put forth by Mr. Deaver and by Lt. Col. Oliver North, whom Iranscam special prosecutor Lawrence E. Walsh is investigating.

When the Attorney General of the United States must dissociate himself from a pivotal decision on a law because he personally is being investigated under its provisions, the circumstances ironically emphasize the law's usefulness.

## St. Petersburg Times

*St. Petersburg, FL, July 26, 1987*

Lawrence E. Walsh, the special prosecutor in the Iran-Contra scandal, has taken pains to insulate his work from the televised congressional hearings. He ordered his staff not to watch, listen to or read about the testimony of the witnesses. He sealed, dated and filed with the court the results of his investigations into the activities of any immunized witness before the witness testified on the Hill.

Nevertheless, one of the ugliest sideshows of the scandal has been an attempt to bring political pressure on Walsh to affect the way he carries out his duties. It is a blatant effort to distort even-handed law enforcement that deserves to be condemned by the bar and the public.

The most extreme attack against Walsh came last weekend from Patrick J. Buchanan, the former speech writer for Richard Nixon and communications director for President Reagan. Buchanan called on Mr. Reagan to say publicly that "any indictment of Col. North and Adm. Poindexter would be an offense against justice . . ."

Sen. Orrin G. Hatch, the leading apologist for the White House on the special committee, eagerly joined the chorus. He had warned previously that he thought no jury would convict North. This week he said he would support a presidential pardon for North and Poindexter even before any charges were filed. That, of course, would be the ultimate political intrusion into the judicial process: Stopping any investigation before the prosecutor determined whether the law had been violated.

That is not a worthy position for Hatch or any person who believes in the Constitution and the rule of law.

Even before the hearings end, it appears that several laws may have been violated. The first shipment of arms to Iran in 1985 without a presidential finding appears to have violated arms export laws. There may have been a conspiracy to violate the law forbidding direct or indirect aid to the Contras. There may have been a criminal coverup of the scandal, including obstruction of justice by destroying evidence. Perhaps the special prosecutor has evidence of crimes not described in the congressional hearings.

In any case, the prosecutor should make his decision based on the evidence and the law, as we are confident he will. Those who attempt to pressure him probably hurt only themselves in the esteem of a nation with a keen sense of justice.

# The Houston Post

*Houston, TX, June 19, 1987*

President Reagan is getting bad advice from his Justice Department. It wants him to veto an extension of the law under which special prosecutors currently are probing possible wrongdoing by several present and former administration officials. These include Lt. Col. Oliver North and others involved in the Iran-Contra affair.

The law, part of the Ethics in Government Act passed in 1978 to remedy abuses uncovered in the Watergate scandal, will expire at year's end if Congress doesn't renew it. The Justice Department argues that both the present law and bills to extend it are unconstitutional because prosecutors are named by a court instead of by the president. That, Justice contends, impinges on presidential power. Furthermore, the president cannot easily remove a prosecutor or independent counsel.

Though President Reagan agrees with the department's position, the White House says he hasn't yet made a decision on the veto advice. Before he does, he should reflect on the number of times his own administration has invoked the law to ensure an independent, impartial investigation of allegations against top officials — including Attorney General Edwin Meese.

Meese was exonerated in one such probe into alleged financial irregularities, and currently is the object of another concerning his role in a military contracting scandal. In both cases, he requested prosecutors. Two former White House aides, Michael Deaver and Lyn Nofziger, are under separate probes for their lobbying activities after leaving government.

The independent counsel law was intended to prevent executive branch officials from using their positions to avoid investigation or prosecution for wrongdoing, and to allay suspicion that they had. It has worked well. Any question about the constitutionality of whatever new version Congress may pass should be settled in the courts.

# The Chattanooga Times

*Chattanooga, TN, June 23, 1987*

If the Reagan Justice Department were investigating the Iran-Contra scandal that has engulfed this administration, there would be no public confidence in the integrity of the probe. Obviously, the best interests of the public and the administration alike were served by appointment of special prosecutor Lawrence Walsh to conduct an independent investigation. Yet the Reagan administration has escalated its attacks on the law which allowed Mr. Walsh's appointment.

Congress is dealing now with legislation to extend provisions of the Ethics in Government Act which provide for court-appointed independent counsels, like Mr. Walsh, to investigate charges of administration wrongdoing. The Justice Department has urged President Reagan to veto the expected extension, but backers of the legislation claim strong enough bipartisan support to override a veto. That's good news.

The special prosecutor law was passed in the wake of the Watergate scandals to ensure the integrity of investigations into possible misdeeds by officials high in the executive branch. It does that by having special prosecutors appointed by a special panel of judges, thus removing them from control of the administration under investigation. The law alleviates the obvious conflicts of interest in any administration's investigating itself and ensures independent investigations of alleged wrongdoing. That advances the public interest in uncovering official misdeeds. It also protects officials who might be wrongly accused by providing them a credible means for clearing their names.

Reagan administration officials, however, contend that the law is unconstitutional. They maintain that it usurps executive power by making independent prosecutors answerable to the courts rather than the president. The constitutional argument against the law, however, is highly questionable. The Constitution does not specify presidential authority to appoint criminal prosecutors. But it explicitly gives Congress the right to "vest the appointment of ... inferior officers, as they think proper, in the president alone, *in the courts of law,* or in the heads of departments." (Emphasis added.)

Congress exercised that constitutional authority by passing the special prosecutor law and should ignore administration opposition to extending it.

# The Virginian-Pilot

*Norfolk, VA, June 20, 1987*

In 1973, President Nixon fired Watergate special prosecutor Archibald Cox for insisting on access to the White House tapes. Ultimately, Mr. Nixon was forced to resign anyway, but the "Saturday Night Massacre" temporarily stalled the probe of the scandal and exposed to the nation a major weakness in the process for investigating alleged lawbreaking in the executive branch.

To eliminate the potential conflicts of interest when administration officials in the Justice Department, itself an arm of the executive branch, investigate other top administration officials, Congress included in the post-Watergate Ethics in Government Act of 1978 a provision for independent counsel in such cases. Responsibility for appointing the counsel was placed with a special three-judge federal court.

In 1983, the Justice Department expressed doubts about the constitutionality of the statute, but President Reagan signed the legislation that extended the independent-counsel measure for five years.

With the current extension ending in January, Sens. Carl M. Levin, Democrat from Michigan, and William S. Cohen, Republican from Maine, have introduced a bill to make the law permanent. The Justice Department, this time with White House blessing, has renewed its objections, claiming anew that the independent-counsel law is unconstitutional, and has advised Mr. Reagan to veto a further extension.

In a letter to Congress, Assistant Attorney General John R. Bolton faulted performance by independent counsel in several cases. He alleged excessive expenditures, unwarranted delay and "defiance of the most basic principles of diplomatic immunity" and said: "The law creates an opportunity for abuse of prosecutorial power that our constitutional system cannot and must not tolerate."

But how much wrongdoing in government will the people tolerate? The public sector has continued to lose credibility as instances of alleged clandestine operations, influence peddling, conflict of interest and plain old greed have multiplied. Because many such cases have arisen within the federal administrative branch, a system that allows that branch to prosecute its own not only creates opportunity for abuse but almost invites it.

Independent counsel today are investigating the Iran-Contra affair, former White House aides Lyn Nofziger and Michael K. Deaver, Attorney General Edwin Meese III and former Assistant Attorney General Theodore B. Olson.

As Eugene C. Thomas, president of the American Bar Association, suggested: "This is no time for the Justice Department to level an attack on current independent counsel as they investigate or prosecute charges of wrongdoing by administration officials."

Indeed, the list of current cases not only makes it clear that a provision for special prosecution of members of the executive branch is needed; this list makes an insistent argument that counsel be independent in the truest sense. The opportunity for abuse by such counsel exists, of course. But that opportunity seems minuscule next to the apparent opportunities for abuse of power that today's independent counsel are investigating.

## Honolulu Star-Bulletin

*Honolulu, HI, June 26, 1987*

The Reagan administration's Justice Department looked ridiculous when it attacked a bill making permanent the appointment of special prosecutors to investigate allegations of misconduct by high government officials.

The attack was made by John Bolton, assistant attorney general for legislative affairs, who argued that the bill was unconstitutional and said the department would recommend a veto if it passed. Bolton also criticized the counsel in the Iran-Contra affair, Lawrence Walsh.

Bolton's position seemed absurdly self-serving, because his boss, Attorney General Edwin Meese, is himself under investigation by a special prosecutor in connection with the operations of Wedtech Corp., a bankrupt defense contractor.

The special prosecutor law, part of the Ethics in Government Act, will expire at the end of this year unless renewed. It provides for selection of a special prosecutor, or independent counsel, by a three-judge court at the request of the attorney general.

The American Bar Association came to the defense of the prosecutors, asserting that " . . . this is no time for the Justice Department to level an attack on current independent counsel as they investigate or prosecute charges of wrongdoing by administration officials." The ABA said the special prosecutor concept has served the nation well from the time of the appointment of Leon Jaworski during the Watergate scandal.

The reason why independent counsel are needed in the federal government is the same as the reason for an elected attorney general at the state government level. It provides assurance that the prosecutor will be independent of the current administration. This is essential for an investigation to be free of the suspicion of a whitewash.

The special prosecutor law fills the need at the federal level, but Hawaii is one of the few states that does not elect its attorney general. Until it does, an important check on wrongdoing by government officials will be lacking here.

## San Francisco Chronicle

*San Francisco, CA, June 23, 1987*

**THE JUSTICE DEPARTMENT'S** latest attack on the law creating special prosecutors demonstrates flawed reasoning and bad grace. Requesting investigation by an independent counsel is often the best defense an embattled government official can find.

The reason? The public is more likely to believe the conclusion of some distinguished lawyer from outside the Washington hothouse than a verdict concocted from within. The most impeccable approach by a "house" lawyer will inevitably engender talk of an "inside" job carried out with political ends in mind.

That was the whole idea behind enacting such a law after the Watergate scandal. It was to ensure straight-arrow investigations of possible misconduct by high government officials. Generally, special prosecutors have served well in difficult circumstances in Washington.

The U.S. attorney-general's office's contentious attack on the post strikes a sour note when one remembers that Attorney General Edwin Meese said in 1984 it was "essential" such a lawyer be appointed to clear him quickly of allegations of financial impropriety. The law worked well for Meese then. He is now under investigation in the Wedtech situation.

**THERE ARE CLAIMS** that these independent investigators pursue trivia, and spend too much money. Well one man's trivial pursuit is another man's thorough sifting of the facts. And money spent in the proper pursuit of justice is surely well dispensed. This is no time to do away with the role of independent counsel.

# North Testifies; Admits Deceptions, Defends Secrecy

Lt. Col. Oliver North began his long-awaited testimony July 7, 1987 before House and Senate committees investigating the Iran-contra arms scandal. North said he believed that all his activities as a member of the National Security Council staff from 1981 through 1986 had been authorized by his superiors. He admitted deceiving Congress and misusing some funds from the sale of arms to Iran, but he cited national security and the safety of his family to justify those actions.

North was questioned July 7 and 8 by John Nields Jr., counsel to the Democratic majority on the House committee. House minority counsel George Van Cleve took over the questioning during the morning of July 9, providing North with the opportunity to discuss the perceived Soviet threat in Nicaragua. That afternoon, Senate majority counsel Arthur Liman began an intricate cross-examination of North. North testified under a grant of limited immunity (which meant that he could still be prosecuted, but only evidence obtained before his testimony began could be used against him) and under a complex agreement worked out with the committees.

One of the first questions posed to North was whether President Reagan had known that profits (or "residuals," in North's words) from the sale of arms to Iran were being funneled to the contra rebels in Nicaragua. North replied that he had never "personally discussed" the diversion with Reagan, but had "assumed that the President was aware of what I was doing and had, through my superiors, approved it." For many, the question of whether Reagan knew of the diversion had come to be the crucial issue of the hearings. President Reagan had continued to insist that he never knew about the diversion, which magnified the importance of the question in the hearings and in the media. North said that he had prepared five memos recommending the diversion of Iranian funds to the contras, each of which was addressed to then-national security adviser John Poindexter and bore a space for the President's initialed approval. North said that he had destroyed four of the memos, but that one survived to be found by assistant attorney general William Bradford Reynolds on November 22, 1986.

North said July 8 that the idea of diverting funds to the contras had first come from Manucher Ghorbanifar, an Iranian-born arms dealer who acted as a middleman in the transaction. North said he considered the possibility of using Iranian money to fund the contras "a neat idea," adding that he still considered it a good idea. According to North, Poindexter had approved the diversion and William Casey, the late Central Intelligence Agency director, had been "very enthusiastic" about the idea. North said that he had never asked either man whether Reagan had been informed of the diversion in their frequent meetings with the President.

North claimed that he had begun destroying key documents on the arms transactions in October 1986, before the scandal became public and more than a month before previous accounts had said the shredding began. North said July 7 he had continued to shred documents right through the morning of November 25, 1986, when he was dismissed. North could not recall any specific documents he had shredded, except for the four so-called diversion memos. North said he could not remember whether one of those four memos had borne the President's approval.

Liman questioned North more extensively about the shredding on July 9. North revealed that he had shredded documents even as Justice Department officials were looking at other files in his office in November 1986, but insisted that the documents destroyed were not relevant to their investigation. "They were working on their project," he said, "I was working on mine."

North told Liman July 9 that under a "fall-guy plan" created by the administration, he was to be the "scapegoat" shielding his superiors, including Reagan, from blame for the Iran-contra operation. North was willing to be the scapegoat for political purposes, he said, but once a criminal investigation began, he was no longer willing to take all the blame. North July 7 admitted preparing a chronology in November 1986 that contained several falsehoods, but said that former national security adviser Robert McFarlane had told him to include the false statements. North admitted, for what he said were reasons of national security, deceiving Congress on several occasions about the extent to which he was involved in aiding the contras.

"Olliemania" was a widely observed national phenomenon as North parried the committees' lawyers with references to the struggling "freedom fighters" in Nicaragua, to the "vacillating" Congress that would not support the contras, to his wife and daughters, and to his own willingness to take the risks to get a job done.

## The Record

Hackensack, NJ, July 12, 1987

Judging from the flood of telegrams to Congress and the White House, Oliver North is America's newest hero. In one sense, it's hardly surprising. "Ollie," as we've all come to know him, is handsome and engaging, with earnest, soulful eyes and a boyish, gap-toothed grin. He's also eloquent, modest, and as obedient as an Eagle Scout. "I'm not in the habit of questioning my superiors," he told Senate Counsel Arthur Liman Thursday. "If he [National Security Adviser John Poindexter] deemed it not to be necessary to ask the president, I saluted smartly and charged up the hill. That's what lieutenant colonels are supposed to do."

But Ollie North is no hero. He's not even close. He is a zealot who views the world through the distorted lenses of the extreme right. When he defines terrorists as those who kill civilians, destroy property, and blow up power plants for political purposes, it apparently never occurs to him that this is exactly what his beloved Nicaraguan contras have done and continue to do. His notion of unquestioning obedience is simply out of place in a democratic, post-Nuremberg military. Good officers *think*. They know that a soldier's ultimate responsibility is not to his commanding officer but to the larger society of which he and the military are both a part. When confronted with an illegal order, they are legally and morally required to disobey it.

Oliver North questioned nothing and obeyed everything, even when Admiral Poindexter and Central Intelligence Agency Director William Casey ordered him to violate the Boland Amendment prohibiting military aid to the contras — an act of Congress that the president, his own commander-in-chief, had signed into law. Colonel North's support for the roving death squads known as the contras makes him a party to an assault on a sovereign republic and to the death and injury of thousands of Nicaraguans.

•

Finally, his boundless astonishment last Nov. 25 — when Attorney-General Edwin Meese announced that he would be the subject of a criminal probe — makes us wonder whether he understands what government by law is all about. His admission that "there was probably not another person on the planet Earth as shocked as I was to hear that someone thought [the arms diversion] was criminal" is painfully naive. It is sad that he refuses to question Ronald Reagan, William Casey, or John Poindexter for placing him in a position of extreme legal jeopardy and then abandoning him as soon as the scandal broke. He still doesn't understand what he did wrong or how badly he was used by his superiors. A man who invents preposterous schemes to evade the law can be called many things, but "hero" is not one of them.

# the Charleston Gazette

Charleston, WV, July 9, 1987

TESTIMONY by Lt. Col. Oliver North is underscoring that top government officials repeatedly lied to Congress and the American people while waging President Reagan's secret war against Nicaragua.

North says Attorney General Edwin Meese plus White House security chiefs Robert McFarlane and John Poindexter helped draft a false chronology about the illicit delivery of U.S. weapons to Iran. None objected to this lie to U.S. citizens.

North acknowledged that he previously told various falsehoods to advance "the enterprise" of funneling Iranian profits and donated money to the contra raiders. But, self-righteously wearing his uniform and medals, he says there were "good and sufficient reasons" for the deception.

The late CIA Director William Casey apparently lied to the Tower Commission by saying he didn't learn until late 1986 of the diversion of Iranian money to the contras. North says Casey knew from the start.

Meanwhile, North says he lied to Maj. Gen. Richard Secord by telling him that he personally had informed President Reagan of the money diversion. And North says he lied in a letter making it appear he wasn't given a $13,900 home security system by Secord.

Further, shredding documents to prevent the FBI and congressional investigators from discovering the truth is another form of lying.

So far, nearly every major witness before the investigating committee has confessed to previous lies in conducting the White House's covert foreign policy.

McFarlane sheepishly admitted he had testified "inappropriately" by saying he knew nothing of contra fund-raising — when he had just obtained $32 million from Saudi Arabia for the contras.

Assistant Secretary of State Elliott Abrams grudgingly admitted lies to Congress about raising money for the contra — and indignantly blamed it on Congress's refusal to vote taxpayer funds for the guerrillas.

The next scheduled witness is Poindexter — who sent a "well done" memo to North in 1985 after the colonel lied to a congressional committee.

(About that time, North was sending millions of dollars to the contras, and telling them in a secret memo to keep it hush-hush, because "the Congress must believe that there continues to be an urgent need for funding.")

With all the witnesses confessing to previous lies, how can Americans be sure they're telling the truth now? How can the public believe anything that comes out of the White House?

The unfolding evidence shows a sordid corruption of democracy. The American people didn't want to fight Nicaragua, so the administration waged war in secret and lied to America about it.

Charleston, WV, July 18, 1987

HIS testimony at an end, it's worth taking a look at the case made by Oliver North. Permit us to play devil's advocate.

*I was just a simple soldier.* North won the hearts and minds of America thanks in no small part to excellent staging. There sat the beleaguered veteran, chest full of medals, who did as he was told, whose family received no government protection when threatened by terrorists and who, finally, was abandoned as a sacrificial lamb.

Interestingly, North's wasn't nearly as fastidious about appearing in uniform before this scandal broke. In the few existing photographs of him as a White House aide, North never is pictured wearing Marine garb. Simply, he used his uniform as a prop to garner sympathy.

Similarly, the family man vs. terrorists had great emotional pull. North contends he asked the FBI and the White House to protect his family from terrorist threats and was refused. What he didn't bother saying is that the FBI doesn't provide security systems for anyone, nor does the White House have any record of him asking for help. This is no small problem. For accepting such gifts, government officials can be jailed up to five years. North, who took pains to conceal the transaction, obviously knew that.

Yet, this pales next to his overall contention that he was just following orders. As Sen. Daniel Inouye, D-Hawaii, pointed out, that's not a defense for a member of the U.S. military — as it was for those in the dock at Nuremberg. North chose to forget that his oath was to the Constitution, not to Ronald Reagan.

*Our cause was just.* This argument is kith and kin to "the end justifies the means." The colonel would have it that his cause was freedom — freedom for the hostages in Lebanon, freedom for Nicaragua — and that made it all right to subvert freedom at home.

The world according to Oliver North is rule by the colonels, unelected and unaccountable, intelligence agencies independently financed and thus able to do whatever they wish. Call this form of government what you like; it is not what was conceived for this nation.

*I've nothing to be ashamed of.* He has plenty. Lt. Col. North's self-absolution should be compared with his accomplishments. There are more Americans held hostage today than there were before the arms shipments began. Far from freeing captives, the trade was an incentive to take more U.S. citizens.

At the same time, U.S. policy in the Persian Gulf was irreparably harmed. Kuwait's call for a Soviet presence in the gulf was a direct response to its perception of a U.S. tilt to Iran, thanks to the arms sales. America's sons will die in those waters because of North's conspiracy.

Finally, there is the colonel's faithlessness to constitutional government. What's amazing is that so many Americans agree with him. While this country celebrates the Constitution's bicentennial, the outpouring of support for the colonel shows a lot of people don't really care for the burdens of democracy.

Save your prayers for Oliver North; the devil takes care of his own. Say them, instead, for your republic and a people who don't seem to care a damn about their freedom enough to protect it from men like this.

## THE ASHEVILLE CITIZEN

Asheville, NC, July 10, 1987

One of the more curious claims heard from those involved in the Iran-Contra scandal is that money made from the arms sale to Iran was not government money.

Lt. Col. Oliver North has proposed this idea at least twice in his testimony before the committee. Lawyers for Gen. Richard Secord and others who may be indicted have made the same claim. Profits from the sale belonged not to the government, but to Secord and his associates who helped arrange the transaction.

It is clear why they wish to establish this idea. It will be their defense, should they be indicted on charges of misusing public funds. If the money didn't belong to the government, they can't be convicted of turning public funds to private uses.

The Porsche and the personal airplane that Secord bought, the millions of dollars he still has stashed in Swiss banks, the security system purchased for North's home — all of it is legal. And the money diverted to the Contras did not violate the law, because it was a "private donation" rather than public money.

Let's see. Government officials sell government property, in a deal sanctioned by the president, and the money is funneled to a covert, government-run program — yet the money does not belong to the government? Any lawyer who can persuade a court to accept a notion as incredible as this will be an awfully good lawyer indeed.

One reason North and his group were able to make a profit on the sale is that the weapons were undervalued. The Pentagon was reimbursed for the weapons, but it was reimbursed for less than they cost.

What a "neat idea," as North might say. Federal officials, any time they choose, may put an artificially low price on government property, sell it at a standard price to private buyers, and use the "profits" for any purpose they deem worthwhile.

If that is the way our government operated, many of our federal officals could get rich — and Congress' authority under the Constitution to determine public spending would be meaningless.

# The Dallas Morning News

*Dallas, TX, July 14, 1987*

## ST. LOUIS POST-DISPATCH

*St. Louis, MO, July 15, 1987*

Lt. Col. Oliver North has concluded six days of testimony before the special congressional committee investigating the Iran-Contra scandal, and what a show it was The 43-year-old Marine officer proved to be an impressive performer and left no doubt of his keen loyalty to the office of the president. And, the polls show, Americans believe overwhelmingly that he was telling the truth.

Yet beneath the ribbons, the resolute demeanor and the unflinching dedication there lurks a dangerous man. Lt. Col. North is dangerous because two things about him became manifestly plain in the course of his testimony. One: His commitment borders on fanaticism. Two: He has no respect for the constitutional system of checks and balances that seeks to assure that this will be a government enjoying the consent of the governed. That combination augurs poorly for the constitutional safeguards the American people rely on. Unfortunately, this administration was able to recruit many Oliver Norths.

What was equally disturbing was that after six days of testimony, Lt. Col. North remained unrepentant. The lies and the shredding were as staunchly defended at the end as at the beginning. Indeed, he lectured Congress on its failure to grasp America's national interests as he had. He did not understand that what he did cannot be justified by loyalty, patriotism or good intentions. Nor, apparently, do President Reagan and all the others involved in the White House's clandestine policies.

In defending the administration's efforts to keep Congress from knowing what it was up to, Lt. Col. North claimed the lawmakers could not be trusted with secrets. That wasn't the real reason for the deceit, though. The administration knew that trading arms for hostages was shamefully wrong and would never be endorsed by Congress or the public. Accordingly, it decided to disregard requirements for consultation with Congress. By the same token, it knew that shipping weapons to the Contras was illegal; obviously, it was not going to share that kind of secret with Congress.

Once on a morally corrupt course, the administration found it could not contain the corruption. Money passed through many hands and much of it went into the pockets of profiteers, more and more government officials were called on to lie, documents had to be falsified or destroyed. And, before the roof fell in, serious consideration was being given to the creation of a permanent, private, clandestine network funded outside the government but secretly controlled inside it. That such an arrangement — as well as all that went before it — would have done great violence to the principle of accountability, which is at the heart of our system of government, did not cross Lt. Col. North's mind.

Nor, it would seem from all the adulation bestowed on him by the public, has it dawned on many Americans. His testimony was a fearful reminder that the nation's democratic structure is not as unshakably anchored as we like to think.

Lt. Col. Oliver North has been portrayed over the last week as the "Marine who took Capitol Hill." Some might say he's the Marine who has captured a nation. In over a week of testimony before a joint congressional committee, North seems to have stormed not just Congress but also the bastion of public opinion.

While public sentiment on whether North is a hero or a victim is sharply divided, the outpouring of support for him, nonetheless, has been overwhelming: from telegrams to funds for his defense to support for a North presidential race.

This public reaction tells us something not just about Oliver North, the man, but also about today's America — where people may be looking for a hero or a scapegoat, rather than an answer to a perplexing set of questions.

The question that must be raised is whether the substance of the investigation — the dangers of a secret foreign policy outside normal government control — is being overpowered by televised political theater.

Without impugning North's motives, it should be suggested that there are grave policy issues at stake — not the least of which is the operation of a private "CIA outside the CIA." North testified that CIA Director William Casey planned to create "an off-the-shelf, self-sustaining, stand-alone entity" that would carry out covert operations outside normal government control — a shadow government.

Furthermore, these questions remain:

Was the country served by the private foreign policy of North and his rogue patriots? Is foreign policy conducted with non-appropriated funds less accountable than that conducted with appropriated money?

If Congress says "no" to a foreign policy position, can the White House or National Security Council, willy-nilly, say "yes"? Can a president make whatever demands of his staff he so chooses, as North suggested in Monday's testimony, regardless of whether it breaks laws or even rules established by that administration?

The problem is one that may be just beginning if this country allows intelligence agencies to form societies of their own, sealed off by walls of secrecy, to engage in clandestine operations and deceptions — however justified — that defy other principles of democratic government.

No, at issue here is not whether one loves or respects Oliver North, the good Marine who would stand on his head for his commander in chief. At issue is how the country deals with the problems that underlie the behavior of an Oliver North. Congressional restraints on executive power and the propensity toward leaks have opened the door to actions such as those conducted by North.

Some means must be found to keep open communication between the executive and legislative branches on matters of foreign policy. Even North has talked of his desire for a small, select committee of Congress, the members of which could be trusted to advise and consult on covert operations.

North's testimony has revealed that he, and others, essentially elevated themselves to the position of appointed guardians of the republic, guardians who believed themselves more dedicated and more knowledgeable than those elected by the people.

Under such a system, the people surely are shortchanged.

# The Boston Globe

*Boston, MA, July 12, 1987*

Until Oliver North spoke of the plan to create a super-CIA, last week's Iran-contra hearings had been like a sea crowded with small boats passing in the night on the Gulf of Olliemania.

Lawyers pursued sometimes obscure objectives; the public reacted viscerally to the television drama; the witness hewed to a planned speechmaking course, turning unexpectedly into an overnight star.

Then, on Friday, in response to the questioning of committee counsel Arthur Liman, the submarine that had been lurking under the hearings rose to the surface. North acknowledged the plan of William Casey, the late CIA director, to create "an off-the-shelf, self-sustaining entity that could," as North put it, "perform functions for the United States."

What North was referring to was a super-CIA. That revelation went to the heart of the Iran-contra matter. It confirmed the unprecedented threat that President Reagan's secret foreign policy represented for constitutional government.

The Orwellian irony of "Project Democracy," as the plan was code-named, is that it would have removed US foreign policy from the purview of democracy. With a secret treasury, army, navy and air forces, this US-sponsored war-making unit would have been exempt from review and regulation by Congress.

"There were no taxpayer funds involved," North insisted, as if that absolved all legal considerations. Indeed, this war-making "enterprise" was disguised as a commercial entity. Yet it was equipped, as North quoted Casey, for "full-service covert action." It was to have been a permanent worldwide system, under the control of the president and the CIA director, but unacknowledged, based outside the United States and utterly beyond the law.

North was well ahead in the contest for public opinion when Project Democracy finally surfaced. The public had been mesmerized, and many Americans consider North heroic. He was an attractive witness, and was coached by an aggressive, skillful lawyer.

Giving general answers to specific questions whose answers might lead toward President Reagan, North showed himself loyal while carefully implicating others in the administration so that he will not have to face charges alone. When fed friendly questions by the minority counsel, North set forth the administration case for covert war, including the attack on Nicaragua.

It was a weird week on the Gulf of Olliemania. The hearing room made North into a pop star. But the question now is when the public will see through the media event to the deadly implications of the plan that feisty, can-do, undemocratic Oliver North worked so selflessly and effectively to develop.

## 🪖 Post-Tribune
*Gary, IN, July 12, 1987*

There stood quiet Sen. Daniel Inouye, a hero before Oliver North was born, saying that the Marine colonel's behavior suggested he was above the law. Everyone linked to the Iran-Contra affair seems to be either above the law or eager to say that "somebody else made me do it."

It is the law, not the question of being for democracy in Central America that is the issue. It is the law, not whether arms sales to Iran got some hostages freed.

### Our opinions

But Lt. Col. North seems to have shredded the issues from his mind — he is an expert on shredding. It must have been like a comedy. Attorney General Edwin Meese's people rummaging around for key documents while nearby, North kept his shredder going, methodically making the evidence disappear.

In the beginning, there was a law that banned dealing with Iran and government aid to the rebels in Nicaragua. President Reagan already has admitted the arms sale goof and it has hurt him. But North and others involved in using the leftover money to help the Contras were contemptuous of both the law and the elementary necessity for keeping some members of Congress briefed on any covert moves.

North undoubtedly has created an atmosphere of sympathy across America. But which Oliver North are we to believe? Surely not all of them. He comes across as the loyal soldier, willing to take the ultimate hit in the service of his country, and the political hit to protect his president. Is that the real Oliver North?

He has used the hearings as a forum in which to lecture members of Congress and the country on war, the communist threat, the failure in Vietnam and Congress' "fickle, vacillating policy" on the Nicaraguan struggle. The debate on those policies has taken place and it is continuing, but it will not be decided in these hearings. It is only a diversion. The real issue is what appears to be law violations in the top levels of government, or at least a contempt for the right of the people's representatives to know what is going on.

North would have us believe that only he and a few others could be trusted to direct the struggle against evil ideological forces. He and his band were patriots, and those who disagreed were fools or unpatriotic. That's the world he pictures. The lieutenant colonel's supercilious attitude toward Congress reflects some of the problem in this whole matter. He apparently thinks that some hot information would be leaked to the world. Sen. Inouye set him straight on that one, in his quiet, believable way.

But if North was earmarked as the fall guy, he does rate some sympathy and those above him rate scorn in full measure. When North's testimony is over and Rear Adm. John Poindexter tells his versions of this bungling performance, the country may know just where the buck stops.

Nobody in this band of self-styled crusading patriots deserves sympathy for their methods. They lied, deceived, subverted and sneered at the principle of a system run by laws instead of men. The world according to Oliver North and others may demand such behavior, but in the real world it is not so. A government of the people, by the people and for the people demands some accountability.

## The Union Leader
*Manchester, NH, July 10, 1987*

Give credit to Senator Daniel "Your-objection-is-overruled" Inouye, chairman of the Iran-Contra panel, for the most subtle joke of the week, however unintentional. The senator wondered aloud at Wednesday's hearing how Lieutenant Colonel Oliver North could possibly have concluded that Congress couldn't be trusted with state secrets since, he claimed, most leaks come from the White House.

But perhaps the problem was far broader than that.

**Perhaps North and others involved in covert operations, where a breach of trust would have had fatal results, fatal for foreign as well as American operatives and interests, simply concluded that a Congress that would sell out the anti-Communist freedom fighters of Nicaragua via the craven Boland Amendment, a Congress composed of large numbers of members who wanted (and probably still want) the Nicaraguan Marxists to prevail over the Contras, is a Congress that couldn't be trusted —period.**

If there is as strong a citizen backlash as indicated against the sad spectacle of these thoroughly politicized hearings, where the daily airing of dirty linen pleases America's enemies and dismays her friends around the world, is there any wonder? It may not be accurate to assume that all of those citizens inundating lawmakers and the news media with their praise of North necessarily agree with all that he did.

**It's just possible that they hold most culpable those who brought about the conditions in which he felt he had to do it.**

Trust Congress? Senator Inouye may not be aware of the true situation! The sleaze-ball political opportunism in Washington, where politics no longer stops at the water's edge, has not gone completely unnoticed outside the beltway. It would be interesting to poll the parents of sons serving in the Persian Gulf as to what they fear most in the long run —Iranian and Iraqi missiles or partisan political opportunism in Congress.

Incidentally, Senator Inouye, who everyone knows served his country magnificently in World War II, was belaboring the obvious when he subtly sought to compare medals with Vietnam veteran North, a comparison irrelevant to the hearings.

But since the subject has been raised, let Senator Inouye recall that Second Lieutenant Inouye at least had the advantage of having the enemy in front of him and a supportive Congress behind him.

## 𝕷os Angeles 𝕿imes
*Los Angeles, CA, July 16, 1987*

The question put to congressional investigating panels by Lt. Col. Oliver L. North's lawyer was both taunting and triumphant. "Why," asked Brendan V. Sullivan Jr., "don't you listen to the American people and what they've said as a result of the last week? There are 20,000 [pro-North] telegrams . . . that came in this morning. The American people have spoken!"

What the people said, as Sullivan would have it, is that they believe in North and are angry that some of their elected representatives have dared to express doubts about his judgment and rectitude. Sullivan's implicit message was blunt: Ollie North has a lot of supporters out there, and members of Congress who value their political futures would be wise to remember that.

If basic questions of legal and ethical responsibility were things to be decided by a public show of hands, then maybe for an emotional day or two Ollie North might indeed have been able to claim popular forgiveness for what he did. But, as his lawyer certainly knows, that's not the way things work. A witness at a congressional hearing is not a contestant on the "Original Amateur Hour," whose fate depends on how well his performance pleases the audience. Our government and its legal system are not run by telegraphic plebiscites.

Frequently invoking God, country and a conveniently selective memory, North insisted throughout six days of testimony that whatever he did while on the National Security Council staff was legally correct, morally proper and always in the best interests of the nation. As various members of the committees eloquently reminded him in their summations, that's not the way it was at all.

By his own admission, North repeatedly lied to Congress on matters about which Congress has both the constitutional right and the responsibility to be kept fully and honestly informed. In so doing he and others involved with him in the misbegotten Iran-*contra* aid venture demonstrated either their ignorance of or—worse—their contempt for the vital bonds of trust that must exist in a democracy between the people and their elected officials and between the co-equal branches of government. Those who celebrate Ollie North as a patriot and a hero ought to be asking themselves what favors did he do for his country by scheming to undercut its democratic values, and exactly how did he serve its interests by conspiring to deceive the American people?

# The Pittsburgh Press

*Pittsburgh, PA, July 8, 1987*

Middle America, which can be defined as the normal part of the country outside Washington, New York, Cambridge, Mass., and Berkeley, Calif., seems to have fallen in love with Oliver North.

The Marine lieutenant colonel's television image of sincerity, patriotism, dedication to mission and loyalty to superiors has won him much public sympathy. That is demonstrated by a tidal wave of telephone calls, telegrams, flowers and money for his defense that is breaking over Capitol Hill.

We Americans are quick to manufacture heroes (and villains) and one feels like a spoilsport to utter three cautionary words: Not so fast.

No one should deny that Col. North is a military hero. The Marine Corps does not hand out the Silver Star and the Bronze Star lightly.

But is he a civic hero, a White House hero, a figure worthy of the adulation that his performance at the hearings has elicited?

First, the matter of shredding. Col. North described his destruction of evidence as necessary to maintain the secrecy of the Iran-Contra operation. A prosecutor, however, may well regard the shredding, after an investigation began, as obstruction of justice.

Second, lying. Col. North is proud that he lied to Congress to protect the resupply of the Nicaraguan rebels. But for the American democratic system to run well, there must be trust among the co-equal branches. Lies from one branch to the other are corrosive.

Oliver North was selflessly dedicated to restoring democracy to Nicaragua. Unfortunately, as Sen. Sam Nunn correctly observed, he abandoned it at home.

# The Miami Herald

*Maimi, FL, July 8, 1987*

**T**ODAY'S THE DAY. Marine Lt. Col. Oliver North, the man at the vortex of the Iran-*contra* storm, is to appear before congressional investigators and a national television audience and answer questions about how this subversion of normal Government operations occurred.

Alas, some members of the investigating committees already have said that they won't believe the colonel no matter what he says. Their skepticism is not unfounded. As Alfonso Chardy of *The Herald's* Washington bureau reported in an exhaustive and chilling account on Sunday, the Reagan Administration at its outset in 1980 began to form a shadow Government that supplanted, undercut, and thwarted traditional Executive and Legislative Branch structures.

Oliver North, a can-do zealot, rose to the top of that penumbral group of conspirators. Yes, *conspirators*. What else to call it but conspiracy when plans are made to suspend the Constitution and declare martial law in the event of nuclear war or national upheaval over U.S. military actions abroad? By participating in this conspiracy, much less by carrying out the Iran-*contra* scam, Colonel North willingly and willfully violated his officer's oath to uphold and defend the Constitution.

When President Reagan fired Colonel North from his National Security Council post last fall, the Justice Department took its sweet easy time sealing the colonel's office. The delay gave Colonel North and his secretary, Fawn Hall, time to shred at least one 18-inch-thick stack of documents, alter others, and spirit others out of the Old Executive Office Building.

Some of the shredded documents were reconstructed from the original computer tapes. No one except Colonel North knows what documents were not recoverable, or who said what to whom in them, or whom — including the President — they might have incriminated.

Will Colonel North testify truthfully? Will his testimony be perceived as truthful? Or will it be perceived as a logical extension of the illogical — not to say illegal — mendacity that describes this whole sordid affair?

Those questions have hung in the air for months as the nation awaited Colonel North's testimony. Today the answers will begin, at last, to emerge.

# The Washington Post

*Washington, DC, July 15, 1987*

**E**VERYONE, or almost everyone, was extravagantly polite to Lt. Col. Oliver North during his testimony; obsequious might be a better word. The proceedings got pretty mawkish, too, as legislators vied with the witness to see who could tell a more stirring tale of his American roots and so forth. Sen. Inouye even told the tale of little George Washington and the cherry tree. But both the general goo and the notion that the telegrams Col. North was getting from people around the country should alter the nature of the inquiry missed the meaning of what was going on. A lot of things Col. North said required challenge—challenge that was buried on the rare occasions it occurred in the legislators' flow of statements about their beliefs and themselves.

First there is the matter of heroism. Col. North, like Sen. Inouye and some of the others on the committee, is a bona fide war hero: he has been heroic in military combat. That is a record that invites respect and awe. But Col. North seemed to want to extend this idea of heroism to everything else he has done, much of which seems anything but heroic. He regularly conveyed the notion, for instance, that there was something valorous about his coming before the committee, about acknowledging under oath that he had lied about his conduct habitually in the past. He even implied that there was something borderline heroic in those previous lies themselves—it wasn't easy for him to lie, he told the committee with the air of a man who had really made a sacrifice.

Come on: everyone over the age of 3 knows that it is generally easier to lie than not to when you've been caught at something, that lying is not so much valorous as self-protective. And Col. North, appearing under hard negotiated terms of limited immunity and in the constant hovering presence of his attorney, was not doing something heroic but something prudent in telling the truth under oath about his prior lies. Col. North availed himself of his rights, just as he did when he took the Fifth Amendment, and to do so was surely legitimate. But noble? Brave? It is to cheapen true acts of battlefield valor to try to extend the aura of heroism to legal maneuverings and manipulations.

Then there is the substance of what Col. North said. His six days of testimony were followed yesterday by a second appearance by his erst-

while superior, Robert McFarlane. The former national security adviser sharply contradicted Col. North on the officer's central and sensitive claim that in all that he did he had had the approval of his superiors—their number presumably including, for a time, Mr. McFarlane. Mr. McFarlane also took issue with some of the specific statements about him that Col. North had made. The point here is that Col. North's testimony, like that of everyone else, remains to be carefully corroborated and reviewed. The committee will have to resolve the contradictions between the two men's testimony.

Finally there is the matter of accountability, which Rep. Lee Hamilton underlined yesterday in the course of a probing and eloquent analysis of the pervasive disrespect Col. North had shown toward the processes of democratic government. Mr. Hamilton got to the heart of the Iran-contra affair: President Reagan's secret, unprincipled and costly reversal of policy on Iran and the hostages. This is the error from which all other errors flowed and the one whose consequences—the new Soviet political leverage in the Gulf, for instance—are still unfolding.

Of five key documents that Col. North said he had written on the diversion of arms sales proceeds, Mr. Hamilton noted, the officer had been unable to recall either whether they had been returned to him or whether they had been destroyed. There had been no accounting, Mr. Hamilton said, for $8 million earned from the sale to Iran of U.S. arms or for a $250,000 sum "available to you." Mr. Hamilton said he believed Col. North when the latter said he never took a penny. "But we have no records to support or to contradict what you say. Indeed, most of the important records concerning these events have been destroyed." Thus had Congress, denied a role in the creating of a "radically changed" policy, been cut out of a role in overseeing its evolution as well.

The question about Oliver North was never his heroism or his personality or his dedication to what he considers right. The question was always the role he had played in the crazy adventure that President Reagan launched when he decided to open arms-for-hostages dealings with Iran. That is the path Congress must keep exploring as the hearings go on.

## The Houston Post

*Houston, TX, July 12, 1987*

Lt. Col. Oliver North has so far won broad sympathy and support in his appearances at the congressional Iran-Contra hearings. How did this clean-cut, articulate Marine officer, and much-decorated Vietnam War veteran, get mixed up in such a mess?

The former National Security Council aide has passionately defended his key role in covertly aiding Nicaragua's rebels, arranging secret arms sales to Iran in exchange for American hostages in Lebanon, and diverting profits from the sales to the Contras. He has professed unswerving loyalty to those he served, particularly President Reagan, who fired him when the scandal broke last fall.

Loyalty, dedication, initiative, imagination — these are, in themselves, commendable qualities. But they do not justify North's lying to Congress, as he admitted he had done previously, or helping prepare false chronologies of events concerning the arms sales. Nor do they excuse his blaming congressional "vacillating" on Contra aid policy for spawning the clandestine supply system he ran.

North has not implicated the president in the funds diversion, at a time when Congress had barred official U.S. aid to the rebels. But he says his activities were approved by his superiors.

All this raises one of the most troubling aspects of Ollie North's testimony. It reflects what appears to have been a prevalent attitude among some in the administration. Congressional obstacles to Contra aid were to be covertly circumvented. In the Iran arms deal, the president secretly violated his own stated policy against dealing with governments that sponsor terrorism.

The goals of these initiatives were arguably worthy — helping Marxist Nicaragua achieve democracy, easing tensions with Iran, freeing U.S. hostages. But policies should be pursued within our system, not in spite of it.

## The News and Courier

*Charleston, SC, July 11, 1987*

Lt. Col. Oliver North may have won one for the Gipper, succeeding where even The Great Communicator failed. He appears to have made the Contras — or, as he constantly refered to them, "the Nicaraguan resistance" — popular.

All the polls so far have shown minimal support from the American people for the Contras, despite President Reagan's description of them as "the moral equivalent of our Founding Fathers" and as "freedom fighters." (Some of the words used by the president to describe the Contras and win support for them from the American people may, in fact, have been coined by Col. North. While testifying at the congressional hearing, he revealed that he helped write some of the president's speeches).

The public's interest span is short and polls have revealed that a majority of Americans were never certain who was who and what was what in Nicaragua. A large percentage thought that the administration was supporting the Sandinistas.

Col. North not only identified himself totally with the Contras, he also challenged Congress by emphasizing that it was its "on again, off again" support for them that forced the administration to seek other ways of keeping the Contras alive.

Although Col. North's charisma may have made the Contras popular, he will have achieved something of much greater importance if he has also managed to get the American people to understand why support for the Contras is vital to the cause of democracy throughout the Americas.

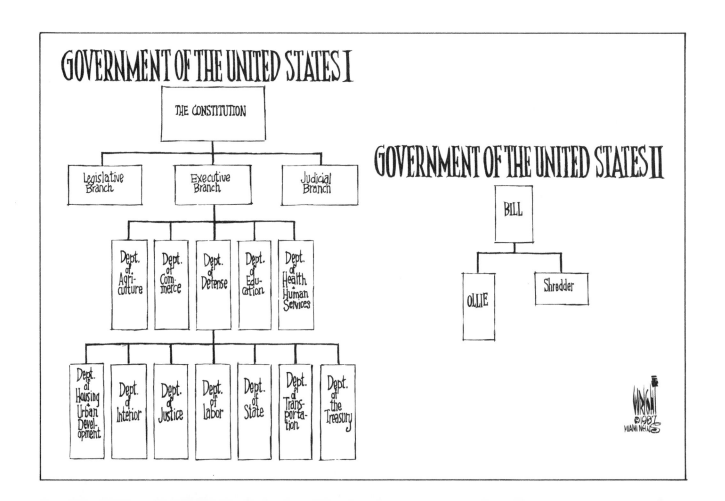

# Poindexter Testifies that Reagan was Unaware of Fund Diversion

Rear Adm. John Poindexter, who served as President Reagan's national security adviser from late 1985 through November 1986, told congressional panels investigating the Iran-contra arms scandal July 15, 1987 that he never told the President about the diversion of funds from arms transactions with Iran to the contra rebels fighting the Nicaraguan government. Poindexter said that he had authorized the controversial diversion and deliberately kept Reagan in the dark in order to "provide some future deniability for the President if it ever leaked out." Poindexter's answer, in response to a question posed by Arthur Liman, counsel to the Senate committee, had been long awaited by a White House wary that Poindexter might say he had briefed Reagan on the diversion. Poindexter testified that he was sure that Reagan would have approved the diversion if he had known of it, an assertion the White House denied. "What's new about that," Reagan said after being told that Poindexter had said he was unaware of the diversion. "I've been saying it for seven months."

Poindexter's testimony followed six days of testimony by Lt. Col. Oliver North, who had served on the National Security Council staff under Poindexter and his predecessor, Robert McFarlane. McFarlane testified briefly July 14, pointing out conflicts between his account of events and North's. Liman's first question to Poindexter July 15 concerned a presidential finding prepared in November 1985 that authorized the arms sales to Iran as a strict arms-for-hostages trade. Although several officials had testified to the existence of the finding, no copy of it signed by Reagan had turned up, and Reagan himself had consistently said that he did not recall signing such a finding. Poindexter said he had watched the President sign the finding, but that he, Poindexter, destroyed it after the arms transactions became public in November 1986 because it was "politically embarrassing."

On the issue of the diversion of funds to the contras, Poindexter insisted that he had never seen any of the five memos that North said he had written to Poindexter suggesting that Poindexter get presidential approval for the diversion. As for telling the President of the diversion, Poindexter wavered between saying that he had withheld the information because it was a low-level detail in the implementation of a presidentially approved policy and saying that he was seeking to maintain "deniability" for Reagan.

# The TENNESSEAN

*Nashville, TN, July 21, 1987*

ADM. John Poindexter has managed to derail any "smoking gun" theory, but his testimony has been no less dismal than that of Lt. Col. Oliver North in picturing an inner world where anything went.

In his days of testimony the admiral said he approved Colonel North's plan for diverting Iranian arms-sale profits to the contras but did not tell the President. He said he wanted to insulate Mr. Reagan from political problems.

Yet the fact he realized there would be problems if it came out was surely something he should have shared with his commander in chief. It was as if he didn't trust the captain's judgment and left him to putter about his cabin while the admiral took the helm. After all, the venerable captain's detailed knowledge of navigation wasn't too sharp. He knew vaguely where he wanted to go, and Admiral Poindexter took it upon himself to find the way.

Mr. Poindexter and the black bag boys in back of the ship were filling in the details they figured the captain didn't want to be bothered with. The "details" involved secrecy, lies to almost everybody, coverups, law breaking and, in effect, setting a course of danger for the President and American foreign policy.

Yet Admiral Poindexter said he had no regrets about anything he did, and he has no apologies to make. Taking a page from Colonel North's book, he blamed the Congress for inaction on the contra funding, and even took a shot at former Speaker Thomas P. O'Neill for holding up approval.

The admiral denied misleading the Congress but complained that too much detail is already provided the lawmakers. Even the Republicans on the panel found that a little much. Sen. William Cohen, R-Maine, said he found it troubling that the admiral admitted withholding information from Congress and yet insisted that was not an act of misleading lawmakers.

Senator Cohen said it would be "suicidal" if Congress and the executive branch continue to "lie to each other... or withhold information or ...alter or shred documents," and if the administration wants to regain support of the American people, "it stops insulting their intelligence and tells them the direct, unvarnished truth."

Admiral Poindexter's testimony has hardly been "unvarnished" and all of it may not be the truth, except in his mind. In his mind, he was on the bridge making decisions while the captain dozed off below. But the captain, he thinks, would have approved of his decisions. ∎

The Grand Rapids Press

*Grand Rapids, MI, July 17, 1987*

As a witness, Rear Adm. John Poindexter has been as phlegmatic as Lt. Col. Oliver North was charismatic. But his testimony has had the pizzazz his personality lacks. He has come to President Reagan's rescue in a way that Col. North didn't, or couldn't.

Adm. Poindexter, in his first day before the Iran-contra select committees, testified that he deliberately withheld from Mr. Reagan information about the diversion of money from the arms sales to Iran to the Nicaraguan contras. The admiral neatly corroborated the president's repeated assertions that he didn't know about the diversion until the scandal was uncovered.

That testimony, unless contradicted, takes some of wind out of the committee's sails. The primary purpose of the congressional investigation was to learn the president's role in the arms-sale-and-diversion scheme, some parts of which may have been illegal and all of which was ill-advised.

Adm. Poindexter has absolved the president of the most serious charge, and the committee seems to have run out of key witnesses. If information about the diversion plan was as well-guarded as Adm. Poindexter contends, then only three knew the details: Col. North, Adm. Poindexter and the late William Casey.

But for the president to claim vindication from Adm. Poindexter's testimony is like the battered prizefighter lying on the canvas raising his arms in triumph. Much in this week's testimony was damning, for the president and for the administration he heads. Adm. Poindexter said Mr. Reagan approved of the arms dale to Iran as a straight arms-for-hostages deal, which contradicts Mr. Reagan's public statements that the arrangement was not made to free the hostages but to build bridges to moderate elements in Iran.

The president says he doesn't remember such an approval. If that's true, then the president has been running the ship of state blindfolded. For a president not to recall such an important policy directive is more than troubling.

The Tower Commission report, remember, found tnat the president had delegated too much authority and that many of the shenanigans took place behind his back. Mr. Poindexter's testimony and Mr. Reagan's explanation suggest otherwise, that the president was briefed but that he doesn't recollect what he was told or did.

On matters besides the diversion, Col. North's and Adm. Poindexter's testimony indicated that the president was not as insulated or divorced from the actions of an ambitious staff as the Tower Commission thought. The president was involved, it seems, and kept from knowledge only about those matters that could destroy him or his administration.

And the admiral reinforced earlier testimony revealing that the administration withheld from Congress information about the operation — information that should at least have been disclosed to members of the leadership. The North-Poindexter-Casey tandem, in fact, deliberately deceived congressional committees in order to keep them in the dark. That attitude is fundamentally at odds with our system of shared power and of checks and balances in representative government. The odds are high that congressional involvement and a fuller discussion of the wisdom of the arms sale venture would have stunted this plan before it grew into a monster.

The tendency in the post-Poindexter days may be for the president and the Congress to declare a draw: To expound, explain, excuse and finally to declare an end.

These hearings will have served no good purpose, however, if the American people ignore the essential lesson that the democratic process is more important than a president or a policy, even one as well-intentioned as freeing hostages.

# Los Angeles Times

## Los Angeles, CA, July 17, 1987

The nation now has sworn testimony that the secrecy that obsessed the Reagan Administration officials most deeply involved in the Iran-*contra* scandal was in fact carried to its ultimate extreme. No one, it seems, bothered to tell the President in whose name all the jiggery-pokery was taking place that profits from the Iran arms sale were skimmed off to support Nicaraguan insurgents. Rear Adm. John M. Poindexter, national-security adviser at the time, says that it was his decision not to burden President Reagan with this information. A relieved White House has hailed as welcome news the assurance that the President didn't have the foggiest idea what his subordinates were up to.

Poindexter says that he kept Reagan in the dark so as to afford him "deniability" if the diversion ever became known, and because he regarded the covert shift of funds to the contras as a mere "detail" in the implementation of the President's policy to keep the insurgency alive. This matter-of-fact acknowledgement of a startling assump-tion of authority raises the inevitable question: If Reagan wasn't told about something as legally consequential and politically explosive as the diversion of funds to the contras, what else might his staff have kept from him over the more than six years of his presidency?

Poindexter indicates that he was quite comfortable with hiding information from Reagan, since he was convinced that the President "would approve it [the diversion] if asked." White House officials insist that Reagan would have rejected the diversion scheme if confronted with it. Poindexter, if he is telling the truth, says he believed that he knew his boss' mind—a conviction presumably based on Reagan's insistence that the contras had to be kept going. Reagan's current aides say that he would never have approved such underhanded methods. There, unresolved and probably un-resolvable, the matter rests. To the White House it adds up to a political plus for the President. Sometimes it indeed pays to be ignorant.

# The Hutchinson News

## Hutchinson, KS
## July 19, 1987

If you don't want to call a tax hike a tax hike, you call it revenue enhancement.

If you don't want to call a thief a thief, you just say he ripped off something.

And if you want to fix it so a liar can lie, you give him deniability.

The Iran-Contra hearings didn't create any of these dismal techniques of modern-day language and living. The hearings have provided, however, new meaning to the deceit of deniability in a nation that treats vulgar dishonesty as a semantic inconvenience.

They were out to give the president deniability, Admiral John Poindexter repeatedly asserted. With enough of that deniability, no matter what happened, the president could always claim he didn't know anything about it. Nobody could prove otherwise.

So far the president has made use of the deniability because nobody has found a tape recording, memo, or other direct order from Ronald Reagan indicating that he knew what was going on in the White House.

What a tragic descent into know-nothingness this represents for the conservative movement.

Ignorance is crowned with virtue, lies are festooned with garlands of state, and stupidity becomes a national treasure so long as nobody finds the true confession chiseled into granite.

And nobody yet wonders how many innocent victims were slaughtered by the missiles we sent to the Iranian thugs ... the same thugs who slaughtered our Marines in Beirut and tortured to death a senior American CIA leader.

But then, of course, the ayatollah probably has deniability, too.

# St. Petersburg Times

## St. Petersburg, FL, July 22, 1987

Is Adm. Poindexter telling the truth?

That is a key question about the Iran-Contra scandal, in particular whether he decided on his own, as he claims, to divert money to the Contras. With Poindexter's five days of public testimony ended, it appears that the question may never be answered with certainty.

Much of the testimony suggests that Poindexter, arrogant and unrepentant, is lying. His superior officers in the Navy have repeatedly praised his intellect and his photographic memory, yet he has testified that he recalls very little about the crucial events of the scandal. For example, Poindexter held an enormously important lunch meeting with CIA Director William Casey on Saturday, Nov. 22, 1986, two days before Poindexter resigned, one day after he learned that the Justice Department was beginning an investigation and one day after he destroyed a presidential finding on the arms swap. Oliver North happened to drop in on the meeting. Yet Poindexter remembers nothing of the discussion except that Casey told him about his testimony to Congress. Did they talk about the destruction of documents? Poindexter doesn't recall. Did they talk about the Justice Department investigation? Poindexter doesn't recall. That simply isn't credible.

Poindexter did not recall seeing five memos written by North specifically requesting presidential approval for the diversion. Nor did Poindexter recall Casey's desire for an independent, private intelligence agency apart from the CIA.

Poindexter's account of two more meetings on Monday, Nov. 24, don't have the ring of truth. The first was with Attorney General Edwin Meese, whose investigators had just discovered the incriminating diversion memo. Here is Poindexter's description of that important meeting: "My recollection is that he started off by saying, I assume you are aware of the memo we found in Ollie's files. And I said yes. He said, were you aware of this? And I said that I was generally aware of the transfer of funds. And then I told him that I was prepared to resign and that I trusted him to recommend to me the timing of my resignation." Did Poindexter tell Meese he had approved the diversion? No. Did he tell Meese that North was acting under his orders? No. Did Meese ask the key question, whether Poindexter had told the President? No. This sounds like a meeting of morons. It just is not the way most people would act under those conditions.

Another strange meeting followed at 9:30 that morning, by Poindexter's account. Poindexter went into the Oval Office to resign. The President, George Bush, Donald Regan and Meese were there. Poindexter claims he offered the President his resignation, explaining that he wanted "to give you the necessary latitude to do whatever you need to do." Poindexter said "the President responded and said that he had a great regret. And that this was in the tradition of a naval officer, of accepting responsibility. And I shook hands with everybody and left the office."

This is the departure of an aide who has usurped the power of his boss, failed to inform him of vital foreign policy decisions and almost destroyed the Reagan presidency? And still no one had asked Poindexter about the diversion decision and about informing the President.

What an odd statement by Mr. Reagan! Poindexter claims the President praised him for acting "in the tradition of a naval officer, of accepting responsibility." In truth, Poindexter had done the opposite. If he is telling the truth, he had violated the military imperative of keeping superiors informed. He had made an important decision without specific authority. That's conduct for the President to praise?

All of these events, as well as Poindexter's willingness to deceive the Congress and those around him, suggest that he is not telling the truth.

But suppose he is. Suppose this well-trained and highly praised admiral did decide to divert funds on his own. This suggests that such a secretive and suspicious climate existed in the White House that his conduct was acceptable, as Poindexter says. Approval of Poindexter's claims would constitute one of the most chilling challenges in American history to the bedrock principle of civilian control of the military.

## The Honolulu Advertiser
*Honolulu, HI, July 24, 1987*

Nothing yet to be said in the Iran-Contra hearings is likely to top what Hawaii Senator Dan Inouye called the "incredible, mind-boggling, chilling" testimony of Admiral John Poindexter.

Certainly, the words of the former national security adviser gave many people a frustrating sense the truth will never be fully known.

Poindexter said he did not tell the president about diverting Iran arms sales profits to the Contras, but a 47- to 33-percent plurality of Americans in one poll just don't believe him.

It's not Poindexter's lack of charm that makes people doubt him but his too-convenient lapses of memory and logic. To charges he withheld information from Cabinet members, he said, "I didn't withhold anything that they didn't want withheld from them."

Secretary of State George Shultz disputed that yesterday, suggesting there were voices of reason in the Reagan administration if only they had been consulted and heeded.

If he is to be believed, Poindexter usurped rights and responsibilities that a military officer and mid-level appointee had no business to. He intended to protect the president's "deniability" and in his testimony he continued to shield the president from active complicity in the scandal.

But the picture of a president with no control over his administration may be equally embarrassing.

Even staunch Reagan supporters found it frustrating that Poindexter remained complacently convinced he had done what Reagan would have wanted and there was nothing wrong with the whole "neat" scheme except that it failed and Congress and the media exaggerated its importance.

The only real regret Poindexter admits to is that he and his fellow schemers were caught without a good enough cover story for "damage control."

It remains to be seen whether a special prosecutor will show Poindexter broke the law. But it's clear that his understanding of the Constitution and the system of democratic government it was meant to create is faulty.

## The Washington Post
*Washington, DC, July 21, 1987*

SEN. ORRIN HATCH elicited from Rear Adm. John Poindexter yesterday a statement that the decision to explore an opening to Iran 1) was the president's and 2) was the product of serious study and review. Evidently Mr. Hatch meant to be establishing Mr. Reagan's capacity for staying on top of policy in his own government. Actually he was establishing the president's responsibility for the basic flaw of the Iran-contra affair, the source from which all else flowed.

Of course, it was reasonable for the American government to be looking to establish some better relationship with Iran in time and also to explore any openings toward moderation that were possible. But the judgment made and the arrangements entered into on the basis of a reading of some of the most exploitative elements in Iran as "moderates" all but define the problem. It was thought that if these fake "moderates" were carefully cultivated, they could either (depending on your reading of the president's purpose) produce the hostages or restore a hostile Iran to a political and strategic situation consistent with the American interest.

At this point it should be evident that the narrower purpose, of dealing with certain elements in Tehran in order to get back the hostages, was quickly discredited. The few hostages who were released were quickly replaced by new Americans seized in Lebanon. That Adm. Poindexter destroyed the presidential finding authorizing such an exchange suggests that he came to understand the futility of this exercise, if he did not start with it.

The United States was not able to make a good test of the broader purpose of the Iran opening, to explore avenues for moderating Iranian policy. But a full-fledged test subsequently was made by France—to which, by the way, Ayatollah Khomeini owed a great debt for its hospitality in his years of exile. As Flora Lewis usefully recalled on Monday in The New York Times, the French, seeking to "normalize" relations with Iran, kicked out another Iranian exile, a leading rival to the ayatollah, and settled a third of a billion dollars upon Iran in partial repayment of an old loan. The Iranians responded by giving refuge in their Paris embassy to an embassy translator (not a diplomat) wanted for questioning in some terrible bombings; this is the incident that triggered the current explosive crisis in French-Iranian relations.

In light of the centrality of the opening to Tehran, by the way, it is especially unfortunate that the congressional committees apparently do not intend publicly to question Michael Ledeen. As the first American to discuss an opening to Iran with the Israelis and the first to meet with a supposedly moderate Iranian, Manucher Ghorbanifar, Mr. Ledeen is in a unique position to inform Congress about the launching of the policy whose crash is absorbing its attentions day after day.

## The Register-Guard
*Eugene, OR, July 22, 1987*

The testimony of Rear Adm. John Poindexter is the most important — and the most troubling — of all so far in the Iran-Contra hearings.

The former national security adviser says that he authorized the diversion of arms sale "profits" to the Contras on his own, purposely choosing not to tell President Reagan about it. He did not tell the President while the operation was carried out. He did not tell him after parts of the story were exposed, creating a public sensation. He did briefly acknowledge knowing about the diversion when he met with the President to submit his resignation, but did not volunteer and was not asked for any details.

Despite Poindexter's persistently calm demeanor, his story is very hard to believe.

It's hard to believe that a military man with such respect for the chain of command would have denied his own commander in chief the option of making such a momentous decision. He did understand the significance of the decision and its potential political explosiveness. It was that understanding, he explained, that caused him to want to protect the President by providing him the ability to say honestly that he knew nothing about it.

Poindexter's credibility is strained by contradictions between his testimony and that of his subordinate, Lt. Col. Oliver North, on a variety of points. When the questioning got sharp, the admiral often took refuge behind the claim that he could not recall an event, an incident, a memo or a conversation. Yet his Navy personnel file is filled with commendations for his meticulousness and his remarkable memory.

Central in this respect are the several memos that Colonel North recalled submitting to Poindexter with requests that he pass them on to the President to obtain approval for things related to the diversion. With the exception of the single memo that survived North's shredder and was found by investigators, Poindexter could not recall any such. He finally said he thought North was simply "mistaken on that point" and that the memos simply did not exist.

While it is difficult to believe that the buck stopped with Poindexter on the Contra diversion, it is also difficult to see how the investigating committee or anyone else can prove otherwise. If Poindexter did tell the President, only he and Ronald Reagan know that for sure, and both have publicly denied it. Oliver North assumed all along that Reagan knew and approved of what was being done, but he has no hard evidence to confirm his assumption.

Ironically, Poindexter's credibility was enhanced most by his straightforward statement that he believed at the time and continues to believe that if he had raised the diversion issue with the President, Reagan would have enthusiastically approved — notwithstanding the fact that the White House says now that the President would not have allowed the project to go forward. On that point, Poindexter is wholly believable and White House spokesman Marlin Fitzwater is not.

As frustrating as Poindexter's spear-taking stance is, the picture will get truly messy if the administration or its supporters pursue foolish proposals for a presidential pardon for either Poindexter or North. Of course a pardon will be possible, and logically will be considered, if either is indicted on criminal charges.

But it's premature even to debate the merits of a hypothetical pardon now. And a pre-emptive pardon before the fact of any indictment, quashing the investigation by the special prosecutor, would be unpardonable.

The Honolulu Advertiser
*Honolulu, HI, July 16, 1987*

**I**t was said that former National Security Adviser John Poindexter would be the most important witness at the congressional Iran-Contra hearings, and so he may prove to be.

Lt. Colonel Oliver North captivated much of the nation, and he remains most memorable. His lasting impact is hard to measure, although he clearly boosted chances for more Contra aid.

But it was Poindexter whose testimony could have led to Ronald Reagan's impeachment, if he had testified the president had authorized the diversion of profits from arms sales to Iran to the Contra rebels in Nicaragua. That is something Reagan has repeatedly denied.

Now Poindexter has taken the blame — or the spear, as some would say — and testified he deliberately didn't tell Reagan about the funds diversion to protect the president from political harm.

And it will be interesting if public opinion polls — which have shown most Americans think Reagan knew and lied about the diversion — will show a major change.

But even if Poindexter is to be believed, that is far from a happy ending to a bad situation. Some points:

● Reagan was damaged a bit by Poindexter's testimony that the president had at first approved an arms-for-hostage trade with Iran. That is contrary to what Reagan claims.

● In Poindexter's version of events, the president comes across as a chief executive who is uninformed and not in control of a key foreign policy move with grave implications. It's hard to imagine other American presidents tolerating such a situation.

● The operation was not only inept — like something invented by Rube Goldberg and executed by Inspector Clouseau, as historian Arthur Schlesinger Jr. put it — it was also a disaster.

We gave the Iranians arms to continue their war with Iraq, paying ransom to terrorists at a time Reagan was urging other nations to embargo arms. Iran's allies in Lebanon now hold more hostages than before.

**A**mericans may be relieved to be told the president was not a liar. But there is plenty of reason to doubt his foreign policy skill and judgment at this crucial time for us when he is planning another controversial venture in the Mideast.

## DAYTON DAILY NEWS
*Dayton, OH, July 23, 1987*

Adm. John Poindexter is not an easy man to give a break to.

If you believe his most important testimony — that he did not tell President Reagan about the diversion of Iranian funds to Nicaragua — then he has caused the President an enormous amount of trouble, precipitated two major investigations and kept the country hanging for months, while the President's popularity and credibility have slumped.

The admiral's valiant defenders point to his distinguished career and say he should not be judged too harshly for one or a few mistakes.

Trouble is, the admiral himself sees no mistake. 'I'm not going to be apologetic about it," he says, noting that he has "no regrets for anything I did." He even denies that the President's credibility has suffered because of his claimed behavior.

He has, it seems, buried his head in the sand.

If, indeed, Adm. Poindexter did keep the information from the President, that's not surprising. He was, after all, working in an environment in which keeping information from central players had become a way of life.

Moreover, his insistence that the President would have approved the diversion if he had known about it is entirely credible. Former White House speechwriter Pat Buchanan — a spokesman for the President's most ardent admirers (the let-Reagan-be-Reagan people) — agrees.

Nevertheless, the admiral definitely does have some apologizing to do. If his story is to be believed, he assumed a degree of responsibility way beyond that appropriate for a staff person, and the harm he has done could not be more obvious.

## Shultz Cites White House Infighting Over Iran Arms Sales

Secretary of State George Shultz July 23, 1987 told the Senate and House committees investigating the Iran-contra affair that his strong opposition to the secret arms sales to Iran had sparked a "battle royal" and "guerrilla warfare" within the White House. He angrily testified that former Central Intelligence Agency Director William Casey and ex-national security advisers Robert McFarlane and Rear Adm. John Poindexter had lied to him and withheld information from President Ronald Reagan in order to continue the Iranian initiative and ultimately protect themselves.

Shultz denied charges that he had deliberately kept himself uninformed about the operation and the covert effort to resupply the Nicaraguan rebels, and then tried to distance himself from the policies once the scandal broke. He said he had argued strenuously against the arms sales and worked to try to end them from the inside. He added that he had offered to resign three times: the first in mid-1982 when he found that McFarlane had made a secret Middle East trip without telling him, the second in 1985 over the administration's plans to require lie detector tests for high officials, and the third in August 1986, when White House and CIA officials made it clear they were not "comfortable" with him. He described the period after the arms sales were revealed in November 1986 as "traumatic" for him. "Everybody was saying I'm disloyal to the President," Shultz said, because he did not defend the Iranian initiative. "...I frankly felt that I was one who was loyal to the President, because I was the one who was trying to get him the facts so he could make a decision."

While he portrayed the President as having been misled and badly served by some of the President's key advisers, Shultz also depicted Reagan as having been the driving force behind the Iran arms-for-hostages deal. Shultz's testimony conflicted with a number of Reagan's public remarks about his knowledge of the affair and his reasons for authorizing the arms sales. In addition to charging Casey with deception, Shultz said that under his direction, the CIA had often skewed its intelligence in favor of administration policy.

# THE PLAIN DEALER
### Cleveland, OH, July 25, 1987

What's Secretary of State George Shultz got that Oliver North and John Poindexter haven't? Credibility. Why? Because he shows remorse. Both Poindexter, a former national Security adviser, and North, his heavily medaled hatchet-man, admitted that they lied about the Iran-contra scandal—to Congress, other administration officials and, indeed, to just about everybody else. They said it was their duty to lie, and thus their confessions were without regret. Shultz, on the other hand, openly admits to having lost major policy battles that he shouldn't have lost. In so doing, he has expressed anger, frustration and dismay. Who sounds more credible to you?

The picture Shultz paints of a White House humming with internecine power struggles and low backstabbing is too vivid to be discounted. His blunt assessment of the hostage ransom as idiotic is not designed to defend himself or anyone else. Indeed, his failure to thwart the plan provokes questions about his fitness to be the nation's top diplomat. If Shultz isn't a wimp (a question that, in those exact words, is being asked in Washington) why didn't he do more to dissuade President Reagan? Why didn't he resign? He said he tried, three times, although not after the scandal went public.

Anybody who tries to resign three times and fails is trying to play a game of chicken without possessing the requisite commitment. Clearly, any secretary of state who is refused an airplane by a White House flunky has obviously been too meek. But the rage Shultz displayed before the committee hints at tremendous pride, and no one with such pride would stay on at the White House simply for the perks and power. It's easier to believe that Shultz remained because, as he has indicated, he thought he could best serve the president and the nation from within the administration.

Shultz's own testimony, however, suggests that such a belief was partly self-delusion. If it isn't now, the White House was until very recently a place of foreign policy chaos. To hear Shultz tell it, miniature Machiavellis were forever slinking through White House corridors and computer links: cutting the State Department out of the foreign policy process; whispering poisons in the president's ear; expanding their authority and power and influence. For Shultz to think that he alone could stem such plotters when he couldn't even get an airplane was—how to say it?—naive.

Regardless of how appealing Shultz seems, you can be sure he has other agendas. Political infighting is characterstic of every administration, and Shultz knew that better than anyone else in the White House. Why is he recounting it with surprise and regret now? Because to distance himself from the disaster of the Iran-contra mess, he must admit to having lost a titanic struggle against it. Moreover, it strips some of the sheen off North and thus helps discourage White House ideologues from rallying to the lieutenant colonel's defense.

Whatever the motive, Shultz's bitter testimony can only lead the Iran-contra committee closer to its final goal—that of determining how such policy failures occur. The testimony shows clearly that Reagan knew what the purpose of the arms sales to Iran was, and that he lied about it last November. Moreover, if he didn't know about the diversion, it was because he was too disassociated. He let moderates and hard-liners battle over important policy decisions and actions, then heeded the victor's advice. That's a sure prescription for policy chaos.

## THE SAGINAW NEWS
### Saginaw, MI, July 27, 1987

So far during the Iran-Contra hearings, the man who knew the least has said the most.

After his initial objection to the arms-sale deal as "a bad idea," Secretary of State George Shultz was virtually cut out of subsequent proceedings. His testimony to Congress last week was painful to hear. It had to hurt him deeply to give it. Shultz is the officer responsible for conducting foreign policy.

But he did not testify out of personal pique. In his slow, measured, tones, this decent man spoke up for the processes of democracy, the responsibility of the presidency, the legitimate concerns of Congress, the primacy of the people. The blind ideologues had childishly harassed him for "letting down the White House." This conservative responded with an eloquent definition of the nature of true loyalty to a president — and it is not the definition of Adm. John Poindexter.

On television he comes across as somewhat gray. The screen can't show the substance in his character and beliefs. But his words embodied a genuine and refreshing belief in the American system as it ought to work. There was no mistaking his dismay that it did not work in this affair, and his quiet anger at those responsible. The weakness in his account is that at the beginning, he, too, was responsible, but unable to persuade the president.

The hearings are fascinating to follow not only for what they reveal about the scandal, but about the figures on the witness stand. Lt. Col. Oliver North was the obedient servant who forgot that he took an oath to defend the Constitution. Poindexter was the calm, precise operative who forgot where Harry Truman said the buck should stop.

And Shultz? He sought to assure Americans that "nobody has to think they have to lie and cheat" to serve in the government.

Near the close of his session, one member of the committee said he wanted to "stand up and cheer." If Americans are looking for a hero out of these hearings, George Shultz would make a fine nominee.

# Richmond Times-Dispatch

*Richmond, VA, July 28, 1987*

From Secretary of State George Shultz's testimony in the Iran-*contra* hearings, President Reagan has emerged stronger than ever. Members of the congressional investigating committees were openly skeptical of assertions from Adm. John M. Poindexter and Lt. Col. Oliver North that they had not informed Mr. Reagan of their plans to aid Nicaraguan rebels with proceeds from the sale of arms to Iran. But the secretary's insistence that the president did not know of the diversion was far more credible because he is highly esteemed by Democrats and moderate Republicans on the panels.

The secretary also expressed the firm belief that Mr. Reagan's sound judgment would have led him to reject the plan had his approval been sought. Mr. Shultz portrayed the president as a "very decisive person," who, when given all the facts, is "a very strong president who is very willing to take un-popular positions and provide leadership to the country." These could not have been welcome words to those congressional liberals who have hoped the Iran-*contra* hearings would prove Mr. Reagan to be intellectually or ethically incapable of providing effective leadership.

In essence, Mr. Shultz's testimony

**Shultz**

confirmed the findings of the Tower commission, which concluded that Mr. Reagan had been poorly served by subordinates who kept him in the dark about the diversion of funds. Justifiably, the commission criticized the president for sloppy management, saying he should have insisted on a greater degree of accountability from his aides. But administrative carelessness does not convict Mr. Reagan of congenital indecisiveness and stupidity.

As secretary of state, Mr. Shultz also should have known about the diversion of funds. But he insisted to the committees that Adm. Poindexter and others involved in the scheme had kept it a secret from him, too. They were motivated to do so partly by the fact the secretary had opposed the arms sale to Iran because, as an attempt to purchase the release of American hostages, it violated the president's vow not to bargain with terrorists.

That members of the president's staff failed to inform him and his top foreign affairs adviser about the diversion scheme is the most deplorable aspect of the Iran-*contra* affair. Decisions on such proposals should be made at the top, not by aides at a tertiary level.

But it is not likely that the investigating committees can find a legislative remedy for the administrative weaknesses the affair has revealed. It would be silly for Congress to try to solve the problem by enacting a law requiring presidential assistants to be honest and candid with their boss at all times. Only the chief executive himself can hope to avert trouble of this kind by choosing his aides with great care and establishing rigid standards for their performance.

# The Pittsburgh PRESS

*Pittsburgh, PA, July 26, 1987*

George Shultz is an honest, dedicated, loyal public servant, and in his straightforward way — without a lawyer whispering in his ear — he explained to the Iran-Contra hearings how the White House stumbled into humiliation and scandal.

In the most believable testimony given to the congressional investigating committees by a major witness, the secretary of state said he and President Reagan had been lied to and deceived by National Security Council officials and the late CIA Director William Casey.

The president was fed bad intelligence and misleading information, Mr. Shultz said, and thus he made the bad decision to trade arms for hostages. Mr. Shultz had opposed the ill-fated deal, and because of that "disloyalty" was kept in the dark by national security advisers Robert McFarlane and John Poindexter and arch-conspirator Casey.

Mr. McFarlane, Rear Adm. Poindexter and Lt. Col. Oliver North, all "can-do" military men, had contempt for the cookie-pushers in the State Department and dealt with their Iranian "moderates" on their own and in secret.

If they had consulted any career Foreign Service officer with experience in Iran, they would have been told: Get the hostages first, before you deliver the arms. As it turned out, Mr. Shultz said sadly, "They got taken to the cleaners."

Mr. Shultz included a shocker in his testimo-

ny: The NSC gang tried to persuade Kuwait to release 17 convicted terrorists as a trade for American hostages taken in Lebanon — a gross violation of stated U.S. policy not to bargain with terrorists.

The veteran Cabinet officer's testimony — he also has served as secretary of labor and of the Treasury — contained valuable advice for Mr. Reagan and future presidents.

One, if the secretaries of state and defense both strongly oppose a foreign policy initiative, the president should give great weight to their counsel.

Two, a president should feel compassion for Americans taken hostage but should not allow that feeling to drive foreign policy, giving kidnappers a lock on America's actions.

Three, no CIA director should become as involved in policy as Bill Casey was, because he will be tempted to tailor intelligence to support the policy, as Mr. Casey did.

Four, the White House national security staff has become too big and powerful. It should coordinate the work of the various departments, and not itself gather intelligence, make policy and implement policy as it did in Iranamok.

Finally, a president should not see his national security adviser every day and his secretary of state only when the poor chap can get an appointment. That gives the wrong official access and power.

# The TENNESSEAN

*Nashville, TN, July 28, 1987*

IN the weeks of testimony before the Iran-contra committees, Secretary of State George Shultz's appearance brought the voice of candor in a veritable sea of admitted lies from the other witnesses.

Mr. Shultz is familiar with the U.S. Constitution and his concept of law wasn't shared by Lt. Col. Oliver North or Adm. John Poindexter. The two were at least contemptuous of the Congress and the normal processes of government. Colonel North acted in the direction of his own moral compass, which pointed in a different direction than that of Mr. Shultz.

Mr. Poindexter took upon himself the responsibility for approving the fund diversion and said he never told President Ronald Reagan because he said he wanted to insulate his commander in chief from political criticism if the story got out. For a man who was known since the Naval Academy for his sharpness of memory, his testimony showed that his recall of critical weeks of November simply went blank.

He couldn't remember, for instance, what transpired when he had lunch with the late William Casey, the CIA director. He did remember having sandwiches, but that was about all.

Mr. Shultz recalled some bitter White House infighting, in which he and Defense Secretary Caspar Weinberger argued against the Iran arms sales. Both lost. The secretary remembered he had been kept in the dark about most things that were going on. And he said that not only had he been deceived, so was the President.

At one point, when he had learned of the bizarre plan to get Kuwait to free imprisoned terrorists as a means of getting the release of hostages, he told the President, who he said was "stunned and furious." Being furious didn't seem to move Mr. Reagan into asking Admiral Poindexter what was going on.

In fact, Mr. Shultz's picture of the White House and its "guerrilla warfare" between officials was bizarre. Not only did some of them not trust Congress, they really didn't trust each other.

Although Mr. Poindexter said he tried to shield the President from knowing too much, apparently Mr. Reagan did know more than he first admitted. According to hand-written notes of a high White House meeting, he ordered his aides not to discuss the TOW anti-tank missiles and other weapons that had been sent to Iran, suggesting that a statement was needed that would reflect two main points: "no bargaining with terrorists, no ransom for terrorists."

But as Mr. Shultz testified that was precisely what was taking place — although, he said, the President rationalized it as not being a "swap."

Rational citizens will identify with Mr. Shultz, whose testimony was thoughtful, candid and, at times, provocative. He separated himself from Admiral Poindexter, former National Security Adviser Robert McFarlane, Mr. Casey and Colonel North.

His appearance helped remind the public that for a time our skewed foreign policy was enough to make *Looney Tunes* look like serious drama. ∎

# The Sunday Oregonian

Portland, OR, July 26, 1987

After an emotional Oliver North and a smug John Poindexter, an angry George Shultz was a refreshing change for the congressional Iran-Contra hearings.

That's not to say that Shultz himself looked refreshed. The secretary of state had the appearance of a weary, troubled man, as well as one still upset at his exclusion from critical foreign policy decisions — and at the hash North, Poindexter and then-CIA Director William Casey made of them.

For those who would glorify North, Shultz added a succinct perspective: "Our guys ... got taken to the cleaners." This was an effort that failed.

Shultz gave clues about why it failed: Basically, the effort was a bad idea in the first place, and it was concealed from the people who might have pointed that out.

His comments brought the hearings back to what should be the core concern of the investigating committees: how these blunders occurred, and how to prevent similar ones happening again. Directly or indirectly, he offered several answers:

• Involve all the people who should be involved: the president, responsible Cabinet members and the Congress.

• Give them the information they need for a sound decision, including intelligence data not skewed by the CIA director's preferences on policy direction.

• Recognize the legitimacy of congressional action — such as the ban on aid to the Contras — rather than ignoring it as misguided.

The reality that, after North and Poindexter's testimony of evasion and secrecy, this sort of basic advice sounds profound is chilling. The highest level of government should not need retroactive civics lessons, or elementary advice on how decision-making should be structured.

The Iran-Contra affair, as described by Shultz, reflected what can happen when the system of checks and balances breaks down. His testimony portrayed President Reagan as a firm, capable decision-maker who needs no protection by his staff, so long as the facts are presented to him. But Shultz also revealed a president impatient with advice — from Shultz and Secretary of Defense Caspar Weinberger — that went against his leanings on the hostage deal.

There is room to ask whether Shultz suffered too much in silence, rather than following through with his thrice-proffered resignation or insisting the president put a halt to the White House effort to isolate the secretary of state.

Whether he could have done more to change the system is a separate question. Shultz, at least, emerges from the hearings, unlike North or Poindexter, as a man who understands, and cares about, how the system is supposed to work.

# The Dallas Morning News

Dallas, TX, July 25, 1987

Secretary of State George Shultz has emerged from the Iran/contra hearings as a far more loyal member of the president's staff perhaps than John Poindexter and Oliver North, who went to such great lengths to conceal from even President Reagan the details of the covert arms deal. Shultz also has shown himself to be a persuasive advocate for major structural changes in the way U.S. foreign policy is managed.

But seen in context, the State Department and George Shultz's administration of it bear at least some share of responsibility for precipitating this foreign policy crisis in the first place. The State Department has from one administration to the next operated on what can only be termed a 19th-century model of state-to-state diplomacy that bears very little relation to the current needs of foreign policy. Its entire apparatus is geared to reinforcing the political status quo. The Foggy Bottom headquarters traditionally has been peopled with career bureaucrats who feel it is *their* foreign policy, not the president's. For example, in many instances where U.S. interests would be far better served in nurturing and supporting the democratic opposition to established governments — be they Afghan freedom fighters, the contras in Nicaragua, or Angolan anti-Marxist rebels — the State Department has vigorously fought such efforts, fearing that its neat diplomatic ties to the established governments would be jeopardized.

As a consequence, the National Security Council, in the case of the hostage and contra issues, assumed an activist role in foreign policy totally unsuited to either its mandate of advising the president or its technical and staff-level capabilities. But it was attempting, with admittedly disastrous results, to grapple covertly with issues that the State Department had failed to address openly and more judiciously, given the very extensive staff and research facilities at its disposal.

The White House has in the wake of this scandal outlined new procedures to rectify the problems presented in Shultz's testimony. Top aides with direct access to the president would be prevented from promoting policies to the president in the absence of other high-level aides. This is a sound step. But if intended to prevent problems like the Iran/contra scandal from reoccurring, it somehow misses the point.

Until the State Department is reorganized or redirected to be part of the solution rather than part of the problem, its influence may continue to be limited, and very little will have been corrected.

# Winnipeg Free Press

Winnipeg, Man., July 25, 1987

Those who expected that the Irangate hearings would end in anti-climax after Admiral John Poindexter testified that President Reagan had no knowledge of the shenanigans going on around him were mistaken. U.S. Secretary of State George Shultz, usually the most restrained and moderate of men, was unabashedly angry and sarcastic when his turn came to testify this week.

It appears that he, as well as the the president, had been lied to and misled by the gang that plotted the fantastic Iran-Nicaragua caper. The result of the ill-conceived venture was that the Iranians took the Americans to the cleaners.

When Mr. Schulz finally learned some of the details of the amateurish bungling that seems to have characterized the whole sorry mess from the beginning, he felt, he said, like wringing somebody's neck.

Such down-to-earth common sense is a welcome relief after the contrived histrionics of Col. Oliver North and the haughty disdain of Admiral Poindexter. It offers some hope that things are not as wildly out of control in Washington as might have been feared and that there are still rational people with some wisdom and integrity left in charge.

Troubling questions remain. It is difficult to imagine some of Mr. Shultz's predecessors as secretary of state — Dean Acheson, for instance, or Henry L. Stimson — allowing themselves to be hoodwinked so blatantly on matters vitally affecting their own department. There are already those who maintain that Mr. Shultz should have resigned when he discovered the devious manoeuvrings that had been going on behind his back. He did, he claims, offer his resignation to Mr. Reagan on three occasions but none of these were directly connected with the Iran-contra affair.

It may well be that his strong sense of loyalty to the president convinced him of the need to stay at the helm during these troubled times. In any event, resignation from the cabinet over differences of policy is not an established tradition in the United States. Cyrus Vance's resignation from Jimmy Carter's cabinet was one of the few instances in modern times.

Mr. Shultz's testimony paints a grim and murky picture of a Washington where top government officials engage in a ruthless struggles to preserve their turf and to advance their policies, and are prepared to go to extreme lengths to pursue these objectives. Prevarication and deceit are almost considered normal.

It is also true, however, that older traditions of integrity and honor have not completely vanished from Washington. The presence in the government of a man of the calibre of George Shultz testifies to this.

# San Francisco Chronicle

*San Francisco, CA, July 27, 1987*

**IN HIS UNDRAMATIC**, thoughtful — and obviously anguished — Iran-Contra testimony, Secretary of State George Shultz came across as an admirable man. There was no lawyer to whisper in his ear; none of the zealousness, evasion and porous memory that distinguished some of his predecessors on the stand. What you saw was what you got, and it was believable. If an American hero is really to be found in this lamentable affair, George Shultz so far best fits that uneasy role.

The secretary's mild and deliberate responses to questioning served to give fiber to his anger at CIA and Security Council shenanigans. "It made me sick to my stomach," said Shultz about news that private U.S. businessmen were negotiating to free 17 Shiite terrorists in Kuwait. You could feel that. And you could believe the president's flashing fury on being told.

Here was an honorable man beset by White House intriguers, by those afflicted with political tunnel vision and convinced of the righteousness of their renegade foreign policy. With a characteristic touch of rueful humor, Shultz rubbed his bare pate and said people were always "after my scalp."

**SHULTZ MADE A POINT** of quoting one of his mentors, the able Bryce Harlow, as having told him: "Trust is the coin of the realm." Trust, loyalty, and accountability; these qualities were lacking in those who undercut their president. The honorable Secretary of State showed us how important they are.

# The Seattle Times

*Seattle, WA, July 25, 1987*

**S**ECRETARY of State George Shultz restored focus to the Iran-contra hearings this week when he emphasized that an important lesson to learn from the entire saga is that decisions must be vested in officials who can be held accountable for them.

There are no Shultz T-shirts on sale, no billboards calling upon him to run for president. He never will become an instant TV star like Lt. Col. Oliver North. But those members of Congress hailing Shultz as a "real American hero" are closer to the mark than those people all over the nation who showered North with telegraphed applause.

Shultz and North have much in common. Both are former combat Marines. And they are unabashed flag-waving patriots. But they found themselves on opposite sides of what Shultz testified was a "battle royal" and "guerrilla warfare."

For many months, Shultz was on the losing side in that battle of the bureaucrats. North's side — commanded by Central Intelligence Agency chief William Casey and Adm. John Poindexter, head of the National Security Council — had the ear of President Reagan far more often than did the secretary of state. Casey wrote a letter suggesting that Shultz be fired for disloyalty to the president. The secretary felt "estrangement" at the White House.

There is nothing novel about that. Blistering agency rivalries are endemic to the capital scene. And Shultz is far from being the first secretary of state to find himself outmaneuvered by other officials with more ready access to the Oval Office.

The major problem with the situation that Shultz faced was that his inner-administration opponents not only kept secrets from him but from the president himself. An explosion at some point was inevitable.

It is amply clear by now why Poindexter and North testified with grants of immunity, while Shultz felt no need of such a shield.

# Meese Admits '86 Probe Was Cursory

U.S. Attorney General Edwin Meese 3rd testified July 28-29, before 1987 before the House and Senate committees investigating the Iran-contra arms scandal. Meese defended his own brief probe of the affair, which had led to his announcement on November 25, 1986 that funds from arms sales to Iran had been diverted to the Nicaraguan contra rebels, but he admitted that he had failed to ask some critical questions of key participants. Meese's appearance was a good deal calmer than had been expected, given that Meese's relations with Congress had long been uneasy. He was also currently under investigation for questionable financial dealings, and his November 1986 investigation of the Iran-contra affair had been widely criticized. Republican Sen. Warren Rudman of New Hampshire had called it a "case of gross incompetence." But rather than a stormy confrontation, Meese's give-and-take with committee members and lawyers was generally calm and convivial.

Meese took great pains to avoid suggesting that anyone in the White House had deceived him in his investigation, but was compelled to admit that discrepancies between Lt. Col. Oliver North's comments to him and North's testimony to the committees meant that North had deceived one or the other. For example, North had told Meese that former Central Intelligence Agency Director William Casey had not known of the diversion, but he had told the committees that Casey had known and was very enthusiastic about the potential for funding other secret operations in the same way.

In general, Meese portrayed a White House in the early days of the scandal that was confused but cooperative and determined to make public the truth—a very different picture from the "battle royal" of deception and power-plays that Secretary of State George Shultz had described in testimony the preceding week.

## BUFFALO EVENING NEWS
### Buffalo, NY, July 31, 1987

IN SHARP CONTRAST with several other witnesses, Attorney General Edwin Meese III exploded few if any bombshells during his two days of testimony on the Iran-contra affair. On the contrary, his low-key manner and speech seemed designed to smooth the waters and play down controversy.

In the process, however, he left important questions unanswered. And he raised others concerning the restrained, almost leisurely manner in which he conducted the inquiry for President Reagan last November that came up with the sensational discovery that proceeds from the secret sale of arms to Iran had been diverted to the contra rebels in Nicaragua.

His was a mixed performance during those critical days.

He left members of the Iran-contra congressional committees rightly critical and perplexed about his tardiness in moving to protect potentially significant documents later shredded by Marine Lt. Col. Oliver North; about his failure to ask seemingly relevant questions or to take notes during many of his interviews; and about his delay in bringing the FBI or members of the Justice Department's criminal division into the inquiry.

Meese's explanation for his relaxed methods that eventful November weekend was simply that this was not initially intended to be a investigation; he had merely been complying with a request from Reagan to sort out the confusion over U.S. participation in a 1985 arms sale by Israel to Iran, did not know about the fund diversion when he began his inquiry and had no reason to suspect criminality. But none of this effectively rebuts the objections to his handling of the matter.

Sloppy as Meese's four-day inquiry was, it did have its positive side, of course. Congressional interrogators conceded what Meese emphasized — that it was his inquiry that had discovered the key document on the diversion and that he had promptly notified the president. This led to the departure of North and Poindexter from the NSC and public disclosure of the diversion as well as the appointment of a special prosecutor to explore possible criminality.

The testimony of Meese and others nevertheless makes it plain that the attorney general ought to have pressed more vigorously for a clarification of details, that he apparently trusted too much and suspected too little.

Meese's mixed performance in this drama, and the doubts it can raise, highlight a frequent failing of presidents of both political parties: that of appointing close friends and important political supporters as attorneys general.

Such appointments inevitably lend the appearance of favoritism or political shadings at the Department of Justice. Right from the start, that can begin to erode public confidence in the single federal agency entrusted with fair-minded enforcement of the nation's laws.

This helps justify, of course, the 1978 law providing for the appointments of independent special prosecutors to look into allegations of wrongdoing in high administration places.

It also supplies a central reason why presidents, charged with faithfully executing the laws, should look outside their circle of old friends and political advisers when searching for an attorney general.

## The Star-Ledger
### Newark, NJ, July 23, 1987

The Wedtech story is a fable with a moral. The moral, simply put, is: There is no idea so good that greed and government interference cannot corrupt it. Wedtech was a small machine shop in the Bronx until government officials began to "adopt" it. Then it blossomed as a military contractor, getting an extraordinary share of government contracts.

The company was founded by John Mariotta. Mr. Mariotta was born in New York but his parents came to New York from Puerto Rico. That made Wedtech eligible to benefit from a federal law intended to assist companies owned by members of minority groups by giving them access to government contracts without competitive bidding.

This was a well-intentioned law designed to achieve an important goal. But government officials soon found a way to divert and corrupt these worthy purposes.

The large number of political figures under indictment or investigation for allegations involving Wedtech contracts is extraordinary and perhaps unparalleled. In a field—military contracts—known for its wastefulness and vulnerability to corrupt practices, Wedtech became a textbook example of what's palpably wrong with the system.

The latest indictment involving allegations of misbehavior in connection with Wedtech contracts was returned against Lyn Nofziger, the former senior political adviser to President Reagan. He was accused of conflict-of-interest charges related to his lobbying on behalf of Wedtech.

Among others indicted in connection with Wedtech contracts are Rep. Mario Biaggi (D-N.Y.), former Bronx Borough President Stanley Simon, two nephews of former Rep. Parren Mitchell (D-Md.) and the former commander of the New York State National Guard. In addition, an investigation is under way into the activities of Attorney General Edwin Meese on behalf of Wedtech and the fact that a blind trust set up on behalf of Mr. Meese showed a profit in Wedtech stock.

Wedtech is now in receivership. Four former officials of the company have pleaded guilty to a variety of charges and, according to prosecutors, have implicated numerous other officials.

All the individuals indicted or investigated in the scandal are entitled to a presumption of innocence. But the system that spawned the Wedtech scandal and the various other scandals involving defense contracts is guilty beyond a reasonable doubt. The procurement process needs a thorough overhaul to prevent the recurrence of Wedtechs.

# THE DENVER POST

*Denver, CO, July 22, 1987*

THE REAGAN administration claims to stand for law and order. Just ask the president's attorney general, Ed Meese, and he will reassure you.

It is more than just curious, then, why Meese's bureaucracy has delayed for more than two years the process of filling three vacancies on the federal court bench in Denver.

The delays in filling the vacancies long ago transcended any reasonable excuse. In the meantime, thousands of innocent and guilty people are having their day in court postponed — which is good news for the wrongdoers and bad news for the law abiders.

As U.S. District Judge John Kane explained in a decision last March, the delays in filling the two district court vacancies had at that time resulted in a loss of 51 months of judicial time, enough to have disposed of 1,530 cases. "Since there are always at least two sides to a case, at the very least, 3,060 people and businesses have been deprived of their day in court during the past 29 months," Kane noted.

That is a strange pattern of behavior in a Republican administration that prides itself on law and order. Unfortunately, there is little sign that the bottleneck may be opening up.

U.S. Attorney Bob Miller was nominated to take one of the two jobs in the U.S. District Court on Dec. 10, 1984. The seat already had been vacant for five months. Since then — 36 months ago — there has been another vacancy on the district bench and one on the 10th U.S. Circuit Court of Appeals. All have been open for more than two years.

These delays are unconscionable. Obviously, there are cases to be heard and work to be done. But the U.S. Justice Department and the Senate Judiciary Committee have put off hearings on Miller's confirmation because of a failure to complete routine pre-hearing investigations.

Apparently, some concern has arisen over Miller's lack of enthusiasm in 1984 for a Justice Department investigation of a Fort Collins paving company. Miller refused to sign the indictment, calling the case "unprosecutable." His legal judgment was vindicated when the case eventually was dismissed by the trial judge.

Apparently, investigators have been trying to define the extent of the problem — to let Miller know in advance so he can prepare himself for committee hearings or, if it's serious enough, withdraw his name from consideration. But Miller apparently hasn't been kept informed of the progress of that investigation, and he's growing weary and discouraged.

Such shoddy treatment is an insult to the integrity of a fine public servant. The investigation and the confirmation hearings must be expedited — not just for Miller's sake, but in the interests of a reasonable workload in Denver's U.S. District Court and 10th U.S. Circuit Court of Appeals.

While Miller is eager to begin working, the other federal judges are laboring for long and tedious hours just trying to keep from falling further behind. It's mostly a losing battle — the only winners are those criminals whose cases are languishing because of the Justice Department's inexcusable dilly-dallying.

## Arkansas Gazette

*Little Rock, AR, July 31, 1987*

Sometimes truth really is stranger than fiction, as Attorney General Edwin Meese III assured the congressional committees that are trying to follow the tangled trails of the Iran-contra scandal. Truth also can be more elusive than the plot of a Faulkner novel.

Senator Warren B. Rudman, a New Hampshire Republican in good standing, was puzzled by the casual manner in which Mr. Meese had questioned Rear Adm. John M. Poindexter, the national security adviser, and Lt. Col. Oliver L. North, a National Security Council aide, after the diversion of funds to the contras was revealed. He noted that the attorney general took no notes and only asked for a "chronology" of events. Mr. Rudman thought the two men should have been required to write a report on "who did what to who and when and how it was paid for."

Colonel North had emphasized his loyalty to the president and his willingness to "stand on his head in the corner" if his commander-in-chief gave the order. The senator said he believed an order to reveal the whole story would have eliminated a need for the lengthy hearings.

Mr. Meese explained that he already knew a great deal about the affair. By the time he suspected criminal violations, he realized the FBI should be asking the questions. The interlude gave Admiral Poindexter and Colonel North time to take the Fifth Amendment and line up their lawyers.

Mr. Rudman was puzzled by the delay in taking control of Colonel North's office after the "major alarm bells went off." The colonel returned to his office and shredded documents from 11 p.m. until 4 a.m.

"I dare say," Mr. Rudman remarked, "there might have been something there that you would have found interesting."

Mr. Meese admitted that was possible but insisted, in a remarkable display of naivete, that Colonel North could have been shredding documents that had nothing to do with the Iran-contra scandal.

Mr. Meese seemed to hold Colonel North in low esteem, particularly after he learned that testimony before the committees contrasted sharply with the findings in his casual inquiry.

"The discrepancies bother me," he admitted. "Two things were different when he made his statements to the committees. One, he was under oath and, secondly, he was under a grant of immunity."

The detached style of the administration may be contagious. Mr. Meese must have caught it (or learned it) in his long association with President Reagan. In his two days of testimony, he seldom showed that the questioners had succeeded in getting under his skin.

Representative Les Aspin of Wisconsin said he believed he knew how the attorney general remained confident. He suggested the White House was relying on "Plan A and Plan B" to escape blame for the scandal.

"Plan A is: We cannot tell a lie. Ollie did it. Plan B is: We cannot tell a lie. John Poindexter did it."

Mr. Aspin did not invent the concept. Colonel North explained it in some detail when he told the committees he had been prepared to accept "political" responsibility for the whole initiative if the scheme unraveled. Someone said he probably lacked stature for the role. The country would never believe a mere lieutenant colonel could make and execute the foreign policy of the United States. If a higher-level fall guy were needed, Admiral Poindexter would draw the assignment.

It should be remembered that the committee hearings are supposed to uncover the facts. The criminal aspects of the scandal (if any) will be handled by the special prosecutor. Therein may lie the best opportunity for revealing the stranger-than-fiction story.

Colonel North said he was prepared to absorb the political heat but he did not bargain to take the criminal rap. If the special prosecutor closes in, he may be able to recall many things he forgot in his extended testimony.

Apparently, there is much to be remembered. One columnist reported that he counted 184 times when Admiral Poindexter answered questions by saying he could not remember. Mr. Meese, according to the same meticulous report, used the ploy 350 times.

If the forgotten details are revealed, the Meese appraisal could be confirmed. The tale, indeed, may be stranger than fiction.

# ARGUS-LEADER
*Sioux Falls, SD, July 31, 1987*

Attorney General Edwin Meese takes offense at suggestions that his investigation into the Iran-Contra scandal was less than thorough.

No apologies are necessary, though. Meese's investigation was not complete, and he must take most of the blame. The rest of the blame is rooted in the nature of his job.

As critics in Congress have noted during the Iran-Contra hearings, Meese wears too many hats. In addition to being the nation's chief legal officer and one of the top law enforcement officials — a demanding job in itself — Meese, like other recent attorneys general, serves as a close personal friend and adviser to the president. Those roles can clash. They did in this case. **Editorial**

The conflicting nature of Meese's duties might explain why, for example, he failed to ask President Reagan whether he knew about the diversion of profits from Iran arms sales to the Contra rebels fighting in Nicaragua.

Meese handled two days of questioning before congressional committees calmly this week, and he deserves credit for uncovering the diversion. But Meese's note-taking was spotty, and his questioning of top administration officials, including John Poindexter, was casual. Poindexter is Reagan's former national security adviser.

Sen. Sam Nunn, D-Ga., brought out during questioning that Meese failed to ask Poindexter who approved the diversion or why Reagan wasn't told about it.

Sen. George Mitchell, D-Maine, appropriately criticized Meese's failure to quickly seal and guard records in Lt. Col. Oliver North's office to prevent the destruction of possible evidence.

In fairness to Meese, he apparently had to sort through lots of lies and deceit from North and others. That, however, does not excuse shortcomings in Meese's investigation. After all, Meese is the attorney general of the United States, a job that should represent the ultimate in thorough but fair law enforcement.

Reagan and future presidents should help keep their attorneys general out of such messes by not considering the nation's attorney general a personal legal adviser.

An attorney general's first loyalty must be to the Justice Department, not to politics or the White House. Nominees to the job should be held to at least as high a standard as the head of the CIA or the FBI.

In addition to criticism about his inquiry into the Iran-Contra affair, Meese suffers the added burden of being mired in problems involving ties to the scandal-ridden Wedtech Corp., a defense contractor.

Meese, one of Reagan's oldest and closest followers, came to the Justice Department in 1985 as a conservative point man for much of the president's political agenda, including proposed constitutional amendments to allow organized prayer in schools and to outlaw abortion. But Meese's image is so tarnished now that he probably never again will be an influential voice in government, at least during the 17 months remaining in Reagan's term.

Meese never should have been attorney general in the first place. Since he is, he'll have to live with the criticism of the job he's doing. It's not off target.

# Newsday
*Long Island, NY, July 17, 1987*

After Attorney General Edwin Meese's messy personal finances were exposed in all their embarrassing detail during his confirmation hearings, you'd think he would have taken great pains to keep his business relationships and disclosure forms in impeccable order once he was in office.

Not so. At best Meese is incredibly sloppy; at worst he's deliberately trying to conceal some of his financial activities.

If Meese is to be believed, stocks he listed as no longer in his possession weren't actually sold because he couldn't find the certificates. In fact, he admitted last week that he still owns 10 separate stocks and an investment fund that were listed as sold on his 1985 disclosure form. And three bank accounts were omitted from earlier forms.

But bad as those errors and omissions are, they pale by comparison to the arrangements concerning his "limited blind partnership" with W. Franklin Chinn, an investment adviser and onetime director of the scandal-plagued Wedtech Corp. Meese's dealings with Chinn came to light in connection with the Wedtech bribery investigations. The attorney general, who intervened on behalf of Wedtech while he was a top adviser in the White House, insists that the $54,000 he gave Chinn to invest was in no way connected to Wedtech.

Whether it was or not, the money definitely wasn't in a blind trust; that would have meant denying the investor knowledge of any transactions to avoid real or apparent conflicts of interest. Meese had access to periodic reports on the transactions.

Meese conceded under questioning that the partnership wasn't blind "in a technical sense" and agreed that he should have included it in documents accompanying his financial disclosure statements.

Slipshod practices like these would be hard to swallow even if Meese were an ordinary lawyer. In an attorney general, they should be grounds for departure from office.

# THE PLAIN DEALER
*Cleveland, OH, July 31, 1987*

As bland as his tie, Attorney General Edwin Meese finished testifying before the joint congressional Iran-contra committee Wednesday night. Lt. Col. Oliver North testified with pious patriotism. Rear Adm. John Poindexter used cold calculation. Secretary of State George Shultz demonstrated rare and billowing anger. By comparison, Meese was to the hearings what vapor lock is to a car engine.

Like Poindexter before him, Meese's testimony contained convenient gaps. But unlike Poindexter, who relied on a faulty memory to get him through sticky questions, Meese resorted to the inconsistency of his note-taking. Meese could testify at length about some relatively inconsequential meetings because he had the minutes in hand. But he remained unspecific about other, far more important discussions because no notes were taken. Key conversations with President Reagan, Vice President George Bush, former CIA director William Casey and Poindexter had to be reconstructed from memory.

Still, one fact has been made plain. The administration was, from the very first, loathe to investigate charges of ransom and diversion. Meese did not assign the initial inquiries to criminal investigators even though it was quickly apparent that criminal activities most likely had taken place. Meese already has testified that in his opinion, the National Security Council was covered by the Boland Amendment, which restricted aid to contra insurgents. Yet, in the face of a multimillion-dollar diversion, he still entrusted the probe to himself and a handful of political appointees. Why delay calling in the FBI? Why avoid the use of seasoned Justice Department investigators?

Even more puzzling, why didn't Meese directly ask North, Poindexter and Casey who authorized the diversion? Perhaps because no one in the administration wanted to hear the answer. Poindexter has testified that when he went to the Oval Office to resign, no one quizzed him. Instead, investigator Meese accepted misleading answers to imprecise questions. That's consistent with his passive approach to the protection of evidence and the pursuit of contradictions, all of which gave North and Poindexter ample opportunity to destroy key documents. How would you describe such a lackluster performance by an attorney general? Try slipshod, unprofessional and convenient.

THE ONLY THREE PEOPLE IN THE U.S. GOVERNMENT NOT SEEING THE IMPLICATIONS OF THE DIVERSION MEMO.

## Roanoke Times & World-News

*Roanoke, VA, July 31, 1987*

**A**MERICANS should sleep better at night knowing that Edwin Meese III is the nation's top law-enforcement officer. The crime rate has to go down when the country's attorney general can recognize only certain kinds of behavior as potentially criminal, and doesn't know how to investigate others.

Granted, Meese had an inkling something was amiss when an assistant of his found that memo in Lt. Col. Oliver North's files at the National Security Council. The paper said that profits from the arms sales to Iran were being diverted to help the Contras. That would have been a time to marshal all available investigative strength. The FBI offered its resources to the attorney general.

Meese declined this expert assistance; it didn't seem, he now says, that any laws had been broken. He kept the investigation in his own hands and those of his lieutenants at the Justice Department. He talked to other top people in the administration and, it appears, was entirely credulous when they protested that they knew nothing or had done nothing wrong.

Contrary to sound prosecutorial practice, he took no notes during interviews with many important witnesses — including Adm. John Poindexter, the national security adviser. Why? Because Poindexter's story simply confirmed what Meese already had heard. Although Ollie North was known to be in the thick of possibly illegal activities, for a few days Meese allowed him free access to his National Security Council office, where the colonel destroyed reams of evidence — by North's testimony, even while Justice Department investigators were on hand.

Meese now says "it does bother me" that in some statements, North apparently lied to the attorney general. But although North has admitted trying to destroy sensitive papers, Meese isn't bothered; those documents, he says, probably were "irrelevant." Presumably, a man who shreds papers from 11 p.m. to 4:15 a.m. is obsessively tidy.

No wonder Meese is known around Washington as "No Problems" Ed. Few things disturb his composure. Few things penetrate his tunnel vision. Street crime of course is bad, and people accused of such offenses are probably guilty; otherwise, he has said, they wouldn't be suspects.

But there's nothing wrong when a man accepts financial and other favors from friends and rewards them with federal jobs — not when the recipient of the favors is Ed Meese. There's nothing wrong with helping a company get a federal contract and then investing your money with that company — not when you're Ed Meese. And when someone turns up an incriminating memo in the White House, you talk to a lot of people, but you assume that they're all telling you the truth and that no laws have been broken. Then you expect other investigators, including members of the Iran-Contra congressional panel, to believe you.

The American Civil Liberties Union has long roused Ed Meese's ire because of what he considers its excessive concern about personal rights; he once called it "a criminals' lobby." The White House staffers incriminated in this scandal didn't need the ACLU; the attorney general was there to make sure that no one trampled on their rights. This is a man whom Ronald Reagan once dearly wanted to wear Supreme Court robes. He should be wearing a clown hat.

## The Philadelphia Inquirer

*Philadelphia, PA, July 29, 1987*

There's a bit of bulldog in the visage of Attorney General Edwin Meese 3d, chief law-enforcement officer of the United States. But the story he told Congress' Iran-contra panels yesterday of his inquiry into the diversion of profits from the Iran arms deal to the Nicaraguan contras was hardly a tale of an aggressive investigator straining at the leash.

In fact, if there was palpable suspicion before his appearance that Mr. Meese had been more on a mission of political damage control than hard-nosed investigation, that suspicion grew as the day wore on. Radio commentator Daniel Schorr, in fact, noted at midday that there seemed "an element of see-no-evil" in the attorney general's effort to find the facts, even as smoke began billowing from the disintegrating Iran "initiative."

That's a gentle way to put it.

Did Mr. Meese move to secure Lt. Col. Oliver L. North's files after a memo was discovered in them disclosing the possibly illegal diversion of money from the Iran arms sales? No, the attorney general said. Why? Because he saw "no hint" that documents might be destroyed.

Did he mention the bombshell memo to CIA Director William J. Casey when he dropped by his home for an evening chat? Well, no. He didn't want to disclose the memo prematurely.

Here was Mr. Meese — one of President Reagan's oldest counselors — alternately trusting a National Security Council colonel not to destroy incriminating material, and then not fully informing the director of the CIA about a budding scandal.

By that time, the Iran-contra affair had ceased being simply a murky bit of policy blundering. The attorney general was confronting a diversion "scheme" (his word) to get around congressional bans on arming the contras. It was a scheme so patently illegal that if the President's complicity had been established cries for impeachment would have shortly followed.

Yet Mr. Meese kept his own criminal division investigators at bay, not to mention the FBI, asserting that it was not clear at first that federal laws had been broken. Caution flags, of course, were being wigwagged in his own department in the form of staff legal opinions that the NSC was covered by the Boland amendment prohibiting lethal aid to the contras, opinions that Congress needed to be notified of significant covert activity by the NSC.

The attorney general *did* find and eventually disclose the North diversion memo. But not before, according to his testimony, he had done a bit of hasty office-to-office shuttling, shoring up possible gaps in the President's deniability.

It appears he performed the job of presidential adviser with distinction. How well he performed as chief law-enforcement officer, however, remains a very open question as he resumes testifying today.

# Iran-Contra Public Hearings End; Panel to Conduct Closed Sessions

The House and Senate select committees investigating the Iran-contra arms scandal ended three months of joint public hearings August 3, 1987. Former White House chief of staff Donald Regan testified July 30-31, and Defense Secretary Caspar Weinberger, the final witness, appeared July 31 and Aug. 3. The committees then planned to hear testimony in closed session from three officials of the Central Intelligence Agency, and possibly a few other witnesses, before the August congressional recess began. Upon returning to the Capital, the committees would begin work on a report that was scheduled for release in October 1987.

The hearings moved quickly and quietly to a close following testimony of Lt. Col. Oliver North and former national security adviser John Poindexter, who told the committees that the long-anticipated "smoking gun" did not exist—President Reagan was never told of the diverion of funds from the Iranian arms transactions to the contras, they said. After North and Poindexter appeared, the committees decided to call only three remaining major figures in the administration: Regan and two cabinet officials.

The final statements by the chairmen and ranking Republicans on the two committees were brief and sounded much like their previous statements, assailing deceit and secrecy in general terms. Sen. Daniel Inouye (D, Hawaii), chairman of the Senate panel, was the most critical of what he called a "flawed policy kept alive by a secret White House junta, despite repeated warnings and signs of failure." Inouye, in his closing statement, acknowledged the widespread perception that the hearings had failed to get to the heart of the scandal, saying, "We may never know, with precision and truth, why it ever happened." The ranking Republican on the House side, Rep. Dick Cheney of Wyoming, defended the administration to some extent and sought to place the scandal in the context of the "traditional struggle between the President and Congress over policy-making and implementation."

In sorting through the 250 hours of testimony and 200,000 documents about the scandal, the committees would have to reconcile dozens of contradictions and fill in dozens of gaps where witnesses had said they could not remember what happened.

## The Virginian-Pilot
*Norfolk, VA, August 5, 1987*

Now that the public Iran-Contra hearings are ended, it may be appropriate to consider to what extent candor can comport with diplomacy.

Wrote the secretary of state:

*I had an immediate objective — the establishment, on our part at least, of a permanent policy of absolute candor and trust in our relations with other countries. I hoped that other nations would adopt a similar policy of candor and trust toward us and one another. Perhaps they might thereby gradually establish confidence and genuine friendliness between themselves and us and other nations. . . . I received at the State Department the initial visit of sixty ambassadors and ministers comprising the entire diplomatic corps; and thereafter I began seeing them individually. In each of these first conversations I told the ambassador or minister, "I intend to be completely frank with you in all our conversations. I intend to tell you the exact truth. You will see that it is the truth." I also required all my subordinates to practice this policy religiously in their dealings with foreign representatives.*

George Shultz, in January, 1981? No, Cordell Hull, in March, 1933. Considered in light of the Iran-Contra hearings, this statement makes interesting reading. Does it demonstrate naivete? Or does it point to an altogether different lesson?

Mr. Hull became secretary of state at age 61, at the end of a long career that included service as Tennessee state legislator, circuit judge, congressman and senator. This is hardly the background likely to breed a starry-eyed idealist, knowing nothing about "the real world."

Yet Mr. Hull came into the office of secretary of state believing that honesty and candor were not incompatible with the goal of conducting the nation's foreign policy. Indeed, he believed that such means made for a *more effective* foreign policy, in that — in time, after good faith had been demonstrated in practice — those he dealt with would come to trust his word.

Rather remarkable, that faith in the sustaining power of integrity. Equally remarkable is the fact that he emerged from nearly 12 years of service as secretary of state (resigning, because of ill health, in November 1944) with this conviction unchanged. This after years of battling Japanese, German and Italian duplicity and aggression in the 1930s, followed by six years of global warfare, four of which actively included the United States.

Those ideals, and Mr. Hull's audacity in carrying them into effect upon taking office, remain relevant today. Are these times difficult and dangerous for the United States? Of course. But ideals that must be thrown out the window in time of danger are sad ideals indeed. In the long run it is still true, a> Ben Franklin had it long ago, that honesty is the best policy. Not only best *morally* but in practice. As Mr. Hull's career testifies.

## Bangor Daily News
*Bangor, ME, August 4, 1987*

Much of the Iran-Contra controversy boils down to the issue of who do you trust. The Reagan administration didn't trust congressmen charged with keeping track of covert activities. Meanwhile, congressmen believe they have a stake in keeping track of what the administration is up to. Currently, a vaguely worded law requires "timely" notification of Congress on such matters.

While congressmen and administration officials point the finger concerning who does the most leaking of classified information, at least one study indicates that the executive branch wins the loose-lip prize hands down. The man on the street can take whichever side he trusts the most, but he also should concede that leaks have their place.

It was John F. Kennedy who said he wished someone had leaked information about the abortive Bay of Pigs invasion before it was launched, so that that debacle might never have happened. Likewise, if somebody had planted a timely leak about the Iranian arms deal before it happened, that outrageous gesture might never have sent the Reagan administration into a tailspin.

There's a good reason why Edmund Burke called the press the Fourth Estate, and why Jefferson said that if forced to make a choice between government and press, he would choose to preserve the latter. Leaks of information can provide a rein on bad government by stimulating the action of the ultimate tribunal in a democracy, the people.

Congress and the president must attempt to pick up the pieces now that the Iran-Contra scandal is winding down by establishing an atmosphere of trust, to the extent that is possible within this volatile arena of power sharing. The issues are old, and so are the solutions.

The solution this time is not new laws. For example, a mandate that the president inform key congressional leaders of covert activity within 48 hours sounds too rigid. Besides, according to the lead actors in the Iran-Contra drama, it wouldn't have prevented the scandal: They claim the president wasn't aware of their activities.

The answer? Both sides must plug up their leaks, purge themselves of their self-righteous loose cannons, and turn to open communications. Congressmen who are entrusted with secrets of state must be respected national leaders, and they in turn should let the executive branch function as only it can.

It's a matter of trust.

## The Dallas Morning News
*Dallas, TX, August 5, 1987*

The Iran/contra hearings are now a footnote to history. But what has been learned from the 29 witnesses and 250,000 pages of testimony that was generated by this three-month session? The foremost question has been answered to the public's satisfaction. President Reagan had no direct knowledge of the illegal diversion of arms to the Nicaraguan contras.

If the aim of the Democrats involved in the hearings was to embarrass the president, they failed. But that is not to say that the president emerged unscathed; his image has been tarnished. And there is little doubt that in choosing the next president, the public will seek candidates exhibiting strength where Reagan proved weakest: a management style that demands accountability from subordinates.

The hearings also pointed out flaws in our foreign policy apparatus that invited abuse. Congress vacillated on aid to the contras, an issue of vital importance to U.S. interests in Central America, and exhibited an inability to keep secrets. This prompted the National Security Council to overstep its legal mandate — and competency — in fashioning the ill-fated Iran/contra affair.

The National Security Council must bear the lion's share of the blame for conducting a foolhardy policy that involved deception at the highest levels of government and a reckless disregard for the rule of law. The most damaging element in the affair was the use of covert action as a means of circumventing the checks and balances that inject sound judgment into difficult policy decisions. It is an open question whether public confidence in the government's ability to properly employ covert action in crisis situations will be repaired.

These hearings also scrutinized and measured the durability of our democratic values. Events already may have proved former National Security Adviser John Poindexter and media hero Oliver North wrong. Their narrow-sighted strategy to win the release of American hostages by selling arms to Iran encouraged the terrorists to seize even more hostages. And the 3,300 TOWs and 50 Hawk anti-aircraft missiles which they illegally sold to Iran fortified the forces that now are menacing U.S. escort ships in the Persian Gulf.

The hearings should act as a reminder that circumventing the law is a shortcut that will backfire sooner or later.

## The Register-Guard
*Eugene, OR, August 5, 1987*

Forty days of public testimony before Senate and House committees filled in the details of what was already known or suspected about the Iran-Contra affair but yielded few earthshaking revelations. Yet the hearings were a valuable use of the committees' and the nation's time. The sale of arms to Iran and the diversion of profits to the Contras was an ill-conceived and unaccountable venture that demanded the thorough ventilation it received.

At the heart of the affair was a secret foreign policy-making group that answered to no one but itself — not to the Congress, not to the Cabinet, not even to the President. The existence of the group and the outlines of its operations were revealed last fall and examined in the Tower Commission report. But only public hearings like those that concluded Monday could have exposed the intricacies of the group's activities and opened an informed public debate on their consequences.

Congress deserves credit for its conduct of the hearings. Combining the House and Senate committees into a joint panel was a major and underappreciated achievement, one that prevented an intramural competition for public attention that would have dragged on through the summer. The committees' chairmen, Sen. Daniel Inouye, D-Hawaii, and Congressman Lee Hamilton, D-Ind., showed commendable restraint, even when witnesses challenged Congress' judgment and trustworthiness. They and the committees' leading Republican members preserved a remarkable degree of bipartisanship through most of the stormy sessions.

President Reagan both gained and lost as a result of the hearings. No "smoking gun" that might have threatened his presidency was found in his desk drawer. But the testimony was damaging nonetheless. Reagan should have known more than he did about the initiatives being launched in his administration's name. The President should be angry and alarmed at having been kept in the dark by subordinates, and he should express his feeling strongly when he addresses the nation next week.

The scorecard is similarly mixed for other current and former administration officials. Secretary of State George Shultz and Defense Secretary Caspar Weinberger came across as loyal, seasoned but ultimately unsuccessful voices of reason on the Iran arms sales. Adm. John Poindexter emerged as an arrogant man with a selective memory who thought he knew without asking what was best for Reagan. Attorney General Edwin Meese was shown to be the sleepiest of watchdogs. Lt. Col. Oliver North starred as a daring operative who valued results more than constitutional processes. And the late CIA Director William Casey, with his passion for intrigue and skill at infighting, remains a mysterious figure.

Attention will now shift to Lawrence Walsh, the independent counsel investigating the Iran-Contra affair. He may file criminal charges against some of the characters in the drama — charges that could include conspiracy, obstruction of justice and violations of laws limiting arms exports and aid to the Contras. Any prosecutions would, of course, open a new and controversial chapter in the story.

Also still to come is the committees' final report, based on the public testimony of 29 witnesses, 500 private interviews and 250,000 pages of documents. But the close of the hearings marks the passing of the climactic event in the drama. Though some questions may never be answered, it is now reasonably clear who did what and who knew about it. That's what the American people needed to find out, and the hearings served that purpose well.

## The Courier-Journal & Times
*Louisville, KY, August 4, 1987*

WHATEVER the Iran-*contra* hearings disclosed about recklessness and obsessive secrecy in the White House, they haven't made a conclusive case either for or against U. S. help for the Nicaraguan rebels. The question of *contra* aid still confronts Congress, no matter how much some lawmakers would prefer to duck it.

What, then, should be done? Public opinion provides no clearcut answer. Polls conducted shortly after Oliver North's testimony last month showed increased support for the *contras*, but more Americans still oppose U. S. aid to President Reagan's "freedom fighters."

Nor has the situation inside Nicaragua changed much. The *contras* escalated the fighting but still lack broad support. Except for a few *contra* leaders, almost no one is predicting the guerrillas can topple the Sandinista government in Managua — even with U. S. aid.

Some Reagan administration supporters argue that the *contras* don't need to win on the battlefield. It's enough that they bleed the Nicaraguan economy and force the Sandinistas to give up whatever dream they may have had of fueling revolution in Central America.

This argument cannot be lightly dismissed. The *contra* war has undermined support for the Sandinistas. Many reports indicate that the Nicaraguan people are growing war-weary. And the Sandinistas are too busy defending themselves to help Marxist rebels in El Salvador.

Nevertheless, there is no indication the Nicaraguan economy and government are about to collapse. And the longer the war grinds on, the more likely it becomes that the Sandinistas will launch major strikes at *contra* sanctuaries in Honduras and Costa Rica. That, in turn, would increase the risk of direct U. S. intervention.

Meanwhile, support for the *contras* is hurting the United States in Latin America and Europe in much the same way Soviet occupation of Afghanistan has tarnished Moscow's image in Moslem lands.

Finally, there is the moral question. While the Sandinista regime is in some ways as repressive as the Somoza dictatorship it replaced, how can the United States justify supporting forces that murder, rape and terrorize the very people to whom we claim to want to bring the blessings of democracy?

This dirty war isn't necessary to protect U. S. security. It isn't necessary to protect our friends in Central America and may even increase their danger. The sooner Congress pulls the plug on the *contras*, the better.

# The Idaho STATESMAN

Boise ID, August 6, 1987

As the Summer of Irangate fades into history, Americans who watched the drama unfold have to be wondering what the congressional hearings accomplished.

Besides giving the country an unpleasant picture of an administration run from the bottom up, the hearings presented a televised textbook on civics. In this bicentennial year of the Constitution, Americans received a 41-day lesson in what it's all about.

In this school put on by Congress and beamed into millions of living rooms and offices across the country, we learned that President Reagan, intent on springing American hostages, illegally sold weapons to Iranian zealots.

As for the diversion of arms profits to the Nicaraguan contras, we learned that the smoking gun was held by an underling; the president apparently did not know or approve of the decision.

But he did, according to former National Security Adviser Robert McFarlane, instruct his staff in 1984 to find ways around a congressional ban on aid to the contras.

They did, all right.

We watched this congressional classroom with a keen interest in the players. Who was believable; who wasn't? Who were the guilty; who were the innocent?

No one emerged very clean. Lt. Col. Oliver North made himself an American hero by testifying that he lied to Congress and shredded government documents to cover his trail. Assistant Secretary of State Elliot Abrams acknowledged misleading Congress about soliciting aid for the contras. Former CIA chief lawyer Stanley Sporkin prepared a presidential authorization of the arms-for-hostage deal after it was already underway.

Former National Security Adviser John Poindexter took it upon himself to set foreign policy by approving the diversion of funds to the contras.

Secretary of State George Shultz tried to talk the president out of trading arms for hostages. So did Secretary of Defense Caspar Weinberger and former Chief of Staff Donald Regan. None, however, punctuated their objections with a resignation.

And the man who sits where the buck once stopped? Can he, with any pride, be content to assert that he didn't know what was going on within his administration?

Irangate was not a miniseries of villains and heroes, but a disturbing look at what happens when men and causes are allowed to supercede the law.

It was a scandal because people given a trust acted outside the law. A constitutionally set process was ignored, lied to, misled and circumvented. What we should have learned this summer, once again, is that we are a nation of laws and that no one is above them.

# The Charlotte Observer

Charlotte, NC, August 7, 1987

Now that hearings have ended, Congress's select committees investigating the Iran-contra affair have retired to write a report on their findings and consider whether legislation is needed to prevent similar scandals in the future.

While most errors revealed in the hearings resulted from poor judgment or the misplaced loyalty of a few presidential assistants, the findings indicate a need for tighter regulation. At least three recommendations come to mind, all intended to strengthen constitutional government.

First, Congress needs to clarify the rules under which covert operations are conducted in the name of the American people. Given today's geopolitics, some covert activity is essential to national security. But the American people cannot allow any agency with the imagination to do so to foment covert activity against a foreign government.

Such activities should be limited to agencies that can be held accountable. In the past, covert activities have been a function of the Central Intelligence Agency, which had to get special permission to engage in such missions and to report them to Congress. The law should be amended to restrict such action to the CIA and prohibit it anywhere else.

Covert activity by the National Security Council, a White House agency created to advise the president, should not be tolerated. In fact, the National Security Council should be denied *any* operational functions. The NSC should stick to analytical and advisory functions.

Second, the procedure for informing Congress of covert activities needs tightening. At present, covert actions must be reported to intelligence committees in both the House and the Senate. Evidence in the Iran-contra hearings suggests that involving too many people weakens security — not so much because of a history of leaks from Congress as because of executive branch *fear* of leaks from Congress. Perhaps the two committees should be collapsed into a joint committee whose membership would be limited to a handful of the most trusted members of Congress. That would fill the need for accountability, yet protect the secrecy of covert action.

Finally, Congress should consider requiring the national security adviser to be confirmed by the Senate, as are other key presidential appointees. Since its creation, the office of the national security adviser has caused friction within the executive branch and confused foreign governments about U.S. intentions. National security advisers not only advise presidents, they also deal directly with foreign nations, in the name of the American people. Giving the people's representatives a voice in examining their views and confirming their appointments might impress upon national security advisers that they are accountable to the people, not just the president.

# The Miami Herald

Miami, FL, August 7, 1987

**T**HOUGH public testimony before the Iran-*contra* committees ended this week, closed sessions on sensitive information continue. The secret testimony, the conflicting versions of who did what on whose authority, and the destruction of documents means, in the words of Chairman Daniel Inouye, Democratic senator from Hawaii, that "We may never know, with precision and truth, why it ever happened."

"It" is the Reagan Administration's secret sales of weapons to Iran in exchange for hostages in contradiction of U.S. policy, and the diversion of some profits to the *contras* in Nicaragua when U.S. law forbade direct aid. Some say that the hearings haven't accomplished much, that they only reiterated what the Administration revealed when it went public on Iranscam in November 1986. Not true.

The hearings met their purpose. They established a public record of how policies so antithetical to the people's will came about without Congress's advice and consent.

The U.S. Government's policy-making mechanism is by nature one of tension because the Constitution makes the Executive and Legislative branches share power. The Founding Fathers knew that giving one branch, such as the Executive, sole power to decide domestic and foreign policy would create a tyranny. The President formulates policy but needs the purse and therefore the consent of Congress to implement it.

It is natural for a President to want to lead according to his views. It is as normal for Congress to be reluctant to yield its ability to constrain unwise policy. The tug-of-war between two powers is kept in balance by the Constitutional checks on each.

The committees' final report is due after the Labor Day recess, giving time to ponder this system. Imperfect? Yes, but it works to the country's advantage most of the time when *both* branches heed the Constitution. In Iranscam, the Administration did not.

Perhaps, despite all the testimony, the full truth is beyond knowing. But, almost coincidentally, the hearings emphasize that, in the Constitution's 200th year, its ability to balance still endures.

# The Washington Post
### Washington, DC, August 5, 1987

NOW THAT PEOPLE in Washington are being retrained for life without the televized Iran-contra hearings, taking crafts classes in the afternoons or possibly getting reacquainted with their office routine, the grim conclusions are pouring forth. What was all that about? it is asked rhetorically, or sort of rhetorically, since the implied answer is: not very much. Some are afraid the culprits got away with too much, that they snookered theamericanpeople (this became one word, totally stuck together, fairly early in the proceedings and applied to all American people not in the room who shared one's point of view). Others assert, in the booming, resonant voice you use when you're not so sure, that all has been explained and that all have been proved innocent, including of course the guilty who were only guilty of an extravagant love of country or an admirable excess of loyalty to the boss.

But surely theamericanpeople and a few others as well know what those hearings were about. Yes, as it is pretty much with all our politics, the event itself seemed to be made up in equal parts of serious endeavor and shameless play. But what emerged was clear: deepened evidence of and insight into a gigantic and persisted-in political mistake (the Iran hornswoggle) and a subconspiracy by incompetent dolts to run a private government, answerable to no one, on the side—and to cheat and trim and lie when their activities began to become known. Now some of the parties are accusing one another of being the one that doctored the documents or suggested the cover-up, but we do certainly know that there was such activity and that in some degree, anyway, there still is. We know the latter from, among other things, the night-and-day contradictions between certain witnesses' testimony. So, of course the public hearings did not answer all the questions. But they did confirm the outlines of what was suspected and provisionally known.

The ironies—so large and weird they are almost impossible to assimilate—abide. Israel, for example, whom the Iranians affect to abominate above all others—except, perhaps, us and Saddam Hussein—was deeply engaged in the arms dealings with the ayatollah's gang and an encour-

ager of and partner in our debacle. Here at home, more recently, there is another savage irony: the pathetic efforts of the titans of law and order to extenuate and excuse the lying and cheating and other sharp practice of those in and around the administration who were caught out. The arguments become hilarious, as the defenders of men who bent the Reagan administration out of shape with their misguided plots, their deceptions and their destruction of documents fall back on what they would, in other circumstances, denounce as "permissiveness" toward lawbreakers or "situational ethics" as alibi. Those poor fellows wouldn't have had to sneak around so much and violate the law if the law had not been there in the first place, we are accusingly told. We should understand how frustrated they were and how they had to act in secrecy because otherwise they couldn't have done the dingbat things they were doing. We should understand that the money raised for the contras is . . . well . . . somewhere. We should understand (this was the attorney general's stunning contribution) that all those government papers Oliver North reduced to a fine dice in his busy Cuisinart—five hours of shredding—may not have been relevant to the Iran-contra diversion . . . who is to say, since these documents are no more?

But finally the supreme irony and an especially mean one is that within much of Ronald Reagan's constituency and among many who think they are doing him a service, the particular men who have done him more political damage than the Democrats could ever have begun to are being lionized. Whether he led them or merely allowed them do this damage and whether by direction or default is almost beside the point. The damage has been done, and it is not only to Mr. Reagan's political standing and interests but also to the country's standing and interests overseas. We have never held with those who wanted Ronald Reagan to abase himself, to "apologize" for what happened. We think most people probably feel that way. The truth is that there is no satisfactory conclusion to this affair possible any longer. What is wanted is simply an acknowledgment, a sign that the president knows what has been brought about by these men and what was wrong with it.

# News-Tribune & Herald
### Duluth, MN, August 13, 1987

Just as sure as Duluthians will feel a nip in the air one of these days, someone will point to the $4 million-plus cost of the Iran-contra hearings as proof they were a mistake. After all, only $3.5 million in Iran arms sales profits were diverted to contra rebels in Nicaragua.

But such arithmetic compares apples and oranges — and fails to get at the purpose of the hearings. They were, after all, not held to track down improper uses of public money.

Though they focused at times on the money trail, the hearings were about a secret foreign policy, flawed accountability, executive branch distrust and similar big-picture topics — none of which can be measured in dollars.

Actually, figures given Wednesday by federal officials show examples of frugality we hadn't expected from a federal operation.

John W. Nields Jr., chief House counsel, was paid $51,000 for the first seven months

of 1987, while Senate counsel Arthur Liman is to get about $60,000 for his work through the end of October. Anyone who's priced — let alone paid — an attorney from a top law firm knows those salaries are a bargain.

And officials said plywood used to remodel the hearing room had earlier been used as a temporary fence for a Senate Office Building project several years ago. Now that is parsimony beyond what most of us expect when we send tax dollars to Washington.

We don't cry as the criminal justice system spends thousands of dollars to investigate, try and jail someone for a $300 stickup. It's a price paid to encourage obedience to the law.

And such hearings are a price a democratic society pays to inform its citizens, to encourage obedience to the law by government officials and to keep fine-tuning our 200-year-old experiment in good government.

# FORT WORTH STAR-TELEGRAM
### Fort worth, TX August 6, 1987

Through the pain and passion of the Iran-contra hearings, Americans should have learned some things about themselves and about the risks of placing their trust in men rather than in democratic institutions and constitutional requisites.

The hearings were important because they were broader than Independent Counsel Lawrence Walsh's inquiry into possible criminal conduct. They aired fundamental issues of responsibility and accountability that go beyond contra aid or trading arms for hostages, and they did it out in the open.

The airing may prove more important than any legislation that results. Surely the American public is capable of recognizing the stark contrast between the secrecy (withholding information from the American people and even from the highest government officials) espoused by Adm. John Poindexter and Lt. Col. Oliver North and the let-the-people-know openness of the hearings — an openness supported by even the president.

From a substantive standpoint, the public hearings expanded upon the Tower Commission's portrait of a presidency remote from the details of policy and of misused government agencies.

The framework of what happened, and how, and why, has now been presented from the viewpoints of those who overstepped their authority and those whose authority was ignored in the process.

Clearly, despite the fad popularity of North, very little glory was uncovered. Clearly, an ill-advised secret policy went awry and was abused. Clearly, the lines between intelligence analysis and policymaking were obscured. Clearly, the channels of legal process, statutory oversight and democratic accountability were evaded. Clearly, a confused and poorly counseled president allowed lower-level staff members to assume national policy responsibilities that should reside with the president alone.

As a result of the hearings, the American public should better understand the dangers of power exercised without accountability and of creating policy without either consensus or proper foundation.

These bitterly learned lessons can be used in the near future.

America faces another presidential election in 15 months and has some new questions to ask of candidates in that election: What style of leadership will they provide? How deep is their dedication to accountable government? What measures would they employ to safeguard against abuses of delegated power?

America still doesn't have all the answers. But if America has learned the right questions, the hearings will have been worth the anguish.

## Reagan Responds to Hearings in Brief Speech

In a nationally broadcast address August 12, 1987, President Reagan asserted that he "was stubborn in pursuit of a policy that went astray" in selling arms to Iran. The address was Reagan's response to the recently concluded House and Senate hearings on the Iran-contra arms scandal. Reagan's speech was conciliatory in tone, but he went no further in accepting responsibility for the scandal than he had in his previous statements. He said that the first contacts with Iran were purely diplomatic but that they "rapidly got all tangled up in the sale of arms, and the sale of arms got tangled up with the hostages." He said his "preoccupation with the hostages" had influenced his decision to go ahead with the arms deals, adding, "This was a mistake." Reagan's assertion that arms and hostages over time "got tangled up" in a purely diplomatic initiative differed sharply from the testimony the committees heard. Most of the witnesses said that the deal was arms-for-hostages from the very beginning.

During the hearings, which lasted from May through July, Reagan had refused comment on the scandal but promised that "you won't be able to shut me up" after the hearings ended. The speech was Reagan's third on the scandal since November 1986, and he had also held two press conferences since then. The latest speech lasted 15 minutes but only half of it was devoted to discussion of the scandal. In the second half of his speech, Reagan recounted his agenda for the remaining 17 months of his term, which included winning confirmation for Robert Bork as a Supreme Court justice, reaching an arms-control pact with the Soviet Union, amending the U.S. Constitution to mandate a balanced budget and stemming communism in Central America.

## The Hutchinson News

*Hutchinson, KS*
*August 14, 1987*

Ronald Reagan still doesn't understand.

After all the lies and stupidity that have slithered from the slimy rocks around him, President Reagan now can only go on sterile television to declare there is nothing he can say "to make the situation right." And that the buck really does stop with him.

Of course the buck stops with him.

Nobody, other than the forgetful Adm. John Poindexter, ever thought otherwise. But what has Ronald Reagan done to show that he understands what the noise was about, or what he did wrong? He has done little.

There is a great deal he could do "to make the situation right."

1. He could say his fundamental decision was wrong. His decision, not somebody else's decision. His reversal of foreign policy and perversion of the truth did not, as he claimed, get "all tangled up" by some mischance of history.

The tooth fairy wasn't involved. The idea of trading arms to one of the world's most heinous collection of thugs was deliberately put in motion by Ronald Reagan, and Ronald Reagan alone.

2. He could say Oliver North is not one of America's greatest heroes. Lt. Col. North is still bemedaled with President Reagan's commendation of heroic stature, though the colonel has been unmasked as a liar, a thief and an officer eager to provide more arms to thugs who previously slaughtered his fellow Marines.

3. He could order courts-martial for the men whom he accuses of betraying him. He should. If he's as "mad as a hornet," as he claims, what's holding him up? Why is John Poindexter still an admiral instead of seaman recruit, or Oliver North still a lieutenant colonel instead of a private?

An error is understandable. Learning from the error should be expected.

But before there can be any learning from an error, the error itself must be recognized for what it was.

## THE SUN

*Baltimore, MD, August 14, 1987*

White House Chief of Staff Howard Baker reflected on President Reagan's speech this way: "Did he put Iran-contra behind him? I'd guess not. But this is certainly not the last word the president will ever say on the subject." We hope it's not the last word. After promising for weeks that once the hearings were over, "you won't be able to shut me up," the president was curiously close-mouthed in his speech. By our stopwatch he only devoted six minutes and five seconds to Iran-contra.

It wasn't six minutes that indicated the president has been paying attention to the hearings or the reaction to them. He still can't bring himself to face the facts. He still would have the nation believe this was a policy of establishing relations with receptive Iranian moderates.

Wednesday night he said, "Secretary [of State George] Shultz and Secretary [of Defense Caspar] Weinberger both predicted that the American people would immediately assume the whole plan was an arms for hostages deal and nothing more." He implied this was their only objection. But Mr. Shultz testified on the Hill, "I felt underneath it *was* arms for hostages." And Mr. Weinberger testified, "We simply cannot deal with people like that [the Iranians]."

The president displayed a dismaying lack of outrage at usurpation of his authority by underlings. He said, "I've been as mad as a hornet." But there was no evidence of anger when he said of

the illegal funds diversion to the contras: "Colonel [Oliver] North and Admiral [John] Poindexter believed they were doing what I would've wanted done"; and, "The admiral testified he wanted to protect me, yet no president ever should be protected from the truth." Very low key and tolerant. This from the man who, when a debate manager usurped his authority, blew his stack on camera, and the public loved him for it.

During the course of the congressional hearings, questions about the late Director of Central Intelligence William Casey's role in planning and managing the diversion of funds were raised but not answered. So were questions about the investigation by Attorney General Edwin Meese. So were questions about the nature of presidential access to information. These are questions the president should deal with in public.

The best way to open up would be to have a press conference. There have been only two in the 10 months since this story broke. That is disgraceful. If the prime minister of Great Britain were in the midst of a crisis of public opinion like this, she would be answering questions of opposition party members in public almost daily. No president has ever shied away from the press to the degree Mr. Reagan has in 1987. A press conference may not supply the last word on Iran-contra, but it would certainly answer a lot more of the public's questions than speeches like Wednesday's ever will.

## Minneapolis Star and Tribune
*Minneapolis, MN*
*August 14, 1987*

In accepting responsibility Wednesday night for the Iran-contra fiasco, President Reagan has done what every chief executive must be ready to do: He has taken the rap for the blunders of his underlings. But Reagan treated the affair as an unpleasant incident rather than the scandal that it was. Little in his mea culpa showed the reflection and repudiation that were due.

Reagan explained the secret sale of weapons to Iran as a consequence of his stubborn pursuit of a "policy that went astray." But that defense skirts the embarrassing fact that the "policy" in question was an arms-for-hostages swap — a deal the president authorized, then denied or forgot, and only grudgingly admits. Whether born of stubbornness or sloppiness, the ransom deal compromised U.S. credibility and encouraged kidnapping.

But Reagan still seems not to appreciate those consequences, just as he continues to minimize the seriousness of the scheme to prop up the Nicaraguan contras. He said he should have been told about the funneling of arms-sale profits to the rebels. But that detail should not foreclose a presidential assessment of his own role in encouraging subordinates to find a way around the Boland Amendment. Americans deserve to know what Reagan thinks about the implications of the Iran-contra conspiracy: for the rule of law, for the relationship between the executive and Congress for public confidence in government.

Conspicuously absent from the president's speech was an explicit condemnation of his subordinates' errors. And he did not say whether he would have approved of the diversion of money to the contras. In declining to denounce that lawlessness and folly, Reagan leaves the false impression that it is excusable. And in opting to forgo a forthright apology, the president suggests that his assumption of responsibility is a mere formality.

Though the president on Wednesday omitted much that should have been said, his actions the previous week are encouraging. He alluded to them in his speech: a vow to mend fences on Capitol Hill, to work for a settlement in Nicaragua and to pursue a U.S.-Soviet arms treaty. All reflect an admirable resolve to reclaim lost respect and political ground. Those steps could go far toward mending the damage inflicted by the Iran-contra affair.

## The Boston Globe
*Boston, MA, August 14, 1987*

President Reagan, still a master of words, used many of them properly Wednesday night. He took the buck away from Admiral Poindexter's desk and placed it on his own, where it belongs. The most important thing he did was reassert his authority and responsibility. In some countries, this task is accomplished through force of arms. In this democracy, the president's words do the job.

Yet words failed Reagan when, in describing the heart of this crisis of authority, he lapsed into the subjunctive mood. "Colonel North and Admiral Poindexter believed they were doing what I would've wanted done," he said. But Reagan, even at this point, did not specify whether he would have supported the diversion of the arms-sales profits to the contras.

An old poetic lament states that "of all sad words of tongue or pen, the saddest are these: It might have been!" This regret also applies to "should," "could" and "would."

The president's speech was not an apology nor even an explanation. Why did his "preoccupation with the hostages" make him blind to his own responsibilities? How could he make thunderous declarations about "terrorist states" while shipping arms to the most terroristic regime of all, in Iran? He never explained.

In the more upbeat, forward-looking part of the speech, Reagan promised that any covert operation in the future "must be legal, and it must meet a specific policy objective." Yet just last week he had suggested no illegalities were involved in the arms transfers, a speculative legal point of view that no one else in Washington seems to share. If nothing was illegal, why promise that future operations will be legal? He did not explain.

This speech could be code-named "Operation Legality" in the style of one of former President Nixon's initiatives during the Watergate scandal. In the 1970s, the Nixon White House launched with a solemn, straight face "Operation Candor," as though candor were a novel notion that deserved an occasional try.

The response to the president, from Democratic Sen. George Mitchell of Maine, was low-key, but did not shrink from pointing out that the scandal was not just in the execution of the policies, but was the policies themselves, which were the president's. This is not a bookkeeping error, Mitchell seemed to be saying.

Several networks Wednesday night identified Mitchell's speech as the "Democratic Party reply." This is incorrect. It was the Democratic *congressional* response. Paul Kirk, chairman of the Democratic National Committee, does not choose the speaker. The leadership of the House and Senate do because they share a constitutional duty to deal with the president. As Reagan said Wednesday night on another matter, lobbying for an unlikely constitutional amendment, "Only the Constitution – the document from which all government power flows, the document that provides our moral authority as a nation – only the Constitution can compel responsibility."

The constitutional process has been compelling responsibility from Reagan. The process involves hearings being held by Congress and an investigation being conducted by a special prosecutor. As these enterprises continue, it seems unlikely that Reagan understood or will ever understand that process.

The buck-stops-here message sounded like a slogan. When Reagan reported the opposition of Secretaries Shultz and Weinberger, it was in the context of their prediction of disaster – not a formal note of opposition but rather like an office betting pool. Why did the president ignore these two senior Cabinet officers? He did not explain.

The president is off on vacation now, and the speech seems to mark his last word on this crisis of authority. He wandered in and out of the subjunctive mood and used some words that were half apology and half explanation, but the truest words he spoke were addressed to the Americans who elected him. "I respect you too much to make excuses," he said. "The fact of the matter is that there's nothing I can say that will make the situation right."

## MILWAUKEE SENTINEL
*Milwaukee, WI,*
*August 14, 1987*

"The image — the reality — of Americans in chains, deprived of their freedom and families so far from home, burdened my thoughts."

With those words Wednesday night, President Reagan gave the nation the most plausible explanation for his approval of the sale of arms to Iran.

While Reagan seemed intent on making it clear that he did not know of the subsequent diversion of some of the proceeds from those sales to the Nicaraguan contras, history probably will record the actual decision to transfer arms to Iran as his most colossal blunder.

The president, obviously, would have been better off had he made this statement earlier rather than trying to obscure the real reason for the arms sales. But his admission now that it was a mistake of the heart, so to speak, takes some of the onus out of that act.

Post-speech critics noted that while Reagan accepted accountability for the fund diversion as a presidential responsibility, he did not say what he would have done had he known of the fund transfer. But Reagan has enough to answer for without speculating on what he might have done.

Indeed, anyone who followed the events since the disclosure of the arms sales could recite a litany of legitimate questions that remain unanswered. But the president may have responded to all when he said: "The fact of the matter is that there's nothing I can say that will make the situation right." Such an admission by a president certainly must be unprecedented.

Whether the president can follow his intention to focus on his agenda for the rest of his term — including an arms-control agreement with the Soviets and Central American peace — depends on the support he will be given by Congress.

"We need to find a way to cooperate while realizing foreign policy can't be run by committee," Reagan said, striking right at an issue that was near the heart of the Iran-contra controversy. Significantly, Sen. George Mitchell (D-Maine) speaking for the Democrats, welcomed the offer of cooperation.

A good start would be for the congressional leadership and the president to reach a meeting of minds on US policy in the Persian Gulf.

## THE ATLANTA CONSTITUTION
*Atlanta, GA, August 14, 1987*

The man who explained what he himself called "the Iran-contra mess" was a sadder Ronald Reagan. The jury is still out on the question of whether he's wiser.

Oh, there were glimmerings that he may be. He struck an appropriate tone of regret, without apologizing. He admitted a policy misjudgment and owned up to the sin of stubbornness. He acknowledged that he was accountable for the mistakes of his subordinates as well as his own. He took vigorous exception with Rear Adm. John Poindexter's contention the president could be kept in the dark so as to be insulated from political embarrassments. He ticked off a series of commendable steps he's taken to improve decision-making and restore a bond of trust between the White House and Capitol Hill. All to the good.

But the president would be kidding himself if he thought the Iranamok stain had been thoroughly rubbed out with just six minutes' worth of his speechwriters' elbow grease. On that score, it's good to hear White House Chief of Staff Howard Baker concede a day later that his boss hasn't heard the last of the affair and to promise that the American public has not heard the final, definitive word from Reagan.

That's a relief. And not because critics of the president want to gloat over his discomfort and gum up his agenda, either.

However much thought and polish went into the president's speech, it was so brief that it left thoughtful Americans wondering:

• Doesn't Reagan realize, even in retrospect, that the simple act of selling arms to Iran, whether to retrieve hostages or to improve relations, was a terrible mistake, one that was compounded again and again by efforts sanctioned by him to buy off the Iran-associated abductors in Lebanon?

• Though his aides have rebutted Poindexter's claim that the president would have approved an unquestionable impropriety — the diversion of Iranian arms profits to the contras — doesn't he see the necessity to speak to that issue himself?

• While it would be imprudent, legally, for him to comment specifically on the evasive actions taken by his subordinates, Poindexter and Oliver North in particular, doesn't he have any general misgivings about lying to duly constituted government bodies and the destruction of official files?

• Isn't it possible — taking national security considerations into account, of course — to shed light now on former CIA Director William Casey's part in this drama?

• Finally, perhaps most intriguingly, since the president spoke only in the most general terms about the whole Iran-contra business making him at times as "mad as a hornet," what was it precisely that made him angry? The answer to that question might be as good a clue as any as to what wisdom he has gleaned from Iranamok.

# THE TENNESSEAN
*Nashville, TN, August 14, 1987*

FOR months President Ronald Reagan promised to comment fully on the Iran-contra scandal once the hearings were finished, but Wednesday night he said little more than he had last March.

He said he would be shouting from the rooftops, but it was more a murmur from the front porch. It was bland. He devoted less than half his speech to the Iran-contra affair and then turned to other things. What he did say about the arms deal seemed to be recycled from earlier comments.

He accepted responsibility, but had no apologies for the sale of arms to Iran. "I let my preoccupation with the hostages intrude into areas where it didn't belong," he said. "This was a mistake."

He reiterated his past statements that he didn't know of the fund diversion to the contras. He took a swipe at his former National Security Council aide. "Yet the buck does not stop with Adm. [John] Poindexter, as he stated in his testimony," Mr. Reagan said, "it stops with me." He said that no operation is so secret it must be kept from the commander in chief. "I had the right, the obligation, to make my own decision."

But Mr. Reagan offered no clue as to what his own decision might have been. He offered no suggestion as to which individuals in his administration were to blame for errant policies. He didn't touch on why he failed to ask Mr. Poindexter or Mr. Oliver North what was going on, up to the day one was fired and the other allowed to resign.

In fact his speech seemed to be a studied effort to get the Iran-contra affair behind him, so the less said the better. Yet Mr. Reagan is well aware that the polls show most Americans don't believe he is telling the full truth. The latest poll put that finding at nearly 60%.

He made indirect reference to that by saying, "These past nine months have been confusing and painful ones for the country. I know you have doubts in your own minds about what happened in this whole episode."

The last nine months have been painful to Mr. Reagan. He has clearly aged in that time when his administration has been brought to a low point. Unfortunately, his speech didn't erase the doubts in the minds of most, nor did it slam the door on a controversy that will still linger hauntingly to underscore his lame duck status. ∎

## THE CHRISTIAN SCIENCE MONITOR
*Boston, MA, August 14, 1987*

PRESIDENT Reagan made more than half a turn in the right direction Wednesday night in acknowledging his administration's mistakes in the Iran-contra affair, and in taking direct responsibility for what went wrong.

Recovering full confidence with the public and allies must wait on the proven sensibleness of future action, as the President and his advisers themselves admit.

Nothing the President might say now can stop a wider process of evaluation and correction going on in the special prosecutor's office, congressional committees, Central Intelligence Agency – in every government office touched by the Iran-contra scandal.

"I was stubborn in my pursuit of a policy that went astray," the President said. This was an extraordinary admission in its first part: More than one top Reagan aide has broken his pick trying to change the President's mind.

The second part was mistaken. For a policy to go astray would imply that it started out aright. Mr. Reagan's arms sale to the Iranians was wrong from the beginning. What Mr. Reagan is still trying to say is that his intention was right, but that people and events messed up. Again, as pointed out by Sen. George Mitchell of Maine in the Democratic response, the problem lay not with people but with policy – and this is the buck that stops in the Oval Office.

Senator Mitchell also said that Americans, Democrat or Republican, want their presidents – this President – to succeed. The Democratic response was, like the President's own talk, constructive. Bygones won't be forgotten until fully aired and corrected. But a big democracy has a big plate of things to get on with. It would be as foolish for the President's opposition – Congress as an institution, not just the Democrats – to spend the next year quibbling over every Iran-contra inconsistency as for the President to think the whole affair will simply sink from sight.

In a democracy there is no one right side. In this democracy, the President cannot claim all right is his. He was elected decisively but still by a minority of Americans, with the greatest energy on his behalf coming from one wing of the political spectrum, the right. That wing is a permanent part of the American electorate. It will not be gone when Mr. Reagan is gone. It will have had two Reagan White House terms to test the market value of its beliefs about strength through arms, populist and conservative family values, the need to downsize the federal government, the Soviet threat, and so forth. It has had an effective champion in Mr. Reagan, but a champion nonetheless with his own Achilles' heel: A stubborn man in the White House can cause a lot of trouble.

Politics tends to exaggeration. It would make mythic figures of people who, like the rest of us, walk the earth without making it tremble.

Nothing has really changed in Americans' common-sense expectations for their presidents. They never expected a Harry Truman, for example, to increase his stature an inch or two. In a democracy, a few individuals rise for a while to run things and then rejoin the rest of the populace.

Strength is in the people. After Mr. Reagan's Wednesday speech, with 17 months to go in his second term, the people may be reassured that this President is seeing things more clearly.

## Wisconsin ▲ State Journal
*Madison, WI, August 13, 1987*

As expected, President Reagan didn't deliver a cascade of apologies for the Iran-Contra affair in his Wednesday night speech to the American public, but he did concede he's "ultimately accountable" for the misdeeds of his subordinates, and he served notice that he's anxious to focus on the future.

Is there any choice? For Reagan, certainly not. Even if his credibility had not been harmed by revelations that his administration violated its own no-deals-for-hostages rules, shipped arms to the pariah nation of Iran, lied to Congress and deceived even its own cabinet members, his time in office is running short.

This fall represents the last best chance for the Reagan White House to produce in some crucial areas — arms control, deficit reduction, trade reform, relations with Central America and the confirmation of Supreme Court nominee Robert Bork — because the new year will bring caucuses in Iowa, primaries in New Hampshire and a public focus on the 1988 campaign.

If Reagan isn't already a lame duck, hobbled by his administration's self-inflicted wounds, historical precedent indicates that his political powers will be greatly diminished in his administration's final year.

Let us hope that Reagan, who has never been accused of being anything less than a crafty politician, and one who is adept at compromise when he so chooses, returns from his California vacation in September ready to do business with Congress and the world.

That doesn't mean caving in to demands to balance the budget by tax increases or passing unwise protectionist trade bills, but it should mean searching for a realistic consensus on issues that directly affect most Americans.

Reagan's attempt to shift public attention away from the Iran-Contra mess will succeed only if people believe that the infamous "buck" has finally stopped and that the president has regained his grasp on reality.

With a little more than a year left in his second term, reality for Reagan means focusing on a few key problems and working toward solutions. Now that we're well into the fourth quarter, the "Gipper" will need to keep his head in the game.

## Honolulu Star-Bulletin
*Honolulu, HI, August 13, 1987*

President Reagan's speech last night was not intended to make any startling disclosures or admissions about the Iran-Contra fiasco. Rather, it was an attempt to put the mess behind him and get on with the business of leadership.

More significant than anything Reagan said about the scandal was this statement: "I have a year and a half before I have to clean out this desk. I'm not about to have the dust and the cobwebs settle on the furniture in this office, or on me." And he went on to list his main concerns for the final months of his presidency: the confirmation of Robert Bork to the Supreme Court, nuclear arms control, Central America and budget reform.

With that declaration the president touched on a serious problem. If the Iran-Contra disaster has left him incapable of effective leadership for the remainder of his term, that is bad news for all Americans.

Obviously Reagan is aware of the problem, and he says he refuses to lapse into passivity. But he's been politically bruised. His confidence is shaken. He has reportedly been depressed — understandably — by the death of Malcolm Baldrige and also by the difficulties of such close associates as Michael Deaver. Moreover, age finally seems to be catching up with him.

It won't be easy for Reagan to stage a comeback. But the president of the United States, whoever it may be, is the most powerful person in the world. To have that office occupied by a political cripple is not in the nation's interest, nor in the Free World's.

For everyone's sake, it's important that Reagan get off the floor and give a good account of himself until the final bell of his term.

# Woodward's Book on Casey's CIA Causes Storm

According to a new book, former Central Intelligence Agency Director William Casey had worked with Saudi Arabia in a bungled attempt to assassinate a Lebanese Moslem leader and had confessed from a hospital bed before his death to having known all along about the diversion of Iran arms sales profits to the Nicaraguan contra rebels. These were among the revelations in *Veil: The Secret Wars of the CIA, 1981-1987*, by investigative reporter Bob Woodward, assistant managing editor of the *Washington Post*. The book caused an immediate firestorm of controversy. Despite the heavy secrecy surrounding its publication, galleys of the book were obtained by *U.S. News & World Report*, which reported key details September 25, 1987. An article in the *Post* Sept. 26 summed up the book's findings, and the *Post* and other publications began running excerpts Sept. 27.

Woodward claimed his book was based on interviews with more than 250 people involved in gathering or using intelligence—including "more than four dozen substantive discussions or interviews" with Casey himself from 1983 to 1987—and hundreds of documents, notes and written materials provided by various sources. Casey had been well-known for his aversion to the press, and the fact that he had established a working relationship with one of the nation's premier investigative journalists startled government officials and other observers.

Of all Woodward's claims, Casey's alleged hospital-bed confession attracted the most attention, even though it played only a minor part at the end of the book. Woodward had used information gathered in the course of researching his book as a basis for a number of exclusive stories in the *Post*, but the Casey confession had not been previously revealed. The extent of Casey's knowledge of the fund diversion had been a key question of the scandal. Prior to his hospitalization for treatment of a brain tumor, Casey told congressional committees that he had first learned of the diversion in October 1986, shortly before the scandal exploded. However, Lt. Col. Oliver North testified that Casey had known of the diversion from the beginning, and a number of lawmakers had reached the same conclusion.

Woodward wrote that he had first tried to visit Casey in his Washington hospital room January 22, 1987 but was barred by CIA guards. He did not reveal details of how he allegedly gained admittance to Casey's room several days later. Woodward said he asked Casey if he had known of the contra diversion all along, and Casey nodded in reply. When asked why, Casey supposedly responded, "I believed. I believed," then fell asleep. He died of pneumonia May 6, 1987 on New York's Long Island.

Sophia Casey, widow of the ex-CIA chief, Sept. 27 denounced Woodward's account as a "lie," saying "he never got in to see my husband." She maintained that either she or her daughter was always at Casey's side, and that he had been incapable of conversation in any event. Woodward stood by his story.

## Minneapolis Star and Tribune

*Minneapolis, MN, October 6, 1987*

Elsewhere on this page columnist William Safire offers sound advice on evaluating "Veil: The Secret Wars of the CIA 1981-87," by Bob Woodward. Safire counsels: Read the full book, not the excerpts; remain skeptical about the finer details, and don't let the book's flaws obscure important lessons it offers about the Reagan administration and the U.S. intelligence community.

The most important lesson is the disquieting one articulated by Sen. Dave Durenberger: Casey has shown that "there are two people that can get away with 'murder' if they want to: One is the president, one is the (director of central intelligence.)"

The significant clause in Durenberger's statement is the last one: "if they want to." Casey obviously wanted to. He was not an evil man, but dangerous, so convinced of the rightness of his anti-Communist crusade that he ignored the laws and protocols of the nation he sought to serve. Casey thumbed his nose at Congress, laughed at the presidency and set about establishing his own foreign policy.

The nature of intelligence work, particularly its secrecy, automatically gives the director of central intelligence an opportunity to get away with murder — if he wants to. Casey has shown the importance of selecting directors who won't want to. Both Congress and the president failed with Casey.

Congress failed by accepting Casey as director of central intelligence despite misgivings and by failing to use its budgeting power to keep him in line. Reagan's failure was more serious. The president may not have sought to get away with murder himself, but was clearly pleased when Casey succeeded. Reagan and his top advisers carefully avoided hard questions about Casey's methods. They didn't want to know. Casey's goals were Reagan's goals.

But Casey's failures were also Reagan's failures. The most spectacular — the Iran-contra affair — has permanently crippled the Reagan presidency and played havoc with American foreign policy.

William Webster, the new CIA director, is undoubtedly every bit the patriot that Casey was. But Webster is a humbler man, a democrat less likely to ignore the rule of law. His appointment perhaps shows that Casey taught America to be wary of intelligence chiefs who do wish to get away with murder. Let that be Casey's enduring legacy.

The Honolulu Advertiser
*Honolulu, HI
October 3, 1987*

Various observers are right in saying that not enough attention is going to the content of Bob Woodward's new book on the CIA and too much is being made of the Washington Post editor's tactic of sneaking into a hospital for a deathbed interview with semi-conscious agency Director William Casey.

That is not a savory scene for most Americans, and the quality of Casey's "confession" is questionable, as Post editors and even Woodward concluded. But that is not the point of the book or typical of the author's extensive research and reporting.

There is plenty of other evidence that Casey knew all about the Iran-Contra dealings and fund diversion. For those who don't like Woodward, there is even the sworn testimony of Lt. Colonel Oliver North that the late CIA director knew.

And, in fact, the book paints a detailed picture of Casey as the mastermind of this and many other frightening and illegal operations. The deathbed scene is almost superfluous, as well as diversionary for much of the public and media.

It is that overall picture of the CIA under Casey that is alarming — an agency covertly operating worldwide in some alarming ways, bending or breaking the law, unchecked and even encouraged by a lethargic president, ignoring and lying to Congress.

And there is little doubt that this book only tells part of what should be a scary tale for Americans.

# AUGUSTA HERALD

*Augusta, GA, October 1, 1987*

It's beyond comprehension why anyone would accept Bob Woodward's word about William Casey's career as CIA director.

**Woodward, of Watergate fame, stands for everything that the late CIA chief opposed — a wimpish agency limited to intelligence gathering and a Neville Chamberlain-style foreign policy based on compromise, retreat and appeasement.**

It strains all credulity to believe Casey, in his dying days, would spill government secrets to a biographer whom he surely knew would do a hatchet job on him, his agency and his policies.

And that's what Woodward's book, *Veil: The Secret Wars of the CIA, 1981-1985* is: a hatchet job, pure and simple. It's designed to discredit Casey's place in history and to energize a skittish, anti-Reagan Congress into another round of CIA-bashing. Clearly, the intent is to strip the intelligence agency of its ability to conduct covert operations, which Casey himself so painfully built up after the disastrous Carter years.

The ruse is working. Even otherwise sane and sensible congressmen, like Sen. Sam Nunn, D-Ga., seem to take the book seriously. The Georgian says he's dismayed to learn that Casey ran off-the-shelf covert operations on his own without approval and against the advice of CIA subordinates.

He ought to be more dismayed that nothing in the book has been confirmed, save a small portion by Lt. Col. Oliver North whose testimony, significantly, came before the book was published.

Even Woodward's tale of Casey's description of President Reagan's condition following the 1981 assassination attempt has been disputed by the doctor involved in the case. Indeed, every tale told in the book is contradicted by the other principals involved. There's not one ounce of supporting evidence to suggest anything Woodward has written in *Veil* is true.

Any editor who published an un-collaborated story like Woodward's would be fired. Maybe that's why nothing was ever published in the *Washington Post* until Woodward's book came out. But then how do you explain the comments of Woodward's boss at the *Post*, Ben Bradlee, who says the newspaper "owes Woodward so much" for his excellent reporting?

**Here's a question for Bradlee: If he believed what Woodward wrote about Casey, then didn't he "owe it" to his readers to publish it in his paper as a running story, like Watergate?**

And if Woodward kept him in the dark about the Casey story, shouldn't the reporter be fired for not sharing his information with his editors?

# The Sun Reporter

*San Francisco, CA, October 7, 1987*

Bob Woodward, an investigative reporter with the Washington Post, seems to take up where he left off in the expose' which ran in the Washington Post which toppled Richard Nixon from office. Woodward was not alone in the Watergate expose', for he coauthored the expose' with a fellow reporter from the Washington Post.

Woodward's latest expose' is in the form of a recently released book entitled *Veil —The Secret Wars of the CIA.*

Mr. Woodward depicts the late CIA director William Casey as a man conducting a cowboy type of operation in direct violation of rules set by the Congress and a past CIA director in which the CIA promised the Congress that it would not indulge in covert activities abroad without informing the Congress.

Woodward said in his book that he had many conversations with Casey, including one in the hospital when Casey was lying on what later proved to be his death bed. In the hospital interview, Casey, according to Woodward, admitted with a nod of his head that he knew of the arms sale to Iran and the transferring of the profits from the arms sale to the Nicaraguan contras.

Reagan said later that Woodward was fictionalizing.

Sophia Casey, the widow of Casey, joined Reagan in denials, and Mrs. Casey even said that Woodward had never been to her home to talk to her husband until Woodward refreshed her memory of the occasion when he was a breakfast guest at her home at the invitation of Casey during the Nightline television program with Ted Koppel.

We have heard the ancients say that whenever someone throws a rock at a pack of dogs, the one that yelps is the one which the rock struck.

Both the President and Mrs. Casey are yelping real loud, so the rock struck them.

Woodward stated that Casey was contemptous of the so called "Reagan laid back style," which infers that, in Casey's view, Reagan has lived in an illusionary world all of his adult life and does not recognize facts when the facts are presented to him.

Casey only joins others who are dismayed with the ineptness of our President.

Mr. Casey, Michael Deaver, Lynn Nofziger and Edwin Meese have tarnished the Reagan administration as much as the sleazy group which Richard Nixon brought with him to Washington did before them.

The difference between Nixon and Reagan is that Nixon had an intellect which, compared to Reagan, makes the incumbent President appear to be a dolt.

Woodward could have triggered a chain reaction with the publication of his book that would have created a Watergate scene on the Potomac.

## The Grand Rapids Press

*Grand Rapids, MI, October 4, 1987*

Washington Post editor Bob Woodward's book on the Central Intelligence Agency is apparently a bargain. Not only does it uncover the covert ways of the late William Casey, but it stimulates debate on journalism ethics and natural security. Only some of this hubbub is flattering to Mr. Woodward and his book.

The book, titled "Veil: The Secret Wars of the CIA 1981-87," is an investigation of Mr. Casey's tenure at the helm of the CIA. It is valuable, insofar as it is accurate, in describing how Mr. Casey ran around the Congress and the president in conducting secret intelligence operations. That Mr. Casey was able, for six years, to conduct a rogue and often brutal foreign policy, to arrange an assassination attempt, to scheme and deal and cover up, should unnerve the American people and wake up the sleepy and gullible in the federal government.

Mr. Woodward's good work aside, it is mildly unsettling that in Washington, glasnost and the Contras and the deficit seem less real and much less interesting than some fiery revelations about a deceased Cabinet officer. If the deep thinkers in the capital showed as much interest in public policy issues as they do in the latest item on the bookracks, then more of the government's daunting problems might be closer to solution.

One topic of conversation centers on Mr. Woodward's reported talks with Mr. Casey before and during his illness. Mr. Woodward writes that he snuck into the hospital room where, he says, Mr. Casey admitted he knew of the diversion of arms money to the Contras. Some properly questioned whether that important ingredient should not have been reported in the Post during the time the Iran-Contra committee was in session. Not to do so seems a breach of the journalistic canon that information be printed when it is learned.

Mr. Woodward and other Post editors say the admission was too vague to use because Mr. Casey might not have been entirely lucid. But if it was too vague for the paper, why is it in the book? And if the Post's standards are too high to admit such vagueness, why has the paper been serializing the book?

More important than this professional dispute is the complaint, from former CIA Director Stansfield Turner and others, that the Woodward book is too revealing of U.S. intelligence secrets. One senior government official compared Mr. Woodward's revelations of secrets to those stolen by convicted spy John Walker. But there's a difference that someone highly perched in government should know. Mr. Walker sold secrets to help the Soviets undermine us — his purpose was sinister. Mr. Woodward's book, besides making the author a large sum of money, is meant to enlighten the public and shake up the policymakers. Thus shaken, they presumably will make better policy.

The intelligence community probably is better off if its dirty laundry is never aired. But that will not and should not happen in a democratic society. If the CIA wants to preserve our way of life, it should know that a free press is essential. The KGB moves more freely than the CIA, but the price of that "freedom" is paid by all Russians.

Two things are certain in all of this. Mr. Casey will not be around to contribute to the debate over the book and the debate will not settle a thing. The book will have to stand alone; it may become part of history or it may slip into the mists. Either way, we must not forget Mr. Casey, or allow his sort of excess again.

# Congressional Iran-Contra Probers Blame Reagan

House and Senate committees that had held hearings on the Iran-contra arms scandal through the summer issued their final report November 18, 1987. The 690-page document chronicled the many questions that remained unanswered about the affair, but placed blame firmly on the shoulders of President Reagan for policies in Iran and Central America that hinged on "secrecy, deception and disdain for the law."

The policies of selling arms to Iran and diverting funds from the arms sales to the contra rebels in Nicaragua was masterminded by a "cabal of zealots" in and out of the White House, the report concluded. "The Iran-contra affair was characterized by pervasive dishonesty and inordinate secrecy." The strongly worded report was endorsed by all 15 Democrats on the two panels and by three Republican senators. Two other Republican senators and all six GOP members on the House panel signed a minority report, released Nov. 17, that rejected the "hysterical conclusions" of the majority report. The minority's report charged that majority's analysis "reads as if it were a weapon in the ongoing guerila warfare [between Congress and the White House], instead of an objective analysis." The scandal stemmed from "mistakes in judgment and nothing more," in the view of the minority. One Republican who signed the majority report, Sen. Warren Rudman (R, N.H.), Nov. 18 dismissed the dissenting report as "pathetic." The other Republicans who joined the majority in signing the report were Sen. William Cohen (Maine) and Sen. Paul Trible Jr. (Va.).

The "central question" of the scandal, the report said, was President Reagan's role. The committees said that question remained unanswered because "the shredding of the documents by [former national security adviser John M.] Poindexter, former National Security Council Aide Lt. Col. Oliver L.] North and others, and the death of [former Director of Central Intelligence William J.] Casey, leave the record incomplete." But "if the President did riot know what his national security advisers were doing, he should have," the report concluded, charging that Reagan had violated the requirement in the Constitution and in his oath of office to "take that the laws be faithfully executed."

On the persistent question of whether Reagan had known of the diversion of Iranian funds to the contras, the committees recounted without comment Poindexter's testimony that he deliberately withheld the information from the President. "The question of whether the President knew of the diversion is not conclusive on the issue of his responsibility," according to the report. Reagan "created or at least tolerated an environment where those who did not know of the diversion believed with certainty that they were carrying out the President's policies." Several of Reagan's advisers "lied, shredded documents and covered up their actions," the report said. "But the President has yet to condemn their conduct."

At the White House the official posture was one of uninterest in Congress's opinion of the scandal. At a public appearance, Reagan's only comment was, "You don't want to know" what he thought of the report. An official statement read by spokesman Marlin Fitzwater quoted Reagan's earlier comments on the scandal and attacked the report as representing "the subjective opinions and not even the unanimous judgment of the committee." The response noted that the President had not violated any laws, concluding: "And now we are through with it."

In a section titled "Who Was Responsible" the committees sought to parcel out blame for the scandal among the various administration officials involved. They began with North, who was the central figure "at the operational level." Throughout the document, the committees assailed North for his elaborate deceits and "obsession" with secrecy. "North, however, did not act alone," the committees concluded, blaming Poindexter for giving "express approval" to North's activities and Poindexter's predecessor, Robert McFarlane, for offering "at least tacit support." McFarlane was criticized further for "embarking on a dangerous trip to Teheran under a complete misapprehension" that all the American hostages held in Lebanon would be freed before he turned over arms he was traveling with.

The committees' several recommendations were less drastic than the report was forceful, but they went further than the Tower commission appointed by President Reagan had gone in proposing changes.

## the Charleston Gazette

Charleston, WV, November 20, 1987

AFTER months of investigation, the main finding of the Iran-contra committees is a simple one: President Reagan bore ultimate responsibility for a policy that was unsuccessful and glaringly illegal.

The committee's majority report doesn't go so far as to accuse the president of an impeachable offense (although Secretary of State George Shultz told Reagan three years ago that solicitation of money from other countries for the covert war against Nicaragua was exactly that). But the report makes clear, by quoting from the Constitution, that Reagan failed in his primary duty, which is that the president "shall take care that the laws be faithfully executed."

It's troubling, then, that White House officials say Reagan probably won't even bother reading the report. His spokesman, Marlin Fitzwater, brushed off the committee's findings as "predictably partisan."

That's typical of the White House. Reagan never liked bad news and he thinks that, by ignoring it, his troubles simply will go away. He refuses to concede the gravity of this scandal, easily the worst since Watergate. Nearly everything he has said about the Iran-contra affair has proved to be untrue.

To this day, he hasn't condemned the actions of his subordinates. As late as July 31, after witnesses before the congressional committees had made it abundantly clear that White House staffers had broken the law, Reagan still claimed "I haven't heard a single word [of testimony] that laws were broken."

Two weeks earlier, Reagan promised to "stand on the roof and yell" his response to the congressional investigation once it ended. "You won't be able to shut me up." But from the Oval Office now there is dead silence.

Reagan still doesn't comprehend that his covert war, concealed from Americans, was wrong. If he hopes ever to regain the support he enjoyed during most of his presidency, he ought to say once and for all that the aides serving under him — no matter their motivations — worked against the democratic ideals they had sworn to uphold.

"By his continuing silence," said Senate Chairman Daniel Inouye, D-Hawaii, "the president creates the impression that he does not find these actions objectionable."

The tragedy, aside from the burden laid on the country, is that the cause of this scandal remains. While three American hostages were freed as a result of the weapons deals with Iran, another three were taken. Their plight has been all but forgotten. And the contra bushwhackers still can't hold any territory in Nicaragua, the tiny nation Reagan wanted to force to "say uncle."

Thus nothing was accomplished by the White House plotting by what the congressional report aptly calls a "cabal of zealots."

## THE SACRAMENTO BEE
*Sacramento, CA, November 19, 1987*

Republican critics of the congressional report on the Iran-Contra affair are correct that the 690-page document contains little that's new, either about the folly of the policy or about the secret organization that carried it out. What may be even more true is that, a year after the first shocking disclosures of the sale of arms to Iran, the whole episode now seems to be only one element in the unraveling of an administration that, with every passing day, looks more irrelevant. But that doesn't make the episode any less frightening.

The major point of the report — that the deficiencies were not in the laws or in the structures of government, but, as Sen. Daniel Inouye said, in those who govern — is incontrovertible. And while the report emphasizes that there is no evidence that Ronald Reagan knew of the diversion of funds to the Contras, it also makes clear, to quote Sen. Warren Rudman, the committee's ranking Republican, that Reagan should have known. Similarly, it pulls no punches about the secret government — the government outside government — that operated out of the White House; about the dishonesty and deception involved in its operations; about the attempts to cover up the story once the affair began to unravel; about Attorney General Edwin Meese's discreditable investigation; and, most of all, about the president's failure, to this day, to condemn what was done.

The eight Republicans who issued a dissenting report tried to politicize their docu-

ment enough to make it look as if the majority report itself was nothing more than politics. But as Republican Rudman said yesterday, the dissenters' effort, which holds Irangate to be nothing more than a political mistake, "is a pathetic report."

The president, the dissenters said, "has already taken the hard step of acknowledging his mistakes and reacting precisely to correct what was wrong," including the appointment of more reliable people as national security adviser and White House chief of staff. But as the record of the past couple of months has made clear, the essential element — the president's lack of interest in, and inattention to, the management of public affairs — hasn't changed at all.

There may be no junta of colonels and arms dealers running its own foreign policy out of the White House these days, and one has to hope that special prosecutor Lawrence Walsh will produce enough indictments and secure enough convictions that the colonels of the future will think twice about trying it again. But things like the Ginsburg fiasco, the president's unwillingness to fire an ethical cripple like Meese and his apparent inability to understand the violations of constitutional government inherent in Irangate provide no assurance that he wouldn't let it happen again. Irangate wasn't just stupid politics, as the Republican dissenters said, or terrible policy, as most Americans knew from the first day; it was a danger to democracy itself.

## Minneapolis Star and Tribune
*Minneapolis, MN, November 20, 1987*

In their report released this week, congressional committees investigating the Iran-contra affair delivered a splendid account of a sorry performance by the Reagan administration. The report gains from its calm, descriptive narration and its avoidance of polemics. It gains, too, from comparison with the minority report. Defenders of President Reagan are undisturbed by the record of White House deception and worse. Their response is similar to the president's complaint last month about the deficit: "It's Congress' fault."

Nonsense. Americans who followed the committees' hearings and now read the report are unlikely to accept the minority's premise: that the president's men acted as they did because congressional leaders can't be trusted to keep a secret.

The National Security Council's covert corps seemed to think their secrets would be kept by private arms dealers, Nicaraguan contras, Israeli and Iranian officials and Iranian Revolutionary Guards. That's more nonsense. Republicans who profess to see in the Iran-contra antics no sign of conspiracy, coverup, lawbreaking and impropriety, and who find only minor errors of judgment, are appropriately the minority. Republicans and Democrats who signed the committees' report are the clear-headed majority.

A year after the Iran-contra scandal began unfolding, it's fair to ask why people should pay attention to still another report on the subject. The

answer, we think, is threefold.

First, the report puts into perspective the information produced in hearings last summer, when the drama of testimony sometimes overshadowed the content. For example, it is easy to recall Oliver North's claim that duty had required him to lie to Congress. It is harder to recall the substance of the lies.

Second, the report offers helpful recommendations, for example urging that the president be required to authorize covert actions. Unfortunately, none of the recommendations would guarantee probity and common sense in high office.

A third value of the report is its usefulness in judging the administration and Congress. The report is unpersuasive on one subject — its tortured justification of Congress' off-again, on-again funding of the contras. But its portrayal of presidential responsibility in general, President Reagan's in particular, is squarely on the mark.

Reagan has "ultimate responsibility for the events in the Iran-contra affair," says the report. We agree. By misdirection, inattention or both, the president encouraged disregard for the laws and for his own stated policies. We also agree with the report's claim that if Reagan "did not know what his national security advisers were doing, he should have." We hope that Reagan has learned and that the next president will not be so lax.

## DESERET NEWS
*Salt Lake City, UT, November 20, 1987*

"There isn't much new in here," said White House spokesman Marlin Fitzwater, dismissing the 690-page congressional committee report on the Iran-contra scandal.

The White House, understandably, may prefer to ignore a report that concludes President Reagan failed to live up to his constitutional mandate to "take care that the laws be faithfully executed."

But the report also contained information never before fully authenticated in the public record:

• Administration officials accepted an offer by Panama's military leader, Gen. Manuel Antonio Noriega, to carry out sabotage operations in Nicaragua, while backing away from Noriega's offer to also undertake assassinations on behalf of the United States.

• Raising money for the contras was an integral part of the operation, not merely a by-product of the arms sales to Iran. It thus violated a congressional ban on such assistance and calls into question repeated public statements by President Reagan to the contrary.

• The secret government-within-the-government was far more extensive than before reported, including underwriting of propaganda efforts, shipments of Soviet arms to the CIA and efforts to channel ransom payments for the hostages through Drug Enforcement Administration agents.

• Top-level administration officials were deeply involved in the operation. The report shows that CIA director William Casey misled Congress on key issues. Attorney General Edwin Meese III undermined the investigation by withholding documents that were later destroyed, and he possibly approved ransom payments to Iran through the Drug Enforcement Administration.

• Specific laws were broken, such as raising money from foreign governments for U.S. government activities; violating the Boland Amendment prohibiting aid to the contras; making false statements to Congress; and obstructing congressional investigations by shredding documents.

Many questions remain unanswered. What was the full scope of the secret government and who — if anyone — was in control of administration policy?

But the most significant revelation is that the American public no longer seems surprised by a report showing that administration officials violated the law, ignored the Constitution, and then tried to cover up their actions. In that sense, Fitzwater's remark that the Iran-contra report is nothing new has a ring of truth — and may be the most damning observation of all.

# Lincoln Journal

*Lincoln, NE,*
*November 23, 1987*

The White House and a number of congressional Republicans are doing their best — and that's pretty good — to minimize the majority congressional report about the Reagan administration's worst foreign policy scandal. We refer to those secret sales of U.S. arms to people President Reagan had identified as terrorists.

Reagan has volunteered no comment on the probe's profoundly critical summary findings even though he once said that when the summer investigations were history, "you won't be able to shut me up."

Presidential associates are shrugging off the majority committee report as nothing new. They want the whole thing to go away. The company line was laid down by one senior White House official:

"The American people have pretty much put this behind them. Most people outside of Washington want to get on with business. Our thought is just to move ahead and not dwell on this."

Probably they are correct in gauging the public attention span. But we hope they err in thinking the public will swallow the adulterated bait that it was nothing but some mistakes in judgments by patriots authorized to make such judgments.

Nothing of the sort.

And if criminal indictments are filed against "the usual suspects" soon, the gravity of the offense of a loose-cannon executive branch should become rather more apparent, even at 1700 Pennsylvania Avenue.

Don't even breathe the word "pardon," as some friends of the administration already are reported doing. (At least they are demonstrating there were more than just mistakes in judgment.)

# The Register

*Santa Ana, CA, November 19, 1987*

If members of Congress took seriously their report on the Iran arms scandal, they would immediately move to impeach President Reagan. Released yesterday, the final 690-page report on the affair concluded: "The Constitution requires the president to 'take care that the laws be faithfully executed.' This charge encompasses a responsibility to leave the members of his administration in no doubt that the rule of law governs."

But though this is the conclusion, the report itself includes no evidence that Reagan violated the law. Therefore, the report's signers have themselves acted with impropriety. They have charged Reagan with violating the Constitution, intending to hurt his credibility, but in the end have produced only a groundless insinuation accompanied by no specific charges.

And to compound impropriety with hypocrisy, House Speaker Jim Wright has in recent days taken over conduct of American foreign policy in Central America, violating the Constitution's strict rule that the president is to conduct foreign policy. Moreover, Article I, Section 8 of the Constitution gives Congress power over the government's budget, yet Congress has yet to pass a budget for the fiscal year that began on Oct. 1. If Congress wants to see a true violater of the Constitution, it should look in the mirror.

What, in the end, does the congressional report on the Iran arms scandal tell us? Nothing we already didn't know. We have long known that the Reagan administration's swap of arms for hostages violated the administration's own stated policy, and that was dishonorable enough. Yet it did not violate the Constitution. Reagan's judgment was bad. But the founding fathers, in giving the president such wide latitude on foreign policy, knowingly took the risk that, in the pursuit of foreign policies necessary to defend America, some bad decisions would be made. Bad judgment doesn't necessarily mean any law was broken.

The same holds true for the $3.8 million diverted from the arms sales to the resistance in Nicaragua — an amount, let us note, less than what Congress wasted in compiling this report. The report concluded that "the question whether the president knew of the diversion is not conclusive on the issue of his responsibility." But it is conclusive. No evidence has ever been presented proving that Reagan knew, and much evidence says that he didn't.

You may conjecture, with some plausibility, that the evidence is defective. But until you explode that evidence, no other conclusion can be drawn but that Reagan truly did not know. By saying otherwise, the congressional report, for a second time, implicitly indicts Reagan.

Moreover, the very point of law at issue, notwithstanding whether Reagan violated the much discussed Boland amendment, is really moot. What does Boland mean? The law exists in several forms, and is completely ambiguous. Any civil law written that way would be thrown out of court as a defective piece of legislation. Indeed, if former White House aides Oliver North and John Poindexter are prosecuted for violating Boland, the law may be nullified.

The Iran arms scandal was a national disgrace. One hopes its lessons have been learned. But instead of cleanly cutting away the canker on the national body politic, this congressional report only grinds salt in the wound.

# Newsday

*Long Island, NY, November 19, 1987*

The U.S. Constitution requires that the president "take care that the laws be faithfully executed." According to the final report of the Iran-contra congressional investigating committee, Ronald Reagan failed to fulfill that responsibility.

Nothing in the 690-page document could be more damning: A president failed his constitutional duty.

Reagan, says the report, led members of his national security staff to believe that their actions were consistent with his desires. And their actions broke the law: Government funds were misappropriated, congressional oversight was deliberately evaded, federal documents were destroyed, perjured testimony was given.

Almost none of this is new — it all came out in excruciating detail during the summer hearings. But taken all together, it is a chilling portrait of arrogance, incompetence and zealotry. The committee concluded that there had been no impeachable offenses, but the damage to the nation, its institutions and its credibility is still enormous.

That eight Republicans felt compelled to issue a minority report is a sad commentary on their sensibilities. They argue that there were only mistakes of judgment and no constitutional crisis, no systematic disrespect for the rule of law. That, of course, is nothing but political palaver. It reflects the same type of extreme partisanship that led Reagan into the morass in the first place.

The report wisely concludes that the Iran-contra affair resulted from the failure of in-

Newsday / M.G. Lord

dividuals to observe the law, not from deficiencies in the existing law or the system. Although there are 27 specific recommendations, many of them have to do with procedure and stronger congressional oversight. Not all of them are warranted. Passing a law, for instance, requiring the president to report to Congress on the organization and procedures of the National Security Council staff might be too much of an intrusion on the executive's prerogative to run his own staff. But recommendations should be carefully considered by both the executive and the legislature.

This report should be required reading for the next president of the United States. The only value of the whole sordid affair is the hope that it won't be repeated.

## Herald News
### Fall River, MA, November 20, 1987

The report by the joint congressional committee probing the Iran-Contras affair has now been made public.

It places the ultimate responsibility for the affair on President Reagan himself, claiming that his administration was at odds with the Constitution and the law and that he failed to execute the law.

Significantly, most of the Republican members of the committee, who were in a minority, are offering their own appraisal which differs from that of the Democratic majority.

In their view the most the President can be accused of is poor judgment in terms of some appointments.

Finally, the difference between the Democratic and Republican reports amounts more to a difference of viewpoint than of substance.

Although both groups may deny it, their split was obviously affected by political considerations, plus the fact that 1988 will be an election year.

The affair and its implications have not yet been used by either party to any marked degree, in part because it is still not known what, if any, indictments will be sought by Special Prosecutor Lawrence Walsh.

But the immediate controversy between the Democrats and Republicans on the congressional committee over their respective reports makes plain that both sides will fight for what they believe is the right interpretation of what went on during the White House's arms dealings with Iran and the diversion of some of the profits from those deals to the Contras.

The real trouble is that there is no way of determining which group is right in its interpretation.

Virtually a year after it became public, the Iran-Contras affair has cast a permanent blemish on the Reagan administration, but it has not yet been settled, and may well never be.

## The Honolulu Advertiser
### Honolulu, HI, November 19, 1987

The final reports of the congressional committees on the Iran-Contra dealings are unlikely to have much immediate impact. But the affair itself still amounts to a stinging indictment of President Reagan as a national leader.

Some are saying that both the majority and minority reports are overblown and shot through with partisanship to the point they cancel each other out. That's debatable. We'd say the majority report is more convincing.

You might say the split decision gives something for Reagan and his partisans to hide behind. But more likely is a point made in an adjoining analysis: The president won't be hurt much because the harm has already been done by earlier Iran-Contra revelations. And he's now on the defense in other damaging battles over the budget and peace in Central America.

Still, the report should serve as a record of what happened and as a reminder later of the period when the Reagan presidency started falling apart through its own mistakes and missteps.

Nobody has the firm evidence or the deep desire to impeach Reagan. Yet it will still be difficult for many to believe that he did not know of the illegal acts being committed by those around him. The hostages and Nicaragua were subjects this often-inattentive president cared deeply about.

At the least, however, he should have known. And worse yet he encouraged those who committed the illegal acts against the advice of Secretary of State Shultz and Secretary of Defense Weinberger. Concludes the majority report:

"The president created or at least tolerated an environment where those who did know of the diversion (of Iran arms sale funds to the Contras) believed with certainty that they were carrying out the president's policies. . . . The ultimate responsibility for the events in the Iran-Contra affair must rest with the president."

So, while Reagan can and will duck again, the judgment of history should end in the Oval Office.

## The San Diego Union
### San Diego, CA, November 20, 1987

The Iran-Contra report documents what was generally known, namely that the Reagan administration went off the rails by trading arms for hostages and secretly diverting arms-sale profits to the Nicaraguan freedom fighters.

In doing so, the administration not only violated one of its fundamental tenets of refusing to pay ransom to terrorists, it may have doomed the Contras, whose chances of receiving continued U.S. aid from a Democratic-controlled Congress, already shaky, have been diminished. If such financial assistance is in fact terminated, another permanent communist beachhead in the Western Hemisphere is all but assured.

Revelations of these amazing episodes and the subsequent political fallout have diminished the President even more than the Contra cause. Although the final report found no smoking gun to link Mr. Reagan with the illegal aid to the Contras, he cannot escape responsibility for this clandestine operation being run by the National Security Council from the White House basement. That the President was in the dark about this wild adventure is altogether damning because it lends credence to charges of a somnolent White House.

The sharply worded report, signed by three of the five Republican senators and all of the Democrats on the special committees, appropriately blames the President for his failure to "take care that the laws are faithfully executed;" the finding unsparingly holds Mr. Reagan fully responsible for the scandal. To his credit, the President has acknowledged that the old Harry Truman buck did indeed come to rest on his desk.

Let it be remembered now that he did appoint a special prosecutor to determine if laws were violated and whether charges should be filed. Having received and examined the congressional report, Mr. Reagan says it's time to move on to other, more pressing issues before the country. We agree.

There has been more than enough partisan posturing on both sides. Some Democrats have exploited the report and now proclaim their intention to use it as a basis to intervene even further in the President's conduct of foreign policy. For example, one of the report's major 19 recommendations would require that Congress be given "timely notice" of all secret operations in advance, or no later than 48 hours after the fact. It should be noted that the President is already required to give Congress timely notification of such activities. The Iran-Contra problem is not so much a lack of laws as a failure to obey the ones already on the books.

The late Sen. Sam Ervin said as much during the Watergate hearings when he noted that the crisis in 1974 could have been avoided had President Nixon simply obeyed the Constitution.

The Ervin principle surely applies to the Iran-Contra affair. And those Republicans who carp that "mistakes in judgment" were made by the administration and nothing more, miss the salient point that the rule of law must not be subverted, no matter how deserving the cause. As the congressional report correctly concludes: "If the government becomes the lawbreaker, it breeds contempt for the law, it invites every man to become a law unto himself, it invites anarchy."

That is the essential moral of the Iran-Contra disaster. It should be heeded by all who take the solemn oath to "preserve, protect, and defend the Constitution of the United States."

# Appendix:
# Chronology of the Iran-Contra Arms Scandal

*Following is a chronology of major events in the Iran-contra affair, based upon the February 26 report of the Tower Commission and on other data reported in news accounts. The commission, formally known as the President's Special Review Board, investigated the role of the National Security Council staff in the Iran-contra affair:*

**Aug. 31, 1984**—National security adviser Robert McFarlane formally requests government agencies to reassess and analyze U.S. policy toward Iran.

**Sept. 2, 1984**—National Security Council staff member Lt. Col. Oliver North suggests to McFarlane that a private donor be found to give a helicopter to the Nicaraguan contra rebels. It is an early indication of the NSC's interest in soliciting private aid for the contras. U.S. military assistance to the contras was barred by the so-called Boland Amendment enacted in 1982.

**April 18, 1985**—Lt. Col. North, according to the commission, sketches a diagram proposing how money from private donors might be channeled to the contras under a program he dubs "Project Democracy."

**May 4-5, 1985**—Michael Ledeen, an NSC consultant, meets with Israeli Prime Minister Shimon Peres. Peres asks Ledeen if the U.S. would approve a shipment of arms to Iran. Ledeen agrees on behalf of McFarlane. In April, Ledeen and McFarlane had discussed a possible Israeli-mediated contact with Iran.

**July 3, 1985**—David Kimchee, director general of the Israeli foreign ministry, tells McFarlane that Iran wants to open a "political discourse" with the U.S.

**Mid-July 1985**—President Reagan, recuperating in a hospital from cancer surgery, authorizes McFarlane to make contact with Iran through the Israelis. McFarlane later says the President was "all for letting the Israelis do anything they wanted" in dealings with Iran.

**Late July 1985**—Ledeen meets in Israel with Iranian-born arms dealer Manucher Ghorbanifar, who says Iran might arrange to release U.S. hostages if the U.S. helps Iran obtain weapons. By September, discussions among Ledeen, Ghorbanifar and Kimchee have progressed to "technical questions" concerning arms transfers and hostage releases.

**August 1985**—McFarlane briefs Reagan on a specific proposal by Kimchee to permit the sale of U.S. TOW antitank missiles to Iran through Israel. McFarlane later says Reagan authorized the sale, White House Chief of Staff Donald Regan says he did not. President Reagan gives conflicting statements to the Tower Commission, first saying he approved such sales, later saying he does not remember doing so.

**Aug. 30, 1985**—Israel sends 100 U.S.-made TOW antitank missiles to Iran through a third party. It is the first of at least eight separate arms shipments over the next 14 months.

**Sept. 14, 1985**—Israel delivers another 408 missiles to Iran, and Rev. Benjamin Weir the same day becomes the first U.S. hostage to be released by pro-Iranian Shiite militiamen in Lebanon. Two more hostages are released over the next year.

**Nov. 22, 1985**—The Central Intelligence Agency arranges for the shipment of 18 Hawk antiaircraft missiles from Israel to Iran. But John McMahon, the agency's deputy director, Nov. 25 says the CIA will not provide any more covert assistance unless President Reagan explicitly authorizes such operations. Iran later rejects the missiles as obsolete.

**Nov. 30, 1985**—McFarlane resigns as national security adviser and is replaced Dec. 4 with his subordinate, Vice Adm. John Poindexter.

**Dec. 7, 1985**—President Reagan holds a meeting in his office with Vice President George Bush, CIA Director William Casey, Secretary of State George Shultz, Defense Secretary Caspar Weinberger, and McFarlane and Poindexter. President Reagan later says he recalls discussing a complex Iranian proposal for release of hostages keyed to arms shipments in installments from the Israelis. Shultz and Weinberger, who have objected to the Iran policy since June, argue strongly against exchanging arms for hostages. Recollections of the meeting are, in the Tower commission's words, "quite diverse." Reagan tells the Tower commission that the meeting ended in "stalemate." But McFarlane and North immediately leave for London and a meeting with Ghorbanifar Dec. 8, in what is later described as an attempt to "unlink" arms shipments and hostages, though no formal record is found.

Dec. 9, 1985—North submits to Poindexter a memo proposing a direct arms-for-hostages exchange, to be handled by retired Air Force Maj. Gen. Richard Secord, a North associate who is also believed to have been running a private supply network for the contras, and Ghorbanifar. North, Ghorbanifar, Ledeen, Secord, new Israeli antiterrorist adviser Amiram Nir—who had taken Kimchee's place—jointly work out an arms-for-hostages plan over the next few weeks. It is not known who took the lead.

Jan. 6, 1986—President Reagan signs a "finding," or order, authorizing covert action including arms shipments to Iran to help secure the release of American hostages. Reagan later tells the commission he does not recall signing the finding; Chief of Staff Regan tells the commission the order "may have been signed in error." The next day, in another Oval Office meeting with Reagan, Bush, Casey, and other officials, Shultz and Weinberger object to the scheme.

Jan. 17, 1986—Reagan signs a second finding authorizing arms shipments, with language only slightly revised from that of the first. But the cover memo now proposes that the CIA purchase TOW missiles from the Defense Department and transfer them directly to Iran. The U.S. for the first time becomes "a direct supplier of arms to Iran," in the Tower Commission's words. Over the next few months, North and Poindexter review a number of plans directly linking the release of hostages to the shipment of U.S. arms. Another shipment of arms, with Saudi billionaire Adnan Khashoggi and Ghorbanifar's middlemen, is arranged in mid-February, and North holds a face-to-face meeting with an Iranian official in Frankfurt, West Germany Feb. 24.

Early February 1986—By this time, the commission says, the CIA has begun acquiring weapons for Iran and has designated a Swiss bank account for the proceeds of the sales. The agency has also put two airplanes "at the disposal of Gen. Secord."

March-April 1986—North is now receiving numerous messages from Secord and CIA field officers on contra operations in and around Nicaragua. The commission says a CIA officer testified that a "private benefactor operation" for the contras was "controlled by Col. North."

April 4, 1986—North writes memorandum for Poindexter to present to President Reagan saying $12 million from the Iranian arms sales "will be used to purchase critically needed supplies" for the Nicaraguan contras. However, the commission says it has no evidence that Reagan saw the memo.

May 15, 1986—President Reagan approves a mission to Teheran by McFarlane. The same day, Poindexter tells North to "generate a cover story" to conceal his heavy involvement with unauthorized contra supply operations.

The next day North sends a note to Poindexter saying the clandestine arms shipments "could well become a political embarrassment for the President." North has "no idea" what Chief of Staff Regan "does or does not know," North writes, but the President "obviously knows why he has been meeting with several select people to thank them" for providing donations to the contras.

May 25-28, 1986—McFarlane, North and other U.S. officials travel to Teheran to meet with Iranian officials. Poindexter has rejected North's request for a prior meeting with the President and other cabinet officers because of potential objections from Shultz and Weinberger. The U.S. entourage shares the plane with a shipment of missile parts for Iran. No more hostages will be released until July 26, however, when Rev. Martin Jenco is freed. On the return trip from Teheran, McFarlane says, North reveals that the proceeds from the arms sales have been used to fund the contras.

June 6, 1986—President Reagan approves military planning to rescue the hostages. North told Poindexter in February that the NSC staff was drawing up plans.

Sept. 9, 1986—North calls Costa Rican President Oscar Arias Sanchez and threatens to "withhold U.S. assistance" if Arias shuts down an airstrip used by the contras. In a note to Poindexter, North admits his call was "well beyond my charter."

Sept. 12, 1986—Israeli Defense Minister Yitzhak Rabin offers "a significant quantity of captured Soviet bloc arms" for use by the contras. Poindexter discusses the offer prior to a meeting between Reagan and Israeli Prime Minister Shimon Peres Sept. 15.

Sept. 15, 1986—North arranges for a Danish ship to pick up weapons in Israel and deliver them to the contras.

Sept. 19-20, 1986—North and Secord meet in Washington with a relative of an unidentified high Iranian official to discuss the hostages.

Oct. 5, 1986—A cargo plane carrying arms to the contras is shot down over Nicaragua and a crewman, Eugene Hasenfus, is captured. The U.S. denies any connection to the operation, but North Oct. 12 tells McFarlane that "we urgently need to find a high-powered lawyer and benefactor" for Hasenfus.

Oct. 7, 1986—A business associate tells Director Casey that money from the Iran arms sales may have been diverted to the contras. Casey in Senate testimony Nov. 21 makes no reference to those suspicions.

Oct. 29, 1986—The CIA arranges for the shipment of 500 TOW missiles from Israel to Iran. This is apparently the last arms shipment. Earlier shipments have taken place in

August, September and November 1985, and in February, May and August 1986.

Nov. 3, 1986—A Lebanese magazine discloses that McFarlane had visited Teheran and that the U.S. had been supplying arms to Iran. A senior Iranian official confirms this Nov. 4.

Nov. 13, 1986—In a television address to the nation, President Reagan acknowledged that the U.S. has sent "less than a planeload" of weapons to Iran but denies they were part of any actual or attempted hostage deal.

Nov. 18-19, 1986—McFarlane and North prepare a chronology of the arms sales for Reagan's reference that obscures the President's approval of the first shipment.

Nov. 25, 1986—Reagan accepts Poindexter's resignation and fires North after it is revealed that profits from the arms sales to Iran have been diverted to the contras. On Nov. 26, he appoints the Tower Commission to review the operation of the NSC and recommend corrective action. On Dec. 2, he asks for an independent counsel to explore charges of illegalities.

Dec. 2, 1986—Frank Carlucci is named national security adviser.

Dec. 4, 1986—House and Senate leaders agree to form separate Watergate-style select committees to investigate the scandal, with work expected to begin in January.

Dec. 6, 1986—Reagan in his weekly radio address acknowledges for the first time that "mistakes were made" in the plan to sell weapons to Iran and funnel profits to the contras. He says the errors occurred only in the execution of policy, not "in the policies themselves."

Dec. 8, 1986—Shultz testifies before the House Foreign Affairs Committee, distancing himself again from the administration's actions concerning arms sales to Iran and the channeling of funds to the contras.

McFarlane testifies before the House Foreign Affairs Committee that North informed him in May that "the U.S. Government had applied part of the proceeds" from the sale of arms to Iran "to support the contras." His testimony contradicts statements by Reagan and Meese that the U.S. was not involved in any transfer of funds to the rebels.

Dec. 10, 1986—William Casey testifies before the House Foreign Affairs Committee that on Oct. 7, 1986 he was told by New York businessman Roy Furmark, a former legal client, about "the whole operation" involving arms to Iran and the possibility that "some of the money may have been diverted for other purposes." However, Casey claims he has no knowledge of the diversion of funds to the contras and repeatedly professes ignorance about CIA cash transactions involving Swiss bank accounts. He says the

first official information he received came from Meese on or shortly before November 25.

Poindexter refuses to testify during a 10-minute appearance before the House Permanent Select Committee on Intelligence.

Swiss officials report the U.S. has failed to provide documentation to back up its request to freeze two bank accounts. As a result, one account effectively remains open to further transactions. Legal experts have expressed surprise at the U.S. delay, one Swiss official hypothesizing that perhaps "the Americans don't really want us to block the accounts at all."

Dec. 15, 1986—CIA Director Casey suffers arm and leg seizures and is admitted to Georgetown University Hospital where he is diagnosed as having lymphoma, a rare form of brain cancer. He is scheduled to testify before Congress the next day.

Regan testifies in closed session before the Senate intelligence committee. He says neither he nor Reagan had any prior knowledge of funds being diverted to the contras, and that the President authorized the Israeli arms shipments after the fact.

Swiss officials say they have received an expanded request from the U.S. government requesting that all accounts associated with North and two others be frozen. On the basis of the request the Swiss government asked the Credit Suisse bank to block the appropriate accounts, and Credit Suisse complies, announcing that at least two accounts have been frozen.

Eugene Hasenfus, who has already begun serving a 30-year sentence for transporting arms to Nicaragua, is pardoned by Daniel Ortega and released to visiting Senator Christopher Dodd.

Dec. 19, 1986—Lawrence E. Walsh is named independent counsel with authority to investigate the Iran arms sales, the diversion of funds to "any foreign country, including, but limited to Nicaragua," and "the provision or coordination of support for persons or entities engaged as military insurgents in armed conflict with the Government of Nicaragua since 1984." Walsh's mandate is somewhat broader than that requested by Meese in his December 4 application.

Dec. 26, 1986—David Abshire, outgoing NATO ambassador, is appointed by Reagan to "coordinate White House activities in all aspects of the Iran matter," effective January 5, 1987.

Jan. 24, 1987—The Army admits it undercharged the CIA $2.5 million for 2,008 TOW antitank missile parts sent to Iran last year. Although the discrepancy was "an honest mistake," according to report, the administration, as a consequence, did not have to report the sale to Congress because it fell below the $14 million cut-off for notification.

Jan. 26, 1987—Reagan meets for 76 minutes with members of the Tower Commission. This is the first discussion of the controversy the President has held with any group other than his staff.

Jan. 27, 1987—In his State of the Union address, Reagan acknowledges that "serious mistakes were made" in the program of selling arms to Iran, but does not disavow the policy itself. He also stands firmly behind the policy of aid to the contras.

Feb. 2, 1987—Casey resigns as director of Central Intelligence.

Feb. 9, 1987—McFarlane takes an overdose of 20 to 30 Valium pills. Police officials, calling it a suicide attempt, say he wrote a note relating to the incident. Friends attribute his action to failing to live up to his own standards rather than fear of pending investigations. McFarlane was to testify before the Tower Commission the next day. He says later he tried to kill himself because he "failed the country."

Feb. 26, 1987—The President's Special Review Board, known commonly as the Tower Commission, releases its report.

Feb. 27, 1987—Reagan meets with Howard Baker to discuss Baker's taking over as White House chief of staff. After the 20-minute session, Baker accepts. Informed of the move, Regan immediately has a one-sentence letter of resignation typed out.

May 5-8, 1987—House and Senate committees investigating the Iran-contra arms scandal open their joint public hearings, devoting their first week to testimony of retired Air Force Maj. Gen. Richard Secord. A skilled covert operator who had been involved in arms shipments to both Iran and the contras, Secord is questioned at length about possible profits he took from the schemes. Much of the questioning concerns minor points in the investigation, and the first week of hearings brought no major revelations.

May 6, 1987—Former CIA Director Casey dies of pneumonia. Because of his illness, which followed surgery to excise a brain tumor in 1986, Casey had not been expected to testify at the hearings.

May 11-14, 1987—Former White House national security adviser McFarlane testifies voluntarily. However, a combination of incomplete or evasive answers by McFarlane and a lack of probing follow-up questions by lawmakers left specific details about Reagan's role still unclear. The major revelation concerns Reagan's 1985 personal involvement in the apparent solicitation of funds from Saudi Arabia to support the contras.

May 14-19, 1987—Robert Owen, describing himself as a courier and "foot soldier" in the Reagan administration's secret contra aid campaign, testifies before the committees under a congressional grant of immunity. Calling North the contras' "quartermaster," Owen testified that he had delivered envelopes full of cash from North's office safe to contra leaders in Washington and Central America in 1984-85, a time when a congressional ban on U.S. aid to the contras was in effect. Owen's testimony was the most explicit to date in specifying the direct role North played in keeping the contras funded.

May 15, 1987—After months of denying that he knew specifics about private aid to the contras, Reagan tells a group of Southern journalists that he had been regularly briefed on contra aid because it was "my idea to begin with."

May 19, 1987—Adolfo Calero, head of largest contra faction, appears before the joint congressional committee. His testimony focuses largely on allegations that North had used about $2,000 in traveller's checks from contra funds for apparently personal expenses, including snow tires and women's stockings. Despite the relatively small sums involved, the suggestion that North might have personally profited from the contras overshadowed Calero's other statements. He revealed that he had worked closely with the CIA.

The Senate confirms the nomination of William Webster as director of the CIA by a 94-1 vote. Webster, 63, had been director of the FBI for nine years.

May 20-21, 1987—Retired Army Maj. Gen. John K. Singlaub, a fiece anticommunist, takes the stand at the congressional hearings. He claims that Assistant Secretary of State Elliot Abrams had agreed to assure two foreign governments—identified elsewhere as Taiwan and South Korea—that Singlaub had the administration's approval in soliciting aid from them for the contras. Singlaub portrays Abrams as more deeply involved in private efforts for the contras than Abrams had admitted.

The committees then hear testimony from three wealthy donors to contra causes: Joseph Coors, former chief operating officer of Adolph Coors Co.; Ellen St. John Garwood, an elderly heiress to the Anderson, Clayton & Co. fortune; and William O'Boyle, heir to a Texas oil fortune. Garwood and O'Boyle describe meeting with North and fundraiser Carl Channell to solicit money directly. According to Garwood, Channell promised that, for $300,000, the donor would get a private, 15-minute meeting with President Reagan.

June 2-3, 1987—Elliot Abrams appears before the congressional committees. His testimony focuses almost entirely on whether he had intentionally deceived the Senate Intelligence Committee Nov. 25, 1986, just as the scandal broke. He admits that he had left a misleading impression with the committee, but insists that his statements had been technically correct and that he had not intentionally deceived the senators. He also contradicts testimony given by Singlaub, saying that he had not met with Singlaub before the general's trip to Asia.

June 3-4, 1987—Testifying under a grant of limited immunity, Albert Hakim, Secord's business partner, appeared before the committees. Considered the person most familiar with the intricate financial arrangements behind the scandal, Hakim detailed for the committees the disposition of some of the profits left over from the sale of U.S. arms to Iran—those that were not diverted to the contras. Hakim said that the structure of front corporations and numbered bank accounts had become so intricate that even he, who had set it up, was often confused. The payment that attracted the most attention was $200,000 in an account that Hakim said was set up for North's family shortly before North travelled to Teheran on a secret, unsuccessful mission to rescue U.S. hostages held in Lebanon. Hakim himself made no secret of the fact that he was motivated by profit.

June 8, 1987—Bretton Sciaroni, counsel to the President's Intelligence Oversight Board, testifies before the congressional committees. Sciaroni had written the legal opinion cited by White House officials, including President Reagan, to support their claim that the Boland amendment banning covert aid to the contras did not apply to the NSC. The questions focus on his qualifications as a lawyer and the thoroughness of his investigation of Boland. Sciaroni admits that he had failed the California bar exam twice and the District of Columbia exam twice before passing the bar in Pennsylvania, where he had never lived or worked. He also acknowledges that his 1985 legal opinion, his first such project as an attorney, was based on brief talks with North and NSC lawyer Cmdr. Paul Thompson, and on quick review of documents that Thompson said were sufficient.

June 8-9, 1987—Fawn Hall, who had been North's secretary at the NSC, testifies before the congressional committees. She offers few new details about her role in the scandal, but because she was a blonde part-time model, her appearance draws more media attention than previous witnesses. Hall defends her actions in altering, shredding, and smuggling out certain documents. "Sometimes you have to go above the written law," she says.

July 7-14, 1987—Lt. Col. Oliver North begins his long-awaited testimony before the House and Senate committees, saying that he believes that all his activities as a member of the NSC staff from 1981 through 1986 had been authorized by his superiors. He admits deceiving Congress and misusing some funds from the sale of arms to Iran, but he cites national security and the safety of his family to justify those actions. North, testifying under a grant of immunity and under a complex agreement worked out with the committees, says that he never "personally discussed" the diversion of funds with Reagan, but had "assumed that the President was aware of what I was doing and had, through my superiors, approved it."

July 15-21, 1987—Rear Adm. John Poindexter tells congressional panels that he never told the President about the diversion of funds from arms transactions with Iran to the contra rebels fighting the Nicaraguan government. Poindexter says that he had authorized the controversial diversion and deliberately kept Reagan in the dark in order to "provide some future deniability for the President if it ever leaked out."

July 23-24, 1987—Secretary of State George Shultz testifies before the congressional committees that his strong opposition to the secret arms sales to Iran had sparked a "battle royal" and "guerilla warfare" within the White House. He angrily testifies that Poindexter, McFarlane and Casey had lied to him and withheld information from President Reagan in order to continue the Iranian initiative and ultimately protect themselves. Shultz denies charges that he had deliberately kept himself uninformed about details of the Iran operation and the covert effort to resupply the contras, and then tried to distance himself from the policies once the scandal broke. He says he had argued strenuously against the arms sales and worked to try to end them from the inside.

July 28-29, 1987—Attorney General Edwin Meese 3rd defends his own brief probe of the Iran arms affair, telling the committtees that funds from the arms sales to Iran had been diverted to the contras, but admits that he had failed to ask some critical questions of key participants. Meese takes great pains to avoid suggesting that the White House had deceived him in his investigation, but is compelled to admit that discrepancies between North's comments to him and North's testimony to the committees meant that North had been deceiving one or the other.

July 30-31, 1987—Former White House Chief of Staff Donald Regan testifies that when no hostages were released following a February 1986 shipment of arms to Iran, Reagan felt that "we'd been had." Regan also blames First Lady Nancy Reagan for his forced resignation. The First Lady had told him that she wanted everyone banished who had "let Ronnie down."

July 31-Aug. 3, 1987—Secretary of Defense Weinberger testifies before the congressional panels that he had repeatedly tried to stop the arms sales to Iran and that he thought he had succeeded each time, only to discover that White House officials had deceived him in order to keep the operation going. Weinberger says that he objected to the sales because they were based on the false premise that a moderate element existed in Iran with which the U.S. could negotiate.

Aug. 3, 1987—Joint congressional committees conclude the public segment of their hearings.

Aug. 12, 1987—Responding to the recently concluded congressional hearings in a nationally broadcast address, President Reagan asserts that he "was stubborn in pursuit of a policy that went astray" in selling arms to Iran. Reagan's speech is conciliatory in tone, but he goes no further in accepting responsibility for the scandal than he had in previous statements.

Sept. 26, 1987—Bob Woodward's book on the CIA is released.

Nov. 17, 1987—The joint congressional panels investigating the Iran-contra arms scandal release their report.

# Cast of Characters

**Abrams, Elliott**—Assistant secretary of state for Inter-American Affairs. Previously served as assistant secretary of State for Human Rights and Humanitarian Affairs. Coordinated inter-agency support for the contras. Worked closely with Lt. Col. Oliver North on the contra aid program, helping to solicit funds from third countries, including Brunei.

**Abshire, David**—Former Ambassador to NATO. Between December 1986 and April 1987, coordinated all White House activities related to the Iran-contra affair.

**Boland, Edward**—U.S. Representative from Massachusetts. Former chairman of the House Select Committee on Intelligence. In December 1982, sponsored an amendment, which bears his name, banning CIA support for groups to overthrow the government of Nicaragua.

**Buckley, William**—CIA station chief in Beirut, Lebanon. He was kidnapped March 16, 1984, and died in captivity in June 1985.

**Calero, Adolfo**—Political director of the Nicaraguan Democratic Force (FDN), the largest contra force. On February 16, 1987, he resigned from the three-man directorate of the United Nicaraguan Opposition (UNO), an anti-Sandinista coalition organized in June 1985 at the behest of the Reagan administration.

**Carlucci, Frank**—Named on December 2, 1986 to succeed Vice Admiral John Poindexter as national security adviser. Former deputy defense secretary and head of Sears World Trade, where he managed a defense consulting group called International Planning and Analysis Center (IPAC). Named November 1987 to succeed Caspar Weinberger as Defense Secretary.

**Casey, William**—Former CIA Director. Resigned February 2, 1987, after entering Washington's Georgetown University Hospital for treatment of cancer on December 15 1986. Campaign chairman for Reagan in 1980. During World War II, served with William "Wild Bill" Donovan in the London headquarters of the Office of Strategic Services (OSS), the CIA's forerunner. He died May 5, 1987 as the Iran-contra hearings commenced.

**Castillo, Tomas**—Pseudonym for the CIA station chief in Costa Rica. Reportedly recalled to Washington for assisting the contra supply network. Said to have relayed messages between the contra groups in Costa Rica and the private force operated by Richard Secord.

**Chamorro, Edgar**—Former public relations official and member of the directorate of the main contra group, the Nicaraguan Democratic Force (FDN). The CIA paid him $2,000 a month plus expenses.

**Channell, Carl R. "Spitz"**—Conservative activist and fundraiser. Founder of the National Endowment for the Preservation of Liberty (NEPL). Publicly lauded for his efforts on behalf of the contras by President Reagan and other administration officials. Worked closely with Lt. Col. Oliver North to raise funds for the contras and to plan and coordinate pro-contra activities. According to one fundraiser, some of the money raised by Channell, ostensibly for humanitarian assistance to the contras, went to provide arms for the contras.

**Clines, Thomas**—Former CIA official in Miami and Laos. Had ties to Richard Secord and convicted arms dealer Edwin Wilson. Allegedly dispatched by Lt. Col. Oliver North for secret missions in the Middle East and Central America.

**Cruz, Arturo**—Former Nicaraguan Ambassador to Washington. Resigned on March 10, 1987, from the directorate of the United Nicaraguan Opposition (UNO). Paid $7,000 per month by Lt. Col. Oliver North between January and November 1987.

**Fahd bin Abd al-Aziz**—King of Saudi Arabia. In February 1984, aboard a yacht off the coast of the French Riviera, CIA Director William Casey reportedly asked him to provide covert funds for the contras and rebels fighting in Angola. Subsequently, between July 1984 and March 1985 over $31 million was deposited in Cayman Island bank accounts that belonged to the contras.

**Ghorbanifar, Manucher**—Iranian arms dealer who served as a middleman in the U.S. arms deal with Iran in 1985 and 1986. Allegedly a former officer of SAVAK, the Shah of Iran's secret police. The CIA and intelligence agencies in Europe considered him prone to exaggeration and unreliable. Nevertheless, CIA Director William Casey and the White House chose to continue using him as a channel to the Iranian government.

**Green, Tom**—Attorney for Secord and Lt. Col. Oliver North. Told Assistant Attorney General Charles Cooper on November 24, 1986, that in proposing the use of Iran arms proceeds for the contras, Secord and Albert Hakim "felt like they were doing the Lord's work."

**Gregg, Donald**—Vice President George Bush's national security adviser and a former CIA official. Informed about the contra aid program by both Lt. Col. North and Felix Rodriguez, a former CIA agent who served with Gregg in Vietnam.

**Hakim, Albert**—Iranian expatriate and Richard Secord's business partner. Together they directed the clandestine contra resupply effort under the auspices of their company, Stanford Technology Trading Group International.

**Hall, Fawn**—Lt. Col. North's secretary, who allegedly helped him destroy and alter documents.

**Hasenfus, Eugene**—Hired in April 1986 to work as a cargo handler for covert resupply flights into Nicaragua from Ilopango Air Base in El Salvador. On October 5, 1986, his plane is shot down over southern Nicaragua and he was the sole survivor. After being tried, convicted and sentenced to 30 years in prison, he was pardoned by Nicaraguan President Daniel Ortega and released.

**Inouye, Daniel**—Democratic senator from Hawaii. Chaired Senate panel investigating the Iran-contra arms affair.

**Khashoggi, Adnan**—Saudi billionaire and arms dealer. Provided bridge financing for the sale of U.S. arms to Iran.

**Kimche, David**—Former Director General of Israel's Foreign Ministry. Got U.S. permission for arms deals with Iran as early as 1981.

**McFarlane, Robert**—President Reagan's National Security Adviser from October 17, 1983 until November 30, 1985. Initiated the review of U.S. policy toward Iran in early 1984 that led to the arms deals and supervised the early NSC efforts to support the contras. Even after departing the White House, McFarlane continued to be involved in the Iran initiative; in May 1986 he led the unsuccessful secret mission to Teheran.

**Meese, Edwin 3rd**—U.S. Attorney General. Conducted the initial probe of the National Security Council cover-up of the U.S. role in arms sales to Iran. At the request of then- National Security Adviser John Poindexter, he asked then-FBI Director William Webster on October 30, 1986, to delay an FBI probe into Southern Air Transport, which had been linked to the contra supply plane shot down over Nicaragua earlier that month.

**Nir, Amiram**—Beginning in September 1984, an adviser on counterterrorism to Israeli Prime Minister Shimon Peres. Reportedly suggested to North in January 1986 that the Iranians be overcharged for weapons shipped to them and the surplus funds be diverted to the contras. Told Vice President George Bush in July 1986 that the U.S. and Israel were dealing with radicals in Iran, not moderates.

**North, Lt. Col. Oliver (a.k.a William P. Goode, Mr. Green, Mr. White)**—Simultaneously managed the covert aid program for the contras and the secret initiatives toward Iran, including the diversion of funds to the rebels, from his post as Assistant Deputy Director for Political-Military Affairs at the NSC. Assisted outside fundraising efforts for the contras and oversaw a private network to supply lethal equipment to the contras.

**Owen, Robert**—Served as Lt. Col. North's liaison to the contras during the congressional ban on aid to the rebels.

**Poindexter, John**—Navy Rear Admiral (demoted from the rank of Vice Admiral after he left the White House) and Robert McFarlane's successor as President Reagan's national security adviser.

**Regan, Donald**—Former White House Chief of Staff. In November 1986, he characterized the arms deals with Iran as a "trade" for hostages, contradicting claims made by other administration officials. Amid widespread doubts about his ability to continue serving the President in the wake of the Iran-contra scandal, he resigned February 27, 1987, immediately after he was informed that President Reagan was replacing him with former Senator Howard H. Baker Jr.

**Secord, Richard**—Retired Air Force Major General. With Iranian expatriate Albert Hakim, was instrumental in the 1984-86 contra resupply effort, which they directed out of the northern Virginia offices of their company, Stanford Technology Trading Group International. The company maintained Swiss bank accounts that were tied to the diversion of Iran arms sales profits.

**Shultz, George**—Secretary of State criticized by the Tower Commission for his passivity in acquiescing in a policy that he disagreed with. Also raised money overseas for the contras.

**Singlaub, John**—Retired Army Major General and chairman of the World Anti-Communist League (WACL) and its U.S. affiliate, the U.S. Council for World Freedom. With Oliver North's knowledge, Singlaub raised money worldwide for the contras. Along with Richard Secord, became one of the major conduits of arms to the contras, providing millions of dollars in arms while a congressional ban on such aid was in effect.

**Tower, John**—Headed President Reagan's special review board that concluded that the Iran-contra arms affair and the National Security Council's covert operations were an "aberration," a failure of people not process.

**Webster, William**—Director of the Central Intelligence Agency and former head of the Federal Bureau of Investigation. Asked by Attorney General Edwin Meese to delay an FBI probe of Southern Air Transport's involvement with contra gun running on grounds that Southern was involved with secret hostage recovery efforts. Then, allegedly agreed with Attorney General Meese that there were no criminal aspects to Meese's probe of the National Security Council cover-up of the role of U.S. arms sales to Iran.

**Weinberger, Caspar**—Secretary of Defense whom the Tower Commission accused of doing a "disservice" to the President for distancing himself from the Iran arms deal instead of fighting it. He left the administration in November 1987.

# Index